INSIDE
REPORTING

A PRACTICAL GUIDE TO THE CRAFT OF JOURNALISM

INSIDE
REPORTING

A PRACTICAL GUIDE TO THE CRAFT OF JOURNALISM

Tim Harrower

Boston   Burr Ridge, IL   Dubuque, IA   Madison, WI   New York   San Francisco   St. Louis
Bangkok   Bogotá   Caracas   Kuala Lumpur   Lisbon   London   Madrid   Mexico City
Milan   Montreal   New Delhi   Santiago   Seoul   Singapore   Sydney   Taipei   Toronto

Higher Education

Published by McGraw-Hill, an imprint of The McGraw-Hill Companies, Inc., 1221 Avenue of the Americas, New York, NY 10020. Copyright © 2007. All rights reserved. No part of this publication may be reproduced or distributed in any form or by any means, or stored in a database or retrieval system, without the prior written consent of The McGraw-Hill Companies, Inc., including, but not limited to, in any network or other electronic storage or transmission, or broadcast for distance learning.

This book is printed on acid-free paper.

4 5 6 7 8 9 0 DOW/DOW 0 9 8 7

ISBN-13:   978-0-07-352614-0
ISBN-10:   0-07-352614-2

Editor in Chief: *Emily Barrosse*
Publisher: *Phillip A. Butcher*
Director of Development: *Rhona Robbin*
Marketing Manager: *Leslie Oberhuber*
Editorial Assistant: *Erika Lake*
Media Project Manager: *Stacy Bentz*
Project Manager: *Brett Coker*
Manuscript Editor: *Patricia Ohlenroth*
Design Manager: *Preston Thomas*
Interior and Cover Designer: *Tim Harrower*
Manager, Photo Research: *Brian J. Pecko*
Production Supervisor: *Randy Hurst*
Printing: *60# Pub Matte Plus by R. R. Donnelley & Sons*

Credits: The credits section for this book begins on page 312 and is considered an extension of the copyright page.

Library of Congress Cataloging-in-Publication Data
Harrower, Tim.
   Inside reporting: a practical guide to the craft of journalism / written & designed by Tim Harrower.—1st edition
      p.cm.
   Includes bibliographical references and index.
   ISBN 978-0-07-352614-0 ISBN 0-07-352614-2 (alk. paper)
      1. Reporters and reporting.   I. Title

PN4781.H343 2006
070.4'3—dc22
         2006046195

The Internet addresses listed in the text were accurate at the time of publication. The inclusion of a Web site does not indicate an endorsement by the authors or McGraw-Hill, and McGraw-Hill does not guarantee the accuracy of the information presented at these sites.

www.mhhe.com

TABLE OF CONTENTS

PREFACE

*S*omewhere, not too far from here, at this very moment, a politician is taking a bribe. A factory is dumping toxic sludge into a stream. A deadly virus is landing at the airport. A high school halfback is bulking up on steroids. Someone's mother is opening a can of contaminated tuna.

Just a typical day in America, in other words, where ordinary folks suffer from a lack of reliable information. What they don't know *can* hurt them.

Who's the watchdog here? Whose job is it to expose the lies, explain the dangers, inform the uninformed?

If you become a journalist, it's *your* job.

Now, I'm a realist. I don't want to fool you into thinking journalism is glamorous. I don't want to dupe dreamy-eyed idealists into believing your deathless prose can slay society's dragons.

Very few news stories will ever change the world.

Still, sometimes a single story — *a single sentence* — can have an effect you never imagined. Put the right facts in the right order and you can make someone laugh. Cry. Reconsider. Understand.

That's how you make a difference in this crazy world: one reader at a time.

*J*ournalism is in flux these days. Experts say that print is dead and TV news is dying, but blogs are big and multimedia is *the real deal*.

You can study statistics and ponder predictions until your head explodes. But if you're considering a career in journalism, where should you begin?

For now — in this book — we'll focus on fundamentals. Not trends. Not theories.

If you want to be a journalist, you need to learn how to gather facts and tell stories. That's basically all there is to it: 1) Gather the facts. 2) Tell the story.

Sure, you can add photos and headlines and Web links and audio sound bites and animated graphics. And we'll get to all that, eventually.

But first, you begin with the basics. That's why this book focuses on news*writing*. It's the traditional, tried-and-true way to master the journalist's craft.

Some of you, I realize, don't want to write for a newspaper. (Some of you don't even want to *read* a newspaper.) You'd rather be webcasters, bloggers, radio anchors, TV correspondents.

I sympathize. As time goes by, I too get increasingly frustrated with slow-motion, old-school, ink-on-dead-tree journalism. But whatever medium you choose for news — text, graphics, audio, video or multimedia — it still begins the same way: Gather facts. Tell stories.

So that's where we'll begin, too.

*S*peaking of multimedia: This book demonstrates what you get when you blend words and visuals simultaneously.

Most authors write the text first, then hand their manuscript to editors and designers who add photos, illustrations and fancy type.

But for this book, I designed each page as I wrote it. Or, rather, I wrote each page as I designed it. Whichever.

It's an unusual way to produce a book, but it's how I like to work. More than 25 years ago, I started designing newspaper pages that way, blending text and images into packages with (hopefully) greater reader appeal.

This kind of "convergence," as it's called, is becoming more common in newsrooms. If you can write and design stories, generate images and create Web pages, you'll be a hot commodity in the journalism job market.

This book, I confess, has been quite a monster to produce independently. But ideally, it will show you how challenging and rewarding and important and seriously *cool* journalism is. Maybe, just maybe, it will even inspire you to become a journalist.

That's how you make a difference in this crazy world: one journalist at a time.

— *Tim Harrower*

THE PRESS ROOM

We hounded these veteran reporters with weekly e-mail questions for nearly nine months. Their expert advice appears throughout this book. Our sincere thanks to our panel:

Andy Alford, *Austin American-Statesman*
JoNel Allecia, *Mail Tribune (Medford, Ore.)*
Ted Anthony, *The Associated Press*
Sarah Bahari, *Fort Worth Star-Telegram*
Erin Barnett, *The Oregonian (Portland, Ore.)*
Jill Barrall, *Hutchinson (Minn.) Leader*
Bob Batz, *Pittsburgh Post-Gazette*
Michael Becker, *Journal-Advocate (Sterling, Colo.)*
Bret Bell, *Savannah Morning News*
Rick Bella, *The Oregonian (Portland, Ore.)*
Matt Benson, *Fort Collins Coloradoan*
Laura Berman, *The Detroit News*
Michael Bockoven, *The Grand Island Independent*
Tim Botos, *The Repository (Canton, Ohio)*
Alex Branch, *Fort Worth Star-Telegram*
Caren Burmeister, *The (Jacksonville) Florida Times-Union*

Steve Buttry, *American Press Institute*
Jim Camden, *The Spokesman-Review (Spokane, Wash.)*
Matt Chittum, *The Roanoke Times*
Carol Cole, *The Shawnee (Okla.) News-Star*
Toni Coleman, *The Pioneer Press (St. Paul, Minn.)*
DeeDee Correll, *The Gazette (Colorado Springs, Colo.)*
Bob Cullinane, *Asbury Park Press (Neptune, N.J.)*
Bryan Dean, *The Daily Oklahoman*
Emily Dooley, *Cape Cod Times*
Paul Duchene
Steve Duin, *The Oregonian (Portland, Ore.)*
Mark Fagan, *Lawrence (Kan.) Journal-World*
Andrea Faiad, *Post-Bulletin (Rochester, Minn.)*
Jesse Fanciulli, *Greeley (Colo.) Daily Tribune*
Todd Frankel, *St. Louis Post-Dispatch*
Mark Freeman, *Mail Tribune (Medford, Ore.)*

Ron French, *The Detroit News*
Ken Fuson, *The Des Moines Register*
John Foyston, *The Oregonian (Portland, Ore.)*
Nancy Gaardner, *Omaha World-Herald*
Steve Gunn, *Muskegon Chronicle*
Heidi Hagemeier, *The Bulletin (Bend, Ore.)*
Don Hamilton, *The Columbian (Vancouver, Wash.)*
Scott Hammers, *Lake Oswego (Ore.) Review*
Kevin Harden, *Valley Times (Beaverton, Ore.)*
Bill Harlan, *The Rapid City (S.D.) Journal*
Jim Hart, *West Linn (Ore.) Tidings*
Kyle Henley, *The Gazette (Colorado Springs, Colo.)*
Doug Hoagland, *The Fresno Bee*
Dave Hogan, *The Oregonian (Portland, Ore.)*
Deb Holland, *The Rapid City (S.D.) Journal*
Karen Jeffrey, *Cape Cod Times*

ACKNOWLEDGMENTS

The author is sincerely grateful to the following friends and colleagues:

◆ **The McGraw-Hill staff:**
Phil Butcher and Rhona Robbin, for their relentless support, patience and good humor through it all; Brian Pecko; Karyn Morrison; Brett Coker, Preston Thomas, Randy Hurst and the San Francisco crew.

This book is based on a proposal and teaching strategy developed with Alice Klement, the former Mildred S. Hansen Professor at the University of Northern Colorado.

◆ **Advice and feedback:**
Marie Naughton and her students at Washington State University Vancouver; Buck Ryan and his students at the University of Kentucky; Linda Vogt and her students at Clackamas Community College; Mark Witherspoon, Brenda Witherspoon and Barbara Mack, Iowa State University; Mark Larson, Humboldt State University; Don Hamilton; Stu Tomlinson; Amy Martinez Starke; Jeff Mapes; James Tidwell; John Zelezny; Jay Bender; Tracy Barry and Joe Donlon at KGW; Melanie Mesaros at KXL; Pete Schulberg; Ken Kahn; Mark Wigginton; Sandy Rowe.

◆ **Morgue annotations:**
Special thanks to the writers who generously shared their insights and expertise: Don Hamilton, Dave Philipps, Jodi Cohen, Alana Baranick, Vanessa Gezari, Sanne Specht, Stuart Tomlinson, Linda Johnson, Kelley Benham, Heather Svokos, Dan Raley, Joe Posnanski, Colleen Kenney, Judd Slivka, Manish Mehta, Mark Morford, Doug Elfman, Claudia Puig and David Sarasohn.

◆ **Illustrations and photography:**
Steve Cowden; Tony Champagne; Joe Spooner; Michael Lloyd; Ross Hamilton; Chuck Kennedy; Marshall Gorby; Monica Lopossay.

◆ **Contributors of words and images:**
Wally Benson; Sheryl Swingley; J. Ford Huffman; Harris Siegel; Steve Dorsey; Tracy Collins; Bonita Burton; Denis Finley; Rob Curley; Lora Cuykendall; Jonathon Berlin; Molly Yannity; Nigel Jaquiss; Michael Gartner; Steve Buttry; Jim Stasiowski; J. Taylor Buckley; Roger Ebert; Susan Mango Curtis; Robb Montgomery; Susan Page; Scott Byers; Diana Sugg; Paul Overberg; Tom Henderson; Greg Esposito; Adam Schefter; Frank Main; David Austin; Amanda Bennett; Kyle Keener; Jeff Hindenach; Ron Matthews; Charles Stough; Rachel MacKnight; researchers Megan DuBois, Bre LeBeuf and Kelsey Warner of the University of Northern Colorado.

◆ **Supplement authors:**
— Paul Kandell, teacher and journalist, for the online workbook.
— David Swartzlander of Doane College for the instructor's manual and test bank.
— Michael Swinford of Saint Anselm College for the learning goals, multiple choice and true-false quizzes, and chapter summaries on the Online Learning Center.

◆ **Student survey coordinators:**
Buck Ryan, University of Kentucky; Mark Larson, Humboldt State University; Lana Jackson, Amarillo College; Rich Cameron, Cerritos College; Beth Dickey, University of South Carolina; Cheryl Pell, Michigan State University; David Swartzlander, Doane College; Mary Arnold, South Dakota State University; Mark Witherspoon, Iowa State University; Lois Breedlove, Central Washington University.

◆ **And most of all:** Without you, Robin, this book — and all the good things in my life — would not be possible.

ACADEMIC REVIEWERS
Special thanks to these instructors for taking time to provide valuable feedback on the text:

Michael E. Abrams, Florida A&M University
Aje-Ori Agbese, Salva Regina University
Candace Baltz, College of Southern Idaho
Linda Thorsen Bond, Stephen F. Austin State University
Jeff Boone, Angelo State University
Candace Perkins Bowen, Kent State University
Mark A. Butzow, Western Illinois University
Betty Clapp, Cleveland State University
Kay Colley, University of North Texas
Steve Craig, University of North Texas
James L. Crandall, Aims Community College
Dale Cressman, Brigham Young University
Kathleen Bartzen Culver, University of Wisconsin
Lori Demo, Ball State University
Eric B. Easton, University of Baltimore School of Law
Amy Eisman, American University
Leo Eko, University of Iowa
Russ Eshleman, Penn State University
Kym Fox, Texas State University
Eileen Gilligan, SUNY Oswego
Mark Hanebutt, University of Central Oklahoma
Cheryl Heckler, Miami University
Lana Jackson, Amarillo College
Richard A. Joyce, Colorado State University, Pueblo
Rachele Kanigel, San Francisco State University
Johanna Keller, Syracuse University
Joel Kendall, Southwestern Oklahoma State University
Teresa Lamsam, University of Nebraska, Omaha
Kimberly Lauffer, Towson University
Alyssa Lenhoff, Youngstown State University
Gary H. Mayer, Stephen F. Austin State University
Frances McDavid, Mississippi State University
Jim Namiotka, Seton Hall University
Patrick Claiborne Neal, Clemson University
Terry L. Renter, Bowling Green State University
Joseph E. Spevak, San Diego State University
Cathy Stablein, College of DuPage
Sara Stone, Baylor University
George Sylvie, University of Texas at Austin
Fred Stewart, Texas A&M University, Commerce
Michael Swinford, Saint Anselm College
James C. Wilson, University of Cincinnati
Linda K. Zeigler, Tyler Junior College
John B. Zibluk, Arkansas State University

Alandra Johnson, *The Bulletin (Bend, Ore.)*
Carla Johnson, *The Spokesman-Review (Spokane, Wash.)*
Lesley Kennedy, *Rocky Mountain News (Denver)*
Jim Kershner, *The Spokesman-Review (Spokane, Wash.)*
Mike Kilen, *The Des Moines Register*
Mike Krapfl, *The Tribune (Ames, Iowa)*
Mary Landers, *Savannah Morning News*
Dion Lefler, *The Wichita Eagle*
Christina Leonard, *The Arizona Republic*
Dave Lester, *Yakima Herald-Republic*
Randy Ludlow, *The Columbus Dispatch*
David Lyman, *Detroit Free Press*
Beth Macy, *The Roanoke Times*
Jeff Mapes, *The Oregonian (Portland, Ore.)*

Joel Mathis, *Lawrence (Kan.) Journal-World*
Monica Mendoza, *The Arizona Republic*
Tripp Mickle, *Tahoe World*
Patricia Miller, *Durango Herald*
Kimberly Morava, *The Shawnee (Okla.) News-Star*
Blake Morrison, *USA Today*
Katy Muldoon, *The Oregonian (Portland, Ore.)*
Tim Nelson, *The Pioneer Press (St. Paul, Minn.)*
Matt Neznanski, *The Tribune (Ames, Iowa)*
Kim Ode, *Star Tribune (Minneapolis, Minn.)*
Kirsten Orsini-Meinhar, *Fort Collins Coloradoan*
Kevin Pang, *Chicago Tribune*
Steve Paul, *The Kansas City Star*
Mike Peters, *Greeley (Colo.) Tribune*
Larry Peterson, *Savannah Morning News*
Phillip Pina, *The Pioneer Press (St. Paul, Minn.)*

Kim Pokorny, *The Oregonian (Portland, Ore.)*
Rita Price, *The Columbus Dispatch*
Aesha Rasheed, *The Times-Picayne (New Orleans, La.)*
Heather Ratcliffe, *St. Louis Post-Dispatch*
John Reinan, *Star Tribune (Minneapolis, Minn.)*
Bill Reiter, *The Des Moines Register*
Judith Reynolds, *Durango Herald*
Peter Rowe, *The San Diego Union-Tribune*
ML Schultze, *The Repository (Canton, Ohio)*
Jerry Schwartz, *The Associated Press*
Kim Severson, *San Francisco Chronicle*
Connie Sexton, *The Arizona Republic*
Deborah L. Shelton, *St. Louis Post-Dispatch*
Sara Shipley, *St. Louis Post-Dispatch*
Melissa Siig, *Tahoe World*

Peter Sleeth, *The Oregonian (Portland, Ore.)*
Judd Slivka
Rachel Stassen-Berger, *St. Paul (Minn.) Pioneer Press*
Ron Sylvester, *The Wichita Eagle*
Stuart Tomlinson, *The Oregonian (Portland, Ore.)*
Julie Tripp, *The Oregonian (Portland, Ore.)*
Kristi Turnquist, *The Oregonian (Portland, Ore.)*
Lee van der Voo, *Lake Oswego (Ore.) Review*
Joe Verrengia, *The Associated Press*
Leah Beth Ward, *Yakima Herald-Republic*
Roy Wenzl, *The Wichita Eagle*
April Wortham, *The Tuscaloosa News*

ABOUT THIS BOOK

*T*his is not your father's journalism textbook. No, times have changed. Reading habits have changed. And journalism has changed, too.

It wasn't always like this. Years ago, people had time. They had patience. Textbooks were exactly that: books filled with *text*, page after page, long rows of type full of deep thoughts.

Today, we process information differently. We need speed. We need visual stimulation. We want a little personality, too (but nothing too goofy or distracting). Nobody likes long, lifeless lectures anymore.

Journalists understand this, or at least they should. They know they're supposed to present information in a visually engaging, reader-friendly way. So we began to wonder:

What if we produced a textbook that presented information in a visually engaging, reader-friendly way?

Wow! Such a radical idea.

To do that, we had to break a few rules and invent some new ones. As you tour this book, you'll notice:

◆ **The design.** There's lots of color, photos and graphics, sure. But the *logic* of the design is more important than the *look*. Though topics are explored in depth, they're arranged into concise, easy-to-digest sections. To free up space, long examples of newswriting have been relocated to the back of the book, the Morgue, as you can see here. •••••••

◆ **The navigation.** Topics are clearly labeled and easy to find. Each two-page spread focuses on a key subject. And a series of links provides cross-references throughout the book.

◆ **The tone.** Most textbooks sound like textbooks. This one reads like a magazine article: concise, practical, informal. That made sense to us. After all, why shouldn't a journalism texbook be designed and written as if it's actually a form of ..... *journalism?*

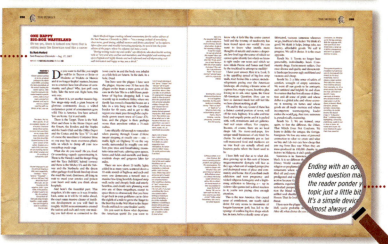

THE THREE MAIN SECTIONS OF THIS BOOK

① *All key topics are presented on two-page spreads like this one, making the information easier to navigate. Subjects are packaged into short, concise sections — like spreads in a magazine.*

Links to related topics are indicated by red arrows here, along the bottom of the page.

② *At the beginning and end of each chapter, pages are framed by a gray border. This makes them visually distinct from the main two-page topic spreads so they'll be easy to find. Look here for exercises, the Press Room and other extras.*

③ *The back of the book is called "the Morgue" — an old newspaper term for a newsroom library. Part anthology, part scrapbook, the Morgue supplements the text by presenting complete stories for detailed analysis.*

We've asked many of the original writers of these stories to provide insights and commentary here, in the margins of the text.

ONLINE EXTRAS

Accessible at **www.mhhe.com/harrower1**, the Online Learning Center Web site provides a wealth of resources for instructors and students that supplement *Inside Reporting*.

The **Student Edition** of the Web site includes a workbook with numerous skill-building exercises and activities, multiple-choice, true-false and grammar quizzes with feedback, annotated links from the book's Webliography, key-term flashcards and crossword puzzles, learning goals, chapter summaries and a glossary.

The **Instructor Edition** of the site includes an instructor's manual that features teaching tips, key points, class discussion topics and activities, suggested homework assignments, a test bank with questions on key concepts, grammar and AP style, and PowerPoint slides.

CHAPTER

The story of journalism

Before you begin learning how to report and write stories, let's look at the heroes and history that brought us this far.

IN THIS CHAPTER:

6▶ Newsroom heroes, legends and folklore
Highlights from the history of journalism, from Mark Twain and Lois Lane to "Citizen Kane."

8▶ The birth of journalism
How newspapers were established in America — and how the fight for a free press led to war.

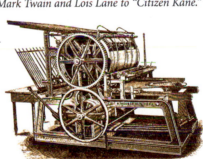

10▶ News in the 19th century
Mass media dominated city streets, while yellow journalism gave reporters a bad name.

12▶ News in the modern age
Magazines. Radio. Television. The Internet. News isn't just for newspapers anymore.

14▶ The student journalists' news attitude survey
Compare your news consumption habits to those of hundreds of other students nationwide.

Newsroom heroes, legends and folklore

Looking for a career that boasts a long, colorful tradition?

Welcome to the world of journalism, where reporters have been digging dirt, raking muck, making headlines and deadlines for centuries now. It's a history full of tabloid trash, of slimy sensationalists, of "drunkards, deadbeats and bummers" (as a Harvard University president once described reporters).

But it's a history full of heroes, too: men and women risking their lives to tell stories of war and tragedy, risking imprisonment to defend free speech. And as you can see here, reporters have become beloved characters in pop culture, too, turning up in movies, comics and TV shows *as if guided by an occult hand.* ▼

In the 1970s, the investigative work of Bob Woodward (left) and Carl Bernstein exposed the Watergate scandal, helped force President Nixon to resign and made the two Washington Post reporters an inspiration to journalists everywhere. Their exploits became a popular book and movie.

FIVE LEGENDARY JOURNALISTS EVERY REPORTER SHOULD KNOW

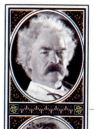

MARK TWAIN (1835-1910)
Twain (real name: Samuel Clemens) is best known as the humorist who created Tom Sawyer and wrote a classic novel, "The Adventures of Huckleberry Finn." But Twain developed his style as a reporter in Nevada and California, writing columns, feature stories, travel pieces and hoaxes that made him one of the century's most popular authors.

NELLIE BLY (1864-1922)
Called "the best reporter in America" in the late 1800s, Bly (real name: Elizabeth Cochrane) pioneered investigative journalism with her bold undercover adventures: getting herself locked up in a lunatic asylum, working in a sweat-shop to expose child-labor abuses. And in a famous publicity stunt, she traveled around the world in 72 days.

H.L. MENCKEN (1880-1956)
Looking for some timeless, biting, brilliantly quotable social commentary? Mencken's your man. Whether ranting about politics ("democracy is the art of running the circus from the monkey cage") or people ("there's no underesti-mating the intelligence of the American public"), Mencken was a hugely influential critic.

ERNEST HEMINGWAY (1899-1961)
Where did this legendary American novelist develop his straightforward prose style? Covering crimes and fires for The Kansas City Star, where the paper's admonitions to use short sentences, short paragraphs and vigorous English "were the best rules I ever learned for the business of writing," Hemingway later recalled.

HUNTER S. THOMPSON (1937-2005)
Hey, we didn't say these were all great writers; we just said you need to *know* about them. And for good or bad, you gotta know about Hunter Thompson and "gonzo journalism," a wacko blend of satire, profanity and hallucinogenic exaggeration. Beware: Gonzo journalism is dangerous, wrong and insanely entertaining.

 Visit **THE MORGUE** to read excerpts from these writers' works:

TWAIN ▶ 190   BLY ▶ 192   MENCKEN ▶ 196   HEMINGWAY ▶ 195   THOMPSON ▶ 198

30 SLANG TERMS FOR "REPORTER"

jotter	ink-stained wretch
ragger	pavement-prowler
scribe	knight of the pen
scrivener	slang-whanger
hoofer	Fourth Estater
hound	bloodhound
snoop	bull shooter
stringer	cover boy/girl
legman	ink slinger
'porter	news grabber
scratcher	nosy newsy
gazetteer	paper stainer
news hack	paragrapher
news hen	pencil pusher
pen driver	wordster

FIVE MYTHS ABOUT REPORTERS

1. Female reporters are gutsy, idealistic, beautiful and single; male reporters are surly, cynical loners who'll lie, cheat and ruin people's lives to get a juicy scoop.

2. Reporters routinely solve mysteries before the cops do, even after their editors yank them off the stories.

3. Reporters spend all of their time either: a) ambushing celebrities outside nightclubs, b) dodging bullets in foreign hotspots, or c) shouting questions at crooked politicians on the steps of City Hall.

4. Reporters celebrate their big stories by drinking whiskey they hide in their desks.

5. All reporters have a liberal bias.

FIVE INSPIRATIONAL BOOKS EVERY REPORTER SHOULD READ

"ALL THE PRESIDENT'S MEN" by Carl Bernstein and Bob Woodward — A gripping tale of politics, scandal, conspiracies, lies and the dogged determination of two heroic reporters. That's right: *heroic*. Watching Woodward and Bernstein unravel the threads that lead to Nixon's downfall is exhilarating. The world needs more gutsy reporters like these guys.

"THE ELEMENTS OF STYLE" by Strunk and White — Lots of books tell you how to write. Most of them make it painful. But this one is full of savvy advice that will stick with you for years, with entries like "Use the active voice" and "Omit needless words." Studying this 100-page mini-manual helps make your prose truly pro.

"WRITING FOR STORY" by Jon Franklin — If you stay in this business long enough, you'll eventually wonder: How do I write a gripping, Pulitzer Prize-winning epic? Franklin's popular feature-writing guide will teach you all the techniques: structure, flashbacks, foreshadowing, pacing. And it's loaded with inspiring examples.

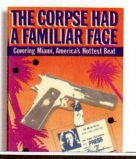

"THE CORPSE HAD A FAMILIAR FACE" by Edna Buchanan — If you wonder what it's like to be a crime reporter in a big city (Miami) full of creeps, crooks and crazies, the legendary Buchanan will not only show you — she'll inspire you to be a cops reporter, too.

"INSIDE REPORTING" by Tim Harrower — Kidding! Just kidding. Instead, find a copy of "The New Journalism," a terrific sampler edited by Tom Wolfe that anthologizes late-20th-century journalistic legends like Mailer, Capote, Didion and Wolfe himself. Don't miss it.

MORE ON **THE OCCULT HAND SOCIETY** ▶ 278   MORE ON **WATERGATE AND "DEEP THROAT"** ▶ 234

FIVE CLASSIC JOURNALISM MOVIES

"CITIZEN KANE" — We all know how crazy reporters can be. This 1941 Orson Welles masterpiece shows you how rich, powerful and loony *publishers* can be. Watching this film transports you back to a golden age of journalism that's gone forever. Film critics agree that "Citizen Kane" showcases some of the most brilliant moviemaking of all time; luckily for us, it's about newspapers, too.

"HIS GIRL FRIDAY" — One of the best of the 1940s screwball comedies: a fast-paced classic starring Cary Grant as a charming newspaper editor matching wits and wisecracks with Rosalind Russell, his star reporter (and ex-wife). Some viewers prefer the 1974 Jack Lemmon/Walter Matthau remake, "The Front Page."

"BROADCAST NEWS" — A smart, comedic look at the personalities in front of *and* behind the cameras in a network newsroom. William Hurt plays an airheaded anchor who represents the brainless artificiality of television news; Holly Hunter plays a producer grappling with her values, her workload and her love life.

"GOOD NIGHT, AND GOOD LUCK" — McCarthy vs. Murrow. Politicians vs. the press. This 2005 drama, set in early days of television news, provides an absorbing introduction to the courage and eloquence of Edward R. Murrow — and a sobering reminder of why democracy requires a free and aggressive press.

Part detective story, part political thriller, "All the President's Men" remains both inspiring and entertaining. Starring Robert Redford as *Woodward (left)* and Dustin Hoffman as *Bernstein*, the 1976 film captures the tireless tenacity that turned these reporters into heroes.

BEST NEWSROOM RANT:
"You know what people use these for? They roll them up and swat their puppies for wetting on the rug — they spread them on the floor when they're painting the walls — they wrap fish in them — shred them up and pack their two-bit china in them when they move — or else they pile up in the garage until an inspector declares them a fire hazard! But this also happens to be a couple of more things! It's got print on it that tells stories that hundreds of good men all over the world have broken their backs to get. It gives a lot of information to a lot of people who wouldn't have known about it if we hadn't taken the trouble to tell them. It's the sum total of the work of a lot of guys who don't quit. It's a newspaper. . . and it only costs 10 cents, that's all. But if you only read the comic section or the want ads — it's still the best buy for your money in the world."

William Conrad,
crusty city editor in the
1959 newspaper movie "30"

FIVE FAMOUS FICTIONAL NEWSROOM CHARACTERS

CLARK KENT and LOIS LANE are the two best reporters at The Daily Planet — though Lois seems to be the only one doing any *actual reporting* at that newspaper. And whenever Lois' nose for news lands her in hot water, Superman (Clark's other identity) conveniently manages to save her before she blows her deadline. Ahh, if only it worked that way in real life. . . .

LOU GRANT was the ultimate surly, burly, gruff-but-lovable editor. On the legendary "Mary Tyler Moore" TV comedy back in the '70s, Lou (played by Ed Asner, at right) ran a TV newsroom; on the "Lou Grant" spinoff, he was the classic crusty, crusading newspaper editor.

BRENDA STARR was a pioneer: a strong female comic-strip character from the 1940s drawn by female cartoonists, which was rare back then. Readers loved the redheaded reporter's far-flung adventures and steamy love affairs, which continue today on newspaper comic pages.

JIMMY was an 8-year-old heroin addict whose heart-wrenching story won a Pulitzer Prize for Janet Cooke and The Washington Post in 1981. The problem? Jimmy didn't exist; the story was a fabrication. Cooke resigned, and her award was revoked in the humiliating scandal that ensued.

What's your JQ?

Think you're pretty smart when it comes to journalism facts, folklore and useless trivia? Prove it. Take this quiz to measure your JQ — your Journalism Quotient.

Answers on Page 284.

1) *"Rock journalism is people who can't write interviewing people who can't talk for people who can't read."* Who said that?
☐ Madonna
☐ Rush Limbaugh
☐ Frank Zappa

2) What cartoon editor used to cry, *"Great Caesar's ghost!"*?

3) In the photo below, President Truman is holding a copy of a famous headline blooper. What did the headline say?

4) Twin sisters born in 1918 became legendary advice columnists known as _____ and _____ .

5) John McMullen, the editor of the Miami Herald, made this prediction in 1982: *"I don't think it has much chance. It won't offer much that's original or different. . . I give it two years."* What was he talking about?

6) Here are slang nicknames for three popular newspapers. What are their real names?
☐ The Urinal and Constipation
☐ The Freep
☐ The Grope and Fail

7) Who used to sign off his newscast by saying, *"And that's the way it is. . ."*?

8) In 1872, Henry Stanley, star reporter for The New York Herald, searched the African jungle for a missing explorer. Stanley's epic account of his expedition climaxed in its final paragraphs, where he uttered one of the most famous phrases in reporting history. What did he say?

9) In what country will you find the world's largest newspaper, with a circulation of 14 million?
☐ India
☐ Brazil
☐ Japan

10) In olden times, reporters typed a certain number at the end of every story. What was that number?

11) Who was the first woman to regularly anchor a nightly network newscast?

12) In 1885, a typical newspaper front page contained 12,000 words. How many words fit on a typical front page 100 years later, in 1985?
☐ 17,700
☐ 9,900
☐ 4,400

13) On the TV show "Sex and the City," what was Sarah Jessica Parker's newspaper job?

The birth of journalism

Every culture seeks effective ways to spread new information and gossip.

In ancient times, news was written on clay tablets. In Caesar's age, Romans read newsletters compiled by correspondents and handwritten by slaves. Wandering minstrels spread news (and the plague) in the Middle Ages. Then came ink on paper. Voices on airwaves. Newsreels. Web sites. And 24-hour cable news networks.

Thus, when scholars analyze the rich history of journalism, some view it in terms of technological progress — for example, the dramatic impact of bigger, faster printing presses.

Others see journalism as a specialized form of literary expression, one that's constantly evolving, reflecting and shaping its culture.

Others see it as an inspiring quest for free speech, an endless power struggle between Authority (trying to control information) and the People (trying to learn the truth). Which brings to mind the words of A.J. Liebling: "Freedom of the press is guaranteed only to those who own one."

In the pages ahead, we'll take a quick tour of 600 years of journalism history, from hieroglyphics to hypertext: the media, the message and the politics.

Presses like this were used to print books and newspapers in colonial times. With skill and arm strength, a printer and a "devil" (his assistant) could produce 200 pages an hour.

❝ *To publish a good Newspaper is not so easy an Undertaking as many People imagine it to be. The Author of a Gazette ought to be qualified with an extensive Acquaintance with Languages, a great Easiness and Command of Writing and Relating Things clearly and intelligibly, and in a few words; he should be able to speak of War both by Land and Sea; be well acquainted with Geography, with the History of the time, with the several interests of Princes and States . . .* ❞

Benjamin Franklin, editor of *The Pennsylvania Gazette*

THE RISE AND FALL OF AMERICA'S FIRST NEWSPAPER

Benjamin Harris was a printer who'd been imprisoned in London for his subversive writings. He fled to Boston in 1686, where he wrote a popular spelling primer, ran a successful bookshop — and, in 1690, produced the first and only issue of Publick Occurrences Both Foreign and Domestick.

It was a small newspaper, printed on three pages. The fourth was left blank, so readers could add news, then pass the paper along. But Harris had failed to obtain a printing license. Worse, authorities claimed the paper contained "doubtful and uncertain Reports," including criticism of military policy. So after one issue, the governor shut it down.

EXCERPTS *from Publick Occurrences, Sept. 25, 1690:*

On a sex scandal involving the King of France: France is in much trouble (and fear), not only with us but also with his Son, who has revolted against him lately, and has great reason if reports be true, that *the Father used to lie with the Sons Wife.*

On a disease epidemic: The Small-pox which has been raging in Boston, after a manner very Extraordinary is now very much abated…. The number of them that have dyed in Boston by this last Visitation is about three hundred and twenty…. It seized upon all sorts of people that came in the way of it, it infected even Children in the bellies of Mothers that had themselves undergone the Disease many years ago.

On the first Thanksgiving: The Christianized Indians in some parts of Plimouth, have newly appointed a day of Thanksgiving to God for his Mercy in supplying their extream and pinching Necessities under their late want of Corn, & for His giving them now a prospect of a very Comfortable Harvest.

On war with the Indians (whom Harris calls "miserable salvages"): When Capt. Mason was at Fort Real, he cut the faces and ript the bellies of two Indians, and threw a third overboard in the sight of the French, who informing the other Indians of it, have in revenge barbarously Butcher'd forty Captives of our that were in their hands.

TIMELINE (1400-1800)

The 1400s: Johann Gutenberg invents the printing press around 1440, printing his famous Bible in the 1450s. William Caxton brings the first printing press to England in 1476.

The 1500s: Henry VIII censors printers by issuing a list of prohibited books and forcing all printers to obtain licenses. Authorities arrest printers for sedition and "unfitting worddes."

1609: Europe's first regularly published newspapers emerge: Avisa in Wolfenbüttel (northern Germany) and Relation in Strasbourg.

1610: Weekly newspapers appear in Cologne and Vienna.

1620s: London printers first distribute "corantos" — small pamphlets summarizing foreign news translated from German and Dutch journals.

1644: English poet John Milton publishes his "Areopagitica," an eloquent plea for free speech. His ideas will be recycled a century later by American revolutionaries struggling for greater press freedom.

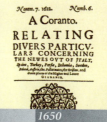

1665: The first true English-language newspaper is printed: twice weekly, the Oxford Gazette prints news of the British court. After 24 issues, it moves to London and becomes the London Gazette.

1690: In Boston, Publick Occurrences tries to become America's first newspaper. It fails.

1600   1625   1650   1675

THE ZENGER TRIAL AND FREEDOM OF THE PRESS

In 1734, when a brash young editor named John Peter Zenger printed accusations of official corruption in his New York Weekly Journal, the angry governor had him arrested for libel. ▼ Zenger's attorney, Andrew Hamilton, argued that citizens have a right to criticize the government, and that libel occurs only when printed words are "false, malicious and seditious." ▼ The jury agreed, and Zenger went free.

MELVILLE E. STONE, *the Chicago publisher who modernized The Associated Press in the early 1900s, on the significance of the Zenger trial:*

The jury took the bit in their teeth and asserted their right to be the sole judges of both the law and the facts. And so it came about that there was a famous revolution in the colonial law. The judge ceased to be the sole arbiter of an editor's fate, and the truth when published from good motives and justifiable ends became an adequate defense for the journalist brought to bar. For the first time in the world's history, the freedom of the press, so far as such freedom was consistent with public rights, was established. The seed which John Milton had sown a century before, when he wrote his famous plea for "unlicensed printing," had come to fruition. Gouverneur Morris said this verdict was "the dawn of that liberty which afterward revolutionized America."

QUOTED

"The question before the court is not just the cause of the poor printer. No! It may in its consequence affect every freeman on the main of America. It is the best cause; it is the cause of Liberty… the liberty both of exposing and opposing arbitrary power by speaking and writing Truth."

Andrew Hamilton,
during the Zenger trial, 1735

J O I N, or D I E.

THE FIRST NEWSPAPER CARTOON

When Ben Franklin ran this editorial cartoon in his Pennsylvania Gazette in 1754, the snake symbolized the American colonies, which needed to unite in self-defense against the French and Indians. It later symbolized the colonies in their fight for independence from the British, and the design was incorporated into the nameplate of the influential Massachusetts Spy (see story below).

Franklin had begun his career as an apprentice on his brother's paper, the New England Courant. He became a witty writer and a bold editor; his Gazette was lively, popular and profitable. "If all printers were determined not to print anything till they were sure it would offend nobody," he said, "there would be very little printed."

"Advertisements are now so numerous that they are very negligently perused, and it is therefore become necessary to gain attention by magnificence of promises and by eloquence sometimes sublime and sometimes pathetick. Promise — large promise — is the soul of advertising. The trade of advertising is now so near perfection that it is not easy to propose any improvement."

Dr. Samuel Johnson,
The London *Idler*, 1758

PATRIOTISM, PROPAGANDA AND THE REVOLUTIONARY WAR

In 1765, the British Parliament imposed a heavy tax on all printed matter: the Stamp Act. Editors protested noisily, and colonists united in forcing a repeal of the tax. That further weakened Britain's control of colonial printers.

As the revolutionary debate heated up, editors grew bolder, exerting political influence and exhorting military action. Objectivity disappeared. Loyalist editors were driven out of business, while patriot editors filled their papers with news of rebellion and commentary such as Thomas Paine's "Common Sense."

One of the most notable journalists of his time, Isaiah Thomas was a master printer and an articulate agitator. When he began publishing The Massachusetts Spy in 1770 it was nonpartisan, but by 1775 Thomas was demanding independence from England. His account of the Battle of Lexington (at right), reprinted in newspapers throughout the colonies, was a mix of outstanding reporting and persuasive propaganda.

ISAIAH THOMAS

EXCERPTS *from The Massachusetts Spy, May 3, 1775:*
Isaiah Thomas launches his eyewitness report on the Battle of Lexington with this: Americans! Forever bear in mind the BATTLE of LEXINGTON! — where British troops, unmolested and unprovoked, wantonly, in a most inhuman manner, fired upon and killed a number of our countrymen, then robbed them of their provisions, ransacked, plundered and burnt their houses! Nor could the tears of defenseless women, some of whom were in the pains of childbirth, and cries of helpless babes, nor the prayers of old age, confined to beds of sickness, appease their thirst for blood or divert them from their DESIGN of MURDER and ROBBERY!

From Thomas's description of the battle:
… The commanding officer accosted the militia, in words to this effect, *"Disperse, you damn'd rebels! Damn you, disperse!"*
Immediately one or two officers discharged their pistols, which were instantaneously followed by the firing of four or five of the soldiers. … They fired on our people as they were dispersing, agreeable to their command, and we did not even return the fire. Eight of our men were killed and nine wounded. The troops then laughed, and damned the Yankees, and said they could not bear the smell of gunpowder.

"Were it left to me to decide whether we should have a government without newspapers, or newspapers without a government, I should not hesitate a moment to prefer the latter."

Thomas Jefferson,
1778

1704: The first successful American newspaper, The Boston News-Letter, is published.

1729: Ben Franklin takes over The Pennsylvania Gazette, making it the boldest and best paper in the colonies.

1765: The Stamp Act forces all papers to display an official British government seal — and to pay a tax that raises prices 50 percent. After violent protest, the act is repealed.

1776: The Declaration of Independence first appears publicly in the Pennsylvania Evening Post and is reprinted in 20 other colonial newspapers.

1783: The Pennsylvania Evening Post, a thrice-weekly, increases its frequency to become America's first daily newspaper.

1700   1725   1750   1775

Throughout the 1700s: Mailmen on horseback ("postriders") play a key role in delivering news and newspapers to editors and subscribers all across New England.

1735: Freedom of the press is strengthened in the colonies when John Peter Zenger, jailed for libel by a New York governor after printing harsh criticism, is acquitted.

1791: The Bill of Rights provides that "Congress shall make no law… abridging the freedom of speech or of the press."

MORE ON **SEDITION AND LIBEL** ▶ 139

MORE ON **PRESS RIGHTS** ▶ 136

News in the 19th century

Technical advances and brilliant ideas forged a new style of journalism.

It was a century of change, and newspapers changed dramatically. The typical newspaper of 1800 was an undisciplined mishmash of legislative proceedings, long-winded essays and secondhand gossip. But by 1900, a new breed of editor had emerged. Journalism had become big business. Reporting was becoming a disciplined craft. And newspapers were becoming more entertaining and essential than ever, with most of the features we expect today: Snappy headlines. Ads. Comics. Sports pages. And an "inverted pyramid" style of writing that made stories tighter and newsier. ▼

The key changes in the 19th century:

◆ *The emergence of the penny press.* In the 1830s a new kind of newspapering emerged, aimed at the interests of the common citizen: local news, sports, human-interest stories about real people and, above all, crime.

◆ *Innovations in printing.* Cheaper paper and faster presses made news affordable and available like never before, especially to America's growing urban population.

◆ *The rise of the modern newsroom.* The biggest and best newspapers hired and trained reporters to cover news in a professional way.

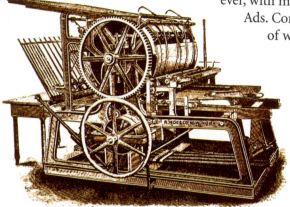

By the 1830s, steam-powered presses could produce 4,000 pages per hour, printing on both sides of long paper rolls. Such technical advances made newspapers cheaper — and thus, more affordable to the masses.

THE PENNY PRESS: MARKETING MEDIA TO THE MASSES

Most colonial newspapers were printed on small presses in small numbers for educated readers. But when Benjamin Day began selling the New York Sun for a penny a copy in 1833, he pioneered the idea of "mass media." As Day put it, the penny press "lay before the public, at a price well within the means of everyone, all the news of the day."

Within two years, the Sun was the top-selling paper in the U.S. with a circulation of 20,000 — encouraging other editors to imitate and improve the format.

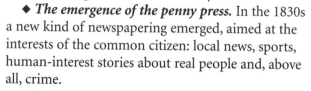

ORDINARY NEWSPAPERS	THE PENNY PRESS
Papers cost 6 cents apiece, usually by subscriptions delivered in the mail.	Papers cost just a penny apiece, usually bought from paperboys on the street.
Political commentary, trade statistics, poetry, letters, secondhand gossip.	Lots of local news, crime coverage, human-interest stories, features.
News is reprinted from government documents and correspondents — or lifted from other newspapers.	Reporters cover a variety of beats: Wall Street, churches, society, sports, and most significantly, crime.
Editors move slowly in responding to events; news is often old and stale.	Editors aggressively compete for and promote big breaking stories.
Promote one political party's agenda.	Independent of any political party.
Funded by political parties or subscribers.	Funded by street sales and advertising.

TIMELINE (1800-1900)

1800: 20 dailies and more than 1,000 weeklies publish in the U.S.

Missouri Gazette.

1825: The New York Advertiser installs the first "cylinder" press in America, allowing faster printing on bigger sheets of paper.

1830s: Editors use homing pigeons and the Pony Express to deliver news from distant points.

1847: Frederick Douglass begins publishing The North Star, an influential paper dedicated to fighting slavery and bringing news to black Americans.

1800

1808: The Missouri Gazette becomes the first paper printed west of the Mississippi as printers accompany settlers into the expanding frontier.

1820

1827: Reporters from three newspapers become the first Washington correspondents, providing Congressional coverage that continues to this day.

1830

1833: The New York Sun becomes the first successful penny paper published in the U.S.

1840

1844: The telegraph is used for the first time to transmit news, making long-distance reporting possible.

MORE ON **THE INVERTED PYRAMID** ▶ 38

BENNETT CRAFTS A NEW STYLE OF JOURNALISM

BENNETT

James Gordon Bennett was a terrific writer and a brilliant publisher. He launched the New York Herald in 1835 with little money and no staff — but by midcentury, the Herald was the biggest newspaper in the world thanks to enterprising reporting, sensational stories and innovative new ideas: interviews, reviews, letters to the editor, money pages, society columns, sports stories, special "extra" editions.

In Bennett's words: "It is my passion, my delight, my thought by day and my dream by night, to conduct The Herald, and to show the world and posterity that a newspaper can be made the greatest, most fascinating, most powerful organ of civilization that genius ever dreamed of."

EXCERPT from The Herald, April 11, 1836:

When a prostitute known as Helen Jewett was murdered, Bennett visited the crime scene. On the front page of the Herald, he provided a description that enthralled readers and helped usher in a new era of sensational reporting:

"Here," said the Police Officer, "here is the poor creature."

He half uncovered the ghastly corpse. I could scarcely look at it for a second or two. Slowly I began to discover the lineaments of the corpse as one would the beauties of a statue of marble. It was the most remarkable sight I ever beheld — I never have, and never expect to see such another. "My God," exclaimed I, "how like a statue! I can scarcely conceive that form to be a corpse." The perfect figure — the exquisite limbs — the fine face — the full arms — the beautiful bust — all surpassed in every respect the Venus de Midici, according to the casts generally given of her....

For a few moments I was lost in admiration at this extraordinary sight — a beautiful female corpse that surpassed the finest statue of antiquity. I was recalled to her horrid destiny by seeing the dreadful bloody gashes on the right temple, which must have caused instantaneous dissolution.

THE GOLDEN AGE OF YELLOW JOURNALISM

As New York's population exploded, the city became the nation's media center. It was an age of publishing legends such as Horace Greeley, the liberal, crusading social reformer, and Henry Raymond, who strove to make his New York Times the most objective and well-written paper of its era.

But two editors rose above the rest in a fascinating struggle for power and influence: Joseph Pulitzer (The World) and William Randolph Hearst (the New York Journal). Both men reshaped American journalism in the late 1800s with a style of newspapering known as "yellow journalism," taking its name from the Yellow Kid, the first color comic, which ran in both the Journal and the World.

What characterized yellow journalism? Loud headlines. Sensational stories on sin and sex. Lavish use of pictures, often faked. Sunday supplements full of crowd-pleasing comics and features. Crusades. Publicity stunts. And rumors disguised as news — such as those that led to war with Spain.

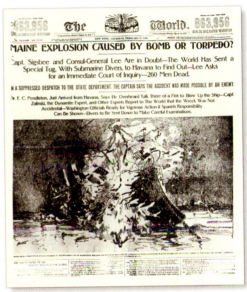

HEARST, PULITZER AND THE SPANISH-AMERICAN WAR

The excesses of yellow journalism reached a climax as Hearst's Journal battled Pulitzer's World for supremacy in New York. Hearst spent millions in family fortune to hire away Pulitzer's top staffers, and he used his genius for sensationalism to concoct bigger, bolder stories. When The World sent correspondents to Cuba in 1896 to dramatize the rebels' fight for freedom ("Blood in the fields, blood on the doorsteps, blood, blood, blood!" one wrote), Hearst dispatched staffers of his own, famously messaging one artist: "You furnish the pictures and I'll furnish the war."

Hearst and Pulitzer inflamed readers, pressured politicians — and the day after a Navy battleship exploded in 1898, they published the two competing pages shown above. War was declared, and circulation skyrocketed. On Page One, Hearst's paper asked, "How do you like the Journal's war?"

In the words of E.L. Godkin, editor of the more restrained, more responsible Evening Post: "It is a crying shame that men should work such mischief simply in order to sell more papers."

1851: Henry J. Raymond founds The New York Times, which becomes one of America's most responsible and respected newspapers.

1867: Emily Verdery Bettey becomes the first woman reporter on a New York paper.

1867: First practical typewriter patented.

1876: Alexander Graham Bell invents the telephone; within seven years, telephone lines will connect New York and Chicago.

1886: Reporters start earning bylines in daily newspapers on the East Coast.

1898: Yellow journalism reaches its heights (or rather, depths) as Hearst and Pulitzer trump up war with Spain.

50 | 1860 | 1870 | 1880 | 1890

1857: Harper's Weekly, the first illustrated paper in America, makes its debut.

1861–1865: For the first time, hundreds of reporters cover a big event: the Civil War. Filing bulletins and stories via telegraph forces reporters to use a tighter writing style that becomes known as "the inverted pyramid."

1878: E.W. Scripps begins building the first newspaper chain; he eventually owns 18 papers.

1880: First photograph printed in a newspaper (of rocks and buildings, right) in the New York Daily Graphic.

1897: The term "public relations" is used, for the first time, by a railroad company.

News in the modern age

Radio and television brought an end to newspapers' media monopoly.

WALTER CRONKITE *recalls announcing the death of President John F. Kennedy on CBS, Nov. 22, 1963:*
I was doing fine . . . until it was necessary to pronounce the words: *"From Dallas Texas, the flash — apparently official. President Kennedy died at 1 p.m. Central Standard Time — a half-hour ago."* The words stuck in my throat. A sob wanted to replace them. A gulp or two quashed the sob, which metamorphosed into tears forming in the corners of my eyes. I fought back the emotion and regained my professionalism, but it was touch and go there for a few seconds before I could continue.

Why? Ask yourself: Which did you look at first — this gray column of text or that dramatic image of Walter Cronkite to the left?

That's basically why, as the century progressed, newspapers surrendered their supremacy: The competition was just too appealing. First came radio, wooing listeners with sound and music. Then movie newsreels added faces to the voices in the news. By 1950, television mesmerized viewers (and advertisers) with sights, sounds and unbeatable immediacy. As the century ended, a new rival emerged: online news via the Internet.

So how did newspapers respond?

◆ *Tighter writing.* Flowery, long-winded prose gave way to a briefer, newsier writing style.

◆ *Better formatting.* Papers became sectioned by topic (sports, features, business), with more columnists, features, calendars and listings.

◆ *Improved design.* Papers ran stronger headlines, bigger photos, more color and graphics.

◆ *Corporate consolidation.* To survive, most big-city newspapers were sold to national chains.

PULITZER SPREADS HIS CRUSADING INFLUENCE

PULITZER

In the years after 1900, Joseph Pulitzer transcended yellow journalism to create a more lasting legacy: He became the model of a passionate, public-spirited modern publisher. His paper, The World, launched courageous crusades against corruption in government and business. Before he died in 1911, he funded one of the first schools of journalism, at Columbia University. And to encourage journalistic excellence, he established the Pulitzer Prizes.

JOSEPH PULITZER's *journalistic credo:*
Our Republic and its press will rise or fall together. An able, disinterested, public-spirited press, with trained intelligence to know the right and courage to do it, can preserve that public virtue without which popular government is a sham and a mockery. A cynical, mercenary, demagogic press will produce in time a people as base as itself. The power to mould the future of the Republic will be in the hands of the journalists of future generations.

When the Pulitzer Prizes were first awarded in 1917, the journalism categories included only reporting, editorial writing and public service. Today, prizes are awarded in 21 different categories.

TIMELINE
(1900-2000)

1900: Satirical political cartoons become a popular way for newspapers to comment on current events.

1920: KDKA-Pittsburgh begins broadcasting the first regular radio schedule.

1926: As radio enjoys growing popularity, the NBC radio network is formed; CBS will begin broadcasting a year later.

1934: The Associated Press begins transmitting wire photos.

1941: FDR declares war on Japan as the largest radio audience in history listens in.

1900   1910   1920   1930   1940

1901: Marconi sends the first radio signal across the Atlantic Ocean.

Early 1900s: The era of "muckrakers" — social reform-minded journalists and magazine writers who expose injustice, fraud and political corruption in government and big business.

1923: Henry R. Luce launches Time magazine, the nation's first newsweekly.

1938: "CBS World News Roundup" debuts; its influential news coverage will make it America's longest-running radio news show.

1939: NBC and CBS begin commercial television broadcasts.

A sniper shot and killed President John F. Kennedy on the streets of Dallas Friday. A 24-year-old pro-Communist who once tried to defect to Russia was charged with the murder shortly before midnight.

Kennedy was shot about 12:30 p.m. Friday at the foot of Elm Street as the Presidential car entered the approach to the Triple Underpass. The President died in a sixth-floor surgery room at Parkland Hospital about 1 p.m., though doctors say there was no chance for him to live after he reached the hospital.

The Dallas Morning News,
Nov. 23, 1963

Man stepped out onto the moon tonight for the first time in his two-million-year history.

"That's one small step for man," declared pioneer astronaut Neil Armstrong at 10:56 p.m. EDT, "one giant leap for mankind."

Just after that historic moment in man's quest for his origins, Armstrong walked on the dead satellite and found the surface very powdery, littered with fine grains of black dust.

The Washington Post,
July 21, 1969

RADIO RULES THE AIRWAVES

In 1920, only a handful of hobbyists heard the first radio broadcasts. But by 1927, 30 million Americans tuned in to celebrate aviator Charles Lindbergh's homecoming. Radio was entering its golden age.

Though powerful publishers at first prevented stations from broadcasting news, radio soon became the first medium to provide a 24-hour stream of news coverage. During World War II, dramatic reporting by legendary newsmen like Edward R. Murrow helped hone the modern newswriting style: concise wording, short sentences, dramatic delivery.

AMERICA TURNS ON AND TUNES IN TO TELEVISION

After World War II ended, Americans began buying televisions — 1,000 sets a day. But in those early years of network TV, programming was primarily devoted to entertainment (Milton Berle and "I Love Lucy"). Ratings for newscasts were disappointingly low.

Television journalism came of age in the 1960s. In 1963, America sat spellbound for four days watching nonstop coverage of the Kennedy assassination. To many critics, it was television's finest hour. And ever since, viewers worldwide have become dependent upon television to cover big breaking stories.

MEANWHILE, BACK AT THE NEWSPAPER...

As the century progressed, newswriting became more focused on facts and less on sensationalism. Shorter sentences and tight writing replaced the flowery prose of the past. Reporters were trained to use the inverted pyramid, a story structure that stacks the big facts first, the lesser facts later.

As the century progressed, newspapers became more readable, more colorful, more objective and more timely than ever before. But their power and prominence gradually faded (along with the attention spans of most Americans.) As you can see in the chart at right, newspapers are no longer Americans' first, or favorite, source of news.

In the 1990s, as computers invaded American homes, a new medium emerged: the Internet. And with each passing day, more and more users now turn

EDWARD R. MURROW *reporting live during the Battle of Britain, Sept. 22, 1940:*
There's an ominous silence hanging over London. Out of one window there waves something that looks like a white bedsheet, a window curtain swinging free in this night breeze. It looks as if it were being shaken by a ghost. There are a great many ghosts around these buildings in London. The

MURROW

searchlights straightaway, miles in front of me, are still scratching that sky. There's a three-quarter moon riding high. There was one burst of shellfire almost straight in the Little Dipper. There are hundreds and hundreds of men . . . standing on rooftops in London tonight, waiting to see what comes out of this steel-blue sky.

LEON HARRIS, *CNN anchor, reporting live, Sept. 11, 2001:*
You are looking at this picture — it is the twin towers of the World Trade Center, both of them being damaged by impacts from planes. We saw one happen at about maybe nine minutes before the top of the hour, and just a moment ago, so maybe 18 minutes after the first impact, the second tower was impacted with a — by another — what appeared to be, another passenger plane. In fact, we've got some tape replay of that. Do we have the tape available right now?

Here is the tape. . . . Incredible pictures. These happened just moments ago.

SURVEY: WHERE AMERICANS GET THEIR NEWS

Minutes Americans spend per day:	**1994**	**2004**
Watching TV news	38	32
Reading a newspaper	19	17
Listening to radio news	17	17

Where Americans say they got news yesterday:	**1994**	**2004**
Watched TV news	72	60
Read a newspaper	49	42
Listened to radio news	47	40
Went online for news	-	24

Source: The Pew Research Center, 2004

to the World Wide Web for news — reading text, viewing video, participating interactively — leaving newspapers to wonder: How do we keep readers interested in ink on paper? Or are we doomed to become dinosaurs?

1952: CBS News coins the word "anchorman." NBC launches the first magazine-format TV program, the "Today" show.

1960: Only 2,000 people owned television sets in 1945; now 90% of American homes have a TV.

1974: President Nixon resigns following dogged investigation of the Watergate scandal by The Washington Post's Woodward and Bernstein.

1982: USA Today makes its debut, shocking the news establishment with shorter stories and bold colors.

950   1960   1970   1980   1990

1963: TV news comes of age with its coverage of the Kennedy assassination; 96% of homes with televisions watch an average of 32 hours of coverage.

Late 1960s: Anti-war and anti-establishment underground newspapers spring up in U.S. cities and on college campuses.

1976: The Apple II becomes a popular home computer; Nintendo starts to sell computer games.

1980: Media mogul Ted Turner launches the Cable News Network (CNN), the planet's first 24-hour news channel.

1990s: The Internet wires the planet; laptop computers, digital cameras and modems allow reporters to file stories and photos from anywhere in the world.

The STUDENT JOURNALISTS' NEWS ATTITUDE SURVEY

In the next chapter, we'll explore how journalists define news — and whether the American public agrees with them. But before we go any further, let's find out how YOU use the news and how you feel about the news media's performance.

Answer the questions below as honestly as you can. (There are no right or wrong answers, of course.) We've given this survey to more than 500 journalism students across the country. And on page 284, you can see how your responses compare to all the rest.

1) I think news stories usually:
☐ Get the facts straight
☒ Contain inaccuracies and distortions

2) I prefer to get my news:
☐ By watching pictures or video footage, with audio narration
☐ By reading printed text
☒ Through a combination of text and images

3) Generally, I think the government:
☐ Should do more to restrict what the news media publish
☒ Should do as little as possible to restrict what the news media publish

4) The president is assassinated. What would you be most likely to do? (You can choose more than one):
☐ Turn on the TV, then leave it on constantly to monitor the situation as intensely as possible.
☒ Turn on the TV, see what's happening, then turn it off and get on with my life.
☐ Track developments online by monitoring news Web sites.
☐ Buy a newspaper as soon as I saw one that had a big assassination headline.
☐ Listen to radio news and talk shows.
☐ Avoid the news as much as possible to escape the annoying hype and overkill.

5) Which of these people do you consider to be journalists? (Check all that apply):
☒ Bill O'Reilly   ☐ Rush Limbaugh
☒ Bob Woodward   ☒ Katie Couric
☐ Oprah Winfrey   ☐ Jon Stewart

6) In general, the news is biased in favor of:
☐ Conservatives
☐ Liberals
☒ Neither

7) If you heard conflicting versions of a news story, which version would you most likely believe?
☐ The local newspaper
☐ The local TV news
☒ The national TV news
☐ Radio news
☐ An independent Web site

8) Which of these adjectives would you generally use to describe most news today? (You can select more than one):
☐ Boring   ☐ Entertaining
☐ Useful   ☒ Sensationalized
☒ Depressing   ☒ Negative

9) How often do you generally watch TV news?
☐ Daily   ☐ Occasionally
☒ Several times a week ☐ Never

10) How often do you generally read newspapers?
☐ Daily   ☒ Occasionally
☐ Several times a week ☐ Never

11) How often do you generally read news online?
☐ Daily   ☒ Occasionally
☐ Several times a week ☐ Never

12) A news reporting career seems like it would be (check all that apply):
☐ Fun   ☐ Frightening
☒ Frustrating   ☒ Important

CONFIDENTIAL SOURCES

Public officials or whistleblowers often slip reporters controversial information secretly — *off the record* — to avoid getting into trouble. In exchange for this information, reporters promise to conceal the identities of these anonymous sources.

In extreme cases, however, a story may trigger a criminal investigation. A reporter could be ordered to testify, to tell a judge the name of his or her confidential sources.

Suppose this happened to you. What would you do? If you reveal your source's name, you break your promise. You expose your source to legal or professional harm. In the future, your reporting ability may be compromised because other sources will distrust you; your colleagues and your news organization may be discredited, too.

BUT if you refuse to name your source, you could hamper a criminal investigation. You could be shielding a lawbreaker. And the judge could send you to jail for days — *weeks* — until you cooperate.

What would you do?

☐ As a reporter, I'm obligated to protect my sources, even if it means going to jail.
☐ As a citizen, I'm obligated to honor and obey the legal system and comply with the judge's request.
☒ It would depend on the circumstances of the case.

WHICH OF THESE STATEMENTS DO YOU MOST AGREE WITH? CHECK EITHER "A" OR "B"; LEAVE BLANK FOR "NEITHER."

☐ **a)** I prefer to read, watch or listen to news that's presented with an attitude, even if it's opinionated, because it makes the topics more interesting.
☒ **b)** I prefer to read, watch or listen to news that is as neutral and objective as possible. I resent it when journalists inject their own opinions into stories.

☒ **a)** I could easily go for weeks without reading any news.
☐ **b)** I couldn't go a day without reading any news.

☐ **a)** Journalists are too critical of public figures and government policy.
☒ **b)** Journalists don't do enough to challenge public figures and expose governmental problems.

☐ **a)** I can usually relate to most news stories I read, see and hear.
☒ **b)** I generally feel that most news stories have little relevance to my life.

☒ **a)** The news media don't do enough to explain the important issues of the day.
☐ **b)** The news media do a good job explaining the important issues of the day; the problem is, people just don't pay enough attention.

☐ **a)** Generally, I prefer to read news about serious issues and major events.
☒ **b)** Generally, I prefer to read celebrity news and lighter, offbeat stuff.

CHAPTER

2

How the newsroom works

Journalism isn't a solo effort. It takes talent, teamwork and training for any news outlet to succeed. Here's a look at the process in detail.

IN THIS CHAPTER:

What is news?

Editors, reporters and readers have asked that question for centuries.

In every newsroom, journalists constantly apply what's called *news judgment:* the ability to determine which stories are most interesting and important to readers.

But which readers? To a 13-year-old boy, the day's biggest story might be the city's new skateboarding ban. To a 70-year-old woman, it might be a new Social Security proposal. The teenager doesn't care about Social Security; the retiree won't read about skateboarding. Whose news interests should prevail?

Take the page at left, for instance. How did those stories get there? Who decided that *those* were the topics most worthy of front-page prominence? Denis Finley, editor of Norfolk's Virginian-Pilot, explains the paper's choices:

1 When the president visits your city, it's a big deal. But it happened in the morning and was all over TV, and we had two big, breaking news stories that day. So we decided to run a photo of Bush that refers to content about his visit on an inside page.

2 A tragedy involving a police officer will almost always lead our newspaper. A public servant who sacrifices his or her life should be honored. Readers instinctively wonder if they're safe while they empathize with the family and friends of the murdered officer.

3 Oceana is the largest jet base on the East Coast, responsible for at least 12,000 local jobs. A base-closing commission ordered the city to condemn homes around the base, but now the city says "No way!" A great example of aggressive, urgent local news reporting.

4 Dick Cheney's chief of staff is indicted. Wow: high-level shenanigans. On most days, this story would lead the paper, but since other stories are more important, interesting and relevant to our readers, the Libby story is played in the lower portion of the page.

5 These are promos to other stories — on the avian flu, falling gas prices and an upcoming election guide — that teach readers something, watch out for their interests and give them something to talk about. And to be useful to our readers, we remind them to set their clocks back to mark the end of daylight-savings time.

So here you see one of the basic facts of life for news reporters: *They* do the research and *they* write the stories, but it's their *editors* who ultimately decide how successful they are — and where their stories run.

Presidential visit

The Virginian-Pilot
SATURDAY, OCTOBER 29, 2005 · 146TH YEAR · NO. 349 · 50 CENTS

Norfolk officer shot to death

COUNCIL WON'T SUPPORT TAKING OCEANA HOMES

Cheney aide, indicted in CIA leak case, steps down

WHO IS LIBBY?

SUSPECT STILL ON THE LOOSE, CONSIDERED ARMED THREAT

2nd recent fatality among local police

ONE ACCOUNT

STILL AT LARGE

IN THE LINE OF DUTY

SPECIAL REPORT

How much should I worry about the threat of avian flu?

COMING SUNDAY
Ready to cast your ballot?

Cheaper gas!

Fall back

THIS JUST IN: MAN BITES DOG!

When Olavi Velkanmaa was attacked by a wolf, he bit back.

Velkanmaa, 33, was opening a workshop last week in a small Finnish town north of Helsinki when he came upon a large male wolf. As the beast lunged at his throat, Velkanmaa grabbed its head. They wrestled for about 10 minutes.

"I was fighting for my life," Velkanmaa said. "I saw its throat and went for it with my teeth, but the wolf's paw got in the way and I bit it instead."

The wolf took off, leaving Velkanmaa with cuts, minor bites — and the taste of warm wolf blood in his mouth.

— The Associated Press

NEWS BY THE NUMBERS I

Percentage of Americans who say they prefer news about serious issues and major events: **63**

Who say they prefer crime and celebrity news: **24**

Percentage who think the media are out of touch with average Americans: **48**

Percentage of stories in a typical newspaper about government or politics: **25**

Percentage of Americans under 30 who have little or no interest in politics: **42**

Percentage of journalists who say they often avoid running stories readers think are important, but dull: **77**

Who say they sometimes ignore stories because readers might find them too complex: **52**

Percentage of Americans who find the news depressing: **84**

Who find the news negative: **77**   Who find the news sensational: **58**

— See page 312 for sources

NEWS BY THE NUMBERS II

"News Arithmetic," from a 1932 editing textbook by George C. Bastian and Leland D. Case:

1 ordinary man + 1 ordinary life = **0**
1 ordinary man + 1 extraordinary adventure = **NEWS**
1 ordinary husband + 1 ordinary wife = **0**
1 husband + 3 wives = **NEWS**
1 bank cashier + 1 wife + 7 children = **0**
1 bank cashier − $100,000 = **NEWS**
1 chorus girl + 1 bank president − $100,000 = **NEWS**
1 man + 1 auto + 1 gun + 1 six-pack = **NEWS**
1 man + 1 wife + 1 fight + 1 lawsuit = **NEWS**
1 ordinary man + 1 ordinary life of 79 years = **0**
1 ordinary man + 1 ordinary life of 100 years = **NEWS**

WHAT'S NEWS? THAT DEPENDS ON THE NEWSPAPER

The New York Times runs "All the News That's Fit to Print," but what fits in one paper may not fit in another. Here's how three mythical Mudflap papers might decide which of these eight stories to run:

STORM WARNING: Dangerous winds and heavy rain are forecast here tonight.
COUNTY FAIR: Pigs! Pies! Polka! The Mudflap County Fair starts this weekend.
TUITION HIKE: Mudflap College will raise classroom fees 10 percent next year.
VOLLEYBALL BILL: Congress passes a bill making Friday National Volleyball Day.
FLU SHOTS: Flu season is coming. Vaccinations now available for senior citizens.
MEXICO BUS CRASH: 30 children are killed as a bus plunges off a cliff in Nogales.
GIRL SCOUT COOKIES: A Mudflap girl breaks the state's cookie sales record.
LOTTERY WINNER: A Mudflap College student wins $90,000 in the state lottery.
EMINEM SEX CHANGE: A celebrity-gossip Web site reports Eminem had surgery.

KEY
👍 YES, RUN IT
👎 NO, DON'T
❓ IT VARIES

THE METROPOLITAN DAILY

We've got lots of pages to fill with a wide range of topics — from local to global, from briefs to long analyses. Here's how our editors would usually vote:

THE STORY	👍	👎	❓	COMMENTS
STORM WARNING	✓			Readers really love scary weather stories.
COUNTY FAIR	✓			Can we find a nice human-interest photo story?
TUITION HIKE	✓			No surprise; run it on the Metro section front.
VOLLEYBALL BILL		✓		Meaningless ceremonial baloney.
FLU SHOTS	✓			Good consumer story for the health/local page.
MEXICO BUS CRASH			✓	Use it only if there's room in "World Briefs."
GIRL SCOUT COOKIES			✓	Maybe; can we make this profile cute enough?
LOTTERY WINNER		✓		Jackpot's not big or juicy enough to be a story.
EMINEM SEX CHANGE		✓		Wait until someone TRUSTWORTHY reports it.

THE COMMUNITY WEEKLY

We have limited space and a tight regional focus — local people, local sports, issues that affect local readers. Here's how our editors would usually vote:

THE STORY	👍	👎	❓	COMMENTS
STORM WARNING			✓	We're a weekly, but we'll monitor any damage.
COUNTY FAIR	✓			Let's go whole hog. Add extra inside pages, too.
TUITION HIKE		✓		Daily paper covered it; nothing new to add.
VOLLEYBALL BILL		✓		Cheesy public-relations stunt.
FLU SHOTS	✓			Good consumer story; possible Page One.
MEXICO BUS CRASH		✓		Sorry, we don't run international news.
GIRL SCOUT COOKIES	✓			Will make an adorable profile, with photo.
LOTTERY WINNER		✓		People win lottery jackpots all the time.
EMINEM SEX CHANGE		✓		None of us have ever heard of this guy.

THE TWICE-WEEKLY CAMPUS PAPER

Space is very tight, and stories focus almost exclusively on campus culture, student sports and academics. Here's how our editors would usually vote:

THE STORY	👍	👎	❓	COMMENTS
STORM WARNING		✓		With our printing schedule, we can't do weather.
COUNTY FAIR		✓		No thanks, unless ag students are involved.
TUITION HIKE	✓			Strong student interest; aim for Page One.
VOLLEYBALL BILL		✓		Nobody cares, not even volleyball players.
FLU SHOTS			✓	How soon until shots are available to students?
MEXICO BUS CRASH		✓		Not even juicy enough for our "World Briefs."
GIRL SCOUT COOKIES		✓		This is SO not interesting.
LOTTERY WINNER	✓			Appealing campus human-interest feature.
EMINEM SEX CHANGE		✓		Can't run it, but we'll e-mail it to all our friends.

WHAT MAKES A STORY INTERESTING TO READERS?

Everybody's different — and what's fascinating to you might be *boooring* to me. Still, these values figure most prominently in stories that qualify as "news":

IMPACT: Does the story *matter* to readers? Will it have an effect on their lives or their pocketbooks? The bigger the consequences, the bigger the story needs to be.

IMMEDIACY: Has this story just happened? Is it about to happen? Timeliness is crucial, especially when you're competing against other media.

PROXIMITY: How close is this story? Obviously, events close to home will matter more to readers than events in other cities, states or countries . . . usually.

PROMINENCE: Does this story involve a well-known public figure or celebrity? If so, readers are bound to be more interested or curious.

NOVELTY: Is something new, odd or surprising going on? (Did a man bite a dog?) Readers enjoy news that's intriguing and unexpected.

CONFLICT: Is there a clash of power? A political battle? A sports rivalry? Reporters are constantly on the lookout for dramatic stories to tell.

EMOTIONS: Does this story make us sad? Happy? Angry? Readers respond emotionally to human-interest stories that are poignant, comical or inspiring.

WANT TO TRY A SIMILAR NEWS JUDGMENT EXERCISE? **TEST YOURSELF** ▶ 32

What readers want

You might write terrific stories, but they're worthless if nobody reads them.

So what do readers want? The answers vary at every publication — and those answers determine whether you should emphasize breaking news or thoughtful analysis. Serious issues or lighter features. Politics or entertainment. Objectivity or opinion. Meat or fluff.

Some journalists stubbornly insist that only *they* know what's best for readers (*Here, eat this. It's good for you*). Giving readers what they want is sometimes dismissed as "pandering." That attitude, unfortunately, is what dooms inflexible, unresponsive publications to extinction.

Smart journalists adjust to the tastes, reading habits and news appetites of their readers. And as new media transform the news media, it's essential to monitor how effectively you're delivering your message and satisfying your audience. After all, it's *their* publication . . . not yours.

SO HOW DO WE KNOW WHAT READERS READ?
1. WE ASK THEM.
2. WE WATCH THEM.

Several decades ago, publishers grew concerned about stagnant newspaper circulation, or "dwindling market share," in media jargon. They began hiring market-research consultants to study readers and determine what might sell more newspapers. (In those days, reliable data about reader habits was rare.) As circulation continued to decline, more and more research was commissioned — and today, it's common for large media companies to employ their own research staff, monitoring readers through:

FOCUS GROUPS: Readers convene in small groups (six to 12 people) to discuss and debate a publication. A moderator guides the conversation while editors observe via camera or one-way mirror.
Advantages: You hear ordinary people exchange opinions about what you're doing right and wrong; it's a good way to test new ideas and prototypes.
Disadvantages: A handful of people may not accurately reflect the majority view. Worse, one or two loudmouths can sway everyone else's opinions.

PHONE, MAIL AND WEB SURVEYS: Researchers compile a series of questions (*How often do you read this publication? Which topics are most important to you?*), then mail questionnaires or conduct phone interviews with respondents who have been selected and screened to ensure the survey's accuracy.
Advantages: Data can be quite detailed; the more questions are asked, the more comprehensive the findings. Results are generally reliable and accurate.
Disadvantages: Respondents do lie ("Yes, I always read editorials"). And editors often don't know what to do with statistical results. Suppose 39 percent of your readers want more crime coverage. Is that a mandate? Or a minority?

MONITORING DEVICES:
Cameras embedded in computer screens track users' eye movements as they read Web pages (above). Cameras can monitor readers' eyes as they scan newspaper pages, too.
Advantages: The eyes don't lie. We can *see* what people actually read.
Disadvantages: The testing occurs in unnatural conditions, which pressures readers to read differently than they might if they were outside the lab.

OTHER WAYS TO GAUGE READER RESPONSE:
◆ **Ethnography.** Acting much like anthropologists, researchers study the habits and rituals of media consumers (often observing them in the field) to learn what, where, when and especially *why* readers read what they read.
◆ **Sales/Web views.** It's simple math: Track which papers sell more than others, or which Web pages generate more hits.
◆ **Reader response.** Monitor phone calls, e-mails and letters to the editor in response to topics and stories (both pro and con).
◆ **Anecdotal feedback.** It's not always trustworthy, but reporters rely on word of mouth to gauge which stories strike a chord with sources, friends and colleagues.

FASHION CORNER

Update Spring Wardrobe on Budget

A revealing page from a reader survey at a Nebraska paper, showing how people often skip over text to view reader-friendly bullet items instead.

HOW TO CONDUCT A QUICK, CHEAP AND UNSCIENTIFIC READER SURVEY

STEP 1: Recruit 10 to 20 volunteers. (The more people you enlist, the more reliable your survey will be.) Aim for a representative mix of readers: by age, gender, lifestyle, etc.

STEP 2: Ask your volunteers to read the next issue of your paper as they would typically do — but tell them to circle everything they read with a dark felt-tip pen as they go through the paper. That may mean just a headline, a photo caption or the first two paragraphs of a story. (By "reading," we mean *tracking words in a meaningful way,* not just *glancing.*)

STEP 3: Ask your recruits to do this for several issues of the paper. If you're a daily, have them read for a week; if you're a weekly, ask them to read for a month. When they're done, have them return the papers to you.

STEP 4: Mark each pile so you know who's who (i.e., "25-year-old female grad student"). Then ask: What did they consistently read? What *didn't* they read? What topics or story treatments had the most (or least) success? Identify patterns and problems. Make changes. Then try another survey.

5 THINGS EVERY REPORTER NEEDS TO REMEMBER ABOUT READERS

1 READERS ARE IN A HURRY

The average reader spends just 26 minutes a day with a newspaper, according to recent surveys by the Readership Institute, a media research center at Northwestern University.

And when they cancel their subscriptions, the reason readers most frequently give is this: *I just don't have time to read a newspaper.*

"Readers use a wide variety of media," says Mary Nesbitt, the Readership Institute's managing director, "and there is a finite amount of time in their day. There is no dearth of news and information, but there is a dearth of time.

"You are competing for their attention, so stories need to be clear, focused and to the point."

2 READERS HAVE SHORT ATTENTION SPANS

"Nine times out of 10, readers prefer short stories to long stories," Nesbitt says, "and they rarely read past the jump."

Why? They're impatient. They're dog-paddling in a sea of information, much of it meaningless. They're distracted, too: According to a 2003 study, 74 percent of Americans regularly watch TV *and* read the newspaper at the same time.

It's frustrating to admit it, but many readers just can't seem to process long, complicated stories. So what's a reporter to do?

"Start with the idea that the story will be short, then think about whether something longer is needed," says Michele McLellan, director of Tomorrow's Workforce, a newsroom training center. "Journalists often get this backward."

3 READERS WANT STORIES THAT PERSONALLY CONNECT

"Readers want to see themselves in the newspaper," McLellan says. Unfortunately, though, "newspapers focus heavily on the power structure and that means middle-aged, white, male, official perspectives dominate."

That's why successful reporters craft stories that focus on *you*, the reader, instead of *them*, those politicians and strangers *over there.*

"Institutional stories — stories about the actions of city council, the planning commission or the school board, for instance — are ignored," Nesbitt says, "unless the reporter makes it clear why it really matters.

"People like to feel smarter about things that matter to them, not necessarily what *you* think should matter to them. Understand what people really care about, and then in your work help them to smarten up."

Readers want news that's both as *local* and as *personal* as possible.

HOW TO READ THE NEWSPAPER FASTER

Tips from Esquire magazine

For news stories, read the first three paragraphs. Or read slate.msn.com's Today's Papers, a quick summary of what's in the major newspapers.

For feature stories (trends and profiles), skip the anecdote at the start and go straight to the third or fourth paragraph — what journalists call the "nut graph" — which sums up the article in a couple sentences.

For movie reviews, go straight to the last paragraph. Or visit rottentomatoes.com, which compiles dozens of reviews and distills them into an easy-to-digest rating.

For the gossip page, scan for the bold-faced names.

4 READERS WANT STORIES TOLD IN A COMPELLING WAY

Dry, detailed summaries of news events are a staple of journalism, but if that's all you give readers — an endless parade of facts, paragraph after paragraph after paragraph — you'll sap all their stamina.

Given a choice, readers generally prefer *stories*: real narrative dramas starring real people. Research shows that feature-style writing — with more personality, more *why should I care* attitude — often has more appeal than standard, "inverted pyramid"-style newswriting. ▼

Readers will always want solid, accessible facts. If you're smart, though, you'll develop a versatile repertoire of reporting approaches.

"Readers respond to a variety of story forms," Nesbitt says. "If a story can be more effectively told with a bulleted list, a series of photos, a Q-and-A format or a graphic, so be it."

5 THERE'S MORE THAN JUST ONE TYPE OF READER

Some readers are hard-core news junkies. Others are casual browsers. Some love long, in-depth profiles. Others hate them. Some read the paper simply out of fear that they'll miss something and feel left out of conversations. (Researchers call them "anxiety-driven" readers.)

Can you please everybody? No. But keep your ideas fresh. Keep your topics diverse. Stay out of ruts.

And remember, readers who call or write to say your story offended or enthralled them *do not necessarily* speak for the majority. So don't let random criticism intimidate you; don't let flattering fan mail steer you into safe, predictable formulas.

MORE ON **THE INVERTED PYRAMID** ▶ 38   MORE ON **FEATURE AND NARRATIVE WRITING** ▶ 118

How a story gets written

News events can occur suddenly and unexpectedly — and when they do, you can't always predict where they'll lead. Here's an example of one such story, another thrilling newsroom adventure from the files of...

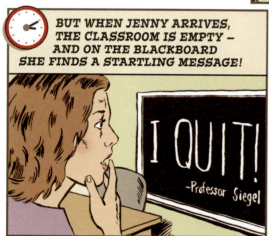

JENNY TALKS TO DR. HUGH LYON SACK, THE PROFESSOR TAKING OVER SIEGEL'S CLASSES.

DR. SIEGEL IS A BRILLIANT SCHOLAR. I'LL DO MY BEST TO FILL HIS BIG SHOES.

BUT OFF THE RECORD? I HEARD HE GOT A FEMALE STUDENT PREGNANT. I CAN'T SAY ANY MORE.

IN THE HALLWAY, JENNY INTERVIEWS TWO GRAD STUDENTS WHO HAD WORKED CLOSELY WITH DR. SIEGEL.

THE **REAL** REASON HE LEFT WAS THAT HE WAS ABOUT TO BE FIRED FOR SEXUALLY HARASSING ONE OF HIS STUDENTS! WHAT A **PIG!**

WELL, I THOUGHT HE WAS THE **BEST TEACHER** I EVER HAD! I WOULDN'T BE GOING TO MED SCHOOL IF IT WEREN'T FOR DR. SIEGEL.

BACK IN THE NEWSROOM, JENNY KICKS AROUND THE STORY WITH HER EDITOR.

SO HAS ANY STUDENT FILED A HARASSMENT COMPLAINT AGAINST SIEGEL?

NONE THAT I KNOW ABOUT. AND ALL CAMPUS OFFICES **CLOSED** AT FIVE O'CLOCK!

LET ME CALL DR. SIEGEL ONE MORE TIME.

NO COMMENT? OK, WHAT ABOUT THE RUMORS THAT YOU'RE QUITTING TO AVOID HARASSMENT CHARGES?

CLICK!

RATS! HOW CAN I WRITE A STORY WHEN I'M MISSING SO MANY FACTS?

JUST WRITE UP WHAT YOU'VE GOT! LET'S **GO!** I'M SAVING A 4-INCH HOLE FOR YOU ON PAGE ONE!

SO WITH 20 MINUTES UNTIL DEADLINE, JENNY TYPES HER NOTES INTO A STORY.

LISTEN, JENNY -- I CUT OUT THAT REFERENCE TO SEXUAL HARASSMENT. UNTIL WE GET OFFICIAL CONFIRMATION, IT'S JUST AN UNFOUNDED **RUMOR!**

OK, CHIEF. BUT SAVE ME SPACE TOMORROW — I'M COMING BACK WITH THE **REST** OF THE STORY!

SO WHAT DID JENNY LEARN TODAY?

1. YOU OFTEN SPEND 90 PERCENT OF YOUR TIME CHASING A STORY, AND JUST 10 PERCENT WRITING IT.

2. NOT EVERYTHING A REPORTER HEARS MAKES IT INTO THE FINISHED STORY.

3. NOT EVERYTHING IS WHAT IT SEEMS. IN THIS CASE, IT TURNS OUT DR. SIEGEL ACTUALLY QUIT BECAUSE

By **JENNY DEADLINE**
Epitaph staff reporter

After two decades in biology classrooms, Dr. Harris Siegel ended his campus career today with two words scrawled on a blackboard: "I QUIT."

Siegel's sudden resignation caught both students and colleagues by surprise.

"I'm shocked and saddened," said Dorsey Stevens, head of the biology department. "Dr. Siegel was a valued member of our faculty for 20 years, and we will not be the same without him."

In a letter sent to Stevens Monday morning, Siegel explained that "for personal reasons, I must resign effective immediately, in order to spend more time with my family."

Contacted by The Epitaph Monday afternoon, Siegel refused further comment, ~~leaving some students to speculate that he had quit to avoid facing a sexual harassment complaint.~~

Students say they'll miss Siegel. "He was the best teacher I ever had," said graduate student Heather Lewis. "I wouldn't be going to med school if it weren't for Dr. Siegel."

Dr. Hugh Lyon Sack will step in to teach Siegel's classes the rest of the term. "I'll do my best to fill his big shoes," Sack said.

HE'D JUST WON $5,000,000 IN THE LOTTERY!
COULD DR. SIEGEL HAVE SUED THE PAPER FOR PRINTING THOSE RUMORS? SHOULD JENNY HAVE DONE ANYTHING DIFFERENTLY?

How the news comes together

It's like an assembly line where workers race the clock to produce a new product each day.

Editors and reporters call it "the daily miracle." And it *does* seem miraculous that despite blizzards, computer meltdowns, editing screwups, power outages and press jams, the newspaper gets printed and delivered day after day, year after year — sometimes century after century. Take The Oregonian, for instance. It's Portland's only daily newspaper and one of the biggest papers in the nation (with a daily circulation of more than 350,000).

What does it take to produce a typical issue of the paper? Here's a look at a typical day in the life of a big-city newsroom as The Oregonian's 465 editors, reporters, photographers and designers race the clock.

Editor selects stories for Street Final

Coordinating desk fields phone calls

Reporter checks sources

News teams plan day

Feature staff plans stories

Reporters and photographers cover incidents

Graphics artist builds maps and charts

6 A.M.
The first editor arrives and begins selecting stories to run in the Street Final edition, which prints at noon for downtown street sales.

7 A.M.
Editors on the coordinating desk field phone calls and sort obituaries. The newspaper publishes 200 obits a week.

8 A.M.
After ingesting large amounts of coffee, editors check wires for stories. Police reporters check sources for overnight news.

9 A.M.
News teams gather to plan the day's news coverage. The editorial board meets to discuss the day's issues.

10 A.M.
Top newsroom editors meet to assess the day's news and begin planning Page One. Reporters call sources and go into the field to cover stories.

11 A.M.
Wire editors begin choosing the top national and world news stories. Feature staffers hold planning sessions to develop future projects. ▼

NOON
Reporting continues. Many reporters remain in the newsroom making phone calls or finishing stories they've previously researched.

1 P.M.
Graphic artists build maps and charts for both news stories and special projects. In the features section, page designers work days in advance on section fronts.

2 P.M.
Reporters update their editors and team leaders, who compile summaries of stories planned for the next day's paper (called "budgets").

INSIDE THE NEWSROOM AT THE OREGONIAN

The Oregonian's news department employs 465 staffers, including 124 reporters, 59 copy editors, 26 team editors and 20 photographers. Most staffers work downtown; dozens more work in small bureaus in the suburbs. Wire services provide most of the world and national news, although the paper also has two reporters covering politics in Washington, D.C.

REPORTERS AND EDITORS

The newsroom is divided into teams based on topics or geography, such as:

Family & Education	Business
City Life	Sports
Crime & Justice	Living

Within each team, reporters are often assigned to beats. The Crime & Justice team, for instance, has beats for prisons, federal court, night cops and family violence.

When a reporter files a story, it first goes to an editor on his or her team, who checks it for accuracy, organization and fairness.

COPY EDITORS AND PRESENTATION

Once stories are edited, they're sent on to copy editors and designers. Copy editors check stories for grammar, spelling and punctuation, add headlines, and then send everything to the presentation team, where designers have laid out the stories — with any additional photos, captions and graphics — on the page.

EDITORIAL BOARD

The 15-member editorial department works independently of the newsroom — on another floor of the building, actually — to produce the paper's opinion pages. The editorial staff writes editorials that present the newspaper's views on current events, selects letters to the editor and edits guest opinion columns. The paper also employs an editorial cartoonist.

PHOTO AND GRAPHICS

After returning from their assignments, photographers review their work and make prints — or rather, printouts, since most of their images are now digital. With the help of photo editors, they select and process the best photos for the newspaper. These are digitally sent to the presentation team for layout.

Nearly a dozen graphic artists receive information from editors and reporters with which they build charts, graphs, maps and other graphic elements to accompany stories (like the illustrations on this page).

MORE ON **PLANNING PACKAGES** ▶ 126

THE MAJOR DIVISIONS AT A DAILY PAPER

Like reporters always do, we've been focusing our attention on the *newsroom*. But all news organizations — whether they're newspapers, TV stations or Web sites — depend on other departments for their survival.

Two-thirds of The Oregonian's employees work outside the newsroom to help produce and deliver the paper each day, selling ads, driving trucks, balancing the books and running the press.

Here's a quick rundown of what goes on in other parts of the building while *you're* busy writing stories.

THE ADVERTISING DEPARTMENT

The Oregonian's staff of 293 works in several key areas:

Classified ads. More than 100 people process ads for real estate, cars, jobs, pets, etc.

Retail and display ads. Nearly 100 employees sell display ads (the ads that run below and beside news stories).

Advertising services. These staffers help clients write, edit and design their ads.

THE PRODUCTION DEPARTMENT

This is where 379 people transfer the words and pictures of news and advertising onto paper:

Camera and composing. These workers prepare pages for printing, turning them into negatives.

Plate making. This crew turns those negatives into plates that are mounted on the press.

The press. These 136 staffers operate the printing press and bundle papers for delivery.

THE CIRCULATION DEPARTMENT

The 155 employees in this department work night and day to distribute the newspaper, recruit new subscribers and respond to calls from customers.

Delivering the paper is their most important job. And most of those papers go to subscribers. (Only about 18 percent of The Oregonian's 350,000 daily papers are sold in street racks and stores.) Most of the deliveries are handled by independent contractors who drive trucks, run distributorships and supervise the carriers who deliver papers to people's homes.

3 p.m. news meeting

Editors pick top stories

Presentation team designs pages

Last deadline for stories, photos and graphics

Editing of stories, photos and graphics

Copy editor checks stories

Slot editor reviews copy editing

Makeup editor checks wires before going home

3 P.M.
The newsroom's top editors meet again to review the day's news and discuss how to treat (and where to run) the day's biggest stories. Copy and layout editors begin editing stories and designing news pages.

4 P.M.
Most reporters are now back in the newsroom, writing to meet a 6 p.m. deadline. Top editors meet one last time to solve last-minute problems and make their final story selection for the front page.

5 P.M.
News reporters continue turning in their stories. Photographers are making final decisions on photos. Meanwhile, the copy desk edits all wire stories.

6 P.M.
This is the deadline for reporters to send their stories to editors (though front-page stories have until 6:30). It's also the deadline for sending photos to the presentation team, where pages are designed.

7 P.M.
Copy editors review stories for accuracy, grammar and style. ▼ Then they add headlines and photo captions. Slot editors finish checking the work of copy editors by 7:45.

8 P.M.
The presentation team sends the last of its pages to composing for the first edition. The presses start rolling at 8:30. This edition is then delivered statewide.

9 P.M.
This is the deadline for getting copy and photos to the presentation team for the second edition, which rolls at 10:30.

10 P.M.
Reporters race to meet the 10:30 deadline for the Sunrise edition (the main morning paper) that prints at 11:45.

11 P.M.
All the editors and reporters have headed home. One makeup editor remains until 1 a.m., checking the wires for late-breaking news.

Information adapted from a timeline prepared by The Oregonian and illustrated by Steve Cowden.

MORE ON **EDITING** ▶ **52** AND **STYLE** ▶ **54**

Who's who in the newsroom

Newspapers are like armies. They need clear lines of authority to avoid chaos.

Like armies, they have powerful generals who call the shots (editors and publishers) while the ground troops (reporters and photographers) rush onto the battlefield. And like armies, newspapers depend on teamwork for their survival. Getting stories assigned, written, edited and published requires a group effort.

So who does what? Journalistic job descriptions vary from paper to paper, depending upon the size of the staff. At a small paper, there's more overlap between jobs. Reporters might find themselves interviewing the mayor one minute, shooting his photo the next, and then designing that story for the front page. At big metro dailies, jobs become more specialized. You might spend years writing only fashion stories, while down the hall someone does nothing but review films.

Still, it all begins with reporters tracking down news. At most papers, writers are either:

◆ *General assignment reporters* who cover a wide range of stories, from chasing breaking news to pursuing tips from sources or editors; or

◆ *Beat reporters* who cover a specific topic: politics, crime, education, sports, movies. Most reporters at most publications are assigned to beats, because that's the most efficient way to ensure coverage of every major news event.

This organizational chart shows the hierarchy in a typical midsized newsroom. The actual number of desks may vary, but the overall system is one that's worked for decades at publications big and small.

THE PUBLISHER
The ultimate boss. Presides over all departments to ensure profitability.

PRODUCTION MANAGER
Oversees the staff and equipment that get the newspaper printed on time.

CIRCULATION MANAGER
Supervises the distribution of the paper for subscribers and street sales.

ADVERTISING MANAGER
Coordinates the sales and production of classified and display ads

THE EDITOR
Runs the newsroom. Has the final say in story selection and news philosophy.

Outside the newsroom, these three departments ensure that the paper gets printed and distributed. The ad staff, in particular, generates the revenue that pays the newspaper's bills. These managers usually have equal clout and report directly to the publisher.

MANAGING EDITOR
Oversees the day-to-day operation of the newsroom; resolves staffing issues.

These editors have equal clout in the newsroom and usually report to the managing editor.

PHOTO EDITOR
Coordinates photo assignments and chooses images to run in the paper.

ONLINE EDITOR
Works with other editors and reporters to develop material for Web site.

COPY DESK CHIEF
Oversees the editing (and at many papers, the layout) of all stories in the paper.

FEATURES EDITOR
Assigns and edits all the stories running in the paper's feature section.

SPORTS EDITOR
Assigns and edits all the stories running in the paper's sports section.

CITY EDITOR
Assigns and edits most of the paper's local "hard news" stories.

These staffers have equal status in the newsroom and report to their department editors.

PHOTOGRAPHERS, GRAPHIC ARTISTS
Photographers shoot photos; artists create graphics or design pages.

REPORTERS & EDITORS
Enhance or expand news stories for presentation on newsroom Web site.

COPY EDITORS
Edit text of stories; write headlines and photo captions; lay out pages.

FEATURE WRITERS & REVIEWERS
Write stories about lifestyles and entertainment; critics write reviews.

SPORTS REPORTERS
Write stories about local teams; at big dailies, they cover national events.

NEWS REPORTERS
Write stories about government, crime, local people, regional events.

ANOTHER SMART OPTION: CREATING A TEAM SYSTEM

There's a major downside to the organizational chart above. The biggest group of news reporters is clumped in one corner of the newsroom, often reporting to just one city editor. On a big paper, that becomes inefficient. It can lead to bottlenecks, power struggles and gaps in local coverage.

In much the same way, the photo staff is often clumped in another corner of the newsroom, off by themselves, while the copy editors all sit together in their corner of the newsroom. That doesn't always promote collaboration and harmony.

One solution? Reorganize staffers into teams. Some big newsrooms have eliminated the city desk and reassigned reporters to teams organized by topic: the government team. The crime team. The sports team. And so on.

Some teams have their own photographers. Bigger teams — the entertainment team, for instance — may have their own photographers, copy editors and designers. The advantage? Staffers learn to work together as a unit, from brainstorming ideas to designing the finished page.

MORE ON **COVERING BEATS** ▶ 90   AN AMUSING LIST OF **UNUSUAL BEATS** ▶ 29   HOW NEWSROOMS WORK FOR **BROADCAST JOURNALISTS** ▶ 164

LIFE AT A SMALL WEEKLY:

Scott Byers, *The N'West Iowa Review*

Scott Byers, 35, is sports editor of the N'West Iowa Review (circulation 5,600). Byers is one of 10 staffers in a newsroom that produces the Review and two other weekly publications (the Sheldon Mail-Sun and an entertainment tabloid).

So what do you do each week?

Primarily writing, quite a bit of editing, contributing to the layout and design. I do the headline writing. I've done photography before, but really, I only do that in a pinch.

How many stories a week do you write?

During peak season — I counted it up one week this summer, when we were doing baseball and softball — I did 106 game stories.

WHAT?? How is that possible?
Organization. *(Laughs.)*

Does it bother you that journalists at weeklies get less respect than, say, journalists at The New York Times?

Absolutely. My assumption is that a lot of them have never been in this situation, so they can't really understand how much work there is, and how much you're on your own. Whereas *there*, it seems you get a lot more help and a lot more time per story

I would argue that, if it's done right, a small-town paper offers you the opportunity to write better stories than you would at a big paper because you have more freedom — you're not restricted by any corporation that tells you "this has to look *this* way," or "this is the formula for how we write things." You're really allowed to use all of your skills.

What's the best thing about working at a small paper?

Total control. I have absolute and total control over everything that goes on in sports, basically. The owners know me and trust me, and they know I know what I'm doing, so pretty much anything I want to do, I can do.

And there's no one looking over my shoulder. I make my own hours; I'm here when I wanna be, I'm gone when I wanna be. As long as it gets done before deadline, it doesn't seem to matter to anyone.

What's the downside to working at a small paper?

You have to do it all yourself. There'll be weeks where you have to write 106 stories. *(Laughs.)* I mean, I *can* do it, but nobody likes to be that busy.

What's the most fun part of your job?

I get to sit around and talk to people about sports all day and get paid for it. I absolutely love sports.

LIFE AT A BIG DAILY:

Susan Page, *USA Today*

Susan Page, 54, first started covering the White House and national politics in 1980. She is now the Washington bureau chief for USA Today (circulation 2.3 million).

How often do your stories run in the newspaper?

If I'm on a news event like we just had — the Republican national convention — I'll write three or four stories a week. But as a general rule, I don't write that often. I might write one or two stories a week, and sometimes I'll work on a story that'll take several weeks to do. But I can say with confidence that there's never been a week when I wrote 106 stories.

USA Today is a huge operation. Do you like working in a newsroom that big?

I do. I like working for a newspaper that has a lot of impact. When you write a story, it gets read across the country. I like that I write for a newspaper that's delivered every day to the driveway of my mother's home outside Wichita, Kansas.

My whole career, I've covered the White House and national politics, where hundreds of reporters cover the same stories I do. And at USA Today, I can cover that area in a way that's different from what everyone else is doing. I try to do stories that connect the dots in a way that other people haven't, or that challenge the conventional wisdom. And to do those stories requires time and resources. Many times, I do stories that involve polling,

and our polling editor knows more about that than I do. Or database manipulation — our database editor does that better than I can. Or presentation, so a story makes a big splash on the front page, which graphic artists are able to do. It's a collaboration that makes the whole greater than any one of us could do by ourselves. It takes a big paper to support that kind of journalism.

Is your job fun?

Yeah, it's great. I really love everything about it. I love going out to see events. I love interviewing people — man-on-the-street kinds of interviews. I love coming back and trying to write in a way that conveys to a reader everything I saw, that's engaging and accurate. And I like going to headquarters and seeing the paper put together at night: the people doing the layout, choosing the pictures. I really feel so fortunate to do something that I like so much. There's just not another thing I'd rather do.

The PRESS ROOM POLL

Results from a survey of the 100 reporters on our Press Room panel:

35% hope to become an editor someday.

42% don't ever want to become an editor.

64% say that in most newsrooms, writing feature stories or sports gets less respect than writing "real" news stories.

17% want the publisher to get involved in the newsroom.

68% want the publisher to stay *out* of the newsroom.

16% believe that most editors are just failed reporters.

77% say they can tolerate loud, ugly ads surrounding their stories because they know newspapers need to make money, but:

70% say they'd rather poke out their own eye with a stick than to write or sell advertising for a living.

62% say that copy editors get the least respect of all newsroom staffers.

68% say that reporters generally work the hardest at small daily papers.
— 24 percent said reporters work hardest at weeklies;
— 8 percent said they work hardest at big dailies.

39% say that reporters generally work harder than anyone else in their newsroom.

90% say that if they had it to do all over again, they'd still become newspaper reporters.

MORE ON **COVERING SPORTS** ▶ 108   MORE ON **COVERING POLITICS** ▶ 106   WHAT DO REPORTERS CONSIDER THE **BEST AND WORST NEWSROOM JOBS?** ▶ 30

What it's called

Want to sound like a reporter? Talk the talk.

When you start writing for a publication, it might be a daily (printed every morning), a weekly (printed, say, every Wednesday) or a newsletter published once a month.

It might be a mainstream newspaper (The New York Times), an alternative publication (The Village Voice) or some specialty publication (Fur & Feather Magazine).

It might be a *broadsheet* (a large-format page, roughly 14 by 22 inches) or a *tabloid* (a format about half that size).

Whatever the publication, your stories will be *spiked* or *killed* if they're unpublishable. If they're too long — if you've written a *thumbsucker* or a *goat-choker* — an editor may *cut* or *trim* a few *grafs* (paragraphs). If a sloppy editor ruins your story, you can moan that it's been *butchered;* if it runs on page 17, you can groan that it's been *buried.*

Yes, it all sounds pretty violent. Want more? Read on.

American news consumers relax at home by reading a **broadsheet** *newspaper.*

American news consumers relax at home by reading a **tabloid** *newspaper.*

THE PARTS OF A STORY

Not all publications use the same jargon, but there's agreement on most terms. Here are some common elements found in a typical story.

BYLINE
The reporter's name, often followed by credentials. Many papers require that stories be a certain length — or written by a staffer — to warrant a byline.

DATELINE
Gives the location of a story that occurred outside the paper's usual coverage area.

LEAD
(also spelled *lede*). The opening of a story. Here, this *news lead* condenses the key facts of the story into the first paragraph.

QUOTE
Someone's exact words, usually spoken to the reporter during an interview.

ATTRIBUTION
A phrase that tells readers the source of a quote OR the source of information used in the story.

Freeway closed as ornery oinker hogs traffic

A pig named Mama falls from a truck and causes commuter chaos

By SUSAN PAYSENO
Staff reporter

PORTLAND — Westbound traffic on Interstate 84 was backed up for nearly five miles early Monday when "Mama," a 600-pound hog on the way to slaughter, fell from the back of a truck.

For two frustrating hours, the sow refused to budge.

Fred Mickelson told police that he was taking six sows and a boar from his farm in Lyle, Wash., to a slaughterhouse in Carlton when Mama escaped.

"I heard the tailgate fall off, and I looked back and saw her standing in the road," Mickelson said with a sigh. "I thought: 'Oh, no. We've got some real trouble now.' "

Mama was "pretty lively and loud" when she hit the ground, Mickelson said, lumbering between cars and causing havoc on a foggy day.

There were no accidents, police said.

After about an hour of chasing the pig with the help of

The Associated Press / KRAIG SCATTARELLA
Highway workers use a loader to lift Mama, a 600-pound sow, onto a truck Monday on Interstate 84. The pig fell from the truck on the way to slaughter.

police, Mickelson began mulling over his options, which included having a veterinarian tranquilize the hog.

About 10 a.m., a crew of highway workers arrived and decided to use a front-end loader to pick up the sow and load her back into the truck.

"That pig was in no hurry to move," said Wally Benson, the highway crew chief. "I think she knew where she was being taken, and she was in no hurry to get there."

Even the police were sympa-

thetic to the pig's plight.

"That pig really honked off a lot of commuters," said trooper Tracy Collins — a vegetarian. "But I was sad to see her go."

Sue Payseno covers traffic and transportation issues in Oregon and Washington. She can be reached at suepayseno@news.com.

"That pig really honked off a lot of commuters."
— **TRACY COLLINS,**
Oregon state police trooper

HEADLINE
The big type, written by copy editors, summarizing the story.

PHOTO
Photos are usually shot by staff photographers, but they can also be bought from national wire services. Photos usually run in black-and-white, since color pages cost more to print.

PHOTO CREDIT
A line giving the photographer's name (often adding the paper he or she works for.)

LIFTOUT QUOTE
(also called a *pullquote*). A quotation from the story that's given special graphic emphasis.

TAGLINE
Contact information for the reporter, enabling readers to provide feedback.

THE PARTS OF A PAGE

Join stories together and you create a full newspaper page. And at most newspapers, no page is more important than Page One, which showcases the most compelling stories and images. Here's a look at the components you might find on a typical front page:

FLAG
This is the one front-page element that never changes: the name of the paper, set in special type.

EDITION
Daily papers often print one edition for street sales, another for home-delivery to subscribers.

INFOGRAPHIC
These *informational graphics* display key facts from the story in a visual way. At big papers, they're created by artists; at smaller papers, they're produced by editors or reporters.

DECK
A subheadline, written by copy editors, that supplements information in the main headline.

TEXT
The actual story. When text is set into columns of type, it's measured in inches. This story runs for about seven inches before it jumps.

JUMP LINE
When a long story is continued on another page, editors run this line to tell readers where the story continues, or *jumps.*

CUTLINE
(also called a *caption).* Information about the photo is often collected by photographers but written by copy editors or reporters.

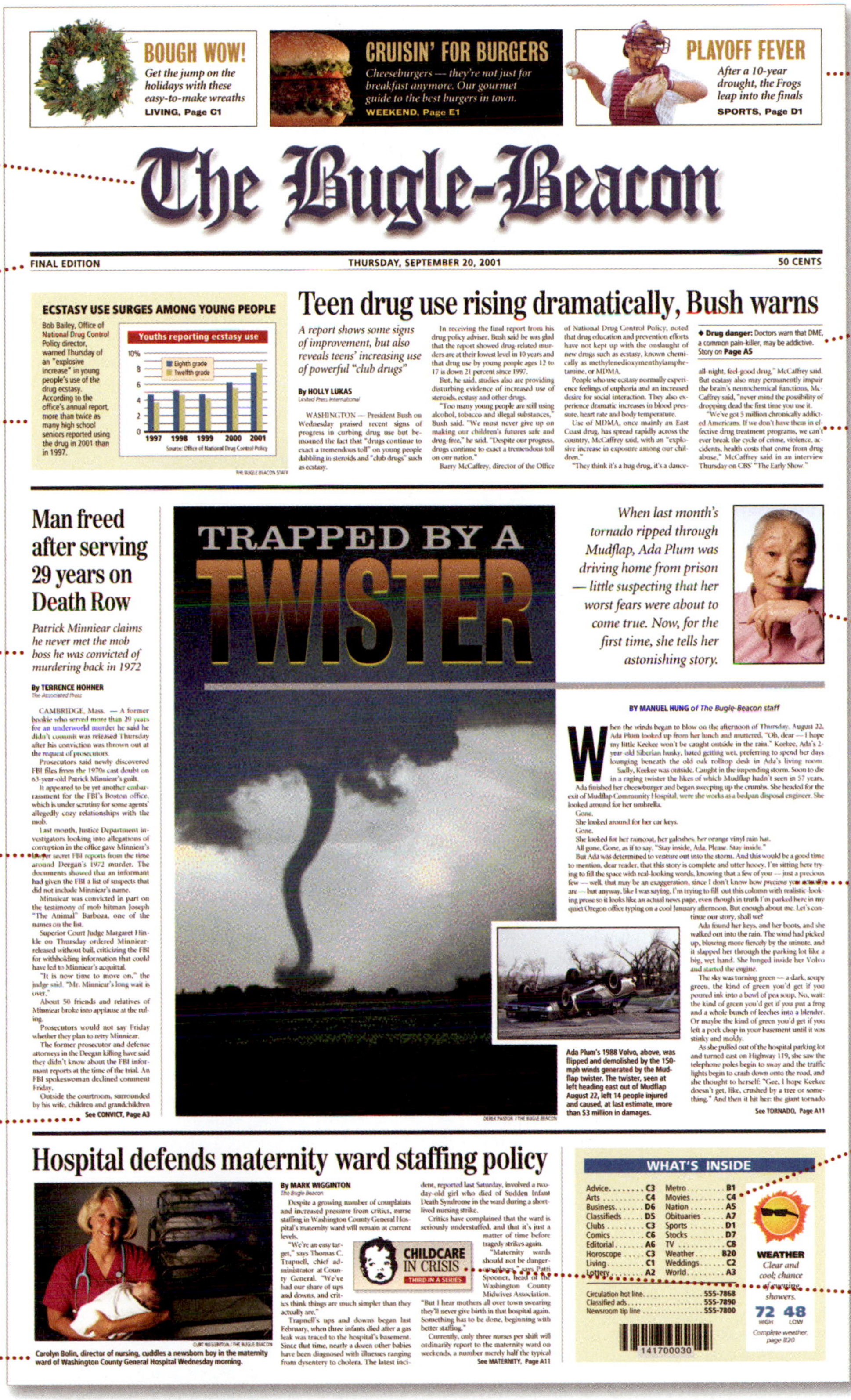

BOUGH WOW! Get the jump on the holidays with these easy-to-make wreaths LIVING, Page C1

CRUISIN' FOR BURGERS Cheeseburgers — they're not just for breakfast anymore. Our gourmet guide to the best burgers in town. WEEKEND, Page E1

PLAYOFF FEVER After a 10-year drought, the Frogs leap into the finals SPORTS, Page D1

The Bugle-Beacon

FINAL EDITION | THURSDAY, SEPTEMBER 20, 2001 | 50 CENTS

ECSTASY USE SURGES AMONG YOUNG PEOPLE

Bob Bailey, Office of National Drug Control Policy director, warned Thursday of an "explosive increase" in young people's use of the drug ecstasy. According to the office's annual report, more than twice as many high school seniors reported using the drug in 2001 than in 1997.

THE BUGLE BEACON STAFF

Teen drug use rising dramatically, Bush warns

A report shows some signs of improvement, but also reveals teens' increasing use of powerful "club drugs"

By HOLLY LUKAS
United Press International

WASHINGTON — President Bush on Wednesday praised recent signs of progress in curbing drug use but bemoaned the fact that "drugs continue to exact a tremendous toll" on young people dabbling in steroids and "club drugs" such as ecstasy.

In receiving the final report from his drug policy adviser, Bush said he was glad that the report showed drug-related murders are at their lowest level in 10 years and that drug use by young people ages 12 to 17 is down 21 percent since 1997.

But, he said, studies also are providing disturbing evidence of increased use of steroids, ecstasy and other drugs.

"Too many young people are still using alcohol, tobacco and illegal substances," Bush said. "We must never give up on making our children's futures safe and drug-free," he said. "Despite our progress, drugs continue to exact a tremendous toll on our nation."

Barry McCaffrey, director of the Office of National Drug Control Policy, noted that drug education and prevention efforts have not kept up with the onslaught of new drugs such as ecstasy, known chemically as methylenedioxymenthylamphetamine, or MDMA.

People who use ecstasy normally experience feelings of euphoria and an increased desire for social interaction. They also experience dramatic increases in blood pressure, heart rate and body temperature.

Use of MDMA, once mainly an East Coast drug, has spread rapidly across the country, McCaffrey said, with an "explosive increase in exposure among our children."

"They think it's a hug drug, it's a dance-all-night, feel-good drug," McCaffrey said. But ecstasy also may permanently impair the brain's neurochemical functions, McCaffrey said, "never mind the possibility of dropping dead the first time you use it.

"We've got 5 million chronically addicted Americans. If we don't have them in effective drug treatment programs, we can't ever break the cycle of crime, violence, accidents, health costs that come from drug abuse," McCaffrey said in an interview Thursday on CBS' "The Early Show."

◆ **Drug danger:** Doctors warn that DME, a common pain-killer, may be addictive. Story on **Page A5**

Man freed after serving 29 years on Death Row

Patrick Minniear claims he never met the mob boss he was convicted of murdering back in 1972

By TERRENCE HOHNER
The Associated Press

CAMBRIDGE, Mass. — A former bookie who served more than 29 years for an underworld murder he said he didn't commit was released Thursday after his conviction was thrown out at the request of prosecutors.

Prosecutors said newly discovered FBI files from the 1970s cast doubt on 63-year-old Patrick Minniear's guilt.

It appeared to be yet another embarrassment for the FBI's Boston office, which is under scrutiny for some agents' allegedly cozy relationships with the mob.

Last month, Justice Department investigators looking into allegations of corruption in the office gave Minniear's lawyer secret FBI reports from the time around Deegan's 1972 murder. The documents showed that an informant had given the FBI a list of suspects that did not include Minniear's name.

Minniear was convicted in part on the testimony of mob hitman Joseph "The Animal" Barboza, one of the names on the list.

Superior Court Judge Margaret Hinkle on Thursday ordered Minniear released without bail, criticizing the FBI for withholding information that could have led to Minniear's acquittal.

"It is now time to move on," the judge said. "Mr. Minniear's long wait is over."

About 50 friends and relatives of Minniear broke into applause at the ruling.

Prosecutors would not say Friday whether they plan to retry Minniear.

The former prosecutor and defense attorneys in the Deegan killing have said they didn't know about the FBI informant reports at the time of the trial. An FBI spokeswoman declined comment Friday.

Outside the courtroom, surrounded by his wife, children and grandchildren

See CONVICT, Page A3

TRAPPED BY A TWISTER

DEREK PASTOR / THE BUGLE BEACON

When last month's tornado ripped through Mudflap, Ada Plum was driving home from prison — little suspecting that her worst fears were about to come true. Now, for the first time, she tells her astonishing story.

BY MANUEL HUNG of *The Bugle-Beacon staff*

When the winds began to blow on the afternoon of Thursday, August 22, Ada Plum looked up from her lunch and muttered, "Oh, dear — I hope my little Keekee won't be caught outside in the rain." Keekee, Ada's 2-year-old Siberian husky, hated getting wet, preferring to spend her days lounging beneath the old oak rolltop desk in Ada's living room.

Sadly, Keekee was outside. Caught in the impending storm. Soon to die in a raging twister the likes of which Mudflap hadn't seen in 57 years.

Ada finished her cheeseburger and began sweeping up the crumbs. She headed for the exit of Mudflap Community Hospital, were she works as a bedpan disposal engineer. She looked around for her umbrella.

Gone.

She looked around for her car keys.

Gone.

She looked for her raincoat, her galoshes, her orange vinyl rain hat.

All gone. Gone, as if to say, "Stay inside, Ada. Please. Stay inside."

But Ada was determined to venture out into the storm. And this would be a good time to mention, dear reader, that this story is complete and utter hooey. I'm sitting here trying to fill the space with real-looking words, knowing that a few of you — just a precious few — well, that may be an exaggeration, since I don't know how *precious* you actually are — but anyway, like I was saying, I'm trying to fill out this column with realistic-looking prose so it looks like an actual news page, even though in truth I'm parked here in my quiet Oregon office typing on a cool January afternoon. But enough about me. Let's continue our story, shall we?

Ada found her keys, and her boots, and she walked out into the rain. The wind had picked up, blowing more fiercely by the minute, and it slapped her through the parking lot like a big, wet hand. She lunged inside her Volvo and started the engine.

The sky was turning green — a dark, soupy green, the kind of green you'd get if you poured ink into a bowl of pea soup. No, wait: the kind of green you'd get if you put a frog and a whole bunch of leeches into a blender. Or maybe the kind of green you'd get if you left a pork chop in your basement until it was stinky and moldy.

As she pulled out of the hospital parking lot and turned east on Highway 119, she saw the telephone poles begin to sway and the traffic lights begin to crash down onto the road, and she thought to herself: "Gee, I hope Keekee doesn't get, like, crushed by a tree or something." And then it hit her: the giant tornado

See TORNADO, Page A11

Ada Plum's 1988 Volvo, above, was flipped and demolished by the 150-mph winds generated by the Mudflap twister. The twister, seen at left heading east out of Mudflap August 22, left 14 people injured and caused, at last estimate, more than $3 million in damages.

Hospital defends maternity ward staffing policy

CURT WIGGINTON / THE BUGLE BEACON

Carolyn Bolin, director of nursing, cuddles a newsborn boy in the maternity ward of Washington County General Hospital Wednesday morning.

By MARK WIGGINTON
The Bugle Beacon

Despite a growing number of complaints and increased pressure from critics, nurse staffing in Washington County General Hospital's maternity ward will remain at current levels.

"We're an easy target," says Thomas C. Trapnell, chief administrator at County General. "We've had our share of ups and downs, and critics think things are much simpler than they actually are."

Trapnell's ups and downs began last February, when three infants died after a gas leak was traced to the hospital's basement. Since that time, nearly a dozen other babies have been diagnosed with illnesses ranging from dysentery to cholera. The latest incident, reported last Saturday, involved a two-day-old girl who died of Sudden Infant Death Syndrome in the ward during a short-lived nursing strike.

Critics have complained that the ward is seriously understaffed, and that it's just a matter of time before tragedy strikes again.

"Maternity wards should not be dangerous places," says Patti Spooner, head of the Washington County Midwives Association. "But I hear mothers all over town swearing they'll never give birth in that hospital again. Something has to be done, beginning with better staffing."

Currently, only three nurses per shift will ordinarily report to the maternity ward on weekends, a number merely half the typical

See MATERNITY, Page A11

CHILDCARE IN CRISIS
THIRD IN A SERIES

WHAT'S INSIDE

Advice	C3	Metro	B1
Arts	C4	Movies	C4
Business	D6	Nation	A5
Classifieds	D5	Obituaries	A7
Clubs	C3	Sports	D1
Comics	C6	Stocks	D7
Editorial	A6	TV	C8
Horoscope	C3	Weather	B20
Living	C1	Weddings	C2
Lottery	A2	World	A3

Circulation hot line	555-7868
Classified ads	555-7890
Newsroom tip line	555-7800

141700030

WEATHER
Clear and cool; chance of evening showers.
72 HIGH 48 LOW
Complete weather, page B20

TEASER
(also called a *promo* or *skybox).* This is designed to grab readers' attention so they'll buy the paper and read this story in the sports section.

REFER
This alerts readers that there's another story on the same topic in another part of the newspaper.

WIRE STORY
A story written by a reporter working for another paper or a national news service, then sent (by wire, in the old days) nationwide.

MUG SHOT
A close-up photo of someone's face. These usually run small — just an inch or two wide.

CENTERPIECE
(also called a *lead story).* Editors decided that this was the top story of the day — either because of newsworthiness or reader appeal — so it gets the best play and the biggest headline on Page One. Notice how this story isn't about a current event; it's a type of feature story called a *follow-up.*

INDEX
One of the last page elements that copy editors produce before sending the paper off to the press.

LOGO
A small, specially designed title (often with art) used for labeling special stories or series.

SO WHO DESIGNS THIS PAGE?

The editors choose the stories and decide which get biggest play. But the actual layout is usually done by a staff designer or copy editor— someone with both design ability and dependable news judgment.

Tools, talent and temperament

A career in journalism can be rewarding and fun, but it's not for everybody.

As a reporter for the New York Herald Tribune put it years ago: "The newspaper business is the only enterprise in the world where a man is supposed to become an expert on any conceivable subject between 1 o'clock in the afternoon and a 6 p.m. deadline."

That's the downside of journalism — but that's its appeal, too. Every day, you learn something new. You meet fascinating people. You get a front-row seat to history, and you never have to dress up, get a license, sell anything or even *know* anything. Just ask a lot of questions and the stories write themselves.

Well, almost.

So what does it take to be a reporter? First, let's go shopping.

THE BASIC HARDWARE: TOOLS EVERY REPORTER NEEDS

In the old days, all you needed was a card that said *PRESS* stuck in your hatband and *presto!* You were a journalist. Nowadays, the standards are higher and the technology is more sophisticated. To be a modern reporter, you need:

NOTEBOOK
Sure, it's the most low-tech tool in your tool-box, but it's also the most essential: cheap, portable, nothing to break, no batteries to fail. Just add a pencil and you're ready to interview anybody, anywhere.
Smart tip: Use only spiral-bound pads; they give you better control as you flip the pages while scribbling notes.
Best bet: Learn speedwriting or shorthand, and you can quote fast talkers much more accurately.

TAPE RECORDER
Why use a tape recorder? As we'll discuss later, you may want to to ensure you quote everyone accurately. You might want to protect yourself from charges that you misquoted somebody. Or maybe you don't want to look too conspicuous while you're reporting a story.
Smart tip: Learn the laws in your state governing taping of conversations.
Best bet: Buy a digital recorder with speech-recognition software and you can convert voices to text as you transfer files to your computer.

COMPUTER
It's hard to imagine anyone who doesn't already use a computer these days. But as a reporter, you'll be plugged in constantly to surf the Internet, send e-mail, take notes and, most importantly, write stories. (And to file reports from the field, you'll use a portable laptop.)
Smart tip: Take a typing class. Once you build up speed, you'll be able to type as fast as you can think — which is *really* handy.
Best bet: Want to make yourself valuable in any newsroom? Get savvy at all kinds of software for page layout, image processing, Web design and video production. (See below.)

CAMERA
At most newspapers, there aren't enough photographs because there aren't enough photographers. So if you want to make your stories more appealing, develop some skill with a camera. Digital cameras are the smartest, simplest option.
Smart tip: Try to carry an extra battery *and* an extra memory card — just in case.
Best bet: Get your newsroom to invest in cameras that shoot video. If the quality's good enough, you can download movies to your publication's Web site.

TELEPHONE
You may think this one is ridiculously obvious. (A *telephone?* Duhhh!) But you would be amazed at the hours you'll spend working the phones once you start reporting full time. A telephone is still the most effective way to pester people for information.
Smart tip: With a cell phone, you can pester people anywhere. (Get the newspaper to supply one; don't use your private line.)
Best bet: Get a cell phone that takes pictures and you can transmit images back to the newsroom. In the not-too-distant future, they may be good enough to run online, or even in print.

AND IF YOU REALLY WANT TO IMPRESS YOUR BOSS...
Imagine a future where cyberjournalists write stories, snap photos and make movies. That future isn't far off. "The people who can shoot video, write stories, do radio on the side, basically do it all — these are the journalists of the future," says John Schidlovsky, director of the Pew Fellowship in International Journalism. So why wait? Start training yourself *now* to be the multimedia reporter of the future.
Smart tip: Shooting video is easy. Editing video is trickier, but just as essential. Learn to use basic editing software so you can tweak what you shoot.
Best bet: Keep abreast of new advances in multimedia storytelling. If you can produce audio, video, animated graphics *and* text, you can get a job anywhere.

QUOTED

"*Journalists should be people in whom there is at least a flicker of hope.*"
Sen. Paul Simon

"*The only qualities essential for real success in journalism are ratlike cunning, a plausible manner and a little literary ability.*"
Nicholas Tomalin,
London Sunday Times writer

"*As I look back over a misspent life, I find myself more and more convinced that I had more fun doing news reporting than in any other enterprise. It really is the life of kings.*"
H.L. Mencken,
legendary journalist

"*A good journalist is a rewarding sight. He must have a zest for events. He must have a dedication to facts and a scent of humbug. He must cultivate skepticism while avoiding cynicism. He must learn to cover causes for which he can have sympathy but must not display loyalty. He must be incorruptible. He must go where he is not wanted, and be resistant to those who are too welcoming. And for all of this, his hours will be long, his pay inadequate, and his standing in the community not particularly high.*"
Thomas Griffith,
Time magazine editor

"*Any idiot can pick up a pen and a notebook and call himself a journalist — and many of them do.*"
Sean Scully,
freelance journalist

"*You go out and meet someone new every day, in a new situation, and they tell you something you've never known before, in a place you've never been. What keeps you alive is the daily surprise. It's a (expletive) joy.*"
Jimmy Breslin,
columnist

GOT WHAT IT TAKES TO BE A REPORTER?

Right about now, you may be seriously asking: *What have I gotten myself into?* But relax. Self-doubt (bordering on panic) is a common occurrence among beginning reporters.

To find out if you have the right stuff to be a journalist — the talent to turn facts into stories *and* the temperament to shove a microphone into a stranger's face — take this test and rate your reporter-osity. Check the appropriate boxes in the left-hand column, then total up your points to see how you scored.

HOW TRUE IS EACH STATEMENT? **TALENT**	HOW TO SCORE YOUR ANSWER	SCORE
1. I enjoy reading. I consume a lot of books and magazines. ☐ MOSTLY TRUE ☐ NOT TRUE	To be a serious writer, you first need to be a serious reader and a student of the craft. *Score 2 pts. if you said* MOSTLY TRUE.	
2. For me, writing is rewarding. And I am confident that people genuinely enjoy the stuff I write. ☐ MOSTLY TRUE ☐ NOT TRUE	The best journalism is a form of creative writing. The most successful reporters enjoy expressing themselves and connecting with readers. *Score 3 pts. for* MOSTLY TRUE.	
3. I don't pay much attention to spelling. My grammar and punctuation probably ain't great, either. ☐ MOSTLY TRUE ☐ NOT TRUE	If you answered "mostly true," it's time to clean up your act. Out in the real world, nobody wants to waste their time fixing the messes you make. *Score 2 pts. for* NOT TRUE.	
4. I'm generally adept at computer technology: sending e-mail, downloading files, shooting digital photos, etc. ☐ MOSTLY TRUE ☐ NOT TRUE	In most newsrooms, you're expected to be computer-savvy. And the more versatile you are, the more successfully you'll be able to adapt and evolve. *Score 1 pt. for* MOSTLY TRUE.	
5. I can organize my ideas and write quickly when I need to. ☐ MOSTLY TRUE ☐ NOT TRUE	If writing is a slow, laborious chore for you, you might consider a career as a tortured poet instead. *Score 3 pts. for* MOSTLY TRUE.	
6. I'd make a good game show contestant because I'm pretty good at remembering facts and trivia. ☐ MOSTLY TRUE ☐ NOT TRUE	Journalism isn't just about writing — it's about gathering and processing lots of information. Not everyone has the knack (or a good memory). *Score 2 pts. for* MOSTLY TRUE.	
7. I'm efficient and self-sufficient when it comes to doing extensive library or Internet research. ☐ MOSTLY TRUE ☐ NOT TRUE	If you become a reporter, you'll be spending *years* of your life doing detective work, searching for files, records and obscure data. It helps if you're good at it. *Score 2 pts. for* MOSTLY TRUE.	

HOW TRUE IS EACH STATEMENT? **TEMPERAMENT**	HOW TO SCORE YOUR ANSWER	SCORE
8. I'm generally more curious than most people I know. ☐ MOSTLY TRUE ☐ NOT TRUE	The best reporters have an insatiable curiosity and a wide range of interests. *Score 3 pts. for* MOSTLY TRUE.	
9. In public situations, I'm pretty shy; I avoid asking questions in class, for instance. ☐ MOSTLY TRUE ☐ NOT TRUE	Reporters need to be bold, aggressive — sometimes even fearless. If you're shy, you can work to overcome it, but the job may be uncomfortable for you. *Score 2 pts. for* NOT TRUE.	
10. I think it's unpatriotic to question or criticize our government. ☐ MOSTLY TRUE ☐ NOT TRUE	It's nice to have respect for authority, but if you're a journalist, it's smarter to be skeptical. Remember, politicians lie. It's their job. Your job is to catch them at it. *Score 1 pt. for* NOT TRUE.	
11. When I choose a career, I'll require a stable, 9-to-5 job where my workday is routine and I make big money. ☐ MOSTLY TRUE ☐ NOT TRUE	Uh-oh. This could be a deal-breaker for you. Reporters work long hours (often at night and on weekends), and the pay's good only at the bigger newsrooms. *Score 3 pts. for* NOT TRUE.	
12. If I really want something, I'm tenacious until I get it. ☐ MOSTLY TRUE ☐ NOT TRUE	If you lack patience and persistence, your reporting career could be very short-lived. *Score 3 pts. for* MOSTLY TRUE.	
13. When I'm under pressure, I can keep my cool and stay focused without losing my temper. ☐ MOSTLY TRUE ☐ NOT TRUE	Journalism is a constant battle against the clock. You're often juggling stories right up until the last minute. You need quick wits and grace under pressure. *Score 1 pt. for* MOSTLY TRUE.	
14. When strangers or teachers criticize what I write, it really bugs me. I mean, who do they think they *are?* ☐ MOSTLY TRUE ☐ NOT TRUE	Being a reporter means rewriting stories to make editors happy — and listening to readers call you a moron. You'll need patience and a thick skin to survive. *Score 2 pts. for* NOT TRUE.	

YOUR TOTAL SCORE

SCORING YOURSELF

30 points: *Congratulations! You were destined to be a journalist. (Or else you lied, which is a heinous thing for a reporter to do.)*
25-30 points: *You're a solid contender for a successful journalism career. You've got the personality and ability a good reporter needs.*
20-25 points: *Journalism is a good fit for you, mostly — but it may require you to change your attitude or improve some skills.*
Less than 20 points: *Think we're grading too harshly? Well, there's a good chance you just won't be happy working in a newsroom.*

AND THE BEAT GOES ON AND ON AND ON...

Not every reporter is cut out to cover hard news. For some of you, covering cops, courts and car crashes may seem like a real *downer.*

Luckily, though, there are lots of newspaper jobs that let you write about the things you enjoy. The San Francisco Chronicle, for example, recently created a sex beat. Get a job in Orlando, and you can work the Disney World beat.

Here's a list of other unusual, intriguing beats gathered from newspapers across the United States:

Shopping malls
Pets
Pro wrestling
Boating
Beer
Wine
Cars and automotive news
Auto racing
Computer games
The porn industry
Death and dying
Golf
Children's books
Book clubs
Weather
Hunting and fishing
Hiking and biking
Gardening
Recreational vehicles
Religion
The environment
Rock music
Classical music
Technology
Children and families
Senior issues
Traffic
Travel
The state fair
Culture, race and diversity
Celebrities and gossip
Military affairs
Gaming
(covering local casinos)
Wal-Mart
(at a paper in Arkansas near Wal-Mart's headquarters)
Olympics
(at a paper in Colorado Springs, home of the U.S. Olympic Committee)

MORE ON **NEWSROOM BEATS** ▶ 90

The PRESS ROOM

ADVICE ON REPORTING AND WRITING FROM VETERAN JOURNALISTS

Welcome to the Press Room, where we turn the tables on journalists by asking THEM the questions. For a complete list of participating panelists, see page 2.

WHAT'S THE BEST JOB IN THE NEWSROOM — YOUR DREAM JOB?

Travel writer: Get paid to see, feel, taste, smell and write about the world's most beautiful and interesting places? Sign me up.

Katy Muldoon, *The Oregonian*

The one I have now: converged reporter, covering a beat for print, TV and online. I get to do everything, except manage. Quite a deal.

Mark Fagan, *Journal-World (Lawrence, Kan.)*

Sports columnist. Are you kidding me? The guys make bank, put their opinion in the paper twice a week and lounge the rest of the time. Plus, they cover all the major sporting events. It doesn't get any easier than that.

Tripp Mickle, *Tahoe World*

I am fairly certain that my job — Metro columnist — is a better fit than OJ's glove. But it is, of course, a living hell of constant, Sisyphean deadlines, irate reader calls and column-idea panic. Be careful with your dreams.

Laura Berman, *The Detroit News*

Full-time outdoor writer. Not only would you get paid to play — fish, hike, hunt, ski, etc. — but there are plenty of opportunities to wade into hard news from public-policy angles and tons of great feature stories related to the tragedy and triumph of the human spirit. Maybe it shows my bias toward outdoor play, but I think you could do everything with this beat.

Kyle Henley, *The Gazette (Colorado Springs, Colo.)*

International reporter for a massive and rich newspaper, able to pick and choose the best stories from all over the world.

Rachel Stassen-Berger, *Pioneer Press (St. Paul)*

Investigative reporter. I enjoy having the freedom to pursue a topic that requires extra effort and expertise. It's also rewarding to be the driving force in making change in people's lives.

Heather Ratcliffe, *St. Louis Post-Dispatch*

Editor, of course. I'd have fewer Federal Reserve and city council stories on 1A; I'd tell my reporters to get out and find quirky, compelling stories about how people *really* live.

John Reinan, *Star Tribune (Minneapolis, Minn.)*

Most will say feature writer. But I say it is the police/courts reporter. I'm fortunate to be doing what I love. You get breaking news, features, meetings/trials, investigative series, excitement and more — all rolled into one beat.

Kimberly Morava, *The Shawnee News-Star (Shawnee, Okla.)*

Special project reporters have the opportunity to dig deep into a story and reflect, outside the pressure of a daily deadline, which makes it the best job in the newsroom by far. Any job that takes you off the treadmill and offers you a chance to think has to be the greatest blessing the gods of journalism can bestow.

Deborah L. Shelton, *St. Louis Post-Dispatch*

WHAT'S THE WORST JOB IN THE NEWSROOM?

I'd hate working on the copy desk because those folks are stuck in the newsroom all day and never meet interesting people.

Heather Ratcliffe, *St. Louis Post-Dispatch*

The job I'd least like to have is crime reporter, which I've already done, thank you very much. It's an extremely important job, obviously. But those cops treat you like crap. You have to have a thick skin.

Deborah L. Shelton, *St. Louis Post-Dispatch*

I think an assistant city editor on a political or city hall beat would suck. In fact, I did it and it did suck. Too much pressure from the top and bottom, no time to reflect and generally bad writers who think they're the Second Coming.

Kim Severson, *San Francisco Chronicle*

Writing obituaries. Get one name wrong (sometimes the family member or the funeral home screws up), and you'll hear about it for days.

Michael Becker, *Journal-Advocate (Sterling, Colo.)*

Overnight editor on the local desk. Horrible hours and numbing routine broken by the terror of huge stories breaking out without anyone at hand to help.

Jerry Schwartz, *The Associated Press*

Editor. It's all tasks, "goal-settings," meetings. You imitate but do not create. You give off heat and light … but so does a trash fire.

Roy Wenzl, *The Wichita Eagle*

Covering courts for a big paper with neurotic editors. No fun getting pulled in a dozen different directions by morons who can't make up their minds.

Judd Slivka, *The Arizona Republic*

Because it's the most difficult job, I vote for city editor. Constant interruptions from reporters and other editors, the need to make quick decisions on coverage and the daily barrage of calls from unhappy or just weird readers make this the toughest task in any newsroom.

Leah Beth Ward, *Yakima Herald-Republic*

Covering the state legislature, because it tends to be the most scrutinized job with the least creative freedom, because editors love taking the trivia of government and forcing it down readers' throats.

Ron Sylvester, *The Wichita Eagle*

The guy who cleans around and under my desk. It really is a landfill of half-used notebooks, old documents and dust-gathering reference books. A mess.

Mark Fagan, *Lawrence (Kan.) Journal-World*

WHAT INSPIRED YOU TO BECOME A REPORTER?

My uncle used to tell me these amazing, compelling, engrossing stories around the campfire. I thought he was the coolest guy ever. Now I get paid to do that every day.

Kevin Pang, *Chicago Tribune*

I never planned on it. In college, I majored in history and even dropped a newswriting course because it was boring. But I still wrote for the college paper and loved seeing *my* written words in print. When I found I could combine the thrill of writing with the ability to ask anyone almost anything, anywhere, I was sold.

Leah Beth Ward, *Yakima Herald-Republic*

I was inspired by the Vietnam War. I believe the American public would have opposed that war from the outset if media had put out better information. That still guides me — giving people information to make decisions about their future.

Rick Bella, *The Oregonian*

I can't do math. I'm horrible, terrible, a disaster with numbers. Journalism seemed to be the only major that didn't require four years of math.

Judd Slivka, *The Arizona Republic*

> **As a young girl, I watched my grandmother read the morning and afternoon newspapers. I asked, why both? Her answer became my goal: "I want to see who tells the better story."**
>
> **Connie Sexton,** *The Arizona Republic*

Here was what was cool about it right away: I, a shy person, had a reason to ask anybody anything. And they would answer!

Jeff Mapes, *The Oregonian*

I decided to become a reporter when I was in the fourth grade. Perhaps it's because I loved writing and grew up on newspapers; my father bought the *Chicago Sun-Times* and *Chicago Tribune* daily. My career plans began to gel when I was in high school. I subscribed to several teen-oriented and women's publications. I never saw people who looked like me, a black woman, in these publications. They didn't speak to my issues and I decided to change that. I settled on newspapering because of Watergate. I just loved the government-watchdog role journalists play and decided I needed to be a part of that.

Toni Coleman, *Pioneer Press (St. Paul, Minn.)*

I'll never forget my reporter father, while covering a coal mine disaster, talking with women making tissue paper funeral flowers. Ever since I was a tag-along toddler, he's been inspiring me.

Bob Batz Jr., *Pittsburgh Post-Gazette* (His father, Bob Batz, is also a feature writer, at the Dayton Daily News)

I was selected to be editor of our Girl Scout Newspaper, a project for some career badge. I was 10, and I loved it. I was much better at that than I was selling cookies.

Jill Barrall, *Hutchinson (Minn.) Leader*

My dad, Jack Kennedy, is a high school journalism teacher and ever since I can remember, I wanted to be just like his student editors. They just seemed so cool to my grade school eyes – there was the gothic girl with the huge black hair and tons of eyeliner, the popular jock, the studious student body president, the freaks, the weirdos and everyone in between. They all flocked to my dad's class, and I did, too.

It must be in the blood: my grandfather was a journalism major, my dad a teacher, my sister and I working journalists. Choosing a different occupation never crossed my mind. And now, at 31, I still look to my dad for advice.

Lesley Kennedy, *Rocky Mountain News (Denver, Colo.)*

WHO'S YOUR JOURNALISTIC HERO?

Edna Buchanan, *Miami Herald*. She brought humanity to cop stories in an accessible way that inspired me to do the same. Following is my favorite lead of hers, about a man shot while in line at a McDonald's:

"Gary Robinson died hungry."

Erin Barnett, *The Oregonian*

Mike Royko. He was funny, fearless and looked out for the powerless. Through his writing, readers learned that the newspaper was on their side. I hope they still feel that way, but I wonder.

Ken Fuson, *The Des Moines Register*

Mike Royko. For humor, grace, outrage, intelligence and his simple, elegant and direct prose.

Don Hamilton, *The Columbian*

Thomas Jefferson, who said that if given a choice between government and no newspapers, and newspapers and no government, he would prefer the latter. His point was that an informed citizenry is more important to a vital democracy than the exact structure of its institutions.

Michael Becker, *Journal-Advocate (Sterling, Colo.)*

Seymour M. Hersh, a man who fearlessly roots out the worst, the hardest stories about the American experience and makes us face the reality. From Vietnam to Iraq, he has been a voice that refuses to be silent when all others are cowed.

Peter Sleeth, *The Oregonian*

David Broder, because in an era of talking-head gas-bag pundits, he remains the political writer that everyone looks to for balanced, insightful coverage.

Jim Camden, *The Spokesman-Review (Spokane, Wash.)*

Don't laugh. My hero is Carl Kolchak, the television character on the 1974-75 show "The Night Stalker."

Kolchak chased down the most wonderful and wild news stories about vampires, werewolves and mummies. I always wanted to do those stories, but unless the mayor sucks some councilman's blood during a city council meeting, or the president of the park district suddenly is seized by the mummy's curse, it ain't going to happen for me.

Here's the clincher: Not one of Carl Kolchak's news stories was ever published. His editor always tore them up at the end of the show and told Carl to go cover something real for a change.

Carl just kept doing what he did without fear or fail. That's the kind of news reporter I want to be when I grow up.

Kevin Harden, *Valley Times (Beaverton, Ore.)*

TEST YOURSELF

Answers to these exercises
are on page 286.

1 WHICH STORY IS MORE NEWSWORTHY?

*Fill in the blank with the word that makes each story more
newsworthy to local readers, and explain your reasoning.*

1. An earthquake struck _____ today, killing at least 50.
   a) Malaysia   b) San Diego

2. The office of _____ was evacuated today after a
clerk opened a letter believed to contain anthrax.
   a) Oprah Winfrey   b) the British ambassador to Egypt

3. Police arrested 20 suspected terrorists in downtown Toronto today _____.
   a) after intercepting suspicious e-mail messages   b) after a three-hour gun battle

4. _____ is being treated at a local hospital.
   a) The governor's son   b) An ebola victim

5. A local policeman died last weekend after _____.
   a) his plane crashed in the Alaska wilderness.   b) he tried to rescue a young boy from drowning.

6. A drunk driver was killed after his car hit a tree _____.
   a) on New Year's Eve   b) on the way to his 100th birthday party

7. Convicted double murderer Arthur Itis escaped from prison _____.
   a) one year ago today   b) last night

8. _____ takes effect at midnight tonight.
   a) A pay hike for state legislators   b) A new local pooper-scooper law

2 WOULD YOU RUN THESE STORIES?

*Not all stories are suited for all news organizations. Take the stories listed below, for instance.
Mark each story with an **A, B, C** or **D** to show whether it's suitable for the following news outlets:*

   A = The Springfield daily newspaper   **C** = The weekly Springfield Community Crier
   B = The Springfield College student radio station   **D** = The Weekly World Enquirer (below)

_____ **1.** Former Yankee legend and baseball Hall-of-Famer Bo Linball died last night in a
Brooklyn nursing home at age 103.

_____ **2.** Rhoda Rooter, a local botanist, stunned the state flower show last weekend by
unveiling Sapphire Serenity, the world's first naturally hybridized blue rose.

_____ **3.** A Springfield College professor
resigned Tuesday after winning $5 million
in the state lottery.

_____ **4.** A man claims that a prostitute he
hired in a Springfield hotel turned out to be
an alien who tried to suck his brain.

_____ **5.** A new fad on Canadian college
campuses: "pumping," where students stick
bicycle pump nozzles up their sphincters
to give themselves a rush of air.

_____ **6.** A typhoon struck Borneo
this morning, killing more than 400 and
leaving thousands homeless.

_____ **7.** The Springfield County
commissioners approved permits for a
new waste-disposal site yesterday.

_____ **8.** A doctoral psychology
student at Springfield College believes
that tattoos lower your IQ.

3 WHAT'S IT CALLED?

1. _____
A sentence or paragraph that
provides descriptive information
about a photograph.

2. _____
A phrase that identifies the source
of a fact, opinion or quote in a
story.

3. _____
The area or subject that a reporter
is responsible for covering.

4. _____
Words in large type running above
or beside a story to summarize its
content.

5. _____
The reporter's name, usually
printed at the beginning of a story.

6. _____
William Randolph Hearst said it's
anything that makes a reader say
"Gee whiz."

7. _____
The first sentence or paragraph of
a story.

8. _____
A graphic treatment of a quotation
taken from a story, often using big
bold or italic type and a photo.

9. _____
Words appearing at the
beginning of the first
paragraph of a story that
identify where the story
was filed.

10. _____
To continue a story on
another page.

Want to try more
reporting exercises
online? Visit the
ONLINE LEARNING
CENTER at
www.mhhe.com/
harrower1

CHAPTER

3

Newswriting basics

Ready to write a simple news story? This chapter introduces you to the concepts and formulas all reporters have learned to rely upon.

IN THIS CHAPTER:

Just the facts

When you write a story, you must try to be objective. Truthful. Fair.

You can't just pull material from your memory, or quote your friends, or make pronouncements about the way things ought to be. You must be *factual* — which means basing your stories on the best facts you can find.

Good reporters respect the integrity of facts. When you select them carefully and arrange them

Facts are simple and facts are straight
Facts are lazy and facts are late
Facts all come with points of view
Facts don't do what I want them to.

Talking Heads,
"Crosseyed and Painless"

skillfully, you can communicate without inserting your own opinions. For instance, this fact by itself seems trivial: *Percentage of Americans who can name two freedoms granted by the First Amendment:* **28.**

But now add this fact: *Percentage of Americans who can name two members of "The Simpsons" cartoon family:* **52.**

Together, those two facts lead to a logical, unspoken conclusion — that Americans pay more attention to TV characters than to government. True? Arguably. But it's a good example of how journalism should work: The *facts* tell the story, and readers draw their own conclusions.

AND NOW, POSSIBLY THE WORST STORY EVER WRITTEN

How many different kinds of errors does it take to screw up a news story? Here's a frightening (but fictional) example:

❶ Unhealthy? Says who? That's an unsupported opinion. Reporters shouldn't take sides on controversial issues.

❺ Bad math alert! The dorm is open 40 weeks per year; that means each resident ate 20 burgers a week. Likely? No. And one carrot does not weigh one pound, so this second statistic is bogus and misleading.

❼ This is pseudoscience. What specific "research" has proven that meat is bad? Which cancer rates are lower in Japan? Aren't other factors (stress, lifestyle, environment) also responsible for causing cancer?

❾ Inserting religious opinion into any news story is a sure-fire way to offend readers. Believe whatever you want, politically or religiously, but never try to pass it off as news.

⓫ June only has 30 days. A mistake as simple (and dumb) as this can cast doubt on every other fact in the story.

❶ Campus vegetarians will hold a puke-in at Turkle Hall Friday to protest the dormitory's unhealthy food policies. All students are encouraged to attend. **❷**

"The menu in that dorm is just meat, meat, meat," said Ben Dover, the highly respected president of Vegetarians Opposed to Meat in Turkel (VOMIT). "That's why so many Turkle residents have been getting sick this year." **❹**

According to Dover, Turkle's 200 residents were fed more than 160,000 hamburgers last year while eating just 1,000 pounds of carrots. In other words, a typical student ate just one carrot for every 160 burgers. **❺**

Dover said the protest was sparked after a student worker in Turkel's cafeteria spotted a crate of beef labeled "Grade D: Fit for Human Consumption." Many colleges try to save money by buying Grade D meat products, which include brains, skin and testicles. **❻**

Research has shown that a diet heavy in meat is bad for you. In Japan, where rice is a staple in people's diets, there is a much lower incidence of cancer. My own health has improved dramatically since I stopped eating meat last year. **❽**

Even spiritual masters like Gandhi and the Buddha proved that a vegetarian lifestyle brings you closer to God. **❾**

"Our puke-in has received letters of support from famous vegetarians like Opra Winfrey and Dwight Yokum," Dover added. **❿**

The event begins at noon Friday, June 31, outside the Turkle Hall cafeteria. **⓫**

❷ Encouraged to attend? By whom? This smacks of partisan cheerleading.

❸ Highly respected? In whose opinion? Objective newswriting should avoid vague, biased generalizations like this.

❹ Says who? According to what statistic? It's irresponsible to quote an allegation like that without adding facts to support it (or a counterargument to refute it). In fact, because this story relies entirely on just one source — Dover — it's far too unbalanced to be trustworthy.

❻ There is no such thing as "Grade D" meat. In fact, this entire paragraph is an urban legend: folklore popularly believed to be true. A good reporter would have checked out this story and discovered that it's a fabrication.

❽ Never inject yourself into a news story. "My" opinions and anecdotes about "me" are irrelevant and unprofessional.

❿ By misspelling *Oprah* and *Yoakam*, the reporter undermines the credibility of this entire story. (Note, too, how many times the reporter has flubbed the spelling of *Turkel.*)

SO WHERE DO OPINIONS BELONG IN JOURNALISM?

Journalism, it has been said, presents a maximum of information with a minimum of opinion. But isn't it sometimes appropriate to add emotion and attitude to newswriting? Doesn't complete objectivity suck the life out of stories? Where do you draw the line?

Journalists debate these questions endlessly. And the answers aren't always simple. Most newspaper stories can be placed on a continuum that ranges from rigidly objective (breaking news) to rabidly opinionated (movie reviews). Here's what we mean:

NO OPINION

An earthquake measuring 7.4 on the Richter scale shook western Japan on Sunday, forcing hundreds to evacuate as quake-generated tsunami waves approached. *(Reuters)*

This news story is straightforward, factual and unemotional — even though this event resulted in deaths and injuries. The reporter makes no attempt to overdramatize the situation or to philosophize about the human tragedy.

President Bush roared out of his New York convention last week, leaving many Democrats nervous about the state of the presidential race. Gov. Edward Rendell of Pennsylvania said Kerry "has got to start smacking back." *(The New York Times)*

In political news stories like this one, reporters must be careful not to inject their own political views. It's OK to use colorful descriptions if they're accurate (Bush "roared," Democrats are "nervous"), but opinions should be expressed only by people quoted in the story.

Tom Brady was uncannily accurate as usual, throwing for 335 yards and three touchdowns, but that wouldn't have been enough if not for two big plays by a defense that had been pushed around all night. *(The Associated Press)*

Sports stories often add flavor and attitude to the reporting. Like a play-by-play announcer, this reporter blends fact ("335 yards") with interpretation ("uncannily accurate as usual"). Sports fans — unlike readers of hard news — accept some colorful spin on their stories.

Only in an election year ruled by fiction could a sissy who used Daddy's connections to escape Vietnam turn an actual war hero into a girlie-man. *(The New York Times)*

Opinion columns must be truthful, but they can be partisan and passionate, too, like this excerpt from a column critical of George Bush's 2004 campaign against John Kerry. Readers understand that this is commentary, not news.

STRONG OPINION

Shamelessly devoid of intelligence, interesting characters, scares or gore, "Alien vs. Predator" is a concept that fails to deliver on any of what made the original films so great. *(Willamette Week)*

This movie review doesn't pull any punches. And that's what readers expect from critics, whether they're reviewing music, food, drama or video games. Reviewers, like columnists, are expected to mouth off in provocative ways.

OBJECTIVITY VS. OPINION — HOW TO GIVE LINCOLN HELL

Distorting the news with your opinions is as damaging — and unprofessional — as defacing a photograph. Still need convincing? Read the following excerpt from the Staunton Spectator, Oct. 7, 1862. This is how a typical Virginia newspaper reported that President Lincoln had issued the Emancipation Proclamation to free the slaves. Here's what results when reporters dispense with facts:

LINCOLN'S FIENDISH PROCLAMATION

Since the time our first parents were expelled from Paradise, and

"They hand in hand, with wandering steps and slow,
Through Eden took their solitary way,"

there has not been as much joy in Pandemonium as at this time. The Arch-Fiend in the regions of woe "grins horribly a ghastly smile," for he and his emissaries upon earth — the extreme abolitionists — have succeeded in prevailing upon "Old Abe" to issue a proclamation of emancipation which will send a thrill of horror through all civilized nations. . . .

Before he committed this act of atrocity, in reply to the Committee sent by a meeting of the "Christians (!) of all denominations" of Chicago, who were, at the instigation of Satan, urging upon him to

perpetrate it, he said that "he had been considering it night and day for some time . . . ."

In a word, the devil triumphed, and Lincoln issued his proclamation, which has "crowned the pyramid of his infamies with an atrocity abhorred of men, and at which even demons might shudder."

After the Committee of abolitionists from Chicago had retired, and when he was in some perplexity as to the course he should adopt, Satan, his potential ally, "squat like a toad at his ear," addressed him, as Milton represents Death as addressing Sin within the gates of Hell. . . .

Think you can write a better lead? Try the exercise on page 64.

The five W's

Facts usually fall into these main groups.

And your success as a journalist depends upon your ability to keep your facts straight. In the early 1900s, cards were posted in the newsroom of Joseph Pulitzer's New York World that shouted:

ACCURACY! ACCURACY! ACCURACY!
WHO? WHAT? WHERE? WHEN? HOW?
THE FACTS — THE COLOR — THE FACTS!

Now, you can argue about the number of W's here. (Are there four? Or five? Does "how" count as a W?) But you can't argue that good journalism combines facts and color, as Pulitzer observed. By "color," he meant description and flavor. But in the example at right, we'll take "color" even more literally:

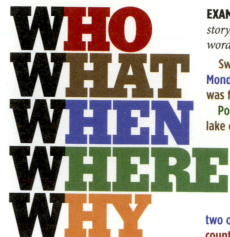

WHO WHAT WHEN WHERE WHY

EXAMPLES OF THE FIVE W's in a typical story, with facts color-coded to match the words in the headline at left:

Swimming was prohibited in Cooper Lake Monday after a dangerous amount of algae was found in the water last week. Polk County health officials declared the lake off-limits because of blue-green algae blooms. Ingesting the water can make people ill and kill small pets. The restrictions include windsurfing and sailboarding but not boating. "We hope it won't last longer than two or three weeks," said Robin Fox, the county's director of environmental health.

POPE JOHN PAUL II | 1920-2005

Church's shepherd, world's statesman

No, we're not talking about that legendary 1960s rock group, The Who — although we *could* be, if we were writing a story about classic rockers. And that story might be popular, too, because readers love stories that focus on people: Celebrities. Movers and shakers. The rich and powerful. The weird and wacky.

THE WHO

Reporters generally love writing "people profiles," too, because it's so fun to interview fascinating folks. Journalism provides a perfect excuse for letting you ask intimate questions of total strangers.

When you start assembling facts for even the hardest hard-news story, always look for the "who" elements: Who's involved? Who's affected? Who's going to benefit? Who's getting screwed? No matter how abstract the topic, it's the "who" angle that keeps it real.

◀ **THIS OBITUARY** *from the San Jose Mercury News explains who Pope John Paul II was, who's mourning his death around the world and who might replace him as the next pope.*

EMPHASIZING THE "WHO" ANGLE:

This lead from the Medford (Ore.) Mail Tribune makes it instantly clear what the story's about:

A self-described miser who drank outdated milk, lived in an unheated house and held up his second-hand pants with a bungee cord has left a $9 million legacy that will benefit Southern Oregon social service agencies.

This feature story centers on a number of "whos" — film critics, film characters and film actors:

The Online Film Critics Society, an international association of Internet-based cinema journalists, is sharing its love with the character we're supposed to hate.

The society has announced its new list celebrating the Top 100 Villains of All Time.

The greatest screen villain, according to the 132 members, is Darth Vader, played by David Prowse and voiced by James Earl Jones in the original "Star Wars" trilogy.

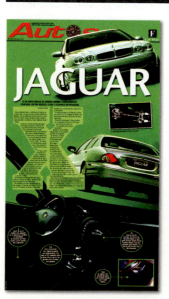

What's "what"? It's the stuff that news is *about* — events and ideas, projects and problems, dollars and disasters. And it's your job, as a journalist, to monitor and explain the stuff that matters most to your readers, whether you

THE WHAT

find it in a classroom, dig it up on a government beat or watch it on a football field.

Now, here's something you may not have realized before: The "what" gives news its substance; the "who" gives news its humanity and personality. Why does that matter? Because news stories become dry and dull when they focus too much on, say, meetings and money (the "what") and forget to connect them to real people (the "who"). Which is one reason why business reports and scientific papers are so boring: They're all "what" and no "who."

◀ **THIS CAR REVIEW** *from La Voz is unconcerned with who, when or where. It's all about what the car looks like, what its features are, what works, what doesn't — and what everything costs.*

EMPHASIZING THE "WHAT" ANGLE:

Notice how this USA Today business story begins with a list of famous "whats":

The Empire State Building. The SUV. The Incredible Hulk. The Boeing 747.

When it comes to big, no place does it better than the USA. But after a 34-year run, one of these icons is starting to see its popularity fade.

The 747 — synonymous with "huge" as the world's largest commercial jetliner — is increasingly being pushed out of airline fleets worldwide for being too expensive to operate and too hard to fill. . . .

Here's a Toronto Star story about a pop-culture trend:

Plastic surgery reality shows are setting a frightening example, bringing the practice of cosmetic surgery into disrepute, doctors say.

"It is barbaric, the whole premise of changing the way they look completely," says Dr. Frank Lista. "It's turned plastic surgery into a freak show.". . .

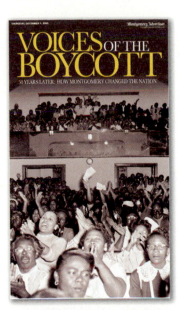

VOICES OF THE BOYCOTT

50 YEARS LATER: HOW MONTGOMERY CHANGED THE NATION

Some news stories happened in the past (*The Beavers lost Friday night's game*). Some will happen in the future (*The Beavers play the Warthogs next week*). And some go on and on, through the past, present and future

THE WHEN

(*The Beavers are in the midst of a 20-game losing streak. When is it ever going to end?*).

Timeliness is essential to every story. In this media-saturated, 24-hour cable-network-and-online-delivery culture we live in, readers want news that's fresh and immediate. They depend on you to tell them *when* events happened, when events *will* happen and how long they'll last.

Being a reporter, then, means constantly keeping your eyes on the clock, for two reasons:

1) so you can include the "when" in every story, and
2) so you can finish every story before deadline.

◀ **THIS SPECIAL SECTION** *from the Montgomery (Ala.) Advertiser, published on the 50th anniversary of the Montgomery Bus Boycott, examines life in the 1950s, a key period in civil rights history.*

EMPHASIZING THE "WHEN" ANGLE:

This story from the Las Vegas Review-Journal is all about holidays, so it begins:

Clark County public school students don't go to class on Labor Day, Nevada Day, Veterans Day, Thanksgiving, Christmas, Martin Luther King Jr. Day, Presidents Day or Memorial Day.

In the past, they've had to go to school on the Jewish holy day of Yom Kippur, when it fell on a school day.

This year, the district's 258,000 students will have Monday off because administrators deliberately scheduled the first of four teacher training days to coincide with Yom Kippur. . . .

Here's how a British newspaper starts a story headlined, "The twilight angels who come out after hours":

While most of us are just settling down for a night in front of the TV at seven o'clock in the evening, for a special team of Plymouth nurses work is only just beginning. . . .

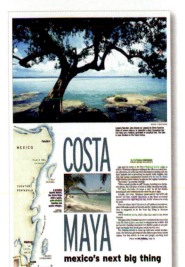

COSTA MAYA

mexico's next big thing

The bigger the news organization, the broader its coverage area. USA Today, for example, calls itself "The Nation's Newspaper," and it covers the entire world.

But most American newspapers are small dailies and weeklies that focus exclusively

THE WHERE

on their cities, counties or school campuses. Which means the "where" of every story is crucial: the closer the event, the more relevant it will be to readers.

But explaining the "where" of a story isn't always easy. That's why the more complex a topic is, the more you need to supplement your reporting with visuals such as a map (*Where will they build the new airport?*), a diagram (*Where will they expand the gym?*) or a photo (*Where did police find the body?*).

◀ **THIS TRAVEL STORY** *from The Oregonian focuses on a specific place — Costa Maya — relying on maps, photos and detailed description to paint a picture for would-be visitors.*

EMPHASIZING THE "WHERE" ANGLE:

This story from the Washington Post immediately transports you to a dramatic destination:

Fishermen call it the "Hell Hole," this place of whistling winds and smashing waves in the north Atlantic Ocean. Above a chasm in the Northeast Channel, which runs between the submerged Georges and Browns banks off Nova Scotia, fishermen catch cod, haddock and other fish with hooks at the ends of long lines, and by dragging nets along the sea floor.

"It takes guts to fish 'Hell Hole,' " said Sanford Atwood, a 54-year-old fisherman who has braved Hell Hole's elements aboard his boat, the Ocean Legend. . . .

And here's a classic "where" lead by Bob Batz:

When it comes to advertising the location of its monthly meetings, the Global Positioning System Users Group is different than most groups.

They gather on the fourth Thursday of the month at N 40 37 18 W 80 02 50 W. . . .

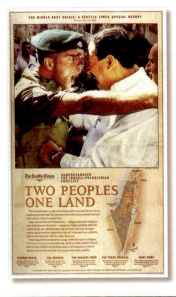

THE MIDDLE EAST CRISIS: A SEATTLE TIMES SPECIAL REPORT

TWO PEOPLES ONE LAND

UNDERSTANDING THE ISRAELI-PALESTINIAN CONFLICT

Good journalism reports the news; great journalism explains it. And explaining the news requires asking, over and over, the question

THE WHY

"why": *Why is this law necessary? Why will it cost so much?* And most important of all: *Why should we care?*

When news breaks suddenly, finding the explanations for events can be difficult. But for most stories, remember, the "why" is what makes the news meaningful.

◀ **THIS SPECIAL SECTION** *from The Seattle Times explains the causes of the Israeli-Palestinian conflict.*

Good reporters are good teachers. They know how to explain things in a clear, concise way. And explaining the "how" of a story often requires detailed explanation:

THE HOW

How will this plan work? How did that prisoner escape? How do I decorate my dog for Halloween?

For short stories and news briefs, the "how" is often omitted to save space. But readers love a good "how-to" story, especially in the feature section.

▶ **THIS FEATURE STORY** *from the Marion Chronicle-Tribune provides a beginner's guide to doing the laundry.*

Laundry 101

How to do your own laundry
A step-by-step guide

It's like death and taxes... Doing laundry is just one of those things everyone has to do. So, whether you're just starting college or just a big momma's boy, here's some things you should know before doing your first load:

The inverted pyramid

This newswriting format summarizes the most important facts at the very start of the story.

It may seem like an obvious idea to us nowadays — getting *right to the point* when you start a story — but it didn't occur to most reporters until midway through the 19th century. For example, here's the lead from a Fourth of July story in the Massachusetts Centinel in 1785:

> Monday last, being the anniversary of the ever-memorable day, on which the illustrious Congress declared the then Colonies of North-America to be Free, Sovereign and Independent States, all ranks of citizens participated in the celebration of the happy event, and even Nature put on more than usual mildness, expressive of her joy on the occasion — Ere the Eastern ocean was yet bordered with the saffron hue, the feathered choristers sang their early matin, and to usher in the auspicious day, Aurora unbarred the ruddy gates of the morn, with sympathetic smiles.

Flowery enough for you? By 1898, however, the Chicago Tribune was opening stories this way:

> GUANTANAMO BAY, Cuba — The first heavy fighting at close quarters between the American marines and the Spaniards took place here today.
> As usual, American pluck and discipline won. The little invading force showed splendid courage and spirit. . . .

What changed? Sentences got shorter. Writing got tighter. And reporters developed a formula for compressing the most newsworthy facts — the who, what, when, where, why — into the opening paragraphs of a story. That formula lives on today. It's known as the *inverted pyramid*.

According to newspaper folklore, the inverted pyramid was first developed during the Civil War by correspondents like these from the New York Herald. Reporters transmitted their battlefield stories via telegraph, which was expensive and unreliable. Stories could be cut off in midsentence, before the reporter had gotten around to saying who'd won the battle. So frustrated editors started urging writers to file fact-filled summaries of their stories FIRST, then fill in the lengthier details.

Before long, the inverted pyramid became the standard structure for most news stories.

WHY, IT <u>DOES</u> SORT OF LOOK LIKE AN UPSIDE-DOWN PYRAMID, DOESN'T IT?

The problem is this: How do you structure a news story so that readers quickly understand what's going on — without having to read a mile of text?

The answer: Summarize first. Explain later.

Whenever you write a story, you have to decide how to stack the facts. One solution, used for centuries by storytellers, is to stack facts *chronologically:* first one thing happened, which caused another thing to happen, which caused something else to happen, and then the princess married the prince. The End.

Sure, those types of stories are entertaining, but only if you stick with them from start to finish — which makes them an annoyingly slow, inefficient way to deliver breaking news. See for yourself:

THE CHRONOLOGICAL STORY
On Sept. 20, Pete Moss bought some marijuana from Lynn C. Doyle. But Moss's dog bit Doyle in the leg during the transaction. So Doyle grabbed a shotgun and killed Moss's dog.
Moss was furious. He got in his car, chased Doyle into an alley and crushed him against a dumpster. Doyle died.
The next day, Moss confessed to police that he had run Doyle over. He was arrested and charged with second-degree murder.
Yesterday, Moss pleaded guilty in court. The judge sentenced him to 10 years in prison. On his way to Jackson State Prison, Moss leaped from a police van and escaped. A search is under way.

THIS IS THE LEAD, WHICH SUMMARIZES THE STORY'S MOST IMPORTANT FACTS.

THIS PARAGRAPH ADDS MORE DETAILS OR BACKGROUND.

THIS PARAGRAPH ADDS EVEN MORE DETAILS.

THIS ADDS MORE DETAILS.

MORE DETAILS.

MORE DETAILS.

MORE DETAILS.

As the story goes on, the facts become less essential and the text becomes more cuttable — which lets editors trim the story to fit on the page.

To tell that same story using the inverted pyramid, you'd stack the facts in the *opposite* order, putting the final facts first:

THE INVERTED PYRAMID STORY
A search is under way for a criminal who leaped from a police van outside of Jackson State Prison yesterday.
After pleading guilty to second-degree murder in court, Pete Moss was on his way to begin serving a 10-year sentence when he escaped.
Moss had been arrested Sept. 21 after confessing to killing Lynn C. Doyle by running him over in an alley with his car. Moss admitted he had been furious with Doyle for shooting Moss's dog during a marijuana deal.

See the difference? In chronological stories, things slowly get resolved at the *end*. In the inverted pyramid, things quickly get summed up at the *beginning*. You start as strong as you can, summarizing what's most newsy — then you add additional facts in descending order of importance.

The inverted pyramid helps readers scan news stories quickly and efficiently. But it helps you *write* news stories quickly and efficiently, too. Once you train yourself to organize facts this way, you can apply this formula to almost any breaking news event — which is why the inverted pyramid has been a cornerstone of newswriting for the past century.

HOW A TYPICAL NEWS STORY USES THE INVERTED PYRAMID

As we've seen, the main advantages of the inverted pyramid are:
◆ It condenses information efficiently, so readers can grasp facts quickly.
◆ It allows editors to trim stories from the bottom, since the details in the text become gradually less essential. Now, reporters certainly *don't* want their stories cut carelessly (or prematurely). But sometimes it's necessary. Take this wire story, for instance. It could be cut after the second paragraph. Or the third. Or . . . .

Here's the main point of the story, engagingly summarized. Notice how the lead is crafted to start with the "who" of the story, a name you'll recognize: Arnold Schwarzenegger.

The second paragraph elaborates on the "birthday gift" mentioned in the lead. It also adds more details about the "when" and "where."

The third paragraph fills in the rest of the "what" details, describing the stamp and the series it's a part of.

This final paragraph supplies relevant but less essential background information: a quick recap of Schwarzenegger's stampworthy career and his latest Austria connection. Is there more to this story? We don't need it. This is enough.

VIENNA, Austria — California Gov. Arnold Schwarzenegger is getting a birthday gift from his home country: a stamp in his honor.

The Austrian post office announced on its Web site that the $1.25 stamp will be released on the actor-turned-politician's birthday, July 30. Schwarzenegger, who will be 57, was born in the Austrian village of Thal near the southern city of Graz.

The stamp — which shows Schwarzenegger in a suit and tie, with the U.S. and Austrian flags in the background — is part of a collectors series called "Austrians living abroad," the post office said.

Schwarzenegger moved to the United States in 1968 to pursue a career as a body builder and movie star. He made his first visit to Austria as California governor last weekend, when he represented the United States at the state funeral of President Thomas Klestil.

— *The Associated Press*

SO SHOULD YOU USE THIS FORMAT FOR EVERY STORY?

Not every journalist is a fan of the inverted pyramid. Writing coach Don Fry called it "the worst form ever invented by the human race for explaining anything in words." And Bruce DeSilva of The Hartford Courant once complained that "the inverted pyramid remains the Dracula of journalism. It keeps rising from its coffin and sneaking into the paper."

What's the problem? Why do some journalists get so honked off at the inverted pyramid? Two reasons, usually:

◆ *It gets repetitive.* And stale. And repetitive. Who wants to read a paper where story after story looks like this?

THE MOST IMPORTANT FACTS
A LESS IMPORTANT FACT
AN EVEN DULLER FACT
A BORING FACT
ZZZ-ZZZ-ZZZ
BLAH, BLAH,
BLAH

◆ *It doesn't always organize story material logically or engagingly.* If you're not careful, complex stories may start with a bang but end with a whimper as facts stack up and bog down in a "muddle in the middle."

The solution? Don't get lazy; don't let your writing fall into a rut. As we'll explain later, you have a wide range of options for structuring stories and making complex material reader-friendly. ▼ (Take this book, for example. Notice how it combines visuals with short-form writing to keep things interesting.)

Bottom line? The inverted pyramid is valuable for helping you arrange the facts in breaking news stories quickly and efficiently. Will you use it on every story? No. But it's still an essential tool in every reporter's toolbox.

WHY WRITING A GOOD LEAD ACTUALLY MATTERS TO READERS

No reporter would ever deliberately try to bore or confuse readers. But sometimes it happens: A story takes too long to get going. Readers struggle to make sense of it. They get impatient. They bail.

And that's why it's *crucial* for you to realize how important your lead is. If you take too long to make sense, your readers will flee like rats from a sinking ship. Take the story below, lifted from the front page of a Colorado newspaper. Try making sense of it by reading just the text. By the time the story jumps to page 7, you'll be moaning, *What's the point?* Fortunately for most readers, the headline tells what the story's about long before the writer does.

Drew Carey, improv group to headline at UCCC

It was just a trip to blow off some steam from the constant pressures of filming "The Drew Carey Show," but Kathy Kinney is glad her cast members made the trip.

Kinney, who plays the mascara-encrusted Mimi on the long-running sitcom that will finally end this summer,

Kinney

attended a comedy improvisational act in Cleveland, and they called for Drew Carey to do the show. Carey didn't feel like it, but he did do some improvisational comedy. And this is where Kinney fit in perfectly.

Kinney, along with another cast member, Ryan Stiles, made their living on improvisational

SEE UCCC, PAGE A7

Writing basic news leads

It's the essence of journalism: the key facts summarized in a concise way.

Some journalism experts insist that the lead (or "lede") of a story must be *just one paragraph*. And that paragraph must use *just one sentence*. And that sentence must be *25 words or less*. And if you violate that formula, angry readers will scoff. Your story will be doomed.

Charles Dickens

Fortunately — or unfortunately — it's not that simple. As we'll see in the pages ahead, you have many, many options for writing smart, engaging leads.

Let's begin by focusing on the most fundamental option, the basic news lead for inverted-pyramid stories. It's the style of newswriting that comes closest to using a dependable formula. And here's the good news: If you can master the process of writing leads — identifying key facts and expressing them concisely — you'll have a solid command of the craft of journalism.

Still, learning to write even the simplest leads takes time and practice. For many writers, just *starting* the story is the most agonizing, time-consuming part of the job. But that's why they pay writers the big bucks. So start honing your speed and skill now.

HERE'S WHAT HAPPENS WHEN YOU "BURY THE LEAD"

Every so often, a surly editor may tell you to rework a story because you *buried the lead*. Which means, basically: You blew it. You thought *that thing* was the most important part of the story, but it's actually *this thing* — the news you buried down in the twelfth paragraph. So fix it, you knucklehead.

Here's a memorable example of a buried lead that actually ran in a New Jersey paper a half-century ago. This paper had recruited secretaries from local organizations to report on their groups' activities. But because these women weren't trained reporters, they didn't know how to write news stories — or more importantly, how to write news *leads*. So they ended up with this:

The Parent-Teacher Association of Cornelis Banta School held its regular monthly meeting Tuesday evening in the school cafeteria, for the election of officers for the coming year, with Mrs. Noah ten Floed, president, in the chair. The nominating committee proposed Mrs. Douwe Taleran for president, Mrs. David Demarest for vice president, and Mrs. Laurens van Boschkerken for secretary-treasurer. It was moved and seconded that the nominations be closed.

Mrs. Gianello Venutoleri arose and said that she wanted to nominate Mrs. Nuovo Cittadino, Mrs. Giuseppe Soffiate, and Mrs. Salvatore dal Vapore. Mrs. ten Floed ruled Mrs. Venutoleri out of order. Mrs. Venutoleri appealed to the parliamentarian, Miss Sarah Kierstad, who sustained the chair.

Mrs. Venutoleri took a small automatic pistol from her handbag and shot Mrs. ten Floed between the eyes. Constable Abraham Brinkerhoff came and escorted Mrs. Venutoleri to the county jail. The body of Mrs. ten Floed was removed to Van Emburgh's Funeral Parlor.

There being no further business, the meeting adjourned for refreshments, which were served by Mrs. Adrian Blauvelt's committee. The next meeting will be held on Friday evening, Sept. 10, for the installation of officers.

HOW TO WRITE AN EFFECTIVE NEWS LEAD

 COLLECT ALL YOUR FACTS

This is essential, for two reasons:
◆ If you don't know the whole story, your lead can't accurately summarize what's going on.
◆ The more you know about the story, the easier it will be for you to sum it up and boil it down.

 SUM IT UP, BOIL IT DOWN

If you had just 10 seconds to shout this story over a cell phone with dying batteries, what would you say? If it helps you organize your thinking, jot down the five W's in a list, like so:

WHO: Three Mudflap passengers were injured.
WHAT: A private plane crashed.
WHEN: Friday night, 9:12 p.m.
WHERE: The Mudflap River behind Mudflap Airport.
WHY: A bolt of lightning struck the plane, killing the engine.

 PRIORITIZE THE FIVE W's

The lead needs to contain the facts that are most important — and *only* those facts that are most important. So evaluate each of the five W's. Ask yourself: Which facts must be in the lead? Which can wait a paragraph or two? And which of the key facts deserves to start the first sentence?

 RETHINK, REVISE, REWRITE

Write a first draft, even if it's not perfect, just to get things rolling. Then ask yourself:

Is it clear? Are the key points easy to grasp? Is the wording awkward in any way?

Is it active? Have you used a strong *subject-verb-object* sentence structure?

Is it wordy? Do readers trip over any unnecessary adjectives or phrases?

Is it compelling? Will it grab readers and keep them interested?

A PLANE CRASHES. WHICH LEADS ARE BEST (OR WORST)?

Writing leads is often a process of trial and error. You try stacking different facts in different ways until you find the most concise, effective combination. Let's use that plane crash (from tip #2 at left) as an example. You work for a weekly paper in a town near the airport. What's the best lead for that news story? Here are some of the solutions you might create when you emphasize each of the five W's:

LEADING WITH THE WHO

In news stories about accidents or disasters, leads often begin by stating the number of deaths or injuries. It may seem morbid, but it helps readers gauge the seriousness of the event. So let's try that:

> Clark Barr, 45, Leah Tard, 42, and Eileen Dover, 17, of Hicksville, were injured when a bolt of lightning struck their private plane, a Cessna 812, at 9:12 p.m. Friday. Barr suffered a fractured leg, Tard cracked several of her ribs, and Dover, who remains in intensive care at Mudflap Hospital, broke both her wrists and ankles after nearly drowning in the river after the plane crashed.

Is this overkill? Yes. There's *way* too much detail too soon. Readers' eyes will glaze over as they try to digest all those facts. The lead should summarize, not itemize; even the names of the victims should wait a paragraph or two. One exception: a recognizable name can leap to the lead if that person is newsworthy —

> Hicksville mayor Clark Barr and two other passengers were injured Friday night when their private plane crashed into the river behind Mudflap Airport after being struck by lightning.

— but ordinarily, nonrecognizable names don't belong in the lead. Besides, that paragraph is still too wordy. Can it be trimmed even more? How about this:

> Three people were injured Friday when a plane crashed at Mudflap Airport.

It's shorter, yes. But now it's *too* short. There's just not enough information. It's vague. Dull. Undramatic. We need a few more details — but not *too* many — to tell the story and capture some of the drama:

> Three passengers were injured Friday when lightning struck their private plane, plunging them into the river behind Mudflap Airport.

Success! This lead gets the job done. It emphasizes the "who" (the three injured passengers) and conveys just enough of the key facts without becoming too wordy.

LEADING WITH THE WHAT

There are three "whats" in this story: the plane, the crash, the lightning. Which "what" is most lead-worthy? Let's begin with an obvious (but bad) idea:

> There was an accident at Mudflap Airport Friday when a plane crashed after being struck by lightning, resulting in injuries to three passengers.

Dull? Yes. Why? Beginning a lead with a tired phrase like "there was" or "it is" makes the sentence flat and uninspired. It's almost like we're *backing into* the story. Better to use a more specific noun, like:

> A private plane crashed at Mudflap Airport Friday after being struck by lightning. Three passengers were injured.

Not bad. But "a private plane" isn't the most exciting phrase to start the lead with. ("A hot-air balloon shaped like SpongeBob SquarePants" — now, *there's* a phrase that could grab readers' attention.)

Notice, too, how that lead uses two sentences. That's acceptable. There's no rule that requires a lead to be only one sentence. BUT if you can write a single clear, compact sentence, do it. Let's try again:

> A private plane was struck by lightning and crashed at Mudflap Airport Friday, injuring three passengers.

This lead has a new problem. Know the difference between active and passive voice? Active voice uses strong subject-verb-object phrasing: *"lightning struck a plane."* Passive voice uses weaker phrasing: *"A plane was struck by lightning."* Good writers avoid the passive voice, especially in leads, because it lacks punch. Train yourself to recognize and avoid passive phrasing. Which means rewriting the lead like this:

> A bolt of lightning struck a private plane as it landed at Mudflap Airport Friday, causing a crash that injured three passengers.

Good. We're using the strongest "what" to start the lead. We're using active voice. We're supplying enough of the key facts without getting too wordy.

LEADING WITH THE WHEN

The plane crashed on Friday — but does the date have any major significance? No. The "when" is not a crucial part of this story. (In fact, do we even have to specify it was Friday *night*?). Thus, this lead —

> On Friday night, three passengers were injured when their private plane crashed at Mudflap Airport after being struck by lightning.

— is a bit weak. Like that first "what" lead at left, it backs into the story, which often happens when you begin the lead with a prepositional phrase.

Now, suppose it had been a tragic week at Mudflap Airport. You *might,* in that case, call attention to that fact by crafting a "when" lead like this:

> For the third time this week, a private plane crashed at Mudflap Airport. On Friday, three passengers were injured after their plane was struck by lightning.

But that's not the case. So that's not our lead.

LEADING WITH THE WHERE

How important is the "where" of this story? Is it more important than the injuries or the lightning?

> At Mudflap Airport, three passengers were injured Friday when their private plane crashed into the river after being struck by lightning.

No. The "where" is crucial, but it's just not the juiciest fact. (Plus, we're assuming that Mudflap is nearby. If we lived farther away, we might also need to add more geographic detail, like what *state* Mudflap is in.)

LEADING WITH THE WHY

What caused this crash? Lightning hit the plane and killed the engine. The story will go into greater detail, but a lead like this gives readers a quick grasp of what went wrong. So this "what" lead is also a good "why" lead.

WHICH LEAD IS BEST? Most reporters (and editors) would choose either that final "who" lead or that final "what" lead. Both are effective. Which do you prefer?

Beyond the basic news lead

It's not mandatory to begin every story with a roundup of essential facts.

As we've said, for most breaking news events, you need leads that are quick. Factual. Concise. You need leads that summarize the *who-what-when-where-why*. And being able to write solid news leads on deadline is one of the most valuable skills a reporter can possess.

But not every story is a timely news event. Some stories explore social issues. Some profile interesting people. Some provide previews of coming attractions.

And for those, a basic news lead may be too dull and dry. You may need something livelier, snappier, more creative, a lead that doesn't just *summarize*, but amuses. Astonishes. Intrigues.

Now, it's impossible to specify *what* kind of story requires *what* kind of lead. That's what makes reporting so creative. When the right story comes along, instead of writing this —

> A Hicksville man has been sentenced to life in prison for murdering his girlfriend.

— you might lead with this:

> Lincoln Mabry Jr. so loved Becky Kerr that he beat her in the face with a pistol barrel and shot her to death.

Over the years, reporters have devised dozens of oddball names for offbeat leads: pssts, zingers, sing-alongs, riddle-posers, God-Only-Knows. Call them whatever you like; the fact is, all good reporters spend countless hours searching for the Perfect Lead. Now it's your turn.

Edgar Allan Poe

ONE OF THE LONGEST (AND MOST MEMORABLE) LEADS EVER WRITTEN

After a surprisingly warm March day in 1995, feature writer Ken Fuson wrote this piece in The Des Moines Register. One sentence, 290 words. Gimmicky, yes. But irresistible.

Here's how Iowa celebrates a 70-degree day in the middle of March: By washing the car and scooping the loop and taking a walk; by daydreaming in school and playing hooky at work and shutting off the furnace at home; by skateboarding and flying kites and digging through closets for baseball gloves; by riding that new bike you got for Christmas and drawing hopscotch boxes in chalk on the sidewalk and not caring if the kids lost their mittens again; by looking for robins and noticing swimsuits on department store mannequins and shooting hoops in the park; by sticking the ice scraper in the trunk and the antifreeze in the garage and leaving the car parked outside overnight; by cleaning the barbecue and stuffing the parka in storage and just standing outside and letting that friendly sun kiss your face; by wondering where you're going to go on summer vacation and getting reacquainted with neighbors on the front porch and telling the boys that — yes! yes! — they can run outside and play without a jacket; by holding hands with a lover and jogging in shorts and picking up the extra branches in the yard; by eating an ice cream cone outside and (if you're a farmer or gardener) feeling that first twinge that says it's time to plant and (if you're a high school senior) feeling that first twinge that says it's time to leave; by wondering if in all of history there has ever been a day so glorious and concluding that there hasn't and being afraid to even stop and take a breath (or begin a new paragraph) for fear that winter would return, leaving Wednesday in our memory as nothing more than a sweet and too-short dream.

...AND ONE OF THE SHORTEST LEADS EVER WRITTEN

James Thurber was a popular humorist and cartoonist in the mid-20th century. He started out as a newspaper reporter, where an editor told him to write shorter, more dramatic leads — which prompted Thurber to begin a murder story this way:

Dead.
That's what the man was when they found him with a knife in his back at 4 p.m. in front of Riley's saloon at the corner of 52nd and 12th Streets.

THE CITY INSTALLS NEW PARKING METERS. WHAT KIND OF LEAD SHOULD YOU WRITE?

The city council met Tuesday. The proposal: install parking meters on Boinck Street, the road that runs alongside the school campus, where students have always parked for free. Angry students argued against the plan: "It's just greedy," said Dan DeLyon. "It's slimy," said Isabelle Ringing. "It's a stab in the back," said May K. Fist.

"It's long overdue," said the mayor, and the measure passed. Effective Jan. 1, the meters will cost 50 cents an hour — and parking violations will result in a $50 ticket.

Suppose you're covering this story for the campus newspaper. What kind of lead would you write? A basic news lead? Or something more provocative? Here are some options:

> The city council met Tuesday to discuss . . .

Wait! Stop! This is boring. What's the *news?* Try again:

> A proposal to install parking meters on Boinck Street was a topic of hot debate at Tuesday's city council meeting.

Still too dull. Why? It misses the point. The *proposal* isn't the story. The *meeting* isn't the story. The *impact on your readers* is the story. That's got to be the main emphasis.

> Students will pay to park on Boinck Street starting Jan. 1, thanks to a measure passed by the city council Tuesday.

Better. It's still a standard news lead, but it does a good job of answering the question, "Why should I care?" (although some editors might challenge the use of the word *thanks).* But must this story use a serious lead? Or could we try:

> There's no such thing as a free parking space. Not after Jan. 1, anyway. That's when students will start paying 50 cents an hour to park on Boinck Street.

Clever? Or cliché? This lead adds some extra attitude, but is it too much? And should it say "students will start paying" — or "*you* will start paying"? If you like the idea of aiming this story at "*you* the student reader," then how about:

> Starting Jan. 1, it'll cost you $50 if your parking meter expires on Boinck Street. Happy New Year.

Is it OK to featurize the lead like that? If so, why not show how the parking plan would affect a typical student —

> Dan DeLyon's job at Stinky's Pizza barely pays him enough to gas up his '87 Camaro every day. So starting Jan. 1, he'll be taking the bus to school.
> "They're sticking meters on Boinck Street," he said. "I can't pay 20 bucks a week to park."

— and then segue into the details of the plan that passed last night. Is that an engaging way to humanize the topic?

> "It's long overdue," said mayor Lilac A. Rugg, describing a new measure passed by the city council Tuesday authorizing the installation of parking meters on Boinck Street.

Ugh. A dull quote makes a dull lead — and so do phrases like "authorizing the installation." (Notice, too, how deeply buried the phrase "parking meters" is.) Now, some editors say it's lazy to start *any* lead with a quote. But how about:

> "It's slimy," said Isabelle Ringing.
> "It's just greedy," said Dan DeLyon.
> "It's a stab in the back," said May K. Fist.
> During an angry debate at Tuesday's city council meeting, students voiced their anger at a plan to install parking meters on Boinck Street. But the plan passed, and students will start feeding meters Jan. 1.

These quotes are strong, but those student names are a bit distracting (besides, the story's not about them). What if we edited the quotes for greater impact? Like this:

> "Slimy."
> "Greedy."
> "A stab in the back."
> Students voiced their anger at the city council's plan to install parking meters on Boinck Street on Tuesday. But the plan passed, which means students will start feeding meters Jan. 1.

Those opening quotes now have more punch. But:
◆ It sounds like they'll install the parking meters *Tuesday.* That sentence needs rewriting to eliminate confusion.
◆ Many editors (and readers) would feel this lead is unfairly negative. It seems to side with the angry students. True?

The most effective lead, then, may be one that combines the meters, the meeting and your money. How about:

> The meters are coming.
> Despite opposition from students, the city council approved a new parking plan Tuesday — which means that starting Jan. 1, you'll pay 50 cents an hour to park on Boinck Street.

As you can see, you've got lots of options, depending on your taste and news judgment. Which version would you choose?

✓ CHECKLIST

◆ **Be concise.** Streamline your ideas, your words, your sentence structure. Think *subject-verb-object.*
  The biggest problem with most leads? They're too wordy. Remember, most news leads are just one sentence. Most use fewer than 30 words. That's not an ironclad rule — just an observation *based on millions of successful news stories.*

◆ **Be accurate.** Get your facts and spelling right. One mistake in the lead will sabotage the entire story.

◆ **Remember what day it is** when readers read your story. If there's a chance of confusion when you write about *tomorrow's concert* or *last night's game,* use the names of the days to be safe.
  And speaking of days: Be careful to put the date in the right place.
  Wrong: *The panel will meet to discuss drug use on Friday.*
  Right: *The panel will meet on Friday to discuss drug use.*

◆ **Don't name names.** Don't say *John Smith was hit by a bus* in your lead, unless everyone knows who John Smith is. (Don't just say *A man was hit by a bus,* either. Try to add a touch of description, like *An elderly Mudflap man was hit by a bus.)*

◆ **Use strong verbs.** Which means rewriting that sentence above to make it active, not passive: *A bus struck and killed an elderly Mudflap man Tuesday. . .*
  Beware of soft, mushy verbs like "be," "try" and "plan" — or dull, bureaucratic verbs like "considered," "met" and "issued." Don't let your leads bog down in meetingspeak. And speaking of meetings:

◆ **Ask "Why should I care?"** Write from the reader's point of view as often as possible. Don't just report — *explain.* Explaining why things matter often makes the best lead.

◆ **Sell the story.** Find out what makes *this* story different or special, and use that to punch up the lead. Who wants to read another ordinary meeting/game/speech story?

◆ **Don't get hung up** by a problem lead. Unsure of how to start the story? Just jot something down and move on. Finish the story, then loop back around and revisit the lead.

◆ **Move attributions to the end of the sentence,** the reporting textbook said. Not: *The reporting textbook said to move attributions to the end of the sentence.* ▼

WANT TO TRY WRITING SOME LEADS? **TEST YOURSELF ▶ 62**   MORE ON **ATTRIBUTIONS ▶ 82**

HOW TO WRITE A GREAT LEAD

WRITE   TOSS IT OUT   REWRITE   TOSS IT OUT   REWRITE

Leads that succeed

A roundup of the most popular, commonly used options.

Writing is a creative process, so there's no possible way we could list every conceivable category of lead. (Many have tried; all have failed.) Instead, this collection of favorites is just a beginning. And remember, there's no type of lead that *always works,* just as there's no type of lead that *always fails.* The success of every lead depends on how well you write it. And rewrite it. And rewrite it.

Want more ideas? Browse our collection of inspiring leads scattered throughout **THE MORGUE**

① BASIC NEWS LEADS

◆ **The summary lead** begins the majority of news stories by combining the most significant of the five W's into one sentence:

> The Pentagon has ordered 1,500 additional troops to Iraq to provide security in advance of the upcoming election, military officials announced Wednesday. — **THE ASSOCIATED PRESS**

◆ **The delayed identification lead** is a type of news lead that withholds a significant piece of information — usually a person's name — until the second paragraph:

> A Smallville man escaped injury Saturday after plunging over Wohelo Falls in a kayak.
> Lance Boyle, 27, was treated for cuts and bruises at Mercy Hospital after what he called a "wild, boneheaded ride."

Spreading the information through two short paragraphs makes it easier to digest than if you crammed it all into one long paragraph.

By structuring that same information a bit differently — still using a delayed-identification lead — the story takes a different tone:

> Lance Boyle will never forget the "wild, bone-headed ride" he took Saturday.
> The Smallville man escaped injury after plunging over Wohelo Falls in a kayak.

Most news stories won't name names in the lead unless they belong to recognizable public figures or celebrities. A lead that does that, however, is called — what else? — an **immediate identification lead:**

> Actress Scarlett Johansson was involved in a minor car crash near Disneyland last week while trying to elude photographers.

② ANECDOTAL/NARRATIVE LEADS

Some stories unfold slowly, as the writer eases into the topic with an engaging and meaningful anecdote. This *anecdotal lead* begins a story on adult skateboarders:

> About five years ago, architect Mark Seder was reading the morning paper and watching his 10-year-old son riding at a local skate park. As he kept looking up from the paper to his son, something dawned on him.
> "I realized that I was getting out of shape and I thought, 'Why in the world don't I join him?' "
> Soon afterward, armed with a board, a helmet, and knee and elbow pads, Seder took his first tentative ride. He was 49 years old.
> Today, Seder is 54 and still skating . . . .
> — **STEVE WILSON,** *Portland Tribune*

Ideally, the anecdote will have a beginning, middle and end; it will be a mini-story with symbolic resonance for the *bigger* story you're about to tell.

Some feature stories begin by dropping you right into the action — action that often continues throughout the entire story. These are called *narrative leads.* If anecdotal leads are like snapshots, narrative leads are movies:

> "Oh, Jesus," she moaned softly. She squeezed my hand.
> The vacuum machine purred steadily and the fetus that was her unborn child was sucked through a clear plastic hose and into a large glass bottle.
> "Oh," she said again, and scratched my forearm.
> "We're almost done," the doctor said. "I just have to check and make sure you're all clean and empty."
> She squeezed my hand harder. . . .
> — **BOB GREENE,** from a column called "Kathy's Abortion"

③ SCENE-SETTER LEADS

In 1941, *Time* magazine wrote a story on America's reaction to the attack on Pearl Harbor. It began with a description:

> It was a Sunday morning, clear and sunny. Many a citizen was idly listening to the radio when the flash came that the Japanese had attacked Hawaii. . . .

Scene-setter leads lack the urgency of hard-news leads. They're a device borrowed from fiction ("*It was a dark and stormy night. . .*"), and they're usually reserved for long feature stories, where descriptions of sights, sounds and smells transport you to another place:

> The stink. That hits you first. Like a furnace blast. Now notice the mirrors spackled with dried mucous, sweat and spit, the faint arcs of blood that speckle the walls behind the ring. The portrait of Jesus as a boxer watching over the heavy bags. The ring, with its ropes that sag like a sad smile.
> It doesn't get any more authentic than an old boxing gym. As real and as honest and as raw as the paint peeling from the walls. . . .
> — **INARA VERZEMNIEKS,** *The Oregonian*

⑥ DIRECT ADDRESS LEADS

Virtually all news stories are written in an objective, third-person voice; stories refer to *him, her, they, them.* But feature stories often use the second-person voice to speak directly to *you,* the reader:

> If you've been waiting for a chance to collect every episode of "Buffy the Vampire Slayer" in one boxed DVD set, you're finally in luck.

For a feature about "missed connection" classified ads, a *direct address lead* may be the best way to explain the story's topic:

> You're at a party when you spot a stranger across the room. You feel a spark, a moment when your eyes lock with his. But your friends are tugging at your sleeve, ready to leave, so you head out the door. Now you can't get Mr. Fascinating Stranger out of your mind. Why didn't you just go over and talk? What if he felt the same connection?
> Some people don't just wonder — they advertise. . . .
> — **KRISTI TURNQUIST,** *The Oregonian*

REWRITE   TOSS IT OUT   REWRITE   TOSS IT OUT   REWRITE   FINISHED

④ BLIND LEADS

These are more extreme versions of the *delayed identification leads* mentioned earlier. You deliberately tease readers by withholding a key piece of information, then spring it on them in a subsequent paragraph. Like this:

> The most valuable consumers in the apparel business right now are people who carry no cash, have no credit cards and often spit up dinner on their new clothes.
> They're infants and toddlers — and at a time when sales in many apparel categories are flat, they're fueling a major boom in baby clothes.
> — JOHN REINAN, *Star Tribune* (Minneapolis)

Here's a terrific blind lead for a sports story:

> First the pale pink nail polish. Then the gold stud earrings and the monogrammed purse.
> Is this any way for a football player to dress?
> It is if she's a girl.
> Meet Erin Shilk, 5-foot-3 and 108 pounds: lover of the Aggies, boys, soccer, cooking and chemistry. She's a girl blazing a trail for the '90s. . . .
> — BONNIE GANGELHOFF, *The Houston Post*

⑦ THE STARTLING STATEMENT

One in four Americans will be infected with a sexually transmitted disease at some point in their lives. Did that grab your attention?

That's the goal of the *startling statement* (also called a "zinger" or a "Hey, Martha!"). It's used to begin this story from Romania. We dare you — *try* to stop reading:

> Before Toma Petre's relatives pulled his body from the grave, ripped out his heart, burned it to ashes, mixed it with water and drank it, he hadn't been in the news much.
> That's often the way it is with vampires here in Romania. Quiet lives, active deaths.
> Villagers here are outraged that the police are involved in a simple vampire slaying. After all, vampire slaying is an accepted, though hidden, bit of national heritage, even if illegal.
> "What did we do?" pleaded Flora Marinescu, Petre's sister. "If they're right, he was already dead. If we're right, we killed a vampire and saved three lives. Is that so wrong?"
> — MATTHEW SCHOFIELD, Knight Ridder Newspapers

⑤ ROUNDUP LEADS

Sometimes, instead of focusing on just *one* person, place or thing in the lead, you want to impress the reader with a longer list. Take the *roundup lead* on this legislature story:

> Gamblers get more choices. Smokers inhale cheaper cigarettes. And tipplers can hoist a round to Oregon lawmakers who kept state alcohol taxes among the lowest in the nation.
> Even gluttons came out OK in the just-ended legislative session, which rejected efforts to require more nutritious school lunches and more time in PE classes.
> "Sin had a fabulous session," summed up Sen. Ginny Burdick, D-Portland.
> — HARRY ESTEVE, *The Oregonian*

This feature story uses a blind roundup lead:

> Sherlock Holmes did it. So did Albert Einstein, Hugh Hefner, Bing Crosby, Gen. Douglas MacArthur, President Gerald Ford and Popeye the Sailor.
> Yes, they all discovered the secret of looking smooth, suave and utterly sophisticated:
> Pipe-smoking.

⑧ WORDPLAY LEADS

This catch-all category encompasses a wide range of amusing leads, including bad puns:

> For Germans trying to lose weight, the wurst is yet to come.

Or this scene-setter with sound effects:

> *Kawhooooooooomp!* The Hell Candidates' twin flame cannons torch off like the burners igniting in a jet engine and flames spike 20 feet up into the lights above the stage of the Paris Theatre.
> — JOHN FOYSTON, *The Oregonian*

Or this portrait painted with typography:

> Most dogs have upper teeth shaped something like this: VVVVVVVVVVV.
> Buster Finkel, sad-faced pet of Max Finkel, has upper teeth something like this: UUUUUUUUU.

Or witty wordplay like this, from a story about a mother caught in the middle between the police and the welfare system. Here's how reporter Heather Svokos started that story:

> Rock. Susan McQuaide. Hard place.

. . . AND THREE LAZY LEADS YOU SHOULD USUALLY RECONSIDER

◆ *Topic leads.* It's not enough to simply state that a game was played —

> The Swamp Toads battled the Mudhogs in a crucial conference playoff Saturday.

— or that a meeting was held:

> The school board convened Tuesday night to discuss complaints about the cafeteria.

Those are called *topic leads.* And they're lazy. The news is *not* that a game was played; what matters is the *outcome* of the game. Who won? And yes, the school board met. Big deal. What happened?

Topic leads are weak because they convey no actual news. Instead, they say to readers: *Maybe something happened. Or maybe not. We're trying to decide.*

◆ *Question leads.* Some editors *loathe* sports stories that begin with questions —

> Did the Swamp Toads finally figure out how to reverse the Mudhog curse Saturday?

— or meeting stories, too, for that matter:

> What has the school board decided to do to reduce complaints about cafeteria food?

Get. To. The. Point.

Question leads are just weak, irritating stalls — sometimes. But does that make *all* question leads taboo? No. It's possible to craft clever, engaging questions that hook us into reading further. But beware; you may need to convince grumpy editors that a question lead is the best option.

◆ *Quote leads.* Seldom is a quote so terrific that it becomes the smartest, most appealing way to launch a story. Instead, what usually happens is this:

> "The cafeteria food is awful, and it costs too much," said sophomore Anne Chovey at the school board meeting Tuesday.

The problem? The quote doesn't fairly summarize the story. It's an opinion, not a fact. We don't immediately know who's speaking. The sentence ends awkwardly.

That quote would work well in the second paragraph — following a newsier lead.

After the lead...what next?

Just write another paragraph. Then add another. And another. . . .

Writers spend lots of time and energy crafting and polishing their leads. Which is good, especially when it forces you to evaluate your material and prioritize your facts.

Yet writing a lead is just the beginning. A lead may hook readers into starting a story; it may brilliantly distill crucial data. But you have to follow the lead with good material, too.

Call me Ishmael.

That's right, Ishmael! Rhymes with "whale," and that reminds me of a story.

You'll probably want to know where I was born and what my lousy childhood was like and all that David Copperfield kind of crap...

Herman Melville

So how do you do that? How do you decide *what* facts go *where*? And *when*? And all those other *W's*?

It mostly depends on how long the story will be. That's why it's essential to discuss assignments with an editor before you start writing. You may think a story has awesome potential, but your editor may decide it's only worth a 6-inch brief. Or conversely, that innocent-looking little feature story could blossom into a prize-winning epic.

Once you know a story's length, you can estimate how tightly you'll need to condense your material. Some things will fit; others won't. Not a problem: Even the Book of Genesis squeezes the creation of the universe into just seven paragraphs.

And it's got a great lead.

BRIEFS AND BRITES: NEWS STORIES IN A CONDENSED FORM

The best way to get the hang of writing news stories is to start small, with *briefs*. A brief is any news story that's — well, *brief*. Some briefs are just a paragraph long (like the smartly crafted news summaries on the front page of The Wall Street Journal). Longer briefs may contain five or six paragraphs; if they're bigger than that, they're called *stories*.

Some briefs are written as entertaining little featurettes. They're called *brites,* and they're usually odd or amusing news nuggets told in a humorous or ironic way, as an alternative to ordinary briefs.

Here's an example of each.

A BRIEF: *Most standard news briefs are written using the inverted pyramid structure: a summary lead followed by additional details in descending order of importance. That's true for this example, as well. It's a typical news brief summarizing the key facts of a local bank robbery.*

A man robbed a Lake Grove-area bank Monday, making off with an undisclosed amount of cash.

No weapon was seen, and no one was hurt in the incident.

According to Lake Oswego police records, a man entered the Key Bank branch at 16210 S.W. Bryant Road about 3:15 p.m. and presented a teller with a note demanding money. The man then left the branch's back door and rode away on a bicycle.

Police described the man as in his 20s, about 5 feet 10 inches tall and 180 pounds. He was last seen wearing a baseball or fisherman-type cap, jeans, and a black, long-sleeved, quilted jacket.

A BRITE: *Brites provide more personality and more comic relief than standard news briefs. The lead tries harder to provoke interest; the ending often serves as a "kicker," providing a whimsical or unusual punch line. The key is keeping everything as short and tight as possible.*

It's enough to bring tears — or milk — to your eyes.

In Istanbul Wednesday, a Turkish construction worker poured milk into his hand, snorted it up his nose and squirted it 9.2 feet out of his left eye in what he hopes will be recognized as a new world record.

"I'm happy and proud that I can get Turkey in the record book even if it's for milk squirting," said Ilker Yilmaz, 28, who is able to perform the unusual feat because of an anomaly in his tear gland.

Guinness World Records will officially verify Yilmaz's record after reviewing documents from witnesses at the event, which was sponsored by Kay Sut, a Turkish milk company.

THE SECOND PARAGRAPH (THE NUT GRAF) AND WHY IT'S IMPORTANT

As we've seen, there are basically two types of leads:

1) Those that summarize the story, getting *right to the point,* and

2) Those that don't.

Now, there's nothing wrong with writing a punchy lead that teases or amuses readers. Like this:

Want to live longer? Have another beer.

Fun stuff! But readers will quickly ask, *What's this story about?* Which is why the next paragraph says:

Researchers from Laube University say beer has antioxidant boosters that could help fight cancer, heart disease and diabetes.

Aha! *Now* we see.

That paragraph — the one that condenses the story idea into a nutshell — is called the *nut graf.* And it's vital. Without a nut graf, impatient readers may wonder *What's the point?* and drift away, no matter how clever your lead is.

MUST EVERY STORY CONTAIN A NUT GRAF, THEN?

No. Nut grafs are helpful for feature stories (see examples at right). But for news stories, your second or third paragraph may have other duties to perform. You may need it *to supplement any of the five W's missing from the lead:*

A Salem golfer is recovering after being hit by lightning Friday morning.

Wally Benson, 53, is in fair condition at Mercy Hospital after being knocked unconscious on the third hole of Salem Golf Club during a sudden thunderstorm.

Or *to provide background for the action described in the lead:*

Electricity was finally restored for 3,000 shivering Loften residents Friday.

Repair crews worked for more than 72 hours after Monday night's ice storm downed dozens of power lines.

Or *to add a supporting quote:*

It's official: Ferris Wheeler, the Stars' star shortstop, is out for the season.

"My doctor said he's never seen a wrist as badly shattered as mine," said Wheeler, who was hit by a pitch in Saturday's game against Lincoln.

EXERCISES IN **WRITING BRIEFS AND BRITES** ▶ 63, 64

NO DOGS ALLOWED

THE PARTS OF A STORY:
HOW TO ORGANIZE YOUR FACTS EFFECTIVELY

You've written a terrific lead. You've added a solid nut graf. Congratulations. Now what?

Try outlining your story. Review your notes. Organize your material into sections. Then try sequencing those sections in different orders to see what's most logical.

For instance, suppose a college is debating whether to ban dogs on the school grounds. Here's two different ways to organize that story. Both work fine. Which do you prefer?

How to read these stories:
In the first story (left), we labeled each paragraph **A**, **B**, **C**, **D**, etc. In the second story, notice how we've rearranged those same paragraphs.

VERSION ONE *Here's a straightforward story written as an inverted pyramid. (Notice how you could cut the text after paragraphs E, G or H.) As you read the story, pay attention to its structure. Does the material flow logically from point to point?*

VERSION TWO *This story uses all of Version One's material but arranges the paragraphs in a different order to produce a different effect. Notice how this version begins and ends with Juliet, the dog owner. Does this structure seem more appealing?*

VERSION ONE

THE LEAD
A humorous approach to the dog problem.

(A) Dog poop. It's everywhere: on the sidewalk, on the lawn, on the soles of your shoes.

THE NUT GRAF
This is the essence — the *so what?* — of the story: *Dogs may soon be outlawed.*

(B) But that may soon change. The Bilford College board of trustees, in response to hundreds of complaints, is considering a new regulation declaring the campus off-limits to dogs.

THE PROTESTER
We now hear from an anti-dog spokesman who addresses the *why* question.

(C) Ferris Wheeler, president of Students Against Dogs (SAD), has collected nearly 300 signatures on a petition calling for a campus dog ban.
"This stinks," Wheeler says. "I mean, this school smells like dog doo. Irresponsible pet owners are letting their dogs chase cyclists, bark and crap all over campus."

RECENT DEVELOPMENTS
This describes *when* and *how* students and staff are reacting.

(D) Last week, the school's landscaping crew — which students call the "poop patrol" — tried posting signs saying "NO DOGS ALLOWED." Students tore them down. Tempers have started to flare.

SIMS QUOTE #1
To balance the argument, Juliet now expresses the views of student dog owners.

(E) "This proposal is ugly and unfair to responsible dog owners like me," says junior Juliet Sims. "I admit there's too much poop on the sidewalks, but it's wrong to let a few bad apples ruin it for everybody."

SIMS QUOTE #2
With quotes this juicy, we're happy to let her keep talking....

(F) Sims lives off-campus with a golden retriever named Romeo. "He's my sweetie," she says. "He sleeps with me, eats with me, showers with me. He even goes to class with me."

SIMS QUOTE #3
Another juicy, dramatic sound bite.

(G) A ban on dogs would pose a painful dilemma for dog-lovers like Sims.
"I hate locking Romeo up all day," she says. "I'd rather quit this stupid school."

THE CURRENT LAW
This provides more context about pet rules on campus.

(H) Campus regulations currently require all dogs to be leashed, but the rule is rarely enforced. And while pets are prohibited in campus dormitories, no law has ever banned them from school grounds.

WHAT NEXT?
We finish by sending readers to the big meeting.

(I) To resolve the dispute, the board will hold a public hearing at 7 p.m. Thursday in Bilford Union, Room 11.

VERSION TWO

(F) Juliet loves Romeo.
"He's my sweetie," she says. "He sleeps with me, eats with me, showers with me. He even goes to class with me."

THE LEAD/ SIMS QUOTE #2
This lead starts the story with a more human angle.

(B) But that may soon change. The Bilford College board of trustees, in response to hundreds of complaints, is considering a new regulation declaring the campus off-limits to dogs.

THE NUT GRAF

(E) Which means that Juliet Sims may have to bid farewell to Romeo, her golden retriever, whenever she goes to school.
"This proposal is ugly and unfair to responsible dog owners like me," says Sims, a junior living off campus. "I admit there's too much poop on the sidewalks, but it's wrong to let a few bad apples ruin it for everybody."

SIMS QUOTE #1
Now the reader gets the joke: Romeo is ... a dog! This device is called a *blind lead* — where readers have to wait a few paragraphs for the setup to pay off.

(H) Campus regulations currently require all dogs to be leashed, but the rule is rarely enforced. And while pets are prohibited in campus dormitories, no law has ever banned them from school grounds.

THE CURRENT LAW
This info now appears sooner than it did in the previous story.

(C) But lately, some anti-dog activists have started to bark. Ferris Wheeler, president of Students Against Dogs (SAD), has collected nearly 300 signatures on a petition calling for a campus dog ban.
"This stinks," Wheeler says. "I mean, this school smells like dog doo. Irresponsible pet owners are letting their dogs chase cyclists, bark and crap all over campus."

THE PROTESTER
Notice how the anti-dog argument comes later in this version. Does that seem to tilt the story in favor of Juliet? Is it fair?

(D) Last week, the school's landscaping crew — which students call the "poop patrol" — tried posting signs saying "NO DOGS ALLOWED." Students tore them down. Tempers have started to flare.

RECENT DEVELOPMENTS
Notice how the line about "tempers" leads into the next paragraph.

(I) To resolve the dispute, the board will hold a public hearing at 7 p.m. Thursday in Bilford Union, Room 11.

WHAT NEXT?

(G) A ban on dogs would pose a painful dilemma for dog-lovers like Juliet Sims.
"I hate locking Romeo up all day," she says. "I'd rather quit this stupid school."

SIMS QUOTE #3
Like closing a circle, the story ends where it began: with Juliet. ▼

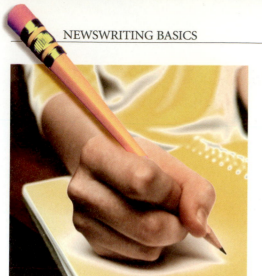

Story structure
Giving an overall shape to your writing.

Let's be clear: There's no simple, droolproof, one-size-fits-all solution for organizing stories. Every story unfolds in a different way.

Still, there's nothing random about good writing. Every story needs a beginning, middle and end. You can't just toss facts together as if you're flinging spaghetti against the wall. If you want readers to stick with you, you've got to organize each story's overall structure. Here's how.

ORGANIZING YOUR STORY: THE MOST COMMON SHAPES

You may think newswriting is a free-form, seat-of-the-pants, spur-of-the-moment, sit-down-and-start-typing kind of thing.

Wrong. Write that way, and your stories become clumsy, rambling jumbles of random facts and quotes.

Readers hate chaos. If you confuse them, you lose them.

So think before you write. Organize your ideas. Plan your story, whether by sketching a quick outline, visualizing a mental image or brainstorming with an editor — whatever helps you draw a road map for your story to follow.

If you get stuck, try carving your story's structure into broad sections, such as:

   I. The Problem
   II. What It Means
   III. What Happens Next

Or try something like this:

   I. Look: This Person Has a Problem
   II. Uh-oh. The Problem Is Everywhere
   III. What the Experts Say
   IV. What the Future Holds
   V. What It All Means for That Person We Met at the Start of the Story

That structure, it turns out, is quite popular with journalists — especially feature writers at the Wall Street Journal. To save time and effort, many crafty reporters automatically pour their stories into that tried-and-true shape (just like they pour breaking news into inverted pyramids).

Yes, we know: Every story is different. Still, if it helps you to visualize stories in physical shapes like pyramids, circles or martini glasses, consider the options at right.

THE INVERTED PYRAMID

Best for: News briefs, stories about breaking news events.
Not recommended for: Anything else.
How it works: Summarize the key facts in a concise lead. Then organize the story as logically as possible, arranging paragraphs in descending order of importance. End the story when you run out of facts (or you run out of room on the page).

MOST IMPORTANT FACTS
ADDITIONAL FACTS
MORE FACTS
ETC., ETC.
ETC.

THE MARTINI GLASS

Also known as: The hourglass.
Best for: Crimes, disasters or other dramatic news stories where you want to include a chronology to show how events unfolded.
How it works: Begin with an inverted-pyramid summary of the story's most important facts. Once that's done, shift into a chronological narrative. (Try setting it up with a phrase such as *Police gave this account of the accident:*). Then detail what happened, step by step. If possible, end with a *kicker* (a surprise twist or strong closing quote).
Example: See "Check-writer sets off clerk's internal alarm" in the Morgue, page 223.

THE LEAD
KEY FACTS IN INVERTED PYRAMID FORM
CHRONOLOGY OF EVENTS
KICKER

THE KABOB

Also known as: The Wall Street Journal formula or the circle.
Best for: Stories on trends or events where you want to show how *actual people* are affected or involved.
How it works: The story begins with a quote or anecdote about a *specific* person. Then it broadens into a *general* discussion of the topic. It ends by returning to that *specific* person again.

Think of it as arranging meat and veggies on a shish kabob skewer: Start with a juicy red tomato (an anecdote). Follow that with a nut graf. Then add meat — chunk after chunk after chunk — until you reach the end, where you reprise with another tomato (a final quote or anecdote).

OPENING ANECDOTE → NUT GRAF → DETAILS → CLOSING ANECDOTE

The Wall Street Journal is well known for writing stories this way. Some also view it as a circle like the one at left. Whatever.

Example: See "For those cut off, a life primeval," page 213.

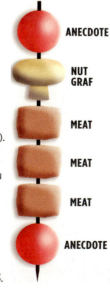

ANECDOTE
NUT GRAF
MEAT
MEAT
MEAT
ANECDOTE

AND AS YOU MOVE FROM PARAGRAPH TO PARAGRAPH, REMEMBER:

◆ *Keep paragraphs short.* Short, punchy paragraphs are *much* easier for readers to scan and absorb.

Really.

Some reporters have even trained themselves to write just one sentence per paragraph.

Like this.

Think of it this way: In a thin newspaper column, thick paragraphs (like the one you're reading now) get dense and daunting as long, wordy sentences stack up, giving your eyes no place to rest. Deep paragraphs may actually discourage readers from sticking with your story. So you should also try to:

◆ *Write one idea per paragraph.* Keep your focus tight, especially when explaining complex material. Parcel out your information in short, paragraph-sized chunks. Think about hitting the return key every time you type a period.

◆ *Add transitions.* To keep your story flowing, guide the reader from one idea to another with carefully placed transitions — words or phrases such as:

*However,   Meanwhile,
In addition,   Previously,
Finally,   On a related issue,*

In this example, notice how transitions (in italics) help connect the ideas from sentence to sentence:

Police will cast a watchful eye on downtown revelers this New Year's Eve.

But police admitted they will not be as prepared for trouble as they had hoped. *For one thing,* backups from the state highway patrol will probably not be available.

Instead, Police Chief David Barker said he will rely on reservists to augment the city's regular officers.

SO WHAT CAN YOU DO TO KEEP READERS FROM GETTING BORED?

See these two guys here? See how they're reading their newspaper with excited grins on their faces? Well, nobody does that anymore. Sorry.

Nowadays, readers are in a hurry. They're impatient. They're easily bored. And your job is to deliver the news to them in the most appealing, accessible, easy-to-digest way. In fact, we could argue that the modern journalist's job basically boils down to:

1) *teaching,* and
2) *storytelling.*

Which means that anytime you have a wonderful narrative story to tell, by all means *tell it.* Weave your magic. Paint a picture. Make us laugh. Make us cry.

But how often will you find those wonderful narrative stories? Unfortunately, they're pretty rare. Which means that most of the time your job is to teach readers about complex issues and events. You'll have to *think* like a teacher; you'll have to constantly ask: What's the most effective way to convey this material?

For today's readers, gray pages packed with paragraph after paragraph of long-winded narrative text simply *isn't* the most effective way to convey information anymore.

Later on, we'll explore this topic further.▼ But for now, before you unleash any mile-long narratives, consider these alternatives:

ALTERNATIVES TO LONG, GRAY NEWS STORIES

BULLETS

One effective way to emphasize a series of items is to add *bullets,* which help to highlight key points so they "pop" out of the text. For best results:

◆ **Start with a boldface phrase,** like this, to make your main points easy to scan.
◆ **Use parallel construction.** Here, for example, every bullet item is a handy tip, and each one begins with a verb.
◆ **Run at least three items.** Fewer than that, your list will look odd or incomplete.

Throughout this book, we use bullets (with boldface type and diamond-shaped dingbats) to highlight and summarize tips and lists. Bullets work for news stories, too.

SIDEBARS

A *sidebar* is any short feature written to accompany a longer story. Sidebars usually run in boxes beside or beneath the main story, like the one you're reading now. They help you reorganize complex information into smaller sections, to which you can add graphics, photos, etc.

As it turns out, sidebars often have higher readership than the stories they accompany simply because they're shorter and easier to access.

SUBHEADS

Ours are boldface, underlined and gray (but they work in plain black, too). Notice how they *instantly* show you that the text in this sidebar is divided into four sections.

Subheads break long stories into short, accessible chunks. They can be inserted whenever there's a shift in topics — which means that anytime you want to make complex material more reader-friendly, you can build subheads into your story as you write it. Like we've done here.

OTHER STORYTELLING ALTERNATIVES

Not every story requires paragraph after paragraph after paragraph of text. Take this book, for example. Have you noticed how there's virtually *no* long-winded text anywhere in this thing?

You be the judge: Has this format made the information easier for you to absorb? Or have we *dumbed it down too much?*

You can approach news stories the same way we've structured this book. You can break complex material into lists. Quizzes. Q and A's. Timelines. Chronologies. First-person flashbacks. Diagrams.

In Chapter 6, we'll show in more detail how these alternative story forms work. ▼

THE ENDING. THE CLOSER. THE KICKER. THE BIG FINISH.

Good writers agonize over their endings as much as they agonize over their leads. They often save their best stuff for last: a juicy quote. A revealing anecdote. An amazing fact. A clever pun. The goal is to give the story a climax, a punch line — what writers call a *kicker.*

"You should hear it echoing in your head when you put the paper down," says Bruce DeSilva of The Associated Press. "It should stay with you and make you think a little bit."

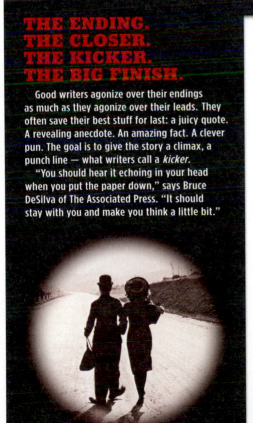

SAM STANTON *of the Sacramento Bee concluded his story about the execution of a murderer this way:*

A guard read the wordy announcement that contained a simple message:

Robert Alton Harris had been declared legally dead at 6:21 p.m.

The witnesses filed outside, into the bright sunlight.

After 25 years and nine days, California's gas chamber was back in operation.

DON HAMILTON *covered the dedication ceremony at a Vietnam War memorial. His story ended:*

Toward the end of the ceremony, Lee Ripley looked down and shook his head. Ripley served in the Air Force in 1968 and 1969.

"I hope we don't have to do this again anytime in the future," he said quietly. "But I bet they said that after Gettysburg. We still haven't learned anything."▼

ERIN BARNETT *wrote about a woman caring for her failing husband, an Alzheimer's victim:*

She pulls a turtleneck over John's wiry gray hair. Then she brushes his teeth and his wet hair before pulling him up. He looks down at her. She looks up at him.

"There you go sweetie," she says. And John is off. He strides back through the bedroom. He passes a watercolor of maroon, yellow and brown on the wall. Nellie says it is nasturtiums climbing out of their planter box. Like all her paintings, this one has a name. She calls it "Breaking Free."

RICK BELLA *begins his story about a seaside sand-castle contest with a biblical reference:*

In the beginning, there was mud.

The story concludes this way:

Finally, as the crowd retreated, the Pacific lapped at the creations, reclaiming the sand to re-create the familiar beach.

Ashes to ashes, mud to mud.

✓ CHECKLIST

◆ **Plan ahead.** Don't just stop a story because you ran out of material. Write the ending right after you write the lead, then work on the middle. Think of the lead and the ending as bookends.

◆ **Don't end stories by summarizing** what we've learned, like term papers do. There's no need to revisit or rehash points you've previously made. We don't need any sermonettes, either.

◆ **Avoid cute clichés** like *That's all, folks,* or *And that's the way it is.*

◆ **End with a bang** (a strong word or phrase), not a whimper (a weak attribution like "he said"). Effective writers try to place their most emphatic words **here, at the end.**

READ THIS ENTIRE STORY ▶ 202   MORE ON **SHORT-FORM ALTERNATIVES** ▶ 128

Rewriting

Your story's good. Now make it better.

Observe, at right, Ludwig van Beethoven struggling to write one of his orchestral works. Notice how the brilliant composer wrote and rewrote and rewrote note after note after note. And even after he *died,* Beethoven kept on decomposing.

Ba-da-*boom.*

No, but seriously . . . any serious journalist will tell you that writing, as the old adage goes, is *rewriting.* Very few stories arrive fully formed and perfectly phrased; most require rethinking, restructuring, rewording and a lot of other *"re"* words.

"There's no rule on how it is to write," Hemingway once said. "Sometimes it comes easily and perfectly. Sometimes it is like drilling rock and blasting it out with charges."

We could explain further, but first we've got to go back and polish up that Beethoven joke.

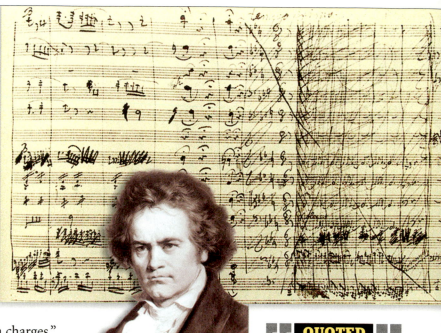

BEFORE & AFTER: A REPORTER'S EARLY DRAFT AND FINAL STORY

Stories don't always start out *bad.* They don't always end up *good.* The goal of rewriting is to make things a little better, then a little better, then a little better — until you run out of time.

Take the story below, part of a Labor Day package on people with odd jobs. Compare the before-and-after changes that make it more readable:

No, no, no. This lead is too cutesy.

Sentence is long and dull, with weak verbs, clunky phrasing *("as such")* and redundant wording *(grading, inspecting, monitoring).* Very slow going.

Such a weak cliché. And *"cuts the cheese"?* Please. Are we trying to embarrass this woman?

"Carefully inspects" seems redundant. (Can you *carelessly* inspect something?)

The word *"which"* is used the same way in two consecutive sentences.

A nice quote, but it rambles on for too long.

That phrase *"put on a lot of weight"* sounds a bit harsh and insensitive.

BEFORE

Linda Marvin is a cheese whiz.

For the past four years, Marvin has been a cheese grading analyst for the Tillamook County Creamery Association, and as such, she is responsible for inspecting and monitoring the quality of Tillamook cheese.

As quietly as a mouse, she cuts the cheese, chews it, smells it and rubs her fingers in it.

Marvin carefully inspects the color, texture, odor and flavor of the cheese, which other cheese makers don't do. That lowers their quality, she says, which hurts the industry overall.

"I'm very proud of my work," she says. "People say, 'I don't know if I could chew cheese every day.' But luckily, I love cheese. I really do. And I really don't mind doing this."

So with all this constant cheese-chewing, has Marvin put on a lot of weight?

"I spit it out," she says, "so I haven't gained any weight."

AFTER

Linda Marvin's nose knows cheese.

As cheese grading analyst for the Tillamook County Creamery Association, she spends each day smelling and squeezing chunks of Tillamook cheese.

She chooses some cheese, then chews it. Sniffs it. Snaps off a slab. Rubs her fingers in it.

Marvin gives that cheese a complete physical checkup — color, texture, odor, flavor — something lesser cheese makers don't bother doing. Which cheeses her off.

"I'm very proud of my work," she explains. "People say, 'I don't know if I could chew cheese every day.' But luckily, I love cheese."

After four years of cheese-chewing, has Marvin packed on a few extra pounds?

"I spit it out," she says with a laugh, "so I haven't gained any weight."

This lead is better (or, at least, it's fun to read aloud).

This paragraph is now tighter and punchier. Verbs are stronger and more colorful.

Another sentence that's fun to say aloud. These short sentence fragments speed the read.

A change in wording.

Another sentence fragment. And an attempt at humor.

Those last two extraneous sentences have been removed from this quote.

The reference to *"four years"* has moved here, from the second paragraph. *"A few extra pounds"* is kinder and gentler.

① PASSIVE VERBS

There is a problem many reporters struggle with. The sentences that are written by them are passive. Their phrasing is made awkward because of this, and — wait! *Stop!*

Let's rewrite that paragraph to make it less *passive:*

Many reporters struggle because they write passive sentences. This makes their phrasing awkward.

See the difference? We've strengthened our syntax by starting sentences with their subjects. We've eliminated that clunky phrase *there is.* And we've replaced the verb *to be* (words such as *is* and *are*), with stronger verbs.

You don't have to be a grammar geek to see our point here. Make your sentences *emphatic.* Avoid weak, flabby verbs. No — don't just avoid them. *Zap* them. *Whack* them. Give them the *heave-ho. Gun them down* and *snuff them out.*

② REDUNDANCY . . . AND REPEATING YOURSELF

Sorry. Obviously, we got carried away just then.

But sometimes it's not so obvious that you're using unnecessary words and phrases. Why say that someone is *currently* president of the club? Or that the game is *scheduled for* Friday night? Or that the victims were burned *in the flames?*

Those italicized words add bulk, but no extra meaning. Just as bad are phrases such as these, which are simply doublespeak:

grateful thanks	true facts	personal opinion
all-time record	end result	serious danger
totally destroyed	very unique	first time ever

Be on the lookout for unnecessary modifiers that *sound* logical but add nothing. Eliminate waste. Edit yourself ruthlessly. As Mark Twain once advised: "When in doubt, strike it out."

5 REASONS TO HIT THE DELETE KEY

③ LONG, LONG, LONG, WORDY SENTENCES

It should be pointed out that many writers, in order to make themselves sound much more profound and scholarly than perhaps they actually are, use flabby, inflated wording such as "it should be pointed out" and "in order to" and "perhaps" — which we just did ourselves, in fact, earlier in this sentence — in addition to piling up clauses (some using dashes such as those a few words back) or parentheses, such as those in the line above, not to mention semicolons, which often suggest that the writer *wants* to end the sentence, but just can't bring himself to actually type a period; nonetheless, today's busy readers are too impatient to tolerate the sort of 18th-century pomposity wherein writers, so in love with the sound of their own voices, just go on and on and on and on and and on and on and on and on and and on and on and on and on and and on and on and on and on and on

④ JARGON AND JOURNALESE

Bureaucrats love to use words like *utilize, finalize* and *structured.* Cops like to say suspects are *apprehended* and *incarcerated.* And if you're a campus spokesman, why say *"the school can't afford the pay raises"* when you could say *"the salary scale revision will adversely affect the university's financial stability"?*

Good reporters relentlessly strive to filter out bloated, convoluted jargon and officialese. And those who don't should be *redirected, transitioned* or *subject to personnel surplus reduction* (i.e., fired).

But reporters often lapse into "journalese" without realizing it. Journalese, as veteran editor Joe Grimm puts it, is the peculiar language that newspapers have evolved that reads like this:

> Negotiators yesterday, in an eleventh-hour decision following marathon talks, hammered out agreement on a key wage provision they earlier had rejected.

That's not as bad as bureaucratic gobbledygook. But it's still a problem because it's full of:

⑤ CLICHÉS

Beyond the shadow of a doubt, you should work 24/7 to avoid clichés like the plague. Hel-*lo?* It's a no-brainer. Go ahead — make my day.

Tired, worn-out clichés instantly lower the IQ of your writing. So do corny newswriting clichés (a form of journalese) like these:

> The *close-knit community* was *shaken by the tragedy.* *Tempers flared* over a *laundry list of complaints.*

> The *embattled mayor* is *cautiously optimistic,* but *troubled youths* face an *uncertain future* sparked by *massive blasts* in *bullet-riddled, shark-infested waters.* So *now begins the heartbreaking task of cleaning up.*

Yes, clichés *can* come in handy. And yes, a skilled writer *can* use them in clever ways.

Once in a blue moon. ▼

Is your writing murky? Dense? Too wordy and complex? Test it and see. The Fog Index, developed by Robert Gunning 50 years ago, measures the readability of your prose. It assumes that the longer your sentences, and the bigger the words you use, the tougher your stuff is to read.

Here's how to calculate your Fog Index:

1) Find a typical sample of your writing, one that uses around 100 words.
2) Count the average number of words you use per sentence.
3) Now count the total number of "hard" words you use — those with three syllables or more (not counting proper names).
4) Add those two figures together.
   Example: If you average *12* words per sentence and use *10* big words, *12+10=22.*
5) Multiply that sum by 0.4.

The resulting number is your Fog Index: the number of years of schooling a reader needs to understand what you've written.

THE FOG INDEX

Since most Americans read at about a 9th-grade level, experts advise aiming for a Fog Index of 7 or 8, just to be safe. The Bible, Mark Twain and TV Guide have Fog Indexes of about 6. (So does this Fog Index story.) Gassy academic papers and foggy government reports score in the — ugh — twenties.

Consider this example:

> "The developments in the reconstruction project come after revelations that an extensive effort by the Goode Administration to repair damages at 82 houses near the destroyed homes has been plagued by shoddy workmanship, double-billing by contractors, inadequate management controls and ongoing disputes over how much damage was caused by the May 13 siege in which a police bomb ignited a blaze that killed 11 people."

That paragraph has a Fog Index of 30. Now consider this from Winston Churchill:

> "We shall go on to the end. We shall fight in France. We shall fight in the seas and oceans. We shall fight on the beaches, in the fields, in the streets, and in the hills. We shall never surrender."

Like it? It has a Fog Index of 3.4.

Editing

Who's going to clean up the errors in your story?

For centuries, reporters have had a love-hate relationship with their editors. On the one hand, reporters see editors as "the boss" — barking orders, spiking stories and mangling their exquisite prose. "I am not the editor of a newspaper," Mark Twain said, "and shall always try to do right and be good so that God will not make me one."

But on the other hand, where would you be *without* editors? Who would calm the newsroom chaos? Pacify angry readers? Fix your clumsy spelling? Delete that innocent-looking phrase in your story that might get you sued?

Every story needs editing, and every newsroom needs good editors. Copy editors, photo editors, design editors, online editors — they all play a part in making your efforts as effective as they can be.

HOW EDITORS PLAY A PART IN THE STORIES YOU WRITE

Every story you ever write will be edited. By an editor. Or perhaps many editors. It varies from newsroom to newsroom. On a small weekly, one editor may write, proofread and design every page in the paper. At a big daily, you might find an "assistant night editor for sports" who never writes a word and relies on a dozen other editors to process the reporters' finished stories.

Generally, though, editors are responsible for a) managing the newsroom staff, and b) making sure every story is as error-free as possible. For example:

Don Colburn, a reporter covering health issues at The Oregonian, discusses a story idea with his editor, Sally Cheriel.

BEFORE YOU WRITE THE STORY

◆ **Assigning the story.** Editors try to match the story to the right reporter, weighing factors such as workload, beat, writing style, prior stories, etc.

◆ **Planning the angle.** Editors will often urge you to focus on a particular aspect of the story: *"Let's look at the effects of this tax on part-time workers."*

◆ **Estimating the scope.** How long should each story be? Editors will often decide *("just give me 10 inches")* based on a story's impact, the amount of news traffic that day or how much space is available in the paper.

◆ **Anticipating the packaging.** Some stories are simple: just text and a headline. Others require photos, sidebars, charts or graphs — and the best time to plan a complex package is before you start writing. ▼

As deadline approaches, Cheriel works with Colburn on the final draft of his story, making comments and suggesting changes.

WHILE YOU WRITE THE STORY

◆ **Adding new details.** Editors will notify you of new developments *("the mayor just got arrested")* that require you to revise your story.

◆ **Monitoring your speed.** *"When's that tax story gonna be done?"* With many stories in progress, editors always keep one eye on the clock, guiding the staff's work flow as deadline approaches.

◆ **Fine-tuning your approach.** Before you veer in the wrong direction, editors try to ensure your story answers the right questions. ("The lead isn't that *they lost the game*, it's that *the quarterback broke his leg*.")

◆ **Monitoring layout changes.** If a new ad comes in, your 20-inch story may suddenly get cut in half. Or the story may hold for a day, waiting for a late photo.

Copy editor Kay Mitchell follows behind The Oregonian's reporters and editors, making last-minute corrections and writing headlines.

AFTER YOU WRITE THE STORY

◆ **Editing the content.** Several editors may examine the structure and substance of your story to ensure it's readable, logical and fair.

◆ **Copy editing.** This is where any errors in spelling, grammar, punctuation or style get fixed. When that's done, a copy editor writes a headline that summarizes your story.

◆ **Cutting or padding to fit.** Once all the photos, ads and stories combine on the page, some elements may need to grow or shrink. On deadline, the easiest solution may be to cut the bottom off your story.

◆ **Assigning follow-up stories.** Often, one event *("the mayor resigns")* flows into another *("meet the new mayor")* — and the whole process begins again.

MORE ON **PACKAGE PLANNING** ▶ 126

HOW MUCH EDITTING DO YOU NEED?

How's your spelling? Grammar? Punctuation? Know much about style, usage or libel? Take this test and see if you're ready to write a printable story.

Answers on Page 292.

1 *Which would you print?*
___ **a)** Police arrested the rapist, Levon Coates, who sheriff Smith described as a homeless drug addict.
___ **b)** Police arrested the alleged rapist, Levon Coates, whom Sheriff Smith described as a homeless drug addict.
___ **c)** Neither of the above.

2 *Which would you print?*
___ **a)** The $4,400,000 grant is allocated into three areas: $1,700,000 for research, $1,900,000 for new oscilators, and $1,800,000 for salaries.
___ **b)** The $4.4 million grant is allocated into three areas: $1.7 million for research, $1.9 million for new oscilators and $1.8 million for salaries.
___ **c)** Neither of the above.

3 *Which would you print?*
___ **a)** The terrorist will be hanged at midnight.
___ **b)** The condemned terrorist will be hung at 12 midnight.

4 *Which would you print?*
___ **a)** By the time Lincoln became President, seven states had succeeded from the union: South Carolina, Mississippi, Alabama, Florida, Louisiana and Georgia.
___ **b)** By the time Lincoln became president, seven states had seceded from the Union: South Carolina, Mississippi, Alabama, Florida, Louisiana and Georgia.
___ **c)** Neither of the above.

5 *Which would you print?*
___ **a)** Melman is the candidate that is very heavily favored.
___ **b)** Melman is the heavily-favored candidate.
___ **c)** Neither of the above.

6 *Which is correct?*
___ **a)** Between you and me, she is a better reporter than I.
___ **b)** Between you and I, she is a better reporter than me.

7 *Which would you print?*
___ **a)** Jim and his friend, Jack, were chased by his dalmatian puppy, Rex, which bit him.
___ **b)** Jim and his friend Jack were chased by his Dalmatian puppy, Rex, who bit him.
___ **c)** Neither of the above.

8 *Which would you print?*
___ **a)** The boys' golf team won their first play-off.
___ **b)** The boys golf team won its first playoff.

9 *Which would you print?*
___ **a)** 20,000 helpless villagers died in the tragic volcano eruption.
___ **b)** Twenty thousand helpless villagers died tragically in the volcano eruption.
___ **c)** The volcano killed 20,000 helpless villagers.
___ **d)** None of the above.

10 *Which would you print?*
___ **a)** More than 50 anti-war churchgoers carried handmade signs.
___ **b)** Over 50 antiwar church-goers carried hand-made signs.

11 *Which would you print?*
___ **a)** Prof. Anne Benson said, "Dr. Wormer is a blackmailing faggot, like my ex-husband."
___ **b)** Professor Anne Benson alleged that Dr. Wormer was "a blackmailing faggot" like her ex-husband.
___ **c)** Neither of the above.

The PRESS ROOM

WHAT DO YOU MOST RELY UPON EDITORS FOR?

I have learned — after many years of proud ignorance — that I am only as good as the editor working with me. A good editor can do everything from offer emotional support on a tough story to help you reshape the inevitably bad first draft of a long story. Conversely, a bad editor can lead you down the road to hell.
Peter Sleeth, *The Oregonian*

Making sure the narrative of the story flows, finding any holes in a story, and — yes — catching spelling, grammar and punctuation boo-boos.
Michael Becker, *Journal-Advocate*

I rely on editors to save me from myself. After a year writing for The Associated Press, I generally write pretty cleanly. Then there are those days when I produce massive brain farts and I hope and pray they yank my copy back from the writing abyss.
Carol Cole, *The Shawnee News-Star*

More than anything, I need an editor to find the holes in my stories. My copy is pretty seamless, and it can disguise a lot, even from me.
Jerry Schwartz, *The Associated Press*

When you get stumped on something or run into a reporting or writing problem, an editor can stand back and provide ideas you haven't considered. It's easy to get blinded when you've been working on a story for a long time, and a good editor will help you get through that.
Sarah Bahari, *Fort Worth Star-Telegram*

I rely on editors to determine which stories I need to tackle first, which ones deserve the most (or least) space and which ones I can shelve. This is important input for busy journalists who have ever-growing lists of story ideas.
Jesse Fanciulli, *Greeley Daily Tribune*

Catching tiny details like "Is it *Elisabeth* or *Elizabeth?*"
Patricia Miller, *Durango Herald*

The best editors inspire, energize, constantly question my copy and edit within the tone and cadence of my stories. Only one has done that in my career.
Mark Freeman, *Medford Mail Tribune*

This is something that is universally underappreciated and overlooked and, dammit, for me it's the most important thing *ever*: enthusiasm. I want an editor who invests as much energy and enthusiasm and spirit in a story as I do. Most of the other stuff I can get on my own (even my husband — a TV guy! — can line-edit with the best of 'em). Big-picture editing — the kind where *thinking* and brainstorming are required — is a very close second.
Beth Macy, *The Roanoke Times*

Newswriting style

You say "Mister Potato Head," I say "Mr. Potatohead." Who's right?

Historical footnote: Years ago, editors wore green eyeshades to shield their eyes from the glare of harsh newsroom lights.

When you write stories, some things are certain: how to spell *paraphernalia*, for example. As you type the letters, they'll either be right or wrong.

But other writing questions can't always be answered so easily. For instance, one reporter might choose to write *The six-inch T.V. costs ninety dollars.* Another might say *The 6" TV costs $90.* Both sentences seem correct, but which version is preferable? And who decides?

That's where style guidelines come in.

When journalists talk about "style," they mean either:

◆ the way you write (in a "breezy, comic style," say, as opposed to a "wordy, intellectual style"), or

◆ the rules that govern punctuation, capitalization and word usage (writing *the president was born Jan. 1* instead of *the President was born January first.)*

Every news outlet customizes its own style guidelines. Some newspapers, such as *The New York Times,* require reporters to refer to men as *Mr.* throughout a story; most other papers discourage using such "courtesy titles." Some capitalize the *W* in *Web site*; others say *website*.

It's the copy desk's job to standardize the style in your stories — but it helps if you know the rules, too.

THE ASSOCIATED PRESS STYLEBOOK: AN INDUSTRY STANDARD

WHAT A STYLEBOOK ENTRY TELLS YOU

Entries are alphabetical, as in a dictionary. But the listings include topics such as **days of the week,** as well as specific words.

Cross-referencing helps you learn more about a topic elsewhere in the book.

Some entries simply show you the corrrect spelling, capitalization or hyphenation.

Italicized text provides examples of correct and incorrect usage.

These boldface entries show you the correct punctuation — but they also provide background information to help you verify facts.

days of the week Capitalize them. Do not abbreviate, except when needed in a tabular format: *Sun, Mon, Tue, Wed, Thu, Fri, Sat* (three letters, without periods, to facilitate tabular composition). See **time element**.

daytime

day to day, day-to-day Hyphenate when used as a compound modifier: *They have extended the contract on a day-to-day basis.*

D-Day June 6, 1944, the day the Allies invaded Europe in World War II.

DDT Preferred in all references for the insecticide *dichloro-diphenyltrichloroethane.*

Over time, every newsroom develops style guidelines for writing about local people, places and things. Suppose the center of your campus is officially called Smith Quadrangle, but students call it "the quad." Should you refer to it that way in print? And should *quad* be capitalized?

Most publications don't have the time, energy or grammatical wisdom to grind out a comprehensive guide to the English language. So they select a proven, professional manual to serve as their official arbiter of style — and the American news industry standard is "The Associated Press Stylebook and Briefing on Media Law."

The Associated Press is a news cooperative providing state, national and international stories, photos and graphics to more than 15,000 news outlets around the world.

Newsrooms do use other stylebooks (The New York Times markets its style manual, for instance). But if you pursue a print reporting career, the AP stylebook is the one that will eventually wind up on your desk.

NUMBERS

◆ Spell out *one* through *nine,* then go to figures for *10* and up. If a sentence begins with a numeral, either spell it out or rewrite the sentence. Figures for years, however, are an exception: *2004 was an election year.*

◆ Always use numerals for ages: *He's an 8-year-old genius. The law is 1 year old.*

◆ Always use numerals in ratios: *She won the election by a 2-to-1 ratio.*

◆ For dimensions, use figures and spell out inches, feet, etc.: *She is 5 feet 9 inches tall.*

◆ Write *percent*, not *per cent* or *%*. Depending on the sentence, you may use either a singular or plural verb. Both of these are correct: *The teacher said 75 percent was a failing grade. As a result, 25 percent of the students were failing the class.*

◆ *Dollars and cents:* Both are written lowercase. Use a dollar sign ($) and numerals for an exact figure: *The hamburger cost $3.99.* For amounts less than a dollar, use numerals: *It cost 99 cents.* Use a $ and numerals to two decimal points for amounts of $1 million and up: *The plan costs $79.31 million.* Spell out casual uses: *I loaned her a dollar. She looks like a million bucks.*

TITLES

◆ Titles generally are capitalized only when used before a name: *President Roosevelt, Professor Tate, Pope John.* But when used otherwise, do not capitalize: *The president spoke to Congress. The professor scheduled a committee meeting.*

◆ Some titles are descriptive of occupations and are not capitalized: *astronaut Tom Swift, assistant coach Janet Johnson.*

◆ *King, queen* and other royal titles follow much the same guidelines. Capitalize them only directly before a name. *If I were a king, I'd want to be like King David.*

◆ Some titles are a bit more complicated, such as *former President Gerald Ford* or *acting Mayor Jill Fox.* Note that the qualifying word is not capitalized.

◆ For long titles, it's best to put them after a name for easier readability: *Jim McMullen, president of the association, wants taxes lowered.* Or, if you prefer, you can say *The president of the association, Jim McMullen, wants taxes lowered.*

CAPITALIZATION

◆ Always capitalize proper nouns: *Wally, Nike, Boston.*

◆ Capitalize common nouns when they're a part of the full name for a person, place or thing: *Republican Party, Dixon Lake, Benson Boulevard.* In other references, the nouns are not capitalized if they stand alone: *the party, the lake, the boulevard.*

◆ Some words derive from a proper noun and depend on that word for their meaning. They should be capitalized, as in *Christian, English, Marxist.* But other words no longer depend on the proper nouns for their meaning: *french fries, pasteurize, venetian blind.*

◆ The first word in a sentence is always capitalized, even if it is a proper noun that otherwise is not. For instance, *e.e. cummings* is all lowercase, but at the beginning of a sentence it would be *E.e. cummings,* which looks odd and should be recast to avoid.

◆ In composition titles, the principal words in a book title, movie title and the like are capitalized, including prepositions or conjunctions of four or more letters: *"Gone With the Wind."*

AP STYLE
HIGHLIGHTS

*"The Associated Press Stylebook"
is the ultimate desktop reference
for print reporters and editors.
It's the book you'll turn to first when
you're unsure about usage, grammar,
capitalization and punctuation.
There's a lot to learn in its 400 pages,
but here's a roundup of the guidelines
you'll use most often. (To save time
later, commit these to memory.)*

ABBREVIATIONS

◆ Abbreviate these titles before a full name, except in quotations: *Dr., Gov., Lt. Gov., Mr., Mrs., Rep., the Rev.* and *Sen.* When used before a full name in a quote, spell out all except *Dr., Mr., Mrs.* and *Ms.*

◆ After a name, abbreviate *junior* or *senior* as *Jr.* or *Sr.* After the name of a business, abbreviate *company, corporation, incorporated* and *limited.*

◆ Always abbreviate *a.m., p.m., A.D.* and *B.C.*

◆ When a month is used with a specific date, abbreviate *Jan., Feb., Aug., Sept., Oct., Nov.* and *Dec.* Spell out months when used alone or with a year only: *We met in December 2000, then got married on Dec. 14, 2002.*

◆ Spell out the names of all states when they stand alone. Eight states are never abbreviated: *Alaska, Hawaii, Idaho, Iowa, Maine, Ohio, Texas* and *Utah.* The others are abbreviated when used with the name of a city, town, etc., whether in datelines or in text. See the stylebook for the acceptable state abbreviations.

ADDRESSES

◆ Abbreviate *street, avenue* and *boulevard* when they're used with a specific address, such as *1234 Della St.,* but spell them out otherwise: *We took a drive down Electric Avenue.* Other designations, such as *court, lane* and *road,* are always spelled out.

◆ Always use figures for the address number.

◆ Spell out *First* through *Ninth* if they're street names, then go to figures after that: *222 10th Avenue.*

◆ If you have a complete address, abbreviate any compass points, such as *712 Jones St. S.E.* But without an address, it's just *Southeast Jones Street* (note *Street* is spelled out and capitalized).

THE INTERNET

◆ Some basic styles: *Internet, the Net, World Wide Web, the Web, Web site, dot-com, JPEG, DVD, CD-ROM, online, cyberspace, e-mail.*

◆ When listing Web addresses, use this format as a guideline: *http://www.timharrower.com*

PARENTHESES

◆ When a phrase in parentheses is inside a sentence, place the closing parenthesis inside the period: *They gave everything they had (but they still lost).* If it's a separate thought, the closing parenthesis goes outside the period: *They gave everything they had. (Unfortunately, they still lost.)*

◆ Use parentheses to insert a state name or similar information within a proper name: *She's a sports reporter at the Allentown (Pa.) Morning Call.*

◆ Do not use parentheses to set off a political designation. Instead, use commas: *Joan Jeffries, D-Fla., said Thursday that she would run for re-election next year.*

POSSESSIVES

◆ For plural nouns not ending in *s,* add *'s: men's clothing.* If they end in *s,* add only an apostrophe: *the dogs' leashes.*

◆ For singular nouns not ending in *s,* add *'s: the school's playground.* This applies to words ending in *x* or *z* as well.

◆ For singular common nouns ending in *s,* add *'s* unless the next word begins with *s: the waitress's order book, the waitress' sugar.*

◆ For singular proper names ending in *s,* use only an apostrophe: *Jones' music, Phyllis' car.*

◆ *It's* is not a possessive; it means only "it is." *Its* is a possessive: *A dog likes its food,* not *it's.*

PREFIXES

◆ Use a hyphen if the prefix ends in a vowel and the word that follows begins with the same vowel: *re-entry, anti-inflammatory.* (*Cooperate* and *coordinate* are exceptions.)

◆ Use a hyphen if the word that follows is capitalized: *The song was written by ex-Beatle Ringo Starr.* Guidelines for specific prefixes:

pre- : The stylebook does list exceptions to Webster's New World Dictionary, including *pre-empt, pre-exist* and *pre-election.*

co- : For nouns, adjectives and verbs that describe a partnership, use a hyphen: *co-author, co-worker, co-pilot.* Do not use a hyphen in other cases: *coexist, coeducational, cooperate.*

sub- : In general, no hyphen is needed: *subtotal, subcommittee, submachine gun.*

A FEW OTHER NITPICKS WORTH REMEMBERING:

◆ It's *adviser,* not *advisor.*
◆ *amid,* not *amidst.*
◆ *ad nauseam,* not *ad nauseum.*
◆ *minuscule,* not *miniscule.*
◆ *doughnut,* not *donut.*
◆ *amok,* not *amuck.*
◆ *Smithsonian Institution,* not *Institute.*

Further/farther:
◆ *Further* is an extension of time or degree: *We need to take this idea further.*
◆ *Farther* is used to show physical distance: *I live farther from school than you do.*

Imply/infer:
◆ You *imply* something by what you say or write.
◆ People *infer* something by reading your words.

Making deadline

When you're a reporter, you live by the clock.

In broadcasting, you measure stories in minutes and seconds. At newspapers, you measure them in inches — but still, those presses roll at a set time. Which means every page must be designed and finished at a set time. Which means every story must be edited and proofed at a set time. Which means *you* must turn in your story at a set time — otherwise, you cause serious problems for lots of people.

Which makes them angry. And gets you fired.

Meeting your deadline isn't optional. It's mandatory. Oh sure, stories sometimes straggle in, a few minutes late. Once in a while, they even fall through at the last minute. But every reporter knows how deadly it is to blow a deadline.

Now, if you plan to write for online publications, you could argue that there *are* no deadlines in cyberspace — that news is updated around the clock. Which is true. Nevertheless, editors will always be pushing you to finish your stories; you'll always need to write with speed and efficiency, because the beast will always need feeding.

> *"In real life I am basically shy and can't do a lot of things, but on the job, the story is all that matters — the deadline is coming at you, unstoppable, like an avalanche down a mountain. You brave the wrath of crooks and cops and bad crowds and mean dogs without even seeing them. There is no time. Do what you have to and worry about it later. And fortunately, you do not worry even then, because later arrives with the hot breath of a new deadline on its heels."*
>
> **Edna Buchanan,**
> legendary crime reporter

IDEA FILE

TIPS FROM THE PROS TO HELP FINISH THAT STORY BY DEADLINE

Bob Batz,
Pittsburgh Post-Gazette:
I always tell people who are stuck, including myself: Breathe, think, and then just write down the story like you'd tell it to a friend. You can always go back and fine-tune it if you have time.

Peter Sleeth, *The Oregonian:*
It helps when you are stuck on a story to realize there are just three boxes to fill: The lead, the nut graf and the explanatory body of the story, in that order. If you write each one as a stand-alone, it can help the biggest weenie get through deadline.

Jesse Fanciulli,
Greeley Daily Tribune:
Write a super-fast first draft: Just let the words tumble out, write as fast as you can and don't let your inner critic prod you into self-editing. Once you have everything you want to say down, look it over, pinpoint the angle, write the lead, reorganize, insert quotes, facts and figures, rewrite where necessary and check the facts.

Kevin Pang, *Chicago Tribune:*
If you're stuck staring at your monitor, walk away from the computer. Grab a pen and steno pad. Go to the break room and write out your story. When you're typing, the words fly on the screen almost reflexively. By writing each word out, you'll have time to think and process what you want to say, and how to say it.

Kevin Duchschere, *Star Tribune:*
Assemble the story in your head even as you're reporting it. Make mental notes to match the jottings in your notebook: an apt quote, the best scene-setter, telling details.

Jim Souhan, *Star Tribune:*
Some people freeze on deadline. My cure for that: Start typing. The simple act of typing in possible leads or details frees you up. Sometimes writing a bad lead on deadline helps you remember what a good lead looks like, and allows you to jump-start your writing.

YEARS AGO, IN WARTIME, PRISON GUARDS WOULD DRAW A LINE AROUND A CAPTURED SOLDIER AND TELL HIM...

YOU CROSS THAT LINE AND YOU'RE DEAD!

THIS LINE BECAME KNOWN AS THE DEADLINE.

DEADLINES... THOSE PRISONERS ONLY HAD TO WORRY ABOUT GETTING SHOT — I'VE GOT AN EDITOR!

Your story's not finished until it passes the . . .

DEADLINE CHECKLIST

ACCURACY

YES NO

☐ ☐ Have you checked the spelling of every name? Double-checked it with the actual person? (Is it *Christyn? Krystin?* Or just *Kris?*)

☐ ☐ Have you verified all dates, places and times of events?

☐ ☐ Have you personally tested all phone numbers mentioned in your story, using what you actually typed on the screen? Did someone answer and approve the number for publication?

☐ ☐ Have you personally tested any Web or e-mail addresses in your story? Are you sure all Web addresses will still be valid when the story is published?

☐ ☐ Have you double-checked every job title? Company name?

☐ ☐ Have you run spell check? Double-checked all unusual spellings (*Smyth, Millar*)? Caught any homonym mix-ups (*their, there*)?

☐ ☐ Have you tested all the math in your story? Do the numbers and percentages correctly add up? (If in doubt, ask a colleague to recalculate your figures for you.)

☐ ☐ Have you checked the accuracy of facts or claims made by sources quoted in your story?

☐ ☐ In reviewing all the sources of information you used, are you sure that everything is reliable and up to date?

☐ ☐ For stories on complex topics that are new to you, have you tried running your story by an expert on the subject?

☐ ☐ Have you checked the accuracy of all information in related sidebars or photo captions? Does everything match what's in the story?

☐ ☐ Do all quotes accurately capture what was said, and convey what was *meant?* Are they clearly and correctly attributed?

☐ ☐ Have you added middle initials where appropriate (especially crime or court stories)?

FAIRNESS AND BALANCE

YES NO

☐ ☐ Is the story fair? Are all sides of the issue represented?

☐ ☐ Have you given all your sources an opportunity to respond to any negative charges or opinions?

☐ ☐ Can readers clearly tell *fact* from *opinion* in your story? Are you sure that your story doesn't disguise opinion as fact?

☐ ☐ Have you clearly labeled any facts that may be in dispute?

☐ ☐ Is there a diversity of voices quoted in the story: a representative mix of genders, races, ages, etc.?

☐ ☐ Have you avoided unnecessarily alluding to anyone's race or religion unless it's relevant to the topic?

WRITING STYLE

YES NO

☐ ☐ Does the lead or nut graf clearly state what the story's about?

☐ ☐ Does the story back up what's said in the lead?

☐ ☐ Is your lead concise? Fewer than, say, 30 words?

☐ ☐ Are all the five W's clearly explained without making readers dig through the rest of the story to find them?

☐ ☐ Does the story convey *why readers should care?*

☐ ☐ Have you taken pity on your readers and explained complex/inside information in a way that ordinary folks can understand?

☐ ☐ Do you personally understand everything in the story?

☐ ☐ If appropriate, does the story give readers enough tools to get involved (phone numbers, Web sites, event information, organizations to contact)?

☐ ☐ Have you gone through the story to weed out all excess flab, like unnecessary adjectives and adverbs?

☐ ☐ Are sentences short enough?

☐ ☐ Are paragraphs short enough?

☐ ☐ Are sentences written in the active voice, with strong verbs?

☐ ☐ Have you corrected all grammar and punctuation problems?

☐ ☐ Have you removed all jargon and journalese?

☐ ☐ Have you made all clichés as scarce as hen's teeth?

☐ ☐ Have you ever actually seen hen's teeth? You know why you haven't? Because they are so freaking *scarce,* that's why.

☐ ☐ Have you eliminated inappropriate slang, such as *"freaking"?*

☐ ☐ Does your story avoid unconscious sexist or racist phrasing?

☐ ☐ Have you eliminated all dull, meaningless, say-nothing quotes?

☐ ☐ Have you clearly sourced and attributed all information that's not general knowledge?

☐ ☐ Have you considered how your sources will react to this story? Are you sure you haven't violated their trust, included any information without their consent, or caused them any embarrassment?

☐ ☐ Have you refrained from mentioning yourself in the story or using "I," "me," "we" or "us" (except when quoting others)?

☐ ☐ Have you alerted your editors to anything in your story that readers may find offensive or objectionable?

☐ ☐ Have you read a printout of your story? (This will help you view the story with fresh eyes, and it may reveal errors you missed on the computer screen.)

MORE ON **SOURCES** ▶ 68   MORE ON **QUOTATIONS** ▶ 80   MORE ON **ATTRIBUTIONS** ▶ 82

66 newswriting tips

Boring-but-important advice every reporter should memorize.

Luckily for you, this book won't bog itself down analyzing grammar, syntax and punctuation. Instead, on these two pages we've summarized key principles every reporter should know — adapted from the "Hot 100" tips compiled by Sheryl Swingley of Ball State University.

WRITING LEADS

1) Keep leads short. The first paragraph should usually be 35 words or fewer.

2) Try to limit leads to one or two sentences.

3) Avoid starting leads with the *when* or *where* unless the time or place is unusual. Most leads start with *who* or *what*.

4) Avoid beginning leads with *there, this* or *it*.

5) Use quote and question leads sparingly.

6) The first five to 10 words determine if the lead will be an attention-getter.

7) Remember, *what happened* makes a better story than the fact it did.

THE REST OF THE STORY

8) Vary your sentence lengths. Stories become dull when sentences are all the same length. If you notice that happening, try turning one long sentence into two or three shorter ones.

9) If you must write a long sentence, try using a short sentence before or after it.

10) Avoid using several prepositional phrases in a sentence. Prepositional phrases start with some of the following words: *about, above, against, at, between, by, down, during, for, from, in, like, on, over, through, to, toward, under, up, until, upon, with.*

11) Remember that short paragraphs encourage readers to continue reading.

12) Try to limit paragraphs to:
- 60 words or fewer, or
- no more than 10 typeset lines, or
- one to three sentences.

13) Paragraphs should generally contain only one idea.

14) Avoid introducing new information at the end of a news story. All aspects of a story should usually be introduced or outlined in the first few paragraphs.

15) Transitions — linking words such as *but, and, also, besides, however, meanwhile, subsequently, finally,* etc. — are necessary to show the reader that the writer has a sense of direction. Carefully placed transitions guide the reader from one thought to another.

EDITING AND STYLE

16) Eliminate words such as *when asked* and *concluded*. These are weak transitions. Just report what was said.

17) Whenever possible, omit the word *that*.
Example: *The quarterback says he's ready,* not *the quarterback says that he's ready.*

18) The correct order for writing *when* and *where* is time, day (date) and place: *The concert begins at 8 p.m. Friday in Fox Hall.*

19) For a past event, say it happened *Tuesday,* not *last Tuesday.* For a future event, say it will happen *Monday,* not *next Monday.* Eliminate the words *last* and *next.*

20) Use the day of the week for events occurring within six days of a specific day; use the date for events occurring seven or more days before or after a specific day.

21) On first reference, identify a person by his or her first and last names. On second reference, refer to the person by his or her last name only.

22) On second and all other references, don't use *Miss, Mrs., Ms., Mr.* or *Dr.* unless it's a style requirement of the news outlet you're writing for.

23) A long title should follow, not precede someone's name. A title that follows the name should be lowercased and set off in commas.

24) Short titles may precede names and usually are capitalized. See *titles* in the AP Stylebook.

25) Always double-check the spelling of all names.

26) Use the computer's spell-checker. When in doubt, consult a dictionary. The latest edition of "Webster's New World College Dictionary" is the preferred reference.

27) For style questions, consult the AP stylebook. If the answer cannot be found there, consult a dictionary or a grammar guide.

28) Ask for help. Public library information desk personnel can be resourceful and helpful in person or on the phone. (University librarians are usually better at offering advice face to face.)

RULES OF GRAMMAR

29) If *none* means *no one* or *not one,* use a singular verb.
Example: None *was* found guilty.

30) When you use a pronoun to refer to a team or a group, the proper pronoun to use is *its,* not *they.*
Example: The *team* wants to improve *its* record.

31) Use parallel construction for verbs in lists or sequences.
Example: He likes camp*ing,* fish*ing* and hunt*ing.*
NOT: He likes camp*ing,* fish*ing* and *to hunt.*
Example: The fire *killed* six people, *injured* 60 more and *forced* hundreds of residents to leave their homes..
NOT: The fire *killed* six people, *injuring* 60 more, and *will force* hundreds of residents to leave their homes.

32) When using *either...or* and *neither...nor,* the verb agrees in person with the nearer subject.
Examples: Either the coach or the *players are* to blame. Neither the players nor the *coach is* to blame.

33) Know the difference between *its* (no apostrophe for possessive pronoun) and *it's* (the contraction for *it is*).
Examples: The dog has a thorn in *its* (possessive pronoun) paw, and *it's* (contraction) time to remove it.

34) Know the difference between *whose* (possessive pronoun) and *who's* (the contraction for *who is*).
Examples: *Whose* (possessive pronoun) coat is this? *Who's* (contraction) wearing it?

35) Know when to use *their* (possessive pronoun), *there* (adverb) and *they're* (the contraction for they are).
Examples: It is *their* (possessive pronoun) project. The project is over *there* (adverb). *They're* (contraction) working on it.

36) When making comparisons, *as* and *such as* are generally preferable to *like.* Use *like* as a preposition, not to introduce clauses.
Examples: It tastes *like* a peach. The farmer grows peaches, *as* he did last year.

WORD CHOICES

37) Eliminate lazy adverbs. Let strong verbs do their jobs. Instead of *the radio played loudly,* write *the radio blared.*

38) Eliminate lazy adjectives. Let strong nouns do their jobs. Instead of *the gang members created a chaotic scene,* write *the gangsters created chaos.*

39) Choose strong verbs that suggest what they mean. Active verbs add pace, clarity and vigor to writing. Avoid *be* verbs.

40) Use simple words. Don't send readers to the dictionary. Odds are they won't bother looking up definitions; worse, they might quit reading.

41) Words such as *thing* and *a lot* annoy many readers and editors. Choose better synonyms. (Note correct spelling of *a lot.*)

42) Be careful using the word *held.* Make sure the object can be held physically.
Weak: *The Rotary Club meeting will be held at noon Monday in Room 125.*
Better: *The Rotary Club will meet at noon Monday in Room 125.*

43) Avoid using words that qualify how someone feels, thinks or sees. Qualifiers include the following: *a bit, a little, sort of, kind of, rather, around, quite, very, pretty, much, in a very real sense, somewhat.*

44) If you use jargon that won't be understood by a majority of readers, be sure to explain each term used.

45) Writing *yesterday* or *tomorrow* may be confusing to readers. Use the day of the week. (*Today* may be used with care.)

46) Give a person's age if necessary for identification or description; it's preferable to saying *teenager* or *senior citizen.* Write *Jim Shu, 30,* instead of *30-year-old Jim Shu.*

47) For suicides, until the coroner completes his or her investigation, it's best to say the person *was found dead* or *fell* or *plunged to his death.* (Some papers avoid using the word *suicide;* check with your editor.*)

48) For arrests, write *arrested in connection with, sought in connection with, charged with* or *arrested on charges of.*

49) For murders, write that arrests are made *in connection with the death of.* Do not report that a victim was murdered until someone is convicted of the crime. In obituaries, it may be said the victim was *killed* or *slain.*

50) For fires, write that a building is *destroyed,* not *completely destroyed.* Buildings also are damaged *lightly, moderately* or *heavily.* A fire may *gut* or *destroy* the interior of a building. To *raze* a building is to level it to the ground.

NONSEXIST, NONAGEIST, NONDISCRIMINATORY WORD CHOICES

51) Avoid words that reinforce ethnic, racial, gender or ageist stereotypes.

52) Avoid referring to someone's ethnicity, race, gender or age unless it's essential for the clarity of the story. (Race might be relevant when a criminal is at large; referring to ethnicity, race, gender, age or disability might be appropriate when an achievement or event is a first.) Use the substitution test: If you wouldn't say it about a Caucasian man, then don't say it about a woman, people of other races or people with disabilities.

53) Use *he or she* instead of *he.* Women do notice the difference. If using *he or she* or *him or her* is awkward, try a plural pronoun: *they, them, their* or *theirs.*

54) Substitute asexual words for sexist *man* words. For example:

QUESTIONABLE	BETTER
mankind	people, humanity
man-made	synthetic, manufactured
manpower	workers, work force, staff, personnel
founding fathers	pioneers, colonists, patriots, forebears
anchorman	anchor
cleaning woman	housekeeper, custodian
coed	student
fireman	firefighter
foreman	supervisor
housewife	homemaker
postman	letter carrier
policeman	police officer
salesman	salesperson
stewardess	flight attendant
weatherman	meteorologist
the girls (for women over 18)	the women

55) Respect people with disabilities:

crippled	impaired, disabled — or be specific: paraplegic
deaf and dumb, deaf mute	hearing- and/or speech-impaired
crazy, insane, half-witted, retarded	mentally ill, developmentally disadvantaged, disabled or limited — or be specific: emotionally disturbed

Separate the person from the disability.

Mary, an epileptic, had no trouble doing her job.	Mary, who has epilepsy, had no trouble doing her job.

— Examples adapted from an International Association of Business Communicators' book called "Without Bias."

PUNCTUATION

56) No comma should appear between time, date and place.
Example: *The fire started at 4:32 a.m. Monday in the kitchen of Bob's Bakery.*

57) In a series — *red, white and blue* — a comma is usually not needed before *and* unless the series is complex or confusing.

58) Use a comma with *according to.*
Example: *Dogs are becoming more intelligent, according to researchers at Penn State University.*

59) Avoid comma splices: joining two independent clauses with a comma.
Example: *Half the company's customers lost power after the ice storm, power was restored to most of them quickly.* (A period or semicolon should replace the comma.)

60) Another common problem: adding a comma between the subject and the verb.
Example: *About half of the company's customers, lost power after the ice storm.* (The comma is not needed.)

61) When in doubt about using a comma, leave it out.

62) Quotation marks always go outside commas (,") and periods (."). They always go inside semicolons (";) and colons ("":). They may go inside or outside of question marks. Check the AP stylebook.

63) The dash is a long mark (—) most often used to separate a list or series in sentences where extra commas might be confusing. **Example:** *All these punctuation marks — commas, periods, dashes, hyphens — have their own peculiarities.*
Dashes also provide a way to insert interruptions or dramatic phrases.
Example: *All these tips — don't worry, we're nearly done — are important to know.*

64) The hyphen is a short mark (-) used in hyphenated modifiers (*two-week workshop, well-read student),* in words that break at the end of a line of type (like this *hyphenated* word here), in telephone numbers and Social Security numbers. Don't hyphenate adverbs ending in "ly" paired with adjectives: It's a *freshly painted room,* not a *freshly-painted room.*

65) Use an exclamation point only after brief expletives.
Examples: *Fire! Run! Goal!*
Exclamation points often demonstrate a lack of control (or excess of emotion) on the writer's part. Use them sparingly.

66) If you ever catch yourself overusing a particular set of punctuation marks — dashes, parentheses, semicolons — force yourself to stop. Remember, simple sentence structures are always best.

IF YOU COULD OFFER ONE PIECE OF ADVICE TO A REPORTER JUST STARTING OUT, WHAT WOULD IT BE?

Read voraciously. Find the best reporters and read every word they write. Try to figure out how they do what they do, and then incorporate what you want into your own style.

Another piece of advice: Take a typing class. I'm not even sure if they offer them anymore, but I've always been jealous of the reporters whose fingers absolutely fly on deadline.

Bret Bell, *Savannah Morning News*

Reading upside-down and backward is a skill worth cultivating, and not at all hard once you catch on. I once picked up a scoop on who would be the new city manager of Cincinnati with a little furtive desktop perusal while interviewing the mayor. I confirmed the name, obviously, with other sources.

Randy Ludlow, *The Columbus Dispatch*

I didn't go to j-school, but the best advice I ever got was from a crusty editor who told me to carry a pencil, because a pen won't work in rain or cold. That advice saved me one rainy night when I covered a fatal plane crash.

John Reinan, *Star Tribune* (Minneapolis, Minn.)

I wish I would have learned shorthand.

Nancy Gaarder, *Omaha World-Herald*

At my first journalism job, we were taught: *If your mother says she loves you, check it out.* It sounded harsh at the time, but the hard truth is, you've got to get confirmation and documentation. Don't believe it until you've checked it out yourself.

Deborah L. Shelton, *St. Louis Post-Dispatch*

If you ever, ever get a niggling feeling about something in a story, even the faintest of niggles, don't ignore it. For it almost always comes true the next morning. So make that extra phone call and sleep better.

Leah Beth Ward, *Yakima Herald-Republic*

The PRESS ROOM

ADVICE ON REPORTING AND WRITING FROM VETERAN JOURNALISTS

Professor Halvorson, formerly of the University of Oregon j-school, had the best advice I ever heard. He advised every young journalist to put 10 percent of his net paycheck each week into a "Go To Hell Fund." The good and wise professor reasoned — and it is true — that there will be times when you are asked to do unethical things in your career and you need to be able to tell your editor to go to hell, and take a walk.

Peter Sleeth, *The Oregonian*

Take your vacation time.

Andy Alford, *Austin American-Statesman*

◆ Spend less time with journalists and more time with people who read the paper. They have better stories to tell.
◆ Spend less time in the office.
◆ Call fewer corporate executives. Call more employees who work for those executives.

David Lyman, *Detroit Free Press*

With rare exceptions, by the third paragraph of every story, answer the two questions that readers doubtlessly are asking:
  1) What's this story about?
  2) Why should I bother reading it now?

Katy Muldoon, *The Oregonian*

Got an interview subject who's nervous and intimidated? Ask where their bathroom is and go use it. That's right, go potty. With this simple act of humility, you'll break the tension, give the subject a chance to relax, and most importantly, let the subject know that you're a regular, humble person like them and no one to be feared.

Matt Chittum, *The Roanoke Times*

Write as you report. Don't wait until you've finished all your interviews and gathered your information to start writing. Write when you get the idea. Write after your first interview and after your second and after you gather some information online. You'll be a better writer and a better reporter.

Steve Buttry, *Omaha World-Herald*

Remember that the story is not about YOU. Whatever fears, hopes and opinions you harbor about the subject, the sources, how you're feeling, whether you had lunch, whether your photographer is a jerk — *they do not matter*. The important thing is to be a true representative responsible to the integrity of the story.

JoNel Aleccia, *Mail Tribune* (Medford, Ore.)

Don't turn in a story you wouldn't read. And when they tell you newspapers are a business, believe them.

Ken Fuson, *The Des Moines Register*

Don't lean on "quotes." Focus too much on finding them during reporting and you'll miss more telling details. Good quotes are rare. You can tell the story better than the characters in it. So after writing, go back and take out half the quotes. And don't quote me on this.

Bob Batz, *Pittsburgh Post-Gazette*

Editing is incredibly subjective. One editor's idea of great versus so-so journalism can be entirely different. Don't let any editor have you believing you are too good or too bad. It's all perspective.

Alex Branch, *Fort Worth Star-Telegram*

You see a child crushed by an 18-wheeler while sledding, turning beautiful snow into a slushy red crime scene. You see the charred remains of a body. You smell death. You listen to those who grieve. You tell their stories. Dealing with trauma isn't always taught — or learned — in journalism school. It's experienced on the job.

Kimberly Morava,
The Shawnee News-Star (Shawnee, Okla.)

WHAT'S THE WORST PIECE OF JOURNALISTIC ADVICE YOU EVER GOT?

"If you can't spell, you will never be a reporter," said a journalism prof who sent me home crying. Now that I've been a reporter for nearly 15 years, I think maybe I should give him a call.

Rachel Stassen-Berger, *Pioneer Press* (St. Paul, Minn.)

The worst advice I ever got was a warning that anyone who wanted to speak off the record probably was lying. This was from a veteran assistant city editor. I quickly learned that people will tell you the truth in a lot of different settings for a lot of different reasons under a lot of different conditions.

Rick Bella, *The Oregonian*

Most idiots deal in absolutes. For example, I've heard "Never write to be cute," or "Never end a story with a quote." The only black and white in journalism should be the ink and paper.

Michael Bockoven, *The Grand Island Independent*

The inverted pyramid. What a crock.

Alex Branch, *Fort Worth Star-Telegram*

The worst advice I ever got is to pay attention only to the stories I write. True, we control only our own efforts, but a newspaper is a shared endeavor. We sink or swim together.

JoNel Aleccia, *Mail Tribune*

Bad advice: No one will read a story longer than 30 inches. Correction: No one will read more than two inches if it's poorly written; they will read 100 if it's well written.

Mike Kilen, *The Des Moines Register*

I do remember some bad "advice" that I gave myself. I failed miserably when I tried to emulate the gruff, cynical veteran reporter sitting next to me. I learned I had to be myself, even if it meant being bumbling and insecure.

Nancy Gaarder, *Omaha World-Herald*

Worst advice: Always outline. It's just not true.

John Foyston, *The Oregonian*

The worst piece of advice imparted to me as a reporter: There's no room for compassion in journalism.

Karen Jeffrey, *Cape Cod Times*

One "dumb editor" told me never to use brand names in stories. I think he actually changed a DQ Blizzard in a feature to "ice cream product." Tasty! (I changed it back.)

Beth Macy, *The Roanoke Times*

Never start a story with a question?????? In my 20 years, I've used probably five question leads. Sometimes it works. This was the lead to one of my stories that won the state AP contest:

The average adult human heart is about the size of a clenched fist and weighs only 11 ounces. So why, when a parent loses a child, does the hole in their heart feel like an abyss?

Deb Holland, *The Rapid City Journal*

HOW MUCH REWRITING DO YOU GENERALLY DO?

A reporter who doesn't rewrite has tight deadlines, bad habits or both. (In fact, I rewrote the above sentence twice.)

Writing can always be made better and tighter. I've won a lot of awards for writing, and I can't recall any for stories — deadline stories included — that I didn't rewrite to some degree. Good reporters don't wait for their editors to tell them to improve their copy — their satisfaction is not what you should be aiming for. You should be trying to satisfy your own standards, and that involves tinkering with your copy as long as is humanly possible.

Ron French, *The Detroit News*

I rewrite constantly, but a paragraph at a time. The first paragraph has to be exactly as I want it before I go on to the second. Once the second is finished, I revise the first two, and so on. It's incredibly inefficient, but that's how I do it. I've never been able to write a rough draft. I've tried, but it always just reads like another version of my notes.

Ken Fuson, *The Des Moines Register*

I don't write. I rewrite. My stories come about more like rocking a car back and forth in a ditch than a train going down the track. Eventually it gets out and I'm on my way.

Tim Nelson, *Pioneer Press* (St. Paul, Minn.)

Who has time to do much rewriting? I think it's valuable to be able to let complicated stories sit overnight and tackle rewriting with a clear head the next day, if time permits. If it doesn't, you find out how good you really are.

Carol Cole, *The Shawnee News-Star*

If I have the lead down — and the tone established, complete with nut graf at the end of a great scene — I'm in. If not, I'm in hell. Tip: If it's impossible to do a nut graf, your story (and maybe even your reporting) lacks focus. I had to re-learn that one again, just this week.

Beth Macy, *The Roanoke Times*

I almost never rewrite. But I never start writing a story until the reporting is complete and the story is developed. Why waste time half-writing a half-reported story?

Mark Freeman, *Mail Tribune*

I'm a rewriter. I think it's fun. Honest. I love getting a second shot at something, and am still shocked by how much better I can make a piece I thought was ready to go.

It's best if I have a night away from it. Unfortunately, that's rarely the case. Arggh and damn. But even stepping away for an hour or two gives me fresh eyes. I can come back and distill a watery paragraph to a more potent thought, or simply see the shortest distance between two points.

Kim Ode, *Star Tribune*

Tons of re-writing. The first crack never works. Playing with a story helps you say what you really want to say. Getting it out ain't that hard. The trick is getting it to sound right. (I'd like to go back and revise this.)

Todd Frankel, *St. Louis Post-Dispatch*

Answers to these exercises are on page 287.

1 CHOOSE THE BEST LEAD

Decide which lead is preferable and describe precisely what's wrong with the others.

1. ___ a) At Lyman Airport, a helicopter crashed Friday night, killing the pilot.
___ b) A helicopter pilot died after crashing at Lyman Airport Friday night.
___ c) A helicopter pilot died in a tragic crash at Lyman Airport Friday night.

2. ___ a) The Oakdale City Council met Tuesday to approve a plan to increase residential water rates.
___ b) The Oakdale City Council voted 4-3 to approve a 20 percent increase in residential water rates on Tuesday.
___ c) If you live in Oakdale, your water bill will increase by 20 percent — an average of $12 a month — beginning Oct. 1.

3. ___ a) On Saturday, June 3, two local students won a statewide dance championship.
___ b) Lena Genst and Nadia Hedd twirled to victory Saturday at the prestigious FSSA State Dance Championships.
___ c) Two Kennedy High seniors won $1,000 Saturday after finishing first in a statewide dance contest.

4. ___ a) A Spudville man named Robbin Banks was arrested after robbing a bank Friday.
___ b) Police arrested a Spudville man Friday and charged him with bank robbery. The man's name: Robbin Banks.
___ c) Spudville police arrested a man named Robbin Banks Friday. His crime: robbing banks.

5. ___ a) Pneumonia has taken the life of Justin Case, the oldest prisoner in Florida history.
___ b) Justin Case, the oldest prisoner ever to serve in a Florida prison, died Sunday of pneumonia.
___ c) Florida's oldest prisoner has died at 93.

2 TOO MUCH OPINION?

Read the following excerpts and decide: Is the wording appropriate, or has the reporter colored the story with too much opinion?

1) Moe Mentum's futile campaign came to a disappointing end last night as the candidate conceded defeat before 200 loyal supporters.

2) Moe Mentum's grassroots campaign came to an end last night as the exhausted candidate conceded defeat before 200 cheering supporters.

3) Logging continued in Conifer National Forest yesterday, despite howls of protest from liberal legislators and environmental radicals who assailed timber workers as "rapists."

4) Legendary geezers the Rolling Stones will rock Memorial Coliseum tonight as they kick off the first of three highly anticipated weekend concerts.

5) *From "The Daily Show With Jon Stewart":*

Jon Stewart: What's your overall sense of the mood down on the Republican convention floor? How did it feel to be there last night during the speech?

Stephen Colbert: Well, John, as a journalist I have to maintain my objectivity, but I would say the feeling down here was one of a pervasive and palpable evil: a thick demonic stench that rolls over you and clings like hot black tar, a nightmare from which you cannot awaken, a nameless fear that lives in the dark spaces beyond your peripheral vision and drives you toward inhuman cruelties and unspeakable perversions — the delegates' bloated, pustulent bodies twisting from one obscene form to another, giant spider-shaped and ravenous wolf-headed creatures who feast upon the flesh of the innocent and suck the marrow from the bones of the poor.

3 UNSCRAMBLE THE FIVE W'S

We've scrambled the basic facts for four different news stories. Sort them out to determine which facts most logically belong together — then write the leads for each of these stories for a publication in Dayton, Nebraska.

WHO	WHAT	WHEN	WHERE	WHY
Abner Hoobler	Was swept over Niagara Falls and lived	Tuesday night	The Living Jungle at the Dayton Zoo	Claimed he spends too much time clowning around with his friends
Victor, a labrador retriever	Glued a clown mask to her husband's face while he was sleeping	Easter Sunday	The bedroom of a house in North Dayton	Becomes the first Nebraskan to be 115 years old
Carlotta Tendant	Bitten in the leg by a lion	Midnight tonight	Niagara Falls, N.Y.	Jumped out of a pickup truck while his family stopped at Waffle Hut
Rev. Faith Christian, minister at the Dayton Zealotic Church	Celebrates birthday	7 a.m. Saturday	Twilight Nursing Home in Dayton	Says she leaped over the wall to convert the beast to Christianity, shouting "Jesus will save you"

4 BOIL DOWN THESE LONG-WINDED LEADS

Here's how two different news stories actually started. Can you condense their essential facts into tighter, more effective leads?

1) The Rev. Thomas J. Reese, an American Jesuit who is a frequent television commentator on Roman Catholic issues, resigned Wednesday under orders from the Vatican as editor of the Catholic magazine America because he had published articles critical of church positions, several Catholic officials in the United States reported.

2) What should have been a fun and exciting weekend turned into a destruction derby for some PCC students. It is a norm for students to gather to celebrate the weekend. Excessive damage was caused to the campus this weekend when some parties got out of control. What was the main cause of it all?

"It's typically directly related to alcohol consumption and too much of it," Nate Buseman, Director of Housing, said.

The suites were the main site of destruction over the weekend. Buseman said bannisters were splintered, emergency lights broken, a window shattered and one of the doors was damaged due to abnormal bending at the top of the door frame.

5 SUPPLY THE MISSING NUT GRAF

Study this story. It's missing a nut graf. Write one and stick it where it belongs.

When Tad Pole left the Lawton Library last Tuesday afternoon, he couldn't believe his eyes.

"My bike was gone," he said. "That's the third bike I've had stolen this year. I had a huge honkin' lock on it, too."

Lynn O'Leum had an expensive mountain bike stolen from outside Hoobler Hall last week. "I know at least three other people whose bikes have been boosted this year," she says. "That's it. From now on, I'm walking."

Even Helmut Laws, president of the campus cycling club, had his bike stolen during a club meeting last month.

"I've never seen anything like this," said Seymour Butts, campus security chief. "Whether it's one thief or a whole gang, we can't be sure. But it's an epidemic."

In an average year, 50 bicycles are reported stolen. So far this year, that number is 230, an all-time high. …

6 WRITE THIS NEWS BRIEF

Here are the facts for a short news story. Decide what's important and write the story.

- Laura Lynn Hardy is 19.
- She's a yoga instructor with red hair.
- She lives in Locust Valley, 10 miles west of Lincoln, in an old farmhouse.
- She ate lunch in Lincoln on Friday, Dec. 24, with her ailing grandfather.
- After lunch, while cycling past Lincoln Federal Savings, she saw a thick manila envelope on the sidewalk.
- She was in a hurry, so she stopped, put it in her backpack and bicycled home.
- When Hardy opened the envelope at home, she found it contained a total of $300,000 in cash and checks made out to Fenster Ford.
- Fenster Ford is owned by Fred Fenster. It's the area's largest car dealer.
- Hardy immediately phoned the bank and told them about the envelope.
- She then rode her bike back to Lincoln.
- It was snowing. A total of six inches of snow eventually fell by morning.
- Around 5 p.m., Hardy arrived at the bank. Xavier Mooney, president of Lincoln Federal Savings, was there. So was Fred Fenster.
- They thanked Hardy and shook her hand while posing for photos.
- Hardy then rode back home.
- When contacted by phone, Hardy said, "It's enough just to do the right thing."
- When contacted by phone, Fenster said, "She's a great little girl, the kind of girl we in Lincoln should be proud of."

7 CHOOSE THE CORRECT GRAMMAR, PUNCTUATION AND STYLE

Which of these versions is correct? (These exercises use "The Associated Press Stylebook" to settle all disputes.)

1. __ a) It's not OK to wear T-shirts at practice, coach Carter said.
__ b) It's not okay to wear tee shirts at practice, Coach Carter said.

2. __ a) General Myers met ten times with former vice president Gore.
__ b) Gen. Myers met 10 times with former Vice President Gore.

3. __ a) He drove East from Seattle, Washington to Boise, Idaho.
__ b) He drove east from Seattle, Wash., to Boise, Idaho.

4. __ a) The FBI office has moved to 1250 Third Ave.
__ b) The F.B.I. office has moved to 1,250 3rd Avenue.

5. __ a) In the 90's she received mostly A's in school despite being a rock-and-roll groupie.
__ b) In the '90s, she received mostly A's in school despite being a rock 'n' roll groupie.

6. __ a) Aaron C. Reskew Jr. is the candidate who will be elected mayor.
__ b) Aaron C. Reskew, Jr. is the candidate that will be elected Mayor.

7. __ a) 17 clerks worked from 7-10 a.m. in the morning, and were paid just five dollars an hour.
__ b) Seventeen clerks worked from 7 to 10 a.m. and were paid just $5 an hour.

8. __ a) Over 16,000 attended Game 1 of the world series to see the Tiger's 5-to-2 victory.
__ b) More than 16,000 attended Game One of the World Series to see the Tigers' 5-2 victory.

9. __ a) Nearly 50 percent of adults say they're concerned about developing Alzheimer's disease.
__ b) Nearly 50% of adults say they're concerned about developing Alzheimers Disease.

10. __ a) The nineteen-year-old girl was born September 20.
__ b) The 19-year-old woman was born Sept. 20.

CRAFTING CLEVER LEADS FOR BRITES

An amusing brite deserves an amusing lead. Write a catchy, clever lead for each of these four stories.

1) A sheriff's deputy in Ridge-crest, Calif., ticketed Linc and Helena Moore Friday after one of their chickens allegedly impeded traffic on the road near their farm. A police spokesman said that chickens in the roadway have been a problem in this small community, but verbal warnings have failed to resolve the problem.

2) Steve Relles lost his computer programming job three years ago when it was outsourced to India. Now he earns a living as a dog butler, scooping up dog droppings. Relles has more than 100 clients in Delmar, N.J., who pay him $10 a month to clean the poop out of their yards.

3) Rick O'Shea, an electrician, was admitted to Mercy Hospital Saturday morning after being electrocuted. Doctors failed to revive him, and he was declared dead at noon. But at 12:15, a nurse noticed O'Shea's hand twitching — then his eyes popped open. He's now listed in serious condition at the hospital.

4) The London Zoo recently opened an exhibit featuring three men and five women (all swimsuited British volunteers) caged on rocks behind a sign that reads "Warning: Humans in Their Natural Environment." The exhibit will teach the public that "the human is just another primate," a zoo spokesman said.

---

9 REWRITING THE EMANCIPATION PROCLAMATION LEAD

THE PROBLEM:
Modern news leads didn't exist in 1862. So when Lincoln issued his Emancipation Proclamation, some newspapers wrote garbage like this:

"The Arch-Fiend in the regions of woe grins horribly a ghastly smile, for he and his emissaries upon earth — the extreme abolitionists — have succeeded in prevailing upon Old Abe to issue a proclamation of emancipation which will send a thrill of horror through all civilized nations. . . ."

YOUR ASSIGNMENT:
We fired the reporter who wrote that terrible lead above. We need *you* to rewrite the top of this news story – just the lead and the first few paragraphs – to run in tomorrow's paper (Tuesday, Sept. 23, 1862).

First Reading of the Emancipation Proclamation of President Lincoln
Francis Bicknell Carpenter, oil on canvas, 1864

THE HEADLINE:
Lincoln Issues Emancipation Proclamation

WHO: President Abraham Lincoln

WHEN: Monday, Sept. 22, 1862

WHERE: Washington, D.C.

WHAT: An executive order that outlines what will happen three months from now: On Jan. 1, 1863, all slaves in states which have seceded from the Union will be freed.

THE CONDENSED VERSION:
"I, Abraham Lincoln, President of the United States of America, and Commander-in-Chief of the Army and Navy thereof, do hereby proclaim. . . that hereafter . . . the war will be prosecuted for . . . the immediate or gradual abolishment of slavery. . . . That on the first day of January, in the year of our Lord one thousand eight hundred and sixty-three, all persons held as slaves within any state, or any designated part of a state, the people whereof shall then be in rebellion against the United States, shall be then, thenceforward, and forever, free."

WHO WILL BE AFFECTED:
At least 4 million slaves in only those states that have seceded from the Union.

WHO WON'T BE AFFECTED:
Slaves in the border states (Delaware, Kentucky, Maryland, Missouri and West Virginia) which remain loyal to the Union.

THE CATCH:
If any seceding state rejoins the Union before this measure takes effect, it can keep slavery — at least for now, until a Constitutional amendment can be passed. Secretary of State William Seward criticized this loophole by saying, "We show our sympathy with slavery by emancipating slaves where we cannot reach them and holding them in bondage where we can set them free."

OTHER RELEVANT FACTS:
◆ Slavery was introduced to America in 1619.
◆ The war between the states started April 12, 1861.
◆ The Union army's victory last week at the battle of Antietam gave Lincoln the confidence to move forward with this preliminary announcement.
◆ The final, official proclamation will be issued three months from now, on Jan. 1, 1863. (It will be more detailed but will essentially make the same points.)
◆ In the short term, the proclamation may have more symbolic value than actual impact. But it clearly proclaims to the South (and the world) that the war is being fought not just to preserve the Union, but to end slavery.

Hopefully, as Union armies occupy more and more Southern territory, the Proclamation will enable Federal troops to free thousands — perhaps millions — of slaves.

Reporting basics

Now that you're familiar with the fundamentals of newswriting, you're ready to gather information and interview newsmakers.

IN THIS CHAPTER:

Where stories come from

Stuff happens constantly. So how does it become a story?

When most readers talk about stories, they may be thinking of fictional novels or childhood fairy tales like "Goldilocks and the Three Bears." But when journalists talk about *news* stories, they mean real people and real events: "Bears Terrorize Lost Girl in Abandoned Cottage."

Where do news stories come from? They usually originate:
- ◆ from events that are sudden and unpredictable;
- ◆ from events that are scheduled and predictable;
- ◆ from news releases alerting the media to noteworthy events or topics;
- ◆ from ideas generated by readers, editors or reporters.

BREAKING NEWS EVENTS

When terrorists attacked America on Sept. 11, 2001, it was sudden, violent, horrific, painful — the biggest breaking news event in decades. Reporters from big papers swarmed onto the scene; reporters from small papers explored the shock waves that rippled through their own communities.

Fortunately, most breaking news stories aren't that earth-shaking. But wherever you are, you need to be ready when a dorm catches fire. Or a professor quits. Or a blizzard strikes. Or three crazed bears corner a little girl in a cottage in the forest.

And in the aftermath of major news events — storms, tragedies, political crises — you may need to write what's called a *follow-up* or *second-day story,* to further explain what happened and what it all means.

So be prepared. At any moment a phone call, the police scanner, even campus chatter may send you running. As foreign correspondent H.R. Knickerbocker observed years ago: "Whenever you find hundreds and thousands of sane people trying to get out of a place and a little bunch of madmen trying to get in, you know the latter are reporters."

 REMEMBER:

◆ The bigger the story, the more you need to be on the scene as it happens. Nothing beats firsthand, eyewitness reporting.

◆ Move fast. For breaking news stories, quick reflexes and writing speed are crucial.

◆ Always carry a cell phone so you can call for instructions or backup.

◆ Carry a camera, too. Shoot images to jog your memory or to fill for photographers who may not arrive in time.

SCHEDULED EVENTS

Many events happen on schedule, recurring predictably: The mayor campaigns for re-election. The semester ends. The swallows, or cicadas, return. And every concert, court case and football game is scheduled weeks (or even months) in advance.

In many ways, then, scheduled events are easier to cover than breaking events. You know when they'll start and finish; you can generally predict what will happen; you can decide in advance how important the event is. That allows you to plan the timing and scope of your coverage. Better still, you can write *advances, precedes* or *previews* that explain the "who, what, when and where" for readers ahead of time.

But beware of becoming a publicity pawn for every speech, debate, meeting, march and press conference. Historian Daniel Boorstin called these "pseudo-events": illusions created for the media that crowd out real issues and real events. If stories that simply rehash meetings and speeches are filling your newspaper and boring your readers, try generating your own ideas about issues and newsmakers (see the lower section of the next page).

REMEMBER:

◆ Make sure your newsroom keeps a long-range calendar of upcoming events: games, elections, anniversaries, etc.

◆ Bone up on history *before* events occur. Search the Internet or back issues of your paper to see how your staff handled things in the past.

◆ For big events, team up with editors, photographers and other reporters to plan your coverage and package your stories in advance.

A TYPICAL DAY, A TYPICAL PAPER — AND WHERE THE STORIES CAME FROM

Let's analyze a typical issue (Dec. 30, 2004) of a small-town Oregon weekly newspaper: the Lake Oswego Review.

We itemized every bit of news in the paper — every story, every brief, every calendar notice — exactly 100 items in all. What we found:

4 COVERED BREAKING NEWS EVENTS

The lead story on Page One recounted a brutal dog attack. But beyond that, only three other stories dealt with breaking news (although we *did* count the "police blotter" listings as one big item.)

82 COVERED SCHEDULED NEWS EVENTS

By far, most of the items involved planned events, from high school basketball games to yoga classes at the senior center.

Of those 82 events,

65 ORIGINATED FROM PRESS RELEASES

Like most papers, the Review is quite dependent on news releases: The majority of items printed in the paper were rewritten from material sent in by local agencies and event organizers, from gallery openings to obituary notices.

14 ORIGINATED FROM STAFF/READER IDEAS

Several of these were columns about local issues. Several others were year-end retrospective features. The rest were mostly profiles of local movers and shakers.

NEWS RELEASES

Day after day, bureaucrats, event organizers and public relations experts send their news releases (also called press releases) to newsrooms big and small. They arrive by phone, fax, e-mail and snail mail; many elaborate releases use video production and Web sites.

In a flow so constant,

PRESS RELEASE

FOR IMMEDIATE RELEASE — Sept. 20, 2005

Media Contact: Eamonn Hughes, Dublin Marketing, 503-554-5455, hughes@barbecue.com

Public Contact: Student Barbecue Association, 503-555-6655

Student Barbecue Association

CAMPUS CLUBS COMBINE TO SPONSOR BINGO & BARBECUE BASH

...part of Ringworm Awareness Week, students from the Mountain Biking Club ...he Student Barbecue Association will sponsor a Bingo and Barbecue Bash ...y, Sept. 29, at 7 p.m. in Gilligan Hall. ...ofits from the barbecue, which costs $10 per person, will be donated to the ...worm Prevention Cooperative. ...ne barbecue will offer diners a choice of chicken, ribs, shrimp, roasted corn ...the cob, coleslaw and chocolate cake. And at 9 p.m., immediately following ...a bingo tournament will offer participants the chance to compete ...chairperson Kate Minniear, who has ...ree years. "And with the ...ine how this

some news releases are sure to end up on your desk. Those announcing tryouts for "Our Town" or soliciting baked goods for a Humane Society fundraiser may become calendar items. Others get routed to the copy desk to become news briefs and short features.

But many handouts are genuinely newsy: the golf team hires a new coach; an old professor retires; a student wins a prestigious scholarship. They may contain useful bits of biography, background or statistics. To develop these into legitimate stories, however, you'll need to add your own research.

Sometimes the news-release volume is so large, and the flow so persistent, that staffs feel besieged by publicists selling a cause, image or event.

Newsroom folklore tells of a frustrated editor at The Washington Post who once banned all publicity handouts. That lasted one day. Because even a big paper with a big staff needs to know where the bingo games, boat shows and bulimia support groups will be. ▼

YOUR OWN STORY IDEAS — OR SUGGESTIONS FROM READERS AND EDITORS

News stories typically focus on events. Feature stories, on the other hand, often focus on issues, trends or people. And the ideas for feature stories can originate in surprising, unpredictable ways.

Maybe you're walking down the street and you realize, "Everybody's wearing a nose ring these days. I should do a story about *nose rings.*"

Or maybe you're talking to a friend who says, "My mother just went on a pork-and-pineapple diet and lost 300 pounds" — and you think,

"Whoa. That's *bizarre.* Maybe I should do a story about that."

Yes, when you're a reporter, helpful story tips pop up everywhere: in meetings with editors, in phone calls from readers, in the pages of every magazine and Web site you browse. For many reporters, dreaming up cool story ideas is the most rewarding part of the job.

Take the three engaging features shown below. Here's how the reporters came up with those ideas:

DAVE PHILIPPS *on the idea for this story about sending critters through the mail, in the Colorado Springs Gazette:*

"An AP story about an alligator chomping its way out of a box in a post office ended with this matter-of-fact gem: *Alligators longer than 20 inches long cannot be sent through the mail.* When I stopped laughing, I called the post office and got a copy of the rules. From there it was just a matter of fishing out the ridiculous in the book's vast reservoir of mundane regulations."

FASHION FOOTNOTE

'YOU WORE FLIP-FLOPS TO THE WHITE HOUSE?!'

By Jodi S. Cohen and Maegan Carberry
Tribune staff reporters

THE FLIP-FLOP FLAP: As she sat in bed reading the newspaper, Chicago Tribune editor Ann Marie Lipinski spotted a photo of Northwestern University's championship lacrosse team posing with President Bush at the White House. Lipinski's eyes were drawn to the women's shoes: in the photo, four of the women were wearing flip-flop sandals. *Flip-flops? At a White House ceremony?*

"I ripped the picture out, set it aside and wondered if there was a story there," Lipinski said, "or if I just needed to get some sleep."

The next morning, Lipinski showed the photo to other newsroom colleagues — and a story was born. A team of reporters interviewed fashion experts, members of the lacrosse team and their mortified family members. The story created a national sensation, inspiring follow-up coverage from Newsweek to the "Today" show.

DON HAMILTON *on the idea for this package on baseball gloves — a blend of nostalgia, history and advice — in The Oregonian:*

"It was winter, I was cold and I needed some baseball in my life. So I conjured up this opening day story only to immerse myself in the game. I wanted history, lore and colorful characters. I wanted readers to smell the leather, hear the *thwock* of the ball and remember running onto the field with a new glove with all the other kids. And I wanted to learn how to spell *thwock.*"

🪦 **R.I.P.** Visit **THE MORGUE** for the complete text of these stories:

MAIL SPECIES ▶ 203   YOU WORE FLIP-FLOPS TO THE WHITE HOUSE? ▶ 208   GLOVE STORY ▶ 205

MORE ON **GENERATING STORY IDEAS** ▶ 114

MORE ON **NEWS RELEASES** ▶ 180

Finding and using sources

They provide the raw material that reporters turn into stories. Without them, there's no news.

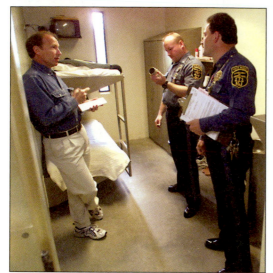

Asbury Park Press reporter Bob Cullinane (left) talks to corrections officers in a New Jersey state prison cell.

To write a story, you gather information. And the success of your story depends on the quality of your information. As the newsroom adage goes:

A reporter is only as good as his sources.

So what are sources? They can be government officials. Facts in an almanac. Records in a courthouse. Numbers on a Web site. They can illuminate and explain — or they can confuse, distort and lie. Which is why every reporter must learn how to:

◆ *select sources* for relevance, to focus each story on what's most important;

◆ *check sources* for accuracy, to ensure all facts and statements are true;

◆ *balance sources* for fairness, to represent all sides of every issue;

◆ *cultivate sources* for tips and story ideas in the future.

All stories require sources, but the types and numbers of sources vary from story to story. A single source might supply all the information you need for a short feature or news brief. But to get the best possible information for longer stories on more complex topics, you'll need to contact a wide variety of sources.

In the pages ahead, we'll examine how to get information *out of* your sources and *into* your story — whether you're researching data or conducting face-to-face interviews.

USING SOURCES TO WRITE A BREAKING NEWS STORY

You're in the newsroom late at night when you hear the first clues: chatter on the police scanner. Sirens echoing across campus. *Fire!*

Yes, a dormitory is burning. And since stories like this don't come to you, you've got to sprint to the scene. It's there you'll find many of the sources that will give your story its credibility and color: injured students, frantic parents, stunned neighbors, exhausted firefighters, beleaguered administrators.

So *go!* Drop this book and get moving!

Later, back in the newsroom, you can phone the campus spokesman and look through your paper's archives to learn: When was the last fire on campus? What's the history of the dormitory? Who are the best contacts to pursue?

Campus and hospital officials may hold back specific information about injured students, citing legal statutes. But many local and state reports will be public, and some may even be online: the fire alarm log, the fire marshal's recent safety inspections, reports on previous fires, statistics for the campus and the community.

Tracking down the best sources before deadline will depend, as always, on your instincts and initiative.

THE STORY

(1)(2) Two students were injured Friday evening when a fire gutted the third floor of Gilligan Hall, forcing almost 100 students into the chilly autumn air and temporary housing.

(1) One student is being treated for second-degree burns at General Hospital, university spokesman Wayne Dwops said. The other, treated for smoke inhalation, was released before midnight.

(1) Neither Dwops nor hospital officials would release student names or hometowns.

(3) The fire started in the northeast corner of the dorm's third floor, and firefighters spent 10 minutes rousting students from all four floors, according to city police reports.

(3) Campus police logs show that emergency teams responded quickly, first to an alarm at 7:19 p.m. and then to a 7:20 p.m. call from an unidentified resident assistant.

(3) The city's fire department also recorded a 911 call from a cell phone at 7:23 p.m., and two engines arrived within 10 minutes.

(4) Six city firefighters finished dousing flames shortly after 8 p.m., and police investigators began sifting through rubble immediately.

(1) The cause of the fire was not clear. "It's too early to speculate," Fire Capt. Dwayne D. Pipes said shortly before midnight.

(7) Constructed in 1924, the building houses 300 students in 150 rooms. Half of its residents are now boarding elsewhere, campus administrators said.

(5) "Thank goodness my roommate is on a date. She doesn't know we're homeless yet," said Barbara Seville, an exchange student from Italy who lived on the third floor.

(5) Farley Davidson invited Seville to bunk at his house at 1515 Maple Ave., adding: "I just wish I had room for everyone."

(3) The dorm was last inspected in April, with a May 19 report from a city fire marshal showing no safety code violations.

(6) A police official indicated that an arson investigation is under way.

THE SOURCES

1 Officials at or near the scene, speaking on the record.

2 Reporter's direct observation on the scene.

3 Routine police and fire reports, all public records.

4 Staff photographer's direct observation.

5 Ordinary people at the scene, speaking on the record.

6 A police official, speaking anonymously.

7 A news release posted on the university's official Web site.

READ THE COMPLETE TEXT OF A DORM FIRE STORY ▶ 216

THE WIDE WORLD OF SOURCES: A SURVEY OF WHAT'S AVAILABLE

The more sources you use, the better your reporting's:

◆ *Depth.* Your story will provide more information and insight.

◆ *Context.* The reader hears more points of view while approaching the topic from different perspectives.

◆ *Reliability.* There's less chance of inaccuracy or bias when you gather facts from a variety of sources.

Take that dormitory fire, for instance. Suppose you're writing a follow-up story on the fire: how it occurred, who's been affected and what happens next. Here's a look at the main types of sources you might consult for this (or any) story:

NEWSMAKERS

These are the people who, willingly or not, take part in news events: the firefighter who battles the blaze; the player who scores the big goal; the singer who headlines the concert. Their recollections, opinions and emotions validate stories and give them life. Who wants to read a story about a dramatic rescue without hearing from the hero?

EXAMPLE:
Firefighter Dwayne D. Pipes raced into the burning kitchen to carry 3-year-old Jim Pansey to safety.
"I heard a child screaming," Pipes said, "so I hacked through a wall and found him huddled in a closet. The poor kid was frozen in terror."

SPOKESPEOPLE

Who speaks for institutions? Big corporations? Or public agencies like the police or fire departments? Usually one person (or office) is responsible for disseminating information to the media. This helps streamline the process and eliminate confusion, but it also gives those organizations more opportunity to control or "spin" the facts.

EXAMPLE:
University spokesman Wayne Dwops said the fire damaged the Human Resources offices on the ground floor, but 99 percent of their computer files had been saved.
The dorm will remain closed for at least two more days, Dwops said.

EXPERTS

Whatever the story topic, you can usually track down an expert — a professor, a scientist, an author — to offer some opinions or expertise. Not all "experts" have official-sounding credentials (someone might be an expert in Elvis trivia, for example) — so anytime you interview experts, make sure their insights are reliable and relevant.

EXAMPLE:
Justin Case, a Harvard law professor and author of "Death in the Dorm," calls the issue "a ticking time bomb."
Every dorm fire, Case argues, "proves that administrators would rather spend your tuition on sports than make campus buildings safer."

OFFICIAL RECORDS

All institutions compile and store massive amounts of information. In most cases, all you have to do is ask (or know where to look), and you can unearth helpful statistics, reports, court records, etc. Private companies are often secretive, but most public records are available under the Freedom of Information Act. ▼

EXAMPLE:
In 1977, according to university records, junior Claire Voyant sued the school for $1.7 million after suffering third-degree burns in a dormitory fire that spring. Voyant convinced the jury that the fire had left her "too traumatized to continue her studies."

REFERENCE MATERIAL

Before the Internet came along, most research relied on printed materials. But nowadays, it's faster and more efficient to explore encyclopedias, almanacs, dictionaries and phone books online. (For more on Web research, see the next page.)
For instance, an Internet search for dormitory fire statistics found:

EXAMPLE:
According to the National Fire Protection Association, more than 2,000 fires occur at U.S. colleges and universities each year, resulting in three deaths and 102 injuries annually, on average. Most of those fires occur early in the morning.

ORDINARY FOLKS

Not every source in every story *has* to be an authority with an official-sounding title. Sometimes you want to hear the opinions or anecdotes of the man in the street or the woman on campus. Whether reacting to an event or typifying a trend, quotes from ordinary people add authenticity that resonates with readers.

EXAMPLE:
"I'm moving out," said sophomore Grace Quirrel. "Next term, I'm renting an apartment off campus.
"This dorm isn't safe. There's too much drinking, too many parties where yahoos go nuts and make life dangerous for everybody else."

QUESTION & ANSWER

What does it mean to "attribute" something to a source?

It's a common journalistic term, so get used to using it. Take this sentence:
Sen. Smith said the war is a reckless mistake.
The phrase *Sen. Smith said* is called an attribution. It identifies where the idea that *the war is a reckless mistake* came from. And that's important to specify.
Attributing facts and opinions to their sources shows readers that you're *reporting* what's been said, not saying it yourself. ▼
Look at the examples in the white boxes at left. See how every fact and quote is carefully attributed?

What do journalists mean when they talk about "anonymous" sources?

Some sources are reluctant to be named or quoted in a story. They're afraid they'll be fired, embarrassed — even arrested. So reporters will sometimes word an attribution this way:
One prominent senator called the war "a reckless mistake."
Granting anonymity to nervous sources is often the only way to get information into a story. But it can undermine your credibility, too, which is why editors generally discourage it. ▼

How do you decide whether a source is reliable?

Be wary of *every* source you use. Ask yourself:
◆ How does this person know what he/she knows?
◆ What's the past record of this source's reliability?
◆ Does this source have some bias or self-interest that compromises the integrity of what he/she says? Am I being manipulated for some reason?
◆ Is this information available from other sources that would allow me to verify or refute what he/she is saying?

MORE ON **OPEN RECORDS LAWS** ▶ 137   MORE ON **ATTRIBUTIONS** ▶ 82   MORE ON **ANONYMOUS SOURCES** ▶ 79, 107

Using the Internet

The World Wide Web is every researcher's dream come true.

With a few clicks of the mouse, you can scan the latest headlines. You can dig up terrific story ideas. You can gather statistics, quotations, facts and opinions from every corner of the globe.

The Internet is unquestionably the most valuable reporting tool ever created.

By now, you've probably already spent endless hours exploring the Web. But if you've never used the Internet for serious research, you may need to increase your efficiency — and your skepticism. As the AP stylebook points out, "The Web is a sprawling database that's about one-quarter wheat and three-quarters chaff." You can't always find what you need, and you can't always trust what you find.

Keep in mind, too, that no matter how useful the Internet may be, it's no substitute for reality — for *real* discussions with *real* human beings. Look at the woman in this photo. She's been staring at that monitor for hours, mesmerized into a stupor. Don't let that happen to you. At some point, you need to get away from your desk, get out of the office and *do some actual reporting.*

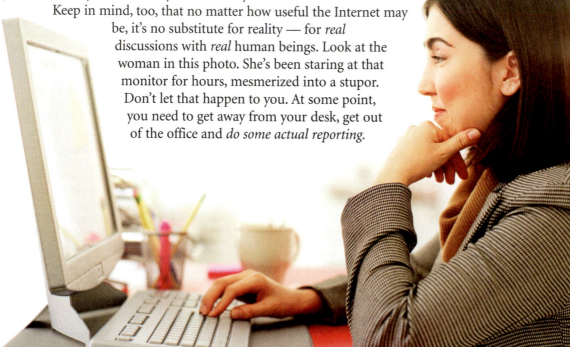

THE ELEVENTH COMMANDMENT

You're surfing the Web. You stumble on a sentence, a paragraph — *maybe even an entire story* — that is so exquisitely right, so swipe-ably perfect, that you copy and paste it into your files and pretend you wrote it.

You've just plagiarized. It's lazy. It's wrong. And if you're caught, it could end your journalism career.

With proper attribution, to quote another's thoughts and words is appropriate; plagiarism, however, is cheating, and it may break copyright law as well.

UH-OH! PLAGIARISM ALERT! Yes, we must confess: *That entire preceding paragraph was plagiarized.* It's true. As we were researching plagiarism on the Web, we found that quote and lifted it into our story.

So what should we do with that paragraph? We should either **quote and credit the source —**

As grammarian Kenneth G. Wilson once said: "With proper attribution, to quote another's thoughts and words is appropriate; plagiarism, however, is cheating."

— or paraphrase, while still crediting the source —

Quoting someone's thoughts and words is appropriate, grammarian Kenneth G. Wilson says — provided you attribute them properly. But plagiarism, he says, is cheating.

— or rework and reword the idea until it's more ours than theirs. But remember, readers deserve to know where facts and ideas originate. So when in doubt, cite your source. ▼

THE REPORTER'S WEBLIOGRAPHY

Ready to do some online reporting? Here's a select list of recommended Web sites to get you started.

RESEARCH & REFERENCE

Bartleby.com
www.bartleby.com
The one-stop site for all your reference needs: dictionary, thesaurus, almanac, Bible, quotation finder, encyclopedia — and more.

State and Local Government on the Net
www.statelocalgov.net
The fastest way to link to all city, state or county agencies, wherever you're searching.

ProfNet
www.profnet.com
Need an expert? ProfNet connects reporters with thousands of experts and spokespeople.

Urban Legends and Folklore
www.urbanlegends.about.com
The best place to verify or debunk those dubious "stories" that circulate via e-mail.

SEARCH ENGINES

Google
www.google.com
The most impressive all-around search site, whether you're looking for Web pages, newsgroups, images or news updates.

Yahoo
www.yahoo.com
The best directory site, with links to maps, phone books and thousands of topics.

Webcrawler
www.webcrawler.com
A "meta" search engine that compiles results from a half-dozen other engines.

For a more comprehensive list of the best Web sites for reporters, see page 310.

JOURNALISM TIPS & TOOLS

National Press Club online library
www.npc.press.org/library/reporter.cfm
The ultimate clearinghouse of resources for reporters, everything from phone directories to FBI crime reports. Truly the motherlode.

Newslink
www.newslink.org
Looking for a newspaper, magazine, TV or radio Web site? You'll find the link here.

Poynter Institute for Media Studies
www.poynter.org
Helpful advice and engaging discussions on all aspects of the journalist's craft.

A Journalist's Guide to the Internet
www.reporter.umd.edu
Another handy guide providing links to hundreds of online resources for reporters.

MORE ON **PLAGIARISM** ▶ 147 AND **COPYRIGHT** ▶ 143

INTERNET SEARCH TIPS FROM THE PROS

Our number one Internet research tip: Make friends with a librarian. No matter how savvy you think you already are, a smart librarian can help you save time and search more effectively with tips like these, compiled from a variety of library Web sites:

◆ **Try using directories AND search engines.** They're both handy. A *directory* provides a huge list of Web sites organized by topics that get more detailed the deeper you dig (**Yahoo.com** and **Excite.com** are good examples). A *search engine* lets you enter key words or phrases, then scours the Web to provide links to sites using those words. (The top search engines include **Google.com** and **alltheweb.com**).

◆ **Bookmark your favorite search sites and get familiar with them.** Don't limit yourself to one search site. They all have strengths and weaknesses. Directories are generally best for providing broad context; search engines are best for zeroing in on specifics.

◆ **Keep keywords as specific as possible.** When using search engines, avoid common words like *money* or *sports*. For best results, enter several keywords at a time. Or use phrases. Then keep refining your keywords as you monitor results, adding new words, deleting others, testing synonyms.

◆ **Study the site's search syntax.** In other words, learn a few tricks to increase your efficiency. Take a moment to review the tips on the search site's "help" page to find out if you should type quotation marks around phrases, or if capital letters matter. At some search engines, typing *Miami heat* will dig up sites about basketball; typing *Miami AND heat NOT basketball* will show you sites about Florida weather.

◆ **Watch your spelling.** A misspelled word forces your search engine to ignore the results you really want. But keep in mind that some words (*theater* and *ecstasy*) may yield useful results if you deliberately enter alternative spellings (*theatre* and *ecstacy*).

◆ **Before you link to Web sites, study their addresses.** Do they look professional? Reliable? Visit the most credible sites first.

FAKES, FLUBS, SPOOFS, GOOFS AND HOAXES

When a massive tsunami struck South Asia in 2004, several newspapers printed this "exclusive" front-page photo showing a crowd fleeing the wave.

The problem? This photo, forwarded around the world via e-mail, was actually taken in 2002 on a beach in China, where tourists flock to watch the giant surf.

"Mistakes like this make a mockery of the media and damage the image of journalists being trustworthy selectors of news," said Guy Berger, a journalism professor in South Africa, upon seeing this photo in the Johannesburg paper.

Bogus Web material appears in stories, too. In 1998, The New York Times explained how popular movie titles had been translated into Chinese:

◆ *The Crying Game* became "Oh No! My Girlfriend Has a Penis!"

◆ *George of the Jungle* was "Big Dumb Monkey Man Keeps Whacking Tree With Genitals."

◆ *Batman and Robin* was "Come To My Cave and Wear This Rubber Codpiece, Cute Boy."

Sadly, the joke was on the Times. Those titles were all spoofs from TopFive.com, a humorous Web site.

"I made a mistake," the reporter later lamented. "I should have checked each of these out."

WHO DO YOU TRUST? EVALUATING A WEB SITE'S RELIABILITY

A reporter is only as good as his (or her) sources. So when you use a Web site as a source, you entrust your credibility to faceless strangers.

You can get burned doing that. How? By reprinting information that *looks* reliable, but turns out to be:

◆ fabrications or distortions disguised as truth, or

◆ statements misquoted or wrongly attributed to someone.

As you gain experience in online research, you'll see that the closer you get to the original source, the more trustworthy the facts. You'll also find that institutions (whose site's addresses often end in *.gov, .us* or *.edu*) are more credible than personal pages.

How do you assess the reliability of a Web site? By evaluating its authority, accuracy, objectivity and timeliness.

AUTHORITY

◆ Are you sure of the author's identity, reliability and credentials?
◆ Is the site sponsored by a reputable institution or organization?
◆ Does the information seem to be comprehensive and complete?
◆ Is there a way to contact the author to verify or challenge information?

ACCURACY

◆ Did the information originate with this source — or does the author say where the information was obtained?
◆ Can you verify this information from another reliable source?
◆ Are there spelling/grammar/factual errors that cast doubt on this source's professionalism or reliability?

OBJECTIVITY

◆ Is this site affiliated with a sponsor or group with a slanted agenda?
◆ Can you trust this site to distinguish between facts and opinions?
◆ Does this site present feedback from readers who challenge its accuracy or correct mistakes?
◆ Might this be satire or a hoax?

TIMELINESS

◆ Has this site been updated recently?
◆ Are there publication dates on all pages containing timely material?
◆ Can you ensure that all information is up to date?
◆ Are the links to and from this page updated regularly?

BEYOND THE BASICS: E-MAIL, NEWSGROUPS AND BLOGS

Instead of gazing passively at Web pages, try using the Internet to interact more productively with news sources. Here's how:

◆ **NEWSGROUPS.** Newsgroups are online bulletin boards organized by topic. They're a great place to find story ideas and eavesdrop on conversations relevant to your beat. If you have questions about a specific topic (and you have time to wait for a response), newsgroups can help you track down experts or generate authoritative answers to the questions you pose. Caution: *Don't trust anyone whose identity you haven't verified.*

◆ **E-MAIL.** It's the most efficient way to contact the experts you find mentioned on Web sites you visit. (Search engines can help you track down their e-mail addresses.) It's also a great way to conduct interviews with multiple sources simultaneously. And of course, reporters use e-mail to receive press releases, tips and feedback from readers, colleagues and sources.

◆ **WEBLOGS.** Most Web logs dispense opinions. Some spread rumors. But many do a fine job covering news events, refining and refuting facts presented by mainstream media. Monitoring blogs can produce terrific story ideas; information from blogs, if verified and cited, can run in your stories. And *writing* your own blog establishes a dialogue with sources and readers. ▼

READ HOW INTERNET REPORTING HELPED CAPTURE **AN ESCAPED MURDERER** ▶ 224   MORE ON **BLOGS AND WRITING FOR THE WEB** ▶ 159

Observation

To bring news stories to life, you need to engage your senses — and the reader's, too.

There's an ancient adage that editors and reporters love to quote over and over: *Show,* don't tell.

Suppose you're covering a dorm fire. You talk to the fire chief, the cop, the students. They tell you about the blaze, the building, the damage — but where's the drama? The realism? The human cost?

Show, don't tell.

When you're at the fire scene, engage your eyes, your ears, your journalistic radar. Where are the victims? What are they doing? What are they wearing? Are they clutching pets? Possessions? Each other?

As a reporter, you're not simply a stenographer. You're an eyewitness, a spectator with a front-row seat. You're the eyes, the ears, the *senses* of the reader who visits the scene through the power of your words.

The ability to observe accurately — to record events so faithfully that details jump right off the page — is the secret to great reporting. In fact, it's the key to success in *any* kind of writing, which explains why so many successful novelists — Mark Twain, Stephen Crane, Dorothy Parker, Ernest Hemingway, Carl Hiaasen — began as reporters.

Show, don't tell. So rather than tell you any more, we'll show you some classic examples.

SIGHT

Yes, it's time to retrain your eyeballs to notice the little things: the bald spot on the back of a man's head; the tattoos on a woman's hands; the exit wound behind the dictator's ear.

In the examples at right, notice how vividly the visual details capture what the reporter is seeing. Some of these descriptions seem almost too poetic to be real. But the attention to detail lets you view the scene as if you're looking through the reporter's eyes.

CHARLES WALLACE *eavesdrops on a pearl merchant in Bahrain:*

Hassan Arrayed opened a ragged square of red felt on the desk in front of him and lowered his face like a falcon swooping on its prey.

With a cackle and a gapped-tooth grin, Arrayed held his prize out to a woman customer who, as tradition still dictates in conservative corners of the Arab world, was enveloped in gauzy black silks down to her tattooed hands.

"This one is $6,000," he said proudly.

Clutched in Arrayed's hand was a lustrous pearl the color of Devonshire cream. The pearl, which caught the sunlight flooding in from the streets of Bahrain's gold market outside the stall, was the size of a grape.

TOM WOLFE *describes the hair of an aging American author:*

As we approach from the rear, we notice a bald spot on the crown of his head. It's about the size of a Sunshine Chip-a-Roo cookie, this bald spot, freckled and toasty brown. Gloriously suntanned, in fact. Around this bald spot swirls a corona of dark-brown hair that becomes quite thick by the time it completes its mad Byronic rush down the back of his turtleneck and out to the side in great bushes over his ears. ▼

MILTON BRACKER *describes the scene in Italy in 1945 after dictator Benito Mussolini was executed:*

Mussolini had changed in death, but not enough to be anyone else. His closely shaved head and his bull neck were unmistakable. His body seemed small and a little shrunken, but he was never a tall man. At least one bullet had passed through his head. It had emerged some three inches behind his right ear. There was another small hole nearer his forehead where another bullet seemed to have gone in.

As if he were not dead or dishonored enough, at least two young men in the crowd broke through and aimed kicks at his skull. One glanced off. But the other landed full on his right jaw, and there was a hideous crunch that wholly disfigured the once-proud face.

MORE ON TOM WOLFE AND **FEATURE WRITING STYLE** ▶ **116**

SOUND

Capturing sounds on the printed page isn't easy. In fact, you'll find some stories (say, a profile of a comic who does celebrity impressions) may be better suited for radio or TV if they're dependent on sound for their success.

Still, skilled writers employ all their senses to capture the smells, tastes and (yes) sounds of their stories. Notice how the descriptions at right range from subtle to extreme as they try to paint sonic pictures for readers.

TOM WOLFE *profiles a woman attending a new-age seminar in a California hotel:*

The trainer had said, "Take your finger off the repress button!" Let it gush up and pour out! . . . So she starts moaning.

"Oooooooooooooooooooohhhhhhhhhhh!"

And when she starts moaning, the most incredible and exhilarating thing begins to happen. A wave of moans spreads through the people lying around her, as if her energy were radiating out like a radar pulse.

"Oooooooooooooooooooohhhhhhhhhhh!"

So she lets her moan rise into a keening sound.

"Oooooooooooooooooooohhhhhhhhhhh-eeeeeeeeeeeeeeeeeeeeee!"

And when she begins to keen, the souls near her begin keening, even while the moans are still spreading to the prostrate folks farther from her, on the edges of the room.

"Eeeeeeeeeeeeooooooooooohhhhheeeee-eeeeeeeeeoooooooooooooh!"

So she lets her keening sound rise up into a real scream.

"Eeeeeeeeeeeeeaiaiaiaiaiaiaiaiaiaiaiaiai!"

And this rolls out in a wave, too, first through those near her, and then toward the far edges.

"Aiaiaiaiaiaiaiaiaiieeeeeeeeeeeeeeeeohhh-hhhheeeeeeeeeeaiaiaiai!"

And so she turns it all the way up, into a scream such as she has never allowed herself in her entire life.

"AiaiaiaiaiaiaiaAAAAAAAAAAAAARRRRRR-RRRGGGGGGGGGHHHHHHHHH!"

And her full scream spreads from soul to soul, over the top of the keens and fading moans —

"AAAAAAAARRRRRRGGGGGGHHHHaiaiai-aieeeeeeeeoooooohhhheeeeeaiaiaiaiaiaia-AAAAAARRRRRRRRGGGGGHHHHHHHHH!"

— until at last the entire room is consumed in her scream.

SUSAN ORLEAN *describes an African record store in Paris:*

If you walk down the Rue des Plantes, you will at first hear just the usual rumbling and tootling and clattering sounds of a Paris street, and then, as you pass the open door of Afric' Music, you will be blasted by a few bars of a Congolese ballad, and as soon as you step past the door, the ballad will suddenly be out of earshot, and the Paris street sounds will resume, as if you had walked through a harmonic cloudburst.

JUSTIN DAVIDSON *reviews a classical musician in concert:*

The pianist Evgeny Kissin propelled himself stiffly onto the stage of Avery Fisher Hall on Thursday, looking rather as if his joints needed oiling. He dutifully bent his mouth into a labored and momentary smile, gave a quick jerk of his torso in lieu of a bow, and then sat at the piano where, in an instant, all his discomfort melted into power and control.

Watching the awkward young pianist plunge into music was like seeing a seal slip into water, and in the 40 mesmerizing minutes that followed, Kissin gave one of the most lissome and lyrical performances of Beethoven's Piano Concerto No. 5 that I have ever heard.

BILL BLUNDELL *wrote this lead to a story on the vanishing American cowboy:*

The lariat whirls as the man on horseback separates a calf from the herd. Suddenly, the loop snakes around the calf's rear legs and tightens. Wrapping a turn of rope around the saddle horn, the rider drags the hapless animal to his crew.

The flanker whips the calf onto its back, and the medicine man inoculates the animal. Amid blood, dust and bawling, the calf is dehorned with a coring tool, branded in an acrid cloud of smoke from burning hair and flesh, earmarked with a penknife in the ranch's unique pattern and castrated. It's all over in one minute.

DAVID RHODE *watches a street dentist at work in Pakistan:*

As Mr. Sajjad sat on a small stool on a pedestrian bridge over a set of railway tracks, Mr. Jameel pried out brown chunks of dead tooth and flicked them onto the red plastic tarp spread out under the stool. At one point, the amateur dentist lit up a cigarette to smoke as he worked. At another point, a locomotive passed under the bridge, belching black diesel smoke onto the instruments and into the patient's mouth.

The factory worker showed no sign of discomfort as Mr. Jameel filed down his false tooth. He did not even complain when his gums started bleeding. Throughout the ordeal, he winced just twice. Afterward, he admired his new tooth in a small hand-held mirror and thanked his dentist.

ACTION

Why are so many newspaper stories so boring? It's because nothing ever *happens*. There's no action.

If you want to write a dull sports story, for example, just quote the coach and spout some statistics. But if you want to bring that story to life, describe how the Big Play unfolded, how the touchdown got scored, how the players celebrated and the fans went nuts.

Verbs add *verve*.

EMOTION

It's not easy. Capturing the moods and emotions of strangers, without adding inappropriate goo or schmaltz, is terrifically difficult to do. And it's usually best reserved for the right moment in the right feature story.

But notice, in these examples, how the writers *show* you the scene, in simple and direct language, without *telling* you how to feel.

COREY KILGANNON *writes about Hermine Wilber, who has just undergone surgery to end a lifetime of deafness:*

"Are you ready?" asked the technician, named Sara Morton, who specializes in cochlear implants.

"Am I ready?" answered Mrs. Wilber, after reading Ms. Morton's lips. "55 years."

Then Ms. Morton held a piece of paper in front of her mouth so that Mrs. Wilber could not see what her lips were doing. "Bop, bop, bop," Ms. Morton said.

Right away, Mrs. Wilber repeated the sounds she had just *heard*. "Bop, bop, bop."

Everyone around her, all these people who loved her, started to cry.

"Come on," Mrs. Wilber said with a happy smile. "Talk to me."

Her oldest daughter, also named Hermine, put her hand gently over her mother's eyes and said words Mrs. Wilber had never heard before: "I love you, Mom."

Her grandson, Thomas, who is a teenager, tried to speak, but he was crying too hard with happiness to get any words out.

Her husband, Bill, walked up to her and said, softly, "I met you in 1946." It was the first time she had ever heard his voice. He asked her if he sounded as she had imagined. Yes, she said, his voice was low and strong.

BOB GREENE *describes the scene as a daughter visits her mother, who's dying of cancer:*

It was a Friday night. Her mother was in bed; she was hooked up to an oxygen tank by a long cord. The daughter climbed onto the bed next to her mother, just as she had as a little girl. The daughter sensed that her mother was thinking something but not saying it.

The mother looked over. She said the words:

"I just don't want to leave yet."

The two women both started to cry. They held each other, and the daughter could not tell who was rocking whom: the mother rocking the daughter, as in days long ago, or the daughter rocking the mother?

FOR TWO EXAMPLES OF STORIES USING DETAILED OBSERVATIONS, SEE **OREGON PAYS TRIBUTE TO ITS VIETNAM VETS** ▶ **202** AND **FOR THOSE CUT OFF, A LIFE PRIMEVAL** ▶ **213**

Taking notes

What's the best way to record the facts and quotes you gather for a story?

It seems ridiculously simple: People talk to you. You write it down. You type it up. Done! Next!

Not so fast, Lois. Reporting may not be rocket science, we admit, but the truth is: If you don't take

Christina Leonard takes notes and makes a backup tape recording while interviewing a county official for an Arizona Republic story.

good notes, you cannot write a good story. And good note-taking isn't easy. It involves major multitasking — lots of listening, interpreting, observing, evaluating, writing and thinking in a hurry. Under pressure. About unfamiliar topics. In strange places.

If you're not careful, your notebook can become a confusing, chaotic mess, which is why every good reporter needs a system for recording data quickly and organizing it smartly — a system that guarantees that the data you put in your story exactly matches the data your sources give you.

And it all starts with your notebook.

WHAT YOU MIGHT FIND ON A TYPICAL PAGE IN A REPORTER'S NOTEBOOK

Suppose you're covering a Memorial Day parade in Dayton. Here are some notes you might gather:

1 A running log of the time.

2 Joe Hyatt, 63, lives in Dayton. He was a Marine lieutenant colonel in Vietnam. Hyatt said, *"This is a proud and sacred day for Dayton, a day when we celebrate what it means to be American."* Notice how, without learning shorthand, you can speed up your transcribing by:

◆ Skipping small words (*a, the*).
◆ Using symbols instead of common words (*"2b"* for *"to be,"* *"w/"* for *"when,"* and so on).
◆ Abbreviating long words (*"D"* for *"Dayton,"* *"Am"* for *"American"*). But it's wise to review your notes and spell out those abbreviations while your memory is fresh to avoid confusion. (Did he say *"Americans"* or *"an American"*?)

3 Carefully spell out all important facts: names, phone numbers, statistics. Double-check them with your sources as you write them down. When in doubt — if you gather material that you might want to check later — circle it. Or draw a box. Or put question marks beside it. Or add a phrase like *sp?* (check spelling) or *cq?* (check the accuracy).

4 As soon as you have a free moment, review your notes to clean up any sloppy shorthand and to add details that you were too busy to record at the time: physical descriptions, emotions, tone of voice. (For instance, Little Mary here was a curly-haired blonde in a red-white-and-blue dress, clutching small American flags in each hand.) Fill in any gaps in your data collection. Don't worry about gathering too much material. You may not use it all, but you'll regret what you *don't* have.

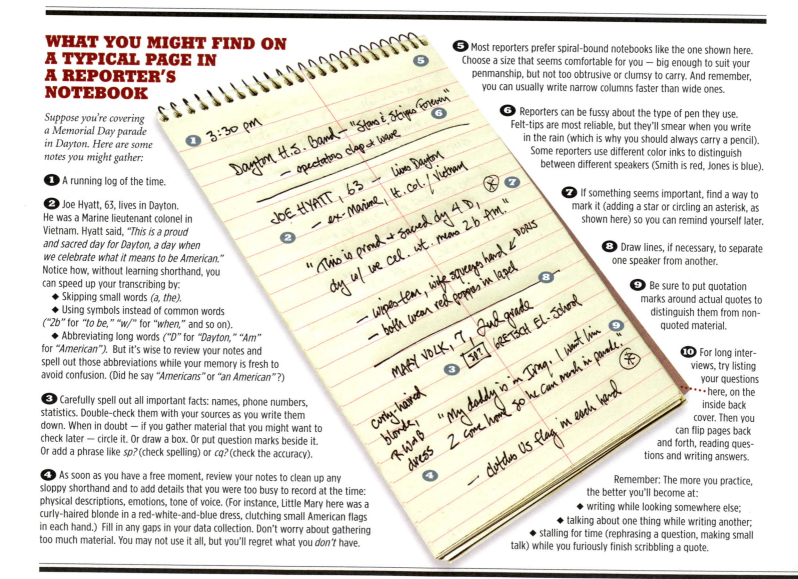

5 Most reporters prefer spiral-bound notebooks like the one shown here. Choose a size that seems comfortable for you — big enough to suit your penmanship, but not too obtrusive or clumsy to carry. And remember, you can usually write narrow columns faster than wide ones.

6 Reporters can be fussy about the type of pen they use. Felt-tips are most reliable, but they'll smear when you write in the rain (which is why you should always carry a pencil). Some reporters use different color inks to distinguish between different speakers (Smith is red, Jones is blue).

7 If something seems important, find a way to mark it (adding a star or circling an asterisk, as shown here) so you can remind yourself later.

8 Draw lines, if necessary, to separate one speaker from another.

9 Be sure to put quotation marks around actual quotes to distinguish them from non-quoted material.

10 For long interviews, try listing your questions here, on the inside back cover. Then you can flip pages back and forth, reading questions and writing answers.

Remember: The more you practice, the better you'll become at:
◆ writing while looking somewhere else;
◆ talking about one thing while writing another;
◆ stalling for time (rephrasing a question, making small talk) while you furiously finish scribbling a quote.

WHICH IS THE BEST WAY TO TAKE NOTES? A LOOK AT THE PROS AND CONS

Ah, the simple notebook. It's the most indispensable, tried-and-true tool in your toolbox. No matter how high-tech you **NOTEBOOK** try to be, you'll always end up someplace where your only option is scribbling notes in a notebook (or, if you're really desperate, on gum wrappers, envelopes, toilet paper — or your arm). So you might as well get good at it, to avoid being caught unprepared.

ADVANTAGES	DISADVANTAGES
◆ It's low-tech. Nothing to break, no batteries to fail. Worst case: Your pen runs out of ink, so you have to borrow another one.	◆ Since most people talk faster than you can write, quotes may be inaccurate (unless you learn shorthand).
◆ Written notes are easy to access and transcribe later.	◆ Standing still to write can be cumbersome and restricting.
◆ You keep a permanent record of what you heard and saw.	◆ Some of your scribblings will later seem illegible to you.

Taping interviews is the best way to ensure accuracy, especially for lengthy Q-and-A's with fast talkers. Some careful reporters even take additional **TAPE RECORDER** notes while they're taping (as backup, and to add comments and observations). But remember: Recorders make some interviewees uneasy. And in some states, taping people without their permission is illegal. Always ask first.

ADVANTAGES	DISADVANTAGES
◆ It's the most accurate way to capture every word spoken during an interview.	◆ Replaying and transcribing tapes takes lots of valuable time.
◆ If anyone tries to challenge your story, you have actual proof of what was said.	◆ If the machine fails, the tape jams or the battery dies, you've got a serious problem.
◆ It lets you post interview audio on your paper's Web site.	◆ Unless you save every tape, you won't have a lasting record of your interviews.

Some reporters lug their laptops everywhere, taking notes and writing stories while they interview newsmakers or **TYPING** watch the Big Game. But laptops are still buggy and delicate, and their batteries can die unexpectedly. That's why most computer note-taking occurs in the newsroom, where reporters sit at their desks and work the phones *hard,* typing up what they need as they talk.

ADVANTAGES	DISADVANTAGES
◆ It's the fastest way to turn your notes into a story, since it's all right there on the screen.	◆ Since most people talk faster than you can type, quotes may be inaccurate (unless you learn to type with blazing speed).
◆ It's the most efficient way to gather last-minute details or plug holes in a story on deadline.	◆ Computer problems can ruin an interview or destroy a file.
◆ You can conduct an entire interview using chat or e-mail.	◆ You're stuck sitting in one place, staring at the screen.

Arm yourself with a small tape recorder, but keep it in its holster and take notes. The tape recorder is often intimidating and you don't have time to transcribe the tapes. If you discover, however, that you can't keep pace with your subject's logic or eloquence, fire up the recorder.
Steve Duin, *The Oregonian*

I became dependent on tape recorders as a cub reporter and had to wean myself from them. I never use tape recorders. I only take notes.
Deb Holland, *The Rapid City Journal*

Use a tape recorder. Only by listening to the tape later can we be properly appalled at how badly we misheard a quote and/or bungled it in our notes.
Jim Kershner, *The Spokesman-Review* (Spokane, Wash.)

I detest tape recorders. They set an adversarial tone and make interview subjects less inclined to relax and open up. Only the killer quotes need be used and they can be accurately captured with pen and paper.
Randy Ludlow, *The Columbus Dispatch*

The PRESS ROOM
WHICH DO YOU PREFER: TAKING NOTES OR USING A TAPE RECORDER?

Once I interviewed Ralph Nader for a story about a congressman. "His problem is he has no political guts," Nader said into my tape recorder. "Are you referring to his work on health care?" I responded. "Yes." The quote ran and the congressman's chief of staff hit the roof. "Nader says you misquoted him," he said. "You tell Nader I've got it on tape," I said. Half hour later he called again. "Nader says you took it out of context." When I stopped laughing, I told him about the context.
Don Hamilton, *The Columbian* (Vancouver, Wash.)

For a series on adolescent girls, I recorded, to ensure I could capture the way girls talk. If the person speaks fast, I record. If the person has a habit of changing their story or stretching the truth, I record. In interviews for daily stories, however, I don't record, unless it's the governor.
Monica Mendoza, *The Arizona Republic*

Both. Take the tape recorder, turn it on and set it aside. Take clear notes. When you hear that perfect quote, check the meter on the tape recorder and write it in your notes, so you can find the exact quote when you need it.
Phillip Pina, *Saint Paul Pioneer Press*

Tape recorders always fail (at the *worst* moments). Tape recorders make sources talk funny. Recorders encourage lazy notetaking. Recorders encourage lazy listening.

Clip and paste on your tape recorder:

 WARNING! Tape recorders may be dangerous to your professional health.
Don Fry, *writing coach*

Interviewing

Interviews, like stories, come in an endless variety of shapes and sizes.

They can be fast five-minute phoners where you ask a senator for a sound bite (*"What do you think of the new tax proposal?"*). Or they can be intimate interrogations of the rich and famous (like the 1977 Playboy interview with Barbra Streisand that took nine grueling months to complete*).

Writing may be a solitary art, but interviewing is a social skill. You must be friendly, but aggressive.

Orlando Sentinel reporter Ken Ma takes notes during an interview with former heavyweight boxing champion Evander Holyfield.

Polite, but probing. Sympathetic, but skeptical. You need to hurl hard questions at complete strangers who may be shy, sneaky, suspicious of the media or emotionally distraught from the car crash they just survived.

But for many reporters, it's the most fun part of the job. It offers you a fascinating opportunity to pick the brains of the stupidest and smartest and most successful people you'll ever meet. If you're a good listener, you can be a great interviewer.

*Each month, the Playboy Interview provides a fine example of a celebrity Q-and-A. In fact, many men read Playboy just for the interviews. No, really.

ASK YOURSELF: WHICH TYPE OF INTERVIEW SHOULD THIS BE?

Anytime you talk to someone to gather material for a story — facts, quotes, opinions, reactions — it's called an interview.

But no two interviews are alike. They'll vary according to the time you have, the facts you need and the accessibility of the interviewee. You might wind up with:

◆ *A long, formal interview* where you sit privately in a room, asking probing questions and getting revealing answers.

◆ *A quick phoner* where you seek fast facts to plug into a story.

◆ *A walkaround* where you accompany your interviewee as he/she does that newsworthy thing you're writing about.

◆ *An on-the-fly chat* with a newsmaker (say, a politician or athlete) where you fire off questions as they walk through a public place.

◆ *A backgrounder* where you informally pick an expert's brain on a topic you're researching.

But before you start asking any questions, decide whether it's best to conduct your interview in person, over the phone or via e-mail.

	ADVANTAGES	DISADVANTAGES
IN PERSON	◆ It's the best way to build rapport and encourage sources to cooperate. ◆ A subject's physical surroundings often provide useful information. ◆ You can pick up cues by watching a person's gestures, body language. ◆ People take you more seriously when you're right in front of them.	◆ You can waste time setting up a meeting, traveling, waiting, making friendly small talk, etc. ◆ Distractions (people, phone calls) often interrupt the interview. ◆ If *you're* uncomfortable (or not a pleasant person to be around), it soon becomes obvious.
BY PHONE	◆ Fast, efficient way to get answers (IF they answer their phone). ◆ For many people, talking to a reporter isn't as intimidating when they can't see you taking notes. ◆ With cell phones, conversations can occur anytime, anywhere — no advance notice is even necessary.	◆ It's impersonal. You can't tell what people look like, what they're doing, how they're reacting. ◆ It's difficult to record a phone conversation without buying a reliable recording gizmo. ◆ You're much more likely to mishear or misquote someone.
BY E-MAIL	◆ Gives interviewees time to ponder and construct intelligent responses. ◆ Offers the most flexibility; you can ask and answer questions whenever it's most convenient. ◆ Since responses are typed, they're easy to copy and paste — and they provide a record of all that's said.	◆ There's no personal interaction. ◆ The lag time between questions and answers makes it hard to ask immediate follow-up questions. ◆ It takes people an hour to type what they could say in five minutes. ◆ Are you sure this is really the person he or she *claims* to be?

TIPS FOR SUCCESSFUL INTERVIEWS:
BEFORE, DURING AND AFTER

You're a reporter now. You've got stories to write. You need to interview people who possess information your readers require. So what do you do? Here's how the process works.

A British reporter climbs a rope to interview an acrobat practicing a circus routine in London in the 1990s.

SETTING UP THE INTERVIEW

◆ **First, do your homework.** Get familiar with your subject. Read old news stories. Do online research. Check with affiliated organizations. Talk to your editors. Then:

◆ **Think through your story.** Decide who your best sources will be. Who are the experts? Who's in charge? Who's being affected? Who has strong opinions? How many sources do you need to contact?

◆ **Determine the best way to interview those sources.** Who's your key source? Should that interview be done face to face? Should others be done by phone or e-mail?

◆ **Set up the interview(s),** usually by phone or e-mail.

Be persuasive and polite; if necessary, be nicer *than you actually are.* Act like you need help (which you do) and describe what you want. People are more likely to assist you if they know what you're looking for.

◆ **Decide where and when to meet.** Find a quiet, convenient location — or should you meet them in their native habitat (a doctor in a hospital, a mechanic fixing a truck)? Would background activity help your reporting, or would it be distracting?

◆ **Ask if photos will be allowed** or if tape-recording is OK. It's always smart to clear these issues in advance.

PREPARING FOR THE INTERVIEW

◆ **Continue your research.** The more you learn about your subject, the more productive your interview will be. DON'T waste people's time forcing them to explain basic stuff you should already know; instead, use interviews to collect details, insights and opinions.

◆ **Organize your questions.** For your first few inter-

views, you may feel more confident writing out entire questions ahead of time. Some veteran reporters do that; others simply itemize key topics on the covers of their notebooks, glancing at them as they scribble notes.

◆ **Prioritize.** Decide which questions require simple yes-or-no answers (to quickly nail down essential info) and which should be phrased more open-endedly (for more detailed, thoughtful answers).

◆ **Rehearse your interview with a friend** if you're not feeling comfortable with the process. See how questions sound when you ask them. Fine-tune your phrasing.

◆ **Get to the interview on time.** And another thing:

◆ **Dress appropriately.** Don't wear jeans and a T-shirt to interview a banker; don't dress like a banker when you interview a poor farmer. Remember, your appearance can help you gain the confidence of the people you interview.

DURING THE INTERVIEW

◆ **Relax.** Be friendly and curious. Don't be afraid. Granted, interviews aren't exactly casual conversations, but the more comfortable things feel, the more success you'll have loosening your interviewee's lips.

◆ **Never forget: You're in charge.** Once the interview starts, it's *your* show. *You'll* ask the questions, and *you'll* keep asking until you're satisfied. Don't let anyone intimidate you, not even powerful bigshots. Remember, there's real power in that story you're going to write.

◆ **Start with the basics:** name, age, address, title, etc. Be sure to double-check spellings as you jot them down.

◆ **Budget your time.** If you've only got five minutes, don't waste time with chitchat or inessential facts. Get right to the meat of the matter. If it's a longer interview:

◆ **Begin with softball questions.** Warm up with the big-picture, nonthreatening stuff. Save the complex, controversial topics for later.

◆ **Focus your questions.** Broad, vague queries *(What's it like being on the soccer team?)* aren't as effective as precise ones *(How'd it feel to score that winning goal?).*

◆ **Keep it simple.** Avoid long, rambling, two- or three-

part questions. It's more efficient to ask one question at a time, about one thing at a time.

◆ **Limit questions that can be answered simply "yes" or "no."** Questions like *"Were you worried on election night?"* are called close-ended questions, and they often yield dull answers: *"No, not really."*

Instead, ask open-ended questions — *"What was going through your mind as you waited for the election results?"* — to reveal the thoughts and feelings that explain *why* and *how* things happened.

◆ **Make sure every question gets answered.** Pay constant attention. Listen closely. Don't let interviewees out-clever you and sidestep sensitive issues.

◆ **Rephrase questions** when you think an answer is unclear or contradictory, or if you think you'll get a more quotable response.

◆ **Ask follow-up questions.** The best ones are:
1) How do you know that?
2) Can you give me an example?
3) *And…?*

◆ **Stay flexible.** Sometimes an interview takes a turn you never predicted. Go with the flow. Some of your best material may come out of deep left field.

◆ **Ask people to slow down** if you're falling behind in your notes — or slow them down deliberately when they get to the good parts of their stories, so you can gather more interesting details ("What were you thinking? So *then* what happened?")

◆ **Don't worry about asking dumb questions** if they lead to smart answers. Better to sound stupid in an interview than to write a stupid story later. Don't ever be ashamed to say, "Sorry . . . you lost me."

◆ **Remember to look around** and note what you see. What gestures, physical descriptions or activities will add color to the story — or trigger new questions?

◆ **Use reassuring body language** (facial expressions, nodding, making friendly eye contact, etc.). But keep unnecessary comments to a minimum.

◆ **Try using silence as a tactic** to prod people into saying more. Sometimes just gazing blankly at somebody makes them uncomfortable, and they keep talking.

◆ **Don't interrupt.**

◆ **Don't take sides.**

◆ **Save your toughest question** – "the bomb" – for last. If they trust you, they'll answer. If they stomp off in anger, at least they answered all your *other* questions.

AFTER THE INTERVIEW

◆ **Review your notes with the interviewee.** Recap what you've discussed to fill in gaps, correct errors or clarify any confusion.

◆ **Ask, "Who else should I contact?"** Often, the most valuable thing you get from an interview is discovering a better source — a person, a Web site or an organization you didn't previously know about.

◆ **Ask permission to call back later** in case you have more questions. If the interview went well, your subject will be glad to help further.

◆ **Ask interviewees to call YOU** if they think of anything else that might be helpful to your story.

◆ **Say thank you.** And mean it. These people have just given you their time, their trust and their information. Show a little gratitude, eh?

◆ **Review your notes again, privately,** to add further observations, clean up illegible entries and mark the most noteworthy passages. That's always a good time to ask yourself: *Do I have the lead for my story yet?*

◆ **Check back with your sources after the story runs.** They may offer useful feedback or tips for new stories.

FOR MORE ON INTERVIEWING, SEE NEXT PAGE ▶

Interviewing *(Continued from previous page)*

GREG ESPOSITO, *The Roanoke Times:* "After a day of covering flooding throughout Giles County, we saw a man standing on his front porch, surrounded by water. We yelled over to him to see if he needed help. Talking to him over the rushing water proved impossible, so I put my hand up to my ear to let him know I wanted to call him. He gave me his phone number by holding up his fingers. I sat down on the edge of the road, pulled out my notebook and dialed my cell phone. The scene of Bill Turner watching ducks swim in his front yard became the lead for the story."

THE Q-and-A FORMAT: CAPTURING CONVERSATIONS VERBATIM

Most interviews are worked into stories. But for an engaging alternative, you can run a transcript as a Q-and-A.

Q-and-A's usually look like the one at right, with questions posed in one font, the answers in another. They can be light or serious, long or short. You can even edit remarks for brevity, as long as you don't distort their meaning.

The best Q-and-A's let us feel like we're eavesdropping on a stimulating conversation. Consider this excerpt from an interview with Mel Gibson.

"My ears were burning with joy!" interviewer Lawrence Grobel recalled. "I've talked to hundreds of movie stars, and not one of them had ever expressed such rigid beliefs on the record. If this isn't manna for an interviewer, I don't know what is!"

Q: *Do you believe in an afterlife?*
GIBSON: Absolutely. There's just no explanation. There has to be an afterlife. Otherwise, where is the evening-out process? There has to be an afterlife because Hitler and I both walked the planet and I'm not going to the same place as Hitler.
Q: *Is there a hell?*
GIBSON: Absolutely.
Q: *What's your image of the devil?*
GIBSON: The beast with eight tongues and four horns and fire and brimstone. Probably worse than anything we can imagine, as paradise is probably better than anything we can imagine.
Q: *Do you believe in Darwin's theory of evolution or that God created man in his image?*
GIBSON: The latter.
Q: *So you can't accept that we descended from monkeys and apes?*
GIBSON: No, I think it's bullshit. If it isn't,

why are they still around? How come apes aren't people yet? It's a nice theory, but I can't swallow it. There's a big credibility gap. The carbon-dating thing tells you how long something's been around, but how accurate is that, really? I've got one of Darwin's books at home and some of that stuff is pretty damn funny. Some of his stuff is true, like that the giraffe has a long neck so it can reach the leaves. But I just don't think you can swallow the whole piece.
Q: *I take it that you're not particularly broad-minded when it comes to issues such as celibacy, abortion, birth control —*
GIBSON: People always focus on stuff like that. Those aren't issues. Those are unquestionables. You don't even argue those points.
Q: *You don't?*
GIBSON: No.

— From The Art of the Interview

...AND REMEMBER: ALWAYS STRIVE FOR RACIAL AND GENDER BALANCE

Look at the photos on these two facing pages. How many women do you see? How many minorities? Children? Poor people?

That's a problem for most publications: the faces and voices look too much alike — usually white and male, in other words. They don't reflect their community's diversity. Too often, minorities appear only on the sports and entertainment pages.

To connect with *all* your readers, try to vary the ages, genders, races and lifestyles of the sources you select for interviews. That often means you'll need to challenge your own subconscious stereotypes. Or venture outside your personal comfort level. Or even monitor the makeup of your sources to ensure you're striking a fair balance.

"ON THE RECORD," "OFF THE RECORD" — WHAT DO WE MEAN WHEN WE SAY THAT?

A soccer star quits the team, but she's afraid to say why. A union boss says the strike is nearly settled, but won't let you quote him. A rape victim is willing to discuss her ordeal, but doesn't want you to print her name.

How do you handle delicate situations like these? Over the years, reporters have adopted the following conventions for conducting sensitive interviews:

ON THE RECORD
The reporter's source agrees that anything said during the interview can be printed, and the source can be fully identified: *"Bush plans to veto that tax bill," said Roy G. Biv, secretary of commerce.*

- ✔ **Use the information?**
- ✔ **Identify the source?**
- ✔ **Run actual quotes?**

OFF THE RECORD
The information cannot be printed in any form. If a reporter is told *off the record* that Bush plans to veto the tax bill, the reporter must confirm it from an entirely separate source before printing it.

- ☐ **Use the information?**
- ☐ **Identify the source?**
- ☐ **Run actual quotes?**

ON BACKGROUND
The information can be used in a story — and can even run as a quote — but the source cannot be identified by name: *"Bush plans to veto that tax bill," a high-ranking commerce department official said.*

- ✔ **Use the information?**
- ☐ **Identify the source?**
- ✔ **Run actual quotes?**

ON DEEP BACKGROUND
The information can be used, but the source cannot be revealed. The reporter could write that *President Bush is expected to veto the tax bill* — but relying on unattributed speculation may be risky.

- ✔ **Use the information?**
- ☐ **Identify the source?**
- ☐ **Run actual quotes?**

Obviously, it's best for all conversations to stay on the record. Uncertainty and mistrust emerge as soon as things go off the record — which is why, to avoid misunderstandings, many reporters refuse to allow it. *Ever.*

Editors are wary of printing information from anonymous sources, too. What if the source is lying? If you're being duped, your paper's credibility could be damaged.

Still, unnamed sources often provide valuable material. They can leak stories you'd never find on your own; they can steer you to other sources you'd never know about. ▼ But before you agree to give any source anonymity, ask:

Can I persuade this person to go on the record? Have I explained the benefits of telling this story openly and the problems anonymous sourcing might create?

Can I obtain this information through another source so I can avoid unnamed sources altogether?

Do we all agree on the ground rules for this interview and exactly how we'll handle any sensitive material?

Is our newsroom policy clear on anonymous sourcing? You may be wise to stop the interview, place a quick phone call to your editor and discuss how best to proceed — *before* you make any promises to your source.

ADAM SCHEFTER, *The Denver Post (in the white shirt and shades):* "I don't ask too many questions in a setting like this. I try to save most of my questions for one-on-one sessions, where I'm not advertising to everybody else what I'm writing about. If there's an issue that everybody knows about — like, say, the status of whether the Broncos signed their first-round draft pick, as was the case on the date of this picture, which was the first day of training camp — I'll ask it in a public setting like this. Otherwise, for more confidential subjects, I wait until I can ask someone in private."

A ONE-ON-ONE INTERVIEW IS YOUR BEST OPTION. BUT IT'S NOT YOUR ONLY OPTION.

Sometimes you just don't have the time, the ability or the *clout* to schedule private interviews with news sources. Depending on your beat, you may frequently find yourself in situations where there are:

◆ *Many interviewers, one interviewee.* You'll find this at formal news conferences (where politicians meet the press) or at informal post-game media mobs like the one shown above. Reporters usually take turns tossing out questions, and everyone gets to share the answers.

◆ *Many interviewers, many interviewees.* You'll find this in the "spin room" at political debates or during media gatherings at trade shows, where impromptu interviews arise in random clumps. (Tip: If you ever find yourself lost and confused at one of these events, just shadow a veteran reporter who knows who's who.)

◆ *One interviewer, many interviewees.* It gets chaotic talking to a crowd (teammates who just won the big game, assembled members of a rock group), so filter out the distractions and keep a careful note of who says what.

Keep in mind that e-mail may be the most efficient way to ask many people the same questions; just duplicate one message to several sources, then wait for their replies.

MORE ON **ANONYMOUS SOURCES** ▶ 107, 234

Quotations

They make stories more appealing and believable — and yes, you can quote me on that.

Of course, you *can* write entire stories in your own words, without quoting a single source. But those stories often sound like dull, dry, fact-filled news releases. Adding *real* words spoken by *real* people gives your stories personality. Authenticity. Humor. Quotes provide the emotions, opinions and flavor often missing from objective newswriting.

So in each interview you do, keep your radar tuned for colorful quotes. But be selective. Don't run every quote you hear, because:

◆ *People lie.* They exaggerate. They fudge facts to make their case; they bend the truth to win our approval. So stay skeptical. Never forget that classic journalistic adage: *When your mother says she loves you, check it out.*

◆ *People yammer.* And stammer. And fumble around trying to express ideas that *you* — a professional wordsmith — could say better. Take the disjointed ramblings of former president George Bush at left. Who'd want to read that stuff in a news story? As writing coach Chip Scanlan once advised:

> *"By all means, fill your stories with voices — but just as you'd steer clear of a windbag at a party, spare your readers those bloated quotes that deaden a piece of writing."*

President George Bush's response when asked if he would look overseas for ideas to improve American education:

"Well, I'm going to kick that one right into the end zone of the Secretary of Education. But, yes, we have all — he travels a good deal, goes abroad. We have a lot of people in the department that does that. We're having an international — this is not as much education as dealing with the environment — a big international conference coming up. And we get it all the time, exchanges of ideas. But I think we've got — we set out there — and I want to give credit to your governor McWherter and to your former governor Lamar Alexander — we've gotten great ideas for a national goals program from, in this country, from the governors who were responding to, maybe, the principal of your high school, for heaven's sake!"

OK, YOU'VE FINISHED YOUR INTERVIEWS. HOW DO YOU USE THOSE QUOTES IN A STORY?

DIRECT QUOTE Direct quotes capture exactly, word for word, what someone said (or wrote). The quoted statements always begin and end with quotation marks. A phrase identifying the speaker — called an *attribution* — usually follows the quote.

> "Without a doubt, we've got the biggest, fastest, best darn team in the league this year," said Bears quarterback Bruce Easley.

Use direct quotes when the speaker's entire sentence presents ideas or opinions in a relevant, concise way; otherwise, one of these other options may be preferable.

PARTIAL QUOTE If a direct quote is too long or awkwardly phrased, you may decide to insert just a part of it — a clause, a phrase or even a powerful *word* — into your own sentence:

> Quarterback Bruce Easley calls this year's Bears the "best darn team in the league."

But beware of overusing *fragmentary quotes.* Using quote marks to "highlight" certain "words" may just make them look "odd."

PARAPHRASE When you summarize what a source told you without using the exact words or adding quotation marks, it's called an *indirect quote* or *paraphrase.* It's a common way to clarify or condense someone else's statements:

> Bears quarterback Bruce Easley claims that this year's football team will be the best in the conference.

Paraphrasing is necessary because — let's be honest — people don't always speak articulately or efficiently. Quoting them *indirectly* lets you rephrase their ideas in a clear, concise way.

DIALOGUE To capture a conversation between, say, two speakers, you can reprint their actual dialogue:

> "We'll be number one in the league this year," Easley said.
> "And in the state, too," added coach Buttkus. He winked at Easley.
> Easley groaned. "Geez, no pressure," he said.
> Buttkus smiled. "You can do it, son," he said, punching Easley's arm. "You can do it."

Avoid "partial quotes." They "get in the way of" the reader, often imparting a meaning to words "not intended" by the "writer." Or "speaker," for that matter. Do you know what I "mean"?

Dick Thien, editor and writing coach

PROBLEMS TO AVOID WHEN USING QUOTES IN STORIES

◆ **Don't bore readers with dull, obvious quotes.**
A cheerleader tells you she's "very excited about our big victory." Uhhhh. . . that's a *surprise?* A pianist says "the concert is at 9 p.m. Friday." That may be factual, but why quote him on it? Use quotes to add color or reveal character — not to state the obvious. (That's your job.)

◆ **Don't rehash what a quote is saying.** For instance:
> Ivan Oder claims that he never uses deodorant.
> "I never use deodorant," he says.

Look — either *you* say it, or shut up and let *him* say it.

◆ **Avoid using a quote as a lead.** OK, we admit it: Occasionally, a wonderful quote will make a terrific lead. But not usually. And most editors think it's lazy. So write the lead in your own voice, *then* let others talk.

◆ **Don't read people's minds.** It drives some copy editors nuts to read sentences like these:
> Barb Dwyer dreams of being a rodeo clown someday.
> She feels certain it's the best career she could choose.

How do you know what Barb feels? Have you actually *observed* her dreams? Don't put ideas in anyone's head if you can't support them with quotes. Instead, say:
> Barb Dwyer says she dreams of being a rodeo clown.

◆ **Beware of monologues.** Most quotes are one, maybe two sentences. Some are one or two paragraphs. Beyond that, it had better be gripping, engrossing stuff — or you risk letting some windbag seize control of your story.

◆ **It's best not to mimic someone's dialect.** Why? Because *eef yoo bungle eet, den dey git veddy, veddy MAD at choo!* You might not think that insults the speaker, but it does. Leave the dialects to novelists and comedians.

◆ **Beware of foul language.** Every publication has its own decency standards, so you constantly need to gauge what your readers will tolerate and where your editors will draw the line. Remember, you're ultimately responsible for every word that runs in your story. If you use a quote that's offensive, you'll be criticized; if you use a quote that's defamatory, you can be sued. ▼

◆ **Don't distort a quote's meaning** by carelessly deleting words or altering any phrasing — but it *is* OK to clean up minor hemming and hawing (see below).

"The most essential gift for a good writer is a built-in, shockproof shit detector."

Ernest Hemingway

▲ This *liftout quote* is a design gizmo all publications use. It's where you pull a catchy quote out of a story and display it in a bold way. Hemingway's advice, incidentally, is worth remembering as you gather quotes for your stories — but what about his language? Is the "s" word too offensive to use in a family paper? A student paper? A magazine? A reporting textbook?

PUNCTUATION ADVICE FOR USING QUOTES IN STORIES

◆ **Use double quotation marks at the beginning and end of direct quotes:**
> "I am not an animal," said John Merrick.

◆ **Use single quotation marks for quoted statements inside other quoted statements.** When one speaker refers to something someone else said, it looks like this:
> "I love that movie," Sarah said, "where the Elephant Man goes, 'I am not an animal.'"

◆ **Put periods and commas inside quotation marks:**
> "I am not an animal," said John Merrick in "The Elephant Man."

◆ **If you're quoting someone's question, put the question mark inside the quotation marks:**
> At one point, John Merrick asks, "Am I an animal?"

BUT: If you're asking a question *about* quoted material, the question mark goes outside the quotation marks:
> When does he actually say, "I am not an animal"?

◆ **Colons, semicolons and dashes go outside quotation marks,** which usually occurs when the quote is part of a longer sentence:
> "I am not an animal": Merrick's plaintive cry still haunts us.
> Merrick cried, "I am not an animal" — a dramatic moment.

◆ **When editing a quote, use an ellipsis (...) to indicate deleted words, phrases or sentences.** But be careful not to distort the meaning:
> "I read no newspaper now but Ritchie's," Thomas Jefferson wrote, "and in that chiefly the advertisements, for they contain the only truths to be relied on in a newspaper."

> **Edited version:** "Advertisements . . . contain the only truths to be relied on in a newspaper," Thomas Jefferson wrote.

When the ellipsis comes at the end of a quote, use four dots instead of three; the fourth dot represents a period ending the sentence.

◆ **Use parentheses to supply missing words.** It's a little annoying, but in small doses this helps add meaning:
> "I think that he (Jefferson) is right about that," Bush said.

◆ **Capitalize the first word of a direct quote —**
> Bush said, "No, Thomas Jefferson was not an animal."

— but you don't need to capitalize partial quotes:
> Are we finished with this "not an animal" quote yet?

The PRESS ROOM

HOW FAR DO YOU GO WHEN IT COMES TO CHANGING (OR CLEANING UP) THE QUOTES YOU GATHER?

Stammering and the like are the equivalent of typos — they can be fixed. But otherwise, I don't mess with quotes, ever. There is no shame in paraphrasing — quotes should be used only when they illuminate, or say something better than the writer can say it.
Jerry Schwartz, The Associated Press

I must admit to an inconsistent approach. I hold politicians, public officials and public figures to a high standard. I generally use their quotes verbatim, unless their quotes will be incomprehensible without paragraph after paragraph of context to set it up. I give private citizens ("civilians") a lot more leeway and generally clean up their grammar.
Rick Bella, The Oregonian

I've interviewed a lot of foreigners whose command of English is not always the best. I have no problem changing a "has" to a "have" on my computer screen if it means letting my subjects keep their dignity.
Kevin Pang, Chicago Tribune

Take out the *um's* and *ah's*, and that's about it.
Jesse Fanciulli, Greeley Daily Tribune

If your source is grammatically challenged, you can better say what he meant to say by paraphrasing. Run quotes verbatim if the manner of speech goes to the essence of the story (i.e., clean up quotes in a story about hip-hop and you lose credibility. KnowwhatImsayin'?). Otherwise, minimally clean up the quote to avoid having the reader stumble.
Toni Coleman, Pioneer Press

MORE ON QUESTIONS OF TASTE ▶ 144   MORE ON LIBEL ▶ 140

"The time has come," **the Walrus said,**
"To talk of many things:
Of shoes and ships and sealing-wax,
Of cabbages and kings —
And why the sea is boiling hot,
And whether pigs have wings."
                              Lewis Carroll

Attributions

Make sure sources get proper credit (or blame) for what they say.

Sources provide you with facts, opinions and quotes. When you write stories, you must clearly indicate where those facts, opinions and quotes came from.

That's the purpose of attributions.

If a statement is considered common knowledge — *the Earth rotates every 24 hours* — it doesn't require attribution because it's widely known and easily verifiable. But when someone says something new and different — *the core of the Earth contains seeds for growing new Earths* — you must source it in a way that's clear to readers:

"The Earth's core contains seeds for growing new Earths," said astronomer Dr. Jean Poole.

Now, Dr. Poole may be wrong . . . or nuts. If so, you should find another source to contradict her. (*"Dr. Poole is sadly mistaken,"* said professor I.M. Shirley Wright.)

The important thing, journalistically, is to keep your own opinions out of the story. You can say that these two sources disagree with each other; you can explain how Dr. Poole's ideas are considered peculiar. But you must stay as neutral as you can.

Collect facts, opinions and quotes from the best possible sources — then attribute them.

NINE GUIDELINES FOR WORDING AND POSITIONING ATTRIBUTIONS

❶ The first time you identify a source, use his/her full name (and title, if needed). After that, use only his/her *last* name.

> **Ralph Nader, consumer advocate and political activist,** urged colleges to focus on academics, not athletics.
> "If Martians came down from space and watched television, they would conclude that universities are sports organizations," **Nader** said.

❷ For most attributions, it's preferable to put the *noun* ahead of the *verb*:

> "I'd rather meet Madonna than the president of the United States," **Britney Spears said.**
> **NOT:** "I'd rather meet Madonna than the president of the United States," **said Britney Spears.**

But put the *verb* ahead of the *noun* if that helps you avoid awkward phrasing:

> "The kids let out an 'oooh' sound," **said James Twomey,** the father of a Kenosha, Wis., third-grader who was accidentally shown a pornographic film in class.

❸ When a quote uses just one sentence, the attribution usually *follows* the quote:

> "I just wish people would love everybody else the way they love me," **Muhammad Ali said.**
> **NOT:** **Muhammad Ali said,** "I just wish people would love everybody else the way they love me."

❹ When a quotation uses more than one sentence, it's often best to put the attribution *at the end of the first sentence:*

> "I like to drive with my knees," **actress Sharon Stone said.** "Otherwise, how can I put on my lipstick and talk on the phone?"
> **NOT:** "I like to drive with my knees. Otherwise, how can I put on my lipstick and talk on the phone?" **actress Sharon Stone said.**

❺ There *are* times when it makes sense to start a quote with the attribution: to set up a partial quote, for instance. Or to avoid forcing readers to scan a long quote without first knowing who the speaker is:

> **Keith Richards, guitarist for the Rolling Stones, explained that** "rock 'n' roll is always considered, quite rightly, a juvenile music. That's because it's young itself. But that doesn't mean it has to be played by young juveniles."
> **NOT:** "Rock 'n' roll is always considered, quite rightly, a juvenile music. That's because it's young itself. But that doesn't mean it has to be played by young juveniles," **said Keith Richards, guitarist for the Rolling Stones.**

❻ It's also acceptable to set up long quotes with an attribution followed by a *colon:*

> **As Dylan told "60 Minutes":** "I never wanted to be a prophet or a savior. Elvis, maybe. I could see myself becoming him. But a prophet? No."

❼ When inserting an attribution *into* a quote, try to find a logical spot for it, then insert additional quotation marks:

> "One of the great things about books," **President George W. Bush once said,** "is that sometimes there are fantastic pictures."
> **NOT:** "It just makes you feel permanently like a girl," **said Brad Pitt, explaining his sex appeal,** "walking past construction workers."

❽ Once you attribute the first sentence of a quote, you don't need to attribute additional sentences that directly follow:

> **WRONG:** "We are the caretakers of God's creation," said Burger King spokesman Rob Doughty. "We have a moral obligation to treat them humanely, and, when we do slaughter them, to do so in a painless manner," **he said.**

❾ Begin a new paragraph whenever you change speakers. To avoid confusion, add new attributions as soon as possible:

> "When a man's best friend is his dog, that dog has a problem," **Edward Abbey said.**
> **Groucho Marx saw things differently.** "Outside of a dog, a book is man's best friend," **he said.** "Inside of a dog, it's too dark to read."
> **NOT:** "You can put wings on a pig, but you don't make him an eagle," **Bill Clinton said.** "I like pigs. Dogs look up to us. Cats look down on us. Pigs treat us as equals," **Winston Churchill said.**

SO SHOULD IT BE <u>SAID</u>? OR <u>SAYS</u>?

News stories are almost always written in the past tense:
*Coach Wormer **said** the victory was "a team effort."*

But sometimes you'll see an attribution written this way:
*Coach Wormer **says** next week's game will be a "motherwhomper."*

So which should it be, **said** or **says**?

That depends on the type of story — and sometimes, the style of your publication. Serious news stories almost always stick to the past tense *(said)*. But the present tense *(says)* is appropriate for:

◆ **Reviews,** which describe music or drama as if it's happening *now:*

> At the start of the movie, Kane says "Rosebud" and drops dead. The film becomes an inquiry into what that word meant, as a way of understanding Kane.

◆ **Feature stories,** especially the "you are there" types of profiles where all the action seems to be occurring *now:*

> Loreen doesn't know where she'll go when the food runs out. "I got a son in Texas," she says. "I used to, anyways." She turns away and starts to cry.

But be careful not to mix past and present tenses carelessly or inconsistently when you write a feature this way.

◆ **Broadcast newswriting,** where present tense is usually preferable. ▼

HOW ABOUT STATED? UTTERED? SNORTED? SPOUTED? SHOUTED?

Paula LaRocque, writing coach —
Stick to plain and neutral verbs of attribution. *Said* is safe and, unless badly overworked, unobtrusive. *Stated* or *added* can work if you've overused *said*. *Explained* and *announced* are fine if the source really is explaining or announcing. Avoid the weird *(opined, averred, snorted, laughed, chuckled, uttered, voiced, shrugged)* or the overly emphatic *(declared, proclaimed)*.

Louis E. Catron, playwright and professor at the College of William and Mary —
Remember that *said* is invisible. ... Familiarity breeds acceptance. That's the way *said* works in dialogue: The reader just doesn't notice the word no matter how often it is repeated.

Like a good actor, the invisible "said" supports the primary lead but never calls attention to itself. Synonyms, however, are like a circus clown with an outlandish red nose, screaming for attention.

Rene Cappon in "The Word: An Associated Press Guide to Good Writing" —
Never use verbs denoting nonverbal processes as attributives, like *smiled, wept, laughed*. You don't smile words; you say them, smiling. *"I'm fond of him," she smiled,* is no less absurd than *"I'm very hot this morning," he radiated.*

Roscoe C. Born in "The Suspended Sentence: A Guide for Writers" —
You seek a better word not for variety or novelty but to report precisely how a person said a thing if he did it in some distinctive way. This from The Detroit News will illustrate:

> Dirty Harry/Clint Eastwood is squinting down the barrel of his .357-caliber Magnum. "Go ahead," Eastwood aspirates, daring the dude to begin shooting. "Make my day."

Have you seen Eastwood in that scene? That is *exactly* what he does: He aspirates. This writer wasn't seeking a cheap alternative to *says* for variety's sake; he wanted the precise verb that would describe how the man said it. And he found it.

Tim Harrower, "Inside Reporting" —
Aspirates? What kind of high-falutin' verb is *that?*

EXAMPLES OF ATTRIBUTION IN A TYPICAL NEWS STORY

A balanced story requires a variety of sources — some providing facts, others providing opinions. But each source must be clearly attributed.

Here's a news story written by Chuck Slothower, a senior at the University of Oregon, while interning at *The Oregonian.* Notice how each fact and quote is attributed. Notice, too, how the emotion in the story comes from one of its participants — not from the reporter.

This incident was first reported in a Friday-morning news release from the sheriff's department that cited findings from the county's animal control officers.

At a news conference Friday afternoon, Serhan and Manley (the spokesman quoted below) answered questions. Notice how this sentence structure requires the verb *(said)* to precede Serhan's name and description.

Details from the news release.

Serhan provides a description of the injuries. There's no need to verify them separately, since they match the sheriff's report.

Note how this attribution combines *Serhan said* with the phrase *choking back tears.* It's more accurate and dramatic than writing *Serhan cried.*

The fact that a hearing is scheduled is a matter of public record and needs no attribution.

Manley explained this process at the news conference. Again, notice the placement of *said.*

Some editors would change this attribution to say *Serhan **said** she wants the dog destroyed.* Some editors might also move the Manley paraphrase to a new paragraph, though it makes sense the way it's written here.

This final paragraph resulted from research to find recent related stories. Because this case is a matter of public record, no attribution is necessary.

A pit bull attacked and mauled a 28-year-old horse so severely that it had to be euthanized, Clackamas County authorities reported Friday.

"I can only imagine the terror she went through," said Tami Serhan, 29, of Boring, who had cared for the mixed Appaloosa-quarter horse since she was a young girl. "To me, this is like losing a child."

A neighbor's 3-year-old male pit bull escaped through an open gate and attacked the horse in its pasture, Clackamas County Animal Control and Sheriff's investigators reported.

The horse suffered extensive injuries to its face and right rear leg, Serhan said. After a veterinarian gave the horse a slim-to-none chance of survival, Serhan decided to have it put down.

"My baby, after 25 years of owning her, ended up in the back of a meat wagon," Serhan said, choking back tears.

A hearing is scheduled March 8 to determine whether the dog should be killed. In Clackamas County, dogs that attack another animal are subject to a hearing. A second attack means automatic euthanasia, said Deputy Joel Manley, a sheriff's spokesman.

Serhan wants the dog destroyed, noting that her neighborhood has a school bus stop and many pets. She also wants the dog's owner charged with a crime. Manley said that isn't likely, but the investigation continues.

Dog attacks against people sometimes result in assault charges against the animal's owner. An Aloha woman was sentenced Tuesday to 18 months in prison after her pit bulls attacked a 7-year-old boy and a woman who came to the child's aid.

One key source *is* omitted from this story: the owners of the pit bull. Slothower said he wasn't able to contact them by deadline. "I didn't want to put their name in the paper without talking to them," he said. "I didn't want to accuse them of being negligent pet owners."

Math for journalists

Understanding the figures that factor in your stories.

Most reporters would rather craft words than crunch numbers. They often shovel math into stories without decoding its meaning, or worse — they skate past numbers they don't understand. But being able to interpret and explain budgets, ballots and statistics is a crucial reporting skill. Otherwise, you're forced to trust the politicians, pollsters and bean-counters who feed you mathbabble like this: *In 2004, imports rose by 12 percent and the company earned $22 million, a 26 percent increase over 2003, when sales fell 37 percent.*

Mind-numbing? Yes. Useful to readers? No. That's why a brief review of basic principles can help make your stories more relevant and readable.

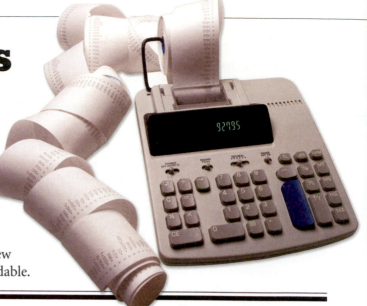

CALCULATING PERCENTAGES

A percentage, to refresh your memory, is the top part of a fraction whose bottom part is 100. Thus, 50 percent ($\frac{50}{100}$) is *half* of something; 200 percent ($\frac{200}{100}$) is *twice* something. Percentages are used to compare the sizes of two different things, or to show how much something increases or decreases over time.

CALCULATING PERCENTAGE INCREASES

Example: The city budget grew from $40,000 one year to $50,000 the next. How much is that?
❶ **Find the difference:** $50,000 - $40,000 = $10,000
❷ **Divide the difference into the original amount:** 10,000 divided by 40,000 = .25
❸ **Multiply your answer by 100:** 100 X .25 = 25

What your story might say: The budget grew by $10,000, a 25 percent increase over last year.

Percentage increases and decreases always measure changes in value by comparing the *difference* to the *original amount.*

CALCULATING PERCENTAGE DECREASES

Example: The budget was reduced from $50,000 one year to $40,000 the next. How much is that?
❶ **Find the difference:** $50,000 - $40,000 = $10,000
❷ **Divide the difference into the original amount:** 10,000 divided by 50,000 equals .20
❸ **Multiply your answer by 100:** 100 X .20 = 20

What your story might say: The budget decreased by $10,000, a 20 percent reduction from last year.

INCREASES OF 100 PERCENT OR MORE

A 100 percent increase is a doubling; a 200 percent increase is a tripling. Thus, if the fire department reported 10 fires in May and 30 fires in June, your story might say:

◆ Fires increased by 200 percent from May to June, or
◆ The number of fires tripled from May to June, or
◆ Three times as many fires were reported in June.

All are correct, but notice how that "200 percent" figure could confuse readers. Those other options present the data more clearly.

FIGURING THE MEAN AND MEDIAN

Suppose you want to find the average IQ, or income, or weight of a group of people. There are two ways to calculate that figure: the *mean* or the *median.*

THE MEAN

This is a simple arithmetic average. Just add up a group of items, then divide that sum by the total number of items in the group.

Example: You want to find the average age of four sisters who are 3, 5, 7 and 9.
❶ **Add** 3 + 5 + 7 + 9 = 24.
❷ **Divide** 24 by 4 (the number of sisters) = 6. The sisters' average age, or *mean* age, is 6.

The mean can be misleading, though — especially if your numbers include some extreme values that distort your results:

Example: A man runs a store and earns $1,000 a day. He has four employees. Each day, he pays the first $10; the second $20; the third $30; the fourth $40. What's the typical daily salary at that store?
❶ **Add** $1,000 + 10 + 20 + 30 + 40 = $1,100.
❷ **Divide** $1,100 by 5 people = $220.

The typical salary is $220? That doesn't seem quite right. Let's try again using the *median:*

THE MEDIAN

The median is the halfway point, the middle number in a series. To find it, sort your list in order, from smallest to largest, then find the value that's exactly in the middle.

In the preceding example, the median daily salary at that store is $30. Two people make more than $30, and two people make less.

Use *medians* when you're averaging a series of numbers that contain irregular extremes: dollar amounts, for example, when you're analyzing typical incomes or housing prices. Use *means* to calculate grade-point averages or determine people's average height, weight or shoe size — whenever the values don't fluctuate too dramatically.

WORKING WITH POLLS AND SURVEYS

All surveys and public opinion polls are estimates. Some are impressively accurate; others are subtly misleading. That's why, as a reporter striving for accuracy, you must keep flawed survey statistics *out* of your stories. Before you publish any poll results, consider:

◆ **The source.** Was the data collected by objective researchers? A smoking survey sponsored by the tobacco industry *might* be less reliable than one conducted by a medical school. And though call-in and write-in polls seem like fun, they're statistically bogus. (For all you know, three bored 12-year-olds repeatedly answered all the questions.)

◆ **The sample size.** The larger the sampling, the more accurate the survey. Or to view it another way: The smaller the sampling, the less you can trust the results. Pollsters use a mathematical formula to determine the *margin of error* for each poll — the plus or minus percentage that indicates the range within which poll results are trustworthy. The more important the survey, the more you need to disclose its margin of error.

◆ **The question wording.** Kill any poll that uses leading, biased questions. Ask someone *Do you feel the government wastes your hard-earned tax money?* and you'll steer them toward a predictable answer. But if you say *Most Americans favor a slight tax increase to strengthen homeland security; do you agree?* you'll steer them the opposite way.

If people don't understand every word or concept in a question, or if the question is too vague, the results are worthless infojunk.

◆ **Other variables.** Is the survey demographically representative (by age, income, gender, etc.)? How many respondents refused to answer questions — or lied? How many might have changed their minds since the poll was taken? Any of those variables could significantly distort the survey's accuracy.

THE REPORTER'S GUIDE TO INFORMATION CHARTS AND GRAPHS

PIE CHARTS

Pie charts depict percentage values or proportions by showing the different parts that make up the whole.

They usually consist of:

1) a circle representing 100 percent of something; and

2) several wedges (like slices of a pie) dividing that circle into smaller percentages. Each "slice" of the pie is an accurate proportion; for example, a section equaling 25 percent of the total would be one-quarter of the pie.

Tips: Too many slices (more than six, as a rule) make pie charts confusing. Apply a different color or shade to each slice, if possible. For variety, you can also try using other shapes: slicing a dollar bill into sections to show where your tax dollar goes, for example.

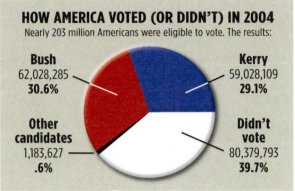

HOW AMERICA VOTED (OR DIDN'T) IN 2004
Nearly 203 million Americans were eligible to vote. The results:

Bush 62,028,285 **30.6%**

Kerry 59,028,109 **29.1%**

Other candidates 1,183,627 **.6%**

Didn't vote 80,379,793 **39.7%**

Source: United States Elections Project

LINE CHARTS

Line charts (also called fever charts) *show connecting points on a graph that measure changing quantities over time.*

They use three basic components:

1) a scale running vertically along one edge, measuring amounts;

2) a scale running horizontally along the bottom, measuring time; and

3) a jagged line connecting a series of points, showing rising or falling trends.

Line charts are created by plotting different points, then connecting the dots to draw a curve. Obviously, a line that rises or falls dramatically will impress readers more than one that barely shows a blip.

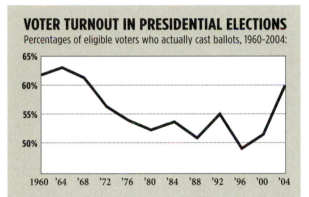

VOTER TURNOUT IN PRESIDENTIAL ELECTIONS
Percentages of eligible voters who actually cast ballots, 1960-2004:

1960 '64 '68 '72 '76 '80 '84 '88 '92 '96 '00 '04

Source: United States Elections Project

BAR CHARTS

Bar charts compare two or more items by depicting data as columns parked side by side.

They use two basic components:

1) a scale running either horizontally or vertically used to measure the data; and

2) parallel bars representing items being measured.

Bars are usually stacked in a logical order: either alphabetically, chronologically or ranked by size.

Tips: Every bar must be labeled clearly. Bars may be screened, colorized or given 3-D shadow effects, as long as the data isn't distorted. To ensure that the bars are accurately proportional, the scale (the vote totals in the chart at right, for example) must always start at "0."

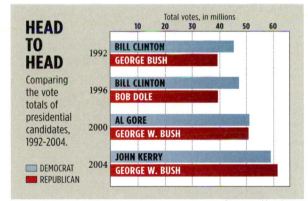

HEAD TO HEAD

Comparing the vote totals of presidential candidates, 1992-2004.

Total votes, in millions
10   20   30   40   50   60

1992   BILL CLINTON / GEORGE BUSH

1996   BILL CLINTON / BOB DOLE

2000   AL GORE / GEORGE W. BUSH

2004   JOHN KERRY / GEORGE W. BUSH

☐ DEMOCRAT
☐ REPUBLICAN

Source: presidentelect.org

FAST FACTS

Sometimes the smartest reporting is also the simplest. And the simplest way to present data is to boil complex topics down to their essential *who-what-when-where-why* — then decide which of those facts are best highlighted in a fast-facts sidebar.

The election-result box at right is one example, but you don't need to save this approach just for big stories. To examine a new property tax, for instance, create a box that simply shows typical homeowners *What It Cost This Year* compared to *What It Will Cost Next Year*. If you conduct a public survey, present the key findings in a sidebar, in big type — then analyze the details and explain what it all means in the main text of the story.

2004 PRESIDENTIAL ELECTION RESULTS
Electoral votes needed to win: 270

	BUSH	KERRY	
	286 ✓ Electoral votes	**252** Electoral votes	
VOTE %	51%	48%	VOTE %
TOTAL	62,028, 285	59,028,109	TOTAL

— Adapted from CNN.com

TO SUCCEED AS A REPORTER, YOU'VE GOT TO HAVE MOXIE. SPUNK. GUTS. YOU'VE GOTTA BE PUSHY. NERVY. BALLSY. FOR EXAMPLE:

Once I wrote a story that fingered a guy as a fish-poacher, and game officers wrote him $913 worth of tickets after it ran. Minutes after the cops left, I went to his house to interview him. He was pounding a hammer on a fence, angry.

After a few questions, he stopped and stared at me. "So you're the reason I got these tickets?" he said.

"Well, yeah," I said.

He stared at me, squeezing the hammer, wondering what to hit next. Then he pounded a board out of the fence.

No matter how angry they get, they never hit the reporter.

Mark Freeman, *Mail Tribune*

When a convenience store owner shot to death a drug dealer outside his business in a rough St. Louis neighborhood, I wanted to ask him what it was like to kill a man.

The cops warned me not to visit the store alone. They suspected the store owner was involved in a variety of crimes. But I went anyway.

I found the owner, Big Mike, with two guns strapped in his shoulder harness and another couple pointed toward me on the table in front of him. He snarled at me while I asked questions.

After about thirty minutes, he decided to cooperate and gave me kudos for having the guts to confront him.

Heather Ratcliffe, *St. Louis Post-Dispatch*

My nerviest moment came when I crashed the wedding of a CEO and his reputed girlfriend/executive.

I insisted that the Free Press put me up in the NYC hotel where the wedding was taking place, so I wouldn't feel like a trespasser. At the appointed hour, I dressed, signed the guestbook, and greeted people I knew or recognized (Gloria Steinem, Jane Pauley, the Detroit People correspondent, an old boyfriend's father.) The BF's father, unfortunately, introduced me to the company's PR guy, who tried to get rid of me. Too late: I had the story.

Laura Berman, *The Detroit News*

The PRESS ROOM

ADVICE ON REPORTING AND WRITING FROM VETERAN JOURNALISTS

Working at a small paper, I have:
◆ been in a car when it was struck by lightning;
◆ had to take cover in a ditch during a tornado;
◆ been shot by a taser gun during a police demonstration;
◆ seen several dead bodies, a compound fracture (bone sticking out of the skin) and found a piece of a person who had been hit by a train;
◆ been kicked out of city hall (three times);
◆ played golf with Alice Cooper.

Michael Bockoven, *Grand Island Independent*

I was once sent to the scene of a police standoff, one of those ugly domestic scenes that spiral out of control until a drunken husband and cops are waving guns at each other.

This happened several counties away late at night, and by the time I arrived the next morning, 1) the man had killed himself, and 2) the police had left.

The door to the mobile home was wide open, and I needed a story. So I crossed the police tape, walked in and wrote down everything I saw: cut-up wedding photos, a shotgun blast through the refrigerator door, blood on a La-Z-Boy and, soon, the bottom of my tennis shoes. Police had fired tear gas into the trailer, and I kept running outside to throw up before returning for more details. A man's life and death were at my feet, and I wasn't going to let a little nausea get in my way.

The kicker: The man's mother-in-law lived nearby, and when I showed up at her door, she spoke to me and no other reporters — the tears in my eyes from the tear gas convinced her I was more empathetic than the other media slobs.

Ron French, *The Detroit News*

Just like there are little white lies, there are little white deceptions that reporters commit to get a story.

Such was the case one frigid night when an explosion at a chemical storage facility in Elizabeth, N.J., rocked the factory town and sent several fireballs into the dark sky.

When I got to the scene, the entrance to the plant was blocked by security guards. Beyond them, I could see the high wall of flames sending embers into the sky and the silhouettes of firemen as they raced about. I had to get inside.

A few weeks earlier, I had purchased a hand-held walkie-talkie at a flea market, and I reached for it now. I drove my car up to the guards and rolled down the window, holding the walkie-talkie to one ear.

"What've we got?" I asked the guard, still holding the official-looking walkie-talkie to an ear.

I could see the momentary hesitation in the guard's face, but then he said: "They said something about benzene."

"Holy cow," I declared. "Don't let anyone in here. This could be trouble." With that, I drove into the plant.

Hours later, I drove out with my story, passing a crowd of reporters huddled behind barricades at the plant entrance. I couldn't resist giving that guard a thumbs-up.

Bob Cullinane, *Asbury Park Press*

A little-known nudist camp let me cover its "Volleyball Superbowl" but suggested I uncover myself. So I revealed more than ever while reporting a story. Conducted my first naked interview. No treat for the nudists, but for readers, it was a quite an exposé.

Bob Batz, *Pittsburgh Post-Gazette*

When I was the new military reporter, I profiled the wing commander for the local Air Force base. His schedule was so busy that he wanted to do part of the interview during his daily three-mile jog on the base indoor track.

I brought my sweats, but forgot my running shoes. I ran it barefoot, which was very hard on the soles of my feet, but convinced the guy that I may be crazy, but I'm dedicated. The blisters healed eventually.

Jim Camden, *The Spokesman-Review* (Spokane, Wash.)

WHAT'S YOUR FAVORITE QUESTION TO ASK DURING AN INTERVIEW?

I always ask, "Is there anything I haven't asked that you'd like to talk about?" Usually, there is, and even if the answer isn't useful, they appreciate the question.

Bob Batz, *Pittsburgh Post-Gazette*

In this part of the country, asking someone about their heritage is a way to endear yourself. "Oh, *Anderson.* Is that Swedish?" The older folks love that one.

Michael Bockoven, *Grand Island Independent*

A question that's saved a few interviews: "Tell me something about yourself (or that situation, or that time in your life) that no one knows/Tell me something about yourself that would surprise everyone, even your mother. . ."

Jim Camden, *The Spokesman-Review*

I love to explore motive in interviews. One of the best questions for me has always been, "Why was that important to you?" If you can discover a person's motive, you can find out what he or she is trying to achieve. And that can form the structure of a story — will this person get what he or she wants?

Ken Fuson, *The Des Moines Register*

I don't have a surefire favorite question, but I do have a favorite technique to reliably soften people up. When getting ready to ask something that is very personal or provocative, I sometimes back into it apologetically and say something like, "This is a real 'journalist' question, but I gotta ask it and let's just see what happens. . . ." Usually, the subjects don't take it so personally and they get chattier than they would've otherwise. It works both for real people — "Tell me why you thought it was a good idea to rebuild your home in the Mississippi floodplain?" — and scientists and physicians who tend to get prickly when their judgment is questioned by journalists and other undereducated people.

Joe Verrengia, *The Associated Press*

When someone seems to be on automatic pilot — you know, the stars who have given this interview a thousand times over — I might ask "What kind of kid were you?" or "If I'd met you as a kid, is there anything I'd have seen that would give me a hint of what you are today?"

David Lyman, *Detroit Free Press*

Silence. This was a hard one for me to learn, because I'm very chatty. But I finally grasped the notion that people feel compelled to fill a silence, and I've gotten better at sitting back and waiting.

John Reinan, *Star Tribune* (Minneapolis, Minn.)

WHAT'S THE DUMBEST QUESTION YOU'VE EVER ASKED DURING AN INTERVIEW?

I was covering a (very bad) college football team for a college newspaper and asked the coach, "Why is it that, when your team was down by 21 with a quarter to go, you called a draw play that failed the three other times you called it? Wouldn't it have been better to call a play that had worked?"

His response: "I'm tired of you people coming in and playing reporter."

My response: "Coach, you're 2-5 on the year. Do you think the alumni are tired of you playing coach?"

His response: "Get out of my office, you little . . ."

Judd Slivka, *The Arizona Republic*

While interviewing the bishop of the Cleveland diocese, a nervous young reporter asked, ``So, was your father a priest, too?" The conversation did not end, but let's just say the bishop was none too impressed.

Rita Price, *The Columbus Dispatch*

I once covered the Miss California Pageant and delicately tried to ask one of the women how much she weighed. She was not amused.

Doug Hoagland, *The Fresno Bee*

> **While speaking with the family of a young man electrocuted in a freak accident, I actually said something about "what a shock" his death must have been.**
>
> **Rita Price,** *The Columbus Dispatch*

A student pilot wrecked a plane. Everybody survived. When I encountered the instructor, I uttered the following rude stupidities: "You the instructor?"

"Yes."

"I guess the instruction failed today, huh?"

Roy Wenzl, *The Wichita Eagle*

The worst and dumbest thing I ever did was fall asleep during an interview while an elderly man was describing how he lost his entire family during the Turkish massacre of Armenians during the early 20th century. My hand kept moving . . . and I awoke to find scribble marks all the way down a legal-size pad of paper. (The man apparently didn't notice because he didn't miss a verbal beat; however, I awoke as his wife nudged my hand with a cup of black coffee.)

Karen Jeffrey, *Cape Cod Times*

While covering a major fashion convention in Montreal for a Chicago weekly, I asked a coat designer if her faux furs were real. The lesson: I was clueless about fashion and should have boned up considerably before taking the assignment.

Erin Barnett, *The Oregonian*

Working with politicians, any time you ask a question that implies wrongdoing on their part, they won't like it. My strategy has always been to pass the blame on the others: i.e., "some of your critics say. . ." or "other elected officials are saying. . . ."

Bryan Dean, *The Daily Oklahoman*

A U.S. Senate aide once fumed to me, "You always begin a question by saying, 'Your critics say. . .' ." He was right. Unless you're quoting a specific critic, just ask the question.

Jeff Mapes, *The Oregonian*

After a school shooting spree, I asked the emergency room manager to detail that workday, but went too far asking him to describe what exactly — clinically — a bullet does to flesh.

The interview resumed after he stopped weeping.

Katy "How Insensitive Could I Get?" Muldoon, *The Oregonian*

TEST YOURSELF

Answers to these exercises are on page 293.

① WHAT WOULD BE YOUR BEST SOURCES FOR THESE STORIES?

a) Cara Mehl, 9, is dying of leukemia. Members of her church raised $10,000 to send Cara and her entire family of 12 to Disney World on her birthday. Who should you talk to for this story, and why?

b) It's early June. The local school board has announced that, due to budgetary constraints, three high-school teachers will be laid off at the end of the school year: English teacher Rita Book; science teacher Molly Kuehl; and computer science teacher Dot Matrix. You're writing a story about the layoffs. Who should you talk to, and why?

c) The local university has suffered a rash of thefts and vandalism, and a violent murder off-campus has everyone asking, "Is this campus safe?" Your editor wants to know how this year's crime compares to previous years — and how it compares to other schools, as well. What would be your main sources for this story?

d) A local man, Hugh Jass, was arrested after neighbors complained that he was keeping a full-grown tiger in his two-bedroom apartment. Who are your best sources for this story?

e) The U.S. Forest Service announced it will begin logging old-growth redwoods in Conifer National Forest to improve the forest ecosystem and protect nearby vacation homes from the threat of wildfires. What sources should you consult before writing this story?

f) Soulful, sensitive singer/songwriter Claire Annette is returning to her hometown (where you're a reporter) for a concert. It's the first time she's been back since graduating from high school 10 years ago; since then, she's sold millions of CDs, toured the world and been on the cover of *Rolling Stone*. What are your best sources for writing an advance for her concert?

③ QUOTES: PUNCTUATION AND ATTRIBUTION

There are at least two things wrong with each of these quotes. What are they?

a) Gov. Lew Swires said he'll support a tax increase on Tuesday. "It's long overdue," said Gov. Swires.

b) "I adore Elizabeth Taylor," gushed student actor Art Major. "Did you ever see her classic performance in "Who's Afraid of Virginia Woolf?"

c) "Assaults on campus increased from 20 in 2004 to 33 in 2005," Penn State University deputy director of university police Ben Z. Dreen said. "That's an increase of 75 percent."

d) The mayor complained, off the record, that Smith was "a rat" for betraying him, he said.

e) Ray Cleaves said, "When I was a boy, I saw Muhammad Ali battle George Foreman on Wide World of Sports. He was always my favorite boxer."

f) "I hate rap music," April Schauer says, "most of the time. It's repetitive and annoying."
   "It's the poetry of the street. It can be hypnotic and imaginative," Mike Raffone says.

Rewrite the following statement: 1) as direct quote; 2) as a paraphrase; and 3) using a partial quote.

"All too often, a story free of any taint of personal opinion is a story with all the juice sucked out. Keeping opinion out of the story too often means being a fancy stenographer." — *University of Missouri journalism professor Geneva Overholser*

② WHAT QUOTES WOULD YOU USE FROM THESE THREE INTERVIEWS?

Suppose you're interviewing sources for that Claire Annette story (see question "f" above). Here are transcripts from three of those interviews. Highlight the passages you would choose to run as direct quotes in your story.

CLAIRE ANNETTE

You reach Claire's manager on his cell phone in an airport somewhere in Japan. You tell him who you are and what you want. He says, "Hold on." And then:

"Hi. This is Claire. I've gotta catch a plane in, like, two minutes. Talk fast."

"OK. Thanks. How does it feel to come back home after all these years?"

"Home? Oh, yeah. We're playing two shows at Adler Auditorium. God, it's gonna be funny. . . I don't know. I mean, I lived there til I was, what? Eighteen? But even though I really needed to get away — to start over, to find my true voice — I've always kept that little town in my heart, I guess, even though it sounds corny to say it. And you know, it's true that everybody sort of fantasizes, you know, about fame and hitting it big. Well, hell, I may be famous, but I'm still basically the same lonely nerd I was back in high school. So, coming home. It's sad. Well, maybe not. See, all my family has sort of moved away, or died, so it's really just sort of a painful reminder of, you know, life goes on, things change.

"I'll tell you, though: I'd love to see Mrs. Washburn again. She was my piano teacher for seven years. I still catch myself, in the middle of a concert, thinking, Boy, if only Mrs. Washburn could see me now. Yeah, I suppose I should really try to get ahold of her. I mean, if I have time. We'll see.

"Anyway, I gotta go catch a plane. Talk to you in a few weeks, OK? Bye."

ANITA BATH, *a devoted local fan:*

"Are you excited about finally getting to see Claire in concert?"

"Oh, come on. I mean, Jesus, this is like a dream come true for all of us here. I can't, you know, afford to fly to Japan or some big stadium concert someplace else."

"What is it you like about her?"

"Oh, gosh, her songs are beautiful. Her lyrics are like poetry. And coming from the same place, geographically, it's like we speak the same language, you know what I mean?"

"Will you get to sit up close for the concert?"

"No. We're in the nosebleed seats. Our tickets suck."

"Any chance you'll get to meet her face to face while she's in town?"

"I've got a friend whose uncle used to live next door to her. But no, Claire's too important, and too busy. We'll go to the airport, though. We'll wave hello when she lands, and we'll wave goodbye when she leaves."

RAMONA WASHBURN,
Claire's childhood piano teacher:

"I taught Claire for seven years. She studied classical piano, along with a little jazz and ragtime. I had a studio in my living room, and she'd come once a week. She was a very . . . a very . . . oh, I don't know . . . a very *clean* girl. I mean, the way she played. I recall she had a very precise way of fingering the notes — she hated to make mistakes — and I used to tell her, Claire, dear, it's not enough just to hit the notes. You've got to put joy, and pain, and love into everything you play. Now, I guess, she's really, you know, gone a little — well, I was going to say overboard, but maybe it's just me. I'm old, and I think perhaps some of her songs are a little too loud and vulgar for my taste. But when she plays soft and slow — oh, it's a sweet thing to hear, isn't it?"

CHAPTER

Covering
the news

*Most news events fall into predictable categories. In this chapter,
we'll offer advice on writing the most common types of stories.*

IN THIS CHAPTER:

Covering a beat

News is everywhere, but beat reporters focus on specific topics or institutions.

Some journalists are free-floating "general assignment" reporters, covering circus clowns one day, bike thieves the next. But most reporters are assigned to beats: Schools. Crime. Sports. Business.

> When I was on a daily beat, some young guy asked me, "Doesn't this become dull?" And I said, "Only to dull minds." **RED SMITH**

Beats vary from newsroom to newsroom. On a small paper with a small staff, the government beat might include everything from courts to school boards. But at a big daily, one reporter might cover only county courts while another covers federal courts; one might work the "night cops" beat while another focuses on gang violence.

At some publications, beat reporters are expected to produce several stories a day *and* shoot photos; at others, reporters might produce just one long story every two weeks. Some editors insist that reporters monitor the bureaucracy and attend every meeting on their beats; others urge reporters to focus on issues, not meetings — to tell stories that involve *real* people.

Like any new job, a new beat can be a strange, scary thing. Here's how to survive.

YOU'VE JUST BEEN ASSIGNED TO A NEW BEAT. NOW WHAT?

1 Do research. Spend time in the newsroom library reading what's been written about the people and agencies on your beat. Check state and local laws to see what their powers and responsibilities are. Learn their history. Study their budgets. Find out what they've been up to — and what they're planning next.

2 Talk to your predecessor, even if he or she has left the newsroom, to get the inside poop you won't read in old stories. Learn who's who, what's what, how information flows through the key organizations you cover. Who's qualified (or allowed) to speak for them? Where will news releases come from — and can you trust them? Who are the players behind the scenes? Which critics, activists and unofficial observers can provide alternative perspectives on controversial topics?

3 Achieve a mind-meld with your editors. Find out what type of coverage they expect — and more importantly, what types of stories *readers* want. Should you cover every public meeting and bureaucratic announcement, or just focus on important issues? Do editors expect a stream of briefs and updates, or longer, more thoughtful analysis? Is the emphasis on breaking news or enterprising features? Talk it all through, then set goals. Establish priorities. Achieve editorial oneness.

4 Meet people. Get out of the newsroom. Hit the bricks. Walk the buildings on your beat and introduce yourself to every potential news source. Obviously that means directors, department heads and other officials, but it also means their underlings: secretaries, clerks, ordinary office workers. Bigshots and bosses may get their names, faces and quotes in the paper, but it's often lowly staffers who provide background information and alert you to stories — once you gain their trust.

Remember that ordinary folks play a role on your beat, too. What nonofficial connections should you make?

5 Make lists. Get organized. Create files and folders full of statistics, quotes, clips and background information. Constantly update your lists of:
◆ *Key sources* — names, titles, areas of expertise, e-mail addresses and phone numbers.
◆ *Upcoming meetings and events* — when sessions will convene, reports will be released, budgets will be prepared, decisions will be due. Stay ahead of the curve; it's your job to notify readers and editors what's coming.
◆ *Story ideas* — profiles, backgrounders, trend pieces, analyses. Don't just cover meetings and wait for news to break (or for editors to tell you what to do). Be your own boss. Take the initiative to produce feature stories that explain issues and capture the flavor of your beat.

LOOKING FOR IDEAS AND ADVICE FOR A SPECIALIZED BEAT?

Good news: You're not alone. A variety of organizations provide advice and resources for journalists covering most common beats. A sampling of what's available online:

BUSINESS
Society of American Business Editors and Writers (*www.sabew.org*)

CHILDREN/FAMILIES
Casey Journalism Center on Children and Families (*casey.umd.edu/index.cfm*)

EDUCATION
National Education Writers Association (*www.ewa.org*)

ENVIRONMENT
Society of Environmental Journalists (*www.sej.org*)

FEATURE WRITING
American Association of Sunday and Feature Editors (*www.aasfe.org*)

HEALTH CARE
Association of Health Care Journalists (*www.ahcj.umn.edu*)

OBITUARIES
International Association of Obituarists (*www.obitpage.com*)

POLICE and COURTS
Criminal Justice Journalists (*www.reporters.net/cjj*)

RELIGION
Religion Newswriters Association (*www.rna.org*)

SCIENCE
National Association of Science Writers (*www.nasw.org*)

STATE GOVERNMENT
Association of Capitol Reporters and Editors (*www.capitolbeat.org*)

SPORTS
Associated Press Sports Editors (*www.apse.dallasnews.com*)

24 ◀ MORE ON NEWSROOM BEATS

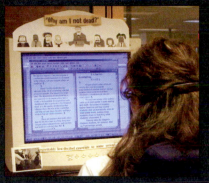

A beat reporter at work: Betsy Hammond, the education reporter for The Oregonian, attends a morning meeting, works the telephone, conducts an interview and visits students in a classroom before sitting down to write a story back in the newsroom.

PHOTOS BY MIKE LLOYD

WORKING A BEAT: DO'S AND DON'TS

Every beat is different — and over time, every reporter develops his or her rules and recipes for success. Still, a few general truths apply:

DO familiarize yourself with your state's open records and open meeting laws. Study how they apply to all governmental organizations on your beat. Understand your legal rights and limitations before disputes arise so you won't get caught flat-footed. ▼

DO follow the money. Who controls it? Where does it go? Study the budgets on your beat to see where the *real* power lies, as well as opportunities for fraud and incompetence. What does it all mean for readers?

DO call sources back to verify facts before stories run. It shows you're serious about fairness and accuracy. It enhances your credibility. And it keeps you humble.

DO write for your readers, *not* to impress the jaded insiders and experts on your beat. Keep things simple. Write with the voice of a teacher, *not* the voice of a bureaucrat. Never assume your readers are as savvy as you are (or that they've studied your previous stories).

DON'T get too cozy with sources. Be careful about promising to spin stories favorably or vowing to keep damaging information off the record. If you make promises you can't keep, you'll burn your sources; if you withhold facts, you'll cheat your readers.

DON'T get used. Public figures attain power and prominence by learning how to spin gullible new reporters like you. Don't be rude or confrontational, but don't let them put you in their pocket, either.

DON'T waste sources' time with idle chitchat when they're working. Focus your questions, get what you need and move along; don't just drop in like some aimless drifter and say, "Uhhh — what's happening?"

DON'T simply mimic what your predecessors did. Maybe they knew the beat better than you do, but that doesn't mean their stories were smarter. Take a fresh approach. Be original. Make the beat your own.

The PRESS ROOM

WHAT ADVICE WOULD YOU GIVE A REPORTER LEARNING A NEW BEAT?

Get your butt out of your desk chair and get out there into your beat. Meet people. Talk to them. Find out how they connect to other facets of your beat. And, above all, do a lot of listening.

Jill Barrall, *Hutchinson (Minn.) Leader*

Always start with the money: Get the budget of whatever department or institution you're covering, start asking on-background questions about how it works and don't quit until you can explain, at least basically, who pays, how

and why. It's the bean counters who run the world. Show your interest in their work.

Tim Nelson, *Pioneer Press* (St. Paul, Minn.)

Coffee and conversation. Once a week, buy a key person coffee. Learn what they want from you before telling them what you want from them. When possible, do interviews in person. Build relationships. While on a story, log contact info for good sources you meet. Then ask them out for coffee.

Erin Barnett, *The Oregonian*

As a crime reporter, I won the hearts and trust of the cops using the three "Bs": baseball, boats and baked goods. I'd bring in fresh-baked cookies to the homicide office and then ask them about last night's game and their latest trip to the lake. Also, make sure you know what kind of weapon they carry in their holsters. They always appreciate a reporter who

takes the time to learn the details of their profession.

Heather Ratcliffe, *St. Louis Post-Dispatch*

Beat Tip 1: Learn the vernacular of the beat. Cops, teachers, soldiers, engineers, politcos all speak in a jargon particular to their field. They have acronyms and abbreviations and other shorthand that you need to know to understand the meaning and the context of their statements.

Tip 2: Be nice to the secretaries, the desk sergeants, the midlevel managers. They know what's going on better than the vice presidents, the chiefs and the CEOs.

Jim Camden, *The Spokesman-Review* (Spokane, Wash.)

. . . Most of all, don't follow the pack. Report on the oddball stuff in the beat and your editors will think you're a genius.

Kevin Harden, *Valley Times* (Beaverton, Ore.)

Be prepared for one of two things from the key sources on your new beat: You might have to take heat for the previous reporter's mistakes — or you might have big shoes to fill.

Either way, get out and meet everyone you can and make connections. Don't be annoying, but stop by often and get to know your main sources *before* that big story breaks. Pass out tons of business cards — give them to anyone who could become a potential source or informant. Everyone's got dirt to share, after all.

Kimberly Morava, *The Shawnee News-Star*

The people you meet and interview regularly on the beat are not your readers. Resist the temptation to write for them. Write for the people whose lives are being affected by the sources on your beat.

Ken Fuson, *The Des Moines Register*

MORE ON **OPEN RECORDS AND OPEN MEETINGS** ▶ 137

Writing obituaries

Death is news. When death occurs unnaturally — by fire, murder, accident or war — you write *news stories*, which usually print alongside other breaking news. But when death occurs naturally — by illness or old age — you write *obituaries*, which are often gathered together on an "obituary page" in most newspapers.

You may think obituaries are just a depressing public service that journalists provide for gloomy old readers. (Writing about *dead people*? How *creepy*. How *morbid*.) But keep in mind that obituaries are read more closely, and by more people, than any other part of the paper. They tell stories. They touch hearts. They honor and inspire.

"There's nothing morbid about a good obituary," a New York Times editor once said, "because a good obit is about life, not death."

What's the difference between an obituary and a death notice?

Obituaries, death notices, funeral notices — the terms mean different things at different newspapers, and they're often used interchangeably.

Generally, death notices are brief announcements providing basic facts about a local person's death (name, age, memorial service). Some publications charge for these; some run them in small type along the bottom of a page, like classified ads.

Obituaries are longer, providing more history and detail. Publications often charge for these, too. They're frequently written by funeral homes or families, not staff reporters. Many short obits follow a standardized format that's simple and goof-proof.

But when prominent citizens die, it's news; their obituaries become news stories written by reporters. Forms from funeral homes provide the basic facts, but interviews with friends, colleagues and family members supply details that are crafted into a fuller story.

OBIT STYLE: WATCH YOUR LANGUAGE

Most publications develop guidelines dictating how reporters handle:

◆ **Addresses.** An obituary may identify the deceased as *Jane Jones of 1234 Main Street*. But is that address necessary? Or does it alert burglars to houses that are now unoccupied? Some editors delete home addresses from obits to protect families from criminals, overeager real-estate agents and insurance salespeople.

◆ **Cause of death.** If a pop singer kills herself or an actor dies of AIDS, it's juicy national news. But what if it's a local cheerleader? Or a beloved pastor? Most families want embarrassing causes of death omitted from obituaries, and most editors agree. (In a national survey of managing editors, 62 percent said they never use the word *suicide* in obits.) Instead of committing suicide, someone "died unexpectedly"; instead of succumbing to AIDS, someone "died after a long illness." Unsure about your newsroom's policy? Check with an editor.

◆ **Past personal problems.** Not everyone leads a blameless life. But is an obituary the proper place to remind readers that John Jones was jailed for drunk driving 20 years ago? Why re-open old wounds for grieving families? Granted, you shouldn't ignore crimes or mistakes made by public figures, but before you dredge up unnecessary dirt about private citizens, weigh the pros and cons. ▼

◆ **Flowery phrases.** Ministers and morticians like to use euphemisms to describe how "our dearly departed brother passed into the arms of the Lord" and now "dwells among the angels." Most editors prefer simply to say "he died." Avoid funeral-home clichés. Don't speculate about the deceased's celestial activities.

◆ **Other terminology.** Funerals are *scheduled*, not *held*. Masses are *celebrated*, not *said* (and *Mass* is capitalized). People die *unexpectedly*, not *suddenly*, since all deaths are sudden. People die *after* surgery, not *as the result of surgery*, unless the surgeon was at fault. A man is survived by his *wife*, not his *widow*.

INFORMATION THAT'S ESSENTIAL IN AN OBITUARY

Write an accurate obituary and families will treasure it forever; write one that contains a sloppy mistake and it'll *annoy* them forever. Not all information sent to you by amateur clerks and funeral directors is accurate; whenever possible, verify it through phone interviews and library research, as you would with any other news story.

Whether brief or in-depth, all obituaries should include:

◆ **Name:** Use full names, including middle name or initial. Nicknames, if commonly used, can be added in quotes. *Please* double-check all spellings.

◆ **Identification:** Find a phrase for your lead that best summarizes who this person was or what he/she did: *John Jones, a prominent local dentist,* or *Jane Jones, author of 29 crime novels.* Later in the story, you can elaborate on the details.

◆ **Age:** State it simply unless the family asks you to omit it: *Jones, 57, died Monday.* Or say *Jones died Monday. He was 57.*

◆ **Day/place of death:** Give the day of the week. Omit the time unless it's relevant for some dramatic reason. If the death occurred out of town, name the city; otherwise, give the local location (hospital, at home, etc.).

◆ **Cause of death:** Some publications omit this out of respect for the family's privacy; some omit it only in certain cases such as suicide or AIDS (see "Obit style" at left). Most avoid grisly details, summarizing by simply saying *he died of lung cancer.*

◆ **Birth date/birthplace.**

◆ **Background:** Education, military service, honors, career achievements — the amount of personal history you include will vary. The more prominent the person, the more in-depth the obit usually is, incorporating anecdotes and quotes from friends, family and colleagues.

◆ **Survivors:** Name those in the immediate family: spouse, children, parents, siblings.

◆ **Funeral/burial information:** Include the name and phone number for the funeral home, so readers can call for details. (You should call, too, to verify that your facts are correct.)

WRITING A STANDARD NEWS OBITUARY

Life isn't fair. There just isn't room, or time, to write a story about everyone who dies. That's why obituaries are generally reserved for prominent or influential people — though in a small town or a school, that may include nearly everybody.

That's also why, in the lead of a news obituary, you want to emphasize the person's significance:

> Edward E. Hughes, founder of the city's oldest and largest law firm, died of pancreatic cancer Tuesday at Mercy Hospital. He was 78.
>
> **OR:** Clifford E. "Duby" Tucker, 101, a classic swamp Yankee who dined on fried eels and delighted in reminiscing beside his potbellied stove, died Sunday at the Westerly Health Center.
>
> **NOT:** Funeral services will be held Monday for Ophelia Pulse, of 1234 Main St., who died of pneumonia Friday.

The lead of a news obituary will usually supply the person's name; major accomplishment or occupation; day, location and cause of death; and age. That's a lot to include, which is why most writers arrange those facts in the same reliable but predictable sequence.

If the cause of death is *natural*, most of the story will focus on the deceased's personal history. If the death is *unnatural* (crime or accident) or the circumstances are unusual, details about the death should precede the deceased's background information.

The more prominent people are, the more you should supplement their histories with quotations (both *about* and *by* the deceased) to both capture their personalities and assess the legacies they leave. Here's an example from the obituary of Gene Miller, a legendary Miami Herald reporter:

> Judy Miller, the Herald's managing editor, called him the "soul and conscience of our newsroom."
>
> "I can't tell you the depth of sadness in this newsroom and in newsrooms around the country today," she said. "He came in my office practically every day he was here, saying, 'Toss me a story.' "

After you've profiled the deceased — recounting all personal/professional highlights — list the names of survivors: spouse, siblings and descendants. (Some publications include "companions.") List the number of grandchildren rather than naming them all:

> Survivors include her husband of 53 years, Daniel Hohn of Madison; two children, Brooke E. Cooper of Lincoln and Jeffrey Darling of Tampa, Fla.; and 12 grandchildren.

Information about memorial services or burials usually runs at the end of the story, though some publications display those details in a separate "fast-facts" sidebar that accompanies the obituary. ▼

ADDING DEPTH AND CHARACTER: THE FEATURE OBITUARY

Some reporters specialize in a popular new style of story: the "common man (or woman)" feature obit. Instead of celebrating the lives of prominent citizens, these tell the life stories of ordinary folks using techniques you'd never see in a standard news obituary:

> She read her Bible and romance novels — nothing too explicit. Reading was OK, but she wasn't much for sitting. TV? A waste of time.
>
> She had no patience with people who weren't productive. She asked what her children had accomplished. She was a little more lenient with her grandchildren. She took in any stray cat that wandered by — too many, actually.
>
> She gardened in her flower bed: hydrangeas, daylilies, honeysuckle, roses and lilacs. Even late at night, there was Judy, out there planting by flashlight.

Notice the difference? The style is looser, friendlier, and full of curiously engaging details:

> Ruby Anderson was a tomboy who ran barefoot through the Minnesota swamps, third daughter of a Norwegian dirt farmer. She used onion tops for straws, scared off lynxes while bringing home the cows and made tepees out of birch bark.

The best feature obits reveal intimate details — so intimate, you can't believe the reporter *didn't actually know the deceased* — along with a surprising candor that captures people as they really were, warts and all:

> During the winters, he did lapidary work, leather craft, and painted by number — tasteful naked women.
>
> . . . Although he adored his daughters, he intimidated his grandkids, and he sometimes drank. He could be ornery and mean, but he loved to sing and mixed up the words to songs: "Chantilly Lace," "Purple People Eater," "God Bless America."

This illusion of intimacy would be shattered if every detail was attributed (*he sometimes drank, his daughter claimed*). So in an unusual departure from newswriting protocol, feature obits omit attributions.

That's risky. But a reporter with reliable radar can, after multiple in-depth interviews with friends and family, discern which details are typical and true.

Amy Martinez Starke is The Oregonian's obituary specialist whose stories are excerpted here. When she writes, she becomes "the god of omniscience," Starke says — "because I know, having talked to enough people, that this is true."

For full-length examples of both a standard news obituary and a feature obituary, visit **THE MORGUE** ▶ 210

HOW TO TALK TO FAMILIES ABOUT THE DECEASED

Writing your first obituary may make you uncomfortable — especially the task of interviewing the family and friends of the deceased. But it's important to verify the facts before printing any obit. Some tips:

◆ Don't be squeamish. People are rarely too upset to talk; in fact, they may appreciate your interest and actually enjoy the opportunity to reminisce.

◆ If you're not sure what to say, try reading from a script. Years ago, a staff memo from the *Amarillo (Tex.) Globe-News* advised reporters to open the conversation this way: *"Hello. This is John Smith with the Globe-News. I have the information about Mr. Lefode from the funeral home, and I wonder if you or someone could go over the facts with me to make sure everything is correct."*

◆ Be supportive. Sympathetic. Human. As veteran obituary writer Robin Hinch suggests, insert yourself into the conversation, when it's appropriate, to let the family know you understand what they're going through: *"Yes, I come from a big family, too."* That may help put them at ease.

◆ "Be willing to listen to the longest, most drawn-out anecdotes or recounting of a long illness," Hinch advises, "even if you know it's stuff you can't use. Good detail can come from those discussions and a comfort level develops for talking to you."

◆ If you're planning to write a long feature obituary, gather as much detail as you can by asking follow-up questions: *What kind of dog did he have? What was its name? What did they do together?* It's the small, telling details that best capture someone's true personality.

◆ Avoid the awkwardly obvious (*"Are you sad that he died?"*), but don't be shy about asking personal questions.

"They can refuse to answer," Hinch says, "but more often than not, they'll tell you lots of interesting things."

If people start to cry, ask a practical question: *What kind of car did she drive?* "It snaps them out of tears," Hinch says.

Covering accidents and disasters

It's tragic, but true — every day, cars collide. Lightning strikes. Planes crash. Homes flood.

Police and firefighters attempt to move the driver of an overturned car after a five-vehicle collision on a New Jersey highway.

Yet if we wrote about every accident and disaster, the news would become an endless torrent of destruction and horror. Critics often accuse the media of sensationalizing tragedy (*if it bleeds, it leads,* cynics say), but most editors maintain standards for deciding which incidents deserve coverage.

One key factor is severity: death, damage or injury. A fender-bender isn't as newsworthy as a fatality; a windstorm isn't a story until it knocks out power or tosses trailers around.

That's another factor: how many people are affected. If a tree falls in the forest, it makes no sound, but if it falls on a school bus, it makes the 11 o'clock news.

Of course, the more local the incident, the more impact it has on readers and viewers. We often become numb to floods, famines and fires in the Third World — at least, until a tsunami devastates entire coastlines — but whenever tragedy strikes close to home, reporters must be ready to tell the story.

GUIDELINES FOR WRITING STORIES ON TRAFFIC ACCIDENTS

WRITING THE LEAD

Begin by remembering that traffic accidents are commonplace, and if this is all that's happened —

> Two cars collided on Walnut Street Friday morning.

— then you might not have a story worth reporting. Though it may sound hard-hearted, several factors are usually required for accidents to become newsworthy: *serious injury* or *death* —

> A Fairfield man was killed in a two-car collision on Walnut Street Friday morning.

— or *unusual circumstances:*

> A school bus collided with an ambulance on Walnut Street Friday morning. No injuries were reported.
>
> ——————— OR ———————
>
> Distracted by a dog fight in the back seat of his cab, a taxi driver crashed into the lobby of Lincoln National Bank on Walnut Street Friday morning.

Notice how that second example leads with the *why.* That approach succeeds only if the *why* is compelling, significant or odd. Accident stories usually lead with either the *what* or the *who.* And unless the *who* is a recognizable name —

> Fairfield mayor Denton Fender escaped injury when his limousine collided with a garbage truck on Walnut Street Friday morning.

— it's best to delay naming the victims until the second or third paragraph.

WRITING THE REST OF THE STORY

As we've previously warned, there's no need to overload your lead with details:

> Laurel Jones, 5, and her parents, John and Jane Jones of Fairfield, were seriously injured on Walnut Street near Third Avenue at 9:35 a.m. Friday when their sports utility vehicle skidded on a grease spill and collided with a garbage truck driven by Thad Hertz, who suffered minor cuts and bruises, police said.

Instead, start with a delayed-identification lead, then distribute the key facts in a logical sequence through the first few paragraphs:

> A child and her parents were seriously hurt Friday morning when their car hit a grease spill on Walnut Street and skidded into a garbage truck.
>
> Laurel Jones, 5, fractured both arms in the collision, police said. Her parents, John and Jane Jones of Fairfield, received head injuries and were rushed to Mercy Hospital, where they were listed in stable condition.
>
> "Some jerk spilled about 50 gallons of industrial lubricant onto the road," said Fairfield Police Officer Stan Dupp, who investigated the accident. "That was enough to turn that patch of street into a skating rink." . . .

In most stories, it's not necessary to identify police officers by name unless they've done something heroic or provided a quote. You can generally refer to them as *police, officers* or *investigators.*

Remember to use caution when explaining what caused an accident. Witnesses may give you distorted, unreliable opinions; even police officers make mistakes. Be sure to attribute all facts and allegations. Use the attribution *police said* as often as necessary. Above all, avoid assigning blame or reponsibility. Don't say *Jones was speeding;* say *police cited Jones for speeding.*

✔ CHECKLIST

When writing a story on an accident, be sure to include:

◆ **Victims:** names, ages, addresses, other relevant personal information. (Double-check all spellings.)

◆ **Extent of injuries/ cause of death.** Identify hospitals where any injured were taken.

◆ **Cause of accident**, according to police, *not* victims or bystanders.

◆ **Location**.

◆ **Time**.

◆ **Circumstances:** road conditions, weather, etc.

◆ **Vehicles:** number, type (i.e., *car, truck, van, bicycle* — not the exact make or model), brief description of damages.

◆ **Arrests or citations** made by police.

◆ **Comments** from police, eyewitnesses, victims or passengers.

◆ **Acts of heroism** or dramatic rescues.

◆ **Relevant facts** about the drivers' destinations, speed, reasons for travel, driving histories, etc.

WHAT TO DO WHEN DISASTER STRIKES

WHAT TO DO TO PREPARE YOUR NEWSROOM

◆ *Anticipate your worst-case scenarios.* Every community is uniquely vulnerable to different *natural catastrophes* (earthquakes, hurricanes, tornados) as well as *man-made disasters* (oil spills, plane crashes, nuclear accidents). Identify the major risks in your region and discuss how your newsroom would cover them. This is also a good time to:

◆ *Check your history.* Do research now, while you have the time and electrical power, to find out your community's worst floods, biggest blizzards, deadliest epidemics. You'll need this information to put breaking news in perspective.

◆ *Obtain information on local agencies' emergency planning.* Identify who's who in emergency response: the local, state and federal authorities responsible for public safety, relief efforts, evacuation, etc. Find out if they're sufficiently prepared for every type of disaster — if not, that's a story worth running *now.*

◆ *Keep a phone list handy* with numbers for editors, reporters, photographers, emergency agencies, even home numbers for public officials.

◆ *Devise a newsroom battle plan* that details who's in charge, where you'll meet, who'll cover what. "The first few hours after a disaster are often the most important in capturing the drama and detail that will be used later," says Josh Meyer, veteran reporter at the Los Angeles Times. "To expect the unexpected and let the news dictate the stories, you must be ready for anything, to go anywhere at a moment's notice."

◆ *Prepare a field kit* with emergency supplies: pencils, pens, notebooks, camera, batteries, bottled water, nonperishable food (a couple days' worth), boots, a change of clothes, a first-aid kit, even business cards (to help those at the scene contact you after the chaos dies down).

DISASTER WEB SITES

Among the best online resources:

www.fema.gov
Reliable information and advice on disaster preparation and relief from the Federal Emergency Management Agency.

www.colorado.edu/hazards
A complete library of disaster data from the University of Colorado Natural Hazards Center.

www.yahoo.com/ Society_and_Culture/Environ ment_and_Nature/Disasters
A comprehensive set of links to every imaginable disaster topic.

WHAT TO DO WHEN YOU ARRIVE ON THE SCENE

◆ *Go where the action is.* "Hit the road immediately and start assessing the damage," Meyer says. "Find out where the dead bodies are and go to them." Or, as a St. Paul Pioneer Press disaster-reporting manual advises, "Head for the biggest mess and look for people who are visibly upset."

◆ *Question authorities first.* Authorities won't have much time to talk, says Steve Lackmeyer, a reporter for The Oklahoman, and what you get in your first few minutes may be the only official information you receive. "Witnesses and victims tend to linger and usually are accessible for a while after the tragedy," Lackmeyer says. "But often times rescuers and emergency responders at disaster scenes can point you to the most interesting situations early on. Do you really want to be spending your first minutes interviewing a victim when you can be witnessing a dramatic rescue effort that is still under way?"

◆ *Talk to victims and eyewitnesses.* Be sure to get their phone numbers in case you need to reach them later. "If you have a chance," Lackmeyer suggests, "walk with them through the disaster scene. Sometimes that will spur more detail and add color to your story."

◆ *Record details that capture the scene* — like the reporter covering the aftermath of a tornado who saw pink insulation scattered everywhere and wrote that the town looked like it was covered in cotton candy.

◆ *Check in often with your editors. And collaborate.* Keep your colleagues apprised of your whereabouts, especially photographers looking for dramatic images. Assess the potential for graphics, too; supply your editors with facts for diagrams, timelines and especially maps. Remember to record the names of streets and buildings so you can later reconstruct the parameters of the scene.

DEALING WITH VICTIMS OF A TRAGEDY? TRY TO USE EXTRA SENSITIVITY

A relative is comforted at the scene of a fire that killed two children in Brockton, Mass.

There's no easy way to interview a mother whose son just drowned in a flood, or a man whose home just collapsed in an earthquake. But it's your job to tell their stories honestly and professionally. Some advice on how to proceed:

◆ *Ask permission.* Identify yourself and your affiliation. Tell them you'll be as brief as possible. Say *"I'd like to talk for a few minutes about what happened,"* or *"I'd like to ask you a few questions about the accident, and I realize this is a painful topic for you. Is that OK?"* If victims refuse, don't press; if they respond with hostility, don't judge. Accept it. Back off and tell them how they can contact you later, if they choose.

◆ *Go slow.* Cover the essentials first (names, ages, addresses, etc.), then ease into more descriptive, emotional details. Be patient; let them ramble.

Give them time to compose their thoughts. If they seem distracted or confused, ask them to repeat facts, double-check spellings. Above all, ensure that everything in your notes is accurate.

◆ *Empathize — but watch what you say.* Treat victims with respect. Control your emotions, no matter how awkward or traumatic the situation may be. Speak calmly, but avoid saying:

▶ *"I'm sorry I have to ask you about this, but"* — Never make your questions sound intrusive. If victims don't want to talk, they'll let you know.

▶ *"I know how you feel"* — No, you don't, as they'll be quick to point out. Don't project.

▶ *"It could have been worse"* or *"You're lucky"* — Blurting out thoughtless, pat responses may provoke anger or frustration. It's better to nod, remain quiet and let the victim fill the silence.

FOR AN EXAMPLE OF ACCIDENT COVERAGE, SEE **THE MORGUE** ▶ 212

More than 70 hogs lost their lives when this barn caught on fire outside of Urbana, Ohio, in 2005.

Covering fires

Some may be harmless, but others make history — and headlines.

The bigger the fire, the bigger the story. Small fires are common in kitchens, barns and grassy fields — and unless someone is injured, they're usually treated as briefs or listed in weekly "fire run" round-ups. You can write these stories without leaving the newsroom, using facts provided in fire department reports or news releases.

But for fires where death, displacement or major damage results, you need to visit the scene — ideally, while firefighters are battling the blaze — to supplement the basic facts with quotes, color and dramatic tales of risk and rescue.

GUIDELINES FOR REPORTING AND WRITING FIRE STORIES

◆ *Identify yourself.* If you're not carrying a video camera with a station logo on it, make sure your press credentials are in plain sight.

◆ *Find the command post* — or "Command," as it's usually called. Look for a car parked beside the fire scene (often with a flashing green light). That's where you'll find the fire battalion chief who's coordinating the operation. If you're not sure where to go, ask directions from a police officer or firefighter.

◆ *Introduce yourself* to Command. They'll either assist you or direct you to a public information officer (PIO). Ask essential questions immediately (Where's the fire? Is it under control? How'd it start? Anyone hurt?), then get out of the way and let the team do its job. Avoid interfering with rescue workers or firefighters unless it's obvious that they're free to talk.

◆ *Get as close as you can,* but protect your own safety. (Fires, collapsing structures, even the blast from a stray fire hose can kill you.) Observe any yellow DO NOT CROSS lines. And unless you're specifically given approval or escort, don't trespass on private property or contaminate crime/fire scenes.

◆ *Wear boots.* And be prepared to go home stinking of smoke.

◆ *Remember, firefighters can provide dramatic details,* but individual firefighters rarely know the whole story. As a rule, only a battalion chief or PIO can be trusted to convey the big picture accurately.

Firefighters can gauge structural damage (i.e., light, moderate, heavy or a total loss). But for the official cause of the fire or estimates of the damage costs, talk to the PIO, the fire marshal or the building's owner. Don't attempt to make guesses yourself.

◆ *Watch your language.* Dramatic fires may inspire you to wax poetic about those *brave heroes subduing the blazing inferno amid rivers of fire.* But stick to the facts. Instead of calling them *towering flames,* be specific and describe them as *flames 50 feet high.*

Other words to use with caution:

▶ *Destroyed* means ruined beyond recovery. A building is either destroyed or it isn't; don't write that it's *partially destroyed* or *totally destroyed.* When in doubt, use the word *damaged.*

▶ *Conflagration* is used to describe a raging, destructive fire that's large (several city blocks) or uncontrolled.

▶ *Holocaust* means "destruction of life by fire." Because of its association with the Nazi's extermination of Jews, avoid using it in routine fire stories.

▶ A fire *guts* a building by destroying its interior. A structure is *razed* when it is leveled with the ground.

Luis Davila carries his 2-year-old son, Abraham, through the charred remains of their home in Medford, Ore., after it was destroyed by fire in 2005. "He was the one inside the house when the fire started," said Davila, cradling the boy. "He had smoke coming out of his nose."

Visit **THE MORGUE** for the full text of this story ▶ **218**

OPTIONS FOR ORGANIZING YOUR DETAILS AND DRAMA

WRITING THE LEAD

As in any other breaking story, if death or injury is the most newsworthy element, it should leap to the top of the lead:

> Six firefighters were injured and nearly 150 senior citizens were left homeless Wednesday night after a fire ripped through a retirement community in west Milford.

If no one was hurt, the lead should focus on the most compelling aspect of the story. And though this works —

> An early-morning fire Friday destroyed a farm-house south of Springfield.

— you don't want to overuse the same basic *what* lead ("A *fire* destroyed a warehouse Monday". . . "A *fire* tore through an Eastview trailer park Friday. . ."). Look for other lead options: the *who* or the *why*, for instance —

> Two Brookdale children escaped a fire that broke out in their bedroom Sunday by leaping out a second-floor window.

> Illegal fireworks sparked a fire that destroyed a South Lyon home Friday afternoon.

If appropriate, you can use an alternative lead approach —

> Terry Hohner left his Portland home shortly before 8 a.m. Thursday to go bowling.
> That might have saved his life.
> Minutes after Hohner drove away, his neighbors heard an explosion and saw flames leaping out of his house on Thurman Street. . . .

— but remember, feature-style leads convey less urgency than news leads. And you must be careful *never* to make light of someone's personal tragedy.

To read how the Newark Star-Ledger covered a fatal fire in a university dormitory, visit **THE MORGUE** ▶ **216**.

COVERING THE AFTERMATH

Some fires are important or emotionally charged enough to warrant follow-up coverage. You may need to report new details about the fire's cause, its impact on the community or the status of its victims. The human tragedy of those victimized by fire produces powerful journalism. (For an example, see the story behind the photo above.)

ADDING DRAMATIC NARRATIVE

Certain events (fires, disasters, crimes) offer opportunities for narrative storytelling. Episodes of struggle and survival provide extra suspense and realism to stories when they unfold chronologically.

You can begin your story with a standard news lead, then segue into a dramatic narrative when it's appropriate. (There's a story form — the Martini — that does this ▼).

OR you can begin the story with the narrative, crafting a suspenseful anecdotal lead as this story does:

> As firefighters finished dousing flames in the wood-frame bungalow Wednesday, neighbors of Clement Williams held their breath.
> Did he get out before the fire consumed his side of the duplex? Had he walked down the street to Abella's restaurant and left his Oldsmobile parked in the driveway?
> Diane Miller held her hand to her mouth and repeated, "Please don't let him be in there," over and over.
> But her husband, David Miller, who kicked in Williams' door but couldn't find anything in the thick smoke, shook his head.
> "I know he's in there," Miller said quietly in the middle of the commotion. "He's always home this time of day, taking a nap."
> Minutes later, as firefighters acknowledged that Williams, 54, had been trapped inside, Diane Miller began sobbing and fell into her husband's arms. . . .   [Angela Moore, *St. Petersburg Times*]

To read the full text of another fire story that effectively incorporates dramatic narrative, visit **THE MORGUE** ▶ **220**.

A TEAM EFFORT:
COVERING CALIFORNIA WILDFIRES AT THE LOS ANGELES TIMES

The deadly wildfires that ravaged Southern California in 2003 were the most destructive in the state's history, taking 26 lives, destroying more than 3,600 homes and causing $2 billion in damage.

At the Los Angeles Times, 76 reporters contributed stories on the fire. As a result, "for its compelling and comprehensive coverage of the massive wildfires," the Times was awarded the 2004 Pulitzer Prize for breaking news reporting.

Geoff Mohan, one of the Times' primary reporters on the story, explains that "a wildfire is just like a war: chaotic, often incomprehensible up close, and dangerous even in its most benign moments."

The hardest part of covering a wildfire? "Fires can overcome and overwhelm you in a matter of seconds," Mohan says. "Over time, the heat and smoke leave you tired, dehydrated and in poor condition to make decisions. Every action must be calculated carefully, and has to include a viable escape route, good communcation about where the fire is (and is going), and teamwork to keep lookout."

And covering a destructive fire is emotionally difficult, too. "Wildfires destroy everything down to the rims of cars, let alone cherished photographs and other mementos," Mohan says. "It is heart-rending to watch someone literally sift through the coals of their former life."

Still, Mohan says, covering a wildfire is an unforgettable experience. "Imagine being paid to witness such an awesome spectacle and in the process getting a close understanding of both human and mother nature," he says. "The ups far outweigh the downs for me."

Los Angeles Times
MONDAY, OCTOBER 27, 2003
A Rampage of Firestorms
13 Die, 700 Structures Are Lost to Wind-Driven Flames

On Foot or in Cars, Victims Had No Escape

The East Is Chic in Germany

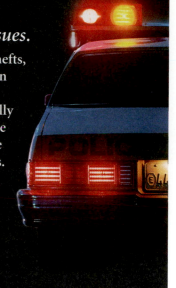

Covering crime

Monitoring criminal incidents and public safety issues.

Crime news both attracts and repels readers. Murders, assaults, thefts, scams — these have real impact and reader appeal, especially when they hit close to *your* home or threaten *your* sense of security.

Yet surveys show that a steady stream of crime reports (especially violent crime, which TV newscasts often thrive upon) prompts the public to accuse the media of sensationalism. Loud, lengthy crime stories create a false sense of danger and crowd out worthier news.

So how much crime coverage is enough? Every newsroom sets its own threshold. Some address every incident, either in stories or briefs; others focus less on random events but instead analyze trends, expose threats to public safety, tell stories about victims, educate readers on how to protect themselves — and cover only crimes so important or unusual that they demand attention.

CRIME-WRITING STYLE AND STRUCTURE

THREE CRIME LEADS BY EDNA BUCHANAN

The Miami Herald's legendary crime reporter Edna Buchanan was notorious for crafting gripping leads like these:

The man she loved slapped her face. Furious, she told him never, ever to do that again. "What are you going to do, kill me?" he asked, and handed her a gun. "Here, kill me," he challenged.
She did.

Gary Robinson died hungry.
He wanted fried chicken, the three-piece box for $2.19. Drunk, loud and obnoxious, he pushed ahead of seven customers in line at a fast-food chicken outlet. The counter girl told him that his behavior was impolite. She calmed him down with sweet talk and he agreed to step to the end of the line. His turn came just before closing time, just after the fried chicken ran out.
He punched the counter girl so hard her ears rang, and the security guard shot him — three times.

Angel Aguada saw a stranger — across a crowded room. Their eyes met. The moment was spoiled when her husband shot Aguada three times.
Romance can be murder, Miami police said Sunday.

Add color, not clutter. Cops have their own lingo. You'll need to learn to decipher jargon and codes before you can talk shop with them, or even monitor a police scanner effectively.

Just don't let copspeak creep into your stories (*the perpetrator was apprehended upon T-boning the vehicle*). Keep your language clear and simple, as Edna Buchanan does in the excerpts at left. Or, if your editors allow it, you can even add some attitude like those excerpts at right.

Crime is serious, yes, but it also provides fascinating glimpses of human behavior. Good reporters learn to add color and drama to their narratives without overdoing it.

Avoid sloppy allegations. Anyone suspected of a crime is innocent until proven guilty — so as you write, keep the suspect separate from the crime. It's acceptable to say that *a robbery was committed. John Smith is being held.* But until he's convicted in court, you must never say that *John Smith committed a robbery.*

Don't write that *John Smith was arrested for robbery*, either. Instead, say that *John Smith was arrested and charged with robbery* — or that *John Smith was arrested in connection with the robbery.* See the difference?

It may not help to add qualifiers like

accused or *alleged,* either. Some editors insist that *accused robber John Smith* still makes him sound like a robber; saying that he *allegedly committed a robbery* seems to imply he's guilty, too.

When in doubt, run it by an editor (or an attorney) to make sure you're using acceptable, neutral wording. ▼

Explore chronological story forms. Most crime stories are breaking news, so they're written in inverted-pyramid style. The lead usually contains the essential *who-what-when-where-how* (though the *whodunnit* and *why* may remain unknown).

Crimes involve dramatic sequences of events, however, and they're often best told chronologically. Note how all three of Edna Buchanan's stories at left use chronological narratives.

So before you commit to writing a traditional just-the-facts news story, consider using an alternative such as the Martini story form, which we introduced back on page 48:

You begin with an **inverted-pyramid lead** ——— to summarize the key facts.

You shift into a **chronology** ——— here, at which point your story recounts the dramatic events step by step.

You end with a meaningful detail or quote: a **kicker** ———

THREE CRIME BRIEFS FROM ARCATA, CALIF.

Newspapers often run "police logs" that summarize the week's most noteworthy law-enforcement activities, such as:

1 p.m. Police received a report of beer cans and other trash dumped behind the Stop 'N' Go.

But in California, the Arcata Eye ("America's most popular obscure small-town newspaper") writes its police-log entries with wit and sarcasm. Readers love them. Three examples:

8:57 a.m. A man in a green hooded jacket carried on the regurgitation tradition down at the Community Center, simultaneously gut-horking and digging through a trash can. Police asked him not to multitask in such a manner — in fact, not to be there at all.

9:14 a.m. A woman experienced the miracle of the digital age when she discovered someone, somewhere making charges on her credit card. And so the paperwork began.

---

11 p.m. On Tavern Row, a traveler apparently dropped a puppy, which died from injuries sustained in the fall, thus avoiding a career as an ill-fed fashion accessory on a string.

For more, visit www.arcataeye.com

 For full-length examples of several crime stories, visit **THE MORGUE** ▶ 222

ADVICE ON COVERING THE CRIME BEAT MORE EFFECTIVELY

◆ Get to know everyone on your beat: cops, coroners, chiefs and *especially* clerks. The public information officer (PIO) will keep you abreast of breaking news, but other sources may provide better scoops and story ideas.

◆ Find out what information is available from the police department and the court clerk's offices. Ask for blank copies of all the forms they keep on file so you'll know what to ask for when researching an incident later.

◆ Get familiar with police procedures. Arrange for ride-alongs with night-shift cops, a tour of the forensics lab, hands-on firearm instruction. Take every opportunity to educate yourself and build relationships with sources.

◆ "The scanner will be the life and death of a good cop reporter," says Kathryn Sosbe of the South Florida Sun-Sentinel. "Do not let it out of your sight or let the battery die." Keep a list of ID numbers and codes handy (and memorize the essential ones) to decipher transmissions.

◆ Be prepared for anything. For ordinary days, wear clear identification; carry a cell phone and camera. For those unexpected big stories, keep an emergency bag in your trunk with a change of clothing, bad-weather gear, boots,

extra batteries, pens, power bars and a flashlight.

◆ Think trends. Look for patterns, connections between crimes. Monitor crime statistics so you'll recognize when incidents — bike thefts, dog attacks, drunk-driving arrests — are on the rise. That's often what the real story is.

◆ Remember, crime isn't just about cops. It's about *real people.* So get out of the office and talk to victims, their families, even the families of the accused. (A good opener: "The police are saying bad things about your son. We just want to get an accurate picture. Tell us about him.")

Convey the human drama that unfolds when crimes occur. Tell stories; capture emotions. Don't view every incident through the cold eyes of law-enforcement sources.

◆ And remember: If a crime involves a teacher, coach, minister or public official, *it's a big story.*

◆ Most papers don't print confessions. Suspects often confess because of misunderstandings or coercion; troubled people often confess to big crimes for publicity or as a *cry* for help. Don't trust confessions until they're admitted as evidence during a trial.

Below, other details you might choose *not* to publish:

WHAT DETAILS SHOULD YOU WITHHOLD FROM STORIES?

When identifying those involved with a crime, especially suspects, use complete names to avoid any misidentification. A middle initial might prevent readers from confusing *Moe D. Lahn* with *Moe A. Lahn,* but for popular surnames like *Smith,* it's wise to add complete middle names, too.

In some cases, however, your publication might omit names altogether. For instance:

Minors: Most people agree that committing a crime in your youth shouldn't wreck your chances of becoming a productive adult. That's why juvenile court proceedings are

kept secret, and why law enforcement agencies are often legally forbidden to disclose the names of minors arrested for crimes. News organizations may choose to withhold the identities of lawbreakers under 18, too, unless the crimes are exceptional or the defendants are tried as adults.

Victims of sensitive crimes: Many state laws forbid police or court personnel from revealing the identities of sexual assault victims, to protect them from public stigma and scrutiny. Newspapers often voluntarily withhold the names of both rape victims and defendants — at least, until defendants are convicted — as well as the names of victims humiliated by financial scams.

Endangered victims: If naming victims threatens their safety or exposes them to further harm, publications may honor their requests to withhold identification.

Suspects: Because it's often difficult to determine *why* police are investigating someone in connection with a case, it's best to avoid labeling anyone a "suspect" until he or she is actually arrested.

And to avoid stereotypes: Referring to a defendant's race, religion or lifestyle may reflect negatively on an entire group of people. Omit that information unless it factors into the crime, or unless police seek the public's help in identifying or locating a suspect by releasing a detailed description.

FRANK MAIN, *crime reporter,*
Chicago Sun-Times (in the suit with red tie):
"I stood at the edge of a forest preserve in Zion, Ill., where two girls had been found bludgeoned that morning. I was waiting for something to happen. That's when I saw a woman approaching, holding a little girl's hand. Her daughter was the best friend of one of the slain girls. The mother had driven her to the crime scene in an attempt to find 'closure.' Other reporters realized the daughter might be able to tell us about the dead girls, who were not yet identified. I felt terrible to be in that pack, questioning a 9-year-old about her murdered friend. I have two boys about the same age and cannot imagine them being grilled by reporters. But professionally, I knew her mother had placed her daughter in that situation, and I had to be in that scrum. The low point: the girl pulled out a photo of her dead friend and the cameramen jostled each other for position to copy it. I saw fear in the girl's eyes. Someone suggested we take turns copying the picture and order was restored. The mother finally stepped in and escorted her daughter away from us."

Covering courts

Tracking and translating trial procedures.

All day, every day, the innocent and the guilty plead their
cases and await their verdicts in county, state and federal
courts. You can't cover every trial — most just aren't
newsworthy — but some cases are exceptions:

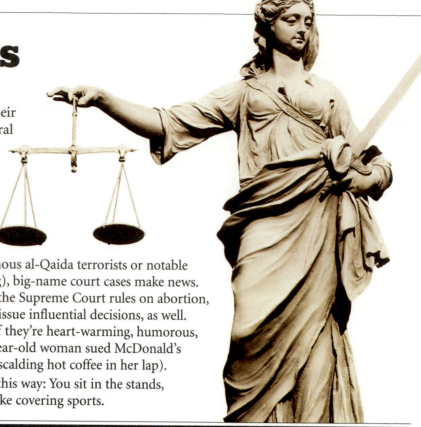

◆ *Murder cases.* Violent life-and-death dramas
resonate with readers. The more compelling the
story and colorful the characters, the more these
trials become headlines.

◆ *Celebrity trials.* Whether they involve famous
faces like Michael Jackson and Martha Stewart, infamous al-Qaida terrorists or notable
local figures (the mayor's wife arrested for shoplifting), big-name court cases make news.

◆ *Important legal rulings.* It's always significant when the Supreme Court rules on abortion,
civil rights or free-speech cases, though lower courts issue influential decisions, as well.

◆ *Human-interest stories.* Cases become newsworthy if they're heart-warming, humorous,
horrifying or odd enough (for example, when a 79-year-old woman sued McDonald's
for millions after she burned herself by spilling their scalding hot coffee in her lap).

If covering courts seems intimidating to you, look at it this way: You sit in the stands,
describe the action and tell readers who won. It's a lot like covering sports.

TIPS FOR REPORTERS COVERING THE COURT BEAT

◆ *Do your homework.* You don't need a law
degree to cover courts, but you *do* need to
understand how the system works, who the
players are, what the terms mean. Study case
histories and key issues. Cultivate sources
(scholars, attorneys) who can translate terms
and technicalities for you — so that you, in
turn, can explain them clearly to readers.

◆ *Learn to navigate court records.* There's a
whole universe of transcripts and dockets to
monitor and decipher, so get familiar with
what you need and where you find it. Some
records are available online; some require a
trip to the courthouse; some are accessible
with a phone call if you make friends with
the right clerks.

◆ *Be vigilant about monitoring future cases.*
Scan the dockets regularly to spot upcoming
trials that look interesting or important. Urge
your contacts (prosecutors, attorneys, even
judges' clerks) to alert you to newsworthy
cases in the judicial pipeline.

◆ *Study the background of every case* before
you enter the courtroom. "You can't raise your
hand to interrupt a district attorney who has
brought up a name or location or date in his
questioning of a witness," AP court reporter
Arthur Everett once said. So it's helpful to
bring background notes or files to the trial.

◆ *Be there for key moments in big trials,* but
don't waste time sitting in courtrooms when

nothing's going on. Study the court calendar so
you can be there when it counts: for opening
and closing statements, crucial testimony, the
verdict and — what's often most important —
the sentencing.

◆ *Don't trust everything attorneys tell you.*
Remember, lawyers are paid big bucks to
manipulate facts and sway people's opinions,
including yours and your readers'. Some
attorneys are *even smarter than you are,* so
stay skeptical. Don't get played.

◆ *Stay neutral.* A defendant might look sinister
and sneaky; a victim might look helpless and
pure. But things aren't always what they seem.
Cops screw up. Witnesses lie. Remind yourself
that what's said in court is an *allegation,* not a
fact. Attribute all testimony accurately: *the
prosecutor alleged, the witness said.* Report the
charges *and* the denials, keeping the coverage as
balanced as you can. Verdicts may surprise you.

◆ *Double-check all your facts.* Make sure all
personal information — names, ages, addresses,
occupations — is accurate, and that all charges
are worded correctly. Charging someone with
the wrong crime (or charging the wrong *person*)
will damage reputations and irritate judges.

◆ *Be a storyteller.* Be balanced and careful,
yes — but if you have dramatic dialogue,
colorful characters or explosive revelations
to report, play them up. Don't bury the good
stuff. People love reading courtroom drama.

BE CAREFUL — OR YOU MIGHT WIND UP IN COURT YOURSELF

Yes, there are ways you can land in court as a
participant rather than an observer. You could be
sued for libel (which might occur, for instance, if
you identify someone as *murderer John Doe*
instead of calling him *defendant John Doe).* Or
you could be called to testify in a case where you
had interviewed confidential sources who possess
crucial information. If you refuse to cooperate,
honoring your promise to protect your sources,
the judge could jail you for contempt of court. ▼

Contempt of court can result anytime a judge
believes you've disobeyed a court order or undermined trial procedure — for example, if you:

◆ Use a camera in a courtroom where photos
have been forbidden.

◆ Talk to jurors or witnesses while a trial is under
way.

◆ Print names (usually of victims, defendants or
witnesses in sensitive cases) or testimony that
the judge has ordered the media not to publish.

◆ Talk loudly, use a cell phone, read the paper or
behave in any rude way that annoys a judge.

Your right to report on a trial might sometimes
conflict with the judge's power to regulate court
proceedings. If you're ever unclear about what's
permissible, contact the judge's office, talk to
your editor or consult an attorney.

Remember, laws may vary from state to state.
And moods may vary from judge to judge.

 MORE ON OPEN COURTROOMS:
What to do when a judge closes
a trial to media coverage ▶ 137

 To compare different treatments of Michael Jackson's trial verdict, visit **THE MORGUE** ▶ 228

A GUIDE TO CRIMINAL AND CIVIL COURT PROCEDURES

To explain judicial proceedings to readers, you need to understand the process yourself. There's a big difference, for instance, between being arrested and being charged with a crime; losing a lawsuit is *not* the same thing as a "guilty" verdict. Though court names and procedures may vary from state to state, this chart illustrates, in a general way, how the criminal and civil court systems work:

MISDEMEANORS

Most states divide crimes into two major categories: misdemeanors and felonies. Misdemeanors are minor offenses (traffic violations, loitering) punishable by fines and/or short jail terms — usually a year or less.

ARREST OR CITATION
A person is either cited (given a traffic ticket, for example) or arrested — that is, taken into police custody. Within 72 hours of an arrest, the government must either file charges or release the defendant.

CHARGES REVIEWED
A prosecutor (or district attorney) reviews the case to decide which charge or charges to press.

ARRAIGNMENT
The defendant appears before a judge to hear the official charges.

PRETRIAL CONFERENCE
The defendant and the prosecutor negotiate the issues or discuss plea bargains; cases are often settled here.

PRETRIAL MOTIONS
Both sides can file requests to narrow the trial's focus or limit evidence.

TRIAL
Both sides argue whether the accused committed the crime; either a judge or a jury decides the verdict.

VERDICT/SENTENCING
Sentencing for misdemeanors usually occurs immediately after a guilty plea or verdict. Punishment may involve fines, jail time, probation, community service, restitution or rehabilitation.

FELONIES

Felonies are serious crimes (such as murder or rape) with more severe punishments: payment of fines and/or imprisonment for a year or more. In extreme cases, some states sentence convicted felons to death.

ARREST OR CITATION

FIRST COURT APPEARANCE
The defendant learns the status of the case. From here, proceedings usually move to either a grand jury, a preliminary hearing or an arraignment.

GRAND JURY
For important cases, prosecutors will convene special juries to meet in secret, examine the evidence and decide whether to file charges (issue an indictment) against a suspect. **OR:**

PRELIMINARY HEARING
A judge hears arguments from the prosecutor and the defendant to determine if there's enough evidence to bring charges.

ARRAIGNMENT

PRETRIAL CONFERENCE/MOTIONS

TRIAL

VERDICT/SENTENCING

APPEAL
Anyone convicted of a crime may appeal the decision, asking a higher court to review the conviction, the sentence or the court proceedings for legal errors. Appellate courts review only the record of court proceedings and don't consider new evidence.

CIVIL SUITS

In criminal cases, the government moves against a defendant for breaking the law; in civil cases, an individual or group moves against a defendant to resolve a dispute, recover a right or obtain compensation for an injury.

SUIT FILED
Attorneys for the plaintiff (the party instituting the action) file a lawsuit. The defendant then files an *answer* admitting or denying the charges.

HEARINGS & MOTIONS
Attorneys may file requests asking the court to limit evidence, issue restraining orders, change the trial's venue or render a *summary judgment* — a dismissal declaring that, even though the allegations are true, the issues don't deserve a trial.

PRETRIAL CONFERENCE
The court encourages both parties to reach a compromise that avoids a trial. By some estimates, 90 percent of all civil cases are settled before trial.

TRIAL
Some actions require court trials (where a judge decides the case), while others permit jury trials.

JUDGMENT
If the plaintiff prevails, the judge may order the defendant either to do something or to *stop* doing something (via an injuction or restraining order). Or a judge or jury may require the defendant to pay damages.

APPEAL
As with criminal trials, this asks a higher court to review the judgment or court proceedings for legal errors.

Covering speeches

Conveying a speaker's remarks fairly—and with flair.

Speech stories are relatively easy to report and write. Unlike breaking news, the events are prearranged; you know in advance *who's* involved, *where* and *when* the speech will occur. Unlike interviews, the speaker does all the work preparing, organizing and explaining the material. You just need to show up on time, pay attention and take careful notes. If everything goes smoothly, an hour later you're ready to write your story. Usually.

Other times — if it's a major address by a political candidate or a passionate plea by a world leader — covering a speech is a stressful test of your ability to process information on deadline, distill what's most important, fact-check what's dubious, sift through a mass of remarks to select the most compelling quotes, then explain to the rest of us why we should even *care*.

United Nations Secretary-General Kofi Annan delivers a speech to the World Economic Forum in 2006.

TIPS FOR COVERING SPEECHES: BEFORE, DURING AND AFTER

BEFORE THE SPEECH

◆ **Research the speaker.** Ask the organizers to send you the speaker's bio. In addition, do online research. Read old news clippings. Then:

◆ **Research the topic.** This will help you to better understand the speech *and* provide you with ammunition if you need to confront the speaker with follow-up questions afterward.

◆ **Request an advance copy of the speech.** It's often available, especially from prominent figures on speaking tours. During the speech, follow along to note where the speaker deviates from the prepared text. Identify quotable excerpts you can transcribe later.

◆ **Ask if picture-taking will be allowed** — and if so, when. Some speakers find photographers distracting.

DURING THE SPEECH

◆ **Grab a good seat.** Sit where you can see and hear well. The front rows are best; an aisle seat will allow you to move freely if you need to take pictures, interview audience members or sprint to the podium to ask questions when the speech is done.

◆ **Estimate the size of the audience.** Better yet, ask the organizers for an official head count. You'll want to include this information when describing the audience and atmosphere in your story.

◆ **Monitor the mood of the crowd.** Gauge how they're responding to the presentation. Are they supportive? Skeptical? Adoring? Hostile? Include examples of colorful crowd behavior in your story.

◆ **Take along a tape recorder.** Even if you only use it for backup, it'll help you quote fast-talkers accurately. But take careful notes, too; always assume your technology will find a way to malfunction.

WRITING THE STORY

◆ **Set up the story with a compelling lead.** Most of the time — but not always — speech stories will conform to a standard formula:

▶ **The lead** summarizes the most newsworthy or provocative point the speaker made, usually presented as a paraphrase or partial quote.

▶ **The second paragraph** is often a powerful quote from the speech that reinforces the point you made in your lead.

▶ **The third paragraph** explains where, when and why the speech was given.

▶ **The rest of the story** combines quotes, descriptions, background information and audience reaction to convey the speaker's message and to characterize how it was received.

This format isn't rigid, of course. For some speeches, the reaction of the audience — booing, cheering, pie-tossing — might be lead-worthy (see example on the next page). Other speeches simply won't yield a single, representative point that distills into a lead. And some speeches may be best served by anecdotal or descriptive leads.

◆ **Put the speaker's name in the lead** *only* if it's familiar to most of your readers: *Globalization has created an "explosion of democracy and diversity," former President Bill Clinton told an enthusiastic audience at Eastern Michigan University on Monday.*

Otherwise, identify the speaker by job title *(the president of the Sierra Club)* or credentials *(the former U.S. ambassador to Mexico),* then name him or her in a subsequent paragraph.

◆ **Avoid topic leads** like this one: *The founder of the American UFO Society spoke Tuesday on the subject of alien abduction.* Remember, the occurrence of a speech isn't your story; the Big Idea of the speech is your story. *One in four of us will be abducted by aliens, the founder of the American UFO Society warned on Tuesday.*

◆ **Include a minimal amount of background/biographical data.** Convey enough details to establish the speaker's credentials, but don't bog readers down in unnecessary history.

◆ **Highlight the speaker's key points.** Use direct quotes, clearly attributed, as often as necessary, especially when statements are phrased dramatically or eloquently. Avoid quoting the speaker if you can paraphrase those ideas more efficiently.

Arrange those points in descending order of importance. You don't need to rehash the speech chronologically, unless the speaker's organization of ideas works best for your story, too.

◆ **Convey the tone of the speech.** If the mood was grim and solemn, your writing should reflect that; if the speaker was zany and irreverent, your story should lean that way, too.

◆ **Beware of false or libelous statements.** If a speaker makes a claim you know to be untrue, you can either omit the remark (especially if it was a simple misstatement of fact) or you can supply facts that refute the claim. If a speaker defames someone in his speech, you and your publication could be sued for libel. ▼ When in doubt, check with your editor or attorney to see if a speaker's allegations cross the line.

✔ **CHECKLIST**

When writing a story on a speech, be sure to include:

◆ **The speaker's name.**

◆ **Relevant credentials** and background information about the speaker.

◆ **The reason for the speech.** Is it part of a series or conference?

◆ **The sponsor** of the speech.

◆ **The time, day and location** of the speech, along with a brief description of the venue, if it's relevant.

◆ **A description of the audience:** the size of the crowd, the type of people, their demeanor, behavior and reaction.

◆ **Quotes** — direct quotes and paraphrases — that convey key points made by the speaker.

◆ **Comments** from those in attendance. The more controversial the material, the more necessary it becomes to collect a representative sampling of quotes and feedback.

◆ **Responses** to critical remarks or allegations, if necessary, from those who are the target of those statements.

◆ **The speaker's fee,** if the amount is exorbitant and newsworthy.

Most speech-story leads convey a newsworthy idea from the speech. This story's lead doesn't, for two reasons:
◆ The polarized, partisan crowd behavior was as newsworthy as the controversial speech that provoked it; and
◆ Coulter's speech was more a collection of jabs and zingers than a comprehensive thesis.

The first three paragraphs capture the flavor of the speech and the activity in the hall. The fourth paragraph gives the crowd size and details on the lecture series.

By now, it's apparent this is as much a *news* story about the behavior of the crowd as it is a *speech* story. The content of Coulter's speech is getting less coverage than the actions of her hecklers and supporters. But fortunately . . .

. . . this sidebar of "Internet Enhanced" extras provides several minute-long audio clips from Coulter's speech, along with a video clip from the local TV news, a reader forum on Ann Coulter, a previous story (with biographical data on Coulter) and a link to Coulter's Web site.

The reporter used a small, handheld recorder to capture the audio clips posted here.

Most speech stories would probably include more quotes from Coulter's address than this story does. But because several speech excerpts are available as audio clips, there's no need to repeat them here, in the text. Instead, the reporter focuses on the crowd, collecting quotes from Coulter fans and protesters.

Ann Coulter causes stir at KU
Heckling, standing ovations interrupt right-wing commentator

By **Mike Belt (Contact)**
WEDNESDAY, MARCH 30, 2005

Conservative columnist and author Ann Coulter was greeted with a mixture of standing ovations and heckling after she took center stage Tuesday night at Kansas University's Lied Center.

As soon as she stepped up to the microphone, Coulter fired off one zinger after another about liberalism while promising to answer questions from left-wing members in the audience who could "thrash their way to a coherent thought."

"I've come to find I like liberals a lot more," Coulter said early in her speech. "They're kind of cute when they're cold, shivering and afraid."

Coulter spoke as the 37th J.A. Vickers Sr. Memorial Lecture Series lecturer to a crowd estimated by KU officials at about 1,800 people. The lectures, which began in 1971, were established through a gift to the Kansas University Endowment Association by the Vickers family of Wichita.

Coulter received several standing ovations during her speech, but she also found herself interrupted several times by a small, scattered group of hecklers.

"I think there are some people in the audience who meant to be at the sexual reorientation class down the hall," Coulter said, in response to the heckling.

Moments later Coulter stopped and called for assistance from students when hecklers started in again and no one of authority was seen trying to stop them.

"Could 10 of the largest College Republicans start walking up and down the aisles and start removing anyone shouting?" Coulter asked. "Otherwise, this lecture is over."

Ann Coulter speaks at the Lied Center as part of the J.A. Vickers Sr. Memorial Lecture Series. Coulter, the 37th speaker in the series, is a right-wing commentator, attorney and author of three New York Times best-sellers.

INTERNET ENHANCED
- 6News video: Coulter visit riles crowd
- Audio: Coulter on the Democratic losses in the election
- Audio: Coulter on Democratic values
- Audio: Coulter on recent scandals
- Audio: Coulter dealing with hecklers and threatening to leave
- Audio: Coulter on the Democratic position on Iraq
- Audio: Coulter on Democratic foreign policy
- On the Street: Why do you think Ann Coulter decided to speak in Lawrence?
- Lecture to feature right-wing commentator (03-29-05)
- AnnCoulter.com

Several people responded, leaving their seats to confront the hecklers, and verbal confrontations erupted in parts of the auditorium. One of those who answered Coulter's call was Michael Conner, a Shawnee freshman.

"All I did was say they shouldn't stop her from speaking," Conner said of confronting some audience members in the back of the auditorium.

Later, when heckling broke out again, a couple of uniformed KU Public Safety Department officers appeared and escorted about six people out of the auditorium.

Coulter resumed her critical remarks, calling Sen. Ted Kennedy a "human dirigible" and the Democrats' "spiritual leader." She also made fun of the Democrats' dalliance with filmmaker Michael Moore and former presidential candidate John Kerry, who she said got away with telling "big, fat, enormous lies."

Despite Kerry's loss, Democrats think their political stances and ideas just "need new labels for their bottles," Coulter said.

Coulter's appearance spurred mixed emotions among those who came to see her. About a dozen protesters stood outside the center before her speech, carrying signs bearing quotes from her books and columns. Ron Warman Jr. dressed up in a clown suit to express his dislike of Coulter.

"I think she's a clown or a witch," the 45-year-old Lawrence man said.

Some of the protesters, such as Robert Richardson, said they were members of the Society of Open-Minded Atheists and Agnostics.

"We're just not open-minded enough to like Ann Coulter," Richardson, 28, of Lawrence, said.

Others, such as Mollie Devine, 26, said she was a big fan of Coulter.

"I love her," the Lawrence woman said. "She doesn't back down. She's also funnier than the other (conservative) columnists."

Mary Anne Smith, 38, said she welcomed a chance to hear a noted right-wing conservative speak.

PRESENTING A MULTIMEDIA SPEECH STORY ON THE WEB

A well-written story can accurately convey the key points of a speech. But capturing the tone, the flavor, the dramatic nuances in a speaker's voice — that's difficult to do in print.

A multimedia package on the Web, however, combines photos, video, audio and text to capture the event in a compelling, multidimensional way.

The story at left appeared on LJWorld.com, the Web site of the Lawrence (Kan.) Journal-World. The text, written and posted immediately after the speech, was the same story that ran in the next day's newspaper.

The Web site's most valuable addition to the reporter's story was a selection of audio clips that let readers listen to Coulter's unfiltered remarks. That enhancement alone made this online version superior to the print version.

But there are other packaging options for online speech stories, too. When Democratic vice-presidential candidate John Edwards made a campaign stop in Lawrence in 2004, LJWorld enhanced its Web coverage with the extras shown in the box below, which accompanied the online Edwards speech story. Along with the text story, the Web site included both audio and video of Edwards' entire speech, a 34-image photo gallery, a 360-degree photo panorama of the crowd, and links to related stories. ▼

INTERNET ENHANCED
Stories:
- Thousands welcome Edwards back
- Audience finds Edwards in touch with concerns
- Police assist Secret Service with security needs
- Downtown businesses profit from thirsty crowd
- Kerry continues campaign on train
- Lawrence has drawn politicians, presidents

Multimedia:
- Photo Gallery: Edwards speaks
- 6News video: Raucous reception for Edwards
- 6News video: John Edwards' speech
Part 1 | Part 2 | Part 3 | Part 4 Part 5 | Part 6 | Part 7
- Audio: Edwards' speech
Part 1 | Part 2 | Part 3 | Part 4 Part 5 | Part 6 | Part 7
- Panorama view: Abe & Jake's Landing before the Edwards speech

Covering meetings

Watching clubs, councils and committees debate and decide.

Government is like an iceberg. It's big. It's slow-moving. And 90 percent of it exists beneath the surface: the secret alliances, the hidden agendas, the partisan deal-making and the bureaucratic wrangling. What's visible to the public is what goes on at *meetings*. Which is why covering meetings is so important.

Private, nongovernmental organizations hold meetings, rallies and conventions, too, and those provide useful material for stories (though you may need special permission to attend). But whether you're covering the school board, the state legislature or the Amateur Orthodontists' Club, it's your job to explain what the issues are, how decisions are made, and what it all means to readers.

TIPS FOR MORE EFFECTIVE MEETING COVERAGE

◆ *Start with research.* Read old news stories to learn about issues, personalities, controversies. Identify the key players, both official and unofficial, on both sides of important issues; call them and ask them to brief you on their goals, projects and problems. For government agencies, review the minutes of previous meetings and study the agenda for the sessions you'll be covering.

◆ *Clarify. Condense. Concentrate.* Meetings often sprawl in 10 different directions, so figure out what's truly significant to readers — and what's meaningless. If you write an advance to explain the goal of the meeting, focus on just one or two key topics.

◆ *Encourage readers to attend meetings* by giving them a graphic nudge. A fast-fact sidebar like the one at left catches readers' eyes and distills the information they need. A format like that is useful for other stories, too: sports events, movie reviews, even obituaries. ▼

CITY COUNCIL MEETING

The Sunnydale City Council invites public comment on the proposed expansion of Sunnydale Airport.

When: 7 p.m. Tuesday.
Where: City Hall, 102 Main St.
For more information: Call 555-1212 or visit the council Web site: www.sunnydale.us

◆ *Go early.* Chat with participants before the meeting starts. Grab a seat where you can see and hear, yet still move freely to interview speakers and spectators. (The quotes you collect are often more lucid than what's said during the proceedings.)

◆ *Dress appropriately.* Blend in as unobtrusively as you can. Dress conservatively if it's a banking conference; skip the tie if it's a labor-union convention. You need to do your job *without* drawing unnecessary attention to yourself.

◆ *Stick around after the meeting.* Ask follow-up questions. Make new contacts. Get reactions from the crowd. Collect names and phone numbers so you can gather additional information later.

◆ *Distill all the meandering malarkey into meaningful news.* Make it *real*. Tell readers why it matters, what it costs, who wins, who loses — and how to get involved at the next meeting.

◆ *Remember, meetings are not automatically newsworthy.* They're often just rubber-stamp rituals or ceremonial displays to placate the public. That's why you must always focus on the *issues*, not the meetings. Partisan quibbling and passionate proclamations are often just superficial drama while the *real* story unfolds somewhere else. Your job — your *real* job — is to dig until you find it.

✓ **CHECKLIST**

◆ **Group/agency name.** Double-check to ensure proper wording (is it the Planning Commission? Planning Committee? Planning Authority?). Explain any acronyms.

◆ **Location and length of meeting.**

◆ **Topics of debate,** including background on any issues unfamiliar to readers.

◆ **Important decisions.** Discuss any significant votes taken or policies adopted. What effect will these decisions have?

◆ **Quotes** from officials, experts or others who addressed the group.

◆ **Reactions** from speakers, spectators — and those affected by decisions, even if they weren't at the meeting.

◆ **Crowd size.**

◆ **Atmosphere.** Was it friendly? Angry? Rowdy?

◆ **Graphics.** Add a map whenever geography plays a crucial role in a story; get drawings to illustrate new design proposals; create charts that simplify budget expenditures.

◆ **Any unusual events** or departures from the agenda.

◆ **What happens next.**

MORE ON OPEN MEETING LAWS:
Reporters have no legal right to attend meetings of private groups, and they must leave if asked. But they are entitled, by law, to attend all public meetings of government agencies and report what goes on there. For more on this often-controversial topic ▶ **137**.

MEETINGS MAY BE DULL AND LONG-WINDED, BUT YOUR STORIES DON'T HAVE TO BE

A few reminders to keep your meeting coverage as compelling as possible — and to help your readers focus on what's most important.

Whether you're advancing an upcoming meeting or covering one that just ended, avoid leads that sound like calendar listings:

> There will be a meeting of the Sunnydale Planning Commission at 2 p.m. Monday in City Hall.
> **OR:** The Lincoln Board of Education met Thursday to review its budget for the upcoming school year.

Dull, dull, dull. Remember, the *meeting* is not the story; *what happens at the meeting* is the story. And in the lead, especially, you must give readers a reason to care. Focus on the issue that dominated the meeting. Place it in context, if you can:

> Long lines at the ticket counter. Frustrating delays at security checkpoints. Lost luggage. Delayed flights.
> Everyone agrees that Jackson Airport is too small and old-fashioned for today's travelers. On Tuesday, county commissioners will debate what to do about it.

Keep your language simple, even when issues are complex. Nothing ruins readability like bureaucratic fuddlespeak. For example, try slogging through this deadly, reader-repelling lead:

> The Lofton City Council voted approval Monday to implement a proposal for restructuring residential water rates as part of a debt restructuring option to offset unexpected consumption increases.

Huh? Instead, try writing your lead in *English*, like this:

> Water rates will increase by 50 percent for Lofton residents next year, the city council decided Monday.
> Angry homeowners immediately vowed to fight the increase. "We've been squeezed out of the process, and that stinks," said Jill Out, one of 60 protesters marching outside City Hall as the commissioners met.

In some cases, the actions or reactions of attendees may be just as newsworthy as the issue being debated. If that's the case, convey those emotions; capture the controversy. Be a reporter, not a stenographer. Your readers don't want the minutes of the meeting rehashed — which is why it's usually best to focus on one or two key topics, itemizing the remainder with bullets:

> In other business at Tuesday's meeting, the council:
> ◆ voted to postpone discussion of the 2009 budget until its June 28 meeting;
> ◆ approved a $410 request from the Safety Committee for new fire extinguishers in the city skating rink;
> ◆ requested additional architectural drawings of the proposed expansion to the Cooper Street transit mall.

PERSONALIZING MEETING STORIES: WRITE ABOUT REAL PEOPLE, REAL ISSUES

There's a danger, when you cover governmental process, that you'll focus only on the politicians and bureaucrats. The movers and shakers. The key players.

But what about ordinary citizens? What about . . . . . . *us?*

Smart reporters find ways to get ordinary people into their stories: their struggles, their goals, and the effects of political decisions on their lives. Telling one victim's tragic tale can personalize a social problem in ways no meeting story ever could.

Many news organizations don't even cover meetings unless they're truly newsworthy. Instead, they write stories that focus on *issues* and *people.* They take the lead in educating readers about community concerns instead of simply rehashing the debate at meetings.

Beware, however. By personifying an issue, you could compromise your objectivity by unwittingly taking sides. You can tell the sad story of a poor grandmother victimized by strict land-use laws — but what about the forests and wildlife those laws helped save?

There are always two sides to every issue. Be careful you don't always choose the most photogenic, feature-friendly side.

HEATHER SVOKOS *began a 1996 story on a West Virginia county commission meeting by focusing on a colorful local character:*

> Dodie Griffin sits on her concrete porch, aims her Mossberg shotgun across the way and blasts her target.
> Over the last few years, she's bagged a slew of snakes and rats that take refuge most of the time in an abandoned house next door.
> She told Putnam County commissioners Monday how she had thought of gathering up her dubious bounty and plopping it onto the desk in their chamber.
> But she thought better of it and addressed the commission without visual aids. This time.
> Griffin recalled creating a stir 20 years ago when she brought commissioners a dead dog. It had apparently been mistreated at the county's animal shelter.
> "I'm gonna be nice about this in the beginning," she said after Monday's commission meeting. "But if something isn't done about this, then I'm gonna be nasty." . . .

PERSONALIZING MEETING STORIES: LOOK FOR WAYS TO INVOLVE READERS

The worst meeting stories aren't just dull — they're irrelevant. They describe unknown officials making unintelligible decisions about unfamiliar problems. Those stories may be well-intentioned, but readers relentlessly ask, *"Why should I care?"* — and if the answer isn't obvious, your audience drifts away.

The best stories engage us. They not only inform us about important issues, they stimulate us to react, to get involved, to *care.* That's why meeting stories should provide tools, explain options, make themselves useful.

Roy Peter Clark, a writing scholar at the Poynter Institute, insists "that journalists must take responsibility for what readers know and understand about the world; that civic clarity is more important than literary grace; and that we need to experiment with the way we tell the bread and butter stories of community journalism — including the dreaded city council budget story." (See story at right.)

"Innovation," Clark concludes, "must attach itself to basic reports, not just surprising stories."

BRYAN GILMER *began a story advancing a 2002 city council meeting by speaking directly to you, the reader:*

> Do you live in St. Petersburg? Want to help spend $548 million?
> It's money you paid in taxes and fees to the government. You elected the City Council to office, and as your representatives, they're ready to listen to your ideas on how to spend it.
> Mayor Rick Baker and his staff have figured out how they'd like to spend the money. At 7 p.m. Thursday, Baker will ask the City Council to agree with him. And council members will talk about their ideas.
> You have the right to speak at the meeting, too. Each resident gets three minutes to tell the mayor and council members what he or she thinks.
> But why would you stand up?
> Because how the city spends its money affects lots of things you care about.
> It's the difference between whether the Walter Fuller Pool is open and heated in the winter or not. It determines whether there will be a new basketball court in North Shore Park. It determines whether the beloved volunteer coordinator at the Office on Aging for senior citizens gets laid off. . . .

 For the full text of these and other meeting stories, visit **THE MORGUE** ▶ 230

Covering politics

Keeping tabs of governmental policies and players.

Government is too important to be entrusted to politicians. That's why the press plays such a critical, controversial role in public affairs. As a political reporter, you'll become part teacher, part watchdog; you'll take a front-row seat from which to scrutinize and demystify key aspects of the government beat:

Decision-making. How issues are debated, how laws are passed, how policies are implemented — and why they matter.

The election process. Who the candidates are, what they do to get elected, and how they perform once they're in office.

Money. Political schemes and dreams all boil down, ultimately, to money — where it comes from, where it goes, and how public policies and programs affect every taxpayer's pocketbook.

Veteran political reporter Helen Thomas interviews President John F. Kennedy in 1960. Thomas, who covered the White House for nearly half a century, once advised young reporters: "Remind the politicians you interview that you pay them, that they are public servants. Remember every question is legitimate. And don't give up. There's always a leak. There's always someone who's trying to save the country."

WHERE DO YOU GO FOR FACTS YOU CAN TRUST?

Smart reporters try to stay one step ahead of the news by monitoring a variety of sources. The usual suspects include:

◆ *Meetings.* As discussed on the previous page, meetings reveal decision-makers in action: city councils, student senates, school boards, even private organizations.

◆ *Speeches.* You can't cover every speech by every public official, but watch for major announcements or policy statements by key players.

◆ *News releases.* These are mailed, e-mailed and faxed by agencies, advocacy groups and political staffers to call attention to issues or alert you to newsworthy events.

◆ *News conferences.* The bigger the story, the bigger the crowd of reporters trying to cover it — which makes press conferences an efficient way for politicians and spokespeople to convey their messages (as well as generate publicity).

◆ *Your network of sources.* Politicians use press releases, news conferences and speeches to tell you what they want you to hear. To uncover the rest of the story, you need to talk to bureaucrats, lobbyists, members of advocacy groups and other public officials to verify and contradict what's being said.

◆ *Documents.* Can you trust all those sources we just mentioned? Not as much as the facts you'll find in government reports and records. Great stories, disturbing trends and shocking statistics are waiting to be uncovered — if you know where to look. When in doubt, follow the paper trail.

Presidential candidate John Kerry talks to reporters during a 2004 campaign stop in Richmond, Va. As candidates travel by bus or plane, they're accompanied by dozens of reporters and photographers — members of the national press corps. At campaign stops, the candidates talk to local journalists.

ADVICE ON COVERING CAMPAIGNS AND ELECTIONS

◆ *Prioritize.* The smaller your publication, the fewer campaigns you can cover. So focus on the races and issues most important to your readers. The bigger your newsroom, the more you can specialize: one reporter covers major races, for example, while another monitors tax proposals and ballot measures.

◆ *Get to know the candidates* up close and personal. What are their goals? What's their message? Who's supporting them? Who's *financing* them? Most importantly: What kind of leaders will they be? Readers depend on you to cut through the campaign rhetoric.

◆ *Do your homework.* Candidates expect to manipulate lazy reporters by feeding them pre-packaged propaganda. Anticipate canned responses; follow up with hard facts and tough questions that demand real answers.

◆ *Line up reliable experts* (professors, activists, retired public officials) who can respond to allegations, explain complex issues and help you avoid being misled or manipulated.

◆ *Decide what really matters.* You're not required to chase every news conference and "Yes On Whatever" rally. "Make the candidates talk about the issues that are important to your viewers," says Frank Wolff, assignment editor at KCRA-TV in Sacramento. "Don't let candidates or spokespeople set the agenda."

◆ *Brainstorm story ideas.* As the campaign season starts, collect ballot information and candidate profiles to see what interesting ideas you can find, Wolff advises: "Maybe it's the first woman to run for judge, a high number of unopposed candidates, controversial or interesting local measures. Include the obvious stories that you know you'll cover, like voter turnout, need for poll workers, third-party candidates."

◆ *Spread onto the Web.* Just because print space is limited (as is the attention span of most readers), that doesn't mean you should boil campaigns down to briefs and sound bites. There's unlimited space on the Web for extended Q-and-A's, speech transcripts, photo essays and in-depth analysis. Create charts that explain the candidates' stands on issues and keep them there, updated constantly, throughout the campaign. Compile your best stories into a handy Web-based voter's guide.

MORE ON OPEN RECORDS LAWS: The press and the public have a right to access nearly all government records. For more ▶ **137.**

THE ADVANTAGES (AND DANGERS) OF UNNAMED SOURCES

Sometimes insiders want to leak information to you, but they don't want to jeopardize their careers by doing so. The only way they'll share what they know is if you promise not to quote them or name them.

Anonymous sources are enormously helpful. Some simply point you in the right direction; others appear in your stories, unnamed: "*According to an administration official . . .*"

Ideally, all information given to you by anonymous sources can be verified by other reputable, named sources — thus eliminating any need to mention "unnamed sources" in your story.

But what if an anonymous source is your *only* source of vital information? Can you trust that it's reliable?

What if the source is simply using you to spread misinformation or take revenge on a political opponent? Won't it damage your credibility if readers think you're in cahoots with partisan gossip-mongers?

Worst of all, suppose a criminal investigation results from a story you write, and a judge orders you to reveal your sources. Will you betray your pledge of confidentiality — or will you risk going to jail for contempt?

Yes, thorny questions arise whenever anonymous sources creep into news stories. That's why many editors forbid them; they're concerned about getting duped into publishing dubious information from deceptive sources.

On the other hand, without Deep Throat, reporters might not have exposed the corruption that plagued President Nixon's administration.

DEEP THROAT: HERO OR TRAITOR?
Visit the Morgue to read commentary on the legacy of the most famous unnamed source in history
▶ 234

5 UNFORTUNATE TRUTHS ABOUT COVERING POLITICS

Advice, commentary and a sprinkling of cynicism from a panel of veteran political reporters:

1 POLITICIANS LIE

Yes, politicians can be honest and trustworthy. But they can also distort, duck and dodge the truth to advance their agendas. So beware.

The best politicians are magicians, masters of illusion. So are their strategists and consultants. Even the nicest politicians lie by omission and spin everything. When you're around them, put up your force fields and activate your BS detector. Then feel free to interrupt their self-serving soliloquies and nail them on specifics. Ask tough follow-up questions. Insist on real answers.

Don't allow juicy "sound bite" quotes to stand alone; provide some rebuttal. This is best done with a declarative sentence that reflects your own authority and knowledge — not a quote from an opponent, which turns the discussion into a *he-said, she-said* mudbath.

2 POLITICIANS WILL SCHMOOZE YOU SO THEY CAN USE YOU

They'll try to charm you just like they charm the voters. "He's my friend," you will say to yourself, "so maybe I shouldn't write anything bad about him."

Well, if they're your friends, you're in the wrong business. And if they think they're your friends, *they're* in the wrong business.

In truth, both sides use each other. Politicians need the press to get their word out; the press needs politicians for comment and access. The trick is in playing the game successfully.

Base your decision on what to write on what you owe your readers. You owe the politicians nothing more than fair and balanced stories.

Don't get too close to your sources . . . ever. There must always be a line.

3 EVERYBODY BELIEVES YOUR STORIES ARE BIASED

Readers and public officials will forever accuse you of distorting the "truth." If no one ever calls your stories biased, you probably aren't doing your job; if, over the long run, you get comparable numbers of complaints from both sides of the

aisle, there's a good chance that you are.

Take pains to be as neutral as possible, even in casual conversations with sources. Listen when they criticize you, but always consider the source complaining. Check your stories to make sure you're reflecting their perspective.

If you've done a diligent job of ferreting out as much truth as you can, then don't let the political players wear you down. Just be ready to defend the process you used to find that truth.

4 PEOPLE DON'T WANT TO READ ABOUT GOVERNMENT PROCESS

They're bored and confused by complicated stories about hearings, partisan bickering and electioneering. Readers want to know how they will be affected by government actions; they don't want to keep track of every turn of the screw. That's *our* job, though it's not what we should automatically write.

Government affects everyone, some more than others. Get out there and find out what happens when the rubber meets the road. Remember, politicians are elected to do the people's work — *people* being the operative word. "You need some RPs," my editor would say. RPs are Real People commenting on how legislation affects them.

5 YOU MUST PEEL AWAY LAYER AFTER LAYER TO GET TO THE TRUTH

In politics, everything important happens behind closed doors. If you're not getting what happened behind the scenes, you're simply not getting the story.

Journalism is one of the few keys that can open those closed rooms. You usually can find what you need if you talk to enough people and ask the right questions — again and again, if necessary. Much of what you need is in plain sight, if you know where to look. The things that aren't are what makes the beat challenging (and fun).

Two good sources for information: Paper records and enemies. The records sometimes reveal key nuggets of information. And no one likes to talk about someone's actions or motives more than their enemies.

— From contributions by Rick Bella, Toni Coleman, Emily Dooley, Harry Esteve, Dave Hogan, Jeff Mapes, Matt Neznanski and Larry Peterson

69, 79 ◀ MORE ON **ANONYMOUS SOURCES**

Covering sports

From the baseball diamond to the ice rink, from the stadium to the speedway—

— sports play a central role in every community, which is why sports coverage is so popular. (It's usually the second most-read topic in most newspapers, behind "general news.")

Sportswriting may seem like fun and games, but it requires accuracy, insight, statistical savvy and cool nerves on tight deadlines. And though sports reporters often explore dramatic issues — drugs, greed, the rise and fall of heroes — their basic mission is to provide a reliable daily accounting of *results* (scores and winners) and *reasons* why teams succeeded . . . or disappointed their devoted fans.

A throng of sports reporters surrounds Muhammad Ali — perhaps the most media-savvy athlete of all time — as he trains for a championship fight in 1965.

CHECKLIST

When writing a game story, be sure to include:

◆ **The final score.** This will usually run in the first paragraph if the story uses a summary news lead; otherwise, it runs as high in the story as possible.

◆ **The teams' names** and the type of sport if it isn't obvious from their names.

◆ **When and where** the game took place.

◆ **The key players** and **the key plays.** If one play or player dominated, that's probably your lead.

◆ **Quotes** from players and coaches on both sides.

◆ **Strategies** that affected the outcome.

◆ **Key statistics,** including any records set.

◆ **Injuries.**

◆ **Both teams' records** and the effect of this game on the standings.

◆ **What this game means** for upcoming games.

◆ **Other relevant factors** such as weather, crowd, noise, athletes who sat out the game, etc.

SPORTSWRITING: THE THREE MOST COMMON TYPES OF STORIES

GAME STORIES

Most sports coverage takes the form of *game stories:* news reports that detail who won and how the action unfolded.

Minor events (prep sports, clubs, recreation leagues) often become short stories or briefs. Many are rewritten from reports phoned in by correspondents attending the events.

But for important games, you need to witness events in person, taking detailed notes, compiling statistics, interviewing players and coaches. (See checklist at right for more details.)

Reporters often write game stories using a traditional summary lead:

> Jason Giambi's four home runs led the New York Yankees to a 17-2 victory over the Tigers in Detroit on Sunday.

But some sportswriters argue that, since fans often know the final outcome before they read your story — they saw the game or caught the score on TV — you should use a more featurized approach:

> Four swings. Four home runs.
> For Jason Giambi, Sunday's 17-2 victory over the Detroit Tigers signaled the end of a frustrating three-week slump. . . .

FEATURE STORIES

You can produce feature stories on any imaginable topic, from a history of team uniforms to How To Throw a Tailgate Party. But the two most common types of sports features are *analysis stories* and *profiles.*

Analysis stories explain how steroids work, why the new coach is a genius, what the new stadium will cost. They can run at the start of a season (*Why the Bears Are Super-Bowl Bound*) or at the end (*How the Bears Can Start Winning Again Next Year*).

Game *advances* are analysis stories that alert fans to upcoming games or matches, explaining who to watch for and what to expect:

> The U.S. Open will begin tonight with aging Andre Agassi playing under the bright lights of Arthur Ashe Stadium, but likely will end in two weeks with Roger Federer lifting the silver trophy. . . .

Profiles are stories that give readers a glimpse of the guy beneath the helmet, the girl with Olympic dreams. A successful profile takes readers behind the scenes, providing a close-up look at athletes' behavior both on and off the playing field. ▼

COLUMNS

The best sports reporting is full of emotion and opinion — though *not* the writer's. Sportswriters can slip a little attitude into their stories, but not too much. If you want to tell readers why the coach is a bum or the goalie got screwed, write a *column.* ▼

Columnists are different from ordinary reporters. It's their job to get fired up and honked off like fans do — only more so.

"You've really got to have flair," says Los Angeles Times sports editor Bill Dwyer. "Then you've got to have innovation and creativity. . . . I need to feel the person's passion or anger. A column needs some emotion."

For example:

> The Royals are never going to win another baseball game. That's clear now. They are going to lose the last 50 games this year. They are going to lose all 162 games next year. After that, it's hard to tell. Maybe they will win a game in May 2009.
> What else can you say after that ninth inning Tuesday night? It was, without question, the worst inning of baseball I have ever seen. There should have been written notes of apology after that inning.

— JOE POSNANSKI, *Kansas City Star*

When writing an advance for a sporting event or game, be sure to include:

◆ **Significance of the game,** match or event.

◆ **History:** rivalries, highlights from the past, won-lost records, results from the most recent matchup.

◆ **Key players** — those most likely to dominate or influence the outcome.

◆ **Records and recent performance** of both teams or key players.

◆ **Quotes** from coaches (and players, too, though coaches may forbid them to speak to the press).

◆ **Strategies** that might affect the outcome.

◆ **Injuries** and players' physical/mental condition.

◆ **Other factors** — venue, weather, atmosphere, crowd behavior — that may come into play.

◆ **Who's favored.**

◆ **Time, place and ticket information** for fans who plan to attend.

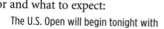

Visit **THE MORGUE** for examples of game stories ▶ 236, 238 . . . a feature story ▶ 240 . . . and a sports column ▶ 242

MORE ON **WRITING PROFILES** ▶ 120   MORE ON **WRITING COLUMNS** ▶ 131

COMPILING & CRUNCHING SPORT STATS

You can't cover a sporting event without including key statistics. A few guidelines on playing by the numbers:

◆ **Conduct solid research.** Before each game, study team and individual records to see who the stars and slackers are, to identify the players' true strengths and weaknesses. Is the fullback carrying the team? Is the goalie skating on thin ice? Numbers don't lie (though coaches and players do).

◆ **Take careful notes.** At most big collegiate and pro events, official scorekeepers provide the press with stats as the game progresses. But at smaller events, you'll have to devise your own system of scorekeeping. If you're new at this — tracking the play-by-play hits, outs, goals or sacks — talk to veteran reporters and get them to share their methods of statistical shorthand.

◆ **Use stats selectively.** How many statistics should you include in a story? That'll depend on how important the event was — and how much space you have. Use stats to highlight trends and turning points *(after going 1-for-12 in the third quarter, Smith scored 24 points in the fourth)* or to quantify pivotal successes and failures *(Jones threw seven interceptions, a team record).* But don't over-do it. Too much irrelevant math turns off ordinary readers and makes you look like a sports-trivia nerd.

◆ **Add charts, graphs or sidebars, if needed.** That's smart for two reasons:
1) They provide a home for bonus statistics that could bog down your story; and
2) They provide visual appeal that attracts readers.
Use sidebars to tabulate team scoring leaders, to sort data by category *(rushing, passing, fumbles, punts),* or to highlight impressive stats:

17 NUMBER OF PENALTIES IN THE THIRD PERIOD

5 NUMBER OF PLAYERS EJECTED FOR FIGHTING

8 NUMBER OF STITCHES IN BENSON'S LEFT CHEEK

MOLLY YANNITY *grew up loving sports and decided at the age of 12 to become a sports reporter. She now writes for the Seattle Post-Intelligencer, covering Washington Huskies football.*

On being a woman covering sports: Female sports writers constantly have to prove themselves to their male peers and readers. I've received several e-mails suggesting I don't know what I'm talking about because I'm a woman and have never played football. Well, Howard Cosell never played football, either, and it didn't hinder his career.

On athletes' attitudes toward women: Athletes and coaches know that I am there to do a job and they respect me for that. Sometimes they're even more open and honest, I've noticed, because I am a woman.

On media coverage of women's sports: I think coverage — for men's and women's sports — is determined by interest and, therefore, money. Events like the Women's NCAA Final Four get great coverage because they are well-attended and there is solid sponsorship. You can't ignore terrific athletes and great storylines, no matter who is the subject. Coverage doesn't have to be equal, but it can't be repressive or ignorant, either.

Her advice to young female (and male) reporters: You have to love this job or you'll never make it. If you love it, anything is possible.

WHO'S ON FIRST. . . . OR IS IT 1st? A BRIEF INTRO TO SPORTS STYLE

"The Associated Press Stylebook" offers comprehensive advice on sports style. (For instance, *coach* is a job description, not a title. It's not capitalized.) But every publication customizes its own rules, which reporters need to learn. Some of the most-used guidelines:

TEAM NAMES

Team names are usually plural, but city names used as team names require singular verbs. *The Yankees are in first place, but Boston is closing in.*

Girls, boys: Refer to athletes in high school or younger as *girls* and *boys;* team names use no apostrophes. *The girls soccer team lost 5-0.* Athletes older than 18 are *men* and *women.*

Leagues: Use abbreviations for all well-known leagues and events: *NFL, NBA, NHL, PGA, NASCAR.*

Indian team names: Some publications maintain that certain team nicknames are racist and offensive to American Indians. Thus, some sports editors refuse to print the Cleveland Indians logo (right); stories avoid mentioning the team name by saying *the Tigers defeated Cleveland 5-1.*

NUMBERS

Most publications observe AP style, spelling out numbers lower than 10: *He threw two strikeouts in the third inning.* But there are exceptions:

Measurements: Use figures. *He ran for 7 yards on third down and was tackled on the 2-yard line. She set a new high-jump record at 7 feet, 1 inch.*

Scores: Use only numerals, adding a hyphen for team scores. *The Bears beat the Lions 7-3. The golfer shot a 5 on the third hole, but was 2-under-par after nine holes. The 6-10 center sank five 3-pointers in the fourth quarter.*

Times: Use numerals, and spell out minutes and seconds on first reference: *2 minutes, 7.5 seconds.* For subsequent times, abbreviate using colons and decimal points: *2:23.6.*

TIPS FOR REPORTERS ON THE SPORTS BEAT

COVERING EVENTS

◆ *Know the sport.* Don't try to fake it. Do your homework. Study clips. Talk to experts. Understand the rules, strategies, players, positions and priorities for each event you cover. True fans can always spot a pretender.

◆ *Cultivate your sources.* Get to know the players and coaches (and the trainers, and administrators, and their secretaries). Get them to know and trust you, too. Get inside their practices. Get inside their locker room. Get inside their *heads.* Great sportswriting is about people; it's not just a rehash of what happened on the field.

◆ *Ask tough, pointed questions.* Find out *exactly* what went wrong, how players *really* felt. Don't be intimidated — but don't be too confrontational or accusative, either. Remember, without colorful quotes and insights, your stories are doomed to dullness.

WRITING STORIES

◆ *Think plot, not play-by-play.* When writing game stories, envision the game as a movie. What's the theme? Where's the drama?

"Boil the sequence of events down to those that are essential to the plot of your story," advises writing coach Steve Buttry. "Identify the most important characters, the key moments, the most telling details."

◆ *Avoid jargon and clichés.* Each sport uses specialized terms (you can't cover baseball without *balks* and *suicide squeezes*), but don't let your story get too technical for ordinary readers. When complexities arise, explain them clearly. And beware of corny, worn-out clichés: *The pitcher served up a lollipop, and Fenster knocked the cover off the ball.*

◆ *Remember, it's a game.* Sports are supposed to be fun. So are your stories. Avoid the somber tone and conventional leads you'd use with hard news. Featurize your writing style; keep your approach lively and informal. A little attitude is acceptable at most publications (check with your editor on this), but if you want to nitpick or offer advice, write a column — not a story.

A FINAL CAUTION ABOUT CHEERLEADING

Journalists shouldn't take sides, even at sports events. Though you're friendly with the players and attend every game, you're *not* an ordinary fan — so don't cheer. Don't boo. Don't write about *our team* or the way *we beat our dreaded archrivals, the Mudhogs.*

For big games, write big stories — but keep your reporting fair and objective. If the fans are joyous, say so; if they're despondent, capture their mood. But keep *your* personal hopes, fears and obsessions to yourself.

TEST YOURSELF

Answers to these exercises
are on page 296.

1 WHAT'S WRONG WITH THIS LEAD?

There are at least two things wrong with each of these leads. Describe as precisely as you can what needs to be changed.

1) The jury reached a shocking verdict Wednesday in the dramatic murder trial of Amanda Lynne.

2) Stan Dupp entertained a crowd of half a dozen spectators at Oak Bank Library with slides of his Hawaii vacation last year.

3) A Honda VTX1800 motorcycle collided with a 2006 Lexus GS sedan at the corner of Fourth and Main Friday, sending the motorcycle's driver to St. Vincent Hospital with a broken neck.

4) After nearly a year of fierce debate, name-calling and pressure from community organizations demanding a return to 1998 tax levels, the Polk County Commissioners met Monday to revise the county's property tax ordinance.

5) "We're taking them one game at a time," coach Rick Shaw said — but for his Mudhogs, it's do or die when they face the Swamp Toads this weekend.

6) Vicksburg police officers were called to a hit-and-run accident at the corner of University Avenue and Second Street at 5:12 p.m. on Oct. 13.

7) Frieda Wales, after suffering from crippling diabetes for five years, finally passed away on Sunday at Golden Slumbers Nursing Home in Durwood.

8) The captain of the 2002 Madison High football team has been arrested for a string of murders, based on confidential tips provided to police by his ex-wife.

2 COVER THIS JOURNALISM SPEECH

In the Morgue, on page 280, you'll find a speech delivered several years ago by Michael Gartner (right).
But suppose that speech was delivered yesterday on your college campus. You were there to cover Gartner's address for your campus newspaper. Using the facts below (plus any other biographical data on Gartner you want to research on the Web), write a 400-to-500-word story on the speech.

WHEN: 10-11:30 a.m. Tuesday.
WHERE: The ballroom at the Memorial Union.
WHO ATTENDED: The crowd of 195 consisted mostly of journalism students.
WHY: Gartner spoke as part of the William Henry Fox First Amendment Lecture Series, a program sponsored by the university's school of journalism that invites journalists to speak several times a year. The series' next featured guest, former NBC anchor Tom Brokaw, is scheduled to speak next month.
THE MOOD OF THE CROWD: Very responsive. Gartner's remarks were greeted with laughter and applause. Nearly 20 students asked questions at the end.
AFTER GARTNER'S SPEECH: Eaton X. Benedict, dean of the journalism school, gave Gartner the William Henry Fox Prize, awarded by the school of journalism each year to a distinguished journalist.
REACTIONS: From Benedict: *"Gartner is a national treasure. His speech hit a nerve."* From sophomore business major Polly Esther: *"I'm not really a journalism major or anything, but he had some pretty good stories to tell."* From junior journalism major Forrest Ranger: *"This is the kind of stuff you never read in textbooks. But it's valuable to hear it."*

3 WRITE THIS CRIME STORY LEAD

It's Thursday morning in Springfield. Local police say they found a body in a downtown alley, and they've identified the victim as Stormy Snowe, the popular weather forecaster on WUGH, Channel 2. Police say that Snowe's ex-boyfriend, Hagar Samuels, has confessed to hitting her with a crowbar after stalking her last night and watching her kiss another man.

1) *What lead would you write for a breaking story published immediately on a Springfield news Web site?*

2) *Local TV and radio stations will give this story big play all day long. What lead would you write for a story appearing Thursday evening?*

4 WRITE THIS ACCIDENT STORY

Here are the basic facts, as provided by the Benson County Sheriff's Office. Write this news brief as tightly as you can. (Aim for 150-200 words.)

WHEN: 10 a.m. Saturday, Nov. 17
WHERE: U.S. Highway 111, as it winds through mountains five miles west of Butteville.
WHO: Cooper Black, 13, of Green Lake in Benson County. Arial Bookman, 14, of Green Lake. Geneva Franklin, 14, of Green Lake. Gill Sans, 16, of Green Lake.
WHAT HAPPENED: Black and Bookman were riding together on an all-terrain vehicle. Black was driving; both were wearing helmets. Heading east on Highway 111, they encountered ice on a curve on the bridge at milepost 23. Their vehicle skidded into the edge of the rock cliff east of the bridge, then hit a tree 20 feet below, which subsequently dislodged both individuals, who fell another 100 feet to the rocky creek bed below.

Following in a second ATV were Franklin and Sans. Franklin was driving; both reported wearing helmets. Their vehicle also skidded on the bridge, but stopped at the edge of the cliff. Seeing his friends unconscious in the creek bed below, Franklin ran for help and called police from a telephone in a house one mile west on Highway 111. Sans attempted to climb down to the creek but fell, injuring his leg.

Rescue crews arrived at 11:13 a.m. Backup workers with ropes and harnesses were immediately requested to access the victims. By 3 p.m., all three victims had been extricated to the roadside, where Black and Bookman were pronounced dead. Sans was treated for a fractured leg and taken by helicopter to Providence Hospital in Dawson. He is currently listed in satisfactory condition.

CHAPTER
6

Beyond breaking news

There's more to journalism than breaking news. Profiles, reviews, investigative reports, columns — the opportunities are endless.

IN THIS CHAPTER:

The world of features

Personalizing the news with stories that educate and entertain.

Some crusty old-timers treat *news* and *features* as if they're two separate things. News, they insist, is the factual reporting of serious events (i.e., *real* journalism), while features involve all that other, nonessential stuff (i.e., fluff).

Ouch. It's not that simple, though. Journalists often find it difficult to distinguish between news and features. News stories usually focus on events that are timely and *public:* government, crime, disasters. Feature stories often focus on issues that are less timely, more *personal:* trends, relationships, entertainment. News stories tell you what happened; feature stories offer you advice, explore ideas, make you laugh and cry. As we'll see in the pages ahead, features include topics, treatments, styles and structures you won't find in standard news stories.

An anonymous editor once observed that when a dog bites a man, that's *news.* How fast the dog was running is *sports.* The litigation that results is *business.* How the man tasted when the dog bit him, and why dog attacks are on the rise, and first-aid tips for treating dog bites . . . those are *features.*

FASHION, FOOD, FITNESS AND FUN: FEATURES EXPLORE A DIVERSITY OF TOPICS

We live in a diverse culture. We all have different interests. Which means that no single subject appeals to every reader. Which means that the more variety your publication offers, the greater its chances of success.

That's why feature stories — and feature pages and feature sections — play such major roles at newspapers and magazines. Take a big-city daily like the Detroit Free Press, for instance. Out of 300 writers, editors, designers and photographers in its newsroom, 60 are devoted exclusively to producing feature pages like those at right.

You can write feature stories on every conceivable topic, of course. But at most publications, features fall into these common categories:

◆ **Lifestyles.** That top page at right is from a Free Press section called "The Way We Live." That's a perfect description of lifestyle features, which explain and explore issues and trends affecting our minds (goals, relationships, jobs, families) and our bodies (fads in fashion and fitness). Since everyone wants to live a longer, happier life, that leads to:

◆ **Health.** Is wine good for your heart? How much sunscreen should you use? Why do we belch? Readers want help improving their health, whether it's a dieting tip, exercise advice or medical news, all of which result from:

◆ **Science and technology.** Readers don't want long-winded research papers, but they *do* want environmental issues and technological breakthroughs explained in an easy-to-understand way, especially when it improves their lives, computers, stereos, TVs or anything else related to:

◆ **Entertainment.** If it's something folks do for fun, it ends up *here,* in the "entertainment" category. Movies, concerts, theater, art galleries, books, recordings, computer games, beer festivals, restaurants — yes, even dining out is considered entertainment, because people love stuffing their faces with:

◆ **Food.** Readers want kitchen-friendly advice on how to buy it, bake it, even *grow* it, though that usually falls into the category of:

◆ **Homes and gardens.** This is where experts tell us how to dig it, weed it, repair, rewire and redecorate it.

In addition, publications often produce specialized pages for kids, seniors, golfers, bowlers, pet owners — the list goes on and on.

Which all goes to show that features mean entirely different things to different people. Stories can be short or long, trivial or profound, serious or funny. Features are fantastically flexible.

"HARD" NEWS, "SOFT" NEWS: WHAT DO THOSE TERMS MEAN?

Think of all stories as a continuum. At one end, you've got *hard news:* serious, timely news events like murder. War. A fire in a nursing home.

At the other end of the scale, you've got *soft news:* lighter, less urgent, less somber topics, like how to buy a puppy. Cookie recipes. A profile of Leaky the Clown.

"Hard" and "soft" are relative terms that describe both the topic and the treatment of a story. For instance, you'd expect a story about *Three Killed as Stage Collapses at Beauty Pageant* to be written in a solemn voice using an inverted pyramid structure. That's appropriate for a hard news story.

On the other hand, a story where the *Rose Princess Shares Her Makeup Secrets* should be lighter. Looser. More casual. That's the style best suited for soft news.

Some stories can go either way: *Springfield Girl Crowned 2006 Rose Princess* could be treated as hard news, as a softer feature, or as some combination of the two, depending on the approach the writer decides to take — and how seriously his readers regard the event.

1 PERSONALITY PROFILE
Readers love reading about famous people. Unusual people. Heroic and idiotic people. They want to know how newsmakers think, talk, act and look. A successful profile, then, combines quotes, facts and descriptions to reveal your subject's true nature.

2 HUMAN-INTEREST STORY
When you've got a tale to tell about *real people* — a situation that's tragic, funny, odd or inspirational — you can unleash your storytelling skills to set the scene, describe the characters, capture the mood and get readers to laugh, cry or tell their friends: *"Hey, did you see that story about . . . ?"*

3 COLOR STORY
"Color," in this case, means *flavor* or *mood.* It's the type of piece you write when you're asked to attend an event — a parade, a strike, a funeral, a disaster — and convey the experience by interviewing participants and describing the sights and sounds.

4 BACKGROUNDER
Also called an *analysis piece.* Through research and interviews, you focus on an issue or event in the news, explaining how it happened, why it matters — and what comes next. It's like teaching a crash course on a complex topic for readers in a hurry.

The Top **10** POPULAR TYPES OF FEATURE STORIES

Features come in all sizes, shapes and styles — brief and in-depth, humorous and heartbreaking — but these reliable formats are the ones feature writers use most.

5 TREND STORY
This type of feature is often more engaging than a backgrounder on a social problem. Trend stories keep readers plugged in to the people, places, things and ideas affecting today's culture — the latest/hottest/coolest/oddest — from fads and fashions to lifestyles and entertainment.

6 REACTION PIECE
When news breaks, or a dramatic issue confronts your community, a reaction story provides a sampling of opinions from experts, victims, even ordinary folks. For controversial topics, it provides a way for key players to tell *their* side of the story.

7 FLASHBACK
Commemorative stories usually run on the anniversary of an historic event — Sept. 11, for example, or the 100th anniversary of City Hall — combining facts, photos and interviews to explain why it was important then, and why it still matters now.

8 HOW-TO
This popular, interactive format teaches readers how to *do* something: Play poker. Buy a house. Invest money. Quit smoking. It often works best presented as an easy-to-follow checklist, diagram, or step-by-step sequence of tips.

9 CONSUMER GUIDE
Readers want to know where to find the tastiest pizza. The hottest jazz. The cheapest shoes. And they expect *you* (the instant expert) to tell them. Almost everything we do, buy or eat can be rated in a way that advises readers what's good, bad and ugly.

10 PERSONAL NARRATIVE
Editors usually discourage stories written in the first person (*"There I was, face-to-face with Bigfoot . . ."*). But if you have a gripping tale to tell — a romantic travel adventure, a brush with disaster, a bout with a deadly disease — writing a personal narrative may be the best way to re-create the drama.

Generating story ideas

There are great stories everywhere, just waiting to be discovered

According to "The Complete Idiot's Guide to Publishing Magazine Articles," the four best angles for stories are 1) how to save time, 2) how to save money, 3) how to be loved, and 4) how to make money.

That may be true — but it's ridiculously oversimplistic, too, because when it comes to feature writing, the varieties of story ideas are endless. As Robert Stein, former editor of Redbook and McCall's, once observed:

"If you gave a dozen writers identical instructions for an article — to report, let's say, on the largest maternity hospital in the city — one writer, whose beat is scientific, would come back with a detailed report on new medical techniques for delivery. Another would write about natural childbirth. A third, with a sense of the dramatic, would bring back a narrative of the hospital's fight to preserve the life of a premature baby. A fourth would string together humorous anecdotes of mothers and fathers who barely got to the hospital on time. A fifth writer might bring back an article on the high costs of maternity care. . . . Send a hundred writers, and no two of the resulting articles will be the same. Because no two writers have identical interests, curiosities, enthusiasms or ways of expressing what they see."

WHERE TO FIND THOSE GREAT (BUT ELUSIVE) STORY IDEAS

You want good story ideas? Solid, sure-fire, crowd-pleasing, award-winning story ideas? Do what every smart feature writer does: Start compiling a list. Look for ideas everywhere you go, then jot them down in a notebook, in a computer, on napkins and matchbooks — but collect dozens. *Hundreds.* Many of them will never pan out; despite your best efforts, they'll be too dull, too dumb or too difficult to do.

Organize your ideas by topic (people, places, trends) or by treatment (profiles, photo stories, how-to guides). Mark timely or seasonal ideas on your calendar or compile what's called a "tickler" file to plan stories months, even years ahead.

The best ideas often pop up unexpectedly, so keep your journalistic radar constantly scanning the horizon. The best places to look for ideas include:

◆ **Your publication's archives.** Stay abreast of local people, trends and events, because they contain the seeds of future stories. Read your own publication (or browse the archives) so you'll know what's been reported — and what tales still need to be told.

◆ **Your competitors.** Just because they beat you to an idea doesn't mean it can't be updated or upgraded. Look for ways to add *your* spin to *their* stories.

◆ **TV, magazines, newspapers, Web sites.** Become a voracious reader. Seek out national trends, issues and statistics you can localize for your own readers.

◆ **News releases.** Your newsroom receives a steady stream of news releases and media kits promoting products, services, activities and awards. Many have the potential to become fascinating features.

◆ **Reader suggestions.** Yes, readers (and editors) will pester you with idiotic story ideas. But believe it or not, they'll have *terrific* ideas, too. So be ready.

◆ **Brainstorming.** Creativity doesn't have to be a solo effort. Bouncing ideas around with friends or colleagues often generates solutions you couldn't produce alone. Here's one way to brainstorm:

HOW TO TELL IF YOUR IDEA IS A GOOD ONE

Here are eight ways to assess a story idea before you try selling it to an editor:

Where did your idea come from?
If it came from reporting, it's probably a stronger idea than one that just popped into your head. Did your reporting suggest a trend? Did it turn up a fascinating person? Did something puzzle or intrigue you?

Is the idea original?
Have you checked the library? If something has been written about your idea already, look for opportunities to find a new angle or local perspective on the subject.

Does the idea surprise you?
If not, how will it surprise your readers? Will they invest the time to read 50 inches of a story if they already know pretty much everything by reading the headline?

Does the idea have movement to it?
What's *movement?* It's change, motion, direction — something that's new, something people are developing interest in, starting to talk about, or think about, or plan for.

Is there a STORY there?
Is there a *tale* in your idea that will draw the reader along — a story that has a beginning, middle and end?

Is there tension?
Tension comes with conflict, a problem to be overcome, a mystery to be solved. Tension is reading the first paragraph of a story and not knowing what the last paragraph is going to say.

Is the story true?
There are an awful lot of compelling ideas — about inventions, and social movements, and diseases, and vitamins, and truisms, and philosophies — that turn out not to be true. Before you propose a story, do enough work to make sure you know what you're talking about. But remember: If something that everyone thinks is true turns out not true in some way you can prove, you've got a great story.

Do YOU like the story?
You're going to be spending a lot of time working on this piece. Shouldn't it be something you love doing? How can you expect your editors and readers to enjoy a story if you haven't?

— Excerpted from "Testing Your Ideas: Ten Pre-Proposal Checks" by Amanda Bennett, editor, The Philadelphia Inquirer

CREATE AN IDEA MAP

Alone or in a group, write your topic in bold letters in the middle of a big sheet of paper. Then start blurting out any related concepts, phrases and terms you can think of — *who, what, when, where, why.* It may seem chaotic, but don't judge. Don't censor. Just brainstorm and jot it all down.

Finished? Now study the results. Identify the strongest themes. Look for "clusters" of ideas. Draw circles or lines to link related words and concepts. On a new sheet of paper, reorganize your key themes into a "map" or "web" like the one at right — then jot down story ideas that explain or illustrate different aspects of those key concepts.

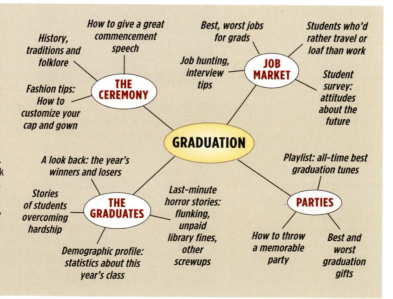

THINK YOU'VE GOT A GOOD IDEA? HERE'S HOW TO TURN IT INTO A STORY

Suppose you discover ants in your house. *Lots* of ants. So you call an exterminator. He says that carpenter ants have been a real problem this year, infesting homes all over town. You think: *Hmmm. This could be a story.*

Now, you *could* just do some research, type up your notes and hand in a story. That's a reliable way to produce a predictable 20-inch chunk of text that nobody needs to read. A *successful* feature — one that's clever, compelling and visually appealing — takes teamwork and planning.

Here's how a good idea expands and evolves into a successful story:

① SEE IF IT'S BEEN DONE

Why waste energy on a story if your publication (or a competitor) already ran it? Check back issues. Do a Web search. Bounce ideas off your newsroom colleagues. Find out what's run and what *hasn't*.

Even if your idea isn't original, it may still have potential. How long ago did previous stories run? It may be time for an update. How was the idea handled last time? Maybe you can add more depth, present fresh facts, give the topic a whole different spin. Old stories often inspire new ideas; just be careful not to recycle outdated material or plagiarize what's been printed.

Remember, some story ideas — like "Hot Toys for Christmas" — never get old, even when they run year after year. After year.

② FOCUS YOUR ANGLE

Let's be blunt: Every reporter is full of ideas doomed to become dull, unreadable stories. Why? Because those ideas are half-baked. Predictable. Fuzzy and unfocused.

Smart writers know how to zero in on an idea, play with it and spin it into something *fresh*. Ask yourself: What's the most compelling way to tell the story? What's the cleverest way to hook the reader? How do I make this information as useful and engaging as possible?

Beware of vague generalizations that sound more like boring essays than inviting features. Don't pitch an idea about *patriotism* — instead, tell the tale of "The Oldest Flag in Town." Don't just ponder the problem of *cheating* — find out "The Top 10 Ways Students Cheat."

③ TALK TO YOUR EDITOR

Whether you work for a newspaper, a magazine, in broadcasting or online, you've got to remember: This is a *collaboration*. You don't own the story. Sure, you're a terrific writer, but you're part of a production team that includes editors, photographers and designers with ideas as valid as yours.

So before you start producing a story, talk to your editor. Once you sell the idea, you need to work out when the story is due, how long it should be, what you must include and what you should avoid. A good editor can shape and steer stories even better than *you* can.

Don't be defensive. Learn how to share. Collaboration makes good ideas better. Selfish isolation makes weak ideas worse.

④ DO YOUR RESEARCH

The fun begins. Phone calls, interviews, library research — you know the drill. This is where you find out how solid your idea actually is. Are your sources cooperative? Facts supportive? Many a good story has been ruined by oververification, as publisher James Gordon Bennett sarcastically noted a century ago.

If the truth takes you somewhere you didn't plan to go, either follow faithfully — or pull the plug if the story seems too shaky to salvage.

This might also be a good time to remind you that feature stories require the same degree of accuracy, fairness and attention to detail as news stories do. Though your topics may be softer, that doesn't mean your reporting standards are any lower.

⑥ WRITE THE STORY

Now you know how long it should be, and when it's due, and what the angle is, and how the package will look. You've done all the research and reporting.

So go write. And rewrite.

And rewrite some more.

But instead of crafting one long narrative story, try turning your research into checklists. Fact boxes. Short copy blocks that dovetail with informational graphics.

And as you work, your colleagues may have further questions, corrections, additions or deletions.

But the biggest challenge still awaits. How well did your ideas score with readers? What clicked? What bombed? The best writers find ways to evaluate the success of every story, relentlessly asking: *How can I do better next time?*

⑤ PLAN THE PACKAGE

Started writing your story yet? Wait! Stop! Hold on for a minute. Before inking your ideas into permanent, perfectly phrased paragraphs, you should take one last whack at collaboration. Some journalists call it a Maestro session — but whatever you call it, this final story conference gives editors, photographers and designers one more opportunity to reshape your story's presentation before you start structuring it in writing.

Should *these facts* be presented as an interactive checklist? Would *this material* work better as a diagram? Shouldn't we shoot photos of *these people* now, before the story gets cold? If you're cooperative and open-minded, you can explore new ideas to make your story as visual and reader-friendly as possible. ▼

MORE ON **PLANNING STORY PACKAGES** ▶ **126**

Feature style

Face it: Some stories require a livelier, looser, more literary voice.

Back in the 1960s, a reporter named Tom Wolfe — that's him at right, in his trademark white suit — got fed up with "the pale beige tone" of standard news writing.

"Readers were bored to tears," Wolfe observed. "This had nothing to do with objectivity or subjectivity or taking a stand...it was a matter of personality, energy, drive, bravura... *style*, in a word." Wolfe began bending and breaking the rules in stories with titles like "There Goes (Varoom! Varoom!) That Kandy-Kolored (Thphhhh!) Tangerine-Flake Streamline Baby (Rahghhh!) Around the Bend (Brummmmmmmmmmmmmmm)..."

So successful was Wolfe's feature-writing style — and the styles of such colleagues as Hunter S. Thompson and Gay Talese — that Wolfe dubbed it "The New Journalism." What was so new about it? Mostly, reporters began borrowing four literary techniques from novelists: 1) realistic dialogue; 2) vivid reconstruction of actual scenes that were 3) viewed through the eyes and minds of the characters, while 4) recording everyday details — clothing, furnishings, gestures, poses — that contained the most symbolic resonance.

The New Journalism is old news nowadays. But successful feature writers still rely on literary techniques you won't find in standard news stories. Some examples:

SYNTAX AND PHRASING

You don't clown around when you write news stories about auto accidents or school board meetings. You write simple, declarative sentences in a solemn, objective tone. Just the facts: no flash, please.

The rules loosen up, however, when you write feature stories. Your editors won't go *freakin' loony* if you use slang or contractions; you can phrase for dramatic effect, even write sentence fragments:

> Ten seconds. Count it: One. Two. Three. Four. Five. Six. Seven. Eight. Nine. Ten. Ten seconds was roughly how long it lasted. Nobody had a stopwatch, nothing can be proven definitively, but that's the consensus. The tornado that swooped through Utica at 6:09 p.m. April 20 took some 10 seconds to do what it did. Ten seconds is barely a flicker. It's a long, deep breath. It's no time at all. It's an eternity.
> — **Julia Keller**, *Chicago Tribune*

Notice how the stylistic flair of those short sentences grabs you while enhancing the story's drama. There's drama, too, when sentences get longer, weaving imagery and details together in an almost poetic way — as in the following example, where the writer describes a photographer climbing to capture the perfect shot:

> Up and up and up, climbing hand over hand into the huge black sky, five stories, then six, up through the dark cylinder of the old ferry terminal, his bulky Linhof lashed to his back, tripod and film holders banging against his sides, crepe-soled shoes slipping on iron ladder rungs spattered with pigeon dung.
> Up and up, until he pushed through the roof flap and popped out into the salty warm July night, scanning the horizon, his brain calculating wind speed and bridge angle and cloud viscosity while the bay breeze dampened his shirt. All thought of work-work-work (this was work, too, but it wasn't) — and of clients and bills was as far away as Timbuktu. It was just him and the camera, way, way out there, like a spinnaker off the bowsprit, a bat on the night breeze, happy, happy to be alive. — **Mary Battiata**, *The Washington Post*

VOICE AND TENSE

News stories are written in the past tense: *The votes were counted. The bill passed.* But features are often written in the present tense, as if you're right there, witnessing the events, and they're happening *now*:

> Let's begin with his pickup truck. It's green, it runs, its windshield wipers don't squeak. Those are the nicest things you could say about it.
> Otherwise, it's noteworthy only for what it contains in the cab, namely, a world. Peter Bacho's world. A quick look-around will give you clues to everything you need to know about the man. Immediately, you might notice his world needs vacuuming. The ashtray overflows with cigarette butts and ashes. He's been smoking a lot lately, a result, he says, of being celibate (more on this later). . . .
> — **Alex Tizon**, *The Seattle Times*

Notice, too, how the reporter puts *you* in the truck and talks to *you* as he writes. News stories don't do that. But feature writers often use the second-person voice to connect more directly with you (or, in "how-to" stories, to offer you helpful advice. This book does that.).

In the excerpt below, notice how the writer uses both the second person and the present tense to put you inside a carnival sideshow:

> Behold the fat man. Go ahead. Everybody does. He doesn't mind, honestly. That's how he makes his living. Walk right up to him. Stand there and stare. Gape at the layers of fat, the astonishing girth, the incredible bulk. Imagine him in a bathtub. Or better, on a bike. Or better yet, on one of those flimsy antique chairs. *Boom!* If you're lucky, maybe he'll lift his shirt. If you're real lucky, maybe he'll rub his belly. Don't be shy. Ask him a question.
> "What's your name?"
> "T.J. Albert Jackson. Better known as Fat Albert."
> "How much do you weigh?"
> "Eight hundred and ninety-one pounds."
> "Gawd! How many meals you eat a day?"
> "Three."
> "What — three *cows*?"
> — **David Finkel**, *St. Petersburg Times*

HELPFUL TIPS FOR SUCCESSFUL FEATURE WRITING

TOM WOLFE *displays his dazzling descriptive flair in this feature on socialite Baby Jane Holzer:*

Bangs manes bouffant beehives Beatle caps butter faces brush-on lashes decal eyes puffy sweaters French thrust bras flailing leather blue jeans stretch pants stretch jeans honeydew bottoms eclair shanks elf boots ballerinas Knight slippers, hundreds of them, these flaming little buds, bobbing and screaming, rocketing around inside the Academy of Music Theater underneath that vast old moldering cherub dome up there — aren't they super-marvelous!

"Aren't they super-marvelous!" says Baby Jane, and then: "Hi, Isabel! Isabel! You want to sit backstage — with the Stones!"

. . . What the hell is this? She is gorgeous in the most outrageous way. Her hair rises up from her head in a huge hairy corona, a huge tan mane around a narrow face and two eyes opened — swock! — like umbrellas, with all that hair flowing down over a coat made of . . . *zebra!* Those motherless stripes! Oh, damn! Here she is with her friends, looking like some kind of queen bee for all flaming little buds everywhere.

◆ **Write tightly.** Keep it short. Select only the liveliest quotes, the most telling anecdotes. As Voltaire said, "The secret of being boring is to tell everything."

◆ **Vary your sentence structure.** Force yourself to avoid ruts in word choice, phrasing and syntax. Deliberately mix it up: long sentences, short sentences. Long paragraphs, short ones.

◆ **Match your treatment to your topic.** Don't inflict a frivolous tone upon a serious issue (or vice versa). Stay versatile; use different styles for different stories. Try to enhance and complement your subject — not overwhelm it. Or to put it another way:

◆ **Don't overdo it.** Yes, it's fun to write colorfully, but using *too* much color is like wearing a clown suit and a big red nose: "Hey, look at me! At *me!!!*" Tone it down, clown. Don't make every story about *you.* And speaking of self-indulgence:

◆ **Avoid first-person stories.** It's always safe to write in the third person (he, she, they). It's often OK to write in the second person (see examples below). But most editors frown upon using the first person (I, we) unless you're recounting some dramatic adventure: *How I Beat Cancer and Scaled Mount Everest.* Got an urgent need to talk about yourself? Write a column or launch a blog.

◆ **Stay objective.** You're writing to serve and inform the reader, not to cheerlead, ridicule or editorialize. Your goal, *always,* is to paint as realistic a picture as possible — not to distort reality or filter it unfairly.

◆ **Either learn shorthand or use a tape recorder.** Two reasons: 1) Good dialogue always flies by faster than you can write it, and 2) Sometimes it's the phrasing and fumbling — *"oh, geez"* and *"yeah, you betcha"* — that capture people's true personalities.

◆ **Find your voice.** Editors (and college professors) have strong opinions and rigid rules about what is and isn't "good writing." Some hate semicolons; some hate dashes — and *italics* — and even exclamation points!!! It's gonna honk you off (they hate slang, too), but your success as a writer depends upon your ability to please your bosses, satisfy your readers *and stay true to your own voice.* That's not easy. But it's the goal of all creative journalists.

◆ **Read.** And read. And read. Find writers you love. Study how they work. Steal their secrets. You can't be a successful writer if you're not an avid reader.

DETAIL AND DESCRIPTION

News stories usually feel like they're written — well, in a *newsroom.* But features attain a *you-are-there* immediacy by carefully detailing people's actions and appearances, as Tom French does here:

> He's in the back seat of the family Volvo, headed to school. His mom and dad are talking up front, but he's not listening. He is still waking up. His light blond hair is uncombed as usual; a micro-pebble of sleep dust clings to the lashes of his right eye. Through headphones, a man is singing into his brain.

See how effectively those details set the scene?

Or take the following example, a description of the guy we met driving that green pickup in the "Voice and Tense" column at left:

> He talks with one hand on the wheel. With or without a cigarette, he has a ventriloquist's way of speaking, as if his teeth have been wired shut. The lips do all the work. He opens his mouth wide only to laugh, which he does often and raucously, mostly at his own jokes.   — **Alex Tizon,** *The Seattle Times*

Now notice how smoothly Katy Muldoon blends all the elements we've discussed — voice, tense, syntax and description — to paint this portrait in a feature about a surfing competition:

> Steve Mikkelsen's chin hasn't communed with a razor in a few days. His unruly graying hair displays spikes of independence. Salt crystals cling to the laugh lines in his face. And yet, when he stands, straightens his back, stretches his arms elegantly north and south, and proceeds to dance, you'd swear this crusty character was Fred Astaire.
>
> A few nimble steps up. A few dashing steps back. A spin. A dip. A headstand. All aboard a 1960s-vintage Corky Carroll model Hobie surfboard — and it's not parked on the beach, but gliding toward shore at the front of a softly breaking wave.   — **Katy Muldoon,** *The Oregonian*

OTHER DRAMATIC TECHNIQUES

When you write fiction, you can dream up colorful dialogue and thrilling action. But in journalism, *everything you write must be true.* You can't fabricate or falsify facts — but you *can* present them in dramatic ways, borrowing techniques from traditional storytelling. For instance, you can hook readers by telling stories chronologically:

> Bam! The blow to the side of her head was quick. Stunned momentarily, she raised the hammer in her right hand and backed Larry into the living room, into the arm of the red velour love seat.
>
> "Larry, don't hit me no more," she screamed. He hit her again, this time on her left temple.
>
> The hammer fell. Larry fell. Blood leapt from the left side of his head, onto the yellow curtains, onto the love seat, onto the brown and yellow shag carpet.
>
> — **Pat Donahue,** *The Stockton Record*

Notice the intense realism of that scene — and its lack of attribution, too. Some editors are uneasy about describing the acts, words, even the *thoughts* of characters without attribution. But it's common in feature writing to capture the "interior monologue" of those in the story, as demonstrated in the Pulitzer Prize-winning example below. It's a risky technique; it's best used *only* when you've extensively interviewed your sources and can vouch for the honesty of every word you write.

> Please, God. Don't let it be kids.
>
> That was Edgcomb's single thought, the one that kept pace with his racing heart as he ran toward Milestone: Please, God, no kids. Please. Please.
>
> He'd been a firefighter for 25 years, he was a powerful, well-built man, a natural leader, and nobody would call Dave Edgcomb weak, no sir. He carried an air of can-do confidence.
>
> But right now he was, in his thoughts, on his knees:
>
> Please, God, just don't let it be kids.
>
> He knew it was bad, real bad, and he knew he could handle anything — but not kids. No dead kids.   — **Julia Keller,** *Chicago Tribune*

Feature story structures

Suppose you want to write a special feature story for Valentine's Day…

Should you organize your text into a traditional structure, or create a short-form package?
As you'll see on these two pages, you have a variety of options — but you've got to plan ahead.

"Feature writing presents you with a choice: You can fight organization as an annoying waste of time, or you can accept it as a challenge that will sharpen both your thinking and your writing. Once you begin to concentrate on organizing, you may amaze yourself by starting to enjoy it — even the outlining. Suddenly an idea will fall into place with an almost audible click, and you'll remember why you wanted to be a writer."

Jane Harrigan, journalism director at the University of New Hampshire

STANDARD STORY STRUCTURES
Using traditional text to convey information

Before you start writing any story, you should review the material you've compiled — your assortment of facts, quotes, opinions and anecdotes — and try to decide:
◆ *How long should this story be?* What's the most appropriate length for this topic? How much depth will satisfy the readers?
◆ *What's my best material?* What needs to run most prominently? What's expendable?
◆ *What key points do I need to make?* And what's the most effective way to make them?

Suppose you've interviewed the oldest couple in town for a Valentine's Day feature. You're ready to write a 15-inch story that includes some history, anecdotes and advice. You outline the story:

  I. A sweet anecdotal lead
  II. A description of the couple
  III. Their history: how they met, courtship, triumphs and tragedies, etc.
  IV. Their advice on love and marriage
  V. Cute ending

That works. *Or* you could arrange the main sections of the story into a different, yet equally logical order:

  I. The lead: a quote or proverb about making love last forever
  II. Romantic advice from our local couple
  III. Their history: how they met, etc.
  IV. A description of the couple today
  V. Cute ending: something anecdotal that shows their love for each other

Same material, different structures. Both versions work just as well.

Notice how writing a simple outline can provide a useful overview of your entire story. If you find you've got more good material to include, just keep adding or rearranging sections until everything's accounted for.

Some stories can be structured in a loose, intuitive way. Others may need to be organized more rigidly, to keep readers from getting distracted or confused.

For a story about "How Local Couples Celebrate Valentine's Day," you could interview three local couples. To organize the story, you could simply move from couple to couple:

  I. The lead / the nut graf
  II. COUPLE 1: Memories, romantic rituals, advice, etc.
  III. COUPLE 2: Memories, romantic rituals, advice, etc.
  IV. COUPLE 3: Memories, romantic rituals, advice, etc.

Or you could organize the story by *topics:*

  I. The lead / the nut graf
  II. GIFTS: anecdotes and quotes from all three couples
  III. WINING AND DINING: anecdotes and quotes
  IV. VACATIONS & GETAWAYS: anecdotes and quotes

Either way, the *body* of your story will progress in a logical way. But you can also add structure to the *beginning* and *ending* of a story, too, by using the "kabob" (or Wall Street Journal) format. ▼

Suppose your topic is "Couples Who Boycott Valentine's Day." To use the kabob format, you would begin with an anecdotal lead:

John and Jenny Smith are madly in love. And for Valentine's Day this Friday night, John's going bowling with his buddies. Jenny's going shopping.

Why? Like a growing number of modern couples, John and Jenny hate Valentine's Day.

The story begins with John and Jenny; it will end by returning to John and Jenny, too. They're like bookends, with the story's key sections stacked in between:

  I. An anecdotal lead introducing John and Jenny
  II. Nut graf (Valentine's Day annoys some couples)
  III. GRIPE 1: It's too commercial (quotes, facts, etc.)
  IV. GRIPE 2: It's too expensive (quotes, facts, etc.)
  V. GRIPE 3: Social pressures (quotes, facts, etc.)
  VI. Ending: We return to John and Jenny for quotes that reveal how they feel

Another popular way to structure a story is to arrange the material in *chronological order.* If you want to write "A History of Valentine's Day," a linear timeline would certainly make sense.

But other stories, too, are truly… well, *stories.* Like movies, they have a beginning, middle and end. Telling the story in a linear, narrative way becomes the most logical and engaging solution.

Many reporters and editors strongly advocate chronological narratives for both news stories (dramatic rescues and crimes) and features (colorful slice-of-life profiles). It's an approach that would work wonderfully for a Valentine feature, of course: *Boy meets girl. They fall in love. They live happily ever after.*

The story at left provides a sweet, heart-rending example.

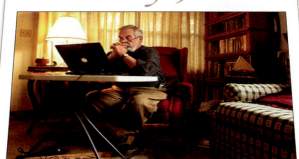

Ed Barber works on this year's public love letter to his wife, Judy. His letters are published annually in the *Independent Florida Alligator* as part of the paper's Valentine's Day tradition called Love Lines.   Times photo — CHERIE DIEZ

In what manner can I describe our love?
Are there enough words in all languages and dialects to do so? (1994)

By KELLEY BENHAM
Times Staff Writer

GAINESVILLE

He knows how the letter will end. Every letter has ended the same way since their letters were high school locker notes.

Always,
Ed

What comes before that is just a fumbling attempt. Ed Barber is 65, and he has loved Judy for 48 years. For more than three decades, he has written her a love letter for Valentine's Day. In his mind, he has never gotten one right.

He's a logical man, and he has tried, in other years, to explain in these letters what can't be explained. He has described love using science and mathematics, compared her to music, wind and water.

But this defies logic. He is just a man. These are just words.

JUDY, it begins.

He plucks softly at the keys. He misses the clattering of manual typewriters. It is so quiet in the house. He stops every so often and puts his chin in his hands, wipes his eyes. Any minute he imagines he might feel her hand on his shoulder. But he is alone in his wingback chair by the big window. Outside the birds are pecking under the tall pine. The humming of the air conditioner is the only sound.

The antique Regulator on the wall has not ticked in almost a year. It is frozen at 9:45. Last March, Ed rewound the hands, a reminder he does not need.

He knows he can't stop time, but he wishes he could. If he

could, maybe he could make it go back.

From chaos you flew to me,
On beauty's butterfly wings. (2004)

When he tells it, and he loves to tell it, he always lingers on the moment he saw her.

She was barely 15, coming back from majorette practice. She was carrying a pile of books, her baton and her crinolines through the empty halls of Hialeah High School. He was a senior, almost 17. He can't say why she stunned him the way she did, why he still remembers the way her curls stuck to her forehead, the way her cheeks flashed pink. She wasn't the girl every guy wanted, but after he saw her, he never wanted anyone else.

He stole her baton to get her to walk with him. The next day he hung around her locker and was late to class. She wouldn't give him her phone number, so his friend Jack spied on her in the phone booth as she dialed her house, copied down the number and auctioned it on the spot. Ed's bid was highest. He asked her out that weekend.

He was her first real date. They saw *The Unguarded Moment* at the theater on Miracle Mile. It was a titillating movie for its time, featuring degenerate youths and a teacher's bra strap.

Ed turned to Judy in the dark and kissed her, a brazen move for a first date in 1956.

"I can't believe it to this day," he says. Just as surprising, she kissed him back.

Please see ALWAYS 8E

Ed and Judy at Ed's senior prom in 1957. The previous fall, Ed had been Judy's first real date.   Family photo

This feature from the St. Petersburg Times uses a chronological narrative to tell a sentimental love story. To read the full text, visit **THE MORGUE** ▶ **246.**

ONE STRUCTURE FEATURE STORIES RARELY NEED: THE INVERTED PYRAMID

For breaking news, the inverted pyramid is your best choice. For features, though, it's weak.

In fact, one of the easiest ways to distinguish news stories from features is this: News stories use inverted pyramids. Features seldom do.

Take the examples at right. A straight news story begins by summarizing key facts, then continues adding facts. And more facts. And more facts.

But a news feature on that same topic humanizes the facts by viewing the event through someone's eyes, embellishing the drama and appealing to our emotions in a way news stories don't.

The inverted pyramid is an efficient way to organize facts in a news story, but it's *not* an engaging way to organize ideas in a feature story.

THE NEWS LEAD

People who smoke marijuana because their doctors recommend it to ease pain can be prosecuted for violating federal drug laws, the Supreme Court ruled Monday, overriding medical marijuana statutes in 10 states.
— *The Associated Press*

THE NEWS FEATURE LEAD

Rebecca LaFore isn't sure the U.S. Supreme Court really considers her a human being. LaFore, who's had five kinds of cancer, carries an Oregon card that gives her access to medical marijuana, which she smokes for pain control.

Monday, the Supreme Court ruled that the federal government may prosecute people who smoke marijuana with a doctor's prescription, as authorized under medical marijuana laws in Oregon and nine other states.

"They've ignored the fact I'm a human being," LaFore said. "They're taking away the quality of my life. I will not die in agony. I'd put a dog down that felt as bad as I do without it."
— *Portland Tribune*

SHORT-FORM STORY STRUCTURES
Using alternative approaches to convey information

Eons ago, when dinosaurs ruled the earth — say, back around 1980 — a "story" had to be a long sequence of paragraphs stacked together in a big gray clump. The more important the story, the bigger the clump.

Unfortunately, many English professors, journalism instructors and newspaper editors believe that's still true today.

So what do you call a . . . thing . . . like the "Perfect Kiss" page reprinted below? Is it less of a story because it doesn't use paragraphs stacked together in big gray clumps?

Pages like "The Perfect Kiss," illustrate the convergence of two key developments in modern journalism:

1) Colorful, creative layouts are easier to produce than ever before, freeing both writers and designers from gray clumps of text and rigid rectangles of art.

2) Readers see layouts like this in books, magazines and newspapers everywhere they go. These packages both satisfy and *encourage* their increasingly short attention spans.

So what does that mean if you're writing a Valentine's Day feature?

If your story is basically a catalog of items or ideas — "Our Favorite Love Songs" or "Most Romantic Gifts for Under $20" — you could write the story in the traditional way, using paragraphs of text that segue from one item (or idea) to another. Nothing wrong with that.

Or, to use a more visual approach:
◆ You could write the story as a series of bullet items, like this.
◆ You could *number* every item, and make the headline numerical, too: "Our 10 Favorite Love Songs," say, or "20 Romantic Gifts for Under $20."
◆ You could write each item as a separate unit to be designed as in the example at right.

On page 128, you'll find examples of 10 popular alternatives to traditional text: lists, quizzes, diagrams, timelines and so on. You can use them to create sidebars for your main story — or you can use them to organize your main story, too, as popular publications such as USA Today have done for years.

The best time to consider using these short-form alternatives is *before* you write. As we pointed out on the previous page, you need to decide: *What key points do I need to make? And what's the most effective way to make them?*

The answer is not always "20 inches of text."

This Valentine's Day page from the Cleveland Plain Dealer views kissing from a dozen different angles. For a closer look, visit **THE MORGUE ▶ 251.**

If your story is significant or appealing enough, editors will make it the *lead story* or *centerpiece* of the page — that is, the story that's the biggest, with the loudest headline and the most compelling design. Thus, the more successfully you plan a story package, the more prominently it will be displayed.

For example, we considered compiling Valentine's Day lists a moment ago. Suppose we create a centerpiece package that *combines* several lists? We could call it "A Global Spin on Valentine's Day." It could consist of:

◆ *how to say "I love you" in 50 languages;*
◆ *how other cultures express affection;*
◆ *how other animals express affection;*
◆ *best romantic foreign-film rentals;*
◆ *the world's most legendary lovers (Romeo and Juliet, Antony and Cleopatra, etc.).*

That package would consist of five different lists designed alongside each other with photos and illustrations. You'd probably write an introductory paragraph or two, too, to explain the concept to readers.

You can also combine different short-form structures into one big feature package. For a Valentine story titled "What Makes a Perfect Lover?", you could combine:

◆ *A* **quiz** *("How Romantic Are You?").*
◆ *A* **checklist** *("20 Blunders Great Lovers Never Commit").*
◆ *A* **quote collection** *with memorable advice from poets, philosophers, films and music lyrics.*
◆ *A* **poll** *— results from a survey you conducted that asked readers for their opinions about romance.*

Creating multi-element packages requires more collaboration and planning. And remember: Though these features may use less text than traditional stories, the same journalistic reporting and writing standards always apply.

MORE ON **SHORT-FORM ALTERNATIVES ▶ 128**

Writing profiles

Capturing personalities by painting word pictures

Everyone's got a story to tell. But some folks are more newsworthy than others, so we write profiles to explore their backgrounds, examine their characters, document their struggles and dreams.

Profiles are biographical, but they're more than a *who-what-when-where-why* rehash of facts. A good profile reveals feelings, exposes attitudes, captures habits and mannerisms. The finished story should be as entertaining as it is informative.

In-depth profiles can take days, even weeks, to assemble. You may need to check someone's credentials, dig up Web documents, read old news clips, consult with colleagues, family and friends.

But in the end, it all comes down to *interviewing*. Profiles provide the ultimate test of your interviewing skills. How well can you coax complete strangers into sharing the details of their private lives?

HOW TO RESEARCH AND WRITE SUCCESSFUL PROFILES

◆ *Solicit your subject's support.* Make preliminary contact with the person you're profiling. Explain who you are, what you're doing, how long it may take. Explain how you'd like to conduct interviews, watch them at work, talk to their friends and colleagues. Be open, honest and nonthreatening.

◆ *Interview and observe.* You'll need *at least* one intensive interview session, if not several. Gather quotes, anecdotes and detailed descriptions: how your subject looks, talks, dresses, acts and interacts with others. (For additional tips, see our section on interviewing ▶ page 76.)

◆ *Find your focus.* After your first interview, review your notes. Reflect. Ask yourself, "What have I got here? What am I missing?" And most importantly: "What's the most interesting angle for this story?" The best profiles are those that focus on an intriguing or newsworthy aspect of your subject's public or private life. Develop a theme that will help you plan your next step:

◆ *Follow up with further interviews and research.* Talk to your subject, and as many other sources as necessary, to flesh out your focus with facts, quotes and anecdotes. Take every opportunity to watch your subject at work or play in a setting that's relevant to your focus.

This is where profiles demand the greatest investment of your (and your subject's) time. Yes, you *can* write single-source, single-interview stories; on a tight deadline, that may be your only option. But the fewer sources you interview and the less time you spend with your subject, the more your profile risks being inaccurate, shallow and dull. In fact, you shouldn't even call a single-interview story a *profile*.

◆ *Structure your story.* Review your material and decide how long your piece deserves to be. Is this a brief vignette? A day in the life? A full-length profile? Before you start writing, organize an outline like the sample story structure at left.

Decide how best to open and close the story. Craft an appealing lead, a solid nut graf, a fitting finish. In the main body, avoid fact-choked chronologies, rambling monologues, meaningless anecdotes. Be fair to your subject — but be kind to your readers.

SAMPLE STORY STRUCTURE

I ANECDOTAL LEAD
An engaging, revealing little story to lure us in.

II NUT GRAF
Summarizes *why* this person matters *now*.

III SCENE 1
We observe our subject in action using dialogue, details and descriptions.

IV CHRONOLOGY
A recap of our subject's past activities using facts, quotes and anecdotes.

V SCENE 2
Another look at our subject in action, leading to:

VI WHAT LIES AHEAD
Plans. Dreams. Goals. Barriers to overcome.

VII CLOSING QUOTE

 For two full-length examples of profiles, visit **THE MORGUE** ▶ 252, 254

J. Kyle Keener, *Detroit Free Press:* "I often shoot symbolically, so a portrait becomes both a likeness of the subject and an icon for the idea I am trying to communicate. This image was part of a photo essay, 'Stars and Stripes Wherever,' about how a diverse group of Americans interpret the flag. Tattoo artist Nate Leintz, 28, represents the idea that patriotism is important to many Americans, not just World War II veterans. Shot from a low angle, with fists clenched, head held high and the classic sky background, Leintz looks strong and proud, almost Superman-like. Often, in both writing and photography, less is more. Showing all of Leintz's tattoos would have made the portrait too visually complex. With one spotlight illuminating the flag tattoo and a second light shining on his face, I can direct the viewer's eye right to the heart of the photograph."

EVERY PROFILE DESERVES MEMORABLE PHOTOGRAPHY

Don't just take our word for it — listen to these words of advice from J. Kyle Keener, chief photographer at the Detroit Free Press and a widely respected photojournalist:

On collaborating with photographers: Talk to a photographer when you're thinking of possible stories to pursue because we're great resources for brainstorming. We tend to be out on the streets nearly all the time with our eyes wide open. Talented photographers see things that other people do not. When you spend your whole life looking, you learn to see better. At the very least, get a photographer involved as soon as you start your reporting so that you two don't miss any key moments to photograph and write about.

On giving orders to photographers: Avoid suggesting exactly what kind of photos we should take. Most photographers and photo editors consider this insulting and a sign of an inexperienced reporter who doesn't have a clue how to function as a team. How would you feel if I gave you a list of questions to ask the subject?

On the time it takes to shoot successful photos: Everyone thinks that we just come in, snap-snap-snap a few pictures, then leave. This is as far from the truth as you can get. Just like you need time to get to know and understand the subject of our profile, we need time to observe and get them comfortable with us hanging around taking photos. Great photographs for a profile don't just happen out of the blue, but evolve as the photographer gains the trust of the subject to get more intimate and storytelling photographs.

On working a story collaboratively: If the story is a long-term, in-depth profile, I want to be there to see and photograph what you see and write about. In this way, our words and pictures will complement each other. High-quality writing and pictures working together have a much stronger power to communicate.

① CAPTURE DETAILS

"If we wanted to spend our time reading resumes, we'd all be personnel managers," says Jack Hart, writing coach at The Oregonian. "And yet the conventional newspaper profile all too often consists of nothing more than a tedious recounting of biographical facts."

Want to bring characters to life? Observe them intently. Use all your senses to paint a revealing portrait:

> Sonny Glick, of St. Helens, stands 5 feet 6. What he lacks in height, he makes up in attitude. He uses volume rather than inflection to make his point.
>
> Most days, the 240-pound man wears muscle shirts, hiking shoes and strong cologne. Court is the only place he forgoes wearing a baseball cap. A thick gold chain hangs from his neck, and a barbed-wire tattoo encircles his fleshy right biceps. He often gets "fired up" and has participated in 28 anger-management classes.
>
> His childhood was as rough as his edges are now. . . .
>
> — Michelle Roberts, *The Oregonian*

But be selective. Give us details that *matter*, that reveal facets of a person's personality. Don't bother describing how *the professor sat in a chrome and black-leather chair gazing at a chestnut-backed chickadee in the 40-foot-tall oak outside his office window.* Those are useless details that go nowhere. All they do is make your story longer.

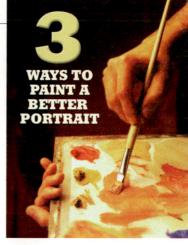

3 WAYS TO PAINT A BETTER PORTRAIT

② RE-CREATE SCENES

These can be slice-of-life moments you actually observe, scenes that catch people in the act of being themselves. Or you can recapture meaningful anecdotes from someone's past:

> Glick remembers going back to the jail dormitory, hoisting himself on the top bunk and pulling the cover over his head. He had hit rock bottom many times. Now he was free-falling into an abyss. He remembers crying for the first time since he was 19, when he'd looked into a coffin at the father he'd never known.
>
> As Glick hid his tears beneath the scratchy jail blanket, something deep inside of him shifted.
>
> "I was a loser, a jerk," he says. "I didn't know how I was going to do it, or if I even had a right to try. But I vowed I would never do drugs again. That I would raise my sons. That I'd be there for them."

It's not necessary, in other words, to write every profile from the detached blandness of a newsroom. Immerse yourself in your subject's world and show us what goes on there. Fill your profiles with *verbs*, not just adjectives.

③ ADD QUOTES AND DIALOGUE

To write a successful profile, you need good quotes both *by* and *about* the person you're profiling.

But as every novelist knows, good dialogue is a terrific device for revealing character and capturing drama, too. You can record dialogue as you hear it or craft it from the anecdotes your sources tell you.

Here's an example from a profile of baseball player Tony Pena:

> They drove around a beautiful community near Santiago. "Isn't this nice?" he asked his mother.
> "Yes," she said. "It is beautiful."
> They then drove through a neighborhood they had driven through before, many times. "I love these homes," Rosalia said.
> "I know," Tony said. "I know."
> And they pulled up to the nicest home. "What do you think of this one?" he asked her.
> "It is the home of my dreams," she said.
> He reached into his pocket, pulled out a key, gave it to her.
> "It is yours," he said. They both cried for a long time.
>
> — Joe Posnanski, *The Kansas City Star*

✔ CHECKLIST

HOW COMPLETE IS YOUR PROFILE?
Questions to ask when reporting and writing profile stories, from Susan Ager, columnist at the Detroit Free Press:

- ☐ Do readers understand why they should care about my subject?
- ☐ What do average readers want to know?
- ☐ What's the payoff for my subject? Why should he/she submit to this process?
- ☐ Can I provide insight and/or inside details about my subject?
- ☐ Can I watch my subject work/live/play?
- ☐ Is my story plump with vivid, memorable details about how my subject works and lives?
- ☐ Do I capture my subject in a real-life scene or two?
- ☐ Can I conduct two, three or more interviews, even if they're brief?
- ☐ Will I keep the interviews conversational?
- ☐ Will my questions be fresh, direct, specific?
- ☐ Will I ask about mundane as well as touchy, intimate matters?
- ☐ Are the quotes spicy and telling?
- ☐ Have I cut out all long, dull and predictable quotes?
- ☐ Have I talked to others who understand my subject or might see my subject with different eyes?
- ☐ Are the turning points in my subject's life obvious to the reader and explored for their lasting impact?
- ☐ Do I, by the end of my reporting, understand what motivates my subject, and will I make that clear to readers?

💡 IDEA FILE

FIND OUT WHAT'S IN THE WAL-MART SACK, AND DON'T LEAVE WITHOUT IT

"I once was profiling a murderer and had an interview with his ex-wife. I established rapport and asked great questions and she gave great answers.

"But I quickly realized what I needed from her wasn't the interview itself. In the chair next to her, she had a plastic Wal-Mart sack, the kind that you haul a couple big toys home in at Christmas time. In it were journals she had written in her grief over the murder of their daughter (he was acquitted), financial records, virtually every piece of paper this woman had dealing with her life with this man. This Wal-Mart sack was her file cabinet.

"I talked her into letting me take the sack back to my hotel. I spent three hours and about $30 at Kinko's that night.

"In addition to providing valuable details such as exact dates, the Wal-Mart sack provided my lead. It came from a letter she had written to her dead daughter in one of the journals, saying she knew he would kill again. (He did, and I was writing the profile to run after his sentencing.)"

Steve Buttry,
writing coach, American Press Institute

Enterprise projects

Special stories allow reporters to reach beyond the routine.

Reporters spend their days "feeding the beast," covering that mix of meetings, events and processes defined as news. Those ordinary news stories are necessary, of course — but few are dramatically different or original.

Enterprise stories, on the other hand, are those that reach beyond the ordinary. They're creative. Ambitious. Unique. They offer reporters a chance to stretch their skills; they give readers a chance to meet colorful characters, to confront complex controversies, to explore the *why*, the *how*, the *what happens next*.

Enterprise projects often become special sections or multipart series that take weeks, even months to research. Most provide in-depth examinations of *people* and *issues*:

HOW DO I FIND TIME FOR ENTERPRISE?

Enterprise stories take time — lots of time — and time is one thing most reporters *don't* have. Covering a beat is a full-time job, and editors are wary of setting you loose to chase down story ideas that may never pan out.

So what's a reporter to do?

◆ *Work with your editors.* Explore ways to maximize your efficiency so you can satisfy your beat's daily demands *and* still seize time for special projects. Decide what's essential and what's optional. Discuss how to shorten routine stories, turn them into briefs — or drop them altogether if they're not worth the effort.

◆ *Make lists.* Long-term: Maintain a list of story ideas you plan to tackle in the near future. This helps you keep projects in the pipeline. *Short-term:* Plan tomorrow's tasks each day before you leave the newsroom; this helps you streamline the time you spend chained to your desk.

◆ *Prioritize.* Manage your daily schedule efficiently and ruthlessly. Eliminate distractions, unnecessary phone calls, office chitchat, time-wasting tasks.

◆ *Devote time each day to enterprise.* Start researching story ideas with small chunks of free time. Once you're sure a story is solid, pitch the idea to editors and enlist their support.

"An hour a day gives you a chance to make steady progress on the long-term goal," says writing coach Steve Buttry. "It also will give the enterprise story momentum that sometimes will help you demand more time for it."

◆ *Keep your project organized.* "Set goals for completion of key tasks, and update those goals as delays occur," Buttry advises. "Don't look at the long-term story as one huge daunting task, but as a series of feasible tasks."

◆ *Don't overwork yourself.* Too many long days and late nights will burn out even the most dedicated reporter. You can ruin a good story by rushing it, so maintain a realistic, reasonable schedule. Allow time to reflect, redirect and rewrite as necessary.

PEOPLE

An in-depth profile of a newsworthy person, family or group, often selected to represent a broader social concern or trend.

IF I DIE

Publication: The Sun (Baltimore, Md.)

Reporter: Diana Sugg wrote the story, with photographs by Monica Lopossay.

The topic: Children die — though our culture has difficulty accepting that fact. As a result, critically ill children often suffer far too much as doctors do all they can to prolong their lives.

To illustrate this problem, Sugg focused on one dying child — 12-year-old cancer victim R.J. Voigt — revealing how his tragic, inevitable death affected his family, the hospital caregivers and R.J. himself.

How long the project took: For two years, while producing other stories, Sugg researched and organized this project. She spent 25 days in the hospital observing R.J. around the clock. Afterward, she spent another three months on additional reporting and four months writing the story.

How it was presented: The finished piece ran as a four-part series on four consecutive days. Each story began on the front page, then jumped to two full inside pages. The series was later reprinted as a 16-page special section.

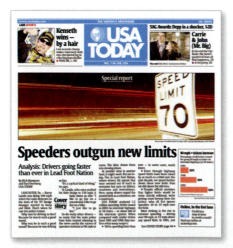

ISSUES

A detailed look at a controversy or problem, exploring what it means and what lies ahead.

WHY DO WE SPEED?

Publication: USA Today.

Reporters: Rick Hampson wrote the story using statistical research provided by database editor Paul Overberg and intern Emma Schwartz.

The topic: More and more Americans drive too fast, resulting in more accidents, more traffic tickets, and more drivers addicted to the thrill of flying along freeways at 100 mph.

How long the project took: Overberg and Schwartz took seven months to collect and crunch data; Hampson spent a couple of months reporting and writing the final story.

How it was presented: The story began at the top of Page One, then jumped inside the section, where the related sidebars and graphics filled an entire page.

 Visit **THE MORGUE** to read excerpts from "If I Die" ▶ 258 and "Why Do We Speed?" ▶ 263

EXPERT ADVICE ON REPORTING AND WRITING ENTERPRISE STORIES

Thinking about undertaking an ambitious project? Before you begin, consider these words of wisdom collected from a panel of veteran reporters:

Reporter Diana Sugg spent a month taking notes in the hospital room of R.J. Voigt, a young boy dying of cancer, for her series, "If I Die." To read an excerpt from Sugg's dramatic story, see page 258.

DOING THE REPORTING

◆ **Start with a thesis.** What are you trying to say? A thesis gives you something to talk about (and you *should* talk about it.) Test it with some initial reporting to find out if you're on target, or if the thesis needs to be changed.

It helps to give the project a name, though you might need to revise that, too.

◆ **Do your research.** Read a lot to get background. Nibble at the edges first; work the peripheral sources before you get to the heart of the matter. For instance, if you're doing a story about a football player who killed someone and his coach was his closest friend, make the coach your last interview. You want to know everything that happened before you talk to that coach.

◆ **Report. Report. Report.** Talk to as many pertinent people as possible. Follow every conceivable paper trail. Identify the experts and understand where conflicts, debate, obstacles and fresh opportunities lie. Read the reports, do the legwork, make the contacts and make a *lot* of them. And then ask those people for more sources. Let them know what your story is about and ask them to contact you if they find something they think is important. Let them know how much effort you're expending.

◆ **Control the material** or the material will control you. If you wait until the writing stage to transcribe or organize your notes, tapes, etc., you will be lost. Devote some time each day to organizing the material. You can do it by date, by subject or by person, but you have to constantly monitor the mountain of information you collect. Doing it daily also helps you spot holes, trends or questions you need to address.

On weekends, do file maintenance: Re-read all your notes and files. (New ideas and connections will emerge each time you read them.) Reorganize the files to better fit your story organization. Make notes to go back and re-interview people based on what you find.

◆ **Look for universal connections.** This is something to think about constantly: What is it about your story that readers can relate to in their own lives?

Remember, the longer your story is, the more compelling your subject needs to be. The best stories are those about people, not about themes.

◆ **Keep a running list of questions and things to do** on a legal pad or on your computer. Don't rely on your memory. Little or big, jot it all down. When you answer a question, cross it out. At the end of the day, it will give you a psychological boost and remind you that you really are making progress even when you don't yet have a story in the paper.

◆ **Talk to your editor every day.** It heads off misunderstandings later. Besides, you sometimes need a fresh and encouraging pair of eyes and ears. Find an editor who wants to hear what you've learned that day. It's invaluable. Remember, too, that when it comes time to edit and design the story, you want somebody in your corner.

◆ **Cooperate with photographers, designers and the graphics staff** — but once you and your editor agree on a focus, enlist her support to prevent other staffers from turning the project into a Christmas tree that adds so many peripheral elements that you lose your focus.

WRITING THE STORY

◆ **Write from the first.** Begin writing as soon as you have your idea for the story. You may start with just a paragraph to yourself or your editor. You may start with a few paragraphs, already starting to resemble a story. You may start with a plan for pursuing the story. Writing at the idea phase helps focus you from the outset on the eventual goal of a story.

◆ **Write after each interview.** Don't simply transcribe your notes (though that would be better than not writing at all). Start writing the story. Work on a lead if you can. If you think the interview might produce just a couple paragraphs for the story, write them.

Writing while the interview is still fresh ensures accuracy, especially if your handwriting is bad or if you have trouble reading old notes. You will be more likely to remember important details about the setting and the speaker's mood and mannerisms.

◆ **Rewrite each time.** Each time you return to the story, read through what you've already written, and rewrite as needed. This will put more polish on your story. It will also help launch you each time, cutting down those long blocks of time where you stare at the screen, waiting for momentum.

◆ **Plan your ending.** Everyone does endings differently, but it's vital in a long or in-depth project to know what your ending is going to be. Otherwise it's like beginning a trip without knowing what the destination is.

◆ **Save often, print a lot.** It seems long projects are destined to be lost. Don't leave at night without printing a copy. It will save your sanity if your files are lost.

◆ **Don't be afraid of the edit.** Good stories need revision. They need an outside force to scrutinize and ask the question your readers will want, not the details you've become obsessed with.

◆ **Seek outside input.** When your project is done, and the editors have read it, ask a friend or spouse to read it. Tell them to mark any spots where they get confused or bored. It needs to be somebody you can trust, who will be willing to hurt your feelings (wives generally have no problem with this, I've found). Don't overdo it, though. This isn't a committee project. But one of the things that will happen is that you will work on this project so long, you will no longer be able to see it the way a first-time reader would. You need a fresh pair of eyes at the end.

◆ **Enjoy the process.** Rare is the reporter lucky enough to focus on one project. Appreciate the opportunity and kick butt. And then come up with another project.

— From contributions by Ken Fuson, Steve Buttry, Emily Dooley, Steve Paul, Judd Slivka, Larry Peterson and Mike McGraw

BUT BEFORE YOU UNLEASH THAT EPIC OF ENTERPRISE, HEED THESE SOBERING WORDS OF CAUTION

From **Jim Stasiowski,** *writing coach*

I always fall back on the wisdom I heard at a panel discussion I attended years ago in Pennsylvania. On the dais were writing-award winners in diverse categories, and sitting side by side were an odd couple. One was a dressed-to-the-hilt big-city reporter, perfectly groomed and filled with more rhetorical gas than the Hindenberg. He talked ponderously for 10 uninterrupted minutes about the cosmic significance of the 12-part series for which he won his award.

Next to him sat a bearded, smirking wiseacre wearing a golf shirt, jeans and sandals, no socks. He probably had won his award for some sarcastic sports column. After Mr. Big City finished pumping the room full of helium, Mr. Wiseacre punctured the presentation this way: "Long stories, huh? I don't write 'em, 'cause I don't read 'em."

My philosophy is this: I'm glad newspapers make room for projects, I'm glad we spend manpower on projects, I'm glad we reach for projects, because if we didn't, no medium would. But we cannot expect people to read them. The best we can hope for is that people will realize we did them and will appreciate that we care enough to try to explain our complicated world.

My one piece of advice for reporters embarking on a project is this: Always, always, always think story-story-story. Never just gather facts. Always see how facts will fit into the story. Don't get caught up in the moment, in the thrill of getting juicy information, a colorful quotation, a touching anecdote. Most stories fail because of too much information, not because of too little.

Investigative reporting

In a free society, some journalists do more than just explain — they expose.

Yes, the stories you publish can inform, educate and inspire — but most nobly of all, they can "comfort the afflicted and afflict the comfortable," as Finley Peter Dunne once wrote. It's the journalist's job, as society's watchdog, to monitor the conduct and *mis*conduct of government and business, the rich and powerful — the "comfortable," in other words.

America boasts a proud tradition of investigative reporting, from Nellie Bly's exposé of 19th-century insane asylums to Woodward and Bernstein's historic revelations about Watergate. ▼

Yet some fear that this noble journalistic tradition is in decline. Though many newspapers continue to publish bold investigative reports (like the Detroit Free Press at right), other editors are increasingly fearful of appearing biased, offending readers, alienating advertisers or instigating messy legal battles. Smaller staffs and shrinking budgets also force publications to curtail the "luxury" of lengthy investigations — no matter how worthy those projects truly are.

DIGGING UP DIRT: ADVICE FOR INVESTIGATIVE REPORTERS

◆ *Be skeptical . . .* Just because documents look legitimate and politicians look sympathetic *doesn't mean* there aren't distortions and deceptions buried beneath the surface. Assume that all public officials and PR spokespeople have hidden agendas. Trust no one.

◆ *. . . but remain objective.* Admit it: As a reporter, *you've* got an agenda, too. So don't let your emotions and biases hijack your news judgment. A sense of outrage and revenge is understandable when you're exposing creeps and crooks, but don't turn into a vigilante. Remain a journalist.

◆ *Focus tightly.* Avoid flat, flabby "umbrella" series on generic topics like teen pregnancy and courtroom corruption. Instead, tell a good story. Focus on just one case, one corrupt official; find ways to make your discoveries resonate with readers.

Above all, avoid the "notebook dump": sprawling stories loaded with unnecessary details. "Ninety percent of your reporting should stay in your notebook," says David Boardman, managing editor of the Seattle Times. "It hurts your credibility to spill a lot of ink over something that isn't worth it."

WHAT IS INVESTIGATIVE REPORTING?

It is the reporting, through one's own work product and initiative, matters of importance which some persons or organizations wish to keep secret. The three basic elements are:
◆ that the investigation be the work of the reporter, not a report of an investigation made by someone else;
◆ that the subject of the story involves something of reasonable importance to the reader; and
◆ that others are attempting to hide these matters from the public.

— *Investigative Reporters and Editors, Inc. (IRE)*

◆ *Cast a wide net.* Collect as much information as you can and cultivate as many sources as possible. "It's important to develop sources before police and lawyers shut them up," says Pulitzer Prize-winning reporter David Barstow. "Be an optimist. You never know when they'll tell you something they'd usually never tell. Put your best efforts into finding human sources, on finding warm bodies, even if they'll only talk off-the-record or on background. They'll give you a direction."

◆ *Keep your nose clean.* "Avoid doing illegal or unethical things that, if somebody found out, could be used against you as blackmail to drop or change a story," advises veteran reporter Jerry Uhrhammer. "You can't worry about threats to yourself and your family. I'm more concerned with being set up. You never know when someone will try to use something against you."

◆ *Work the Web* to connect the dots — to find documents, identify players, study the law. Better yet, go online for help at *www.ire.org/resourcecenter*, the Web site of Investigative Reporters and Editors, to read stories and tip sheets from the pros.

MORE ON **NELLIE BLY** ▶ **192** / ON **WOODWARD AND BERNSTEIN** ▶ **234**

70 ◀ MORE ON **USING THE INTERNET**

UNCOVERING THE BIG STORY:
Nigel Jaquiss, *Willamette Week*

The Pulitzer Prize in investigative reporting is usually awarded to reporters — or teams of reporters — at big daily newspapers. But in 2005, the prize was won by Nigel Jaquiss, a reporter for Willamette Week, an alternative weekly in Portland, Ore. Jaquiss, 44, spent two months painstakingly piecing together proof that Neil Goldschmidt had sexually abused a young girl while he was mayor of Portland in the late 1970s. Jaquiss' bold reporting produced a political bombshell; in fact, Willamette Week first broke the story on the paper's Web site to avoid being scooped by the competition.

Neil Goldschmidt was a beloved political figure in Oregon — until you exposed how, decades ago, he sexually abused a 14-year-old girl. What was the reaction to your story?

Jaquiss: Shock and despair. Goldschmidt put Portland on the national map, earning the loyalty and admiration of Oregonians and people across the Northwest. Some of his allies reacted angrily; Portland's daily paper gave Goldschmidt sympathetic coverage initially and published op-eds critical of Willamette Week for uncovering his secret.

For years, journalists had unsuccessfully chased rumors that Goldschmidt was hiding some dark, dirty secret. How is it that you – one lone reporter on a small weekly paper – succeeded where others failed?

I got tremendous support from my editors and publisher, all of whom were willing to bet the paper on the story. We created a plan, tracked down lots of documents and sources and also got very lucky.

The key evidence in this case came from facts buried in public records. What kind of research did you have to conduct?

Once I learned the alleged victim's name, I made public records requests for court files, arrest reports and every other piece of paper I could think of that might help me find people who knew her and might know her story. I also looked at property records, Goldschmidt's gubernatorial archives, reverse directories and other documents that could provide links between him and his victim.

Are you especially skilled in document research, or is this something most reporters could do?

I don't think I'm particularly skilled, but I am very persistent. I looked at every document, no matter how obscure or seemingly redundant. After having looked at a dozen arrest reports and stacks of court records in Portland, I found a crucial link to key Seattle documents buried in a routine file in a rural Oregon courthouse.

How frustrating was the reporting process? Were there times you wanted to kill the story?

I hit a major dead end when, after I had accumulated circumstantial documents and heard the tale of the victim's abuse at Goldschmidt's hands from several of her friends, both the victim and

her mother swore Goldschmidt never touched her. Lacking a "smoking gun," I assumed at that point Goldschmidt would also deny the abuse, leaving me without a story. I never really considered giving up and soon found other, even more solid confirmations from knowledgeable sources.

You interviewed the alleged victim, but she denied that Goldschmidt ever abused her. You compiled circumstantial evidence against Goldschmidt, but had no confession, no witnesses, no irrefutable evidence. Yet your editors still decided to publish the story. Weren't you worried you might be sued?

Yes, but our libel lawyer, who has represented the paper for 23 years, was closely involved in the last month of my reporting. He and the paper's owners were satisfied that we had enough confirmations — some people provided signed statements; others agreed to various levels of identification — and enough documentation to make the story stand up in court.

There are those who'd say, "Neil Goldschmidt was a distinguished public servant who devoted his life to improving Oregon. Why destroy his career for a mistake he made 30 years ago?" How would you respond?

Goldschmidt did indeed make great and lasting contributions as mayor and governor, but he also ruined a young woman's life — and as I later learned, many people knew of his crime but kept quiet. His "mistake" went on for at least three years; his getting away with it for so long had a corrupting effect on those who knew and created an outrageous double standard.

What advice would you give to reporters working on investigative stories riddled with loose threads and dead ends?

Make a plan that includes finding every conceivable document; approach sources only when fully prepared and in a predetermined order that will allow you to accumulate information steadily and continually re-assess the question of who else might have knowledge.

To ask that question a different way: What's it take to be a successful investigative reporter?

Curiosity, determination and a willingness to persevere in spite of opposition.

When the story of late-20th-century Oregon is written, Neil Goldschmidt will tower over most other public figures. His accomplishments as mayor and governor have stood the test of time.

It is also true, however, that his incomprehensible involvement with an adolescent babysitter changed both of their lives forever and — although few people knew about it — the secret profoundly affected Oregon history. No one can say with certainty how much of the arc of the woman's life was shaped by the man who molested her starting when she was 14. But it is clear that today, on her 43rd birthday, living a thousand miles from her friends and family in Portland, she is a haunted woman.

The woman, whom Willamette Week is calling Susan, suffers from physical and psychological ailments that have robbed her of health and happiness. She weighs little more than 100 pounds; she suffers insomnia, nightmares and a recurrence of flashbacks. Her hands shake constantly, despite the anti-convulsive medicine she takes to control seizures she's experienced.

She didn't change overnight from the bright and beautiful girl her childhood friends remember to the woman who eventually served time in a federal penitentiary. It is undeniable, however, that her future was never again so promising as when Goldschmidt first led her into her parents' basement. . . .

Goldschmidt, who was married, would sometimes hire Susan to watch his two small children. But, according to a cousin of Susan's and more than a dozen of her friends, he used her for much more than babysitting. He would often take her down to her parents' basement, to hotels and other private spots and have sex with her, the sources say.

In Oregon, if an adult has sex with someone under the age of 16, it is considered rape. (According to law-enforcement officials, however, the statute of limitations for prosecution has long since passed.) . . .

To read the complete story, visit
www.pulitzer.org.

Package planning

Teamwork can help turn stories into appealing packages

Most newsrooms are like factory assembly lines: the reporter reports. The photographer photographs. The editor edits. And then — at the last minute — the designer designs.

That assembly-line process works fine if you're making sausages, but it won't consistently produce reader-friendly pages. Lavish layouts rarely succeed when they're slapped together on deadline.

So how do you retool your newsroom to produce packages like *this*? By planning: by instituting a brainstorming process that shapes stories *before* they're written.

A few years ago, Buck Ryan — journalism professor at the University of Kentucky — developed the Maestro Concept, a method of integrating writing, editing, art and design. Ryan proposed that each newsroom appoint a *maestro*, a visual journalist who could orchestrate the interplay of all key staffers. And to guide the process along, participants would use a story planning form like the one reprinted on the next page.

How does it work? Suppose you've just gathered information for a big story. Before you start writing, there's a brief meeting. That's where you, the editor, the photographer and the designer, with the maestro's help, explore the story's potential using a form like the one below to produce a package like the one above.

USING THIS PACKAGE-PLANNING FORM TO IMPROVE A STORY'S PRESENTATION

The story idea: *Can you summarize the story in 25 words or less? That's a good test to see if your focus is tight enough – or if you're still struggling with a fuzzy concept.*

Questions readers will ask: *The first question every reader asks for every story is "Why should I care?" Try to answer this question in a useful, visual way – in the headline, a photo, a sidebar. Now: What other questions will readers have, and how can you best answer them? That list of sidebar options provides alternative ideas for reporting and design.*

STORY IDEA: Carpenter ants are a common pest – so here's a consumer guide to WHAT THEY ARE, WHAT THEY DO – and HOW TO GET RID OF THEM.

QUESTIONS READERS WILL ASK

1 Why should I care? They can cause expensive damage to the wood in your house.
HOW ANSWERED: ☐ HEADLINE ☐ PHOTO/CUTLINE ☐ DECK ☑ TEXT ☐ SIDEBAR: _____

2 How can you identify them?
HOW ANSWERED: ☐ HEADLINE ☐ PHOTO/CUTLINE ☐ DECK ☐ TEXT ☑ SIDEBAR: photo with bio box

3 Where do they invade your house?
HOW ANSWERED: ☐ HEADLINE ☐ PHOTO/CUTLINE ☐ DECK ☐ TEXT ☑ SIDEBAR: cutaway diagram

4 How do you get rid of them?
HOW ANSWERED: ☐ HEADLINE ☐ PHOTO/CUTLINE ☐ DECK ☐ TEXT ☑ SIDEBAR: checklist on exterminators

SIDEBAR OPTIONS
☐ FAST FACTS BOX ☐ GLOSSARY ☐ DIAGRAM
☐ BIO BOX ☐ QUIZ ☐ TABLE
☐ PREVIEW BOX ☐ Q & A ☐ TIMELINE
☐ OPINION POLL ☐ QUOTE COLLECTION ☐ STEP-BY-STEP GUIDE
☐ LIST ☐ RATINGS ☐ EXCERPT
☐ CHECKLIST ☐ MAP ☐ WHERE TO GO/CALL/WRITE
☐ INDEX ☐ CHART

PHOTOS / ART
LEAD ART: Cutaway diagram of a house showing WHERE and HOW the ants usually enter and build nests.
SECONDARY ART: Closeup photo of ants: queen, worker, etc. (If we can't shoot photos, we'll use illustrations.)

HEADLINE / DECK
MAIN HEADLINE: ATTACK OF THE CARPENTER ANTS (sci-fi movie type?)
DECK: The ants crawl in, the ants crawl out. But it's not your snout they're after – it's your HOUSE.

ROUGH LAYOUT

ATTACK OF THE CARPENTER ANTS!

STAFF
KYM
WRITER
REED
DESIGNER
MOLLY
ARTIST/PHOTOGRAPHER
SHAWN
EDITOR/HEAD WORRIER

DEADLINES
Mon. 5/3
INFO FOR SIDEBAR(S)
Wed. 5/5
STORY — FIRST READ
Fri. 5/7
FINAL STORY/ART
Mon. 5/10
RUN DATE

LENGTHS
10"
MAIN STORY
5" each
SIDEBAR(S)
NOTES:
Pete: call agriculture department for ant brochures

Headline/deck: *Why wait until the story is written – and the clock is ticking – to write a headline? Chances are you have enough info to kick around a clever headline right now, or at least generate key words you can refine later. Writing the deck now also helps the team members clearly define the story angle.*

Staff, deadlines, lengths: *One last chance to ensure that everyone agrees on when the different story elements are due, what sizes they'll be, and most important, who's responsible for what.*

Photos or illustrations: *Too often, photographers are excluded from story-planning conferences, then sent out on assignment with hardly a clue what the story's about. But when photographers are included in this preliminary discussion, they can shape the direction of the imagery AND the reporting. By this point in the planning meeting, an attentive photographer should be able to suggest photo ideas – or, if the story is better served by illustrations, staffers can weigh those options instead.*

Rough layout: *While those ideas for photos, sidebars and headlines are being kicked around, the designer can sketch a layout that integrates all the key ingredients with their proposed shapes and sizes. Everything is subject to change, of course, but by the end of the meeting, all the participants should agree on this preliminary vision of the page. Remember, this is just a starting point — the actual page should only get better. After the meeting, this form should be photocopied and distributed for future reference.*

WRITER

DESIGNER

ARTIST/
PHOTOGRAPHER

EDITOR/HEAD WORRIER

DEADLINES

INFO FOR SIDEBAR(S)

STORY — FIRST READ

FINAL STORY/ART

RUN DATE

LENGTHS

MAIN STORY

SIDEBAR(S)

NOTES:

HEADLINE / DECK

MAIN HEADLINE: _____

DECK: _____

ROUGH LAYOUT

STORY IDEA: _____

QUESTIONS READERS WILL ASK

1 *Why should I care?* _____

HOW ANSWERED: ☐ HEADLINE ☐ PHOTO/CUTLINE ☐ SIDEBAR: _____
☐ DECK ☐ TEXT

2 _____

HOW ANSWERED: ☐ HEADLINE ☐ PHOTO/CUTLINE ☐ SIDEBAR: _____
☐ DECK ☐ TEXT

3 _____

HOW ANSWERED: ☐ HEADLINE ☐ PHOTO/CUTLINE ☐ SIDEBAR: _____
☐ DECK ☐ TEXT

4 _____

HOW ANSWERED: ☐ HEADLINE ☐ PHOTO/CUTLINE ☐ SIDEBAR: _____
☐ DECK ☐ TEXT

SIDEBAR OPTIONS

☐ FAST-FACTS BOX
☐ BIO BOX
☐ PREVIEW BOX
☐ QUOTE COLLECTION
☐ LIST
☐ CHECKLIST

☐ INDEX
☐ GLOSSARY
☐ QUIZ
☐ Q & A
☐ RATINGS
☐ OPINION POLL

☐ MAP
☐ CHART
☐ DIAGRAM
☐ TABLE
☐ TIMELINE
☐ STEP-BY-STEP GUIDE

PHOTOS / ART

LEAD ART: _____

SECONDARY ART: _____

Short-form alternatives

To reach readers, sometimes you've got to condense the data.

We've said it before, and we'll say it again: Narrative text is *not* the only way to convey information. It's often slow and inefficient. And if that's all you ever do — forming words into sentences, sentences into paragraphs, paragraphs into stories — your crusty old editors may be satisfied, sure. But what about your audience?

Tomorrow's readers will have shorter attention spans than any previous generation. They'll be more impatient. More distracted. Less tolerant of rambling, bloated text.

Tomorrow's smart reporters will have more tools in their journalistic toolbox; they'll know how to deliver data more efficiently by using alternative formats such as those demonstrated here. These short-form options won't replace narrative stories, but they're an effective way to distill information into reader-friendly sidebars.

Seattle Seahawks vs. Pittsburgh Steelers

Where: Ford Field in Detroit, Mich.
Kickoff: 6:30 p.m. Sunday
TV: Fox, Channel 2
Radio: WUGH (1130 AM)

FAST-FACTS BOX

Readers appreciate it when you distill the *who-what-when-where-why* into a concise package. With a fast-facts box, you can highlight key facts without slowing down the text, or provide compelling data for those who may not want to read the text at all.

Fast-facts boxes can deliver statistics. History. Definitions. Schedules. Trivia. They can update readers on what just happened, or try to explain what happens next:

A FLAWED LAW

The law: A Warrenton ordinance which states, "Riding of bicycles and skateboards is prohibited in certain areas."
Why it was passed: To protect citizens walking on sidewalks.
When: Enacted in 1988.
Fine: $25 to $250.
The problem: Judge H. Dudley Payne ruled that the town cannot enforce such an ordinance because state code permits cities to regulate only bicycles — not skateboards.
What happens next: The General Assembly will consider a bill that will allow towns to prohibit skateboarders in certain areas; if passed, it would go into effect July 1.

— *The Fauquier Citizen*

PROFESSOR'S PROFILE

Susan Mango Curtis

Position: Assistant professor, Medill School of Journalism
Specialty: Visual Journalism
Professional credentials: Design consultant; former assistant managing editor for the Akron (Ohio) Beacon Journal; former art director for the National Rifle Association; active member of the National Association of Black Journalists and the Society for News Design, where she recently completed a one-year term as president.
Currently working on: A design ethics code for the Society for News Design.
Greatest accomplishment: Being part of the Beacon Journal team that won the 1994 Pulitzer Prize for a series titled "The Question of Color."
Greatest passion: To empower visual journalists to become strong voices of change in newsrooms around the world.
Private pleasure: Eating banana pudding.
Nobody knows I'm: very uncomfortable in large groups of people
I've never been able to: learn how to swim.
I'd give anything to meet: Congressmen Adam Clayton Powell Jr.
If I could change one thing about myself: I would like to be taller.
Favorite quote: *"My good friend, I've got a 35-millimeter camera in my pocket. You've got a 45 automatic in yours. But I feel my weapon is probably more powerful than yours."*

— PHOTOJOURNALIST GORDON PARKS

BIO BOX

You can learn a lot about a person — and compress a lot of information into a small space — by distilling biographical data into a *bio box* like the one shown above. Some publications run expanded boxes like this as stand-alone features. (If they're comprehensive enough, they don't require any accompanying text at all.) But most reporters use them to supplement longer profiles, letting you stack personal facts in a tidy, logical way.

MOVING CHECKLIST

One month before you move:
☐ Make arrangements with a rental truck or moving company.
☐ File a change of address with post office.
☐ Transfer children's school records.
☐ Sell or donate unwanted items.

One week before you move:
☐ Contact utilities to change service.
☐ Empty and defrost refrigerator.
☐ Make an inventory list of all your belongings.
☐ Start packing boxes.

The day you move:
☐ Turn off water and lights.
☐ Lock all windows and doors.
☐ Make a final walk-through to check for personal belongings.

CHECKLIST

Want readers to grab their pencils and interact with the guidance you're giving them? Add a checklist. It provides an inventory of activities — but it also makes the information more meaningful, accessible and *personal*.

◀ **MORE EXAMPLES** of checklists can be found in this book on pages **57, 96** and **99**.

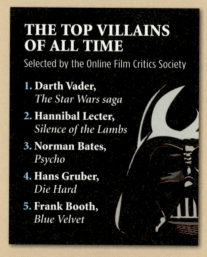

THE TOP VILLAINS OF ALL TIME

Selected by the Online Film Critics Society

1. **Darth Vader,** *The Star Wars saga*
2. **Hannibal Lecter,** *Silence of the Lambs*
3. **Norman Bates,** *Psycho*
4. **Hans Gruber,** *Die Hard*
5. **Frank Booth,** *Blue Velvet*

LIST

What's the best-selling DVD of all time? The biggest fast-food chain? The most popular Christmas toy? The most prestigious college?

Readers love knowing who's the biggest, richest, fastest, best — and the most concise way to convey that data is by compiling a list. Lists can be entertaining (the top movie villains), instructional (the worst local polluters), even spiritual (the Ten Commandments).

◀ **MORE EXAMPLES** of lists can be found in this book on page **6** and **7**. (Even the pages you're looking at *now* are basically just one big list.)

How to care for an amputated body part:

1. Wrap the severed part in plastic kitchen wrap or a plastic bag. Do *not* use cotton on open wounds.

2. Wrap again in gauze or soft fabric, and place the package in a container filled with crushed ice.

3. Mark the container with the time of injury and the victim's name. Give it to medical personnel.

— *ACEP First Aid Manual*

STEP-BY-STEP GUIDE

These simplify a complex process — from baking a cake to adopting a baby — by breaking it down into a logical, interactive series of steps.

◀ **MORE EXAMPLES** of step-by-step guides can be found in this book on pages **40** and **115**.

QUIZ

If you're a student reading this, you're probably sick of quizzes. But readers aren't; they like interacting with stories, whether the topic is health *(Are You Too Fat?)* or sports *(Test Your Soccer IQ)*. True/false, yes/no, multiple choice — whatever the format, tests add interactivity.

◀ **MORE EXAMPLES** of quizzes can be found on pages **29** and **141**.

Average number of hours it takes to read a weekday *Washington Post* out loud: **28**

Percentage of Japanese grade-school children who say they've never seen a sunrise or sunset: **50**

Number of merit badges in Safety awarded to Boy Scouts since 2001: **15,417**

Number in Shotgun Shooting: **65,249**

WHAT'S YOUR ELVIS IQ?

1. How many Elvis albums reached Number One?
2. What was Elvis' major in high school?
3. What was Elvis' middle name?
4. What was Elvis' ironclad rule during concerts?
5. Which of Elvis' records was his own favorite?
6. What was the name of Elvis' flamboyant manager?
7. How much did Elvis weigh when he died?
8. What was Elvis doing when he died?

FACTUAL INDEX

This format — often called a "Harper's Index," after *Harper's* magazine popularized it decades ago — is an appealing way to present statistics: write the setup (in text), then follow it with a "punch line" (usually using a number, in boldface type).

◀ **MORE EXAMPLES** of factual indexes can be found in this book on pages **10** and **25**.

HOW TO TELL A REAL $20 BILL FROM A COUNTERFEIT

Hold the bill up to the light. You should see the words "USA TWENTY" and a small flag on a plastic security strip embedded in the paper.

Hold the bill up to the light. If the bill's authentic, you'll see a *watermark:* a faint image of Andrew Jackson, similar to his portrait at left.

Look for tiny microprinted words, difficult to replicate, on this border beneath the treasurer's signature.

These subtle greens, blues and peaches are tough to copy — as is the "feel" of the paper, a blend of cotton and linen.

When you tilt the bill up and down, color-shifting ink in the number "20" should change from copper to green.

DIAGRAM

Sometimes *showing* is better than *telling.* For instance, you could use words to explain the anti-counterfeiting design features on the $20 bill, but it's much more effective to show an example and point to the parts you want to highlight.*

You don't have to be a skilled graphic artist to create a simple diagram like the one at left. If you want to explain what you'll find on a typical student transcript — or an eviction notice, or the new parking tickets, or a typical painting by a featured artist — all you need to do is reproduce the document and surround it with what are called *callouts* (or *factoids*) to illustrate your points.

◀ **MORE EXAMPLES** of diagrams can be found in this book on pages **27**, **74** and **180**.

* Before attempting to reproduce U.S. currency, be sure to check regulations at www.moneyfactory.com.

QUOTED

H.L. MENCKEN, American journalist:

Love is the triumph of imagination over intelligence.

Democracy is the theory that the common people know what they want and deserve to get it good and hard.

It is the dull man who is always sure, and the sure man who is always dull.

Any man who afflicts the human race with ideas must be prepared to see them misunderstood.

The average man does not want to be free. He simply wants to be safe.

QUOTE COLLECTION

Entertaining and informative, quote collections are usually organized in one of two ways: a sampling of one person's opinions on a variety of topics (above), or a sampling of opinions on one topic from a variety of sources.

◀ **MORE EXAMPLES** of quote collections can be found in this book on pages **34, 35** and **60**.

TIMELINE

It gets confusing when you try to put things in historical perspective using narrative text. But constructing a chronology or timeline can help readers more easily visualize a sequence of events. Timelines usually show the passage of time as a straight line, with key events arranged in chronological order.

◀ **MORE EXAMPLES** of timelines can be found in this book on pages **8-13, 22** and **257**.

MAJOR OUTBREAKS OF FLU IN THE UNITED STATES

1918 **Spanish flu** pandemic kills 500,000 Americans, 20 to 50 million worldwide

1957 **Asian flu** pandemic kills 69,800 Americans

1968 **Hong Kong flu** pandemic kills 33,800 Americans

1998 **Sydney strain flu** epidemic kills 64,700 Americans

1910 1920 1930 1940 1950 1960 1970 1980 1990 2000

Writing editorials and columns

If you have opinions and need to express them, here's your chance.

By now, it's been hammered into you: Reporters must remain neutral. Balanced. Fair.

But opinion-writing is different. In editorials, columns and reviews, the writers' opinions aren't just allowed, they're encouraged. They're *essential.*

Opinion columns appear throughout most publications. Commentary on current events is usually concentrated on the editorial page and the page opposite (called, appropriately, the "op-ed" page). Specialized columnists comment on sports for the sports section, on business for the business page — while in the feature section, you'll find advice columnists, gossip columnists and reviewers. Beyond that, some powerful publications maintain a stable of columnists, each with a distinctive voice, to ponder life, launch crusades or capture offbeat stories that might otherwise fall through the cracks.

Publications need editorials and columns, in short, to provide the personality and passion that news reporting doesn't allow.

COMMENTATORS: ARE THEY TRUE JOURNALISTS?

A 2005 survey revealed that 40 percent of Americans considered talk show host Bill O'Reilly to be a journalist. More than a quarter said Rush Limbaugh was a journalist, too. But only 30 percent thought that Bob Woodward was one.

Professional journalists disagreed. Only 11 percent of polled journalists said O'Reilly was "somewhat close" to being a journalist; 3 percent said that about Limbaugh. But 93 percent called Woodward a journalist. ▼

Are we just quibbling over the definition of *journalist*? Or does this point to a more serious problem: the blurring of the line between objective fact-finding and biased commentary?

We live at a time when 85 percent of Americans believe that news reporting is biased (according to a Missouri School of Journalism study), yet many of these same Americans avoid newspapers and newscasts, getting their news from talk radio, "The Daily Show" and Jay Leno's monologues instead.

So back to the question: Are commentators, columnists and bloggers journalists? Yes. And no. Journalists are those who gather and report facts — ideally, as fairly as possible. Commentators gather facts *selectively*, which isn't fair. (Some ignore and distort facts, which is intellectually dishonest.) Then they mix in their own views to promote their own agendas.

The more comment you insert into your writing, the more you're obligated to label yourself a commentator, not a journalist — out of respect for the ideals of fairness every *true* journalist should have.

EDITORIALS: WHERE PUBLICATIONS TAKE A STAND

❶ Editorials: These columns usually run from 300 to 500 words, commenting on current events, criticizing or praising public officials, endorsing candidates and explaining what issues mean to YOU, the reader. Editorials are usually unsigned, thus appearing to express the opinion of the paper — which means, at small publications, the editor or publisher. At larger publications, an editorial board debates topics as a group, then assigns one board member to distill the discussion into an editorial.

❷ Editorial cartoon: Combining art and commentary, this cartoon renders current events in graphic form, lampooning public figures by turning them into exaggerated caricatures.

❸ Column: Unlike editorials, these opinion pieces are signed. The opinions are solely those of the writer — and the most successful writers are those whose views attract a loyal following. Columnists usually work for one publication, but some sell their columns to national syndicates that distribute them to publications worldwide.

America boasts a proud tradition of opinionated editors dating back to Ben Franklin and Isaiah Thomas, who not only expressed strong political views but ran the presses that printed them.

Today's editors confine their opinions, arguments and recommendations to the editorial page, where space (and reader patience) is limited — which means that, to write an effective editorial, you must:

◆ *Keep it tight.* There's no time for rambling and preambling. Have a point and get to it. Recap key facts and summarize your case like a prosecutor trying to sway a jury.

Or to make this point more visually: The longer your editorial, the more daunting that gray block of text will look, and the fewer readers may read it.

◆ *Keep it relevant.* Select a timely, newsworthy topic that genuinely matters to readers — or, if necessary, explain why it *ought to* matter to them.

◆ *Take a stand.* Craft a strong thesis statement that urges action or invites reaction. Avoid broad, bland platitudes (asking readers to "support America" or "study both sides of the tax plan").

◆ *Attack issues, not personalities.* Avoid name-calling and mud-slinging. If someone's actions are a problem, criticize those actions and tackle the problem *without* cheap shots that make it personal.

◆ *Don't be a bully.* As journalism professor Walter Spearman used to say, "Use the rapier, not the sledgehammer." Be precise, subtle and clever. Sway and persuade, don't bluster and bludgeon.

◆ *Control your anger.* Beginners often find it easier to write an editorial (or a song, or a poem) when they're hurt or angry, Spearman observed. If you're extremely steamed, go ahead and write it — then toss it out and try again without the shrillness.

◆ *Write a strong lead and a solid finish.* Grab our attention at the start, maintain our interest, then wrap things up with a thoughtful ending. Don't let your arguments just dribble away; reward us with a conclusion that smartly caps the case you've made.

COLUMNS: THE OPTIONS ARE ENDLESS

All columnists share the same goal: to build a loyal following. And one way to do that is by specializing.

Some columnists specialize in sports commentary. Others focus only on music. Or movies. Or TV.

Some dispense advice, like Dear Abby, answering readers' questions about relationships. Or cars. Or gardening. Or sex. (Sex-advice columns have become a popular feature in campus publications lately.)

Some columnists become clearinghouses for tidbits on local social events. Others write celebrity gossip columns, dishing dirt about the rich and famous.

Many columnists, however, prefer to tackle a broader range of issues. While their choice of topics may vary, they maintain a recognizable style and voice by adopting one of the common approaches described at right.

Visit **THE MORGUE** for examples of column-writing ▶ 268, 270

TOPICAL COMMENTARY

The most numerous and popular columnists are those who react — with insight, outrage or humor — to political events and social controversies. Over time, readers learn to recognize both their predictable partisan biases and their distinctive writing styles:

> I'm not sure I've ever seen anything as odd as the right wing's insistence that global warming does not exist. I'm not a climatologist, but I can read what they're saying. In fact, they're screaming it. Rush Limbaugh is not a climatologist, either; nor are any of the rest of these pinheads who seem to think the whole thing is some figment of liberals' imagination.
>
> There's nothing liberal about global warming. It's science. There seems to be some element of childish spite in the refusal to recognize it: "Boy, we can drive the liberals crazy by pretending it's not happening, ha-ha-ha."
>
> If you read right-wing blogs, you find a kind of Beavis-and-Butt-Head attitude about the subject, a sort of adolescent-jerk humor. What's astonishing is finding the same attitude among members of Congress.
>
> — Molly Ivins

PERSONAL MEDITATIONS

Some columnists mine their personal lives for universal truths that resonate with readers. Sharing painful, poignant and humorous insights about families, friends and social relationships, their columns often read like diary entries:

> A slate roof is a humbling thing. The one we're putting on the old farmhouse is Pennsylvania blue-black, and it's meant to last at least a hundred years. Jeff the roof guy showed us the copper nails he's using to hang it; they're supposed to last just as long. So will the massive beams upon which the slates rest. "Solid as a cannonball," Jeff says. Looking up at the roof taking shape slate by enduring slate, it is difficult not to think about the fact that by the time it needs to be replaced, we will be long gone.
>
> In this fast-food, face-lift, no-fault-divorce world of ours, the slate roof feels like the closest we will come to eternity. It, and the three children for whom it is really being laid down.
>
> — Anna Quindlen

SLICE OF LIFE

Columnists can be storytellers, too, roaming the streets, eavesdropping on ordinary folks, capturing slices of everyday life you wouldn't otherwise see. The best practitioners of this form use dialogue and narrative in dramatic, evocative ways:

> "I would not say," Scoop said, "that I am the world's greatest shoeshine boy.
>
> "But I have heard it said."
>
> If not the world's greatest shoeshine boy, Wilford (Scoop) Antley is among the world's greatest talkers. Scoop can talk. He can hardly get the shoes shined down at the Tate Barber Shop for talking.
>
> "I am a professional," Scoop said. "I am now 35 years old, and I started when I was 10. I'm better now than I've ever been. I'm at my peak, you might say."
>
> He popped the rag, like the professional that he is. He squirted shoe cream out of an oil can.
>
> "That's the secret," he said. "Plenty of shoe cream, plenty of elbow grease. I take shoes like they come. Lots of boys don't like two-tones. Shining two-tones comes to me like chewing this tobacco."
>
> — Charles Kuralt

WRITING COMMENTARY: ADVICE FOR COLUMNISTS

◆ **Develop a distinctive voice.** "It's not so much what you say as the way you say it," says Keith Waterhouse, a veteran British columnist. "Your column must have a distinctive voice, to the extent that if your byline were accidentally dropped, your readers would still know who was writing. If your style isn't instantly recognizable, what you have there is not a column but a signed article."

◆ **Base your opinions on facts — and present those facts.** It's a delicate balancing act: If you leap to conclusions without providing facts to support them, readers will think you're just a raving loon. Yet if the facts crowd out your commentary, you're just rehashing old news.

Successful columnists know how (and when) to weave facts into their commentary. "It's your voice with facts embedded in it," says political columnist David Sarasohn, "not a huge pile of facts held together by your voice."

◆ **Do your own reporting.** Reading previously printed stories may not tell you everything you need to know. Columnists often research public records, conduct their own interviews with sources and grill reporters for extra details that *weren't* written into news stories.

◆ **Choose worthy topics.** "Feeling passionate about a subject does not necessarily make it interesting reading," Waterhouse observes. "Having something to write about is not the same as having something to say."

◆ **Avoid jumping on the bandwagon** every time a celebrity goes on trial or a scandal erupts. If you don't have fresh insights to share, why add to the media circus noise?

On the other hand, when major news grips everyone's attention — if a terrorist attack or disease epidemic is all anyone can think about — it's your job to come up with fresh insights for your column. "There is no point in writing about anything else," Waterhouse says, "since nobody will be talking about anything else."

◆ **Always have a backup column,** something generic and timeless, ready to run on those days when you simply *cannot* find anything worthwhile to write about. Better still, keeping *two* backup columns handy provides a safety net that greatly relieves the pressure to produce.

But how do readers recognize that THIS story is an opinion column?

Suppose I'm writing a reporting book and I suddenly feel an urge to express my outrage about the *unfair federal laws regulating monkey cloning.* Won't that be confusing to readers? Shouldn't we find a way to differentiate the textbook material from my opinionated commentary?

ME & MY BIG MOUTH

Tim Harrower

Publications usually provide visual cues to help readers identify opinion columns. These include:

◆ **Column logos,** such as the one at left, which label commentaries using the writer's name and photo along with a title or topic.

◆ **A headline font** that's different from the style that standard news stories use.

◆ **An initial cap.** That's design jargon for the big capital "S" that signals the start of this column.

These design devices signal to readers that *this is not just another typical story. It's special — it's opinion, not news.*

Responsible journalists know there's a line between objective facts and personal opinions. It's important to draw that line clearly and visibly for readers, too.

Writing reviews

Readers need your expert guidance to find the best performances and products.

In today's culture, consumers are overwhelmed with choices, bombarded with books, movies, music, TV shows, high-tech gadgets and gizmos — and in their confusion, they seek critics to pick what's good and pan what's bad.

Reviewing is a specialized form of writing: part journalism, part commentary, part nerdy fanaticism. The best reviewers are passionate and knowledgeable about their beats, writing with a critical voice that speaks to both aficionados and ordinary readers.

And while most people use the words "critic" and "reviewer" interchangeably, there is a difference. *Criticism* is the study, evaluation and interpretation of the arts (which is not the same thing as *criticizing*). Criticism ponders the meaning, context and social significance of an artist's work, whether that artist is a poet, a filmmaker or a chef.

Reviews, on the other hand, are less theoretical. They're written on deadline to help ordinary readers answer the question: "Is this thing worth my time and money?"

Most of what you see in newspapers, then, are reviews. And though critics love to unleash lengthy essays pondering the social significance of cultural phenomena, readers are often too impatient for scholarly treatises. They usually prefer a quick "thumbs-up" or "thumbs-down."

> *"I am sitting in the smallest room in my house. I have your review in front of me. Soon it will be behind me."*
>
> — MAX REGER,
> **19th-century German composer,**
> writing a reply to a savage concert review

ROGER EBERT *of the Chicago Sun-Times is one of the best-known film critics in America. In 1975, he became the first film critic to win a Pulitzer Prize. In 1978, he began co-hosting "Sneak Previews," a weekly TV show famed for its thumbs-up/thumbs-down film rating system. (That show has since evolved into "Ebert & Roeper.") Ebert estimates he's viewed more than 8,000 films and considers "I Spit on Your Grave" to be the worst film he has ever seen.*

On his reviewing process: I like to know as little as possible about a movie before I go in. I take notes. If several weeks or months have passed since I saw a movie (at a festival, for example), I try to see it again. I never discuss my reaction with colleagues. Like most newspapermen, I write the review not far in advance, but during the week before it is due.

On rewriting: Most reviews come out first draft. Then what I do is tweak.

On writing to satisfy a diverse audience: I am aware that different readers will be interested in an Iranian art film and a Marvel superhero epic. But in a way I like to think all my readers read everything. My first editor told me: "Anyone who spends the money to buy a newspaper should have a fair expectation of being able to understand just about everything in it."

On being too critical of actors: I try to avoid personal attacks. I am aware that while actors have a lot to do with good performances, they may not be entirely responsible for bad ones.

The three truths he's discovered on the job:
1) The Muse visits during the act of writing, not before.
2) A movie is not about *what* it is about, but *how* it is about it.
3) No good movie is depressing. All bad movies are depressing.

SO YOU WANT TO REVIEW SOMETHING?

Publications always need knowledgeable critics to write reviews of:

◆ **Movies** — theatrical releases and DVDs.

◆ **Music** — concerts and new releases, both classical and popular.

◆ **Television** — new shows and specials, from Oscar telecasts to Super Bowl commercials.

◆ **Theater.**

◆ **Other performances** — dance, comedians, magic acts, circuses, etc.

◆ **Books.**

◆ **Art** — gallery shows and museum exhibits.

◆ **Food** — most reviews focus on restaurants and nightclubs, but in some newsrooms, critics specialize in wine. Or even beer.

◆ **Games** — video and computer games and devices.

◆ **Technology** — the latest audio, video and computer hardware and software. Web sites, too.

◆ **Cars.**

◆ **Consumer goods.** Magazines such as Consumer Reports have shown that readers need help choosing everything from cold remedies and lawn mowers to the best holiday toys for kids.

◆ In addition, many reviewers specialize in **travel advice,** rating hotels, restaurants and tourist spots. Others offer **business advice** on choosing investments: stocks, mutual funds, etc.

GRAPHIC EXTRAS THAT MAKE REVIEWS MORE READER-FRIENDLY

Some critics (not you, of course) have difficulty summarizing what they actually think. This frustrates impatient readers, who often skip to the last paragraph of a review hoping to find a concise verdict.

One solution: Get to the point.

Another solution: Add a rating system. Many reviewers evaluate products or performances by awarding stars (five usually means *excellent*, one means *awful*), while others assign letter grades (from A to F) or graphic icons, such as those forks in the box at right.

To make reviews even more reader-friendly, publications often create fast-fact boxes like those shown here. These provide a way to highlight information that might otherwise bog down your story.

Batman Begins ★★★★☆

Starring: Christian Bale, Liam Neeson, Michael Caine, Katie Holmes.
Lowdown: A dark, dazzling reinvention of the Batman comic legend.
Rated: PG-13 for intense, violent action.
Now showing at: Eastport Plaza.

▲ *A fact box for a movie review.*
A fact box for an automotive review. ▶
▼ *A fact box for a restaurant review.*

McKenzie Grill
🍴🍴🍴

Location: 26 S. Main St. (555-3896)
Cuisine: Seafood in an upscale setting.
Specialties: Crab cakes, pesto-crusted halibut, lobster stew.
Price range: Expensive; most entrees $12-$25.
Extras: Full bar; valet parking; disabled access; all major credit cards.
Serving: Lunch and dinner every day.

2006 Subaru Forester
● ● ● ● ●

What is it? Four-door, all-wheel-drive, compact sport-utility wagon.
How soon? On sale today at most dealers.
How much? Forester 2.5 X starts at $22,390. Loaded, about $31,000.
What's the drivetrain? 2.5-liter four-cylinder rated 173 horsepower at 6,000 rpm; five-speed manual transmission (four-speed automatic is optional).
What are the extras? Climate control; AM/FM/CD stereo with weatherband reception; power steering, brakes, mirrors, windows, locks; cruise control; remote-control locks; fog lights; rear-window wiper, defroster.
How thirsty? 22 miles per gallon in town, 29 mpg on the highway when equipped with manual transmission, 23/28 with automatic.
Overall: A nice small SUV, but there are plenty of those and some are much cheaper.

— Adapted from USA Today

HOW TO WRITE CRITICISM THAT GETS GOOD REVIEWS

◆ **Structure your reviews.** Don't just rant and ramble. Outline and organize your ideas before you write.

You might structure a film review this way: *Lead, Storyline, What's Good, What's Bad, Summary.* For a product review, try this: *Lead, Product Description, Special Features, Performance Pros and Cons, Recommendations.*

Outline the key points you want to make, then spend at least one paragraph analyzing each point. Build your case clearly and logically, like a prosecutor swaying a skeptical jury.

◆ **Balance reporting and opinion.** A successful review combines *fact* and *reaction* — solid information *and* insightful opinion. The trick is finding the right balance.

If you spend too much time regurgitating the plot, for instance, a film review becomes just a pointless rehash. (Two or three paragraphs of synopsis is plenty.) Yet if you spend too much time carping and pontificating, the review becomes a self-indulgent monologue about *you.*

Be a reporter, not just a critic. Provide accurate details (descriptions, background history, sample dialogue, etc.), then explain why things worked — or why they didn't.

◆ **Know your stuff.** Don't try to fake it. You can't survive as a critic if you don't demonstrate an acceptable level of expertise, especially if you're reviewing a specialized topic for a smart audience. In other words, if you don't know Brahms from Beethoven, don't even *think* about reviewing an orchestra; if you can't tell egg from eggplant, don't attempt an upscale restaurant review.

◆ **Be aware of your biases** and compensate accordingly. You may not enjoy science fiction, but that doesn't make *Star Wars* a bad movie; you may love waffles, but that doesn't make Pancake Pit

a five-star restaurant. Rise above your prejudices so you can connect to the broadest possible audience instead of imposing your narrow tastes on readers.

◆ **Eschew pomposity.** Some critics like to show off their erudition with sentences such as: "Patterns of imagery or fragments of significance are oracular in origin and derive from the epiphanic moment, the flash of instantaneous comprehension with no direct reference to time."

Uhhhhhhhhhh . . . . . exactly!

Keep it simple. Strive for clever insights that resonate with readers: "Last night, the Salem Philharmonic played Brahms. Brahms lost." Or how about: "The covers of this book are too far apart" (Ambrose Bierce). Or: "This is not a novel to be tossed aside lightly. It should be thrown with great force" (Dorothy Parker).

◆ **Don't be cruel.** Be tough, yes. But be fair. Use your reviewing soapbox to inform your readers, not to insult their tastes. Nobody likes a grouchy loudmouth.

OTHER DON'TS:

◆ Don't ever reveal surprise plot twists or story endings. (Those are called "spoilers.")

◆ Don't add unnecessary phrases like *I think* or *in my opinion.* The whole review, obviously, is your opinion.

◆ Avoid vague adjectives like *boring, awful* and *fantastic.* Substantiate your opinions with detailed descriptions.

◆ Don't write negative reviews of amateur concerts or children's plays unless you enjoy being a heartless bully.

◆ Don't get personal. Criticize the performance, *not* the performer's private life, appearance, political beliefs, etc.

◆ Don't take it personally when readers point out that you're a clueless idiot. It comes with the territory. These days, *everybody's* a critic.

For three examples of reviews visit **THE MORGUE** ▶ 272-277

Answers to these exercises can be found on page 298.

1 GENERATING IDEAS FOR FEATURE STORIES

The city's oldest church — a huge, Gothic-style Catholic cathedral in the heart of downtown— has been condemned. After two centuries of fires, flooding and rotting timbers, it's ready to collapse. Luckily, the mysterious Elvis Trump, a reclusive billionaire who lives in a nearby mansion, has generously volunteered to reconstruct the cathedral with his own money (though Trump's cathedral will feature ultra-modern architecture).

Next Saturday, a demolition crew, led by famed explosives expert Barney "Boom-Boom" Rubble, will implode the old cathedral by carefully planting hundreds of explosives inside the building, collapsing the structure in seconds with the push of a button. Thousands of onlookers are expected to converge downtown to witness the implosion.

Using the list of feature story types on page 113, generate a list of story ideas — one for each category, and at least 10 in all — that could run both before and after the cathedral's destruction.

2 GENERATING IDEAS FOR SIDEBARS AND INFOGRAPHICS

Take that same story about the imploding cathedral. In a planning meeting, your editor says, "Look — I'm worried that all you reporters are just gonna write long, boring stories that nobody's gonna read. So it's important that you collaborate with the graphics department to create sidebars and graphics as often as you can. Let's hear some ideas. What can you come up with?"

Suggest ideas for:

◆ A fast-facts box
◆ A timeline
◆ A diagram
◆ A step-by-step guide
◆ A map

◆ A list
◆ An opinion poll
◆ A bio box
◆ A checklist
◆ A quote collection

3 HARD NEWS vs. SOFT NEWS

Rank these stories from the hardest to the softest. Give the hardest a 1, the softest a 5 — and explain your reasoning.

◆ A local businessman announced plans to open a new bar called "H-2-Oh!" featuring bartenders and waitresses wearing skimpy bikinis and thong swimsuits. A local church group is planning to protest at tonight's city council meeting.

◆ An angry Burger King customer, upset at getting the wrong order, slashed the throat of an employee in the restaurant's parking lot last night.

◆ A dying woman has decided to will her world-famous collection of Barbie dolls — worth nearly $2 million — to the local Humane Society.

◆ Turkey isn't just for Thanksgiving anymore. Here are recipes and cooking tips to help you give your family the bird all year long.

◆ A line has begun forming at a downtown theater for "Star Wars: Revenge of the Phantom Sith Clones." The movie doesn't open for another three weeks, however.

4 WHAT'S WRONG WITH THESE REVIEWS?

You're free to express your opinions when you write reviews, but there are still a few things you shouldn't do. What's wrong with each of the following excerpts?

1. The Lobster Factory's most popular entree features pan-seared scallops nested on a bed of rice and asparagus — but I've always found the taste of asparagus unpalatable, and this dish did nothing to change my mind.

2. On the CD's third track, "Drinkin', Drivin', Dreamin' About You," guitarist Carson Trucks unleashes a heavily distorted Strat riff obviously inspired by Robin Trower's thunderously Hendrixesque solo on the epic "Whiskey Train" from Procol Harum's otherwise unremarkable 1970 release, "Home."

3. The Farmington Children's Theater Workshop sucked the joy right out of the holiday season with its painfully amateurish, excruciatingly sloppy production of "Rudolph the Red-Nosed Reindeer" last weekend.

4. The orchestra, in my opinion, suffered from Hill Hall's abysmal acoustics.

5. "Recipe for Murder" opens in the stockroom of a Chicago fast-food restaurant. Wally (Jude Law) is romancing the night manager, Wanda (Jennifer Lopez), whose husband, Tito (Don Cheadle), is a hit man for the mob. Tito unexpectedly bursts in, discovers the lovers and shoots Wally between the eyes. The audience is led to believe that Wally is dead — but unknown to Tito, Wanda and the audience, he spends the rest of the movie disguised as Consuella, Tito's mistress, revealing his identity only in the movie's astonishing climax.

CHAPTER

7

Law and ethics

*We interrupt this textbook to warn you about the trouble
that results when you write the wrong thing, intentionally or not.*

IN THIS CHAPTER:

DISCLAIMER: In this chapter, we take an extremely brief look at some extremely complex legal issues.
We've done our best to make this as painless as possible — trust us, this stuff can get *incredibly* tangled
and thorny — but please remember, we're not attorneys (thank God), so do *not* use this book for legal
advice if you find yourself in doubt or in trouble. In the pages that follow, we'll explain broad concepts in
a general way; for detailed answers to specific legal questions, consult a qualified libel attorney.

Press rights

Congress shall make no law respecting an establishment of religion, or prohibiting the free exercise thereof; or abridging the freedom of speech, or of the press….

The First Amendment to the U.S. Constitution

Press freedom is a noble idea, but in reality it's a threat: to shady politicians, bungling bureaucrats, military censors, corporations and crooks and con artists who try to promote their own welfare by restricting the free flow of information.

Which is why journalists constantly fight to protect their rights, rights they've earned through years of court battles and legislation. These rights fall into two main categories:

◆ privileges and protections for journalistic activities, and

◆ access to government operations and records.

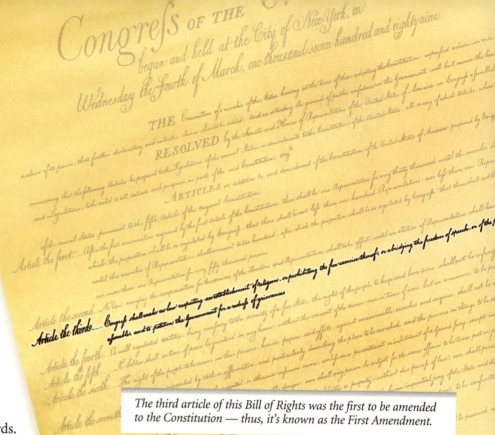

The third article of this Bill of Rights was the first to be amended to the Constitution — thus, it's known as the First Amendment.

QUOTED

"Our liberty depends on the freedom of the press, and that cannot be limited without being lost."

Thomas Jefferson

"The press can be trivial, yes, and it's not always trustworthy. But despite fakery, plagiarism, distortion, lies, government secrecy and media stupidity, there is an ongoing communal drive in the American media to ferret out the truth. This is the single most valuable thing we can do to preserve a free society: protect the right to know what's going on in our world. Argue for it, insist upon it, work for it."

William Kennedy, novelist

"The theory of the free press is that the truth will emerge from free reporting and free discussion, not that it will be presented perfectly and instantly in any one account."

Walter Lippmann, editor and columnist

"Suppression of opinion and censorship of news are among the mortal weapons that dictatorships direct against their own people."

President Franklin D. Roosevelt, in early 1941. Eight days after the attack on Pearl Harbor, he established the Office of Censorship to control the flow of information.

PRIVILEGE AND PROTECTION FOR SOURCES AND STORIES

Over time, laws and precedents have evolved to provide legal protection for journalists as they gather and publish information. The guidelines vary from state to state — but generally, these are the principles every reporter needs to understand:

PRIVILEGE

Privilege is a common legal term (you've heard of *doctor-patient privilege? Attorney-client privilege?*). It's used to describe benefits enjoyed by a specific group — in this case, journalists. When reporters publish their work, they're protected by:

◆ **Fair report privilege.** This allows journalists to report anything said in official governmental proceedings, no matter how slanderous or defamatory the facts or quotes might be, without being sued or censored. The reporting must be accurate and fair, however.

◆ **Opinion privilege.** This protects written opinions (especially insulting ones) from libel suits. It's a bit tricky; it makes a crucial distinction between *facts* and *opinions*. For example, if you write that someone is a thief or a liar, they can sue you for libel (see page 140), and they'll win if you can't offer provable facts to support your claim. *But* if you call someone a knucklehead, or if you claim that "she should be fired" or "he's the worst coach ever" — well, those statements aren't provably true or false. They're just opinions. Thus, they're protected . . . usually.

◆ **Fair comment and criticism.** Like the opinion privilege, this allows you to criticize performers, politicians and matters of public interest (see page 141).

Now, these three privileges apply to material *after* it's printed or published. Other rights and privileges protect the notes you take and the sources you use:

FREEDOM FROM NEWSROOM SEARCHES

Suppose you interview a source who's involved with a crime. You promise not to print her name, but police demand to know who she is. Can they obtain a search warrant to raid your home or newsroom looking for files, notebooks or photos? No. The federal Privacy Protection Act protects you from such searches and seizures *unless* officials suspect you're involved with the crime, you're planning to destroy the evidence, or someone's about to be hurt. You're protected — but you're not off the hook yet . . .

SHIELD LAWS

Suppose a criminal trial results from a story you've written. You're ordered to testify. The judge insists it's in the public interest for you to divulge everything you know; you insist that your credibility *and* your news-gathering ability will be ruined if you break your promises to confidential sources. If you refuse to cooperate, can you be jailed for contempt of court?

Currently, 31 states have "shield laws" that protect reporters by preserving the confidentiality of their notes and sources. But because that protection isn't absolute (no shield laws apply in many states or in federal courts), reporters are often forced to choose: either reveal confidential information or go to jail.

A final question: Are bloggers entitled to the same rights and protections as mainstream media reporters? Some say yes: An independent journalist is just as legitimate as one working for an institution. Others say no: *Any* bozo with a computer can call himself a blogger — and giving protections and privileges to reckless, untrained hacks could encourage abuses that make life difficult for *real* journalists.

JOURNALISTIC ACCESS: LETTING THE SUN SHINE BEHIND CLOSED DOORS

The public has a right to monitor what its government is up to. And you, as a reporter, have the right to cover its trials, attend its meetings and examine its documents. That's called freedom of information or "the right to know" — but it's a right that's often tested and contested.

OPEN COURTROOMS
Access to judicial proceedings

The issues: Does media coverage harm trial defendants? Can it bias a jury? Do cameras turn courtrooms into circuses? Should the press be banned from certain kinds of trials?

Why this matters: In the words of "The Associated Press Stylebook": "The public has a right to know how the court system is handling criminal matters, what kind of deals may be struck by prosecutors and defense lawyers, what kind of evidence may be kept from the jury, and what sort of police or prosecutorial acts or omissions have occurred."

What the law dictates: The Supreme Court has ruled that criminal trials must remain open to the media except for rare instances when an "overriding interest" justifies closure (usually to protect the defendant's fair trial rights).

The confusing gray areas: Some proceedings remain closed: grand jury investigations, military tribunals, etc. And in certain sensitive trials, publishing names of jurors, underage defendants or victims of sex crimes is forbidden.

What you can do: If a judge closes the courtroom, be prepared to make a statement. Reporters often carry cards to read from, which say something like: *"Your honor, I am _____, a reporter for _____, and I object to this proposed closing. I respectfully ask the Court for a hearing at which our attorney is prepared to make arguments that this closure violates the First Amendment…."*

OPEN MEETINGS
Access to official public business

The issues: Should public officials be allowed to make decisions behind closed doors, free from scrutiny? At what point does governmental secrecy become a threat?

Why this matters: It's all about trust. Every citizen has a right to monitor the government's activities and hold public officials accountable for their decisions. And it's the press's job to monitor meetings on the public's behalf. If journalists don't act as watchdogs, who will?

What the law dictates: It varies from state to state. Generally, all local, state or federal boards and commissions that receive revenue from taxes are subject to open meeting laws (or "sunshine" laws, as they're often called). School boards, city councils, student senates, parking committees — they're all required to open their sessions to the public *and* notify the media in advance of all meetings.

The confusing gray areas: State laws are often vague about what constitutes a "meeting." Some are allowed to remain private if they involve legal matters or employee reviews — or if a quorum of members isn't present. Executive sessions (where no votes are taken) may also be exempt.

What you can do: Sadly, many sunshine laws have no teeth. If the law is violated, make noise, in person and in print. Write stories anytime you're denied access. It'll publicize the problem *and* let officials know you're watching them.

OPEN RECORDS
Access to public documents

The issues: Shouldn't all government records be accessible to the public? Who gets to decide what's available — and what's off-limits? Does invoking "national security" simply allow some agencies and officials to operate in secret, free of oversight?

Why it matters: Public officials must be held accountable for the money they spend, the actions they take, the mistakes and corruption they may try to conceal.

What the law dictates: In 1966, Congress passed the landmark Freedom of Information Act (FOIA), requiring all federal agencies to make *most* of their records available upon request. Every state has its own version of FOIA covering schools, courts, cops, government, etc.

The confusing gray areas: The law exempts some material from public access: defense secrets, medical files, sensitive law-enforcement data. etc. *But* most gray areas result from confused bureaucrats and nervous public officials who don't understand or obey the law — and thus deny or ignore legitimate requests for information.

What you can do: To access records, first contact the agency and make an informal request by phone or e-mail. If you hit a wall, submit a written FOIA request (see resources at right). But be patient. Requests can take weeks, months, even years. Improper rejections can be appealed or — if you can afford it — challenged in court.

ONLINE RESOURCES FOR REPORTERS

The Reporters Committee for Freedom of the Press *(www.rcfp.org)* Offers a comprehensive collection of new stories, links and guides to issues ranging from shield laws to media rights. Highlights:

◆ **"How to Use the Federal FOI Act"** *(www.rcfp.org/ foiact/index.html)* An online do-it-yourself booklet giving step-by-step tips on using the federal Freedom of Information Act.

◆ **"Tapping Officials' Secrets"** *(www.rcfp.org/ cgi-local/tapping/index.cgi)* A summary of every state's open records and open meetings laws.

◆ **"Can We Tape?"** *(www.rcfp.org/ taping/ index.html)* A state-by-state guide to laws regulating the taping of conversations and phone calls.

◆ **Legal Defense Hotline** (1-800-336-4243). Offers free advice to journalists and media lawyers 24 hours a day.

Student Press Law Center *(www.splc.org)* Offers help with legal issues facing high school and college journalists.

◆ **"Open Records Law Request Letter Generator"** *(www.splc.org/ foiletter. asp)*. A fill-in-the-blank form to help you request state or local public records.

◆ **SPLC Virtual Lawyer** *(www.splc.org/ virtual_ lawyer)*. Quick answers to press-rights questions.

People say, "Why are you poking your nose into somebody else's business?" My response is, "It's not somebody else's business. It's YOUR business we're poking into. Aren't you interested in our finding out for you what's going on?"
Arthur Sulzberger, publisher, *The New York Times*

YOU'RE A REPORTER. BE TOUGH. DON'T LET THOSE BIG BLOWHARDS PUSH YOU AROUND.

Yes, you should always be polite and respectful, but remember, if you find yourself nose-to-nose with a bald, burly bureaucrat who tells you to bug off because his files are off-limits to pushy reporters like you, instead of slinking away in defeat you should grit your teeth and vow to yourself: *"Listen, pal, just because you work for The Man in this fancy office does not make it YOUR information — it's OURS, we the people, so how dare you keep the public's information from the public? I will not be intimidated; I will get what I need eventually, and if you don't give it to me I will get it another way, even if it makes you look stupid."*

Press wrongs

What happens when your big story leads to big trouble?

"The power of the press" isn't just a noble-sounding cliché. It's real. Journalists *do* have power; their words can comfort the afflicted, afflict the comfortable, educate and entertain audiences of millions.

But power can lead to trouble, too. William Randolph Hearst once boasted that "you can crush a man with journalism," and he was right. You can crush the guilty — but if you're not careful, you can crush the innocent, too. And in return, you can be sued. Disgraced. Dismissed.

Yes, bad things happen to bad reporters who lie, cheat, plagiarize and victimize. But bad things happen to *good* reporters, too. They often pay a price for being society's watchdogs, getting knocked down, locked up, cussed out and hauled into court. Journalism does get dangerous.

We're not trying to frighten you. But if you're willing to exercise the power of the press, you'd better be prepared when things go wrong.

During the funeral of rapper Biggie Smalls in 1997, a scuffle broke out between cops and rowdy fans. Julia Campbell, a freelance reporter for The New York Times, was arrested and charged with disorderly conduct. "I acted as a professional," Campbell insisted, though police claimed she used harsh language and pushed an officer. All charges were later dropped.

TROUBLE IN THE NEWSROOM: WHAT DID IT TEACH YOU?

Only months after entering the newspaper business, I was sued for a million dollars. All I did was create a story logo using a silhouette of our city – sounds harmless, but one reader claimed my logo looked like the copyrighted art on their book cover. Good news: we won the case. For the next year, I studied every aspect of journalism law. I learned I had not paid enough attention to this subject in college and that there are many looking for you to make a small mistake to cash in on.

Scott Farand, visual communications professor, University of South Carolina

---

Community journalism is fun, especially in small towns because people are eager and unafraid to tell you what they think of you and your product. In small towns I've been spit on, told "I wouldn't use your paper to wipe my ass" by a town's mayor, shoved, threatened ("I'd watch your back, boy") and followed out of town to make sure I left. In each case, it was

more a reason to smile than call the police, as most of the people doing the threatening are basically big fish in small ponds who run things the way their idol Boss Hogg did. It's cute, really, as long as they're not armed with projectiles.

Michael Bockoven, *Grand Island Independent*

An alert reader called our college newspaper one day, tipping us off to what turned out to be about a dozen film reviews by a single author plagiarized from other newspapers. Whoops. The plagiarism was blatant and extensive, so we fired the reviewer, who claimed he had been under a lot of stress and didn't know that what he was doing was wrong. We are very deliberate now about about telling new staffers each semester what is and isn't proper. And we made a very embarrassing apology phone call to the most-ripped-off paper.

Lucas Grundmeier, former managing editor, *Iowa State Daily*

While a court reporter in Ventura, Ca., I talked my way inside the courthouse's trial-evidence vault for a feature story. After viewing weapons, bloodied clothing and such, I learned the oldest item still in storage was a $5 bill used in a marijuana transaction decades earlier. I knew I had my lead. I could not find the pot buyer to interview but ran his name in the story. Had I contacted him, I

would have realized he'd kept the bust secret from his family all those years. This I learned from his invasion-of-privacy lawsuit. For outing his secret, the paper settled for an undisclosed sum.

Jeff Sturgeon, *The Roanoke Times*

After readers complained about not enough "good news" in the paper, I once wrote a satirical column filled with obviously bogus "good news," including: *"Due to a computer error, all losing lottery tickets are actually winners this week."* The next morning, I learned the dangers of satire. We were deluged with calls, including one from the State Lottery Office where 30 people were lined up to collect their $1 million. One angry caller said, "So you're telling me that everything in that column of yours is just a bunch of B.S.?"

"No!" I replied. "Well, yeah — that *is* what I'm telling you."

Jim Kershner, *The Spokesman-Review,* Spokane, Wash. (This incident happened at another paper.)

Covering police and courts yields numerous threats in person and by telephone, most often from mothers, wives or girlfriends of the accused or convicted. I use a post office box for an address, use another name in the telephone book, and use my work phone number on personal checks to avoid having angry people show

up on my doorstep or call me at home. The threats range from "I'm going to call a lawyer" to "I'm going to kick your ass."

The mother of a man convicted of child molestation (he and a partner held free puppet shows for children) literally jumped on my back as we exited the courthouse, sending us both tumbling down the steps. An assistant district attorney pulled her off.

Karen Jeffrey, *Cape Cod Times*

Getting sued for libel is a great investigative tool. I learned that when I was sued over a story I wrote in 1990 for Willamette Week, Portland's alternative newsweekly. I wrote that police suspected rock promoter Larry Hurwitz had murdered his publicity director, Tim Moreau. Hurwitz sued Willamette Week and me for libel for $5 million a year later. During the depositions, our lawyers were able to ask Hurwtiz detailed questions about his private and business life that he had to answer, under oath. Among other things, he was forced to reveal he lied on his taxes. After the libel suit was dismissed, I used his answers to continue reporting on the case. Hurwitz was eventually charged with the crime, pleaded no contest and is currently serving time for murdering Moreau.

Jim Redden, *Portland Tribune*

The reporter's guide to
TROUBLE

Reporters enjoy a certain amount of freedom, privilege and power. But there's a downside to reporting, too: you can get into all kinds of trouble. The chart below will help you gauge the severity of common problems that can arise from bad luck, bad judgment or bad intentions. We're not trying to make you *paranoid*; we just want to alert you to some of the dangers you need to avoid. In the pages ahead, we'll explore some of these topics in more detail.

	THE OFFENSE	EXAMPLE	HOW TO AVOID IT
STORIES THAT CAN GET YOU JAILED	**CONTEMPT OF COURT** *Refusing to tell a judge the source of controversial material used in a story.*	With help from a confidential source, you write a story exposing a criminal scandal. During the trial that results, you're ordered to reveal your source. You refuse. The judge jails you for contempt.	Most states have "shield laws" that let journalists protect the confidentiality of most (but not all) sources. If those laws don't protect you, you'll have to choose: name names or do time in jail.
	TRESPASSING *Or, in some cases, it could be called Failure to Obey a Lawful Order.*	You're snooping around a crime scene, or stalking a celebrity's home, or covering a riot, or pestering a tight-lipped politician in his office. The cops ask you to leave. You argue. They arrest you.	It varies. If you're in a public space and you're *not* interfering with police activity, you have a right to be there. Try to reason with the police if you can — but you may still be detained anyway.
	SEDITION *Publishing material too critical of government leaders or policies.*	You're a reporter in a foreign country (say, China or Ethiopia) and you write a story criticizing the government. You're jailed, without trial, for "aiding the enemy" or "conspiring to incite unrest."	Thankfully, sedition is no longer a crime in the U.S. (though it *has* been, as recently as World War I). But overseas, reporters are still imprisoned for attempting to expose official wrongdoing.
STORIES THAT CAN GET YOU SUED	**LIBEL** *Publishing a falsehood that holds someone up to public ridicule or scorn.*	Something in your story — a description, quote, photo, even a headline — insults, misrepresents or defames someone. If they can prove you were careless or malicious, it could cost you *millions*.	Truth is the best defense. As long as you can *prove* that what you wrote is true, you'll win — uhhh, probably. But there are lots of variables that make libel law messy. (See the next page.)
	INVASION OF PRIVACY *Using someone in a story in a way that violates their right to be left alone.*	You write a story called "Who's the Old Hermit in That Creepy House?" with quotes from neighbors and photos peeking into the windows — all of this *without* the owner's consent. He sues.	Always ask: Am I dragging this person unwillingly into the spotlight? Exposing someone's personal secrets without consent? If a story exploits or hurts ordinary folks, it may have crossed the line.
	BREACH OF CONTRACT *Publishing the name of a confidential source after promising you wouldn't.*	You interview a source and agree not to use his/her name in your story. But somehow — by mistake or under legal pressure — the source's identity becomes publicly known.	Avoid promising confidentiality, if you can. Some courts hold that a reporter's promise to conceal a source's name is a legally enforceable contract; others say it's a moral, not a legal, obligation.
STORIES THAT CAN GET YOU FIRED	**PLAGIARISM** *Passing off words or ideas of others as your own, without attribution.*	You're researching a story (or a column, or a review). You find that someone else has already written terrific stuff on this topic, so you "borrow" entire sentences without giving credit.	There's no shame in quoting other sources, so always attribute any words you recycle. Don't forget: Once online, your story will be just as searchable as the text you plagiarized from.
	FABRICATION *Manufacturing or falsifying any facts, quotes or events for a story.*	Maybe you lost your notes for a story, so you try reconstructing them from memory. Or maybe — worse — you need a juicy quote, so you concoct a bogus new source with a likely-sounding name.	Everything you ever write must be provably true (see *libel*, above), no matter how inconvenient that is. Once you lose the trust of your editors, you might as well start cleaning out your desk.
	LAPSES IN ETHICS *Behavior on or off the job that could damage your publication's reputation.*	You're a reporter covering City Hall. Your editor discovers that you've been concealing a sexual relationship with a controversial city council member. Conflict of interest? Yes. You're fired.	As a reporter, you represent your newspaper. To readers, you *are* the newspaper. Thus, editors will hold you to a high standard of behavior *in* and *out of* the newsroom. Don't let them down.
STORIES THAT CAN GET YOU ANGRY PHONE CALLS	**BIAS** *Taking sides in a story, or failing to present both sides of an issue fairly.*	You write a consumer story: "How *NOT* To Get Ripped Off by Used Car Dealers." Angry dealers claim you never contacted them — and because of your one-sided story, they yank all their ads.	Never forget, there are two sides to every story. That's obvious for topics like politics and religion, but your unconscious biases can taint and slant *anything* you write if you're not careful.
	BAD TASTE *Using words or ideas that some of your readers may find offensive.*	At a banquet, a sleazy local politician tells a racist, sexist joke. Your editor says, "Let's teach that jerk a lesson. Print it." Hundreds of readers are now blaming *you* for spoiling their breakfast.	Sometimes you just *know* you'll inflame readers with what you're printing. That's OK, as long as you've cleared it with The Boss. It's far worse to be blindsided by a careless or tasteless slipup.
	BLUNDERS & BLOOPERS *You name it — somebody will find a reason to get upset with your story.*	You misquoted me, you idiot! You misspelled my wife's name, you moron! You printed the wrong address for my bake sale, you nitwit! You claimed Captain Kirk's alias on the planet Organia was	Of all the problems on this page, those inevitable typos, misspellings and factual flubs may be the hardest to avoid, no matter how many editors proofread your stories. Sadly, we're only human.

Understanding libel

It's essential to know the difference between what's acceptable and what's defamatory.

li·bel (lī′bəl) — *n.* Publication of a false statement that deliberately or carelessly damages someone's reputation.

li·a·ble (lī′ə-bəl) — *adj.* To be legally responsible or obligated.

Ben Franklin believed that journalists should be free to write anything they like without fear of being arrested or sued. And if a reporter should abuse his power and damage your reputation? "Break his head," Franklin suggested. "Waylay him in the night, attack him behind, and give him a good drubbing."

Drubbings never really caught on. Instead, we have lawyers. And as a result, if you write something that's damaging and untrue, you can be sued for libel.

Libel's a slippery thing. It's harder to prove in some states than in others; it's harder to win if you're a famous celebrity or powerful politician. The legal boundaries evolve and shift over time, too, as new cases create new precedents.

So what's a reporter to do? The most concise advice we've yet come across is this, written years ago by libel attorney William A. DeFord:

Be sure of your facts. Remember than when you make a statement that might be considered damaging (and, of course, a faithful reporter must often do that), you must not only *believe* it or even *know* it, but *you must be able to prove it.* Remember that "they say" or even that some authority "said" is not sufficient proof, and that the publication of a libel as a rumor, merely, does not make it less a libel.

EXPLOSIVE WORDS: HANDLE WITH CARE

According to legal experts, these common words and phrases, used carelessly, are most likely to lead you into libel litigation:

adultery
AIDS
alcoholic
altered records
atheist
bankrupt
blackmail
blackmail
bribery
buys votes
cheats
child abuse
Communist
con artist
corruption
coward
crook
deadbeat
drug addict
drunkard
ex-convict
fraud
gangster
gay
graft
herpes
hit man
hypocrite
illegitimate
illicit relations
incompetent
infidelity
informer
intimate
intolerance
Ku Klux Klan
liar
Mafia
mental illness
Neo-Nazi
perjurer
plagiarist
prostitute
rape/rapist
scam
seducer
slacker
smuggler
sold out
spy
suicide
swindle
thief
unethical
unprofessional

AT A GLANCE: THE BEGINNING REPORTER'S GUIDE TO LIBEL

Who can sue for libel?
Any living person can be defamed, but dead people can't. Small groups (clubs, businesses, organizations) can be defamed; the government can't.

Remember, getting sued or threatened with a suit doesn't mean you've done anything wrong. But libel suits are costly and time-consuming even if you *win.*

Who is it that gets sued? Me, the reporter?
Usually, it's the publication. But the reporter can be dragged into court as a defendant, too, along with any editors who worked on the story. And if the suit stems from a libelous quote you ran, the person quoted could be a defendant, too.

So what exactly constitutes libel?
All five of these criteria must be met:
1. Statements must be false, based on facts that are wrong or unverifiable.
2. Statements must be defamatory. It can be libelous, for example, to accuse someone of a crime, discredit a person professionally, accuse someone of immorality or imply that a person is infected with a loathsome disease.
3. Statements must be published. Any form of communication counts, whether it's printed, broadcast, posted on the Internet or just typed to a frien
4. Plaintiffs must be identifiable. The must prove that they're the ones name described or pictured.
5. The defendant — that's you — must be at fault either through negligence (failure to exercise appropriate care) or malice (see box at right).

How do I defend myself if someone claims that I libeled him (or her)?
Generally, the best defenses include:
◆ *Truth.* Nothing beats the truth. The plaintiff must prove that what you wrote was false, so you're safe if you can prove your story is true, or substantially true; minor errors sometimes don't matter if the "gist" of a story is accurate.
◆ *Consent.* If someone allows you to publish a libelous statement about him, he can't sue you later — even if the statement starts causing him damage.
◆ *Privilege.* If you don't take sides, the *fair report privilege* allows you to report on newsworthy statements and public controversies. You're entitled to print anything said during most legislative or judicial proceedings, too, as long as your story is accurate and fair. ▼ And you're free to criticize performers when you review their work (see top of next page).

How can I avoid libel?
◆ Verify any questionable material before you print it, whether it originates in a quote or a document, whether it runs in a story, a caption or a letter to the editor.
◆ If people are likely to be offended or damaged by a story, give them a chance to defend themselves in that story.
◆ Remember that public officials often make careless, unofficial claims and charges that can lead to libel, and using words like "alleged" and "reportedly" won't always protect you in court.
◆ If you make a mistake, check with your editor or attorney and respond immediately. Run a correction or retraction to set the record straight. A sincere, printed apology often convinces injured parties to call off their lawyers.

BUT: Don't ever let the threat of a libel suit frighten you into withholding crucial information. Be brave. If it's true, *print it.*

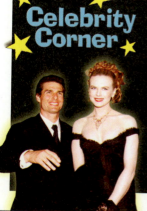

Celebrity Corner

Are libel laws different for famous or influential people?
Yes. For ordinary folks like you and me to win a libel suit, we need to show only that a publication acted negligently. But "public figures" and "public officials" (see definitions at the bottom of the next page) must prove that publications acted with "actual malice" by recklessly deliberately printing lies or disregarding the truth.

Angry celebrities occasionally sue supermarket tabloids for libel. However, those suits can be costly, humiliating and difficult to win — thus, they're commonly resolved with cash settlements. Tom Cruise and Nicole Kidman settled their 1999 suit against the *Star* after it alleged they needed a "sex coach" to make their movie love scenes seem convincing; Martha Stewart settled her $10 million libel suit against the National Enquirer for claiming she was insane.

THE CHERRY SISTERS vs. "FAIR COMMENT AND CRITICISM"

There once was a vaudeville trio called the Cherry Sisters. And they were horrible. In 1901, a critic for a small Iowa newspaper caught their act and wrote:

> Their long, skinny arms, equipped with talons at the extremities, swung mechanically and anon waved frantically at the suffering audience. The mouths of their rancid features opened like caverns, and sounds like the wailing of damned souls issued therefrom. . . .

Reading this review, the Cherrys went bananas. They felt humiliated and degraded. They sued for libel. But they lost.

Why? For one thing, the judge saw them perform. "If ever there was a case justifying ridicule and sarcasm," he said, "it is the one before us now."

The Cherry Sisters appealed to the Iowa Supreme Court — and lost there, too. "Any performance to which the public is invited may be freely criticized," the court ruled. "Also, any editor may publish reasonable comments on that performance."

Thus, the legal principle known as *fair comment and criticism* was established. Because the Cherry Sisters *chose* to expose themselves to public opinion, they had no right to whine when that opinion turned ugly. That's why all critics of books, films, plays, sports events, restaurants or politics are free to publish negative opinions. But they *aren't* free to publish damaging facts that aren't true. That's called libel.

BORING BUT IMPORTANT: FIVE LANDMARK LIBEL CASES

Nothing makes your head swim faster than unraveling knotty legal rulings. But here's a roundup of Supreme Court decisions that helped shape modern libel law:

NEW YORK TIMES v. SULLIVAN

This ruling was a turning point in libel law, so please pay attention:

In 1960, civil rights groups ran an ad in The New York Times describing abuses inflicted upon protesters in the South. The ad contained minor factual errors and made Southern authorities look violent and criminal — so L.B. Sullivan, police commissioner in Montgomery, Ala., sued the Times for libel.

Sullivan lost. The Supreme Court ruled that "debate on public issues should be uninhibited, robust and wide open," even if mistakes sometimes occur. Public officials should be tough enough to take criticism about their conduct while in office. Thus, any public official suing for libel must prove that damage was done with "actual malice" (see lexicon below).

AP v. WALKER *and* CURTIS PUBLISHING v. BUTTS

These two 1967 Supreme Court decisions extended the Sullivan ruling on "actual malice" to cover well-known *public figures*, not just governmental *public officials*.

Walker, a retired Army general, sued The Associated Press for a story claiming he encouraged a riot. The court ruled that the story was written under deadline pressure and its errors were inadvertent. Thus, because the story showed no malice, Walker — a public figure — wasn't libeled.

Butts was a famous football coach who filed a libel suit after a story in The Saturday Evening Post alleged he'd fixed a game. The sloppy reporting had ignored warnings of inaccuracy, the Court said. Thus, it showed malice.

GERTZ v. WELCH

In 1973, attorney Elmer Gertz sued Robert Welch's conservative magazine for libel after it called Gertz a "Communist" for representing clients suing the police.

The Court ruled that Gertz's rights had been violated because, though well known, he was still a private citizen, *not* a public figure; he hadn't actively tried to "engage the public's attention." The Court also ruled that, because private citizens "are more vulnerable to injury," they need more legal protection. Thus, to win a libel suit, ordinary folks need only show that a defamation resulted from negligence, not actual malice.

HUTCHINSON v. PROXMIRE

Sen. William Proxmire used to hand out "Golden Fleece Awards" to agencies guilty of wasting tax dollars. In 1975, he gave an award to Ronald Hutchinson, a monkey researcher at a hospital.

Hutchinson sued Proxmire for libel and won. The Court ruled that Hutchinson was *not* a public figure and his research was *not* a matter of public controversy. Though Proxmire's speeches on the Senate floor were protected from libel suits, his press releases and newsletters were not.

A LEXICON OF LIBEL

Actual malice: It doesn't mean *showing ill will*, as you might think. In libel cases, it means *knowing you're lying* or *disregarding the truth*.

Opinion: It's safe to express ideas (*"John's car is ugly"*) that don't claim to be factual and thus cannot be "false." But saying *"John's car is stolen"* is a statement that's seemingly based on facts — and if false, it can be libelous.

Public official: Someone who exercises power or influence in governmental affairs (a police officer, mayor or school superintendent).

Public figure: A person who has acquired fame or notoriety (a performer or athlete) or has participated in some public controversy (a protester or social activist).

Slander: Defamation that's spoken, rather than printed. (Defamation that's broadcast by TV or radio is treated by the courts as *libel*, however.)

WANT MORE LIBEL PRACTICE? **TEST YOURSELF ▶ 152**

PRINT it or PULL it?
YOU MAKE THE CALL

Here are seven situations you might face as a reporter. What would you do? We asked four prominent legal authorities the same seven questions. Compare your answers on page 300.

1 A football coach tells you he's benching the school's star quarterback because "he's been lazy and stupid. His head's not in the game — he's too busy partying and getting laid." Can you print that quote?

2 Professor Smith publishes a paper theorizing that Asians are genetically superior to blacks. Professor Jones tells you that those ideas are "racist garbage." If you print that, can Smith sue you for calling him a racist?

3 A local jazz musician dies. You're collecting quotes for a profile about her, and one woman says, "She was a brilliant pianist, but the heroin turned her into a thief and a whore." Can you print that comment?

4 After a weeklong manhunt, police finally track down Daryl Lickt and arrest him for murdering his wife. In the story about his arrest, you refer to Lickt as "the alleged murderer." Is it safe to say that?

5 A professor abruptly quits amid rumors that he sexually harassed a student. (See the Jenny Deadline comic on page 20.) Can you report that those rumors exist?

6 A local doctor who specializes in nutrition says that food served in your school cafeteria is unfit for human consumption and that school cooks are unqualified to know the difference between healthy and unhealthy food. Can you print her comments?

7 In your paper's gossip column, you write: "Adam Zapple, that studly quarterback for our fabulous football team, was seen parking his Corvette in front of the Purple Pickle Saturday night. The Pickle, we all know, is the area's raunchiest gay nightclub." The item will run with a photograph showing Zapple in front of the bar. If you print this, can Zapple sue you for insinuating that he's gay?

Invasion of privacy

When unfair reporting victimizes unwilling people.

Some people crave publicity. They *want* to read their names in the paper and see their faces on TV. So they run for Congress, star in musicals, race on the track team or yap happily when reporters ask for their political opinions.

Other people become newsworthy involuntarily. They survive an accident, witness a crime, win the lottery or find themselves embroiled in a scandal. They may not *choose* to be news, but public interest outweighs their desire for privacy . . . for a short time, anyway.

And that's where the problem is. When do ordinary people have a right to be let alone — to stay *out* of the news, if that's what they want? Is there a right to privacy? The courts say yes; unless people are public figures or involved in an event of public interest, you can't drag them into the spotlight without consent.

You've previously seen how libel cases challenge journalistic *accuracy*. As you'll see below, privacy cases challenge journalistic *ethics* and *judgment*.

Fantastic! A libel suit where a reporter plagiarized copyrighted material that invaded my client's privacy. Ka-ching!

THE FOUR MOST COMMON WAYS TO INVADE SOMEONE'S PRIVACY

Though privacy rights and guidelines vary from state to state, most courts recognize four situations that provide grounds for invasion of privacy lawsuits:

❶ INTRUSION

if you gather information unethically — in a situation where someone has a right to expect privacy — you can be sued, even if you never write a story. This might involve:
◆ **Trespass:** walking (or snooping) on private property without the owner's consent.
◆ **Secret surveillance:** using hidden cameras, recorders or other bugging devices.
◆ **Misrepresentation:** disguising yourself to gain unauthorized access to a private area.

FOR EXAMPLE ▶ A journalism professor at a local college abruptly quits her job and drops out of sight. You call her, but she won't answer the phone. You visit her house, but she doesn't answer the door. While standing on her porch, you see her sitting by the window. You snap this picture. But because you trespassed on her property and photographed her without consent, if she sues, you may lose — even if you never print the photo.

❷ PUBLIC DISCLOSURE OF PRIVATE FACTS

Publicizing personal details — about someone's sex life, say, or their medical history — may cause emotional distress if the material is:
◆ **Private:** known only to family or friends and *not* of legitimate concern to the public.
◆ **Intimate:** something personal that people wouldn't ordinarily want revealed.
◆ **Offensive:** liable to humiliate someone if the information became widely known.

FOR EXAMPLE ▶ Suppose you finally interview that professor. She agrees to let you use that photo. You later learn, from her colleagues, the real reason she quit: *severe hemorrhoids*. She asks you not to print the story, but you run it anyway. Though your facts are true, she sues, claiming the story caused pain and humiliation.

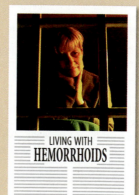

LIVING WITH
HEMORRHOIDS

❸ FALSE LIGHT

This claim arises anytime you run a story, a photo, a headline, even a photo caption that portrays someone in an inaccurate way — as something he or she is *not*. If it can be proven that you acted recklessly and that the portrayal is "highly offensive to a reasonable person," you're guilty of invading privacy — which makes these types of privacy lawsuits similar to libel suits. (In some states, they're considered the same thing.)

FOR EXAMPLE ▶ Months after that photo was taken, a reporter finds it stuck in a drawer and decides it's a *perfect* way to illustrate a story on bankruptcy. But when this woman sees herself in the paper, she says, "What? *I'm* not bankrupt!" If she sues, the paper may lose, because this page is embarrassing and untrue.

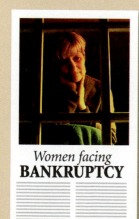

Women facing
BANKRUPTCY

❹ APPROPRIATION

Appropriation is the unauthorized use of someone's name, photo or words to endorse or sell a product or service — a problem that usually occurs more often in advertising departments than in newsrooms. To avoid headaches (and lawsuits), don't use anyone, celebrity or not, to sell *anything* unless they've signed a consent form.

FOR EXAMPLE ▶ Speaking of headaches: Suppose this photo somehow falls into the hands of an ad agency — or a staff artist assigned to design some new ads. This woman *looks* like she's got a headache, so the photo seems to work perfectly. But if the woman sees it and sues, she'll win — because she was used to promote a product without giving her consent.

When headache pain hits, reach for relief.
Odvil.

Years ago, this symbol was required on all printed material in order to establish copyright protection in the United States. Nowadays, it merely serves as a warning. So if you see this —

© 2006 The Daily News

— you've been warned that the attached material legally belongs to someone else.

Copyright law

It protects you from theft (and stops you from stealing).

There are two ways to look at copyright law:

◆ **It's a blessing.** It prevents thieves and plagiarists from stealing your work and publishing it somewhere else — protection you'll be grateful for when you finally write The Great American Novel. But:

◆ **It's a pain.** It makes it dangerous to copy that excellent stuff you find on the Internet: stories, quotes, songs, movies, photos, etc.

As a reporter, you must respect the law. After all, it benefits *you.* Whenever your stories appear in the paper or online, they're automatically protected. (Your publisher usually owns the copyright.)

But that same copyright protection also applies to everything you encounter in print or on the Web. So before you "borrow" someone else's material, you'd better brush up on the rules.

FROM A (APPLE) TO Z (ZIPPER): RESPECTING TRADEMARKS

Just as writers copyright their stories to protect them from theft, businesses register their names and logos as *trademarks* to prevent them from being stolen, too.

Logos are those distinctive designs that companies stamp on their signs and products:

APPLE COMPUTERS MERCEDES-BENZ SHELL OIL

But *names* are registered as trademarks, too. And corporations get *very* protective of their names.

Which is why, if you write a sentence like this, you might actually receive nasty letters from corporate attorneys:

Larry spent the day playing scrabble, eating jello and tossing a frisbee.

The problem? *Scrabble, Jell-O* and *Frisbee* are all trademarks. And corporate attorneys try hard to prevent reporters like you from using their product names in a generic way. Why? If everyone starts refering to all photocopies as xeroxes, for instance, the Xerox trademark loses its uniqueness — which is what happened to words like *aspirin, zipper* and *yo-yo.* They were all company names years ago, until the words slipped into common usage and became worthless as trademarks.

You'll find many commonly used (and misused) trademarks in the AP Stylebook, which advises you to either capitalize the product name or find a generic synonym:

INSTEAD OF:	YOU SHOULD SAY:
Jell-O	gelatin dessert
Band-Aid	adhesive bandage
Realtor	real estate agent
Xerox	photocopy
Jacuzzi	hot tub
Muzak	elevator music

And so on.

Miswording trademarks isn't *illegal,* but it's still wrong — sloppy journalistic manners.

AT A GLANCE: A JOURNALIST'S GUIDE TO COPYRIGHT

What is copyright, exactly?

It's government-approved protection for all forms of creative expression: stories, books, images, songs, Web sites, etc. A copyright legally establishes who owns a creative work — and thus, who controls its sale and reproduction. About 100 years after the work is created (the law gets messy here), the copyright expires and the work enters the public domain.

All work becomes protected by copyright automatically as soon as it appears in concrete form.

What happens if I plagiarize copyrighted material?

If your editors catch you, you could be fired — especially if you stole a *lot* of material in a way that embarrassed your publication. If the copyright holder catches you, you can be sued and forced to pay damages.

Suppose I'm writing a story and I want to run an excerpt from a book — or, say, some song lyrics. How much can I legally reprint?

This is a murky legal area with no precise answers. But generally:

The safest thing to do is obtain permission from the author or publisher by notifying them, in writing, of your intent. The goal, of course, is to get permission *without shelling out any money.*

But consent isn't crucial. As a journalist, you're legally allowed "fair use" of copyrighted material, which boils down to this:

◆ If something is newsworthy (a popular book or controversial photo, for example), then it's

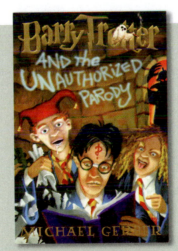

Is it legal to create a parody?

Yes. You're allowed to spoof popular characters and creations as long as you use them as a springboard for your own witty ideas and clever commentary. You can't simply copy the original; you have to add new material for comic effect.

Take this Harry Potter parody (above), in which Barry Trotter helps Hogwash headmaster Alpo Bumblemore battle the evil Lord Valumart. By cleverly transforming the original novel's plot, characters and book cover, the parody becomes new, different — and funny.

"fair use" to show readers what makes it newsworthy by reprinting images or excerpts. However:

◆ The more you excerpt or reproduce, the closer you come to violating copyright. A sentence or two is safe; a paragraph is probably OK. But several paragraphs may be pushing it, especially because:

◆ You must not diminish the value of the original work. If you reprint the juiciest passages from a book, fewer people will buy it, which will greatly annoy the author's attorneys. Remember, too:

◆ You must always credit the source of all excerpted material. Better still, tell readers where they can buy the book or song you're excerpting, thus demonstrating your good intentions.

What about using copyrighted photos or illustrations?

Again, size matters. Small images, like the book cover at left, are usually safe to reprint, as long as they serve a legitimate journalistic purpose.

I write for a small paper. Do lawyers from big corporations really care if I use their material?

That's what everybody thinks — right before they get sued. You may think you're tiny and undetectable, but remember: *Once you publish something, it becomes evidence for all to see.* If a smart lawyer sniffs you out and finds you're attached to a school or publishing company worth millions, you could land in court faster than you can say "My reporting career is over."

Taste and decency (and censorship)

Who draws the line when subject matter becomes offensive?

Even this book is subject to censorship. Take the Dick Cheney story on the facing page. Though The Washington Post printed the actual f-word, our own editors asked us to delete it. That racy magazine cover, too, had to be carefully positioned to conceal the nipple. (We don't want reader outrage to hurt book sales.) See? Issues of taste and self-censorship are a concern for writers *everywhere*.

At every publication, there are restrictions on what you can say. When these restrictions are imposed from *outside* the newsroom — by courts, the military or school administrators — it's called "censorship." When the restrictions originate *inside* the newsroom, it's called "conforming to community values" or "meeting our editing standards" — though some call it "self-censorship."

Self-censorship is common, but is it always necessary? For every ▮▮▮▮▮▮▮ you try to print, there's an editor who'll delete it because it's "too offensive" for readers. For every ▮▮▮▮▮▮▮▮▮ you threaten to expose, there's a nervous publisher ready to spike your story. Journalists constantly debate whether to delete profanities from quotes, remove photos of corpses from war stories, or withhold allegations about ▮▮▮▮▮▮▮▮▮▮ that might anger the administration.

The answers aren't always easy. You'll need to develop radar that senses when you've crossed the line. The problem is, the line's always moving.

YOU CAN'T SAY THAT: FIVE REASONS WHY YOUR STORY MIGHT GET SPIKED

◆ **VULGAR LANGUAGE.** Editors often bleep profanities to avoid offending readers. But which words deserve deletion? Obscenities range from serious (the *f*-word, the *n*-word) to mild (words like *bitch* and *fart*). What about crude phrases (*bite me*)? Racial epithets? Blasphemy? Decisions will depend upon the character of your publication and the context in which words are used. You can argue that slang and vulgarity accurately reflect our culture — but when in doubt, most editors delete.

◆ **OFFENSIVE TOPICS.** Nothing unnerves a squeamish editor faster than a story about sex, drugs or a morally questionable lifestyle (especially if it's accompanied by juicy photos). All it takes is one editor saying, "Oh, that's *sick*," and your story gets tossed on the trash heap whether it's well-written or not. Many publications are either too timid or too conservative to run "threatening" stories about sensitive political or religious issues. Over time, reporters stop arguing and start self-censoring — which is why controversial topics often go unreported.

◆ **CONFLICT OF INTEREST.** At some papers, you can't write a story about "How to Sell Your Own Home" because angry real-estate agents will threaten to pull their ads. At other papers, critics are warned to write only *positive* restaurant reviews so they don't offend advertisers. Yes, stories that anger or embarrass your boss's clients or political allies may get spiked even if they're legitimate news — leaving you to debate whether to quit in protest or become a "team player."

◆ **LEGAL/ETHICAL ISSUES.** Some things are illegal to print: military secrets, copyrighted material, stolen memos. Some things are legally dangerous to print: statements that defame someone or stories that invade a person's privacy. And some things may be unethical to print: the names of sex-crime victims, for example. Should you protect the privacy of those who've been humiliated and hurt — or does the public have a right to know who's making criminal accusations?

◆ **REPORTING FLAWS.** Sure, some stories are too unpolished to print. They suffer from grammatical errors, sloppy fact-checking, unfair treatment of sources. But beware: Occasionally, when editors say "the story wasn't ready" or "it wasn't up to our standards," they *actually* mean they didn't want to risk running it and just won't admit it. So write clean, solid copy — and demand honesty from your bosses.

NOOKY'S BAKERY: SWEET OR TASTELESS?

The story: In a Houston suburb, Charlotte Daingerfield and her daughter Jackie opened Nooky's Erotic Bakery, selling X-rated fortune cookies, chocolate Viagra pills, penis-shaped lollipops (called "Hand Jobs"), cakes shaped like breasts and giant phalluses ("King of the Dickheads"), along with dozens of other crudely comical, sexually suggestive gag gifts for bachelor and bachelorette parties.

The dilemma: Suppose two women opened a store like this in *your* community.
◆ How would local news outlets react?
◆ Is this bakery too offensive to publicize — or could you write an acceptable story in a lighthearted, non-vulgar way?
◆ Would local readers be offended if you accurately described the items for sale? What if you ran close-up photographs?
◆ Could Nooky's buy an ad in your paper?

CASE STUDY #1:
DICK CHENEY DROPS THE F-BOMB

In 2004, Vice President Dick Cheney uttered a memorable obscenity on the Senate floor. As the Washington Post described it:

> A chance meeting with Sen. Patrick J. Leahy (Vt.), the ranking Democrat on the Judiciary Committee, became an argument about Cheney's ties to Halliburton Co., an international energy services corporation, and President Bush's judicial nominees. The exchange ended when Cheney offered some crass advice.
>
> "F●k yourself," said the man who is a heartbeat from the presidency.

Newspapers everywhere faced an awkward decision: Should they print Cheney's obscenity? As it turned out, few did. The New York Times wrote that Cheney used "an obscene phrase to describe what he thought Mr. Leahy should do." Two major news services, the Associated Press and Reuters, wrote that Cheney told Leahy to "f--- off." The Christian Science Monitor said only that Cheney "let rip a vulgar profanity."

After the Post received a few dozen negative e-mails and phone calls, the paper's ombudsman, Michael Getler, defended using the word: "The paper doesn't do it unless it's exceptionally newsworthy and necessary for readers to understand and make a judgment" on the story, he said.

Interestingly, Getler objected to the way that quote was attributed: "F●k yourself," *said the man who is a heartbeat from the presidency.*

"They should have edited that out," Getler said. "After all that long discussion about whether to use the word, the article should've been beyond reproach journalistically. That smart-alecky remark diminishes the paper and weakens the integrity of the piece."

* The Post printed the actual f-word; we deliberately obscured it for your protection.

CASE STUDY #2:
A CONTROVERSIAL CAMPUS COVER

The story explored "erotic body modification": students who pierce their nipples, split their tongues and implant jewelry in their genitals.

But it was the cover that caused the uproar.

The photo showed the breast of an Arizona State University student, pierced through the nipple with a tiny barbell. When ASU's biggest donor saw it, he protested to the university president. The president, in response, tried to intimidate the student paper — even threatening, through a subordinate, to cut off funding and "kick the State Press off campus."

Was the cover image really that offensive? "We felt it was artistic," said Cameron Eickmeyer, State Press editor in chief. "It wasn't lewd, in our opinion. And it was the best way to describe the exact types of piercings students were doing."

The paper's editorial board (a majority of them women) had chosen the cover image after reviewing several photos and discussing their potential impact. As it turned out, the most negative response came from the administration, and even *that* eventually subsided when cooler heads prevailed. Though some students protested the photo, dozens more defended it and supported the paper's right to print it.

"The paper and the administration now have a better understanding of our roles," Eickmeyer said afterward. "And students learned a valuable lesson about the impact of decisions newspapers make."

STUDENT PRESS LAW: HOW MUCH CAN A SCHOOL ADMINISTRATOR CENSOR?

American newspapers are free from virtually all forms of outside censorship. But student publications aren't so fortunate. Consider:
◆ The president of Hampton University confiscated 6,500 copies of the school paper after the editor refused to print her letter praising the student cafeteria on the front page.
◆ A Florida principal outlawed all copies of Wellington High School's Wave when a columnist debated the pros and cons of virginity.
◆ Administrators at Manatee Community College shut down the student newspaper after battling with its editors over access to budget information and conflicts over prior review.

Prior review is the policy that allows (or requires) advisers or administrators to approve

> **Questions about student press law?** The best, most up-to-date source of online information is the Student Press Law Center at *www.splc.org.*

or censor stories in advance of publication — and it's been a source of bitter confrontations. Not all campus newsrooms are free from administration censorship, courts have ruled.

Student press law issues are too far-ranging to discuss in detail here; new court cases constantly challenge students' rights. Bottom line:

Public colleges — Student editors are entitled to control the content of campus publications. School officials cannot fire editors or advisers, discipline reporters, confiscate publications,

withhold funding or make other similar attempts to censor or manipulate content.

Public high schools — Two Supreme Court decisions, *Tinker* and *Hazelwood*, helped establish how much freedom students have and how far school officials can go to control them (see below). But there's lots of gray area here, and a few states have enacted laws to protect public-school journalists from censorship.

Private colleges and high schools — "The First Amendment prohibits government officials from suppressing speech," the Student Press Law Center observes, "but it does not prevent school censorship at private schools." Thus, a private school administrator can act like any other publisher in controlling what's printed.

TWO KEY DECISIONS AND THEIR IMPACT ON STUDENT PAPERS

Where are the limits on First Amendment freedoms for student newspapers? These two landmark Supreme Court decisions help determine what public-school publications can print without fear of administration interference.

TINKER v. DES MOINES SCHOOL DISTRICT (1969)

What happened: Several students (one named Mary Beth Tinker) were suspended from high school for wearing armbands to protest the Vietnam War. The students sued, arguing that their freedom-of-speech rights were violated. The case ended up in the Supreme Court, which ruled in favor of the students.

What it means: School administrators must respect students' rights. Teachers and students, the court said, do not "shed their constitutional rights to freedom of speech or expression at the schoolhouse gate." Free expression — in speech or print — must be allowed, provided it doesn't disrupt school discipline or invade the rights of others.

HAZELWOOD SCHOOL DISTRICT v. KULHMEIER (1988)

What happened: After a high school journalism class created the final edition of its school paper, the principal censored two stories — one on teen pregnancy, another on divorce — saying they were unfair and inappropriate. The students sued, claiming their rights were violated. But the Supreme Court disagreed.

What it means: Censorship is allowed — especially if a story is "poorly written, inadequately researched, biased or prejudiced, vulgar or profane," and if the censorship has a "valid educational purpose." BUT: If a publication is an extracurricular "forum for public expression" where students have been given authority to edit content, it enjoys greater freedom than a classroom activity.

The Seven Deadly Sins

Ethical pitfalls that can lead to trouble.... or termination.

In the Middle Ages, Christian theologians compiled a list of Seven Deadly Sins, those vices most destructive to a monk's spiritual growth: pride, envy, anger, sloth, greed, gluttony and lust.

There are worse sins, of course: rape, murder, incest. But what makes the 7DS so universal is that, as one theologian explained, "they are found on particularly slippery moral slopes." Though we all may flirt with these sins to some degree, when we get in too deep, the consequences start snowballing.

The same is true for journalism's Seven Deadly Sins, those vices most destructive to a reporter's career. All journalists grapple with these sins now and then — but if you indulge too much, your integrity and your reputation will nosedive.

Some might argue that other journalistic sins are just as bad: gullibility, for instance. Or long-windedness. Or brown-nosing politicians and celebrities.

They're bad, it's true. But these can be *deadly:*

DECEPTION
Lying or misrepresenting yourself to obtain information

Is it ethical for reporters to disguise their identities? Many editors say no — never. "Credibility is our most important asset," Henry McNulty once wrote in The Hartford Courant, "and if we deceive people in order to do our job, we've compromised that credibility before a word is written."

Some editors do make rare exceptions. Restaurant reviewers, for instance, can pretend to be ordinary diners, and if you're investigating a con artist or social injustice, it *may* be OK for you to pose as an ordinary citizen. But the rest of the time, you're never allowed to lie.

EXAMPLE:

◆ Chicago police reporter Harry Romanoff was famous for his deceptions. When eight nurses were murdered in 1966, he tricked a policeman into divulging information by claiming to be the county coroner, then scored an interview with the mother of murder suspect Richard Speck by pretending to be Speck's attorney. For other stories, Romanoff made phone calls where he pretended to be a bishop, the chief of police, a White House official, even the Illinois governor.

◆ In the late 1800s, Nellie Bly pioneered the art of undercover reporting by posing as a chorus girl, working in a sweatshop, getting herself imprisoned and being committed to a mental institution. (For an excerpt, see Page 192).

CONFLICT OF INTEREST
Accepting gifts or favors from sources or promoting social and political causes

How much bribery will it take to corrupt a typical reporter? Free meals? Movie tickets? Stock-market tips? How about a cozy job as my "media adviser" after you help elect me?

Yes, gifts and graft can compromise your objectivity and ruin your paper's reputation—which is why editors often insist that reporters avoid any favors, business dealings or political activities that even *appear* to taint their objectivity. TV newscaster Keith Olbermann claims he doesn't even *vote:* "I don't believe journalists covering politics should," he says.

EXAMPLE:

◆ In 2005, columnist Armstrong Williams was scorned and shamed by media colleagues after it was revealed that he accepted $240,000 from the Bush administration to promote the "No Child Left Behind" education-reform law in newspaper columns and TV appearances. "I should be criticized," Williams said. "I crossed some ethical lines." (He *did* keep the $240,000, however.)

◆ In a controversial 2004 decision, The New York Times fired freelance writer Jay Blotcher because he'd been a "public spokesperson for an advocacy organization" (an anti-AIDS group). Though Blotcher hadn't specifically written about AIDS or gay issues, the Times said it acted to avoid any appearance of conflict of interest.

BIAS
Slanting a story by manipulating facts to sway readers' opinions

Columnists can take sides. Cable-news pundits can take sides. But reporters should *never* take sides. Reporters have a duty to tell the truth, the whole truth and nothing but the truth. Deviate from that — by rigging the facts to advance an agenda — and you risk losing the trust of both readers and editors.

In the words of veteran journalist Michael Gartner: "If you have an agenda, you should not be in the newspaper business. . . . If you want to change the world, become a teacher or a politician or a sociologist or a mom. Do not be a reporter." ▼

EXAMPLE:

◆ In 1998, two investigative reporters were fired by a Fox television station in Florida for refusing to distort facts in a news story. The reporters discovered that Florida milk was tainted by the secret use of a bovine growth hormone linked to cancer. When Monsanto, the hormone maker, threatened to sue, the station managers told the reporters they'd be fired unless they either buried the story or edited it to satisfy Monsanto.

◆ CBS News created a scandal during the 2004 presidential campaign when it used dubious documents to dispute George W. Bush's military service record. Many accused CBS of "liberal bias," alleging they had failed to verify the documents because they were too eager to "get" Bush.

130 ◀ MORE ON **OPINION COLUMNS**   MORE FROM **MICHAEL GARTNER** ▶ 280   MORE ON **BIAS** ▶ 182, 275

FABRICATION

Manufacturing quotes or imaginary sources, or writing anything you know to be untrue

"There is one sacred rule of journalism," reporter John Hersey once wrote. "The writer must not invent. The legend on the license must read: *None of this was made up.*"

Ages ago, reporters were urged to fabricate stories to sell more papers. In a famous 1835 hoax, the New York Sun told of a fantastic new telescope that revealed winged creatures on the moon "engaged in conversation."

Try that today — try fictionalizing *anything* in a news story — and you'll be vilified. Every quote, character and event in everything you ever write *must* be verifiably true. Period.

EXAMPLE:

◆ In the most famous case of journalistic fraud, Washington Post reporter Janet Cooke was forced to return her 1981 Pulitzer Prize for a story profiling "Jimmy," an 8-year-old heroin addict. Cooke confessed that the boy was a fabrication, a composite of several child addicts.

◆ Stephen Glass, a reporter for The New Republic, was fired in 1998 after an investigation revealed that 27 of 41 stories he'd written for the magazine contained fabricated material.

◆ In 1998, two award-winning Boston Globe columnists — Patricia Smith and Mike Barnicle — left the paper after it was discovered that each had invented quotes, characters and stories.

THEFT

Obtaining information unlawfully or without a source's permission

As a journalist, you need to be sure about the accuracy and authenticity of every document you use. You also need to be aware of the legal fallout that can result from printing material of unknown or unlawful origin.

Beware of stealing notes, hacking e-mails, snatching papers from a wastebasket. Theft is unethical. It's *illegal.* However, if you legally obtain material without a source's consent, *and* if there's legitimate public interest in the material, *and* if it's not available any other way — then you can evaluate whether the benefits outweigh the potential harm.

EXAMPLE:

◆ In 1998, The Cincinnati Enquirer published an 18-page report exposing corrupt business practices at Chiquita, the banana producer. Editors then found that, in researching the story, reporter Michael Gallagher had stolen 2,000 voice-mail messages from Chiquita. The paper paid Chiquita $14 million and printed an apology; Gallagher was fired. (He later enraged fellow journalists by revealing the name of his confidential source for those messages, who was then arrested.)

Many said Gallagher's Chiquita story was solid, and would have been just as solid *without* using those stolen tapes. But the debacle left readers distrusting what he'd written — and later led to even more firings, lawsuits and embarrassment.

BURNING A SOURCE

Deceiving or betraying the confidence of those who provide information for a story

A source confides in you; you promise confidentiality. But your story reveals her identity. She's fired. Or worse — arrested.

That's the most extreme example of burning a source. But there are lesser levels of betrayal: misleading someone into helping you with a story by distorting what you *really* plan to write, for instance. Or collecting quotes just to make someone sound stupid. Or seducing people into saying things they'll regret, letting them repair the damage after the story runs.

Burn a source just once, and that person may never trust reporters again.

EXAMPLE:

◆ In 1998, a Raleigh News & Observer reporter spent six weeks researching a sensitive portrait of Julio Granados — a typical young, hardworking, homesick Mexican grocery worker. But upon reading the front-page story, federal immigration officials realized Granados had no U.S. work permit. He was arrested and deported. The local Hispanic community felt betrayed and angry.

◆ During Minnesota's 1982 gubernatorial race, a Republican consultant leaked damaging documents about the Democratic candidate to two daily papers. They promised anonymity but later decided his identity was newsworthy, so they printed his name. He was fired — and later won a breach-of-contract lawsuit against both papers.

PLAGIARISM

Passing off someone else's words or ideas as your own

Of all the seven sins, plagiarism is the most loathsome, most shameful, most fatal to your credibility. If you don't understand plagiarism by now, *please put down this book* and go do some research. To explain in a nutshell:

The original. Take these words, spoken by President John F. Kennedy:
"Ask not what your country can do for you — ask what you can do for your country."
The plagiarism. We've changed some words, but they're still Kennedy's ideas:
Ask how you should be helping America. Don't ask how America should be helping you.
The solution. Attribute the ideas to Kennedy using quotes or paraphrases:
Don't ask what your country can do for you, Kennedy said; instead, "ask what you can do for your country."

Thus, to avoid plagiarism: either *rethink* it, *rework* it or *attribute* it.

EXAMPLE:

In 2004, Seattle Times business columnist Stephen H. Dunphy resigned after editors found several examples of plagiarism in his work — in this travel story, for instance:

From the original story, by Robert Selwitz:
"Walk down St. Paul's steps and make a right turn onto the first busy main road. Suddenly you'll be immersed in a series of narrow streets full of shops selling clothing, Chinese art and artifacts, herbal medicines, jewelry, crafts and utensils."

From Dunphy's plagiarized story:
"Upon leaving, walk down St. Paul's steps and make a right turn onto the first main thoroughfare. Suddenly you'll be immersed in a series of narrow streets full of shops selling clothing, Chinese art and artifacts, herbal medicines, jewelry, crafts and household utensils."

JAYSON BLAIR: A "PROFOUND BETRAYAL OF TRUST"

He was a star reporter with a brilliant future at a prestigious newspaper — but now he's a lesson in lapsed ethics, his fall from grace a grim warning to journalists everywhere.

Jayson Blair was just 27 when he resigned in shame from The New York Times in 2003.

"I lied and I lied — and then I lied some more," he later admitted. "I lied about where I had been, I lied about where I had found information. I lied about how I wrote the story. And these were no everyday little white lies — they were complete fantasies, embellished down to the tiniest made-up detail."

Blair's scoops on a variety of national stories at first impressed his colleagues, but later aroused their suspicions. After the San Antonio Express-News caught him plagiarizing one of its feature profiles, Blair's deceptions unraveled. An investigation by Times editors revealed that Blair had committed journalistic fraud in dozens of stories.

"The widespread fabrication and plagiarism represent a profound betrayal of trust and a low point in the 152-year history of the newspaper," the Times admitted in a detailed front-page analysis of the Blair scandal. "He fabricated comments. He concocted scenes. He lifted material from other newspapers and wire services. He selected details from photographs to create the impression he had been somewhere or seen someone, when he had not."

Blair's "tools of deceit," the Times explained, were his cell phone, his laptop computer and his "round-the-clock access to databases of news articles from which he stole." Using those tools, any clever reporter could create a brilliant story anywhere, anytime — just like Jayson Blair.

Journalistic ethics

Reporters and editors must maintain a high standard of professional behavior.

At left, you see an *actual photo* of a reporter taken in 1898, when the news business had sunk to an all-time low.* In that era of yellow journalism, the press's irresponsibility, sensationalism and warmongering dug a deep hole that reporters are *still* trying to crawl out of.

Nowadays, standards have risen. Journalists are better paid, better educated and painfully aware that public opinion will turn against them — swiftly, cruelly, even gleefully — anytime they're caught committing a journalistic sin.

Which is why it's essential that you develop a code of ethics: standards and values that guide your professional conduct. Tough dilemmas await you on the road ahead. How will you decide what to do?

*Some would say we have an ethical problem here ourselves. It's called *excessive sarcasm.*

DOING THE RIGHT THING: IT'S NOT ALWAYS AS EASY AS IT SEEMS

Suppose you discover that the mayor, a married 50-year-old man, has a mistress. Does that deserve a story? What if he's wining and dining her with city funds?

Suppose you find out the mayor was busted for selling pot when he was in college. Does that deserve a story? What if he's currently leading an anti-drug campaign?

Suppose the mayor tells a tasteless, racist joke at a private banquet. Does that deserve a story? If you print the joke, won't it offend readers? If you *don't* print it, won't it seem like a political cover-up to protect him?

Reporters and editors often face tough choices like these: deciding whether to print or withhold damaging facts and quotes, weighing the public's right to know against the harm individuals may suffer as a result.

Answers don't always come easily. But when facing ethical dilemmas, it's essential to ask the right questions. What purpose does it serve if we print this? Who gains? Who loses? Is it worth it? What best serves the readers?

Remember, doing what's *safe* or *legal* or *least likely to cause us trouble* isn't the same as doing what's *right*.

YOU MAKE THE CALL: THREE CASE STUDIES

What would you do if faced with these situations? Like most ethical dilemmas, these scenarios may provoke debate or discussion yet offer no easy answers.

A local grocer and his wife die when they're trapped inside their health-food store during a four-alarm fire. You're writing a follow-up story on the couple (Eaton Wright and Liv Good). You want to show how their family is coping with grief, how the neighbors are reacting to the tragedy, how the store became a local fixture — and you find, while doing your research, that Wright once spent 10 years in prison for child sexual abuse.

Do you include that fact in your story? Is Wright's criminal record relevant here? How do you weigh the value of that information against the pain its publication may cause Wright's family?

An anonymous tip alerts you that someone is mailing gunpowder in letters to the president of a local Bible college, threatening to "blow all you bastard devil-worshippers straight to hell this Halloween." When you contact the president, he urges you *not* to print anything about the threats, for fear of creating panic on campus. Local law-enforcement officials insist that publicity would jeopardize their investigation. Halloween is two days away.

Do you have a duty to warn the community of potential harm? Should you respect the authorities' wishes and hold the story? Or set your own deadline?

A famous major-league pitcher visits a college journalism class as a favor to his friend, the class's teacher. At one point while talking to the students, the pitcher says, "I used steroids for years. Why? Well, I made mistakes. Like all the times I tried cocaine and meth. I have truly used bad judgment sometimes."

Suddenly realizing what he'd just said, he added, "I'm speaking hypothetically, of course. I've always been clean."

Nobody asks a follow-up question. After the pitcher leaves, the teacher tells the class — some of whom write for the school paper — to disregard the drug remarks "out of respect for my friend, who did us a favor by visiting us today."

Should the school paper run a story that accurately quotes the pitcher, or pretend he never made those remarks?

A CODE OF ETHICS:
ESTABLISHING GUIDELINES FOR JOURNALISTS' CONDUCT

Most respectable professions — doctors, bankers, lawyers — set high standards for the behavior of their members. If they step out of line, they lose their credentials.

Journalists, on the other hand, have always included rebels and renegades. For a long time, reporters were uncredentialed and unscrupulous; newspapers were unfair and untrustworthy.

But in the late 1800s, journalists began to grow a conscience. One of the first was William McKean, managing editor of the Philadelphia Public Ledger, who issued a set of ethical guidelines for reporters to follow, with advice such as:

"Let the facts and reasoning tell the story, rather than rhetorical flourish."

"Take care to be right. It is bad to be late, but worse to be wrong."

"Do not say you KNOW when you have only HEARD."

Other newspapers and press organizations soon followed suit. And today, nearly every newsroom has formalized a system of ethical guidelines for all staffers to observe.

One of the best examples is the code of ethics reprinted below, which was created in 1996 by the Society of Professional Journalists.

CODE OF ETHICS
The Society of Professional Journalists

SEEK TRUTH AND REPORT IT

Journalists should be honest, fair and courageous in gathering, reporting and interpreting information.

Journalists should:

◆ Test the accuracy of information from all sources and exercise care to avoid inadvertent error. Deliberate distortion is never permissible.

◆ Diligently seek out subjects of news stories to let them respond to allegations of wrongdoing.

◆ Always question sources' motives before promising anonymity. Clarify conditions attached to any promise made in exchange for information. Keep promises.

◆ Make certain that headlines, photos, graphics and quotations do not misrepresent, oversimplify or highlight incidents out of context.

◆ Avoid undercover or other surreptitious methods of gathering information except when traditional open methods will not yield information vital to the public. Use of such methods should be explained as part of the story.

◆ Never plagiarize.

◆ Tell the story of the diversity and magnitude of the human experience boldly, even when it is unpopular to do so.

◆ Avoid imposing their own cultural values on others.

◆ Avoid stereotyping by race, gender, age, religion, ethnicity, geography, sexual orientation, disability, physical appearance or social status.

◆ Support the open exchange of views, even views they find repugnant.

◆ Give voice to the voiceless; official and unofficial sources of information

can be equally valid.

◆ Distinguish between advocacy and news reporting. Analysis and commentary should be labeled and not misrepresent fact or context.

◆ Distinguish news from advertising and shun hybrids that blur the lines between the two.

◆ Recognize a special obligation to ensure that the public's business is conducted in the open and that government records are open to inspection.

MINIMIZE HARM

Ethical journalists treat sources, subjects and colleagues as human beings deserving of respect.

Journalists should:

◆ Show compassion for those who may be affected adversely by news coverage. Use special sensitivity when dealing with children and inexperienced sources or subjects.

◆ Be sensitive when seeking or using interviews or photographs of those affected by tragedy or grief.

◆ Recognize that gathering and reporting information may cause harm or discomfort.

◆ Recognize that private people have a greater right to control information about themselves than do public officials and others who seek power, influence or attention. Only an overriding public need can justify intrusion into anyone's privacy.

◆ Show good taste. Avoid pandering to lurid curiosity.

◆ Be cautious about identifying juvenile suspects or victims of sex crimes.

◆ Be judicious about naming criminal suspects before the formal filing of charges.

◆ Balance a criminal suspect's fair trial rights with the public's right to be informed.

ACT INDEPENDENTLY

Journalists should be free of obligation to any interest other than the public's right to know.

Journalists should:

◆ Avoid conflicts of interest, real or perceived.

◆ Refuse gifts and special treatment, and shun secondary employment, political involvement and activities that may compromise integrity or damage credibility.

◆ Disclose unavoidable conflicts.

◆ Be vigilant about holding those with power accountable.

◆ Deny favored treatment to advertisers and special interests and resist their pressure to influence news coverage.

◆ Be wary of sources offering information for favors or money; avoid bidding for news.

BE ACCOUNTABLE

Journalists are accountable to their readers, listeners, viewers and each other.

Journalists should:

◆ Clarify and explain news coverage and invite dialogue with the public over journalistic conduct.

◆ Encourage the public to voice grievances against the news media.

◆ Admit mistakes and correct them promptly.

◆ Expose unethical practices of journalists and the news media.

◆ Abide by the same high standards to which they hold others.

IF THE PRESS IS SO DARN WONDERFUL, THEN WHY DOESN'T EVERYONE LOVE US?

Americans love to hate the media. Everybody's a critic — admit it, even *you* — when it comes to the way journalists do their jobs. Consider:

◆ **62% of Americans** say they don't trust the press.

◆ **59%** think newspapers are more concerned about making profits than serving the public interest.

◆ **58%** don't think journalists care about complaints of inaccuracies.

◆ **21%** rate the honesty and ethical standards of newspaper reporters as "high" or "very high." (That same 2004 poll rated 21 professions by their "honesty and ethical standards." Newspaper reporters ranked 16th, behind car mechanics — but ahead of lawyers, at least.)

What's driving this distrust and discontent? Is it a sense of betrayal brought on by a constant parade of media scandals, from Jayson Blair's fabrications to the forged-memo "Rathergate" affair at CBS?

Is it a reaction to the inaccuracies that plague too many news stories?

Is it a "shoot-the-messenger" response to the endless sleaze, gossip, disaster and disease-of-the-week melodramas journalists deliver?

Or are Americans unable to distinguish between serious, objective journalism and the polarizing, hyperbolic bombast of the loudmouths on talk radio and cable TV?

Whatever the reason, journalists are stuck with a negative image — and raising our ethical standards may be the best way to change that.

The PRESS ROOM ETHICS SURVEY

Standards of taste and ethical behavior vary from reporter to reporter. But if you want to see how your decision-making might compare to other reporters', take this survey. We distributed this questionnaire to our panel of 100 professional reporters (and their responses are screened in brown to let you take the survey without being influenced by their answers).

Keep in mind, 100 responses are *not* enough to accurately reflect the views of all reporters everywhere. But it's enough to suggest trends — and to trigger conversations with your colleagues or classmates about where you'd draw the line in your newsroom.

---

1 **You're interviewing a public official in her office. She leaves the room for few minutes. Do you peek at the letters and notes on her desk?**

☐ Yes (if I can read them upside down)
☐ No

Results from our reporting panel survey: 77% of respondents said "yes." As one reporter said, "I refuse to feel guilty about this. The public has a right to know what public officials are doing." Several reporters said they'd walk around the desk, too, but wouldn't actually touch any of the papers.

2 **Some newspapers have a policy forbidding reporters to participate in local political activity — marching in abortion rallies, canvassing for candidates, even sporting bumper stickers. Do you agree with that policy?**

☐ Yes
☐ No
☐ Only if it involves the reporter's beat

Results: 71% of our panelists said they agree with the policy; 29% agree only if it involves a reporter's beat. (Not a single respondent disagreed with the policy.) "When I took the job, I accepted being objective even in public," said one reporter. Another advised: "Join or participate in NO groups or activities that may taint your image to the readers. And all reporters should be registered non-affiliated voters."

3 **Is it OK to accept a gift or free meal from someone you cover on your beat?**

☐ Yes   ☐ No

Results: Only 31% said this was OK. "I let a source buy a meal every so often, as long as it's understood that I buy next time," one reporter said. "Everyone's got their price; mine isn't lunch."

Another reporter admitted that "I will sometimes accept a gift of flowers or a meal from 'civilians,' people who don't have regular contact with reporters who might be offended if I rejected them."

4 **If it's the ONLY way to get accurate information for an important story, would you:**

a) **Claim to be someone else?**

☐ Yes   ☐ No

b) **Avoid identifying yourself as a reporter?**

☐ Yes   ☐ No

c) **Secretly record a conversation without informing the other person?**

☐ Yes   ☐ No

Results: 90% of our panelists said they wouldn't lie about their identity, but 48% *would* avoid identifying themselves as reporters if necessary. And only 37% said they would secretly record a conversation — if it was legal. (Several reporters admitted they weren't sure whether surreptitious recording was illegal or not, since laws vary from state to state.)

5 **Have you ever:**

a) **Fabricated a quote or a fact for a story?**

☐ Yes   ☐ No

b) **Deliberately distorted a fact or quote?**

☐ Yes   ☐ No

c) **Deliberately ignored facts that would have forced you to hold or rewrite a story?**

☐ Yes   ☐ No

Results: 99% said they had never fabricated any facts or quotes; 93% had never distorted facts or quotes; and 94% had never ignored important facts.

6 **Would you approve if your newspaper exposed corruption by printing documents obtained without authorization?**

☐ Yes   ☐ No

Results: 93% said yes. "It depends on the scale of the corruption and how the documents were obtained," said one reporter. "Yes," said another, "as long as we're not talking theft or major deceit."

7 **Do you approve of using anonymous sources:**

a. **When it's the only way to include important information in the public interest?**

☐ Yes   ☐ No

b. **When someone wants to avoid personal or professional embarrassment?**

☐ Yes   ☐ No

c. **When someone gives you a really good quote, but you're unable to verify that person's identity?**

☐ Yes   ☐ No

Results: 93% of our panelists approve of using anonymous sources in example "a." Said one reporter: "If you're right and it's a bombshell, somebody will back it up." Said another: "Yes, but the information must be independently verified."

Only 34% approved of using anonymous sources to avoid embarrassment ("to protect a child's identity, for example," one reporter said). And just 22% answered yes to "c." "Depends on the context," said one. "If it's a conference where someone in the audience makes a statement and you can't find that person later, fine."

8 **Do you approve of news organizations paying money for a crucial interview, if it's the only way to get someone to talk?**

☐ Yes   ☐ No

Results: 86% of our panelists said "no."

9 **Do you think there is too much self-censorship at your newspaper (i.e., editors are too sensitive about offending readers or advertisers)?**

☐ Yes   ☐ No

Results: 65% think there's too much self-censorship. "Absolutely," said one reporter. "As I was told years ago, 'They don't have to like us, they just have to read us.' This is a huge problem!" said another. "We were not allowed to print civil suits of a major grocery advertiser without warning him first!"

10 Thinking back over all the stories you've written, which of the following statements apply? (You can agree with more than one statement.)

- ☐ I have probably plagiarized material, but if I did, it was inadvertent.
- ☐ I have deliberately plagiarized some material.
- ☐ I have never consciously plagiarized any material.

Results: 15% of our panelists said they might have inadvertently plagiarized; 85% said they'd never plagiarized.
None admitted deliberately plagiarizing.

11 In a public meeting, the governor describes a proposed law as "a bunch of bullshit." Your paper's policy would be to:

- ☐ Print the exact phrase
- ☐ Print the word "bull----"
- ☐ Paraphrase with a synonym like "crap" or "manure"

Results: 18% of our panelists said their papers would print the exact phrase; another 18% said they'd use a milder synonym; 62% said they'd print "bull----." Some sample comments from panelists:

◆ "Exact phrase, if it's the governor. For someone not in the public eye, we probably would use the asterisks."

◆ "The fact that he or she publicly used profanity is nearly as important as his or her opinion on whatever the issue is."

◆ "Even those synonyms would likely be considered too unseemly for my newspaper. We'd be more likely to say something like: *The governor strongly opposes the proposed law.*"

12 A friend of yours is the lead singer of a local rock group. Your editor wants you to review the band. Would you agree to do it?

☐ Yes   ☐ No

13 Your editor insists that you review your friend's band. At the show, the singer is stone drunk. It's obvious to everyone. It's a terrible show. If you write an honest review, you could ruin his reputation. He asks you to come back the next night, when he promises to stay sober and do a great show. Do you agree?

☐ Yes   ☐ No

Results: 95% of our panelists said they'd avoid reviewing their friend's band. But if forced to do it, only 31% said they'd agree to return for a second night's show. ("But I'd write about both shows," one said.)

14 A local coach just lost the big game. In a one-on-one postgame interview with you, he utters a racial epithet about his quarterback — an amazingly juicy quote that will outrage the community. He calls you in the newsroom an hour later and says he was distraught about losing, and he begs you not to run the quote. What do you do?

- ☐ Run it
- ☐ Remove it
- ☐ Depends on whether he threatened me or asked me politely

Results: 61% said they'd run it; 17% said they'd remove it; and 22% said it depends. Some sample comments:

◆ "Run it, along with his comments from the phone call."

◆ "Remove it, keep the quote and begin an investigation into the coach's racism."

◆ "Depends. I'm going to assume that I've been covering this team all season. Did the quote reflect ongoing and underlying racial tensions that have been glimpsed throughout the season? If so, print it. Was it truly an aberration, as the coach claims? Then give him the benefit of the doubt."

15 After painstaking research, you write a story implicating a local businessman in a sleazy scandal. Your publisher spikes the story because this man is a major advertiser. Would you leak the story to a friend of yours who works for a competing publication?

☐ Yes   ☐ No

Results: 64% said they'd leak the story — although several reporters said, "No, but I'd start looking for another job."

16 You're writing a story about a local quarterback who was voted the conference's player of the year. You discover he's been arrested for drunken driving. You ask him about this, and he angrily replies that it has nothing to do with his football accomplishments. Do you include this information in your story?

☐ Yes   ☐ No

Results: 78% said yes. Some comments:

◆ "Yes, but not out of spite. You have to get at what it's meant to his career. How has he overcome it?"

◆ "Yes, along with his angry comments. Then I would look more closely at his past and his record and talk to others who have known him."

◆ "Yes, but only if they're relevant (i.e., is he looked to as a leader and exemplar?)"

17 A popular local rapper releases a song that becomes a huge hit, but it contains lyrics that many women find degrading and offensive. You're writing about the controversy. You would:

- ☐ Print the offensive lyrics (so readers can decide for themselves)
- ☐ Avoid printing the lyrics (why give this guy more free publicity?)
- ☐ Paraphrase them and send readers to a Web site that shows the actual lyrics

Results: 31% would print the lyrics; 7% would not; and 62% would paraphrase them and send readers to a Web site for more.

18 You're writing about the outbreak of a new sexually transmitted disease in your city. Would your paper let you write a graphic description of the sexual activity that spreads the disease?

☐ Yes   ☐ No

Results: 52% said yes. "Most papers now will refer to oral and/or anal sex," one reporter observed, "and I wouldn't consider the terms themselves graphic. But how much more would you really need to say?"
"No — that would be *hell* no," said another.
And a final comment: "No," one reporter answered, "but I'd love to give it a shot!"

19 In 1977, a team of undercover reporters from the Chicago Sun-Times opened a bar called The Mirage. For four months, they documented corrupt inspectors asking for bribes and kickbacks. The paper's resulting 25-part series was powerful and popular. It nearly won a Pulitzer Prize — but in a controversial decision, the Pulizer board decided it would be wrong to condone or reward dishonest, deceptive journalism. Do you agree with that decision?

☐ Yes   ☐ No

Results: 64% disagreed with the decision. "If they really opened and ran the bar, it's not deceptive," one remarked. Said another: "Reporters are allowed to own bars, as far as I know."

20 You're the features editor. For a food page running the week before Easter, a reporter wants to print bunny-rabbit recipes. Some staffers feel this a fun, irreverent idea. Others argue that it's an exercise in bad taste that will offend readers. Would you run the recipes?

☐ Yes   ☐ No

Results: 60% said no. "I'm all for being edgy," one reporter said, "but that is just asking for trouble. There are better battles to fight."

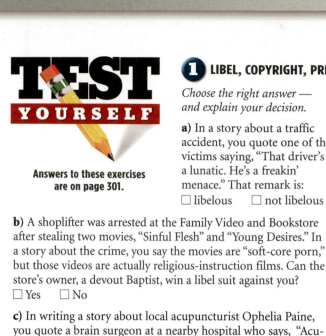

Answers to these exercises
are on page 301.

① LIBEL, COPYRIGHT, PRIVACY: SOME HYPOTHETICAL SITUATIONS

*Choose the right answer —
and explain your decision.*

a) In a story about a traffic accident, you quote one of the victims saying, "That driver's a lunatic. He's a freakin' menace." That remark is:
☐ libelous   ☐ not libelous

b) A shoplifter was arrested at the Family Video and Bookstore after stealing two movies, "Sinful Flesh" and "Young Desires." In a story about the crime, you say the movies are "soft-core porn," but those videos are actually religious-instruction films. Can the store's owner, a devout Baptist, win a libel suit against you?
☐ Yes   ☐ No

c) In writing a story about local acupuncturist Ophelia Paine, you quote a brain surgeon at a nearby hospital who says, "Acupuncturists are all quacks. They'll kill you if you're not careful." Paine considers this defamatory. "Your story will bankrupt me," she says. Could she win a libel suit against your publication?
☐ Yes   ☐ No

d) You write a story describing how Al Bino confessed to police after attempting to murder his wife. After the story runs, a police department spokesman admits they gave you the wrong name; Al Bino was merely a witness to the crime. Could Al Bino win a libel suit against you for the lie you printed?
☐ Yes   ☐ No

e) In a football-game story, you quote the losing coach, who says, "That referee is blind. He cost us the game. He's got no business officiating in this league." Videotapes, however, prove the referee made the right call. Could the referee win a libel suit against you?
☐ Yes   ☐ No

f) You're standing in the hallway, waiting to interview a professor from Iraq. As you lean against the door to his office, you hear him making pro-terrorist, anti-American statements. You take careful notes. Later, you confront him with his remarks. He calls them lies and threatens to sue you if you print them. Could he win?
☐ Yes   ☐ No

g) On his late-night NBC show, Conan O'Brien makes several lengthy jokes about your town and your school. You want to reprint those jokes in your newspaper, but the editor says you can't do it without getting approval from NBC. Those jokes are copyrighted, he says, and NBC could sue the paper if you reprint them verbatim without permission. Is your editor correct?
☐ He's right; you need permission.   ☐ He's wrong; you don't.

h) In writing a story about an outspoken anti-abortion activist, you print that she was once arrested for trying to bomb an abortion clinic. But you've read the court records incorrectly: she only testified at someone else's trial. Your newspaper has run a correction, but she's still furious. Can she win a libel suit?
☐ Yes   ☐ No

i) In that story about the pro-life activist, you reveal that she was once arrested for obtaining an illegal abortion herself, back in 1970 (before Roe v. Wade made abortions legal). She claims that you've violated her right to privacy by revealing confidential information about her medical history. If she takes you to court, can she win her case?
☐ Yes   ☐ No

j) Gossip about your school's cheerleaders is posted on a Web site. You reprint it in your weekly newspaper opinion column, clearly identifying your source. An angry cheerleader reads your column, gets upset and decides to sue for libel. Who is most liable?
☐ You   ☐ The gossip Web site   ☐ Both of you

② LEGAL CONCEPTS AND DEFINITIONS

a) "Libel" is generally defined as any published statement that damages someone's reputation.
☐ True ☐ False

b) It's legal to take photographs of victims at the scene of an accident, even if they specifically forbid you to do so.
☐ True ☐ False

c) As a result of numerous Supreme Court decisions, libel laws are now consistent from state to state.
☐ True ☐ False

d) When writing a news story, it's considered plagiarism to lift sentences verbatim from a press release.
☐ True ☐ False

e) Someone gives you secret information. In return, you promise to conceal his identity. If you suddenly change your mind and publish his name, that's called "burning a source."
☐ True ☐ False

f) Someone gives you secret information. In return, you promise to conceal his identity. If you suddenly change your mind and publish his name, he could sue you for violating a verbal contract.
☐ True ☐ False

g) If you cruelly and unfairly criticize a public figure, that's called "actual malice."
☐ True ☐ False

h) A "shield law" prevents a reporter from being sued for libel.
☐ True ☐ False

i) The Privacy Protection Act prevents the police from confiscating any notes you've taken for a story.
☐ True ☐ False

j) You can publish defamatory statements about people, but as long as you don't identify them by name, they can't successfully sue you for libel.
☐ True ☐ False

k) It's permissible to reprint images you find on a Web site as long as you clearly identify and credit your source.
☐ True ☐ False

l) The "fair comment and criticism" privilege allows you the freedom to say whatever you want when you write a review of a public performance.
☐ True ☐ False

From print to the Web

Will electronic newspapers replace dead-tree newspapers someday? Probably.

Print journalism won't go extinct. But it'll become increasingly difficult to compete against the allure of digital media, where editors can combine text, photos, audio, video, animated graphics, interactive chat and much more.

Online media offer readers more variety — and better yet, more control. Stories, images and digital extras can be linked together in layers, with related options just a click away. That's why *navigation* is a crucial factor on news Web sites. Editors must design sites that are informative, inviting and intuitively logical; sites that let users roam at random, poking their noses into every intriguing corner, following their curiosities to customize their news.

Instead of arranging stories side by side the way traditional newspapers do, like this — 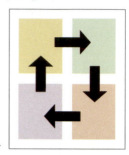 — online news sites link related topics in layers that allow readers to roam from story to story, like this —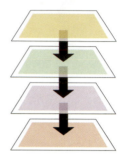

To fulfill the potential of new media — and to satisfy Web-savvy readers — reporters need to develop new storytelling techniques. Why simply shovel long, wordy stories online when you can enhance them with multimedia? Tomorrow's journalists will plan and produce their news stories in dramatically different ways.

WHAT'S THE DIFFERENCE BETWEEN PRINT STORIES AND WEB STORIES?

One crucial difference between print and online stories is *timeliness:* Web stories can be posted seconds after they're written and updated constantly as events unfold, just like news on radio and TV.

Breaking news stories are usually written by the beat reporter who'll produce the final print story, though these "continuous news versions" are often pieced together by staffers using other media sources or the beat reporter's notes.

As New York Times political reporter Richard Stevenson explained, "If I feel that I don't have a story nailed down sufficiently, or that I don't have time … or that taking the time would prevent me from doing the reporting I need to do, then I won't agree to do a continuous news version."

Other differences between the two media are more visibly apparent. Take the newspaper story at left, for example. It uses a big photo to catch your eye. But on Web pages like the one at right, images usually run smaller, since you can't predict readers' screen sizes or connection speeds. (Click on that photo, though, and it will enlarge.)

That printed page uses text that's too small to read on a computer screen. Online text uses bigger type, and stories run in just one column — which forces readers to scroll downward as they read. The story at right would fill two screens; longer stories can fill *dozens.* That's why long stories seem longer (and less reader-friendly) on the Web.

In print, a "story" consists of just text, photos and graphics. Online, though, you can add links to audio, video, other Web sites, archived stories, blogs, podcasts or extra interactive elements. A news *story*, in other words, may become part of a complex multimedia *package.* Though the options are more diverse, the journalistic standards and reporting techniques should remain the same.

Megan Peter (left) and Jennifer Christy block a shot by Central's Amy Bethany in Saturday night's state championship game.

State champs!

The Bugler girls' volleyball team defeats Central to capture title

By LEX MINNIEAR
Bugle-Beacon staff

It took seven long years. But the Lady Bugler volleyball team of Lincoln High School captured the state championship Friday night for the first time since the 1994 season.

The final win against Central High School brought the team's overall record to 22-6, setting a school record.

The Buglers took the match against Central in only two games with scores of 15-7 for each. Teammates Robin Fox, Holly Lukas, Krystyna Wolniakowski and Lorrie Richardson landed 100 percent in serves to help clutch the victory. Patty Snow and Claire Puchy combined for 11 kills while Kathy Hughes and Sue Payseno chipped in with two hits.

Coach Georgia Eldridge was pleased with their performance. "I love these girls," she said. "There was never a point in this tournament when I thought we wouldn't go all the way."

Eldridge credited the Elite Eight seniors, Kathryn Wigginton, Nancy Casey, Holly Lukas, Krystyna Wolniakowski, Lorrie

INSIDE
◆ **Tournament results:** How other local teams fared / Page 7
◆ **The MVP:** Betty Coffman wins for her game-saving spike / Page 8
◆ **Fan reaction:** Bugle supporters celebrate in the streets / Page 9

Richardson, Patty Snow, Claire Puchy, and Kathy Hughes for keeping the team focused and under control.

"They've each done a good job playing important roles for us and I am very proud of everything these kids have accomplished in the last two seasons," said Coach Eldridge.

The Lady Buglers were the runners-up in the state finals last year behind Northville. Nine of the returning players were on the team that advanced to the regional quarterfinals but were defeated by North Farmington.

Returning senior Holly Lukas said, "We determine our destiny. There is no moun-

tain too high if we play as a team."

Freshman team star Lori Robinson proclaimed, "We showed them who's boss out there on the court! Now everyone knows we're back, we're bad — deal with it!"

The team showed a lot of character after coming back to beat North Farmington earlier in the district race. After being defeated by the Lady Eagles previously in the season, they knew the Central matchup would be crucial.

The Central coach was philosophical. "We gave it our best," said Marion Frederick. "But tonight, the best team won. I've got to hand it to the Buglers. They played a heckuva match out there."

The Buglers took the match against Central in only two games with scores of 15-7 for each. Teammates Robin Fox, Holly Lukas, Krystyna Wolniakowski and Lorrie Richardson landed 100 percent in serves to help clutch the victory. Patty Snow and Claire Puchy combined for 11 kills while Kathy Hughes and Sue Payseno chipped in with two hits.

Coach Georgia Eldridge was pleased with their performance. "I love these girls," she said. "There was never a point when I

Sports

PRINT THIS STORY   E-MAIL THIS STORY

Bugler girls' volleyball team wins state championship

By LEX MINNIEAR
Bugle-Beacon staff
8:30 p.m. – Nov. 20, 2005

It took seven long years. But the Lincoln High School Lady Bugler volleyball team captured the state championship Friday night for the first time since the 1994 season.

The final win against Central High School brought the team's overall record to 22-6, a school record.

Megan Peter (left) and Jennifer Christy block a shot by Central's Amy Bethany in Saturday night's state championship game. (Bugle-Beacon photo)

The Buglers took the match against Central in only two games with scores of 15-7 for each. Teammates Robin Fox, Holly Lukas, Krystyna Wolniakowski and Lorrie Richardson landed 100 percent in serves to help clutch the victory. Patty Snow and Claire Puchy combined for 11 kills while Kathy Hughes and Sue Payseno chipped in with two hits.

MORE ON THE MATCH
◆ **Tournament results:** How three other local girls' teams fared.

VIDEO HIGHLIGHTS
◆ **The winning point** and other memorable moments from the match.
◆ **Fan reaction:** Bugle fans dance in the streets.

Coach Georgia Eldridge was pleased with their performance. "I love these girls," she said. "There was never a point in this tournament when I thought we wouldn't go all the way."

Eldridge credited the Elite Eight seniors, Kathryn Wigginton, Nancy Casey, Holly Lukas, Krystyna Wolniakowski, Lorrie Richardson, Patty Snow, Claire Puchy, and Kathy Hughes for keeping the team focused and under control.

"They've each done a good job playing important roles for us and I am very proud of everything these kids have accomplished in the last two seasons," said Coach Eldridge.

The Lady Buglers were the runners-up in the state finals last year behind Northville. Nine of the returning players were on the team that advanced to the regional quarterfinals but were defeated by North Farmington.

Returning senior Holly Lukas said, "We determine our destiny. There is no mountain too high if we play as a team."

The Central coach was philosophical. "We gave it our best," said Marion Frederick. "But tonight, the best team won. I've got to hand it to the Buglers. They played a heckuva match out there."

The Bugle-Beacon's Lex Minniear can be reached at (394)555-8776 or minnear@bugle.com

▲ BACK TO TOP

FROM HOME PAGE TO STORY: NAVIGATING ONLINE NEWS SITES

There's something inefficient — *messy, even* — about the way newspapers are put together. For example:

◆ Unrelated stories and photos are sandwiched together on the page, often colliding in awkward, distracting ways.

◆ Pages are hard to navigate; stories are hard to find. If you're passionate about a particular topic — hockey, for instance, or the environment — there's no easy way to search the paper and discover what subjects have been covered.

◆ Stories are often forced to jump from one page to another. Readers hate when that happens.

◆ Readers are subject to the editor's news judgment. The stories *you're* most interested in often don't make the cut.

◆ Space is limited. And as newsroom budgets tighten, the available space — the "news hole"— shrinks.

Online news sites, however, avoid many of these problems. Pages like the one at right don't exist on the Web, so many of the problems that affect them — like squeezing unrelated stories into a limited space until everything fits perfectly — don't exist, either.

Except on the home page.

Just as the front page is a doorway to the printed newspaper, the home page is a gateway to the online news. And because the home page links users to every related page, it must be comprehensive, yet easy to navigate: busy, yet *clean.* Story links require compelling headlines and concise, engaging summaries.

Here's what you'll find on a typical newspaper home page, as we transform the newspaper at right into an online edition:

This front page uses the same stories as the Web version below. How is it different? It's bigger. More portable. Not nearly as busy, because it offers fewer options to readers. By comparison, the Web site's home page uses little text; to read a story, you must follow its link to another page.

Time/date: Readers need to know how current this news is. Sites updated more than once a day should include the time of the update, as well.

Index (or *navigation bar):* It's easy to get lost in cyberspace. That's why a complete, clickable index is vital on the home page — and on every other page in the site, as well.

Lead story: This text is just a compelling summary, but you can click the headline to link to the full story, or click the icons below to see graphics, photos and a video clip. That lead photo may seem small, but large images take up space and force pages to download much more slowly.

Navigation buttons: These quickly link users to the site's most popular sections; the index down the left side is more complete.

Search engine: This helps users hunt for specific topics, dates, names, etc.

Ads/promotions: These are usually positioned horizontally at the top of the page or (better) in this right-hand rail.

Interactive extras: Online news sites provide features that print media can't: webcams, slideshows, polls, blogs, animated graphics and more. See our list on page 158.

Page depth: This page was designed to fit on one screen so readers won't have to scroll. It's best to avoid never-ending vertically-scrolling home pages (readers don't like to scroll unless there's a good reason) but that's not always easy. Usually, the bigger the site, the deeper the home page.

Footer: Every page on every Web site should include copyright information. But this is also a good spot to solicit e-mail feedback from readers or provide links to other sections of the site.

Links: Click on these headlines to visit the site's other top stories. Many sites add summaries or photos to these headline collections, but those can deepen the page and slow the download time.

Media convergence

Text + photos + audio + video + graphics = multimedia.

Suppose you decided to profile Ludwig van Gogh, a brilliant painter/composer. Which medium, or *media,* would produce the best story?

To display his paintings, you'd use photographs. To present his music, you'd use audio recordings. To show him at work — conducting an orchestra or painting — you'd use video footage. To explain the meaning and impact of his art, you'd use text.

In short, to create the ideal profile, you'd need *multimedia. Cross-platform journalism. Media convergence.* Whatever you call it, it's an idea whose time has finally come. Stories once trapped on paper can now be posted online; stories once confined to text and photographs now incorporate audio, video and interactivity.

Technological innovations are transforming 21st-century journalism. Your job, your newsroom, even the stories you write will soon change dramatically. So get ready.

CONVERGENCE: COMING SOON TO A NEWSROOM NEAR YOU

Different journalists mean different things when they talk about convergence. (Some even avoid the word, preferring to use the term *fusion.*) But generally, convergence takes three forms:

NEWSROOM CONVERGENCE

In a converged newsroom, journalists from different media (TV, radio, newspaper, online) all share the same workspace instead of occupying separate offices in separate buildings.

One of the most notable examples is the News Center in Tampa, Fla. In 2000, the staffs of the Tampa Tribune, WFLA-TV and TBO.com — all owned by Media General Inc. — moved into a huge $40-million facility with a TV studio on the first floor and a joint newsroom above it.

Sharing a newsroom encourages cross-platform cooperation. When editors from different media attend the same meetings and plan coverage together, they can steer each story to the format that tells it best.

NEWSGATHERING CONVERGENCE

Here, reporters, editors and photographers collaborate on story production. In its simplest form, news crews might share a helicopter to report on a flood. A TV newscast might borrow

From a small studio in the business department of the Orlando Sentinel newsroom, Wilma Colon delivers a daily news-headline Webcast that appears on the Sentinel's home page. Colon is a "converged reporter" who also writes for the Web, reports for El Sentinel (a Spanish-language weekly) and produces segments for the local Telemundo telecast.

one of the newspaper's graphics. A TV reporter might cover an event for broadcast, then write a longer story for the Web site.

With training, print reporters learn to deliver TV news reports; photojournalists shoot photos, video *and* conduct interviews.

In other words, journalists *multitask* in *multimedia,* whether it's one story produced by a team of TV, print and online staffers — or one reporter preparing variations of one story for several different media.

CONTENT CONVERGENCE

This is where the final story is presented in multimedia form, combining text, images, audio, video, blogs, podcasts, slideshows — the options are continually expanding. At present, content convergence is still in its infancy, but you can glimpse the future on innovative Web sites.

Imagine, years from now, a new hybrid medium combining the audio and video of TV, the responsiveness and resources of the Web, the portability and print quality of newspapers. Editors and reporters will become "content producers" trained to choose the most effective, entertaining storytelling techniques from a vast menu of multimedia options.

THE CONVERGED REPORTER: MYTH OR INEVITABILITY?

At the News Center in Tampa, Victoria Lim is the consumer reporter for WFLA-TV. But she also expands her TV reports into stories for the Tampa Tribune, where she writes a weekly column. And she wins awards for the multimedia projects she posts on the TBO.com Web site.

Lim is known as a "converged reporter." In the future, will all journalists need to exhibit that much versatility?

Some say yes. They point to Preston Mendenhall, MSNBC's international editor, who traveled to Afghanistan in 2001 lugging a backpack that contained a laptop, a satellite phone, digital cameras and microphones. Transmitting reports from the field, he single-handedly acted as reporter, producer, editor and engineer.

Others are less enthusiastic about "backpack journalism." Some, like online journalist Martha Stone, worry about the "mush of mediocrity" that results when you overtax busy journalists.

"While some multimedia journalists can handle a variety of tasks efficiently and professionally," Stone says, "most will only deliver mediocre journalism. While some may excel at writing the story for print or broadcast, they may produce poor-quality video or still pictures. . . . Quality comes from those journalists who practice a defined job, be it writer, videographer, photographer or editor."

Asking reporters to become do-it-all superjournalists is unrealistic, it's true. Still, as newsrooms evolve, reporters should be prepared to expand their skills, whether that means learning how to post audio interviews, write blogs or record podcasts.

"If I were still reporting," says new-media guru Rob Curley, "I'd be doing everything I could to show just how invaluable I was to a news organization's ability to survive all the changes we're going through."

Search
[Go!]
underwritten by:
Ace Sports & Tickets

NAVIGATION

Sports

Men's B-Ball
↳ Stories
↳ Archives
↳ Schedule
↳ Roster
↳ Statistics
↳ Recruiting
↳ Message Boards
↳ 2003 Media Day
↳ Late Night '03
↳ 2004 NCAA Tournament
↳ '03-'04 Season
↳ '02-'03 Season
↳ Ask Gary
↳ Need Tickets?
↳ New Seating Plan
↳ History
↳ Coaches
↳ Multimedia
↳ Video
↳ Audio
↳ Photo Galleries
↳ Changing of the Court
↳ Self hired
↳ More on Men's Basketball

Women's B-Ball
Football
Baseball
Softball
Track & Field
Cross Country
Men's Golf
Women's Golf
Soccer
Swimming
Rowing
Tennis
Volleyball
Bowling

Miscellaneous
The KU Cheerleaders
New Band Uniforms
Self Hired
AD Lew Perkins
Strength Center
Columns
Chat Transcripts
Schedules
Message Boards
Recruiting
Changing Of The Court
New Seating Plan
Inside Look At KU Football
E-mail Edition
Weather
Handheld Edition
Border War
Jayhawks in the media
Whack Woodling
Multimedia
Photo Galleries
Screensavers

BASKETBALL
Home | Basketball

🗨 Discuss story   ✉ E-mail story   🖨 Printer Friendly   ✉ E-mail editor

UAB's 'hell' hath no fury

Kansas shreds press, rolls into Elite Eight

By **Gary Bedore**, Assistant Sports Editor
SATURDAY, MARCH 27, 2004

Sᴛ. Lᴏᴜɪꜱ — Alabama-Birmingham didn't exactly put Kansas University through 40 minutes of hell Friday night.

Scott McClurg/Journal-World Photo
Kansas University's Aaron Miles (11) blows past UAB's Gabe Kennedy for an easy basket in the Jayhawks' 100-74 rout of the Blazers. Miles finished with 13 points and 10 assists in KU's win Friday in St. Louis.

It was more like 40 minutes of hilarity for the No. 4-seeded Jayhawks, who shredded UAB's vaunted press in racing to a 100-74 victory over the No. 9-seeded Blazers -- KU's most lopsided win in 23 Sweet 16 appearances.

"It was like playing in the rec center -- attack, take it to the hole when you're not guarded and score," KU junior guard Keith Langford said after scoring nine points at the Edward Jones Dome. "We had a lotta easy baskets tonight."

The Jayhawks (24-8), who easily advanced to Sunday's Elite Eight meeting with third-seed Georgia Tech, converted 30 baskets in 56 attempts (53.6 percent) and 36 free throws in 44 tries. The outmanned Blazers resorted to 40 minutes of hacking KU junior forward Wayne Simien.

Simien, 6-for-8 on field goals, hit 18 of 20 free throws. He collected 30 points and five assists.

His 18 free throws made were the most by a Jayhawk since Wilt Chamberlain converted 18 of 23 against Nebraska in 1958. He was four off the school record of 22, set by Vern Long in 1911. In those days, just one player on a team shot free throws, so there's an asterisk by Long's name.

Kansas' 36 made free throws were a school record for the NCAA Tournament.

"It's nice to be up there with somebody as great as Wilt," Simien said. "I knew I was up there, but didn't know I had 18. I'm a pretty big load inside for them to handle matchup-wise."

"I think that (fouling) is all they could do to prevent me from getting to the basket."

Simien, who had 12 points the first nine minutes as KU blazed to a 28-13 lead, was recipient of pinpoint passes from his teammates.

"Collectively we did a great job handling their pressure," Simien said of pressure that UAB used to oust top-seeded Kentucky in the second round. "We went against seven or eight guys on the court all week. You take away three ... and it's like cake with five."

Indeed, KU coach Bill Self looked like a mastermind Friday. His week-long practice tactic of having his starting unit go against eight players at a time prepared the Jayhawks for the Blazers' pressure.

"Our scout team busted our tails all week. They killed us at practice. I give them credit for this win," KU freshman J.R. Giddens said after scoring 18 points off 8-of-14 shooting.

Jeff Graves and Aaron Miles also were in double digits with 13.

"They were on defense the whole time at practice," Giddens added. "They never let up in giving it to us. Tonight when we saw five guys pressing, it was a lot easier."

Point guard Miles, who had 10 assists, six turnovers and four steals, agreed.

INTERNET *ENHANCED*
📷 **See the photos:** KU-UAB photo gallery
🔊 **Hear Bill:** KU-UAB postgame comments
📹 **6Sports video: Jayhawks blaze past UAB**
📹 **6News video: Local fans cheer on the 'Hawks**
📊 **Get the stats:** KU-UAB box score
📊 **UAB animated plays**
📊 **KU animated playbook**

Stories
📄 **UAB's 'hell' hath no fury**
📄 **Woodling: Post-UK Syndrome benefits Jayhawks**
📄 **KU among Elite again**
📄 **Miles has ball breaking press**
📄 **Misses hurt Blazers' press**
📄 **Langford: KU playing its best ball**
📄 **Jackets win game, lose standout**

More Multimedia
📹 **6Sports video: Simien leads team to victory**
📹 **6Sports video: KU trounces UAB, 100-74**
📱 **Sign up for NCAA tournament and KU game cell phone updates**

Beat writers' pre-game chat
💬 **Chat wrap with Bedore, Norris**

MULTIPLATFORM REPORTING: CONVERGENCE AT THE JOURNAL-WORLD

Since the emergence of convergence in the 1990s, most of the pioneering newsrooms have been in Florida: Tampa. Sarasota. Orlando. Naples.

And then there's Lawrence, Kansas.

In downtown Lawrence, a renovated post office has been rechristened the News Center. That's where print, broadcast and online journalists work side by side to produce a daily newspaper, a Web site and TV newscasts for the family-owned World Company.

"The seating areas are not broken down by medium, they're broken down by beat," explained media director Rob Curley, who has since relocated to the Naples Daily News. "So all the political reporters sit together. All the courts and cops reporters — print, television and online — sit together."

The result? The Lawrence Journal-World, a 21,000-circulation daily, prints a story about a basketball victory at the University of Kansas — while LJWorld.com, a partner Web site, offers Jayhawk fans the added value of animated graphics and slideshows, along with audio and video from the local cable channel, 6News Lawrence.

The results are impressive. And popular, too: Those Web pages register up to 13 million views a month.

"We believe it is important to look upon our business as an 'information business,' not merely a newspaper or a cable television operation," publisher Dolph Simons Jr. noted at the paper's 100th anniversary in 1991.

"We want to stay abreast of new developments and be able to deliver news and advertising, as well as other information, however a reader or advertiser might desire." ▼

MULTIMEDIA EXTRAS FOR THIS SPORTS STORY:

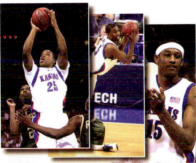

AUDIO CLIPS: A sound file plays post-game comments by the team's coach.

PHOTO GALLERY: In a newspaper, photographers may be able to run only a few of the game photos they shoot. But this popular Web feature provides fans with dozens of extra images of players, coaches and fans.

ANIMATED PLAYBOOK: Click the "PLAY" button and this graphic shows you how one of the big plays unfolds.

MORE STORIES: Related or expanded stories — which may or may not have run in the printed newspaper — offer additional angles on the game.

CELL PHONE UPDATES: If you're a fan but can't watch the games, this service sends scores and stats as text messages to your cell phone.

PRE-GAME CHAT: Sports reporters from the Journal-World and the opposing team's paper (The Birmingham News) went online to answer questions from fans a few hours before the game.

SPORTS VIDEO: This is the basketball story from the Channel 6 newscast, featuring video highlights from the game. For some stories, reporters might tape special webcasts that include additional game footage or interviews with coaches, players and fans.

Online storytelling options

With so many useful options available, why simply shovel text online?

Years ago, Web developers coined a sarcastic term — *shovelware* — to describe text that's lifted from a printed publication, then dumped onto a Web site without adapting or enhancing it. Shovelware is easy. It's a no-brainer. But it's lazy. And ultimately, if you load your news site with shovelware, readers will decide that either you don't care — or you *just don't get it*.

The Web offers vast storytelling potential, but you'll never tap it if you're too dependent on text. So put down that shovel and pick up some of these smart new tools instead.

AUDIO, VIDEO, ANIMATION, INTERACTION: NEW FORMS OF NEWS DELIVERY

Before going any further, let's be clear that *text is a terrific tool*. The printed word remains the fundamental building block of online journalism. So don't discard text; *add* to it. Choose other tools to enhance your storytelling. As your Web vocabulary grows, you'll find you can sometimes even eliminate text — but that's the exception, not the goal.

Choose the right tools for every story. As digital news pioneer Jonathan Dube wisely recommends:

Use print to explain.
Use multimedia to show.
Use interactives to demonstrate and engage.

With that in mind, here's a list of online options to add to your reporting toolbox:

MULTIMEDIA OPTIONS

Video. Some converged news sites repackage clips from TV newscasts. That's a good start, but newscasts may be too brief. Expand your online coverage with video interviews, documentary-style packages, even digital footage submitted by readers. Remember, video is a terrific way to capture atmosphere and action.

Audio. Add audio files of speeches, interviews, musical excerpts — or to demonstrate sounds that play a part in a story. Listen to the radio reporters on National Public Radio for good examples of audio storytelling techniques.

Webcams and webcasts. For many events (parades, political debates, a major storm on the coast), a video camera can provide your site with live, streaming images.

Podcasts. These are basically radio versions of stories for users who'd rather listen than read. They're downloadable, too, for playback at a later time. Like radio news stories, podcasts are most effective when they incorporate sound bites, music and other audio extras.

Animated graphics. These are like the charts, maps and diagrams you see in newspapers — except they're animated to simulate motion. They'll illustrate the path of the hurricane or show, step by step, how a new gizmo works. Some add sound; some are "clickable," giving users more choices and control.

INTERACTIVE OPTIONS

Live chats. These are interviews — of newsmakers, experts, even newsroom staffers — asking questions submitted by readers and moderated by a reporter or editor. To ensure successful reader participation, these Q-and-A sessions should be promoted ahead of time.

Reader feedback and comments. Stories, blogs, editorials, columns — all provide opportunities for readers to post opinions and reactions. But you can also ask readers to send in story ideas, anecdotes, photos, videos, interview questions — or ask them to participate in:

Online polls and quizzes. With the right software, you can conduct reader surveys on any topic (though results may not be statistically accurate). You can integrate tests and quizzes into stories, too, with forms that check your fitness level, test your Grammy IQ or calculate: *What Will This New Tax Plan Cost YOU?*

Downloads. Government records or official documents often play crucial roles in stories. Let readers click-and-download that material right from your story or provide them with links to the original Web sites.

LINKS

If you've done your job and written a good story, readers will want *more*. So give it to them. Provide links to:

◆ *Previous stories, graphics and photos* on this topic (or related topics) from your newsroom's archives.

◆ *Other Web sites* that provide expanded information.

◆ *Organizations or individuals* mentioned in your story whom readers will want to contact.

◆ *Editorials or columns* that offer opinions or insights into topics discussed in your story.

◆ *Additional story elements* you weren't able to include: statistics, quotes, even full-length transcripts or audio of interviews.

For links to Web stories using these options, visit the Online Learning Center at
www.mhhe.com/harrower1

Slideshows (or *photo galleries*) combine a series of photos and captions to illustrate a topic or event. Some slideshows simply provide a variety of images; others are carefully edited and arranged to tell powerful stories. Audio narration, interviews, music, sound effects and visual effects (fades, dissolves, wipes) can be added, too. Photos can even be timed to advance automatically.

At right: from Asbury Park Press online, a slideshow from a Giants-Panthers game.

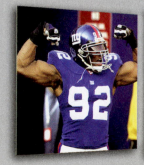

BLOGS: A POPULAR WAY TO ADD VOICES AND VIEWPOINTS

What are blogs? They're Web sites where users post news, comments or links to other sites. Posts appear in reverse chronological order, with the most recent postings on top.

The term *blog* is slang for *Web log.* When *bloggers* post material, it's called *blogging.*

Who creates blogs? Anybody and everybody. For now, let's ignore the millions of bloggers babbling about their proms and pet poodles, and focus instead on blogs produced by:

◆ *Journalists.* Newsroom-related blogs allow reporters to discuss their stories, provide transcripts of interviews, even add supplemental facts. Columnists can test new ideas and defend past columns. Editors can explain the decision-making behind controversial editorials. In each case, readers are invited to enter the discussion, posting questions, comments or corrections arising from their own expertise.

◆ *Participants involved in breaking news.* Bloggers can post minute-by-minute diaries as events unfold, whether they're trapped in a New Orleans flood or standing on the sidelines at the Super Bowl. These writers aren't always trained journalists, but their observations are unique and valuable nonetheless.

◆ *Bloggers who monitor what's new and newsworthy.* Many blogs focus on specific topics (politics, sports, technology, etc.). They provide news updates, forums for discussion and links to other Web sites.

Why are blogs important? Until now, the mainstream media (TV, radio and newspapers) have maintained a newsgathering monopoly. But blogs are slowly turning that one-way monologue into a two-way conversation. Suddenly, everyone has a voice; anyone can contribute facts, opinions, eyewitness accounts and expert testimony.

Bloggers often serve as catalysts for news coverage, too. In 2002, a blog posted offensive comments by Senate Majority Leader Trent Lott, triggering an online uproar that prompted the mainstream media to pursue a story they'd been ignoring.

But is it journalism? Blogging is a form of participatory media, but it isn't always journalism. Consider it a journalistic *supplement* — not a substitute. Few bloggers do their own reporting; many confuse facts with opinions, posting unedited text that's untrustworthy, even libelous.

As Rebecca Blood, author of "The Weblog Handbook," said of bloggers: "Their commentary, done with integrity, can be a great source of accurate information and nuanced, informed analysis, but it will never replace the journalist's mandate to assemble a fair, accurate and complete story that can be understood by a general audience."

BLOG FORMATS FOR JOURNALISTS

Blogs use a variety of formats. Some provide brief notes; others publish long essays. Some are written exclusively by one person; others are collaborative. And some simply list links to interesting items elsewhere on the Web. Here are two examples of formats that journalists might use.

▶ **At right:** This is a terrific format for soliciting reader responses. The writer — in this case Tom Hanson, columnist for the Bonita (Fla.) Daily News — proposes a topic and frames the debate. A discussion then follows, with readers commenting both on Hanson's post *and* on previous responses. Editors screen the public's comments to remove any that are profane or libelous.

▼ **Below:** This approach, used here by Sacramento Bee political columnist Daniel Weintraub, is the most popular format for bloggers. It's a constantly updated notebook of random facts and interesting ideas, a way for reporters to say, "Hey! Look what I just found!" Most items are brief; most link to their original sources on other Web sites.

Politics CALIFORNIA INSIDER

**A Weblog by
Sacramento Bee Columnist Daniel Weintraub**

February 02, 2006

**Daniel Weintraub
Sacramento Bee
Columnist
(916) 321-1914**

**E-mail
Daniel Weintraub**

Recent Columns

Bio

Why a Blog?

RSS feeds
RSS .91
RSS 1.0
RSS 2.0

**Syndicate this site
(XML)**

Search Weblog

February 2006
S M T W T F S
        1 2 3 4
5 6 7 8 9 10 11
12 13 14 15 16 17 18
19 20 21 22 23 24 25
26 27 28

Smart meters

This is long overdue. New electricity meters will let consumers manage their own power load to minimize their bills by using less power at peak times when demand, and cost, is high. Users who can't or won't shift their use to other times will pay more.
Posted by dweintraub at 10:37 AM

Red ink

The final tally from the special election: Schwarzenegger and his allies spent about $76 million. His opponents spent $121 million. The CTA alone kicked in $58 million. Schwarzenegger begins his reelection run with virtually no cash on hand and about a half-million in debts.
Posted by dweintraub at 9:30 AM

Child care fraud

Prosecutors estimate that perhaps half of

Bonita Springs
TOM HANSON COLUMNIST   tahanson@bonitanews.com

Talk of the Town with Tom Hanson

An unregistered sex offender strikes. How do we prevent this from happening again?

JANUARY 30, 2006 (**Posted at:** 10:26 p.m.)

How do we prevent what happened on Saturday from happening again?

A 61-year-old man with a previous conviction for a sexual battery on a child struck again, according to the Lee County Sheriff's Office.

How did he remain undiscovered as a unregistered sex offender?

What can the community do to make sure something like this doesn't happen again?

Are you angry? Let me know.

And how many people blame the parents for allowing their daughter to play unsupervised?

How many people blame the system for not keeping criminals like this off the street?

Post your feelings.

naplesnews.com blogs are collections of short, frequently updated posts by members of the Southwest Florida community. Blog writers, and comment posters, are solely responsible for what they say. (Please take the time to read our full policy.)

If you're interested in writing a blog for one of our sites, send us a couple of sample entries.

COMMENTS

This site does not necessarily agree with comments posted below — responsibility lies with the relevant reader alone. Read our blog agreement.

1 of 1 people found this comment useful.

Posted by **bananas (anonymous)** at 5:57 a.m. on Jan. 31, 2006 (**Suggest removal**)

there is a man sleeping in the dumpster at the construction site of the Beach Walk condominium complex, can a special patrol of the overgrown wooded areas along bonita beach road be put together to roust and out these sometimes dangerous seasonal visitors? what can be done to make property owners clear their vacant lots and trim back and maintain their properites?

0 of 1 people found this comment useful.

Posted by **sdiamond (anonymous)** at 12:59 p.m. on Feb. 1, 2006 (**Suggest removal**)

With all the technology we have why can't we microship these sickos, we microchip animals, we gps systems in vehicles. there has to be a way to monitor these people.

0 of 0 people found this comment useful.

Writing for online media

The Web is changing reader habits and challenging journalistic conventions.

Readers have more options, more control and more sheer *distractions* than ever before —which makes it even harder for news reporters to gain and hold their attention. So what's the answer? In the years ahead, as online reporting continues to evolve, new strategies will emerge — though traditional journalistic standards will remain as essential as ever. In the meantime, try this:

5 TIPS FOR CREATING READABLE, USER-FRIENDLY NEWS STORIES FOR WEB SITES

1 "CHUNK" YOUR INFORMATION

Reading a computer screen is tougher than reading ink on a page. The flickering of the monitor, the distraction of the ads, the wailing of Metallica through your headphones — they all make the Web unfriendly to narrative text.

Surveys repeatedly show that Web users are much more likely to scan stories than read them line by line. A recent Eyetrack study showed that stories with short paragraphs received twice as much attention as those with longer paragraphs. Long grafs discourage extended viewing.

As Crawford Kilian said in "Writing for the Web": "Good writing is good writing, whatever the medium. The difference in Web writing is that good writing is also usually very brief writing. It's clear, concrete, easy to understand without being dumbed down. . . . When the unit of discourse is the *chunk* — the 100 words that fill up a computer screen — every paragraph has to stand on its own without leaning on what the reader *may* have seen in some other chunk."

As you write, force yourself to use shorter paragraphs. Shorter sentences. *Chunks*, in other words.

2 TWEAK YOUR TYPE TO MAKE IT EASIER TO SCAN

Whether you write long paragraphs or short ones, printed text generally resembles a long, gray river — or

worse, an ocean. That undifferentiated grayness can make you look boring, even if you're *not.*

That's why it helps to think like a text designer. You've got to add sub-heads. **Boldface.** Bullets, to help you:
- create lists;
- emphasize key points; and
- make them easy to scan.

Lists, charts, tables, liftout quotes — they're attractive to readers *and* they're smart journalism, too.

As you plan and write every story, look for ways to punctuate ideas, to subdivide content, to add visual appeal to your words. You can't expect an editor to do this after you've finished your 30-inch story; you need to take charge on your own.

3 RETHINK WHAT A "STORY" IS

For print journalists, a "story" means *one long, linear block of text.* Since that's not what Web readers may want, you need to approach Web reporting differently.

Create a *Web package,* not a story. A Web package is a combination of several Web pages linked together.

In a way, this takes the "chunk" concept to the next level: instead of simply rethinking the way you structure sentences and paragraphs, can you rethink the way you structure your entire *story?* Can you break your story into chunks, too?

Suppose, for example, you're covering a mayoral election. Your main

page might analyze the vote totals . . . linked to a page where you interview the winning candidate (with a photo slideshow) . . . linked to a page where experts list the key issues the mayor will face. And so on.

The more complex the topic, the more efficiently this page-based approach will organize your material.

4 ENHANCE YOUR STORY WITH EXTRA ELEMENTS

A story, as we've said, is *not* simply a block of text. Text is a valuable tool, yes, but online journalists have other useful tools at their disposal, too (as we saw on the previous page).

Think *multimedia:* audio, video, graphics, slideshows, podcasts.

Think *interactivity:* polls, reader feedback, live chats, contests.

Think *links:* documents, downloads, blogs, opinion columns.

Different stories demand different storytelling techniques. Smart online journalists find ways to enhance their stories with Web extras every chance they get. You're limited only by your imagination — and by your staff's ability to produce, of course. That's why you need to . . .

5 COLLABORATE

In the past, print reporters trotted off to cover stories all alone. They'd come back to the newsroom and write . . . . big blocks of text.

In the future, reporters (like you) will *still* focus on writing text. But if you want to add audio, video or animated maps to your stories, you'll need to work as part of a team.

Yes, the key is planning. Collaboration. Coordination. An efficient online newsroom is a pool of varied talents, and the more you can tap into that pool for your stories, the better your stories will be.

How best to do that? Plan packages as a team, using a form like this:

ONLINE PACKAGE PLANNING GUIDE

In Chapter Six, we provided a form to help you plan special feature-story packages. ▼

This form works the same way, providing a guide for reporters and editors planning stories for the Web. Here's how it works:

STEP 1:

Photocopy the next page.

STEP 2:

In a team meeting, ask: What's this story *really* about? Boil the idea down to 25 words or less.

STEP 3:

Now think like a reader. What are the most important, interesting questions this story provokes? And where will you answer them? In the main story? In a sidebar? With a photo? Or (better yet) is there an interactive, multimedia extra that best delivers the information? Consult the list at far right for ideas.

Most importantly, ask yourself: Should you break this story into several linked Web pages, each with its own online extras?

STEP 4:

Now it's time to organize the total package, starting with the main page (which may be your *only* page):
- Discuss words and ideas that belong in the headline and deck. You'll need them for home-page promos, too.
- Discuss any photos or artwork you'll need to include on this page.
- Want to incorporate Web extras? Sidebars? Assign these now.
- What links should you include on this page?

STEP 5:

If your story works best as several linked pages instead of just one, repeat Step 4 for each additional page.

After the meeting, make copies of this completed form for everyone involved (or update an electronic version of this form).

ONLINE PACKAGE PLANNING GUIDE

STORY IDEA _____

_____

QUESTIONS READERS WILL ASK

1 _Why should I care?_ _____
  WHERE WE'LL ANSWER: ☐ MAIN STORY   ☐ RELATED STORY   ☐ SIDEBAR/ WEB EXTRA   ☐ PHOTO/GRAPHIC
  DETAILS:

2 _____
  WHERE WE'LL ANSWER: ☐ MAIN STORY   ☐ RELATED STORY   ☐ SIDEBAR/ WEB EXTRA   ☐ PHOTO/GRAPHIC
  DETAILS:

3 _____
  WHERE WE'LL ANSWER: ☐ MAIN STORY   ☐ RELATED STORY   ☐ SIDEBAR/ WEB EXTRA   ☐ PHOTO/GRAPHIC
  DETAILS:

4 _____
  WHERE WE'LL ANSWER: ☐ MAIN STORY   ☐ RELATED STORY   ☐ SIDEBAR/ WEB EXTRA   ☐ PHOTO/GRAPHIC
  DETAILS:

FINAL STORY PACKAGE

MAIN PAGE

HEADLINE/DECK _____

_____

PHOTOS/ART _____

SIDEBARS/EXTRAS _____

LINKS _____

SECOND/RELATED PAGE (OPTIONAL)

HEADLINE/DECK _____

_____

PHOTOS/ART _____

SIDEBARS/EXTRAS _____

LINKS _____

THIRD/ RELATED PAGE (FOR MORE THAN THREE PAGES, USE ADDITIONAL FORMS)

HEADLINE/DECK _____

_____

PHOTOS/ART _____

SIDEBARS/EXTRAS _____

LINKS _____

WEB EXTRAS

SIDEBAR OPTIONS
- ☐ FAST-FACTS BOX
- ☐ Q and A
- ☐ FAQs
- ☐ LIFTOUT QUOTE
- ☐ QUOTE COLLECTION
- ☐ MAP
- ☐ CHART
- ☐ LIST
- ☐ CHECKLIST
- ☐ BIO BOX
- ☐ DIAGRAM
- ☐ TABLE
- ☐ QUIZ
- ☐ TIMELINE
- ☐ STEP-BY-STEP GUIDE
- ☐ GLOSSARY
- ☐ EXCERPT
- ☐ CONTACT INFORMATION FOR SOURCES CITED IN THE STORY

MULTIMEDIA OPTIONS
- ☐ VIDEO CLIP
- ☐ AUDIO SOUND BITE
- ☐ SLIDESHOW
- ☐ NARRATED SLIDESHOW
- ☐ WEBCAM
- ☐ ANIMATED GRAPHICS
- ☐ LIVE WEBCAST
- ☐ PODCAST

INTERACTIVE OPTIONS
- ☐ ONLINE POLL
- ☐ FEEDBACK/COMMENTS
- ☐ LIVE CHAT
- ☐ REQUEST FOR READERS TO SUBMIT:
  - — STORIES
  - — STORY IDEAS
  - — PHOTOS
  - — VIDEOS
- ☐ INTERACTIVE MAP
- ☐ DOWNLOADS
- ☐ CONTESTS

LINKS TO:
- ☐ PREVIOUS STORIES
- ☐ RELATED WEB SITES
- ☐ EDITORIALS/ COLUMNISTS
- ☐ UNEDITED INTERVIEW TRANSCRIPTS
- ☐ OFFICIAL RECORDS AND DOCUMENTS
- ☐ BLOGS

HOW WILL AMERICANS GET THEIR NEWS IN 2025?

How will they get their news? Pretty much the same way they've been getting it in the past 100 years: through newspapers, radio, TV, Web and the gadget of the day (whatever the combination of a phone, PDA, iPod and video player will look like). The only difference that the plethora of distribution will make is that it will increase competition among news gatherers. I'm an optimist, so I'll guess that the competitive pressure will force journalists to improve their craft. I'm hopeful that the works of a few solo journalists — who for the first time have near-equal footing with old-school, massive news organizations — will re-establish the nobility of journalists. And I'm especially hopeful that American-style journalism — which is the lubricant of democracy and equitable capitalism — will spread around the world and take root in places it hasn't before, like China and the Middle East.

Kourosh Karimkhany, Wired News editor

In 2025, only a small group of readers/viewers/listeners will take in what we consider "news" today. The combination of audience fragmentation and increasing desire to tune into like-minded sources will mean more people get information, but fewer people get objective or vetted information. The need for reporters will continue to decrease; the need for pundits will continue to increase. "News" of the WSJ/NYT/NPR variety will be a premium product for an elite audience, like poetry is today.

Jimmy Guterman, writer, magazine publisher and media consultant

People will be getting their news from other people — word of mouth, amplified and distributed by the ubiquitous network. People will be telling their own stories. Much of it will be more true than anything we were able to do with the Old Journalism, but much of it will be false.

The reporting process will be very much about chasing down and killing bad information — debunking — and pointing out the good, and those responsibilities will be taken up by conscientious amateurs as well as professionals. The value of professional journalism will not be so much about providing information, but rather providing clarity. And as William Gibson said, the future is already here — it's just unevenly distributed.

Steve Yelvington,
reporter, editor and Internet strategist
for Morris Digital Works

> **The essence of the reporter's job — learning and telling good stories — won't change, but the tools, context, competition and audience will change vastly.**
>
> **Steve Buttry,**
> American Press Institute

In 2025 people will get their news from a wide diversity of sources, including both old and new media, customized to individual preferences and styles. Among the new media will be miniature wearable devices wirelessly connected to global networks delivering on-demand multimedia news and information.

Reporters will need to focus on original reporting, emphasizing firsthand accounts from the field. They'll need to be comfortable with multiple media and engaging in interactive conversations with audiences, sources and other reporters.

John Pavlik, journalism professor and author of "Journalism and New Media"

Hardware is never as interesting as software.

Hardware will be small, portable, wireless, broadband, multimedia-compatible — and maybe disposable.

The key to what KIND of news is *relevance:* sports for some, big news events for all. But there will be "personal" news — from your family, your friends, your refrigerator telling you to pick up milk on the way home.

Alan Jacobson, newspaper design consultant

I expect we'll all have personalized, intelligent news feeds that give us information wherever we are, on whatever device we happen to have in our hands or in our sight at a given moment.

So, in 2025 I would expect to climb into my car — or settle down into my airline seat — and have the same media experience available to me as if I were sitting in front of my computer. There's my mail; my customized news feeds from a variety of sources, filtered based on my interests and geography; my micro-local news from non-journalist correspondents; etc. I should be able to interact with all that news and communicate (video if I want it) with anyone through that digital portal.

So that's the first key point: my personal media experience travels with me and is accessible from any device I encounter (not necessarily own). Perhaps we'll be freed from lugging around heavy laptops. At the least, they'll shrink to offer all that's described above, but be the size of a magazine.

The second key point is that in 2025 our personal media experiences will be fed by a combination of professional journalists' reports and reports from enthusiastic citizens. I believe that today's "citizen journalism" is the beginning of something big.

So, I envision my 2025 news and information feed to include some detailed news that I and only a few other people care about, in addition to the larger news. My news portal will include news from my child's teacher, with classroom schedules, photos from my kids' day at school, their homework assignment, etc. My running group's news will be included, and I can use the device I'm on to have a video conversation with the group leader to get directions to the next meeting.

Basically, I'm envisioning many layers of My News – some of it sent to me from friends, some from people I don't know but are experts or enthusiasts in something I care about, some of it from professional journalists. I'll select who I receive these feeds from based on topic interest, of course, but also based on their credibility ratings.

At this point, if I had to guess who's going to provide this digital-news/information nirvana to us, I'd say Google. Imagine a Google of tomorrow keeping track of all these news/information feeds for you and delivering them to you wherever in the world you may be.

Steve Outing, interactive media columnist, Editor and Publisher Online

---

Broadcast news

TV and radio journalism is neither better nor worse than print journalism.

It's just different — though critics, pundits and journalists themselves may passionately disagree. Each form of media has strengths and weaknesses. And while obvious, they're worth repeating:

◆ Print journalism provides a level of depth, context and sheer information that television and radio newscasts can't supply.

◆ Broadcast journalism, through the power of dramatic video and engaging audio, offers emotional appeal, realism and immediacy that printed stories can't match.

◆ Watching or listening to a news broadcast generally requires less intellectual effort than reading a complex news story in a newspaper.

◆ Broadcast journalism, critics say, treats news as entertainment, evading complex issues while sensationalizing conflicts, crimes, car chases, etc. Critics of print journalism say newspapers aren't entertaining *enough* — they're full of dull-but-important government stories and serious-but-boring social issues that seldom connect with modern Americans.

Yes, differences exist. But whether you're a print journalist or a broadcast reporter, your goal remains the same: Gather all the information you can, then tell your story in a clear, compelling way.

HOW A TYPICAL BROADCAST NEWS STORY COMES TOGETHER

KXL anchor Sharon Mitchell reads a radio newscast in the station's Portland studio, where all news production is computerized — including the script she's reading.

ON RADIO At most radio stations, especially small ones, the *news director* serves as a one-person newsroom, writing local stories, reworking wire copy and serving as the *anchor* who reads news on the air. At larger stations, news directors supervise a small team of reporters who cover the area's most newsworthy stories.

In a typical day, a reporter might cover from one to five different stories — some by phone, others in the field. Formal beats aren't practical (there's too much news and not enough reporters), so assignments often vary unpredictably, from meetings to murders.

After gathering information, reporters occasionally transmit a live report from the field, especially for big breaking stories. Usually, though, they'll return to the newsroom to review the audio they've recorded, select *sound bites*, write the script and assemble the finished story. It's common for reporters to create several different versions of each story. Some become short, text-only *readers* for anchors to deliver, while others become longer packages *(wraps)* that incorporate sound bites and the reporter's own narrative.

Thus, in an average day, a reporter might file a dozen different stories — although a typical story may combine just 20 seconds of narration and 10 seconds of sound bites. ▼

This is what KGW anchor Tracy Barry sees when she delivers the news. The script scrolls in front of the camera lens; below it, a digital clock tracks the newscast's time.

ON TELEVISION TV reporters (and many radio reporters, too) start their days with a news meeting. That's where the news director and the *producers* (who supervise the newscast material) discuss and select the day's top stories. The *assignment desk* then monitors *who* covers *what* out in the field.

Like radio reporters, TV reporters can seldom predict where they'll be from day to day. They might cover a cat show one moment, a high-speed chase the next. At a big station, a reporter might cover one or two stories daily; at smaller stations, reporters might cover half a dozen. There's often little time to do research or study a story's background, which means reporters must be fast learners.

Unlike radio or print reporters, TV journalists work side by side with photographers, since video is essential for most stories. And stories come together in a variety of ways. Interviews and *stand-ups* are often done *live* — as often as possible, at many stations. Some stories are taped and transmitted to the newsroom from the scene; for others, reporters return to the station, review the video, write a script and assemble a *package* for a later newcast. Producing a typical 90-second story can take hours (during which news crews are often interrupted to go chase yet another breaking news story).

Producers and anchors, meanwhile, do their own writing and editing, too, carefully trimming and timing stories so they'll fit, to the precise second, in the final newscast. ▼

FOR A GLOSSARY OF **RADIO TERMS** ▶ **168**   FOR A GLOSSARY OF **TELEVISIOM TERMS** ▶ **170**

ALL THE NEWS THAT FITS — AND THAT'S REALLY NOT MUCH

Yes, broadcast journalists produce brilliant in-depth reports, from social analysis on NPR to hard-hitting exposés on "60 Minutes." But those are the exceptions. As a rule, most broadcast news stories are brief. *Extremely* brief.

How brief? Instead of measuring stories in words and inches, broadcast journalists measure them in minutes and seconds. A four-minute radio newscast may contain a dozen stories, but many will be just a few seconds long. A typical TV news story may consist of four or five sentences lasting 40 seconds.

Broadcast journalists generally read 150-180 words per minute. At that rate, it would take 28 hours to read a typical edition of The Washington Post. Most half-hour newscasts contain fewer words than one typical newspaper page.

As a result, broadcast news is concise, but shallow. Fast-paced, but superficial. As newscaster David Keith Cohler admitted in his broadcasting textbook:

"Let's not kid ourselves: Any radio or TV newscast that promises to deliver *all* the news is grossly misrepresenting itself. . . . Assume that people interested in a story's wealth of details will read newspapers, because they know radio and TV will usually not take the time to include them."

Want to write TV and radio news? Start the clock. You'll need to think fast, boil issues down to their basics — and write as tightly as you can.

WHAT'S IN A HALF-HOUR NEWSCAST?

According to results from two major surveys of local television news:

◆ Roughly 70 percent of all stories were under one minute long.

◆ Three-quarters of all stories were local.

◆ The most common topic, by a 2-to-1 margin, was crime.

◆ The newscast's lead story involved crime 39 percent of the time.

◆ Most stories that involved controversies gave *only* or *mostly* one point of view.

NEWS, *14 minutes*
Crime, fire, accidents and disasters made up more than a third of all news stories

SPORTS and WEATHER
6.4 minutes

TEASERS/CHAT
1.6 minutes

ADVERTISING
8 minutes

Sources: The Project for Excellence in Journalism and the Lear Center Local News Archive

WHAT A TYPICAL BROADCAST NEWS SCRIPT LOOKS LIKE

If you're reporting live from a news scene or recording your own narration, you can scribble notes any way you like. But if you're writing a story for someone else to read (say, a newscast anchor), your script must be formatted — and formats vary from station to station. Two typical examples:

A RADIO NEWS STORY

At some stations, reporters make each line of a news script 70 characters wide, which equals about 10 words. At a normal rate of speaking, each line would take four seconds to read — making it easy to estimate the story's total running time. But scriptwriting software now calculates the timing of each story as you type it.

This is the *slug* (or name) of the story, along with the writer's initials and date.

Notice how the numbers in this story are written the way they're pronounced. Even the acronym "ESU" is hyphenated to keep the anchor from pronouncing it "Ee-soo."

This indicates a prerecorded quote — called a *cut* or *actuality* — that ends with the phrase "save the planet." In the past, cuts were recorded on tape cartridges. The term *cart* still survives, even though most cuts nowadays are digital files stored in the computer system.

BOTTLE BILL
TALENT: TJH
9-20-06

Students from Eastern State University dumped more than 13-thousand cans and bottles on the Capitol lawn today.
   The cans represent each student currently attending E-S-U. Event organizer Sara May says the group is supporting legislation that would give 10-cents back for every container you recycle.

[Cart No.: BOTTLEBILL1.wav
Time: 13s
Out-cue: "...save the planet."

The group collected 25-hundred bottles and cans while at the Capitol... and gave donors a DIME for each of those containers.

Some radio stations capitalize words that need extra emphasis. Others underline. It's common, too, for ellipses to indicate pauses.

Broadcast scripts avoid hyphenating words. Writers try to make the story as easy as possible to read aloud — even if you've never seen it before.

A TELEVISION NEWS STORY

Television scripts use what's called a *split page*. The right half mimics what anchors see on their prompters; it tells them what to say, when to say it and what's being shown on-camera from moment to moment. The left half displays technical details — for audio, video and graphics — used by the director and production crew.

(ANCHOR ON CAM)

(JOE)
LANDLORDS MAY GET A LITTLE HELP FROM THE STATE IF THEIR PROPERTY IS DAMAGED BY METH MAKERS.
   A NEW BILL INTRODUCED BY STATE SENATOR TED CEARNY (CAR-nee) WOULD GIVE LANDLORDS UP TO 5-THOUSAND DOLLARS FROM THE STATE'S CRIME VICTIMS COMPENSATION FUND.

TAKE SOT FULL
TRT: :09
OUTQ:...NEED OUR HELP."
CG \\ TED CEARNY \\ STATE SENATOR

(SOT)
"A lot of innocent property owners face financial ruin trying to clean up the mess from these meth labs, and they need our help."

This indicates who's speaking, which is especially important for newscasts with two anchors.

In scripts, words that are tricky to pronounce are spelled out phonetically. Notice, too, how dollar amounts are spelled out.

The anchor has stopped talking, and viewers are now watching the senator's sound bite (or SOT, for "sound on tape"). This bite lasts nine seconds, as indicated by the TRT ("total running time") to its left. This transcript, by the way, is used to generate the closed-captioning for this newscast.

This tech talk basically says the sound bite ends with the words "need our help"— and a computer-generated name line appears on-screen.

Some radio and TV stations use ALL CAPS all the time. Some use CAPS for narration, lower case for sound bites. CAPS are easier to read from prompters several yards away.

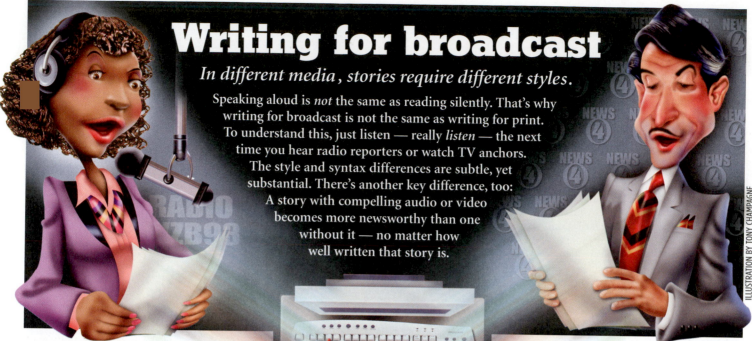

Writing for broadcast

In different media, stories require different styles.

Speaking aloud is *not* the same as reading silently. That's why writing for broadcast is not the same as writing for print. To understand this, just listen — really *listen* — the next time you hear radio reporters or watch TV anchors. The style and syntax differences are subtle, yet substantial. There's another key difference, too: A story with compelling audio or video becomes more newsworthy than one without it — no matter how well written that story is.

ILLUSTRATION BY TONY CHAMPAGNE

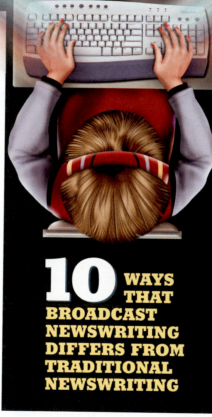

10 WAYS THAT BROADCAST NEWSWRITING DIFFERS FROM TRADITIONAL NEWSWRITING

1 USE A FRIENDLIER, MORE CONVERSATIONAL TONE

When people hear a news announcer's voice on the radio or watch a news anchor's face on TV, they establish a connection that's familiar. Friendly. Almost intimate.

That's why broadcast newswriters are urged to write the way they talk, using simple words in a natural-sounding speaking style — "like you're talking to your mother," it's often said.

Unlike newspaper stories, which generally adopt a proper, official-sounding demeanor, TV and radio newscasters establish a friendly we-you relationship with their audiences, which makes it OK to say, *"Here are the top stories we're following tonight: Watch out for construction delays if you're driving near the river tomorrow. . . ."*

It's possible to overdo it, of course. You'll ruin your credibility with slang, jargon and sloppy speech, *especially* for serious news.

2 KEEP IT SHORT. SIMPLE. AND EASY TO FOLLOW.

You're writing for the ear, not the eye. Your listeners will have a hellish time decoding the tangled clauses in sentences like this:

Warren Peace, a Bloomfied cab driver who claims a passenger was drunk and insulted him last night, was arrested and charged with assaulting him.

Contorted syntax that *might* work in print becomes indecipherable when read aloud over the air. So write in the active voice. Keep your subjects and verbs close together. And avoid the clutter of long clauses and parenthetical phrases. Simplify — like this:

Police are charging a Bloomfield cab driver with assaulting a passenger. The driver, Warren Peace, claims the passenger was drunk and insulting.

To avoid information overload, express one idea per sentence. Limit sentences to 20 words or less. And notice how it's OK to start sentences with conjunctions, like we just did. Or to use sentence fragments. Like this.

Good broadcast newswriting uses simpler words, too: *admit,* not *acknowledge; charges,* not *allegations; end,* not *terminate.* And so on.

Can you streamline your sentences without dumbing down your information? Can you simplify your word choice without becoming simple-minded? That's the real challenge of broadcast newswriting.

3 DON'T STRUCTURE STORIES IN THE INVERTED-PYRAMID FORM

Inverted-pyramid news stories start strong but finish weak, as facts gradually become less crucial. But in broadcast newswriting, every fact is crucial. Every second is precious. Every word counts.

Broadcast news stories need a beginning, middle and *end;* they need to hold listeners from the lead to the final sentence.

So give every story a solid ending, whether it's a zinger (*"It turns out Ralphie is a 400-pound gorilla"*), a summary statement (*"But for now, both sides appear deadlocked"*) or vital details (*"The council will finally vote on the plan at tomorrow's meeting"*).

4 USE THE PRESENT TENSE AS OFTEN AS POSSIBLE

Broadcast news needs to sound . . . *new.* Fresh. Immediate. That's why news stories use the present tense as often as possible.

Newspaper stories are traditionally written in the past tense:

A Lancaster man was hospitalized yesterday after he was attacked by a crazed chicken.

Broadcast stories try to tell people *what's happening right now,* so they constantly recast leads to convey immediacy:

A Lancaster man is recovering this morning after being attacked by a crazed chicken.

This doesn't mean you should avoid using the past tense; it simply means you should seek story angles that emphasize *what's new* and *what's next* rather than rehash yesterday's old news. If a Supreme Court justice resigned yesterday, today's story becomes:

The president is meeting with advisers this morning to begin choosing a Supreme Court nominee . . .

In broadcast news, events happen *late last night, a few hours ago, in a few moments.* (It's OK to approximate.) Even looking toward the future beats dwelling in the past:

> The city is bracing for another winter storm Friday like the one that gave us a foot of snow yesterday.

5 CONTRACTIONS ARE ACCEPTABLE, EVEN FOR HARD NEWS STORIES

Serious newspaper stories are written in a solemn tone that generally avoids the use of contractions: *The mayor said he will not seek re-election.*

But because broadcast newswriting is more conversational, contractions are OK: *The mayor says he won't seek re-election.*

Some contractions, however, are awkward to pronounce: *there're, that'll, it'd, that'd.* Beware, too, of contractions that sound like plurals. To say *the jury's reached a decision* might sound like there's more than one jury; it's more accurate to say *the jury has reached a decision.* Use contraction-free phrases when you need to convey clarity or authority.

6 ATTRIBUTIONS AND QUOTES REQUIRE DIFFERENT TREATMENT

In print journalism, you're trained to place attributions *after* you relay information:

> Jones confessed to murdering his wife, police said. He could face the death penalty if convicted.

But in broadcast stories, that dangling phrase, *police said*, might sound ambiguous. Read it aloud. Did police say Jones confessed, or that he could face the death penalty?

To avoid confusion and make it immediately clear where information comes from, you should generally attribute the source *first:*

> Police say Jones confessed to murdering his wife.

This becomes even more necessary when sources convey opinions. In printed stories, this quote is easy to understand because we can see the quotation marks:

> "I am not a crook," President Nixon said.

But if a newscaster begins a sentence by saying "*I am not a crook,*" listeners will be confused. For a brief moment, they'll wonder, "Why is this newscaster denying that she's a crook?"

Because it's hard for audiences to "hear" quotation marks, it's generally preferable to paraphrase than to use direct quotes (*President Nixon said that he was not a crook*).

If you must quote someone, try this:

> Nixon said — quote — "I am not a crook."

Or:

> As Nixon put it: "I am not a crook."

Of course, your best option is to provide actual sound bites so audiences can hear quotes for themselves. When those bites aren't available, TV newscasts often display the printed quotes as on-screen graphics.

PAM ZEKMAN *was a successful reporter at the Chicago Sun-Times before she became an investigative reporter for WBBM-TV in Chicago. Her reaction to the transition from print to broadcasting:*

"I mourned the lack of space in TV for all the wonderful facts I piled into my newspaper stories. What I didn't realize was how powerful my stories would become when I got rid of a lot of the stuff I thought was so precious.

"Writing for TV forces me to get to the point sooner and to make that point more clearly than I did when I was writing for newspapers. TV taught me to appreciate the power of pictures, and to work with photographers in a collaborative way."

7 ADD PHONETIC PRONUNCIATION WHEREVER NECESSARY

Tongue-twisting words and foreign names can easily trip up an anchor — which is why broadcast news writers often avoid naming names if they're not essential to the story. If it's sufficient to simply say *the president of Iran,* you'll avoid the perils of pronouncing *Mahmoud Ahmadinejad.*

But when complex names are necessary, be sure to add phonetic pronunciations — often called *pronouncers* — each time the word is used, whether it's Joseph Pulitzer (PULL-it-zehr), Senator Daniel Inouye (ee-NO-way) or Mahmoud Ahmadinejad (mah-MOOD ah-mah-dih-nee-ZHAD).

Some stations run the pronunciations *following* the regular spelling, while others run it *in place of* the original word — whichever way the news readers prefer.

8 USE PUNCTUATION TO HELP — NOT HINDER — THE DELIVERY

If you were to read this column of text during a newscast, you might find the use of hyphens at the right edge of each line a bit distracting. That's why you should avoid hyphenation when preparing text for broadcast.

In the same way, you should avoid jumping sentences from one page to another. That's not a problem if you read from a computer screen or teleprompter. But suppose this leg of type was a news story printout. Instead of jumping to the next column in mid-sentence, it's safer to end the sentence here, then add a word like *more.* *(MORE)*

Then you'd begin this next sentence on a new piece of paper. See? There's less chance of stumbling or fumbling that way.

To indicate short pauses, use commas; add them even more frequently than you would in a print news story. (Remember, however, that *lots* of commas may indicate that your syntax is too tangled and clause-ridden.)

Longer pauses help to add emphasis or clarity to spoken news. Use dashes or ellipses to indicate those pauses:

> Quarterback Biff Wellington says he'll be ready to play . . . and <u>win</u> . . . Friday night.

To ensure that important words get the proper emphasis, <u>underline</u> them, as we did in these last two sentences — though at some stations, you might use ALL CAPS.

9 AVOID ABBREVIATIONS AND SYMBOLS

You should spell out nearly all words in broadcast news stories. Why? Well, if you see *ST.* in an unfamiliar story, will it mean *Saint* or *Street*? Does *DR.* mean *Drive* or *Doctor*? Is *REP.* a *Representative* or a *Republican*?

States, months, days, titles — to avoid any confusion, it's best to write them out in full.

One exception: well-known acronyms like *F-B-I, C-B-S* or *Y-M-C-A.* (Notice how we added hyphens to show that each letter is pronounced individually. When acronyms are pronounced like words — *NATO* or *NASA* — hyphens aren't used.)

Generally, avoid using symbols — *$, %, @, &* — but use words instead: *dollar, percent, at, and.* When in doubt, spell it out. If a student has a 3.9 GPA, write that she has *a grade-point average of three-point-nine.*

10 NUMBERS: ROUND THEM OFF AND SPELL THEM OUT

Americans suffer math anxiety. Your audience has a difficult time *hearing* and *comprehending* complex numbers.

Read this sentence aloud: *The thieves stole $397,528.* Notice how the numbers start to jumble when you just *hear* them. That's why most broadcast stories would say *The thieves stole nearly 400-thousand dollars.* Too much precision causes confusion. If precise numbers aren't essential, round them off with phrases such as *nearly, more than, about,* etc.

And to make numbers easy to read, write them this way:

0: Write as *zero.*

1-9: Spell them out as words. (In most newsrooms, spell out *eleven,* too, since *11* could be mistaken for two L's.)

10-999: Use numerals.

Above 999: Use a combination of words and numerals. Instead of *20,130,000,* write *20-million, 130-thousand.* (Or better yet, round off and say *more than 20-million.*)

Radio news reporting

Radio journalism may be the most challenging form of news reporting.

You can't rely on graphics and images as TV reporters do. You can't write long, descriptive sentences and stories as print reporters do.

"When people are listening to your story on the radio, they're doing it while they dodge traffic, talk on their cell phone and do their makeup," says Chris Filippi, a reporter at KIRO radio in Seattle. "Your writing needs to be as direct and attention-grabbing as possible. Word economy is key."

The best radio reporting is snappy, yet eloquent. Conversational, yet concise. Friendly, yet authoritative. And while in-depth reporting still thrives on campus radio and NPR — and whenever big local news events break — most stories at most stations require you to boil everything down to its 30-second essence.

The hours are long, the pay is low, the stress is relentless. Still, radio remains an exciting, dramatic, rewarding way to tell stories.

MELANIE MESAROS, *news reporter, KXL radio in Portland, Ore.:* "One of the things we try to do as journalists is take people places they wouldn't normally get to experience. In this case, I'm behind the scenes at the county 'drunk tank,' where they were preparing to handle a rush of Fat Tuesday revelers. I asked the manager about the process of being brought in but also tried to have some fun. He ended up giving me a colorful sound bite on how everyone seems to be related to the mayor."

TIPS FOR CREATING RADIO NEWS STORIES

◆ *Write to your bites.* Good radio news stories combine *your* narration with *other people's* sound bites — and the more colorful and emotional the cuts, the more impact your story will have. So how does the process work?

First, gather audio. *Lots* of audio. A 10-minute interview may yield just one 10-second cut — but that may be all you need.

Next, select your best bites. How many? That depends. For breaking news, one colorful quote from a newsmaker, eyewitness or official may be enough; for controversial topics, you should provide bites from all sides. Edit them judiciously: use 5- to 10-second cuts for short stories, and cuts up to 30 seconds for long stories.

Now write a strong lead. Your job is to grab listeners while supplying the basic facts; as needed, transition into recorded quotes to bolster those facts with opinions and firsthand details.

◆ *Make every word count.* Your story may consist of just five or six sentences, so edit yourself ruthlessly. Prune to the bone. Kill every inessential syllable.

◆ *Focus on people.* "Find the one element in a story that connects with people," advises Martin Untrojb, a producer at WCBS radio in New York City. "If you can do that, any story will be interesting. For example, budget stories are boring. Sixteen trillion dollars mean nothing to the average Joe, but if you tell them it will mean an increase in *their* monthly taxes by 100 dollars, they will listen."

◆ *Read your stories aloud.* Don't trust anything you've written until you've heard it spoken out loud. Listen for wordiness, clumsy clauses — anything that might confuse listeners or bog down your momentum.

◆ *Record natural sound, too.* Some reporters turn on their recorders once they enter that victorious locker room or that boisterous school playground to capture background sound they'll integrate into their stories.

◆ *Paint word pictures.* Write with color. Drama. Flair. Don't just state dry facts; help your listeners *visualize* your stories. Listen as Edward R. Murrow describes a Berlin bombing raid:

"The clouds were gone....The small incendiaries were going down like a fistful of white rice thrown on a piece of black velvet. ... The cookies, the four-thousand-pound high explosives, were bursting below like great sunflowers gone mad."

IT TAKES PRACTICE TO SOUND LIKE A PRO

Want to develop a smooth, natural-sounding radio delivery?

◆ **Record yourself.** To hear yourself as others hear you, you don't need expensive gear (although the better the microphone, the truer your voice will sound). Record yourself reading text; as you play it back, really *listen* to the way you speak. Then try to:

◆ **Adjust your delivery.** Try raising and lowering the pitch of your voice, adjusting your volume, speeding up, slowing down. When does your voice sound most pleasing? If you hate the sound of your own voice (and who doesn't?) ask friends for feedback.

◆ **Remember,** the most common problems that afflict broadcast journalism students *can* be avoided:
— Speaking too quickly or slowly;
— Emphasizing the wrong words;
— Limiting your vocal range;
— Stumbling over words.

◆ **Study the pros.** Analyze and imitate the diction, inflection and pacing of broadcasters you admire.

◆ **Practice.** It takes years to develop a professional-sounding singing or speaking voice. So keep practicing until you gain confidence and create a delivery style that's uniquely yours.

SOME COMMON RADIO NEWS TERMS & JARGON

Anchor: The person hosting a newscast.

Actuality (also called a *cut, sound bite* or *bite*): The recorded voice of someone in the news, or sound from a news event. Actualities include statements from public officials, interviews with eyewitnesses, comments from experts — even the shouts of an angry mob.

Natural sound (or *ambient sound):* Sounds recorded to capture the flavor of a news scene — birds singing, crowds cheering, planes landing.

Script: The written version of a radio news story.

Voicer: A news story by a reporter that doesn't use actualities. When it's delivered by an anchor reading a script, it's called a *reader.*

Lead-in: Words that introduce some element in the story — identifying the source in a cut, for instance.

Live: Not prerecorded; usually refers to stories filed from a news scene.

Wrap: A story that begins and ends with a reporter's voice "wrapped" around one or more actualities or cuts. (TV reporters called this a *package.*)

Intro (or *anchor intro):* The lead to a reporter's wrap, read by an anchor.

In-cue: The first words of a cut or wrap.

Out-cue (OQ): The final words of a cut or wrap.

Tag (or *sign-off, sig-out, lockout, standard outcue):* The closing line where reporters say their names and station call letters ("Ella Funt, Newsradio 920").

Talent: Reporters, anchors, disc jockeys — those paid to appear on the air (as opposed to engineers or office staff).

Tease: A brief headline or promo for a coming story.

A FIRE AT THE YACHT CLUB: COVERING BREAKING NEWS ON THE RADIO AND IN PRINT

Radio news reporters need to collect facts quickly to file live reports. On Jan. 25, 2006, a fire broke out at a yacht club in Portland, Ore. Three reporters from competing radio stations scrambled to the scene. Here are the wraps they filed during the 8, 9 and 10 a.m. newscasts, along with the full story that ran in the local newspaper the next day.

8 A.M.
The story as heard on KXL (750 AM in Portland):

Anchor: YOU CAN STILL SEE IT -- CREWS BATTLING A BIG HOUSEBOAT FIRE ON HAYDEN ISLAND. KXL'S CHARLIE MAXTON IS LIVE AT THE SCENE AND JOINS US NOW WITH THE LATEST.

Maxton: THE GOOD NEWS IS THAT NO ONE HAS BEEN HURT HERE, REBECCA, BUT THERE ARE A LOT OF WORRIED BOAT-OWNERS LOOKING ON, WATCHING THIS BIG FIRE AT THE COLUMBIA RIVER YACHT CLUB, AT THE EAST END OF HAYDEN ISLAND.

THERE ARE AT LEAST TWO BOATHOUSES ON FIRE, AND FIREFIGHTERS ARE TRYING TO KEEP IT FROM SPREADING TO OTHER BOATHOUSES AROUND THEM. INSIDE THOSE BOATHOUSES ARE SOME EXPENSIVE YACHTS. THE OWNERS CAN ONLY STAND HERE AND WATCH THIS BURN. THEY'RE NOT LETTING ANYONE GET DOWN THERE TO THEIR BOATS.

SMOKE IS STILL POURING OUT FROM THE FIRE. THERE'S A BIG CLOUD DRIFTING OFF TO THE WEST OVER I-5. FIREFIGHTERS HAVE KIND OF AN ACCESS PROBLEM WITH THIS FIRE -- THE DOCK IS ONLY ABOUT SIX FEET WIDE. THAT MAKES IT KIND OF HARD TO GET THEIR EQUIPMENT IN THERE TO FIGHT THIS.

REPORTING LIVE IN NORTH PORTLAND, CHARLIE MAXTON, NEWSRADIO 750 KXL.

NOTICE HOW:

◆ This story is a voicer — a report with no sound bites. The reporter had just arrived on the scene and hadn't been able to record any interviews yet.
◆ Not only are there no interviews, but there are no names, either. Like most news stories that break suddenly, reporters scramble to report the *what, when* and *where* ("Minutes ago, a plane crashed into the World Trade Center"). The *who* usually takes a little longer. And discovering *why* this fire started could take days.

9 A.M.
The story as heard on KEX (1190 AM in Portland):

Anchor: THREE BOATHOUSES ARE A PILE OF SMOKING RUBBLE AT THE COLUMBIA RIVER YACHT CLUB IN NORTH PORTLAND AFTER A FIRE THIS MORNING. 1190 KEX'S MICHAEL DESMOND HAS THE LATEST. HE'S LIVE ON TOMAHAWK ISLAND.

Desmond: FIREFIGHTERS GOT THE CALL ABOUT 6:37 THIS MORNING. THREE OF THE BOATHOUSES WERE DESTROYED. IT'S LIKELY BOATS WERE INSIDE THEM AND ALSO HEAVILY DAMAGED. PORTLAND FIRE LIEUTENANT ALLEN OSWALT SAYS AT LEAST ONE OF THEM IS IN DANGER OF SINKING.

Oswalt: *"Because, of course, you got this boat hull down there that's burning, and we're putting water in it. Eventually, if we put enough water in it, it's gonna sink. But, uh, they switched over to foam."*

Desmond: ALLAN ELI OF VANCOUVER HAS HIS BOAT ONE ROW AWAY FROM WHERE THE FIRE STARTED. HIS REACTION WHEN HE HEARD ABOUT IT?

Eli: *"Well, you don't wanna record that, do ya? It was just kinda, 'Aw, crap,' you know. You can't help but feel sorry for your fellow club members."*

Desmond: NO ONE WAS HURT. THE FIRE WENT TO TWO ALARMS, INVOLVING AT LEAST 70 FIREFIGHTERS. LIVE AT THE COLUMBIA RIVER YACHT CLUB -- MICHAEL DESMOND, NEWSRADIO 1190 KEX.

NOTICE HOW:

◆ Desmond recorded interviews at the scene, edited them into short cuts, then tailored his script to them.
◆ Those two sound bites provide the variety and perspective reporters strive for. In this case, we have one official (Oswalt is the fire department spokesman) and one eyewitness. That's a solid combination.
◆ The second bite shows how inarticulate bystanders can be. You could argue about whether the word "crap" is appropriate for broadcast — but on deadline, you often settle for what you can get.

10 A.M.
The story as heard on KPAM (860 AM in Portland):

Anchor: FIREFIGHTERS CALL IT "OVERHAULING" -- PUTTING OUT THE LAST EMBERS, CLEANING UP AFTER A BIG FIRE. THAT'S GOING TO BE GOING ON ALL DAY AT THE COLUMBIA RIVER YACHT CLUB NEAR JANTZEN BEACH. KPAM'S TIM HOHL WAS THERE ALL MORNING AND JOINS US LIVE.

Hohl: THAT FIRE BROKE OUT JUST BEFORE 6:30 THIS MORNING, MARK. A ROW OF FANCY BOATHOUSES AND EVEN FANCIER BOATS . . . FLAMES SHOOTING 50 FEET INTO THE AIR BEFORE TWO FIREBOATS AND FIREFIGHTERS WHO HAD TO DRAG HAND LINES DOWN UNDER THE DOCKS GOT IT UNDER CONTROL.

Oswalt: *"Investigators, you've seen 'em here, there's three or four of 'em here, they're doing the interviews. That's pretty much what's gonna determine the cause of the fire: the history on each boat, maintenance that was done recently . . . stuff like that."*

Hohl: THREE BOATS WERE DESTROYED, INCLUDING A BRAND-NEW 56-FOOT YACHT LIKELY WORTH MORE THAN A MILLION DOLLARS. FIREFIGHTERS WERE ABLE TO SAVE ONE YACHT BY CUTTING IT LOOSE WITH A LEATHERMAN TOOL.

LIVE IN THE NEWSROOM, TIM HOHL, 860 KPAM.

NOTICE HOW:

◆ Hohl has returned from the fire to the newsroom.
◆ His story offers details lacking in the others: the 50-foot flames, a 56-foot yacht worth a million dollars.
◆ Hohl's second sentence is awkward — a good example of why you should keep sentences simple and position subjects and verbs close together.
◆ Hohl doesn't identify the source of his sound bite. Radio reporters sometimes do that to speed up stories; they assume the sound bite makes sense on its own.

"What gets said in the sound bite is more important than who says it," Hohl explains. "The sound still tells the story, even though the person's not identified."

The story as printed the next day in The Oregonian:

A two-alarm fire early Wednesday morning along the Columbia River's Northeast Portland shore destroyed three boathouses and the pricey yachts they contained, officials said.

Three yachts ranging from 48 to 63 feet long sank hours later, sending cleanup crews scurrying to prevent the escape of hundreds of gallons of diesel fuel, said Lt. Allen Oswalt, a Portland Fire Bureau spokesman.

Damage was expected to be minimal, and cranes are scheduled to lift the sunken yachts today, officials said.

Several Vancouver residents spotted flames at the east end of Hayden Island about 6:30 a.m. Firefighters arriving at the Columbia River Yacht Club a few minutes later saw thick plumes of black smoke billowing from boathouses. Without enough hoses, they called for a second set of crews 12 minutes later.

By the time firefighters could begin dousing one of the boathouses, the fire had spread to the two boathouses a few feet away on either side, Oswalt said.

The flames made the metal sheeting on the yacht garages buckle, then "melt right off like plastic," he said.

Firefighters mostly extinguished the fire by 7:54 a.m. The three yachts and the boathouses charred by the fire sank about 11:30 a.m. Combined, they were worth about $2.5 million, said Chris Mongrain, the Columbia River Yacht Club's rear commodore.

The fire spared four other yachts threatened by flames, Mongrain said. Firefighters cut the mooring lines on another yacht worth $4 million, pushing it out to a rescue boat that towed it to safety, Oswalt said. The yacht club is home to 186 vessels.

"It could've been a lot worse," Mongrain said.

Rescue crews threw three booms into the river to contain the spread of diesel fuel from the sunken yachts, officials said.

Nina DeConcini, a spokeswoman for the Oregon Department of Environmental Quality, said she did not think the fuel caused significant damage.

Television news reporting

It's not simply radio with pictures. TV journalism requires a unique approach.

A successful television reporter needs to move swiftly from story to story, becoming an instant expert who'll condense a confusing jumble of facts into 60 seconds of journalistic clarity. But that's not all. In two critical ways, TV reporting differs from all other news media:

◆ **You talk into a camera.** Live. Without notes. Yes, *anchors* read from a script as they deliver news from the studio — but the trend in local TV news is for reporters to do live stand-ups from news scenes as often as possible. That requires grace under pressure, a rock-solid memory and fluid improvisational skills. Think it's easy getting pounded by a hurricane as you describe the city's evacuation plan?

◆ **You depend on video.** Words are crucial, but images rule. TV viewers want to *view* TV. They want color, action, drama — not talking heads reciting lifeless facts. As veteran newsman Garth Kant warns in "How to Write Television News": *"Talking head bad. Video good. Memorize that."*

TV news isn't just a newspaper with bonus video. To produce a successful newscast you need an entirely different mind-set, from news judgment to storytelling techniques.

CBS reporter Ed Bradley interviews an African AIDS patient for a segment of "60 Minutes."

SOME COMMON TELEVISION NEWS TERMS & JARGON

Television reporters use many of the same terms radio reporters do (see page 168). In addition:

Audio: Sound heard on TV.

Video: Images seen on TV.

Sound bite: A recorded comment from a news source, usually audio *AND* video.

Track: The audio recording of a reporter narrating a story.

B-roll (or *cover*): Video images shot at a news scene that are later used to illustrate (or *cover*) a sound bite or reporter's track that was recorded separately.

Stand-up: A shot of a reporter at a news scene talking into the camera; if it's *live* (not prerecorded), it's called a *live shot*.

Package: A story that's prepared by a reporter, usually taped, featuring the reporter's track, one or more sound bites and often a stand-up.

Anchor intro (or *lead-in*): The lead, read by an anchor, that introduces a reporter's package.

Bridge: A stand-up that moves the story from one angle to another.

Toss: What's said as one anchor or reporter hands off to another.

On cam (or *o/c*): On-camera; the image that's being telecast.

VO, voice-over: When the anchor speaks over video, or when a reporter narrates over video cover.

SOT, sound-on-tape: A recorded sound bite (usually audio *AND* video) played during a story.

Rundown: The order in which stories will appear during a newscast.

Prompter: A device that projects a news script in front of the camera lens for an anchor to read. (*TelePrompTer* is a well-known brand name.)

Talking head: A person being interviewed; a dull sound bite of someone just talking.

SOME ADVICE FOR BEGINNING TELEVISION NEWS REPORTERS

◆ *Collaborate.* Print and radio reporters go solo to news events, but TV news relies on teamwork between you and your photographer. So start thinking visually. Share ideas for story angles, camera angles, where to focus. Remember — the stronger your visuals, the better play your story will get. Learn to respect and *collaborate* with images.

◆ *Write to the video.* Lead with your strongest shot (the car chase, the burning house, the coach's tantrum). Grab viewers' attention with an arresting image, then structure your story from there — like you're storyboarding a movie or sequencing frames in a comic strip. Weave your narration around the images; provide the details and transitions that keep things moving.

◆ *Don't overload with facts.* Keep in mind that viewers must process the images and narration simultaneously. Too much detail will overtax their concentration.

You don't need to explain what's obvious in the video. ("As you can see, dozens of clowns are walking alongside those parade floats.") Instead, provide narration that enhances the images — or use video to enhance your narration. Tell us facts the images can't provide. ("The

VIDEO INTERVIEWING TIPS

◆ **Find a location** free of disturbing background noise and distracting visuals.

◆ **Get to the point.** Savvy TV reporters sense the sound bites they're looking for, and they zip through interviews quickly — collecting pearls, not mining for ore. Steer subjects to where the shortest, sweetest sound bites are.

◆ **Maintain eye contact.** It'll divert your subject's gaze away from the camera gear. Ask interviewees to look at *you,* not the lens.

◆ **Rephrase and re-ask questions** if you think that will help interviewees give you shorter, smarter answers.

◆ **Watch for good sound bites.** Jot down phrases in your notebook that'll help you locate the most airworthy bites later on.

◆ **Avoid "stepping on" sound bites** with questions or reactions (like "uh-huh") as subjects talk. Keep quiet. Nod your head.

◆ **Remember to shoot cutaways** — video that shows you listening attentively to your subject — at the end of your interview.

parade's clowns are actually convicts on leave from Jackson State Prison.")

◆ *Engage viewers' emotions.* Take a wildfire, for example. "Don't just tell them how many homes burned; let them hear the crackle of flames," says Cara Liu, a reporter for KPHO in Phoenix. "Show them the melted windows to illustrate how hot the fire burned. Don't just tell them how many people had to be evacuated; let them hear from a family, scrambling to gather their loved ones and most precious belongings. Television can capture emotion like no other medium."

◆ *Look professional.* That usually means a jacket and tie for men, a dress or suit for women. Wear solid colors; avoid stripes. If bright lights make your skin shine, add makeup. And don't forget your hairspray! (One anchor suggested we devote an entire chapter to "Hair.")

Think that's vanity? Look: If you've got bad hair, an ugly tie or a huge pimple on your nose, viewers will latch onto it and become distracted. You could be announcing a cure for cancer, but viewers will say, "Hey — check out *the zit on his nose.*" That's why you should try to eliminate all distracting flaws. Aim for flawlessness ... not glamour. ▼

COMMON FORMS FOR TELEVISION NEWS STORIES

It's the newscast producer's job to decide how much air time each story deserves — and what format it should use. For short, simple stories, an anchor simply reads the script; for longer, more complex topics, a reporter works with a producer, editor and photographer to produce a *package*. Below are four of the most common story formats, as demonstrated in stories broadcast on KGW in Portland, Ore.

READER

This is the most basic type of story: the anchor simply reads the news script while looking at the camera. Often, an over-the-shoulder graphic (OTS) identifies the topic with an image or caption, as this example shows:

(ANCHOR ON CAM)

VIOLENCE IN IRAQ OVERNIGHT KILLED FOUR U-S MARINES. THE MILITARY REPORTS THAT A ROADSIDE BOMB IN THE ANBAR PROVINCE WEST OF BAGHDAD EXPLODED, KILLING THREE MARINES . . . AND A FOURTH DIED AFTER AN EXPLOSION SUNDAY.

VOICE-OVER (VO)

This format begins with the anchor or reporter on-camera. As she continues to read, her voice overlays videos that illustrate the topic. This is often called video "cover." (In an actual newscast script, the left side of the page would contain detailed information on the type and timing of the video clips.)

(ANCHOR ON CAM)

A SEARCH TODAY FOR TWO MISSING FISHERMEN IN TILLAMOOK BAY HAS BEEN SUSPENDED, AND NOW THE COAST GUARD WILL LAUNCH AN INVESTIGATION TO DISCOVER WHY THAT CRABBING BOAT SANK.

(ANCHOR/VO)

PIECES OF THE BROKEN VESSEL WASHED UP ON THE BEACH YESTERDAY. THE BODY OF ONE FISHERMAN HAS BEEN RECOVERED.

TODAY, SEARCHERS ON 18 BOATS COMBED THE COASTLINE FOR THE MISSING MEN AND FOUND NOTHING.

THE TILLAMOOK SHERIFF SAYS HE DOUBTS THE SEARCH WILL RESUME TOMORROW.

VOICE-OVER TO SOUND ON TAPE (VO/SOT)

This format segues from a VO into a sound bite — usually a brief, edited comment from a newsmaker. (At some stations, this format is called VO/B, for "voice-over w/ bite.") The VO script should segue smoothly into the bite.

(ANCHOR ON CAM)

A PORTLAND WOMAN IS DEAD, HER HUSBAND IN SERIOUS CONDITION TONIGHT AFTER A WRONG-WAY DRIVER SLAMMED INTO THEIR MINIVAN.

(ANCHOR/VO)

THIS IS THE AFTERMATH OF THAT CRASH ON I-205 THIS MORNING. IT SHUT DOWN THE SOUTHBOUND LANES FOR SEVERAL HOURS. POLICE SAY 31-YEAR-OLD VLADIMIR SHINTAR IS THE WRONG-WAY DRIVER. POLICE FOUND BEER BOTTLES INSIDE AND OUTSIDE HIS CAR.

(DOLBEY)

"A lot of leads are still being followed here. Warrants are being written for blood draws. Investigators are saying that alcohol appears to be a factor in the collision."

PACKAGE

A package is a complete story by a reporter, usually combining sound bites, voice-overs and stand-ups. Here's a package with an anchor lead-in:

(ANCHOR ON CAM)

THE COST OF GRAFFITI IN BEAVERTON MIGHT SOON GO TO PROPERTY OWNERS AND BUSINESSES. THE CITY IS CONSIDERING A FINE FOR THOSE WHO LET THE VANDALISM LINGER TOO LONG. NEWSCHANNEL 8'S RANDY NEVES IS HERE WITH REACTION TO THAT PROPOSAL.

(NEVES, LIVE IN STUDIO)

WELL, TRACY, THE REACTION IS MIXED. GRAFFITI CRIMES ARE EXPLODING IN BEAVERTON RIGHT NOW. POLICE SAY THE LONGER A TAG IS LEFT ON A WALL, THE GREATER THE RISK OF GANG VIOLENCE. SOME BUSINESSES ARE FUMING OVER THE IDEA.

(NEVES/VO)

MIKE CLAYBOE HAS COVERED UP DOZENS OF GRAFFITI TAGS AT HIS BEAVERTON GAS STATION. THE CULPRITS NEVER CEASE.

(CLAYBOE)

"They're a bigtime problem. They're a menace. And they need to be dealt with."

(NEVES/VO)

POLICE HAVE DOCUMENTED NUMEROUS RECENT GRAFFITI INCIDENTS. THEY SHOW AN ESCALATION OF RIVAL GANGS ANTAGONIZING EACH OTHER OVER TURF ISSUES.

POLICE INVESTIGATED 80 CASES OF GRAFFITI CRIME IN 2004. THAT NUMBER JUMPED TO 230 CASES IN 2005. THAT'S A 188 PERCENT INCREASE. PROMPT REMOVAL OF THE GRAFFITI IS KEY, THEY SAY.

MAYOR ROB DRAKE IS PUSHING FOR A NEW ORDINANCE REQUIRING PROPERTY OWNERS TO CLEAN UP GRAFFITI WITHIN SEVEN DAYS -- OR FACE A 250-DOLLAR FINE.

(DRAKE)

"It was time to ramp it up and deal with it. The 250 is reasonable. It's enough to get people's attention."

(NEVES/VO)

CLAYBOE SAYS THERE ARE BETTER WAYS TO CURB CRIME THAN PUNISHING ITS VICTIMS.

(CLAYBOE)

"That is silly. This is a public safety issue. We already pay for public safety. To have somebody charge you 250 bucks just because somebody stole your car? Give me a break."

(NEVES/VO)

MAYOR DRAKE SAYS THE CITY WILL HELP BUSINESSES WITH THE CLEANUP PROCESS. BUT WITHOUT A NEW, STRICT POLICY, HE SAYS THE TAGGING EXPLOSION MAY NEVER CEASE.

(NEVES, LIVE IN STUDIO)

THE NEW RULE WILL APPLY TO ALL PROPERTY OWNERS, INCLUDING HOMEOWNERS. MAYOR DRAKE SAYS THEY'LL HAVE 30 DAYS AFTER THE ORDINANCE PASSES BEFORE THE GRAFFITI RULES ARE ENFORCED.

The PRESS ROOM

ADVICE ON REPORTING AND WRITING FROM BROADCAST JOURNALISTS

For this edition of the Press Room, we interviewed dozens of radio and TV professionals across the country. Here's a selected sampling of their responses.

WHAT ADVICE WOULD YOU GIVE SOMEONE JUST STARTING OUT IN BROADCAST NEWS?

Have very thick skin. You will send out a lot of tapes. You need to learn to take rejection in stride.

Melissa Cabral, anchor, KHSL/KNVN-TV, Chico-Redding, Calif.

Ask yourself: how bad do you really want it? Does getting to work at 3 a.m. sound worthwhile? Working X-mas, Thanksgiving, etc.? Are you willing to move out of state for $14,000 a year, before taxes? If not, try something else.

Tyler Lopez, reporter, KMGH-TV, Denver

Wear comfortable shoes, never pass up a chance to go to the bathroom and always carry extra food. You never know when the big story is going to break and you're going to be stuck covering it all day long.

Chris Filippi, reporter, KIRO radio, Seattle

Look at everything and everyone as a possible story or source for a story. Never stop reporting. Whether you're at the supermarket, in your car or at a bar, the guy sitting next to you may be a lead or a feature, but you'll never know unless you look, talk and listen.

Morgan Loew, investigative reporter, KPHO-TV, Phoenix

Be strong, because if you think it's tough now . . . just wait.

Stephanie Abrams, reporter, CBS 3, Philadelphia

Find your own voice and write for it. I always used to recommend interns read Hunter S. Thompson's "Fear and Loathing on the Campaign Trail." Inevitably, someone would ask if reading it would make them better writers. "No," I'd tell 'em. "But it will show you that it is possible to write in an unconventional style more suited to you than to follow any textbook example. And THAT may help make you a better writer."

No one will ever write like Hunter, and maybe that's a good thing. But any broadcast journalist worthy of the name will develop a written style and written voice that's more like them and less like the AP Stylebook.

Bill Clark, consumer reporter (aka "The Consumer Champ"), KMGH-TV, Denver

Practice and practice and practice some more, to get comfortable in front of the camera. The one thing that negatively sticks out more than anything is a young person looking stiff and uncomfortable. Even if you have to practice with a home video camera, just sit in front and tell a story. Don't read. This is not comfortable. Tell a story about a news event or sports event. Tell the story like you're telling it to a group of friends or family members. Use hand gestures. Laugh when it's appropriate. Smile.

The world is full of young news readers who look like they're trying to be as serious as possible. You must have personality and life. You must give the viewer a reason to watch you, or they will not.

Lionel Bienvenu, sports director and main sports anchor, KMGH-TV, Denver

Don't get into radio news. It's notoriously poor-paying (even in union shops). I know I sound cynical, but I've been in the biz for a long, long time. She's a harsh mistress who takes everything you have to give and affords you very little in return. You can have fun doing it . . . just don't plan on making a living at it.

Craig Butterworth, anchor/reporter in Virginia

Focus on the writing. Writing is everything. Good writing will hold together a story with bad video. But good video will never hold a story together with bad writing.

Stefanie A. Cruz, anchor/reporter, KMAX-TV, Sacramento, Calif.

When it comes to getting that first job, don't be afraid to go to a place like Billings, Montana. I had to go to Eureka, California. It was terrible, but I was only there a year. A lot of people have the looks and talent to do the job, but far fewer have the drive to go to some terrible little town. It sometimes comes down to how badly you want it.

Troy Hayden, anchor, Fox 10 News, Phoenix

> **Love what you do. You may be forced to move far away, work holidays, long hours, and make very little money at first. But if you still love it . . . it is the best job in the world.**
>
> **Kim Fettig,** investigative reporter/anchor, CBS 46, Atlanta

Concentrate on learning to write, and read out loud constantly. Also, gather a set of facts and practice ad-libbing. Every broadcaster needs to ad-lib at some point, and it has become nearly a lost art. Learn to think on your feet.

Steve McIntosh, news director, KNSS radio, Wichita, Kan.

You have to love telling stories. If you don't, then you won't be willing to make the sacrifices necessary to achieve any measure of success.

Bob Kealing, reporter, WESH-TV, Orlando, and national hurricane correspondent for NBC

Learn the basics and don't get in a hurry. The smaller markets may not be as glamorous or pay as well, but that's where you'll learn the tools of the trade. A lot of people don't realize just how important working in radio can be. I can tell just by listening who's worked in radio and who's just done television. The people who've spent two or three years in radio write tighter, tell a better story, know more about delivery and how to use their voice. Work on your college radio station, but also work at a commercial station with a good reputation, even if it's part-time. Volunteer if you have to. Once you know how to handle live radio, television's a lot easier.

Jim Craig, news anchor/reporter, WRVA radio, Richmond, Va.

WHAT'S THE BIGGEST MISCONCEPTION PEOPLE HAVE ABOUT BEING A RADIO OR TV REPORTER?

We're all rich, have makeup artists and just sit and read a prompter.

Stefanie A. Cruz, anchor/reporter, KMAX-TV, Sacramento, Calif.

Everyone's wealthy and we all get free clothing.

Tyler Lopez, reporter, KMGH-TV, Denver

There's nothing glamorous about standing in three feet of snow in the howling wind in the dead of winter. Well, unless you're covering the Winter Olympics! Never mind, it *is* pretty glamorous — at least by my standards. Give me hurricanes or give me death.

Russell Haythorn, reporter, KMGH-TV, Denver

Long and crazy hours. Be prepared to miss every birthday, holiday and family gathering as you climb the ladder and even after you've "made it."

Many people are surprised to find out that the top spot in radio means you have to get up at 3 a.m. or earlier.

Chris Sullivan, reporter, KIRO radio, Seattle

I don't think they grasp how demanding it is. I mean mentally, emotionally and physically. Maybe they could add to the old saying, "The news never sleeps — and seldom do you."

Shawna Castellano, anchor/reporter, KLBJ radio, Austin, Tex.

Some people think all journalists do is interview people and show up in front of the camera . . . but the truth is, crafting a great story usually requires you to work much longer than the standard 8-hour day. Sometimes you're working on more than one story at a time, juggling facts, phone calls, scripts and a deadline that never changes.

Terrell Forney, reporter, WPLG-TV, Miami

That we are liberal. It's just that television lends itself to emotion which tends to appear more liberal. Most of us are just going after the bad guys, celebrating the good and telling the stories of the day.

Chris Burrous, weekend co-anchor for "Good Day Sacramento" on KMAX-TV

This business is far from glamorous. What's glamorous about carrying a camera, lugging a 35-pound tripod and running in high heels in 100-degree weather!?

Melissa Cabral, morning anchor, KHSL/KNVN-TV, Chico-Redding, Calif.

HOW IS WRITING FOR BROADCAST DIFFERENT FROM WRITING FOR THE PRINT MEDIA?

In radio, we are writing for the ear. Not the eye. That means we use short, declarative sentences, the active not the passive voice, and we use sound as a metaphor. If we do our job well, the listeners become engaged in the act of imagination. They become complicit in the story. The engaged listener is like the person in the front of a canoe; he or she will paddle while the reporter sits behind, steering.

Jeffrey Dvorkin, ombudsman, NPR, Washington, D.C.

I sometimes think that print journalists write to impress while television journalists write to be easily understood. Try reading a few sentences from The New York Times aloud. How many times did you have to come up for air? Short, direct simple sentences are best for TV.

Larry Mendte, anchor, CBS 3, Philadelphia

TV people are some of the worst spellers on the face of the earth, myself included. Our sentences tend to be fragmented or run-ons. We write conversationally as opposed to correctly, which means we're often grammatically incorrect.

Keli McAlister, reporter, Q13 Fox News, Seattle

When writing for radio, stories must always be brief and generally will not be able to explain the full story but just one part of it — hopefully, the most important part. Even Walter Cronkite once commented on the difference between print and broadcast by saying he was always tempted to end "The CBS Evening News" with the words, "That's the way it is …. for more information, consult your local newspaper."

Ken Herrera, host of Wisconsin's Morning News, WTMJ radio, Milwaukee

In television writing, think about what would get your attention about the story. That's your lead. What's more interesting: "Police are investigating a car crash on Highway 99" or "A family mourns the death of an 8-year-old boy killed in a car crash this afternoon." The lead should capture your attention immediately.

Kelli Saam, anchor/reporter, KHSL/KNVN-TV, Chico-Redding, Calif.

In broadcast journalism, you *have* to write conversationally. Even at this level, a lot of reporters tend to throw in the big words instead of just talking how you would to your mother or father on the phone. Not to say you have to dumb down the audience . . . but conversational speaking is key!!

Yvonne Nava, anchor/reporter, WPLG-TV, Miami

Print journalism requires reporters to fit every detail of what they see, hear and learn into the sentences that fill just a few paragraphs. If they fail, the reader won't see or hear the whole story. With broadcast writing, you have the luxury of letting the pictures and sounds speak for themselves. Your challenge is to write copy that gives meaning to the sights and sounds, without getting in their way.

Morgan Loew, investigative reporter, KPHO-TV, Phoenix

Broadcast writing is much tighter. Write to video. Short, declarative sentences are best.

Russell Haythorn, reporter, KMGH-TV, Denver

The difference between writing in broadcast mode and print mode is pretty much the difference between night and day. Radio, and TV for that matter, is what I call "short-attention-span theater." You have 30 seconds to tell the story and sometimes that includes a sound bite. You have to be concise and to the point.

Writing for broadcast also means writing more conversationally. Print uses words like "Council eyes tax increase." Who talks like that? In broadcast we say, "Your taxes could be going up". You're always trying to relate it to your audience.

Jeff Stapleton, anchor, WRVA radio, Richmond, Va.

Answers to these exercises
are on page 302.

1 WRITE THE LEADS FOR THESE TELEVISION NEWS STORIES

a) You're the anchor of the 11 o'clock news. Earlier this evening, there was a deadly police shooting downtown. A man had a gun and wouldn't put it down, so the officer on the scene shot and killed him.

This is the second time this has happened in the last two weeks.

There's a reporter standing by, live at the scene. What's your lead-in to the reporter's stand-up?

b) Write a one-sentence lead that best boils down this story:

Last night, following an argument, Rocky Beach, 28, attacked his wife, Sandy, with a knife. After severely cutting both her arms, he then doused her with kerosene. As Rocky searched for a match, Sandy fled from the couple's home in suburban Smallville, and is now recovering at Providence Hospital. Police have issued a warrant for Rocky's arrest. He drives a blue 2002 Toyota pickup truck.

c) Here's a summary of a dull academic news release. How would you rework it into a catchier lead?

Results of a yearlong study by the Cooper State University Food Sciences Laboratory were released Wednesday, March 31, indicating that increased consumption of beets can reduce foot odor by more than 50 percent.

2 WHAT'S WRONG WITH THIS BROADCAST NEWSWRITING?

There are at least two problems with the style and phrasing of each of these TV/radio news story excerpts. Identify the problems; rewrite each example to fix it.

a) "I've got a really painful cramp in my groin," said OSU halfback Bud Weiser, explaining why he's sitting out tonight's game.

b) The victims were taken to St. Vincent Hospital, where they are now recovering. The hospital lists them in critical condition.

c) The thieves stole $17,900,500, bank officials reported.

d) Library officials announced that patrons under the age of 18 will no longer be permitted to check out any of the library's movie videotapes or DVDs.

e) A 10-year-old skateboarder was struck and killed by a truck at 1120 Baker St. this morning. Police haven't yet identified the driver of the truck.

f) The earthquake, which struck at 7:01 a.m., caused no reported damage, just rattling windows and setting off car alarms throughout the city.

g) President George W. Bush has announced a new plan to cut estate taxes by 9%.

3 TURN THIS NEWSPAPER STORY INTO A RADIO BRIEF AND A TELEVISION PACKAGE

Back on page 47, you'll see a story (two stories, actually) about a campus dog controversy.

Read the story. Let's assume you've written it, so you won't be plagiarizing if you rework the material. Assume, too, that you have audio and video recordings of all the interviews quoted in the story.

a) *Write a radio story.* For the Bilford campus radio station, WUGH, prepare a 45-second version of this story. Include a cut or two — and in your script, indicate the complete wording and timing of any cuts you use.

b) *Write a television package.* Now rework that story for the Bilford campus TV station. You can recycle any material you used in your radio script. Assume, too, that in addition to those videotaped interviews, you've also shot plenty of video cover of dogs (like the one in the photo above) roaming and sniffing around the campus grounds.

Your producer wants a complete package, which should include an anchor lead-in, SOTs, voice-overs and a stand-up. The whole package, from start to finish, should last 90 seconds.

Outline, step by step, how you'd organize this package. Write a split-page script. On the left half, describe what viewers would see and how many seconds each separate segment of the package would last. On the right half, indicate who's speaking and the precise words they'd say.

4 WHAT'S IT CALLED?

a) In radio news, a recorded sound bite is often called a _____ or _____. In television news, it's often known as _____.

b) Here's a sound bite from President Bush: "Families is where our nation finds hope, where wings take dream." If you're playing that cut on the radio, you'll know Bush finishes speaking after he says those last two words, *take dream.* Those words are called an _____.

c) A news report read by an anchor that uses no sound bites or voice-overs, just pure narration, is called a _____.

d) You're assembling a radio story about some local drag racers. You've recorded interviews with the racers, but you've also recorded lots of motor noise that you can play in the background while you talk about the sport. What do you call that recorded noise? _____.

e) A TV anchor wraps up a story about a woman who owns 37 cats by saying, "Speaking of cats — it's raining cats and dogs out there!" Turning to face the weathercaster, he continues: "How long before the sun comes back out, Larry?" That maneuver is called a _____.

f) A short promo for an upcoming news story is called a _____.

CHAPTER

10

Public relations

How organizations deliver their messages to the media while keeping their public image as positive as possible.

IN THIS CHAPTER:

176 ▶ What is public relations?
It's not journalism. It's not advertising. A look at what PR is and isn't.

178 ▶ Planning a PR strategy
How to implement a successful plan and choose the best medium for your message.

180 ▶ Writing news releases
They're essential for PR communication. Here's advice on writing them right.

182 ▶ Balance, bias and media manipulation
What role do ethics play in a world where everyone tries to spin the truth?

News and Information

OHSU
Contact: Tamara Hargens
503-494-8653
Email Tamara Hargens

FOR IMMEDIATE RELEASE
January 24, 2005

Click Here to download high-res images. | Index of current releases | News Release Archive | News & Pubs Home

Doernbecher To Receive First Specially Designed, Kid-Friendly Ambulance From Metro West Ambulance

The first custom-designed pediatric ambulance in the region features bright colors and fun caricatures to help Doernbecher's frailest patients and their families feel more comfortable

The Pediatric and Neonatal Doernbecher Transport Team (PANDA) at Doernbecher Children's Hospital will receive the region's first kid- and family-friendly ambulance from its vendor, Metro West, at an open house this Wednesday.

The specially designed ambulance will be on display in the Doernbecher Children's Hospital parking lot from 10 a.m. to noon. The public is invited and refreshments will be served.

When PANDA Transport manager, Maureen O'Hara, R.N., requested a new ambulance from MetroWest because the current PANDA ambulance was showing signs of wear and tear, MetroWest representatives gave her team carte blanche to custom design a new ambulance that would be visually appealing to children. The ambulance vendor then contracted with Braun Northwest, an emergency vehicles manufacturer, to create the new design, which features smiling, colorful caricatures of children on the exterior and lively shades of red, yellow and blue on the interior.

"This one-of-a-kind ambulance is designed to be more inviting and less sterile to our pediatric patients and their families," said O'Hara. "We are excited to be able to offer quality, specialized care in an environment that puts our acutely ill patients at ease."

The PANDA team comprises specially trained nurses and respiratory therapists who stabilize and monitor young patients until they reach the hospital's emergency department or intensive care units. Each year the team transports several hundred acutely ill babies and children to Doernbecher Children's Hospital from around the state; 775 children were transported in 2004.

NOTE TO EDITORS: A high-resolution photo of the ambulance is available for downloading. Photos of the ambulance's interior may be accessed at the Braun Northwest Web site.

\###

OHSU Home | About OHSU | Search | Site Map | Contact OHSU
Health Care Services | Research Programs | Academic & Students | Regional Outreach

© 2001-2004, Oregon Health & Science University

PLUS: 184 ▶ The Press Room   186 ▶ Test yourself

What is public relations?

Every organization has a story to tell — and it's the job of PR professionals to tell it.

When businesses and organizations have news to announce — an event to publicize, a product to launch, a new idea to introduce — they need to get their message out. They need to encourage media coverage. They need to project a positive public image. And to do all that, they need what's known as *public relations*.

Here's a simple example to illustrate how the PR process works:

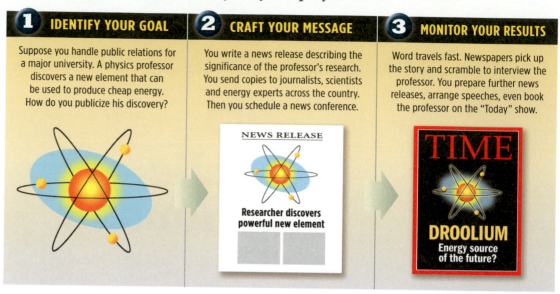

1   IDENTIFY YOUR GOAL

Suppose you handle public relations for a major university. A physics professor discovers a new element that can be used to produce cheap energy. How do you publicize his discovery?

2   CRAFT YOUR MESSAGE

You write a news release describing the significance of the professor's research. You send copies to journalists, scientists and energy experts across the country. Then you schedule a news conference.

NEWS RELEASE

Researcher discovers powerful new element

3   MONITOR YOUR RESULTS

Word travels fast. Newspapers pick up the story and scramble to interview the professor. You prepare further news releases, arrange speeches, even book the professor on the "Today" show.

TIME

DROOLIUM
Energy source
of the future?

WHAT PUBLIC RELATIONS IS . . .

Every organization, big or small, needs to distribute *information:* facts about upcoming events. Details about past accomplishments. Objectives. Opinions. Philosophies. Goals.

All that information ultimately shapes the public's perception of that organization — in other words, its *image.*

Information and *image.* Bottom line, those two things are what public relations is all about.

Useful definitions of "public relations" are hard to create (and often difficult to decipher — take, for instance, the definition at left). But here's one that works, by PR consultant Renée A. Prejean-Motanky:

Public relations is the discipline which looks after reputation, with the aim of earning understanding and support and influencing opinion and behavior. It is the planned and sustained effort to establish and maintain good will and mutual understanding between a business and its public(s).

So how does that translate into an *actual job?* If you work in public relations for a large organization, your responsibilities might include:

◆ Writing news releases.
◆ Organizing news conferences.
◆ Coordinating crisis communications.
◆ Crafting the organization's public identity.
◆ Planning the launch of new products and services.
◆ Producing newsletters and media for employees.
◆ Sponsoring tours, exhibitions and special events.
◆ Attending conferences and delivering speeches.
◆ Acting as the organization's spokesperson (or training others to deal with the media).

. . . AND WHAT IT ISN'T

College students are often attracted to public relations (or avoid it) without really understanding what it *is,* falling victim to these common myths:

◆ *PR is glamorous.* Students sometimes fantasize that PR is a world of celebrities, parties and paparazzi. They dream of careers in tourism (Caribbean cruises!) and fashion (Supermodels!! In sexy swimsuits!!!). Sadly, however, public relations is a business, not a lifestyle. Most PR professionals work for government agencies, high-tech companies, financial corporations — even manufacturing firms. Think industrial solvent is sexy? You may be disappointed.

◆ *PR is easy.* Journalists often quit the newsroom for jobs in public relations, leaving colleagues to grumble, "Aww, she sold out. Went for the easy money. Short days, long lunches." In truth, PR is just as rigorous as news reporting: long hours, relentless pressure to produce. You spend your days researching and writing, planning and strategizing — not schmoozing. Sorry.

◆ *PR is sleazy.* It's all snake oil, subterfuge and spin — at least, that's what some cynics think. And to be fair, the public is weary of cheap publicity stunts, hollow sound bites and gimmicky photo ops. They're sick of doublespeak from politicians and slickly prepackaged lies from greedy corporations.

In reality, however, most PR is useful and welcome, even vital to the community. The Red Cross tells you where to donate blood to earthquake victims. Local police warn you about a ring of car thieves. The city zoo announces its gorilla had a baby. What's so sleazy about that? If you think it's "greedy" for a church group to send out a news release announcing their Christmas clothing drive, then *you're* the Scrooge.

HOW PUBLIC RELATIONS DIFFERS FROM JOURNALISM

If you major in public relations, you're usually required to take at least one reporting class. Why?

For one thing, gaining insight into how the news media operate — how they select, reject and report stories — will help you collaborate more effectively with editors and reporters in any future encounters.

But more importantly, journalism teaches you how to write clean, crisp copy. That's an essential skill for anyone practicing PR. The ability to conduct extensive research, process complex information and communicate it clearly is just as crucial in public relations as it is in journalism.

Beyond that, however, the two occupations take separate but similar paths:

JOURNALISM	PUBLIC RELATIONS
Journalists serve the general public. Thus, they structure their news stories to be as fair and complete as possible.	PR specialists serve organizations. Thus, they structure their messages to be as beneficial to their clients as possible.
Journalists avoid taking sides or advocating action; their job requires independence and objectivity.	PR practitioners promote their clients and advocate action; their job requires loyalty and persuasion.
Journalists control all the information that goes into — and stays out of — their stories.	PR practitioners provide information to journalists, but can't control how those journalists use it.
Journalists depend heavily upon PR practitioners for information (but always remain a bit wary of them).	PR practitioners depend heavily upon journalists for news coverage (but always remain a bit wary of them).
Most journalists specialize in just one form of media: writing stories in newspapers, for example.	PR specialists employ a wide range of media: newsletters, video news releases, brochures, speeches, Web sites, etc.
Many journalists are individualists wary of "selling out" to big corporations. They work in newsrooms where salaries are low and the focus is on journalistic autonomy.	Many PR experts are team players who enjoy working in corporate environments where salaries are higher and the focus is on planning and profitability.
Ultimate goal: informing the public.	Ultimate goal: generating goodwill toward the client.

HOW PUBLIC RELATIONS DIFFERS FROM ADVERTISING

To a casual observer, public relations seems like just another way for businesses to boost sales — like advertising or marketing, but with a more prestigious-sounding name.

Many organizations blur the boundaries, too, with ad and PR staffs sharing the same tools, techniques and job titles.

Yes, advertising and PR both promote an organization to the public. Both seek to improve its success (i.e., its profitability).

But while advertising focuses on *sales*, PR focuses on *public perceptions and attitudes*. Some organizations never advertise, yet every organization needs some kind of public relations.

"Advertising sells the product," says consultant Fraser P. Seitel. "PR sells the organization."

Other differences:

ADVERTISING	PUBLIC RELATIONS
Advertising tries to seduce you with appealing images, catchy music, clever phrases and vague concepts.	PR tries to motivate you with facts, providing explanations and details that withstand scrutiny.
Advertisers control their message: how ads look, where they appear, what they say.	PR specialists provide information to other media, who then control how it's used.
Advertising can be flashy, fantastic and funny. Exaggeration (and distorting the truth) is commonplace.	PR is usually low-key and serious. Exaggeration (and distorting the truth) is damaging, often deadly.
Advertising is expensive. It costs money to run ads in newspapers and magazines, on TV and radio.	PR is relatively cheap. Favorable news coverage can result from news releases, speeches or low-cost publicity events.
Advertising relies upon ads and commercials that run over and over and over and over.	In PR, you write a news release only once. You hold a news conference just once. All your efforts are fresh, not recycled.
Advertising is usually seen and heard by anybody and everybody.	PR is usually aimed at specific targets: journalists, decision-makers. etc.
People try to avoid ads. They tend to distrust or ignore what they see and hear in advertisements.	People seek out interesting news stories (which often originate from PR). They tend to trust what they see and hear in news stories.

Planning a public relations strategy

Without planning, you can't develop a strategy; without a strategy, you can't achieve your goals.

Organizations come in all sizes — but big or small, they need public relations for efficient communication both *internally* (within the organization) and *externally* (with the public).

At smaller shops and offices, one person might manage all the PR efforts, working alongside the business owner or agency director. But larger organizations either hire outside public relations firms or assemble their own PR staff.

The bigger the staff, the more specialized each person's job becomes. Some staffers might be assigned "beats" within the organization, like reporters in a newsroom. At a computer company, for instance, one staffer might specialize in media relations for hardware products, while another focuses on customer service; another might edit the company newsletter, while someone else coordinates outreach projects that provide computers to disadvantaged students.

Still, every successful PR effort requires extensive research, planning and teamwork among the organization's leaders and its PR staff. Here's how the process works:

RACHEL MacKNIGHT, *media relations coordinator, Oregon Health & Science University:* "We spend a lot of our time planning, sometimes in large groups and sometimes in small groups. My colleague Harry Lenhart and I frequently get together to coordinate and plan. We share the South Waterfront beat. The university has entered into a development agreement with the city of Portland and some private entities to help redevelop an underused area along the riverfront. The project is the source of many public relations opportunities and many challenges for a university more accustomed to educating health care providers and the latest advances in research than real estate development."

FOUR STEPS TO CREATING AND IMPLEMENTING A PUBLIC RELATIONS PLAN

Effective public relations is a systematic effort — and whether you're a big organization or a solo enterprise, you need to proceed in a methodical way. Ready to launch a PR campaign? Here's a four-step approach to help you organize the process.

❶ ANALYZE THE SITUATION

First, you need to focus on the issue at hand. Is there a crisis to manage? (Did one of your trucks spill toxic sludge on the freeway)? Or do you just want to increase attendance? Attract voters? Generate interest in your new product?

Try writing a *problem statement* to clarify the issue. Something like:
◆ We need to recruit 100 volunteers for our annual Beach Clean-up Day. Or:
◆ We need to increase our magazine's circulation by 10 percent next year.
To craft a useful problem statement, define the issue as clearly as you can. Try thinking like a journalist —
Who is most affected or involved?
What exactly is the problem?
When and **where** does it matter most?
Why are we concerned?
How does this affect our public?

Extensive research is essential, so start gathering facts. Talk to organization officials and staff members. Analyze trends. Conduct surveys.

When you fully understand the issue, you're ready to ask: *What are our goals? What do we specifically hope to achieve?* Remember, the more clearly you state your goals *now*, the better you'll be able to measure your success later on.

❷ PLAN THE STRATEGY

Sometimes a big problem requires you to answer some big questions: *Who are we? How do we position ourselves in this community? What identity should we project? What's our mission statement?* The bigger your problem or broader your goal, the more essential it becomes to wrestle with those philosophical issues.

But for smaller, short-term goals, you need to determine what your message is — and how best to deliver it. Start with the big picture, then zoom in on specific details by asking questions such as:

Who are we trying to reach? And who can best help us reach them?
What will our message be? What result are we after? What will it cost?
When should we deliver our message?
Where should we target our efforts?
How do we distribute our message most effectively? And how do we want the public to respond?

Ideally, you and your colleagues will craft a detailed, step-by-step strategy that attacks your problem from a variety of angles using a mix of media. (See the next page for a summary of options.) Once your client/employer endorses your plan — and you finalize its budget — you can begin implementation.

❸ IMPLEMENT THE PLAN

This is where your abstract plan becomes reality, taking the form of news releases, speeches, Web sites, brochures, news conferences — the options go on and on. But a skilled PR practitioner knows how best to match the message with the medium to yield the most productive results.

Smart public-relations campaigns may combine a variety of approaches. Why? It's essential to select the most effective format, design and writing style for each type of audience you're trying to reach. A zoo Web site aimed at kids, for example, should be radically different from a fundraising letter aimed at wealthy donors.

Every bit of PR material you generate needs to be clever. Creative. Coordinated like clockwork. And consistent — in look, feel, writing style, color and typography — with all companion efforts.

Most importantly, you've got to craft your message to cut through the clutter. The public (and your media contacts) are buried beneath an avalanche of junk mail and spam. What will it take to get your message noticed? How will you develop news angles that generate the coverage you desire?

❹ EVALUATE THE RESULTS

It's essential to monitor your public-relations efforts to determine how your plan is actually *working*. That's why, before launching any PR strategy, you should establish exactly how you'll evaluate its results — whether by analyzing sales figures, monitoring attendance records, conducting surveys, tracking public feedback, etc.

Remember, statistical data is always preferable to anecdotes, random observations or gut instincts. Everybody has opinions, but you need *objective* answers to such questions as:
◆ What succeeded? What failed?
◆ Did the plan adhere to its objectives?
◆ Did the information reach its target audience? Was our message accepted? Did our message stimulate *action*?
◆ Were the costs worth the benefits?
◆ Has the outcome been affected by factors that our plan failed to address?
◆ Were there unintended, undesirable consequences that need to be mitigated?

Periodic reviews can help you make midcourse corrections while the plan is still in progress. And once a campaign is over, the lessons you've learned can be reapplied to future projects.

MATCHING YOUR MESSAGE TO THE MOST EFFECTIVE MEDIUM

Once you've planned your PR strategy, how do you spread your message? There's no one-size-fits-all solution. Some information is best delivered in a printed text format. For other material, photos and videos may be most effective. And sometimes the human touch — face-to-face meetings, interviews or speeches — will provide optimal results.

Here are the most common options PR professionals employ:

THE NEWS RELEASE

The news release (or press release) is the most useful tool in the PR toolbox. It's the simplest, most popular way for an organization to deliver its message to the media. ▼

In fact, numerous studies have shown that at least half of the content in most newspapers originates from news releases. That's an impressive amount — but keep in mind, those aren't all actual *stories*. News releases supply material for everything from business briefs and police logs to calendar information (club meetings, gallery exhibits, school concerts, etc.).

Some news releases are reprinted verbatim; most aren't. Instead, they provide the facts, ideas or angles for stories that reporters subsequently write.

There's also the **video news release** (VNR): a short, broadcast-quality news package supplied to TV stations, ready to run. It's an effective PR tool, but many critics feel it's "fake news" that blurs the line between advertising and journalism — especially when TV stations use VNRs without identifying them as such.

PRESS RELEASE

FOR IMMEDIATE RELEASE — Sept. 20, 2005

Media Contact: Eamonn Hughes, Dublin Marketing, 503-554-5455, hughes@barbecue.com

Public Contact: Student Barbecue Association, 503-555-6655

CAMPUS CLUBS COMBINE TO SPONSOR BINGO & BARBECUE BASH

As part of Ringworm Awareness Week, students from the Mountain Biking Club and the Student Barbecue Association will sponsor a Bingo and Barbecue Bash Friday, Sept. 29, at 7 p.m. in Gilligan Hall.

Profits from the barbecue, which costs $10 per person, will be donated to the Ringworm Prevention Cooperative.

The barbecue will offer diners a choice of chicken, ribs, shrimp, roasted corn on the cob, coleslaw and chocolate cake. And at 9 p.m., immediately following the barbecue, a bingo tournament will offer participants the chance to compete

OTHER WRITTEN COMMUNICATIONS

Newsletters are distributed to employees or members of special-interest groups. Articles inform and entertain while advancing the organization's objectives.

Pamphlets, brochures and manuals can convey facts about an organization's history, philosophy and facilities (for external audiences) or provide details about employee conduct, pension plans or training programs (for internal distribution).

Position papers or *white papers* explain an organization's stance on topical or controversial issues. These reports are distributed to public officials, financial analysts, special-interest groups and influential decision-makers, often to correct false impressions created by previous media coverage.

Byliners are stories ostensibly written by an organization official — the director or CEO, for example — but in fact, they're ghost-written by trained PR staffers. And **op-ed pieces** are opinionated byliners that run in newspapers on the page opposite the paper's editorials. The credibility of these articles is enhanced by the "expert" byline. More importantly, byliners let officials (not reporters) control the material and carefully craft their viewpoints.

Web sites allow PR practitioners to bypass the news media altogether and control all aspects of the message — while adding images and interactive extras. Many corporate sites now upload all news releases, position papers and promotional images onto a special PRESS section of their sites.

OTHER INTERACTIVE PR OPTIONS

Speeches allow an organization's representatives to deliver key talking points *directly* to interested groups. A well-polished public statement — or a PowerPoint presentation with art and charts — can convey information more persuasively than written text. Speeches personalize the organization, too, while encouraging discussion and debate.

News conferences allow newsmakers and designated spokespersons to speak directly to the media — or directly to the public, if TV news directors find the topic newsworthy. PR professionals coordinate the proceedings and, in many cases, coach company officials on what to say and how to say it.

Special events can include a wide range of publicity efforts: media days, fundraisers, photo opportunities, 10K races — even an outing at the zoo for disadvantaged kids.

Exhibits educate and entertain while raising the organization's profile — whether they're booths at a convention, displays at a fair or signs on the company's factory tour.

Lobbying encompasses all attempts to influence legislation — by letters, phone calls or personal visits. The process is often abused, but for any organization dependent on government funding or support, it's essential to keep legislators well-informed.

THE MEDIA KIT

Media kits (or press kits) compile a variety of promotional material designed to make reporters say, "Hey, this could make a good story!" Whether on paper or online (and digital packages are becoming standard), media kits may include a news release, background info, a biography, photos, even stories reprinted from other news outlets. The goal? Make a wealth of information look as appealing and accessible as possible.

At right are pages from a media kit sent to hundreds of newspapers by a PR firm representing Oreo cookies. A news release announces that "America's Favorite Cookie" will celebrate its 90th birthday with special festivities at a New Jersey shopping mall where the original cookie factory once stood...

... while this next page lists amazing facts that should appeal to feature writers. For instance: *If every Oreo cookie ever made were stacked on top of each other — more than 450 billion — the pile would reach to the moon and back more than six times.*

This fact sheet arranges basic dates and statistics into a timeline.

Another page announces a promotional contest that asks consumers, *"What's Your Favorite Oreo Moment?"* The winners get a trip to the cookie exhibit — and a year's supply of Oreos.

Like many media kits, this one contains photos that editors are encouraged to use, like this classic advertisement from 1924.

MORE ON **WRITING NEWS RELEASES** ▶ 180

Writing news releases

They provide the ideas and information that become news —

— or at least, that's how it's *supposed* to work. You need to spread your message; journalists need material for stories.

So why, then, do most news releases wind up in newsroom junkpiles?

They're too dull. Too long-winded. Too useless, confusing or self-serving.

To be effective, a news release needs two things: newsworthy information and clear presentation. If either is missing, it's doomed to be junked.

Yet even a brilliant news release can't guarantee press coverage. That's why smart PR practitioners build personal relationships with reporters and editors, relationships based on trust and mutual cooperation. They learn *who's* interested in *what* kinds of stories; they understand *where* and *when* those stories are likely to run.

WHY ISSUE A NEWS RELEASE?

◆ To promote an upcoming event or appearance.
◆ To introduce new products, services, projects, campaigns, facilities or fads.
◆ To convey information about a breaking news event that involves your organization.
◆ To announce personnel matters: awards, promotions, hirings, retirements, etc.
◆ To publicize an anniversary, a milestone or a record-setting performance.
◆ To present survey results or statistical data your organization has collected.
◆ To alert citizens or consumers about health or safety issues.
◆ To update the community on worthwhile causes: blood drives, charity fundraisers, etc.

WHAT A TYPICAL NEWS RELEASE LOOKS LIKE

Here's a news release from Oregon Health & Science University (OHSU). Suppose you were a reporter at a local newspaper and you received this. What would you do? Use it as a news brief? Run it as a calendar item?

Turn it into a family-oriented feature story? Incorporate it into a broader feature on the latest ambulance trends and technologies? Or would you toss it in the trash because you just don't think it's newsworthy enough?

This release date is essential. Some releases will be "embargoed" for a later date; they'll say FOR RELEASE MONDAY, JANUARY 30, alerting the media to news that won't be made public for several days.

Most news releases are now sent out as e-mail messages, as this one was. Smart e-mail software lets you add boldface and italic type — even images. The advantages of e-mail releases? They're immediate. They're free. And they allow reporters to copy names, facts and phone numbers right into their stories.

If this were a paper release for mailing or faxing, it would look much the same. But for printed news releases:
◆ Use 8 1/2-by-11 paper.
◆ Print on one side only.
◆ Leave at least a one-inch margin on the sides, top and bottom.
◆ Double-space.

Quotes are often repaired, massaged or manufactured by the PR writer, then approved by the people who allegedly said them.

The final paragraph of the story usually provides basic, boilerplate information about the organization or program.

Contact information is essential, either at the top or the bottom of the release. Make sure the phone is one that can be answered whenever reporters may need to call; use a cell phone number, if necessary.

The headline and deck work together to summarize key points in a compelling way.

This is a low-resolution photo, but a high-resolution image is available for downloading. Notice how much more appealing and effective this news release becomes with the addition of this image. This photo doesn't need a caption, but if it showed a specific person or activity, you'd need to provide names, dates, descriptions, etc.

Most news releases mark the end of the text by typing ### or -- 0 --. If this were a two-page release, you'd need to signal that the story continued, so at the bottom of the first page, you'd type this: (*MORE*). In addition, you'd want to give every additional page a number, along with a short phrase or *slug,* to avoid confusion if pages get shuffled.

News and Information

OHSU

Contact: Tamara Hargens
503-494-8653
Email Tamara Hargens

FOR IMMEDIATE RELEASE
January 24, 2005

Click Here to download high-res images... | Index of current releases | News Release Archive | News & Pubs Home

Doernbecher To Receive First Specially Designed, Kid-Friendly Ambulance From Metro West Ambulance

The first custom-designed pediatric ambulance in the region features bright colors and fun caricatures to help Doernbecher's frailest patients and their families feel more comfortable

The Pediatric and Neonatal Doernbecher Transport Team (PANDA) at Doernbecher Children's Hospital will receive the region's first kid- and family-friendly ambulance from its vendor, Metro West, at an open house this Wednesday.

The specially designed ambulance will be on display in the Doernbecher Children's Hospital parking lot from 10 a.m. to noon. The public is invited and refreshments will be served.

When PANDA Transport manager, Maureen O'Hara, R.N., requested a new ambulance from MetroWest because the current PANDA ambulance was showing signs of wear and tear, MetroWest representatives gave her team carte blanche to custom design a new ambulance that would be visually appealing to children. The ambulance vendor then contracted with Braun Northwest, an emergency vehicles manufacturer, to create the new design, which features smiling, colorful caricatures of children on the exterior and lively shades of red, yellow and blue on the interior.

"This one-of-a-kind ambulance is designed to be more inviting and less sterile to our pediatric patients and their families," said O'Hara. "We are excited to be able to offer quality, specialized care in an environment that puts our acutely ill patients at ease."

The PANDA team comprises specially trained nurses and respiratory therapists who stabilize and monitor young patients until they reach the hospital's emergency department or intensive care units. Each year the team transports several hundred acutely ill babies and children to Doernbecher Children's Hospital from around the state; 775 children were transported in 2004.

NOTE TO EDITORS: A high-resolution photo of the ambulance is available for downloading. Photos of the ambulance's interior may be seen on the Braun Northwest Web site.

###

OHSU Home | About OHSU | Search | Site Map | Contact OHSU
Health Care Services | Research Programs | Academic & Students | Regional Outreach

© 2001-2004, Oregon Health & Science University

10 TIPS FOR WRITING BETTER NEWS RELEASES

1 GIVE YOUR RELEASE AN ENGAGING HEADLINE

Remember, reporters and editors weed out junk mail by scanning news releases before actually reading them. To keep *your* release out of the trash, give it a punchy, active, attention-grabbing headline. Instead of saying *Adam Baum honored at sports banquet,* say *Adam Baum wins $10,000 as Athlete of the Year.*

Use bold type, 10 words or fewer. You can add a deck below the headline, but keep it concise and enticing.

And for e-mail releases, use short, attention-getting subject lines, too.

2 GIVE YOUR RELEASE A COMPELLING LEAD

What's true for news stories is true for news releases, too: a strong lead is essential. This is where you pitch your most newsworthy story angle and condense your most significant facts.

You've got to win over your readers *here,* in the first two paragraphs, so don't hold anything back. Don't be bland or passive; don't save good information for later in the story. Grab your readers' attention immediately, before they hit *DELETE.*

3 AVOID DISTORTION AND EXAGERRATION

You may be tempted to overhype your product or service by using promotional puffery or ad lingo. Don't do it. Avoid words like *famous, unique, cutting-edge, world-class, revolutionary.* If your product is genuinely "groundbreaking" or "first of its kind," prove it with impressive statistics and unbiased quotes.

Remember, journalists are looking for stories, not ads. Their job is to protect readers from lies and scams. Don't set off their b.s. detectors by boasting, bragging or — worst of all — lying. Once you land in their doghouse, you could be stuck there permanently.

4 AVOID JARGON AND TECHNICAL TERMINOLOGY

Your goal is to communicate instantly to the widest possible audience, so avoid specialized jargon, buzz words or acronyms that ordinary folks (or irritable journalists) won't understand. If they can't understand it, they won't read it — or reprint it.

5 USE PROPER NEWSPAPER STYLE

Think of each news release as a blueprint from which reporters will build the actual story. Ideally, a reporter should be able to write a complete news story using *only* the information your news release provides.

That means each release should contain all the five W's, along with useful quotes, facts and statistics. It should be organized in an inverted pyramid, with the most important facts first. It should use active sentence structures and proper newspaper style. It should avoid first-person pronouns (*I, we, my, our,* etc.)

DO'S AND DON'TS WHEN DEALING WITH THE MEDIA

◆ **DO customize your pitch** for different media. Think of good visuals for television, smart sound bites for radio, compelling human-interest angles for print publications.

◆ **DON'T make demands** or dictate how the story should play. Stay flexible; explore new angles. Be willing to reshape your story, if needed, to satisfy journalists' needs.

◆ **DO prepare yourself** for interviews. Rehearse your key talking points in advance (statistics, anecdotes, quotable sound bites) so you'll be ready for any sudden, on-the-record conversations.

◆ **DON'T go off the record** during an interview if you can avoid it; you may blab something you'll regret. If you don't want it quoted, don't say it.

◆ **DON'T keep score.** "Strike the word *favor* from your media relations vocabulary," says PR whiz Richard Laermer. "Just because you gave a reporter a story once, and he covered it once, doesn't mean he owes you."

◆ **DON'T bribe reporters.** They'll get fired if they accept cash, and even small thank-you gifts can create ethical backlash. Send appreciative cards or e-mails instead.

◆ **DON'T be cagey or evasive.** Give straight answers and honest facts, even if they're not always beneficial to you. Saying "no comment" raises red flags that can kill a story.

◆ **And never, ever lie.**

6 KEEP IT SHORT. CRISP. TIGHT.

Reporters receive dozens — often *hundreds* — of news releases, e-mails and phone calls each day. They're racing the clock. So get to the point.

Keep your wording concise. Keep sentences and paragraphs short.

The average news release is around 500 words. (E-mail releases should be shorter than that, in part because some e-mail programs automatically cut off long messages.)

Limit printed releases to one or two pages. Go longer *only* for important news that demands extensive details.

7 STRESS THE BENEFITS TO THE READER (AND THE REPORTER)

As they scan your release, reporters will be asking, "So what? Why should I care?" If you fail to supply a satisfactory answer, your release will be doomed.

The best releases are those that *demand* to be printed. They're useful. Essential. Newsworthy.

So think like a journalist, not like a businessman. If you're describing a new program or product, don't just describe what it is or how it works; explain why it's smarter, better, healthier, more fun, more useful, more valuable. Show how it will engage or help readers *here* (in the local area) and *now* (in a timely way).

8 PROOFREAD CAREFULLY

Journalists are professionals. They don't respect amateurish-looking copy riddled with misspellings and typos. So check and double-check everything, especially names, phone numbers and Web links. Better yet, run all your news releases by objective proofreaders who are unfamiliar with the material. Ask them to check for errors, but listen to their feedback, too, to make sure they correctly "get" your message.

9 DELIVER THE RELEASE AT JUST THE RIGHT TIME

Timing is tricky. Send out a release too soon and reporters will ignore it. Send it too late and they won't have time to verify information or answer questions.

Lead times can vary from several hours (for breaking news announcements) to several weeks (for newspaper calendar listings). Since all news outlets operate on different schedules, study their deadlines closely. As a rule, the bigger the event, the more advance notice you should provide.

10 DELIVER THE RELEASE TO THE RIGHT PERSON

Match your release to the appropriate beat. If you send a story to the business reporter, stress the business angle; for a feature editor, stress the lifestyle angle. Monitor each news outlet to find out who's who, what topics they cover, what types of stories they do. Compile a list of reliable media contacts. Get to know local reporters and their needs, so you can help each other.

Balance, bias and media manipulation

There are two sides to every story — or are there? And who decides?

Journalists may claim to be fair and balanced — they may boast of writing purely unbiased stories — but while objectivity is a noble goal, it's difficult to attain. Every source has an agenda. Every newsmaker has a stake in the story's outcome. Every press release hopes to convince reporters that *these are the facts you need,* whether it's publicizing a free AIDS clinic or unveiling plans for a new Wal-Mart.

Think that's too cynical? Try working in a newsroom for a week and watch the endless parade of puffery, partisanship and self-promotion. You'll quickly realize that news releases, press kits and speeches may inspire news stories, but they always require rethinking. Reworking. Fact-checking. Adding opposing viewpoints.

We're *not* implying that all PR is sinister, or that every press release is a scheme to manipulate the media. We just want reporters to remember: *Everybody spins.*

ONE PRESS RELEASE, ONE NEWS STORY: TWO ATTEMPTS TO DEFINE THE MESSAGE

Brandon Mayfield, an Oregon lawyer, was jailed by the FBI in 2004 after agents linked his fingerprints to terrorist bombings in Spain. But the FBI had the wrong man. After his release, Mayfield claimed the FBI violated his civil rights, targeting and framing him because he's a Muslim.

The Justice Department investigated the case. On Jan. 6, 2006, they issued their report. At left is the FBI's news release responding to the report; at right, the front-page story from The Oregonian. ▼

Here's a textbook example of "positive spin." Notice how all this upbeat phrasing makes the OIG report seem *favorable* to the FBI — as if it's just a helpful collection of friendly suggestions. The news release fails to mention what the report actually said: "We concluded that the examiners committed errors in the examination procedure, and that the misidentification could have been prevented."

Mayfield was detained for two weeks because of errors in the FBI fingerprint lab. The report probed, in extremely technical detail, how those errors occurred and how to avoid them in the future.

More positive spin: The FBI didn't abuse the Patriot Act, the report concluded, but used it only to "share" useful information.

Some nuanced evasion: The report clearly stated that, while Mayfield's Muslim religion may not have been a factor when the FBI first arrested him, it may indeed have slowed his eventual exoneration.

THE FBI NEWS RELEASE

We appreciate the work of the Office of the Inspector General (OIG) in providing additional insights and perspective into how the FBI can strengthen the process of fingerprint identification. Of particular importance, the OIG report confirmed there was no misconduct by the FBI or misuse of the USA Patriot Act. We are confident that the OIG's findings and recommendations, combined with corrective measures already implemented, will significantly enhance our ability to perform our duties to the public. . . .

The OIG report recommends several ways in which the FBI's methodology can be enhanced to minimize the risk of recurrence of the mistake. Several of these recommendations were made previously and independently by the international expert panel. Following that review, we implemented a series of procedural reforms designed to prevent future errors. . . .

The OIG report also includes other important findings about the FBI's initiation of and conduct during this investigation. First, the OIG report concludes that there was no evidence of misuse of the Patriot Act. The report finds, "contrary to public speculation," the FBI did not use certain provisions of the Patriot Act and that the Act did not affect the scope of the FBI's use of FISA surveillance or searches. Instead, the OIG report found that the effect of the Patriot Act on this investigation was to enable the FBI to share lawful information with other members of the law enforcement and intelligence communities. Second, the OIG report concluded that religion played no improper role in the identification or investigation of Mr. Mayfield. Third, the OIG report found no evidence of misconduct on the part of any FBI employees involved in this investigation.

THE NEWSPAPER STORY

FBI fingerprint analysts violated basic rules of their science to wrongly link Brandon Mayfield to the 2004 bombings in Madrid, Spain, and insisted they were correct even after learning the evidence pointed to another man, a Justice Department report said Friday.

The department's internal investigator, Inspector General Glenn Fine, also said that while the FBI did not investigate Mayfield just because he is an adherent to Islam, his religious beliefs and activities made authorities less inclined to re-examine the fingerprint.

The report said one of the fingerprint examiners "candidly admitted that if the person identified had been someone without these characteristics, like the 'Maytag Repairman,' the laboratory might have revisited the identification with more skepticism and caught the error." . . .

In a statement Friday, the FBI pointed out that after the Mayfield case, the bureau invited an independent board of experts to propose changes in how the FBI examines fingerprints, which the FBI has undertaken.

In addition, the inspector general's report "found no evidence of misconduct on the part of any FBI employees involved in this investigation," the statement said. . . .

After the inspector general released the report Friday, two members of Congress issued a letter calling for the House Judiciary Committee to hold hearings on the findings.

"The report raises real and serious questions regarding racial and ethnic profiling by the FBI as well as their competence, veracity and use of Patriot Act powers," said the letter signed by Democratic Reps. John Conyers of Michigan and Robert Scott of Virginia.

Some news outlets drew even harsher conclusions than this. CNN, The Associated Press and The New York Times all stated in their leads that the FBI had done "sloppy work."

Compare the details in these two paragraphs with the highlighted claim near the bottom of the FBI's press release at left.

Here, the story cites that FBI news release, the agency's official response to the report.

We've had to severely shorten this newspaper story, which originally ran about 40 column inches, or 1,600 words. The story included details from the report, background on the case and comments on the findings — including a quote from Mayfield's attorney, who claimed the FBI "misled a judge" to arrest his client. At the end of the story, the final word goes to these Democratic critics. Is that liberal bias?

THE SLIPPERY SLOPE OF SPIN, DISTORTION AND DOUBLESPEAK

Politicians, PR pros and corporate spokespersons are often forced to announce bad news. Explain blunders. Defend unpopular programs.

They know they shouldn't *lie*. Lies, if exposed, produce negative backlash.

So instead, they *spin*.

What's the difference? "When somebody says something of a serious nature that is flat-out untrue and intended to deceive or hurt another person — or keep the public in the dark about an issue of vital importance — that's a lie," explains Bill Press, former co-host of CNN's "Crossfire."

"When somebody twists, bends, toys, exaggerates or plays with the truth in order to make it sound better or give oneself a tactical advantage, that's spin."

But spinning is just the beginning. Here's a roundup of other dubious tricks and tactics both journalists and PR professionals should be wary of:

Scott McClellan relentlessly spun his press conference responses as press secretary for George W. Bush.

SPINNING THE NEWS: COMMON TERMS AND TECHNIQUES

Doublespeak: Any language deliberately crafted to disguise, distort or evade the truth.

Some doublespeak is just gobbledygook — a jumble of buzzwords and bureaucratese. Listen to former Federal Reserve Chairman Alan Greenspan: *"It is a tricky problem to find the particular calibration in timing that would be appropriate to stem the acceleration in risk premiums created by falling incomes without prematurely aborting the decline in the inflation-generated risk premiums."*

Some doublespeak uses cagey syntax to dance around the truth. When caught in a lie and asked, "Is that correct?", President Clinton famously responded with classic doublespeak: *"It depends on what the meaning of the word 'is' is."*

Doublespeak uses prestigious-sounding words to bestow status — calling a garbage collector a "sanitation engineer," for instance. Critics accused President George W. Bush of Orwellian doublespeak when he unveiled his "Healthy Forests Initiative" (it promoted logging, they claimed) and his "Clear Skies" plan (which actually weakened air-pollution safeguards, opponents said).

Then there are **euphemisms:** inoffensive terms substituted for harsher, more disturbing words. In war, *genocide* becomes *ethnic cleansing; civilian casualties* become *collateral damage.* In business, *layoffs* become *downsizing, rightsizing, headcount adjustments* or *reductions in force.*

Cherry-picking: This is the technique of selecting only those facts that support your argument while ignoring the majority that *don't.* It's often done with statistics; you argue that *42 percent of Americans support the president's policy* when polls actually show that 80 percent want him impeached.

A related tactic is **quote mining,** where you dig up statements your opponents have made that, unfairly taken out of context, seem to undermine their arguments.

Glittering generalities: Instead of clearly detailing a specific course of action, you use vague but emotionally appealing abstractions. As John Kerry said: *"I believe in an America that's strong at home and respected in the world. I believe we can have a strong economy focused on good-paying jobs, a health care plan that reduces costs, an energy plan that frees us from Mideast oil, and I believe we can lead a strong military and strong alliances that keep America safe and secure."* Note his repeated use of the word "strong." But what does it mean?

Bridging: This is one of the basic skills that PR coaches teach corporate executives facing hostile press interviews: Instead of directly answering an uncomfortable question, you transition (or bridge) into a more favorable topic. Media trainers suggest such "bridge" phrases as *"Let me put that in perspective"* or *"What's important to remember is...."*

Bridging basically means ignoring the question the reporter asked, and answering the question *you* wanted to be asked.

The nondenial denial: When someone accuses you of wrongdoing, you say, *"I'm not going to dignify that with a response."* Thus, instead of answering the charges (and risking lying), you criticize the criticism, calling it "absurd" or "unprofessional."

Similarly, the **nonapology apology** *("I'm sorry if you were offended by my remarks")* allows you, in the words of humorist Bruce McCall, "to get what you want by seeming to express regret while actually accepting no blame."

Astroturfing: An astroturfing campaign tries to sway public opinion on an issue by creating the illusion of widespread grass-roots support (phony grass = *astroturf.* Get it?). By planting letters to the editor, blog posts, even online reviews, a handful of astroturfers try to pass themselves off as mass numbers of "ordinary" citizens.

Managing the news: Planting questions at press conferences, "dumping" damaging news on Friday afternoons (after people turn off their brains for the weekend), bribing columnists to support certain policies, leaking information (favorable and/or fabricated), threatening editors or sources — these are some of the unethical tactics that help to manipulate media coverage in your favor.

ETHICS IN THE PRACTICE OF PUBLIC RELATIONS

What would you do if a company asked you to promote a product that was unsafe or had been produced using child labor overseas? How far would you twist the truth in a press release defending a corrupt client? Is it ethical to shower senators with gifts and cash so they'll pass legislation that helps your cause?

PR professionals frequently confront these issues. And after years of scandals and ethical lapses, the PR industry realizes that, ironically, it has a public-image problem of its own. In a 2005 poll by the Public Relations Society of America (PRSA), 85 percent of Americans agreed with the statement that *"People who work in the PR industry sometimes take advantage of the media to present misleading information that is favorable to their clients."*

That's why PR firms and associations often adopt codes of ethics.

The PRSA, for instance, urges its members to:
◆ Be honest and accurate in all communications.
◆ Act promptly to correct erroneous communications for which the practitioner is responsible.
◆ Avoid deceptive practices.

PR professionals understand that organizations maintain the public's respect only when they behave ethically. Lies, spin and distortions may temporarily deflect a crisis — but they ultimately cause worse damage once the truth becomes known.

"Public relations professionals are often the conscience of a company," says media relations consultant Steven R. Van Hook. "It's not always a popular spot to be in, but it is our duty. It's what we're paid to do. And, as we sometimes confess to one another, it's what we largely love most about our job."

The PRESS ROOM

ADVICE ON PUBLIC RELATIONS FROM VETERAN PRACTITIONERS

For this PR edition of the Press Room, we interviewed dozens of public relations professionals across the country. Here's a selected sampling of their responses.

WHAT ADVICE WOULD YOU GIVE SOMEONE JUST STARTING OUT IN PUBLIC RELATIONS?

Get some experience in media relations. It's an absolute must. If your client is the media, you need to know how reporters think, what makes a good story, how to pitch so you see what's in it for them and not you.

Julie Hansen, public relations director, Mall of America, Bloomington, Minn.

Learn to write and write well. The fundamental skill for success in public relations is the skill of writing. Writing is a long-term art. The more you read, the better you write. The more you write, the better you write. And practice makes perfect.

Gerard Corbett, vice president of the branding and corporate communications group of Hitachi America Ltd.

Don't take no for an answer. Turn "no" around and you've got "on."

Miriam Silverberg, publicist/owner of Miriam Silverberg Associates

Throughout your entire career, always have at least one mentor. And try to choose people who are tops in their field. This will shorten your learning curve, you'll learn from the very best people in the PR field, and you will become far more successful than if you were left to learn on your own.

Become a sponge and never, ever stop learning.

Joan Stewart, The Publicity Hound, Port Washington, Wis.

Get some sales experience! The principles of public relations are also the principles of salesmanship. Learning the fundamentals of customer characteristics, buying motives, product performance, sales aids, overcoming customer objections and closing the sale are all essential to public relations.

Patti D. Hill, president and founder of Blabbermouthpr.com, Austin, Texas

Spend time in a newsroom. Doesn't matter what kind — TV, print or radio. Don't try to pitch someone in a newsroom if you don't know what their life is like.

Tracy Kurschner, director, Weber Shandwick, Minneapolis

Understand what public relations is and what it is not. It's not just event planning, it's not just publicity and it's certainly not hype. Public relations is a relationship-building function. It has a critically important social role to play, so learn all you can about people.

Yes, writing is important. Writing and editing are the fundamental skills for this field but they will only take you so far — into the role of the communication technician. If you have ambitions as a public relations manager, then you'll need to understand social psychology, organizational communication, sociology, business management and economics as well.

Dr. Larissa A. Grunig, professor emerita, University of Maryland

Be a journalist first. It gives you instant credibility with a reporter. My fastest wins happened when I could tell a reporter about my background, assuring him/her that I knew a story from fluff, that I wouldn't waste their time pitching something that didn't have news value.

Vicki Carlew, VP of Marketing for the Cerner Corporation, Kansas City, Mo.

Stay calm, no matter what happens. It's your job to stay calm in the eye of the storm, especially if your client or your colleagues panic over potential bad news or a big setback in a project. Your job is to make everybody stop, sort out the implications and look at options for dealing constructively and quickly with the problem. I like to ask, "What's the headline going to be?"

Nancy Conner, director of publications and media relations, Minnesota State Colleges and Universities

Credibility is the most important quality one can possess in the public relations field. Without credibility, why should anyone listen to what we have to say, let alone believe it or act upon it? Maintaining one's credibility means constantly being open, honest and accessible.

Lt. Randy Force, public information officer, Maryvale Precinct, Phoenix Police Department

Study the art of writing — and I don't mean "creative" writing. Study the art of writing simple, concise sentences that communicate clearly. Make sure the words are spelled correctly. This seemingly simple act will propel you above most of your peers. Great communication makes things happen. It sells product. It changes minds. It motivates people to action.

Tim McIntyre, vice president, communications, Domino's Pizza Inc.

Read the paper — your local daily newspaper, and a national paper like the Wall Street Journal, New York Times or even USA Today. Better yet: read all of them. Reading the nationals helps you identify trends and potential for stories in your market — positioning your clients as sources — that reporters often don't have time to read.

Sara Fleury, president, BJ Communications, Phoenix

Shut up. Shut up and listen instead of talking. Yes, you rarely will find a savvy and wise person from whom you can learn the secrets of the universe. But you still can learn a lot even from the idiots. What are they idiotic about? What form does their idiocy take? Are there common forms of idiocy? How can you work best with idiots? How can you help them do their best work? What patterns of idiocy do you now recognize in yourself?

David Oboyski, CEO, The Utopia Group

WHAT'S THE BIGGEST MISCONCEPTION PEOPLE HAVE ABOUT PR?

That it is spin and lies. I think they forget about all the PR done for non-profits, education, advocacy, hunger, AIDS, breast cancer — all of that is PR.

Linda Aldoory, editor,
Journal of Public Relations Research

◆ **That you can precisely tell the media what to print and when to print it.** Coverage has to be earned. It cannot be ordered.
◆ **That you can make bad "things" go away.** Bad deeds and bad products can't be covered up; they have to be addressed and addressed straight on — quickly, honestly, accurately.
◆ **That liking and manipulating people makes you a good PR person.** Public relations is a mixture of solid journalism, management philosophy, psychology and sociology.

Andy Marken, president,
Marken Communications, Santa Clara, Calif.

The biggest misconception is perhaps about the nature of the business. It's a two-way street. It's not just pushy publicists vying to persuade a reporter to run a story on their clients or air their clients' side of that story. Nor is it overworked reporters looking for a press release they can insert into unused space on their page. Reporters value their PR contacts (almost) as much as the PR folks value their media contacts.

PR serves a purpose. No, strike that. *Well-executed* PR serves a purpose: It helps journalists do their job.

Andy Garlikov, president,
Proadvance, Los Angeles

That our relationship with journalists is always antagonistic. Professional journalists and public relations practitioners should understand and respect the different roles the two functions play in society. They can work together productively to help report meaningful and accurate stories.

Dr. Linda Hon, professor, University of Florida

We are all glorified car salesmen. I have no problem with car salesmen, but I mean the stereotypical ones who are depicted as sleazy, greasy, and who will sell you a lemon for way too much. We're just trying to get our clients recognition for the great and unique things they're doing.

Aileen Burdock, account associate, Elizabeth Christian & Associates, Austin, Texas

People make the mistake of viewing public relations professionals as "fluff" or unnecessary. When a true public/media relations crisis hits, an organization quickly realizes the value of having the ability to manage a message and utilize strong media relationships.

Liz McClung, communications director,
Department of Corrections, St. Paul, Minn.

The biggest misperception about the PR business is that it is fun and that it is only about people.

Gerard Corbett, vice president of the branding and corporate communications group of Hitachi America Ltd.

EVER WISH YOU'D GONE INTO (OR STAYED IN) JOURNALISM?

When I first moved into public relations and marketing, I felt very uncomfortable with the completely new way of thinking that was required. I now know that was the correct career move. PR and marketing allow me to solve problems through creative thinking and strategic action plans. The field has a much longer-range view than journalism, and I've found it to be more intellectually stimulating and exciting.

I do miss covering fires, however. . . .

Steve Buchholz, director of marketing,
Western Dakota Technical Institute

The way I "do" public relations, I haven't actually left journalism. My education is in journalism, not PR. In fact, I've never taken a formal PR course.

I communicate with journalists openly and clearly. When they put forth a question based on a faulty premise, I say so. I respect deadlines. I don't pitch fluff. I recognize that not everything my company does is "newsworthy" — no matter how exciting it might be to us internally.

I tell stories. I offer perspectives. I

provide facts. I consider what I do — which is helping journalists — to be a form of journalism. The best part: I know my "beat" better than anyone else.

Tim McIntyre, vice president, communications,
Domino's Pizza Inc.

No, no, no. Not enough money, not enough innovation. Lots of lockstep professionally, ideologically and practically. Too much navel-gazing and sanctimony, not enough reflection, analysis and improvement. Way too much herd-like behavior. I'd go crazy.

I like what I do. I take integrity seriously. So I can look myself in the mirror every day. And I get to do more good as a PR person than I can as a journalist, despite conventional wisdom.

David Oboyski, CEO, The Utopia Group

Absolutely not. First, because I'm incredibly gullible, so I was a lousy journalist. And while I miss the fun, sophomoric atmosphere, journalism looks to me less and less distinguishable from business or PR these days. God bless the ones who stay and try to be solid journalists. I suspect they fight a daily battle.

Vicki Carlew, VP of Marketing
for the Cerner Corporation, Kansas City, Mo.

No, because PR includes reporting skills. Every day in this job, I use the skills I learned as a reporter and columnist: information-gathering, editing and writing.

Pete Schulberg, public information officer,
Portland Parks & Recreation

I left journalism after a 10-year stint and I haven't regretted it for a moment. It's not a life that is kind to raising a family; no one ever works 9 to 5 in television, there's no such thing as a lunch break, and "holiday" — isn't that a song?

As a reporter, I got to see thousands of things up close and take part in incredible events that most people will never experience in a lifetime, and for that I am grateful. But in PR, you don't just get a front seat to the action, you get to go deep inside.

It's very rewarding to counsel clients in the midst of a crisis on what course of action to take with the media. And as a recovering journalist, my insider's insight into the inner workings of a newsroom adds some real value to what I have to say.

Liz Miklya, senior media relations consultant,
Weber Shandwick

Answers to these exercises can be found on page 303.

1 GENERATE A NEWS RELEASE

You're the public relations coordinator at the Midland Zoo. You just learned that a polar bear was found dead this morning at the zoo. You talk to the zoo-keeper, the veterinarian and the zoo director. Below are your notes. Write a news release (with a headline) that puts the zoo in the best possible light.

Notes from your conversation with zookeeper Sara N. Getty:

◆ Homer was 16 years old — the oldest bear at the zoo. She found him floating in the pool of the polar bear exhibit at 7 a.m., an hour after his feeding.

◆ The other two polar bears, a 9-year-old male named Yukon and a 10-year-old female named McKenzie, were removed from the exhibit and are being monitored by veterinary staff.

◆ Quote: *"Homer was a very curious and playful polar bear and we will miss him terribly."*

Notes from your conversation with Dr. Shanda Lear, senior staff veterinarian:

◆ Quote: *"The zoo will perform a necropsy to try to determine the cause of death. The results will not be available for several weeks."*

◆ A 10-year-old female bobcat named Regina died of renal failure last week. Two weeks ago, a 6-year-old giraffe named Kenya died. Her neck broke when her horns got caught in her stall.

Notes from your conversation from zoo director Chris P. Bacon:

◆ Today's incident will be investigated to determine the exact cause of death.

◆ Quote: *"We will do everything in our power to determine how this bear died. Animal welfare and the preservation of species are our primary goals here at the zoo."*

◆ Confirmed that two other animals had died this month: a giraffe and a bobcat. Said the deaths are unrelated.

Information from a previous news release:
Polar bears have thrived at the zoo since 1985. Our unique exhibit allows the bears to engage in natural behaviors, playing in manufactured snow, digging in gravel and hunting trout in the chilled pool. The bears are ambassadors for their wild relatives, educating zoo visitors about these threatened animals.

2 NOW TURN THAT RELEASE INTO A NEWS STORY

Now assume you're a newspaper reporter. You've received a news release from the local zoo reporting the death of a polar bear. You interview the same three people above, who repeat that same information. Write a news story.

3 WHAT'S WRONG WITH THIS NEWS RELEASE?

Here's the text of a bad news release. It suffers from at least five serious flaws. What are they?

FOR IMMEDIATE RELEASE — May 20, 2006

Rock Legend Dan Druff to Perform Benefit Concert for Hurricane Victims

"I really want to help those people. No one else seems to really give a crap about them, even though we live in the richest country in America," said Dan Druff, lead singer of the Flakes, announcing plans to perform a benefit concert for the victims of Hurricane Katrina.

The Grammy-nominated star has a long history of such selfless activism. "Now it's time for our fans to do their part," Druff said.

Will you do your part? If you love rock 'n' roll and have even an ounce of compassion for victims, you can't miss our concert.

One of the best bands of the century, Dan Druff and the Flakes recently released their latest CD, "Shampoo This," which Rolling Stone magazine called "one of the . . . albums released this year." They're about to launch a 10-city nationwide tour.

The concert will take place on Saturday night at the LaBelle Theatre. Donations of $20 will be taken at the door. Ten percent of the proceeds will go to the American Red Cross. Advance tickets are on sale at http://www.dandruffandflakes.com.

###

4 PLAN A MEDIA KIT

Part One:

Your company is launching a new line of gourmet organic chocolates. This new product launch is being promoted with a chocolate-tasting event in local grocery stores.

You've been asked to mail media kits to help generate interest and publicity. What would you recommend including in each media kit?

Part Two:

You work in a midsize city. You want to promote your new chocolates and the tasting event to the local community. Who should receive your media kit?

The Morgue

In the newsrooms of yesteryear, editors saved copies of old stories, photos and back issues of the newspaper. These archives became known as "the morgue." This book's morgue contains examples of stories discussed in the text — many of them annotated with commentary by their original authors.

Contents

THE DEATH OF GEORGE WASHINGTON

The front page of the Ulster County Gazette — Jan. 4, 1800

▶ MORE ON **COLONIAL NEWSPAPERS** ON PAGE **8**

The Ulster Gazette began publication in Kingston, N.Y., in 1798. When George Washington died on Dec. 14, 1799, the paper first reported the story two weeks later — in its Dec. 28 edition — and followed up with more details on the Jan. 4 page below.

Though most of the text here is dull and pompous, notice how the author of the Washington obituary injects his grief into his reporting ("WASHINGTON will triumph over DEATH!").

Incidentally, this page has been called the most copied and faked antique newspaper in history. Only two original copies of the actual paper remain, but thousands of reprints have been circulating since 1800, fooling many collectors into thinking they own a priceless, authentic piece of American history.

ULSTER COUNTY GAZETTE.

Published at KINGSTON, (Ulster County) By SAMUEL FREER and SON

(Num. 88)

SATURDAY, January 4, 1800

WASHINGTON ENTOMBED

George Town: Dec. 20

On Wednesday last, the mortal part of WASHINGTON the Great —the Father of his Country and the Friend of man, was consigned to the tomb, with solemn honors and funeral pomp.

A multitude of persons assembled, from many miles round, at Mount Vernon, the choice abode and last residence of the illustrious chief. There were the groves—the spacious avenues, the beautiful and sublime scenes, the noble mansion—but, alas; the august inhabitant was now no more. That great soul was gone. His mortal part was there indeed, but ah! how affecting! how awful the spectacle of such worth and greatness, thus, to mortal eyes

· in the long and lofty Portico, whereon the Hero walked in all his glory, now lay the shrouded corpse. The countenance full composed and serene, seemed to depress the dignity of the spirit, which lately dwelt in that lifeless form! There thoes who paid the last sad honours to the benefactor of his country, took an impressive —a farewell view.

On the ornament at the head of the coffin, was inscribed Surge Ad Judicium.—about the middle of the coffin, Gloria Deo—and on the silver plate,

GENERAL GEORGE WASHINGTON

Departed this life on the 14th

On the 5th the Austro Russians were defeated at Glatus, with the loss of 1200 prisoners beside a great number of killed.

At this place there were 1400 Russians wounded and 600 at Multen.

CONGRESS

HOUSE OF REPRESEN-TATIVES

THURSDAY, DECEM-BER 21

Md. Goode from Virginia was questioned and took his seat in the House.

Mr. Marshall with deep sorrow on his countenance and in a low

from his high station to the peaceful walks of private life.

However, public confidence may change and the public affections fluctuate with respect to others, yet with respect to him they have, in war and in peace, in public and in private life, been as steady as his own firm mind, and as constant as his own exulted virtues.

Let us then, Mr. Speaker, pay the last tribute of respect and affection to our departed friend. Let the grand Council of the nation display those sentiments which the nation feels.

For this purpose, I hold in my hand some resolutions which I will take the liberty to offer to the house.

'Resolved, That this House will wait on the President of the United States, in condolence of this mournful event.

'Resolved, that the speaker's chair be shrouded with black, and that the Members and Officers of the House wear black during the session.

'Resolved, that a committee, in conjunction with one from the Senate, be appointed to consider on the most suitable manner of paying honor to the memory of the man, first in war, first in peace, and first in the hearts of his country.'

Resolved, That this House when it adjourns do, adjourn to Monday.

These resolutions were unanimously agreed to. Sixteen members were appointed on the third resolution.

Generals Marshall and Smith

For the Ulster County Gazette

ON THE DEATH OF

GENERAL WASHINGTON

WHAT means that solemn dirge that strikes my ear?
What means those mournful sighs—why shines the tear?
Why toll the bells the awful knell of fate—
Ah!—why those sighs that do my fancy . . .

Where'er I turn the general gloom appears,
Those mourning badges fill my soul with fears;
Hark!—Yonder rueful noise!—'tis done—'tis done!—
The silent tomb invades our WASHINGTON!—

Must virtues yield their breath
Must bright perfection find relief in death?
Must mortal greatness fall?—a glorious name!—
What then is riches, honour and true fame?

The august chief, the father and the friend
The generous patriot—Let the muse not end;
Columbia's glory and Mount Vernon's pride;
There lies enshrined with numbers at his side!

There let the sigh respondent from the heart
Heave in rich numbers!—let the glowing art
Of tears refulgent beam with grateful love
And the sable mourning our affliction proves;

Weep!—kindred mortal—weep!—no more you'll find,
A man so just, so pure, so firm in mind
Rejoicing Angels, hail the heavenly sage
Celestial Spirits greet the wonder of the age.

ment. It becomes us to submit pears in all ages and classes, to with reverence to him, who "mak- mingle these sorrows with mine, eth darkness his Pavilion." on this common calamity to the world.

With patriotic pride we review The life of our WASHINGTON the life of our Washington, and cannot suffer him by comparison with compare him with those of other

—a band of music with mournful melody melted the soul into all the tenderness of woe.

The procession was formed and moved on in the following order:

Cavalry } With arms reversed
Infantry }
Guard
Music
Clergy

The General's horse with his saddle, holsters and pistols

Pall Bearers

Cols	Cols
Sims	Gilpin
Ramsay	Marsteller
Payne	Little

CORPSE

Mourners
Masonic Brethren
Citizens

When the procession had arrived at the bottom of the elevated lawn on the bank of the Potomac where the family vault is placed, the cavalry halted, the infantry marched towards the Mount and formed their lines—freedom. Having affected the Clergy the Masonic Brothers and the Citizens, descended to the Vault, and the funeral service of the Church was performed—The firing was repeated from the vessel in the river, and the sounds echoed from the woods and hills beyond.

Three general discharges by the infantry, and 11 pieces of artillery, which lined the banks of the Potomac back of the Vault, paid the last tribute to the entombed Commander in Chief of the Armies of the United States and to the Departed Hero.

The sun was now setting. Alas! the son of glory was set forever. No—the name of WASHINGTON—The American President and General—will triumph over DEATH! The unclouded brightness of his Glory will illuminate the future ages!

KINGSTON, January 4, 1800

The limits of our paper are too narrow this week for the great variety of foreign news received by the last mailes—We shall however, lay before our readers a short but comprehensive Summary.

French official accounts under the Bernbearh of October 8 state that on the 4th the Austro-Russians were defeated with the loss of several thousand killed, wounded and taken.

more! The hero, the sage and the patriot of America—the man on whom in all times of danger, every eye was turned and all hopes were placed, lives now only in his own great actions, and in the hearts of an afflicted people.

If sir it had not been usual, openly to testify respect for the memory of those whom heaven has selected as its instruments dispensing good to man; yet such has been the uncommon worth, and such the extraordinary incidents which have marked the life of him whose loss we all deplore, that the whole American nation impelled by the same feelings, would call with one voice for a public manifestation of that sorrow which is to deep and universal.

More than any other individual and as much as to one individual was possible, has he contributed to found this our wide-spreading empire, and to give to the Western world its independence and its freedom. Having affected the great object for which he was placed at the head of our armies, we have seen him convert the sword into the plough share and voluntarily sink the soldier in the citizen.

When the debility of our federal system had become manifest and the bonds which connected the parts of this vast continent were dissolving, we have seen him, the Chief of those Patriots who formed for us a Constitution, which by preserving the union will, I trust, substantiate and perpetuate those blessings our revolution had promised to bestow.

In obedience to the general voice of his country, calling on him to preside over a great people, we have seen him once more quit the retirement he loved, and in a season more stormy and tempestuous than war itself with calm and wise determination pursue the true interests of the na-

that the President would be ready to receive them at 1:0? o'clock this day. The house accordingly waited on him.

The Speaker addressed the President in the following words:

"Sir:

The House of Representatives, penetrated with a sense of the irreparable loss sustained by the nation, by the death of that great and good man, the illustrious and beloved Washington, wait on you, sir, to express their condolence on this melancholy and distressing event.

To which the President made the following Answer:

"Gentlemen of the House of Representatives:

I receive with great respect and affection the condolence of the House of Representatives on the melancholy and afflicting event in the death of the most illustrious and beloved personage which this country ever produced. I sympathize with you—with the nation and with good men thro' the world, in this irreparable loss sustained by us all.

JOHN ADAMS

A message was received from the Senate informing the House that they had agreed to the appointment of a joint committee to consider a suitable manner of paying honor to the memory of the man first in war, first in peace, and first in the hearts of his country, and that they had appointed seven members to join a committee for that purpose.

TO THE PRESIDENT OF THE UNITED STATES

THE Senate of the United States respectfully take leave, sir, to express to you their deep regret for the loss their country has sustained in the death of General George Washington—This event, so distressing to all our fellow citizens, must be peculiarly heavy to you who have been long associated with him in deeds of patriotism. Permit us, sir, to mingle our tears; and on this occasion it is manly to weep. To lose such a man at such a crisis, is no common calamity to the world; our country mourns her Father. The Chief Magistrate of a free people, twice unanimously chosen Chief Magistrate of a free people, we see him at a time when his re-election with the universal suffrage could not have been doubted affording the world the instance of moderation, by withdrawing

abashed at the majesty of his virtue. It reproved the temperance of their ambition and darkened the splendor of victory. The scenes closed, and we are no longer anxious lest misfortune should sully his glory, he has travelled on to the end of his journey, and arrived with him an increasing weight of honor; he has deposited it safely, where misfortune cannot tarnish it—where malice cannot blast it. Favored of heaven, he departed without exhibiting the weakness of humanity; magnanimous in death, the darkness of the grave could not obscure his brightness.

Such was the man whom we deplore—Thanks to God, his glory is consummated. Washington yet lives upon earth in his spotless example—his spirit is in Heaven.

Let his countrymen consecrate the memory of the heroic General, the patriotic Statesman, and the virtuous sage; let them teach their children never to forget that the fruits of his labours, and his example are their inheritance.

PRESIDENT'S ANSWER

Gentlemen of the Senate:

I receive with the most respectful and affectionate sentiments in this impressive address, the obliging expressions of your regret, for the loss of our country has sustained in the death of our most esteemed and admired citizen.

In the multitude of my thoughts and recollections on this melancholy event, you will permit me only to say ,that I have seen him in the days of adversity, in some of the scenes of the deepest and most trying perplexities I have also attended him in the highest elevation and most prosperous felicity with uniform admiration of his wisdom, moderation and constancy.

Among all our original associates, in the memorable League of the Continent in 1771, which first expressed the sovereign will of a Free Naton in America he was the only one remaining in the General Government, although with a constitution more enfeebled than his, at an age when he though it necessary to prepare for the retirement I feel myself alone, bereaved of my last brother, yet I derive strong consolation from the events has taken from us our greatest Benefactor and orna-

more expression awhward; it more, had he lived, could hereafter have sullied his glory, only with those superficial minds, who, believing that characters and actions are marked by success alone, rarely deserve to enjoy it. Malice could never blast his honor, and Envy made him a singular exemption to her universal rule.—For himself he had lived enough, to life and glory. For his fellow citizens, if their prayers could have been answered he would have been immortal. For me his departure is a most unfortunate moment. Trusting, however, n the wise and righteous dominions of Providence over passions of men ,and the result of their councils and actions, as well as over their Lives nothing remains for me but Humble Resignation.

His example is now complete, and it will teach wisdom and virtue to Magistrates, Citizens and men, not only in the present day, but in future generations, as long as our History shall be read. If a Trojan found a Pliny, a Marcus Arelius can never want Biographers, Eulogists or Historians.

JOHN ADAMS

United States
December 22, 1799

A BLOODY MASSACRE NEAR CARSON

By Mark Twain

Territorial Enterprise — Oct. 28, 1863

◄ MORE ON **MARK TWAIN** ON PAGE **6**

In 1862, Samuel Clemens landed a job at the Territorial Enterprise, a newspaper in Virginia City, Nev., where he began writing under the name of Mark Twain — often fabricating entire news stories like this one. As he later recalled: "To find a petrified man . . . or massacre a family at Dutch Nick's, were feats and calamities that we never hesitated about devising when the public needed matters of thrilling interest for breakfast. The seemingly tranquil Enterprise office was a ghastly factory of slaughter, mutilation and general destruction in those days."

From Abram Curry, who arrived here yesterday afternoon from Carson, we have learned the following particulars concerning a bloody massacre which was committed in Ormsby County night before last.

It seems that during the past six months a man named P. Hopkins, or Philip Hopkins, has been residing with his family in the old log house just at the edge of the great pine forest which lies between Empire City and Dutch Nick's. The family consisted of nine children — five girls and four boys — the oldest of the group, Mary, being 19 years old, and the youngest, Tommy, about a year and a half. Twice in the past two months Mrs. Hopkins, while visiting in Carson, expressed fears concerning the sanity of her husband, remarking that of late he had been subject to fits of violence, and that during the prevalence of one of these he had threatened to take her life. It was Mrs. Hopkins' misfortune to be given to exaggeration, however, and but little attention was paid to what she said.

About 10 o'clock on Monday evening Hopkins dashed into Carson on horseback, with his throat cut from ear to ear, and bearing in his hand a reeking scalp from which the warm, smoking blood was still dripping, and fell in a dying condition in front of the Magnolia saloon. Hopkins expired in the course of five minutes, without speaking. The long red hair of the scalp he bore marked it as that of Mrs. Hopkins.

A number of citizens, headed by Sheriff Gasherie, mounted at once and rode down to Hopkins' house, where a ghastly scene met their gaze. The scalpless corpse of Mrs. Hopkins lay across the threshold, with her head split open and her right hand almost severed from the wrist. Near her lay the ax with which the murderous deed had been committed. In one of the bedrooms six of the children were found, one in bed and the others scattered about the floor. They were all dead. Their brains had evidently been dashed out with a club, and every mark about them seemed to have been made with a blunt instrument. The children must have struggled hard for their lives, as articles of clothing and broken furniture were strewn about the room in the utmost confusion.

Julia and Emma, aged respectively 14 and 17, were found in the kitchen, bruised and insensible, but it is thought their recovery is possible. The eldest girl, Mary, must have taken refuge, in her terror, in the garret, as her body was found there, frightfully mutilated, and the knife with which her wounds had been inflicted still sticking in her side. The two girls, Julia and Emma, who had recovered sufficiently to be able to talk yesterday morning, state that their father knocked them down with a billet of wood and stamped on them. They think they were the first attacked. They further state that Hopkins had shown evidence of derangement all day, but had exhibited no violence. He flew into a passion and attempted to murder them because they advised him to go to bed and compose his mind.

Curry says Hopkins was about 42 years of age and a native of Western Pennsylvania; he was always affable and polite, and until very recently we had never heard of his ill-treating his family. He had been a heavy owner in the best mines of Virginia and Gold Hill, but when the San Francisco papers exposed the game of cooking dividends in order to bolster up our stocks he grew afraid and sold out, and invested to an immense amount in the Spring Valley Water Company of San Francisco. He was advised to do this by a relative of his, one of the editors of the San Francisco Bulletin, who had suffered pecuniarily by the dividend-cooking system as applied to the Daney Mining Company recently. Hopkins had not long ceased to own in the various claims on the Comstock lead, however, when several dividends were cooked on his newly acquired property, their water totally dried up, and Spring Valley stock went down to nothing. It is presumed that this misfortune drove him mad and resulted in his killing himself and the greater portion of his family. The newspapers of San Francisco permitted this water company to go on borrowing money and cooking dividends, under cover of which cunning financiers crept out of the tottering concern, leaving the crash to come upon poor and unsuspecting stockholders, without offering to expose the villainy at work.

We hope the fearful massacre detailed above may prove the saddest result of their silence.

A PRESIDENTIAL CANDIDATE

By Mark Twain

New York Evening Post — *June 9, 1879*

◄ MORE ON **MARK TWAIN** ON PAGE **6**

By the time he wrote this piece, Twain's writing style had become much more refined and readable than it was in his "Bloody Massacre" story (previous page). He'd spent years writing stories, letters and essays for several newspapers. More importantly, his first major work — "The Adventures of Tom Sawyer" — had recently been published in 1876.

This piece typifies the folksy, sarcastic style Twain popularized in his social satires and political commentaries.

I have pretty much made up my mind to run for President. What the country wants is a candidate who cannot be injured by investigation of his past history, so that the enemies of the party will be unable to rake up anything against him that nobody ever heard of before. If you know the worst about a candidate to begin with, every attempt to spring things on him will be checkmated.

Now I am going to enter the field with an open record. I am going to own up in advance to all the wickedness I have done, and if any Congressional committee is disposed to prowl around my biography in the hope of discovering any dark and deadly deed that I have secreted, why — let it prowl.

In the first place, I admit that I treed a rheumatic grandfather of mine in the winter of 1850. He was old and inexpert in climbing trees, but with the heartless brutality that is characteristic of me I ran him out of the front door in his nightshirt at the point of a shotgun, and caused him to bowl up a maple tree, where he remained all night, while I emptied shot into his legs. I did this because he snored. I will do it again if I ever have another grandfather. I am as inhuman now as I was in 1850.

I candidly acknowledge that I ran away at the battle of Gettysburg. My friends have tried to smooth over this fact by asserting that I did so for the purpose of imitating Washington, who went into the woods at Valley Forge for the purpose of saying his prayers. It was a miserable subterfuge. I struck out in a straight line for the Tropic of Cancer because I was scared. I wanted my country saved, but I preferred to have somebody else save it. I entertain that preference yet. If the bubble reputation can be obtained only at the cannon's mouth, I am willing to go there for it, provided the cannon is empty. If it is loaded my immortal and inflexible purpose is to get over the fence and go home. My invariable practice in war has been to bring out of every fight two-thirds more men than when I went in. This seems to me to be Napoleonic in its grandeur.

My financial views are of the most decided character, but they are not likely, perhaps, to increase my popularity with the advocates of inflation. I do not insist upon the special supremacy of rag money or hard money. The great fundamental principle of my life is to take any kind I can get.

The rumor that I buried a dead aunt under my grapevine was correct. The vine needed fertilizing, my aunt had to be buried, and I dedicated her to this high purpose. Does that unfit me for the Presidency? The Constitution of our country does not say so. No other citizen was ever considered unworthy of this office because he enriched his grapevines with his dead relatives. Why should I be selected as the first victim of an absurd prejudice?

I admit also that I am not a friend of the poor man. I regard the poor man, in his present condition, as so much wasted raw material. Cut up and properly canned, he might be made useful to fatten the natives of the cannibal islands and to improve our export trade with that region. I shall recommend legislation upon the subject in my first message. My campaign cry will be: "Desiccate the poor workingman; stuff him into sausages."

These are about the worst parts of my record. On them I come before the country. If my country don't want me, I will go back again. But I recommend myself as a safe man — a man who starts from the basis of total depravity and proposes to be fiendish to the last.

TEN DAYS IN A MAD-HOUSE

By Nellie Bly

The New York World — *October 1887*

◄ MORE ON **NELLIE BLY** ON PAGE **6**

On one level, this story could be viewed as a shamelessly sensational stunt to sell papers. But what resulted was a historic exposé by ambitious, 23-year-old Elizabeth Jane Cochran — or "Nellie Bly," as she became known to the world. Bly's undercover assignment to Blackwell's Island began as a dare from John Cockerill, managing editor at Joseph Pulitzer's New York World. But once Bly's report was published, it brought funding and reforms to the institution and helped establish a model for investigative reporting that remains inspiring and engrossing to this day.

O n the 22d of September I was asked by the World if I could have myself committed to one of the asylums for the insane in New York, with a view to writing a plain and unvarnished narrative of the treatment of the patients therein and the methods of management, etc. Did I think I had the courage to go through such an ordeal as the mission would demand? Could I assume the characteristics of insanity to such a degree that I could pass the doctors, live for a week among the insane without the authorities there finding out that I was only a "chiel amang 'em takin' notes?" I said I believed I could. I had some faith in my own ability as an actress and thought I could assume insanity long enough to accomplish any mission intrusted to me. Could I pass a week in the insane ward at Blackwell's Island? I said I could and I would. And I did. . . .

"How will you get me out," I asked my editor, "after I once get in?"

"I do not know," he replied, "but we will get you out if we have to tell who you are, and for what purpose you feigned insanity – only get in."

I had little belief in my ability to deceive the insanity experts, and I think my editor had less. . . .

[Using the name "Nellie Brown," Bly rents a room in a boardinghouse and acts like a "poor, unfortunate crazy girl" until, finally, the police take her away. After a judge and a doctor both declare her insane, Bly is shipped to Bellevue Hospital.]

I put the moth-eaten shawl, with all its musty smell, around me, and sat down on a wicker chair, wondering what would come next, whether I should freeze to death or survive. My nose was very cold, so I covered up my head and was in a half doze, when the shawl was suddenly jerked from my face and a strange man and Miss Scott stood before me. The man proved to be a doctor, and his first greetings were:

"I've seen that face before."

"Then you know me?" I asked, with a great show of eagerness that I did not feel.

"I think I do. Where did you come from?"

"From home."

"Where is home?"

"Don't you know? Cuba."

He then sat down beside me, felt my pulse, and examined my tongue, and at last said: "Tell Miss Scott all about yourself."

"No, I will not. I will not talk with women."

"What do you do in New York?"

"Nothing."

"Can you work?"

"No, senor."

"Tell me, are you a woman of the town?"

"I do not understand you," I replied, heartily disgusted with him.

"I mean have you allowed the men to provide for you and keep you?"

I felt like slapping him in the face, but I had to maintain my composure, so I simply said:

"I do not know what you are talking about. I always lived at home."

After many more questions, fully as useless and senseless, he left me and began to talk with the nurse. "Positively demented," he said. "I consider it a hopeless case. She needs to be put where someone will take care of her."

And so I passed my second medical expert.

[At last, Bly reaches the Insane Asylum on Blackwell's Island.]

As the wagon was rapidly driven through the beautiful lawns up to the asylum my feelings of satisfaction at having attained the object of my work were greatly dampened by the look of distress on the faces of my companions. Poor women, they had no hopes of a speedy delivery. They were being driven to a prison, through no fault of their own, in all probability for life. In comparison, how much easier it would be to walk to the gallows than to this tomb of living horrors!

On the wagon sped, and I, as well as my comrades, gave a despairing farewell glance at freedom as we came in sight of the long stone buildings. We passed one low building, and the stench was so horrible that I was compelled to hold my breath, and I mentally decided that it was the kitchen. I afterward found I was correct in my surmise, and smiled at the signboard at the end of the walk: "Visitors are not allowed on this road." I don't think the sign would be necessary if they once tried the road, especially on a warm day.

The wagon stopped, and the nurse and officer in charge told us to get out. The nurse added: "Thank God they came quietly." We obeyed orders to go ahead up a flight of narrow, stone steps, which had evidently been built for the accommodation of people who climb stairs three at a time. I wondered if my companions knew where we were, so I said to

Miss Tillie Mayard:

"Where are we?"

"At the Blackwell's Island Lunatic Asylum," she answered, sadly.

"Are you crazy?" I asked.

"No," she replied; "but as we have been sent here we will have to be quiet until we find some means of escape. They will be few, though, if all the doctors, as Dr. Field, refuse to listen to me or give me a chance to prove my sanity." We were ushered into a narrow vestibule, and the door was locked behind us.

[Shortly after her arrival, Bly is given a bath.]

A few more songs and we were told to go with Miss Grupe. We were taken into a cold, wet bathroom, and I was ordered to undress. Did I protest? Well, I never grew so earnest in my life as when I tried to beg off. They said if I did not they would use force and that it would not be very gentle.

At this I noticed one of the craziest women in the ward standing by the filled bathtub with a large, discolored rag in her hands. She was chattering away to herself and chuckling in a manner which seemed to me fiendish. I knew now what was to be done with me. I shivered. They began to undress me, and one by one they pulled off my clothes. At last everything was gone excepting one garment. "I will not remove it," I said vehemently, but they took it off. I gave one glance at the group of patients gathered at the door watching the scene, and I jumped into the bathtub with more energy than grace.

The water was ice-cold, and I again began to protest. How useless it all was! I begged, at least, that the patients be made to go away, but was ordered to shut up. The crazy woman began to scrub me. I can find no other word that will express it but scrubbing. From a small tin pan she took some soft soap and rubbed it all over me, even all over my face and my pretty hair. I was at last past seeing or speaking, although I had begged that my hair be left untouched. Rub, rub, rub, went the old woman, chattering to herself. My teeth chattered and my limbs were goose-fleshed and blue with cold. Suddenly I got, one after the other, three buckets of water over my head–ice-cold water, too–into my eyes, my ears, my nose and my mouth. I think I experienced some of the sensations of a drowning person as they dragged me, gasping, shivering and quaking, from the tub. For once I did look insane. I caught a glance of the indescribable look on the faces of my companions, who had witnessed my fate and knew theirs was surely following. Unable to control myself at the absurd picture I presented, I burst into roars of laughter. They put me, dripping wet, into a short canton flannel slip, labeled across the extreme end in large black letters, "Lunatic Asylum, B. I., H. 6." The letters meant Blackwell's Island, Hall 6.

By this time Miss Mayard had been undressed, and, much as I hated my recent bath, I would have taken another if by it I could have saved her the experience. Imagine plunging that sick girl into a cold bath when it made me, who have never been ill, shake as if with ague. I heard her explain to Miss Grupe that her head was still sore from her illness. Her hair was short and had mostly come out, and she asked that the crazy woman be made to rub more gently, but Miss Grupe said:

"There isn't much fear of hurting you. Shut up, or you'll get it worse." Miss Mayard did shut up, and that was my last look at her for the night.

I was hurried into a room where there were six beds, and had been put into bed when some one came along and jerked me out again, saying:

"Nellie Brown has to be put in a room alone to-night, for I suppose she's noisy."

I was taken to room 28 and left to try and make an impression on the bed. It was an impossible task. The bed had been made high in the center and sloping on either side. At the first touch my head flooded the pillow with water, and my wet slip transferred some of its dampness to the sheet. When Miss Grupe came in I asked if I could not have a night-gown.

"We have not such things in this institution," she said.

"I do not like to sleep without," I replied.

"Well, I don't care about that," she said. "You are in a public institution now, and you can't expect to get anything. This is charity, and you should be thankful for what you get."

"But the city pays to keep these places up," I urged, "and pays people to be kind to the unfortunates brought here."

"Well, you don't need to expect any kindness here, for you won't get it," she said, and she went out and closed the door.

[Nellie begins to witness acts of cruelty.]

Soon after my advent a girl called Urena Little-Page was brought in. She was, as she had been born, silly, and her tender spot was, as with many sensible women, her age. She claimed eighteen, and would grow very angry if told to the contrary. The nurses were not long in finding this out, and then they teased her.

"Urena," said Miss Grady, "the doctors say that you are thirty-three instead of eighteen," and the other nurses laughed. They kept up this until the simple creature began to yell and cry, saying she wanted to go home and that everybody treated her badly. After they had gotten all the amusement out of her they wanted and she was crying, they began to scold and tell her to keep quiet. She grew more hysterical every moment until they pounced upon her and slapped her face and knocked her head in a lively fashion. This made the poor creature cry the more, and so they choked her. Yes, actually choked her. Then they dragged her out to the closet, and I heard her terrified cries hush into smothered ones. After several hours' absence she returned to the sitting-room, and I plainly saw the marks of their fingers on her throat for the entire day.

[As the days go by, Bly recounts other "unfortunate stories," as she calls them.]

One of the patients, Mrs. Cotter, a pretty, delicate woman, one day thought she saw her husband coming up the walk. She left the line in which she was marching and ran to meet him. For this act she was sent to the Retreat. She afterward said:

"The remembrance of that is enough to make me mad. For crying the nurses beat me with a broom-handle and jumped on me, injuring me internally, so that I shall never get over it. Then they tied my hands and feet, and, throwing a sheet over my head, twisted it tightly around my throat, so I could not scream, and thus put me in a bathtub filled with cold water. They held me under until I gave up every hope and became senseless. At other times they took hold of my ears and beat my head on the floor and against the wall. Then they pulled out my hair by the roots, so that it will never grow in again."

Mrs. Cotter here showed me proofs of her story, the dent in the back of her head and the bare spots where the hair had been taken out by the handful. I give her story as plainly as possible: "My treatment was not as bad as I have seen others get in there, but it has ruined my health, and even if I do get out of here I will be a wreck. When my husband heard of the treatment given me he threatened to expose the place if I was not removed, so I was brought here. I am well mentally now. All that old fear has left me, and the doctor has promised to allow my husband to take me home."

I made the acquaintance of Bridget McGuinness, who seems to be sane at the present time. She said she was sent to Retreat 4, and put on the "rope gang." "The beating I got there were something dreadful. I was pulled around by the hair, held under the water until I strangled, and I was choked and kicked. The nurses would always keep a quiet patient stationed at the window to tell them when any of the doctors were approaching. It was hopeless to complain to the doctors, for they always said it was the imagination of our diseased brains, and besides we would get another beating for telling. They would hold patients under the water and threaten to leave them to die there if they did not promise not to tell the doctors. We would all promise, because we knew the doctors would not help us, and we would do anything to escape the punishment. After breaking a window I was transferred to the Lodge, the worst place on the island. It is dreadfully dirty in there, and the stench is awful. In the summer the flies swarm the place. The food is worse than we get in

other wards and we are given only tin plates. Instead of the bars being on the outside, as in this ward, they are on the inside. There are many quiet patients there who have been there for years, but the nurses keep them to do the work. Among other beating I got there, the nurses jumped on me once and broke two of my ribs.

"While I was there a pretty young girl was brought in. She had been sick, and she fought against being put in that dirty place. One night the nurses took her and, after beating her, they held her naked in a cold bath, then they threw her on her bed. When morning came the girl was dead. The doctors said she died of convulsions, and that was all that was done about it.

"They inject so much morphine and chloral that the patients are made crazy. I have seen the patients wild for water from the effect of the drugs, and the nurses would refuse it to them. I have heard women beg for a whole night for one drop and it was not given them. I myself cried for water until my mouth was so parched and dry that I could not speak."

I saw the same thing myself in hall 7. The patients would beg for a drink before retiring, but the nurses – Miss Hart and the others – refused to unlock the bathroom that they might quench their thirst.

[Finally, Bly is freed from the asylum.]

The insane asylum on Blackwell's Island is a human rat-trap. It is easy to get in, but once there it is impossible to get out. I had intended to have myself committed to the violent wards, the Lodge and Retreat, but when I got the testimony of two sane women and could give it, I decided not to risk my health – and hair – so I did not get violent.

I had, toward the last, been shut off from all visitors, and so when the lawyer, Peter A. Hendricks, came and told me that friends of mine were willing to take charge of me if I would rather be with them than in the asylum, I was only too glad to give my consent. . . .

I had looked forward so eagerly to leaving the horrible place, yet when my release came and I knew that God's sunlight was to be free for me again, there was a certain pain in leaving. For ten days I had been one of them. Foolishly enough, it seemed intensely selfish to leave them to their sufferings. I felt a Quixotic desire to help them by sympathy and presence. But only for a moment. The bars were down and freedom was sweeter to me than ever.

Soon I was crossing the river and nearing New York. Once again I was a free girl after ten days in the mad-house on Blackwell's Island.

OLD CONSTAN
By Ernest Hemingway
The Toronto Daily Star — Oct. 28, 1922

◀ MORE ON **ERNEST HEMINGWAY** ON PAGE **6**

If you're seriously considering a writing career, you owe it to yourself to become familiar with the work of Ernest Hemingway. His fiction is universally acclaimed, but his earlier stories deserve study, too — particularly the dispatches he wrote as a reporter for The Toronto Daily Star. Many of Hemingway's stories, such as "Old Constan," use a first-person narrative that's discouraged in modern reporting, but his descriptions and insights remain impressive.

This is one of those stories that demonstrate how journalism provides a rich training ground for writers who romanticize about becoming novelists.

CONSTANTINOPLE — In the morning when you wake and see a mist over the Golden Horn with the minarets rising out of it slim and clean towards the sun and the muezzin calling the faithful to prayer in a voice that soars and dips like an aria from a Russian opera, you have the magic of the East.

When you look from the window into the mirror and discover your face is covered with a mass of minute red speckles from the latest insect that discovered you last night, you have the East.

There may be a happy medium between the East of Pierre Loti's stories and the East of everyday life, but it could only be found by a man who always looked with his eyes half shut, didn't care what he ate, and was immune to the bites of insects.

No one knows how many people there are in Constan. Old-timers always call it Constan, just as you are a tenderfoot if you call Gibraltar anything but Gib. There has never been a census. Estimates of the population give a million and a half inhabitants. This does not include hundreds of battered Fords, forty thousand Russian refugees in every uniform of the Czar's army in all stages of dilapidation, and about an equal number of Kemalist troops in civilian clothes who have filtered into the city in order to make sure that Constantinople will go to Kemal no matter how the peace negotiations come out. All these have entered since the last estimate.

If it doesn't rain in Constan the dust is so thick that a dog trotting along the road that parallels the Pera hillside kicks up a puff like a bullet striking every time his paws hit the ground. It is almost ankle-deep on a man and the wind swirls it in clouds.

If it rains this is all mud. The sidewalks are so narrow that everyone has to walk in the street and the streets are like rivers. There are no traffic rules and motor cars, street cars, horse cabs and porters with enormous loads on their backs all jam up together. There are only two main streets and the others are alleys. The main streets are not much better than alleys.

Turkey is the national dish of Turkey. These birds live a strenuous life chasing grasshoppers over the sun-baked hills of Asia Minor and are about as tough as a race horse.

All the beef is bad because the Turk has practically no cattle. A sirloin steak may be either the last appearance of one of the black, muddy, sad-eyed buffalo with the turned-back horns who sidle along the streets drawing carts or the last charge of Kemal's cavalry. My jaw muscles are beginning to bulge like a bulldog's from chewing, or chawing, Turkish meat.

The fish is good, but fish is a brain-food and any one taking about three good doses of a brain-food would leave Constan at once — even if he had to swim to do it.

There are one hundred and sixty-eight legal holidays in Constan. Every Friday is a Mohammedan holiday, every Saturday is a Jewish holiday, and every Sunday is a Christian holiday. In addition there are Catholic, Mohammedan and Greek holidays during the week, not to mention Yom Kippur and other Jewish holidays. As a result, every young Constaner's life ambition is to go to work for a bank.

No one who makes any pretense of conforming to custom dines in Constantinople before nine o'clock at night. The theatres open at ten. The night clubs open at two, the more respectable night clubs, that is. The disreputable night clubs open at four in the morning.

All night hot sausage, fried potato and roast chestnut stands run their charcoal braziers on the sidewalk to cater to the long lines of cab men who stay up all night to solicit fares from the revelers. Constantinople is doing a sort of dance of death before the entry of Kemal Pasha, who has sworn to stop all booze, gambling, dancing and night clubs.

Galata, halfway up the hill from the port, has a district that is more unspeakably horrible than the foulest heyday of the old Barbary Coast. It festers there, trapping the soldiers and sailors of all the allies and of all nations.

Turks sit in front of the little coffee houses in the narrow blind-alley streets at all hours, puffing on their bubble-bubble pipes and drinking deusico, the tremendously poisonous, stomach-rotting drink that has a greater kick than absinthe and is so strong that it is never consumed except with an hors d'oeuvre of some sort.

Before the sun rises in the morning you can walk through the black, smooth worn streets of Constan and rats will scuttle out of your way, a few stray dogs nose at the garbage in the gutters, and a bar of light comes through the crack in a shutter letting out a streak of light and the sound of drunken laughing. That drunken laughing is the contrast to the muezzin's beautiful, minor, soaring, swaying call to prayer, and the black, slippery, smelly offal-strewn streets of Constantinople in the early morning are the reality of the Magic of the East.

THE CONSTITUTION
By H.L. Mencken
The Baltimore Sun — Aug. 19, 1935

◄ MORE ON **H.L. MENCKEN** ON PAGE **6**

Henry Louis Mencken was one of the most influential journalists of the last century, but unlike news reporters — whose personal views should be excluded from their stories — Mencken was renowned and reviled for his cynical and satirical social commentary. With brilliant ferocity, his editorial columns attacked social injustice, religious extremism and the endless imbecility of politicians. Writer P.J. O'Rourke called Mencken the "creator of a new and distinct style of journalism I like to call 'big-city smartass.' "

All government, in its essence, is organized exploitation, and in virtually all of its existing forms it is the implacable enemy of every industrious and well-disposed man. In theory, it invades his liberty and collars his money only in order to protect him, but in actuality it always makes a stiff profit on the exchange. That profit represents the income of the professional politicians, nine-tenths of whom are simply professional rogues. They employ a great many technicians to carry on the ostensible functions of government, and some of those technicians are honorable and competent men, but the politicians themselves are seldom either. Their only object in life is to do as little honest work as they can for the most profit, whether in money, in power or in mere glory. The typical politician is not only a rascal but also a jackass, so he greatly values the puerile notoriety and adulation that sensible men try to avoid.

The prevailing view seems to be that the lower orders of the governmental camorra are the most parasitical and antisocial, but this is not really the case. The minor jobholders that everyone disdains are actually much better fellows than the political bigwigs that most people find it so hard not to venerate. Consider, for example, the post office. Its rank and file is made up of poor men who work hard for every nickel they get, and are so closely watched that the slightest aberration means disaster to them. In return for the relative security of their jobs they have to show a constant competence, and to submit, more often than not, to brutal overloading. But as one goes up the line one finds less and less diligence and less and less capacity for the work in hand, until at the top one commonly encounters a professional politician of the most crass and shameless sort, bent only upon serving his party machine.

It is the same in the City Hall. People who go there on business for the first time are usually greatly surprised to find so many polite, industrious and expert men behind the desks. They expect a gang of lazy, impudent ward heelers, but what they discover is a body of functionaries at least as well qualified as those they are used to meeting in stores and banks. But the higher offices are seldom so decently manned, and in the highest of all, that of the Mayor, it is so rare to find reasonable real and genuine competence that when they happen to be encountered, as in the case say, of the Hon. Mr. Jackson, it seems almost a miracle. When the governor of an American state turns out to be a man of ability and honesty it is a miracle indeed, and of a very rare sort, for most American governors are shabby and scurvy politicians, and some of them are obvious knaves.

II

The one aim of all such persons is to butter their own parsnips. They have no concept of the public good that can be differentiated from their concept of their own good. They get into office by mailing all sorts of fantastic promises, few of which they ever try to keep, and they maintain themselves there by fooling the people further. They are supported in their business by the factitious importance which goes with high public position. The great majority of folk are far too stupid to see through a politician's tinsel. Because he is talked of in the newspapers all the time, and applauded when he appears in public, they mistake him for a really eminent man. But he is seldom anything of the sort, and when he loses his office his eminence usually vanishes instantly.

But while it lasts it is very useful to him, and he is well aware of it. One of the favorite devices of politicians whose stupidity or roguery gets them into trouble is to call upon all good citizens to sustain them as a patriotic matter. This is done not only by the President of the United States, but also by all sorts of lesser functionaries, down to the members of school boards and county road boards. It commonly works pretty well, for most people are flattered when anyone who seems to be distinguished asks for their aid. So they go on whopping up their own creature until in the end his unfitness for his job can be concealed no longer, and then they turn him out in anger, and put in someone still worse.

Here the public gullibility is reinforced by the common notion that government is a kind of separate and autonomous entity, standing from all other institutions. People constantly speak of "the government" doing this or that, as they might speak of God doing it. But the government is really nothing but a group of men, and usually they are very inferior men. They may have some better man working for them, but they themselves are seldom worthy of any respect. Not many of them have ever been able to make their marks at any reputable trade, and not many of them know anything worth knowing, or ever have a thought that is worth having.

III

At intervals in the history of the world, the people of some country or other, or, more accurately, a relatively enlightened and resolute faction of them, become unhappily aware of the nature the government they live under, and undertake measures to improve it. Sometimes those measures take the form of assassinating its principal dignitaries, or of driving them into exile, but more often the thing is done more gently. There was a good example, known to every schoolboy, in England in the year 1215, when the barons of the realm, tiring of the tyrannous exactions of King John, corralled him at Runnymede, and forced him to grant them a long series of liberties, some of which remain the common liberties of every Englishman to this day. John kept his throne, but only at the cost of surrendering most of his old prerogatives.

At such times, not unnaturally, the concessions wrung from the tyrant brought to bay are commonly reduced to writing, if only that the parties of both parts may remember them clearly. A writing of that sort is variously known as a charter, a constitution, or a bill of rights. In a few countries, notably England, some of the principal articles in the existing Constitution are not written down at all, but only generally understood. But whether they are written down or not, they have a kind of force that is greatly superior to that of all ordinary law, and changing their terms is looked on as a very grave matter, to be undertaken only on long consideration, and after getting the consent of all the persons, or at least of a majority of them, whose rights it is proposed to modify.

In brief, a constitution is a standing limitation upon the power of the government. So far you may go, but no farther. No matter what the excuse or provocation, you may not invade certain rights, or pass certain kinds of laws. The lives and property of the people are at your disposition, but only up to a plainly indicated point. If you go beyond it, you become a public criminal, and may be proceeded against, at least in theory, like any other criminal. The government thus ceases to be sovereign, and becomes a creature of sharply defined and delimited powers. There are things it may not do.

> Beware of all politicians at all times, but beware of them most sharply when they talk of reforming and improving the constitution.

IV

This device is probably the greatest invention that man has made since the dawn of civilization. It lies at the bottom of most of his progress. It was responsible for the rise of free government in the Greek city states, and it has been responsible for the growth of nearly all the great nations of modern times. Wherever it has passed out of use there has been decay and retrogression. Every right that anyone has today is based on the doctrine that government is a creature of limited powers, and that the men constituting it become criminals if they venture to exceed those powers.

Naturally enough, this makes life uncomfortable for politicians, and especially for the more impudent and unconscionable variety of them. Once they get into office they like to exercise their power, for power and its ketchup, glory, are the victuals they feed and fatten upon. Thus it always annoys them when they collide with a constitutional prohibition. It not only interferes with their practice of their nefarious trade — to wit the trade of hoodwinking and exploiting the people: it is also a gross affront to their high mightiness. Am I not Diego Valdez, Lord Admiral of Spain? Why, then, should I be bound by rules and regulations? Why should I be said nay when I am bursting with altruism, and have in mind only the safety and felicity of all you poor fish, my vassals and retainers?

But when politicians talk thus, or act thus without talking, it is precisely the time to watch them most carefully. Their usual plan is to invade the constitution stealthily, and then wait to see what happens. If nothing happens they go on more boldly; if there is a protest they reply hotly that the constitution is worn out and absurd, and that progress is impossible under the dead hand. This is the time to watch them especially. They are up to no good to anyone save themselves. They are trying to whittle away the common rights of the rest of us. Their one and only object, now and always, is to get more power into their hands that it may be used freely for their advantage, and to the damage of everyone else. Beware of all politicians at all times, but beware of them most sharply when they talk of reforming and improving the constitution.

THE KENTUCKY DERBY IS DECADENT AND DEPRAVED

By Hunter S. Thompson
Scanlan's Monthly — June 1970

◀ MORE ON **HUNTER S. THOMPSON** ON PAGE **6**

Hunter S. Thompson personified the crazed extremes of journalism. He was a terrific writer but an unreliable reporter — which made him a brilliantly entertaining commentator but a dangerously degenerate role model. (You've been warned.)

Here's an excerpt from one of Thompson's first successful stories: "a classic of irresponsible journalism," he called it. It demonstrates his legendary vulgarity, his shocking behavior and his maddening delight in dancing around the actual facts of the story. No matter what the topic, the main character in any Hunter S. Thompson story is always Hunter S. Thompson.

I got off the plane around midnight and no one spoke as I crossed the dark runway to the terminal. The air was thick and hot, like wandering into a steam bath. Inside, people hugged each other and shook hands . . . big grins and a whoop here and there: "By God! You old *bastard! Good* to see you, boy! *Damn* good . . . and I *mean* it!"

In the air-conditioned lounge I met a man from Houston who said his name was something or other — "but just call me Jimbo" — and he was here to get it on. "I'm ready for *anything*, by God! Anything at all. Yeah, what are you drinkin'?" I ordered a Margarita with ice, but he wouldn't hear of it: "Naw, naw . . . what the hell kind of drink is that for Kentucky Derby time? What's *wrong* with you, boy?" He grinned and winked at the bartender. "Goddam, we gotta educate this boy. Get him some good *whiskey* . . . ."

I shrugged. "OK, a double Old Fitz on ice." Jimbo nodded his approval.

"Look." He tapped me on the arm to make sure I was listening. "I know this Derby crowd, I come here every year, and let me tell you one thing I've learned — this is no town to be giving people the impression you're some kind of faggot. Not in public, anyway. S--t, they'll roll you in a minute, knock you in the head and take every goddam cent you have."

I thanked him and fitted a Marlboro into my cigarette holder. "Say," he said, "you look like you might be in the horse business . . . am I right?"

"No," I said. "I'm a photographer."

"Oh yeah?" He eyed my ragged leather bag with new interest. "Is that what you got there — cameras? Who you work for?"

"*Playboy*," I said.

He laughed. "Well, goddam! What are you gonna take pictures of — nekkid horses? Haw! I guess you'll be workin' pretty hard when they run the Kentucky Oaks. That's a race just for fillies." He was laughing wildly.

"Hell yes! And they'll all be nekkid too!"

I shook my head and said nothing; just stared at him for a moment, trying to look grim. "There's going to be trouble," I said. "My assignment is to take pictures of the riot."

"What riot?"

I hesitated, twirling the ice in my drink. "At the track. On Derby Day. The Black Panthers." I stared at him again. "Don't you read the newspapers?"

The grin on his face had collapsed. "What the *hell* are you talkin' about?"

"Well . . . maybe I shouldn't be telling you . . ." I shrugged. "But hell, everybody else seems to know. The cops and the National Guard have been getting ready for six weeks. They have 20,000 troops on alert at Fort Knox. They've warned us — all the press and photographers — to wear helmets and special vests like flak jackets. We were told to expect shooting. . . ."

"No!" he shouted; his hands flew up and hovered momentarily between us, as if to ward off the words he was hearing. Then he whacked his fist on the bar. "Those sons of bitches! God Almighty! The Kentucky Derby!" He kept shaking his head. "No! Jesus! That's almost too bad to believe!" Now he seemed to be sagging on the stool, and when he looked up his eyes were misty. "Why? Why *here*? Don't they respect *anything*?"

I shrugged again. "It's not just the Panthers. The FBI says busloads of white crazies are coming in from all over the country — to mix with the crowd and attack all at once, from every direction. They'll be dressed like everybody else. You know — coats and ties and all that. But when the trouble starts . . . well, that's why the cops are so worried."

He sat for a moment, looking hurt and confused and not quite able to digest all this terrible news. Then he cried out: "Oh . . . Jesus! What in the name of God is happening in this country? Where can you get *away* from it?"

"Not here," I said, picking up my bag. "Thanks for the drink . . . and good luck."

He grabbed my arm, urging me to have another, but I said I was overdue at the Press Club and hustled off to get my act together for the awful spectacle. At the airport newsstand I picked up a *Courier-Journal* and scanned the front page headlines: "Nixon Sends GI's into Cambodia to Hit Reds" . . . "B-52's Raid, then 2,000 GI's Advance 20 Miles" . . ."4,000 U.S. Troops Deployed Near Yale as Tension Grows Over Panther Protest." At the bottom of the page was a photo of Diane Crump, soon to become the first woman jockey ever to ride in the Kentucky Derby. The photographer had snapped her "stopping in the barn area to fondle her mount, Fathom." The rest of the paper was spotted with ugly war news and stories of "student unrest." There was no mention of any trouble brewing at a university in Ohio called Kent State.

I went to the Hertz desk to pick up my car, but the moon-faced young swinger in charge said they didn't have any. "You can't rent one anywhere." he assured me. "Our Derby reservations have been booked for six weeks." I explained that my agent had confirmed a white Chrysler convertible for me that very afternoon but he shook his head. "Maybe we'll have a cancellation. Where are you staying?"

I shrugged. "Where's the Texas crowd staying? I want to be with my people."

He sighed. "My friend, you're in trouble. This town is flat *full.* Always is, for the Derby."

I leaned closer to him, half-whispering: "Look. I'm from *Playboy.* How would you like a job?"

He backed off quickly. "What? Come on, now. What kind of a job?"

"Never mind," I said. "You just blew it." I swept my bag off the counter and went to find a cab. The bag is a valuable prop in this kind of work; mine has a lot of baggage tags on it — SF, LA, NY, Lima, Rome, Bangkok, that sort of thing — and the most prominent tag of all is a very official, plastic-coated thing that says "Photog. Playboy Mag." I bought it from a pimp in Vail, Colorado, and he told me how to use it. "Never mention *Playboy* until you're sure they've seen this thing first," he said. "Then, when you see them notice it, that's the time to strike. They'll go belly up every time. This thing is magic, I tell you. Pure magic."

Well . . . maybe so. I'd used it on the poor geek in the bar, and now humming along in a Yellow Cab toward town, I felt a little guilty about jangling the poor bugger's brains with that evil fantasy. But what the hell? Anybody who wanders around the world saying, "Hell yes, I'm from Texas," deserves whatever happens to him. And he had, after all, come here once again to make a 19th-century ass of himself in the midst of some jaded, atavistic freakout with nothing to recommend it except a very saleable "tradition." Early in our chat, Jimbo had told me that he hasn't missed a Derby since 1954. "The little lady won't come anymore," he said. "She just grits her teeth and turns me loose for this one. And when I say 'loose' I do mean *loose*! I toss ten-dollar bills around like they were goin' outa style! Horses, whiskey, women . . . s---t, there's women in this town that'll do *anything* for money."

Why not? Money is a good thing to have in these twisted times. Even Richard Nixon is hungry for it. Only a few days before the Derby he said, "If I had any money I'd invest it in the stock market." And the market, meanwhile, continued its grim slide.

*　　　*　　　*

By noon on Friday I was still without credentials and still unable to locate Steadman. For all I knew he'd changed his mind and gone back to London. Finally, after giving up on Steadman and trying unsuccessfully to reach my man in the press office, I decided my only hope for credentials was to go out to the track and confront the man in person, with no warning—demanding only one pass now, instead of two, and talking very fast with a strange lilt in my voice, like a man trying hard to control some inner frenzy. On the way out, I stopped at the motel desk to cash a check. Then, as a useless afterthought, I asked if by any wild chance a Mr. Steadman had checked in.

The lady on the desk was about 50 years old and very peculiar-looking; when I mentioned Steadman's name she nodded, without looking up from whatever she was writing, and said in a low voice, "You bet he did." Then she favored me with a big smile. "Yes, indeed. Mr. Steadman just left for the racetrack. Is he a friend of yours?"

I shook my head. "I'm supposed to be working with him, but I don't even know what he looks like. Now, goddammit, I'll have to find him in that mob at the track."

She chuckled. "You won't have any trouble finding him. You could pick *that* man out of any crowd."

"Why?" I asked. "What's wrong with him? What does he look like?"

"Well . . ." she said, still grinning, "he's the funniest looking thing I've seen in a long time. He has this . . . ah . . . this *growth* all over his face. As a matter of fact it's all over his *head*." She nodded. "You'll know him when you see him; don't worry about that.

Creeping Jesus, I thought. That screws the press credentials. I had a vision of some nerve-rattling geek all covered with matted hair and string-warts showing up in the press office and demanding *Scanlan's* press packet. Well . . . what the hell? We could always load up on acid and spend the day roaming around the clubhouse grounds with big sketch pads, laughing hysterically at the natives and swilling mint juleps so the cops wouldn't think we're abnormal. Perhaps even make the act pay: set up an easel with a big sign saying, "Let a Foreign Artist Paint Your Portrait, $10 Each. Do It NOW!"

*　　　*　　　*

I took the expressway out to the track, driving very fast and jumping the monster car back and forth between lanes, driving with a beer in one hand and my mind so muddled that I almost crushed a Volkswagen full of nuns when I swerved to catch the right exit. There was a slim chance, I thought, that I might be able to catch the ugly Britisher before he checked in.

But Steadman was already in the press box when I got there, a bearded young Englishman wearing a tweed coat and RAF sunglasses. There was nothing particularly odd about him. No facial veins or clumps of bristly warts. I told him about the motel woman's description and he seemed puzzled. "Don't let it bother you," I said. "Just keep in mind for the next few days that we're in Louisville, Kentucky. Not London. Not even New York. This is a weird place. You're lucky that mental defective at the motel didn't jerk a pistol out of the cash register and blow a big hole in you." I laughed, but he looked worried.

"Just pretend you're visiting a huge outdoor loony bin," I said. "If the inmates get out of control we'll soak them down with Mace." I showed him the can of "Chemical Billy," resisting the urge to fire it across the room at a rat-faced man typing diligently in the Associated Press section. We were standing at the bar, sipping the management's Scotch and congratulating each other on our sudden, unexplained luck in picking up two sets of fine press credentials. The lady at the desk had been very friendly to him, he said. "I just told her my name and she gave me the whole works."

*   *   *

Later Friday afternoon, we went out on the balcony of the press box and I tried to describe the difference between what we were seeing today and what would be happening tomorrow. This was the first time I'd been to a Derby in ten years, but before that, when I lived in Louisville, I used to go every year. Now, looking down from the press box, I pointed to the huge grassy meadow enclosed by the track. "That whole thing," I said, "will be jammed with people; fifty thousand or so, and most of them staggering drunk. It's a fantastic scene — thousands of people fainting, crying, copulating, trampling each other and fighting with broken whiskey bottles. We'll have to spend some time out there, but it's hard to move around, too many bodies."

"Is it safe out there? Will we *ever* come back?"

"Sure," I said. "We'll just have to be careful not to step on anybody's stomach and start a fight." I shrugged. "Hell, this clubhouse scene right below us will be almost as bad as the infield. Thousands of raving, stumbling drunks, getting angrier and angrier as they lose more and more money. By midafternoon they'll be guzzling mint juleps with both hands and vomiting on each other between races. The whole place will be jammed with bodies, shoulder to shoulder. It's hard to move around. The aisles will be slick with vomit; people falling down and grabbing at your legs to keep from being stomped. Drunks pissing on themselves in the betting lines. Dropping handfuls of money and fighting to stoop over and pick it up."

He looked so nervous that I laughed. "I'm just kidding," I said. "Don't worry. At the first hint of trouble I'll start pumping this 'Chemical Billy' into the crowd."

He had done a few good sketches, but so far we hadn't seen that special kind of face that I felt we would need for the lead drawing. It was a face I'd seen a thousand times at every Derby I'd ever been to. I saw it, in my head, as the mask of the

whiskey gentry — a pretentious mix of booze, failed dreams and a terminal identity crisis; the inevitable result of too much inbreeding in a closed and ignorant culture. One of the key genetic rules in breeding dogs, horses or any other kind of thoroughbred is that close inbreeding tends to magnify the weak points in a bloodline as well as the strong points. In horse breeding, for instance, there is a definite risk in breeding two fast horses who are both a little crazy. The offspring will likely be very fast and also very crazy. So the trick in breeding thoroughbreds is to retain the good traits and filter out the bad. But the breeding of humans is not so wisely supervised, particularly in a narrow Southern society where the closest kind of inbreeding is not only stylish and acceptable, but far more convenient — to the parents — than setting their offspring free to find their own mates, for their own reasons and in their own ways.

So the face I was trying to find in Churchill Downs that weekend was a symbol, in my own mind, of the whole doomed atavistic culture that makes the Kentucky Derby what it is.

On our way back to the motel after Friday's races I warned Steadman about some of the other problems we'd have to cope with. Neither of us had brought any strange illegal drugs, so we would have to get by on booze. "You should keep in mind," I said. "that almost everybody you talk to from now on will be drunk. People who seem very pleasant at first might suddenly swing at you for no reason at all." He nodded, staring straight ahead. He seemed to be getting a little numb and I tried to cheer him up by inviting him to dinner that night, with my brother.

Back at the motel we talked for a while about America, the South, England — just relaxing a bit before dinner. There was no way either of us could have known, at the time, that it would be the last normal conversation we would have. From that point on, the weekend became a vicious, drunken nightmare. We both went completely to pieces. The main problem was my prior attachment to Louisville, which naturally led to meetings with old friends, relatives, etc., many of whom were in the process of falling apart, going mad, plotting divorces, cracking up under the strain of terrible debts or recovering from bad accidents. Right in the middle of the whole frenzied Derby action, a member of my own family had to be institutionalized. This added a certain amount of strain to the situation, and since poor Steadman had no choice but to take whatever came his way, he was subjected to shock after shock.

Another problem was his habit of sketching people he met in the various social situations I dragged him into — then giving them the sketches. The results were always unfortunate. I warned him several times about letting the subjects see his foul renderings, but for some perverse reason he kept doing it. Consequently, he was regarded with fear and loathing by nearly everyone who'd seen or even heard about his work. He couldn't understand it. "It's sort of a joke," he kept saying. "Why, in England it's quite normal. People don't take offense. They understand that I'm just putting them on a bit."

"F--k England," I said. "This is Middle America. These people regard what you're doing to them as a brutal, bilious insult. Look what happened last night. I thought my brother was going to tear your head off."

Steadman shook his head sadly. "But I liked him. He struck me as a very decent, straightforward sort."

"Look, Ralph," I said. "Let's not kid ourselves. That was a very horrible drawing you gave him. It was the face of a monster. It got on his nerves very badly." I shrugged. "Why in hell do you think we left the restaurant so fast?"

"I thought it was because of the Mace," he said.

"What Mace?"

He grinned. "When you shot it at the headwaiter, don't you remember?

"Hell, that was nothing," I said. "I missed him . . . and we were leaving, anyway."

"But it got all over us," he said. "The room was full of that damn gas. Your brother was sneezing and his wife was crying. My eyes hurt for two hours. I couldn't see to draw when we got back to the motel."

"That's right." I said. "The stuff got on her leg, didn't it?"

"She was angry," he said.

"Yeah . . . well, okay . . . Let's just figure we f--ked up about equally on that one," I said. "But from now on let's try to be careful when we're around people I know. You won't sketch them and I won't Mace them. We'll just try to relax and get drunk."

"Right," he said. "We'll go native."

OPENERS
AN ANTHOLOGY OF LEADS

DEWILDT, South Africa – The cheetahs converged on the old woman in two bounding strides. First one, then two, then five big cats emerged from the tall golden grass, tails twitching and eyes bulging with dreams of meat.

Ann Van Dyk beckoned them with a freckled hand.

"Come here," she purred, "and bite my finger."

Van Dyk, 73, is Africa's original cheetah guardian. Among the continent's more illustrious khaki-clad conservationists, she is an enigmatic, almost mythical figure. To armchair adventurers glued to "Animal Planet," she is a virtual stranger.

Yet thousands of times since 1968 — 47 times in 2002 alone — Van Dyk and her team have rescued hungry and cornered cheetahs with little more than a stick and a scowl.

Six hundred times she has successfully bred the notoriously fickle and high-strung hunters. It's a record that zoos and universities with state-of-the-art embryo labs can only envy.

But it's not enough.

Joe Verrengia, The Associated Press, using a startling-statement lead to begin this profile of a cheetah specialist

This is a murder mystery.

The victim is a tree. Not just any tree, but a 500-year-old live oak, which Texans like to brag is "the most perfect tree in America."

It is 50 feet tall. The branches reach out 127 feet. Its picture has hung in the Tree Hall of Fame in Washington. It is revered because of a legend that is probably untrue — that Stephen F. Austin made peace with the Indians in its shade.

Anyway, that is why it is called the Treaty Oak. Marriages have been held under its canopy. Nearby cafes and office complexes have taken its name.

Now someone is trying to kill it.

Lisa Belkin, The New York Times

Derrick Hanna, 16, would-be car thief, pointed a .357 magnum at a kid in a driver's seat one night. "Get out!" he screamed at Lazaro Gutierrez, 17. Lazaro flinched. Derrick squeezed the trigger five-eighths of an inch.

The upshot:

For Derrick, 50 years in prison.

For Lazaro, life in a wheelchair.

For the rest of us, $661,534.83.

Forget, for the moment, the wasted lives. Forget the argument about gun control.

Think about the money.

The bullet that fragmented inside Lazaro's neck the night of Oct. 21, 1988, set off an awesome run of expenses, mostly underwritten by taxpayers with little idea of the medical-legal costs of America's gun culture.

Patrick May, The Miami Herald, from a story that tabulates in great detail the medical and legal costs of a typical crime

STROUDSBURG, Pa. — Everything was set for Brian Storm and Angela Harms to say "I do" until their pastor said "I won't."

Ted Anthony, The Associated Press, opening a story about a minister refusing to perform a wedding for an interracial couple

OREGON PAYS TRIBUTE TO ITS VIETNAM VETS

By Don Hamilton

The Oregonian — Nov. 12, 1987

◀ MORE ON **STORY ENDINGS, 49** / **OBSERVATION, 72**

On Memorial Day in 1987, reporter Don Hamilton was assigned to cover the dedication of Oregon's Vietnam veterans memorial, a wall in a city park inscribed with the names of Oregon's war dead. Hamilton wasn't sure what kind of story he wanted to write, but after seeing the impact of the Vietnam Veterans Memorial in Washington, D.C. — and knowing Oregon had been a hotbed of antiwar sentiment two decades before — he knew the story would carry a huge emotional wallop.

HAMILTON'S COMMENTARY:

I had no clear plan when assigned a sidebar at the dedication of Oregon's Vietnam memorial. But right away I saw a target-rich environment: a big crowd, intense emotions, thick fog and soaking rain that got worse and worse. I knew my eyes and ears would be my best assets. I'd describe what I saw and heard and let the readers know what it was like to be there.

Reading this story later, I was glad I included the veterans' ages. For some reason, it intrigued me to know the stage of life these guys were in while experiencing these memories.

The story needed to see the intensely personal little dramas taking place that day as well as the war's complicated impact. I found what I needed walking up the spiral path when I glanced up to see an Air Force lieutenant pinning a medal on a soldier's uniform. Even in the rain, I could see the tears streaming down the soldier's cheeks as he saluted. I stopped dead as the scene registered in my brain and turned back to catch them before they vanished into the crowd.

Gary Thompson finally had his Vietnam medal pinned on his chest. It wasn't easy, but then nothing about Vietnam had come easy.

It was a quiet ceremony on a Veterans Day filled with powerful emotions as Oregon paid tribute to its 791 residents lost in the Vietnam War and to all those who served. Thompson didn't lose his life or any limbs in Southeast Asia. He lost some self-respect, but he regained a bit of it Wednesday in the quiet, wet moment before the dedication of the Oregon Vietnam Veterans Living Memorial in Portland's Hoyt Arboretum.

Like many veterans on this Veterans Day, Thompson, a 42-year-old forestry consultant from Springfield, confronted his past. He also hasn't completely come to terms with what happened to him as a Air Force medic in 1967 and 1968.

But he found an officer he didn't know, had a ceremony he hadn't really planned, witnessed by the names of dead men he had never met. In a small way, the tearful ceremony in the driving rain helped Gary Thompson come to terms with his private Vietnam war.

On the long, gently sloping spiral walkway that makes up the memorial, retired Air Force Lt. Col. Tom Hiestand pinned the yellow-and-blue ribbon of the Air Force Commendation medal on Thompson's fatigues.

It happened very quickly next to the alcove bearing the names of 374 Oregonians who died in Vietnam in 1968 and 1969. It took place while they were surrounded by scores of people hustling by, oblivious to the small ceremony being played out.

The nation is grateful to you, Hiestand told him, shaking his hand in the rain. Thank you. His cap dripping wet, his uniform soaked, and his eyes red, Thompson snapped off a salute and then wiped the rainy tears from his face.

Through a bureaucratic mix-up, Thompson hadn't received the medal until March. And he hadn't pinned it on until Wednesday. In fact, when he carried it in his pocket to the memorial, he still wasn't sure what he would do with it. But when he saw Hiestand — they'd never met — he decided to go ahead with the ceremony in the rain.

"It was about coming to terms with what I did in Vietnam," Thompson explained. "You keep asking yourself, did I do enough? You keep thinking you could have made more of a difference. And when you come back, you think you deserted them. Now I feel a lot better about myself."

He wasn't alone. Small dramas were performed throughout the foggy, wet day along the five alcoves bearing the names of Oregon's Vietnam War dead. They came in wheelchairs, on crutches, some missing arms and legs. There were bikers and men in suits. There were widows and wives and fathers and mothers and children and grandchildren of the men and women whose names were etched in the hard black granite. They gently reached out to touch the letters. They took rubbings off the wall. They took pictures of each other standing next to names. They left flowers and little scrawled notes and told each other stories and wondered out loud about the 40 Oregonians listed as still missing.

Grim, tight-lipped men stood rock-still before the wall, examining names of lost buddies. They searched their minds to bring back their memories, the color of their eyes or the crook of a smile or the sound of a voice or the way they smelled after a few days in the mud. Sometimes they remembered how they died, but mostly they remembered the way they had lived.

The sights and the sounds and the memories were stirred in powerful ways by the

The two men were both a little uncomfortable. They'd never met and the lieutenant didn't really know what to say. They probably never saw each other again. The episode was sad and ambiguous, a lot like the war, and intensely personal, just like the events of the day. And it went completely unnoticed by anyone else.

Here are my eyes and ears at work again: a look at the great mosaic of things going on that day. I wanted these images to fly by quickly, reflecting the busy crowd and intense emotions. Any one of these events could have become greater fodder for the story. But there were just so many and they reflected so many different emotions.

Back in the office, I wrote this sequence not so much from notes but from what I remembered watching people who didn't know they were being watched. I tried to read what they were thinking and feeling in these private moments at the wall. This just poured out of me, a genuine, out-of-body writing experience.

events of the day. Sometimes the men with the eagle-eyed pride stared blankly and scowled and swallowed hard lumps in their throats. Sometimes they could do nothing but silently weep under the bleak sky.

"It easily could have been me on that wall," said Jay McAlister, 44, a mail handler from Clackamas.

After searching for names, they stood on the muddy hillside and looked down into the wide bowl that is the memorial and heard the band and the speeches and the slow, solemn thumping of the snare drum. The rain beat so hard against their faces and heads and umbrellas, and it was hard to hear. As the ceremony started, the rain fell harder and it got darker and the fog seeped even lower and misted over the tops of the

trees above the memorial.

"Look at this weather. It reminds me of monsoon up north," said Tom Arnholtz, 38, a farmer from Dundee.

"Naw. It's not that bad. Nothing's that bad," responded Bill Reed, 41, of Portland.

"I've never been so wet as when I was over there. Never," Arnholtz said, wiping the rain from his face.

Toward the end of the ceremony, Lee Ripley, 39, president of Mail Handlers Local 315 in Portland, looked down and shook his head. Ripley served in the Air Force in 1968 and 1969.

"I hope we don't have to do this again any time in the future," he said quietly. "But I bet they said that after Gettysburg. We still haven't learned anything."

MAIL SPECIES
By Dave Philipps
The Gazette — Dec. 11, 2003

◀ MORE ON **STORY IDEAS**, PAGE **67**

This lighthearted story is the kind feature sections do best, and it succeeds on a number of levels. First, there's the inviting writing style: short words, short sentences, short paragraphs. There's the helpful Christmas-shopping angle (introduced in the third paragraph), enhanced by a sidebar list of Web sites that sell critters through the mail.

Finally, there's the humor. Philipps doesn't try to be laugh-out-loud funny, but takes a more subtle, rolling-your-eyes-in-disbelief approach to the topic. "The secret to writing about the hilarious is to play it totally straight," Philipps says. "Let the readers laugh at the subject matter, not at you."

True story: A few weeks ago, in a post office in Milwaukee, Wis., an alligator tried to chew its way out of an Express Mail box bound for Colorado.

The toothy snout of the 4-foot gator chomped through the cardboard even as workers tried to seal it back in the box with tape.

Since it's that package-sending time of year, it might be a good idea to take this pop quiz. It was illegal to send this alligator through the U.S. Postal Service because:

A. Any knucklehead knows not to mail a living creature.

B. Reptiles must be detoothed for mailing.

C. The gator was more than 20 inches long.

If you answered anything but C, you are in danger of letting logic get in the way of postal codes.

The rules are clearly spelled out in the Postal Service Domestic Mail Manual's

chapter on live animal mail-ability. Any alligator or crocodile under 20 inches can travel through the mail with the proper postage.

Not that you should mail an alligator, but you could.

Surprised? Maybe we, as a nation, need to bone up on animal mail-ability.

If we don't, we'll have no one to blame but ourselves if our alligators don't arrive on time so they can be chewing through bows and ribbons on Christmas morning.

SQUIRMY THINGS

First rule:

No snakes.

It doesn't matter if it's a poisonous viper addressed to a personal enemy (which actually happened this year in Arkansas) or a saintly little garter snake that catches pests in the garden. No snakes, period.

And no turtles either, snapping or non. Newts, crickets, horned toads, millipedes

The unusual quasi-biblical bossy tone I used here was quite accidental, but it works well to lead the reader right into the regulations. If I'd used a more bemused "Isn't this strange?" tone, I would have sounded more removed from the material.

These are real rules. Of course, I had to translate them from some of the dullest regulatory language imaginable. These days, it seems like everybody with a desk and an official title talks like a mix between a cop and a tax lawyer. The journalist's job is to translate into real English.

In selecting animals, the sound of language and the wealth of images is important. Since I could pick anything in the world, I didn't want to choose boring animals. Notice how the rhythm of "ocelots, elk, flying foxes and flamingos" feels very natural while creating a wild kingdom rainbow in the reader's head.

and other small, cold-blooded animals are allowed and will be welcomed with open arms at the post office, so long as they aren't snakes or legless lizards that could be confused with snakes. Snakes, we repeat, are not allowed.

Although yeast qualifies as a small, cold-blooded animal, one cannot send home-brew through the mail.

STINGING, BITING THINGS

Poisonous spiders have no place in an envelope, nor do any poisonous or disease-carrying insects. This is the law.

But bees may travel the United States, provided they use ground transportation and not air. Only queen bees may take a plane, accompanied by no more than eight attendant bees. No kidding.

If a package contains one queen and nine attendant bees, the sender will be in violation of postal codes.

Scorpions are quite all right to mail, even deadly, venomous scorpions that hide in people's shoes, as long as they are being sent for the purpose of making antivenin, which makes perfect sense. Please, seal them in an escape-proof package marked "LIVE SCORPIONS."

Dead scorpions can be mailed without special labeling. So can dead eels, seals and cockatiels, so long as they have been obtained legally and are packaged to prevent oozing and obnoxious smells. No funny business.

FEATHERED AND FURRY THINGS

Do not mail ocelots, elk, flying foxes or flamingos. In fact, do not mail any warm-blooded animal, horned or hoofed, furry or feathered, mammal or marsupial, that crawls the earth, not even the slightest shrew, unless it is specifically named in the postal codes.

Swans are perfectly fine to mail, as long as they weigh more than 6 ounces and are in an approved container. This goes for guinea fowl and quail, too. But do not try to ship a

roadrunner. A box marked "LIVE ROADRUNNER" will be refused.

Don't joke around, either. If you mail a box marked "LIVE ROADRUNNER" or "LIVE SWAN" that actually contains snakes, you will be sent to lick stamps at a federal prison.

If you need to mail baby pheasants, that's fine, but send them only between April and August, or else. Adult pheasants can be mailed year-round.

Small sharks are OK. Squirrels are not. Hummingbirds are not. Pigeons are OK. Snakes are not OK. No snakes.

It may seem strict, but calling birds cannot be mailed under any circumstances, not even in the name of true love on Christmas. With the right vaccinations, however, geese a-laying, swans a-swimming, French hens, turtle doves, partridges and pear trees are allowed.

These rules are made to protect mail carriers and ensure your packages arrive safely.

So mail your legal animals early to beat the holiday rush — though maybe you'd be better off giving gifts of food instead of scorpions or some other living creature. Even the snakes will appreciate it.

The third reference to snakes officially makes them a running gag, which means I can mention them sparingly from now on and get a good chuckle. I'm not sure if this is a rule of journalism or vaudeville, but it works.

I could have done a story about why these rules are in place. Would that have been much fun?

GLOVE STORY

By Don Hamilton

The Oregonian — *April 8, 1986*

◀ MORE ON **FEATURE STORY IDEAS** ON PAGE **67**

It's easy to write a baseball story that appeals to sports fans. It's much harder to write one that will appeal to everybody. But this story won a presitigious Penney-Missouri award for feature writing because of the engaging way it combined nostalgia, folklore and useful consumer information. The design for this story nearly filled a broadsheet page; the package included an illustrated glove timeline, shopping tips and a baseball-mitt diagram loaded with history and fun facts.

HAMILTON'S COMMENTARY:

Yeah, I know. A grammatical error to start, and — gasp! — I'm using the first person. But the weird syntax echoes baseball's rural roots, while writing first-person lets me personalize it, lets me brag and provides a nice bracket at the close of the story. The voice shifts between first, second and third person, done more by instinct and intuition than design. The rhythm and the voice felt right.

When I was a kid, I heard Casey Stengel tell an incomprehensible story about players ripping their gloves open. I wanted weird tales, the anecdotes, dugout babble and oddball history that baseball does so well. I wanted this to be fun and interesting.

This ran on Opening Day 1986. I wanted to establish the hold baseball has on me and on America. It has, I've always believed, magical powers that heal the sick and raise the dead. Or something.

I wanted people who knew little about baseball to learn something, even starting with obvious observations like this.

Me and my Mel Stottlemyre glove were big heroes one day when I was 13.

If I hadn't dropped to my knees and stuck my Spalding right down onto the brown dirt of the infield, that line drive would have skipped through for a hit.

It didn't. I caught it for the last out of the game. I glanced down into the pocket, saw the ball snugly covering Stottlemyre's signature and trotted casually to the bench, only vaguely hearing the cheers and whistles of amazement from my teammates and the few fans. Cool. I had the right glove.

Things like that happen with the right glove. The right glove went with Willie Mays to the deepest part of center field for The Catch in the 1954 World Series. Graig Nettles was wearing the right glove when he performed his astonishing acrobatics near third base in the 1978 Series.

With the right glove, anything is possible: great catches. big contracts, World Series heroics. The world is an infield fly when you have the right glove.

And this week it is only fitting that we turn our attention to the care and feeding of the right glove. Monday was the opening day of the major-league baseball season, a holiday of the mind, an unofficial school holiday in many big-league towns.

On opening day, we celebrate eternal youth. On opening day, everyone's in first place.

Celebrate now, because it won't last.

The right glove

If you want to be a big hero like me with my Mel Stottlemyre, you've got to start by getting the right glove. What surely will follow is the right skills, the right insight and the right attitude for baseball and for life.

The first thing you need to know about the right glove is that it's usually a left glove. Right-handed gloves go on the left hand, and left-handed gloves go on the right hand. The glove is named not for the hand it is worn on, but for the hand that throws the ball.

There are black gloves, red gloves, brown gloves, green gloves and blue gloves. The color makes no difference, except that everything but brown looks stupid. Especially green.

There are lots of different kinds of gloves and mitts, and there is a difference between the two. Gloves have fingers; mitts don't. Therefore, we have outfielder's gloves and infielder's gloves — with fingers — but catcher's mitts and first baseman's mitts.

That pie-shaped catcher's mitt may not have fingers, but it has a lot of padding. Good thing. Genetic selection hasn't brought us to the point where the hand is naturally formed to accept 100 mph fastballs without protection. Legend has it that in the days before the heavily padded catcher's mitt, Cy Young's first catcher would line his glove with a hunk of beefsteak. Messy, but safe.

Finding a left-handed catcher's mitt is nearly impossible; so don't try. There have been only two left-handed catchers in the major leagues since the World War I era. No one can come up with a really good reason why. Perhaps it has something to do with a left-handers' inability to get off a quick throw to third base.

Generally, outfielders and pitchers wear the biggest gloves while infielders — except the first basemen — wear smaller ones.

The big gloves are allowed to be as big as one foot. These are favored by pitchers because they can hide the throwing hand from the batter. Outfielders, too, like the big glove, because it gives them an extra inch or two when leaping, diving or jumping after a ball.

It takes all kinds

Infielders tend to like smaller gloves because they make it easier to reach in and

The difference between gloves and mitts was an editor's question. I sputtered and guffawed before realizing I didn't know the answer. OK. Good question. By the way, green gloves still look stupid.

I loved some of the old baseball history I dug up. The beefsteak was one of the more pungent factoids and helped show how brutal the game was 100 years ago.

Not "perhaps" — that IS why there are so few lefty catchers. I shouldn't have hedged.

These four grafs really explain which fielders wear what kind of gloves and why, a very practical explanation. By the way, I hated how that subhead broke up what I saw as a unified, coherent section.

grab the ball for a throw. A baseball can get lost in one of those small tents worn by outfielders.

First basemen wear long, padded mitts designed for scooping low throws out of the dirt. This is very important to the fans sitting behind them.

A baseball glove triggers an incredible array of senses.

Well, I used to do that. I love the smell of a new baseball glove.

Walk quietly through a sporting goods store and spot someone examining gloves. Maybe he'll glance from side to side and, when no one's looking, he'll smash the glove into his face and take a deep breath, inhaling the aroma of the leather.

The mere sound made by a ball hitting a glove evokes a whole world of emotions. In the winter, the fist is pounded repeatedly into the glove's pocket, not only to improve the pocket but also to evoke the memory of catching a ball.

The ears and eyes are a reporter's best friends and I wanted to employ the senses here to summon simple and evocative baseball images. And I liked the word "thwock."

By spring the solid "thwock" sound a ball makes when hitting a glove can be heard in fields all over the country. There's a studied concentration in the simple, casual act of tossing a ball — no talking, just *thwock, thwock, thwock*. It's a nice sound, the sound of summer.

But while the sound never changes, some very strange things have been happening in the appearance of gloves lately,

This is the traditionalist in me getting grumpy and sarcastic about all those new-fangled modern conveniences. Haven't heard a word about these so-called innovations since.

Now there are gloves with little dimples in the pocket — supposedly to help you catch the ball. There are gloves with little electronic scoreboards — supposedly to help you understand that you must catch the ball. And there are gloves with electronic beepers to warn you when you're getting dangerously close to the outfield wall — supposedly to keep you safe while you are catching the ball.

There are gloves with Velcro strips and gloves with miles of leather thongs just great for tying and untying. Which you choose depends on whether you like to tie or rip.

When I was first starting to play baseball, I really thought Mickey Mantle used a glove like mine. Yeah, right.

The signature in the glove really means nothing. Because Stottlemyre's name was in mine didn't mean he used a glove like mine, designed my glove or even knew what my glove looked like. All the signature means is that the player gets money from the glove company.

Generally, though, you'll find a catcher's name on a catcher's mitt and a first baseman's name on a first baseman's mitt.

Even so, a player can become famous for his glove. Of course, that's got nothing to do with what's on his hand: it refers to how well he fields. Or sometimes how badly he fields. Dick Stuart, for example, was known for his glove. He was known as "Dr. Strangeglove." Or "Clank," for the sound of a ball hitting metal. That's what teammates said they heard when balls came his way.

A glove can tell you more about a player than his fielding average. Third baseman Graig Nettles, for example, is self-effacing and needs to concentrate. We know that because he has "Think" written on each finger of his glove. He also has "E-5" on it, the scorekeeper's mark for an error by the third baseman.

In some cases, the glove is used for something other than fielding. Something like terror.

"After it rains in Midland, Texas, the tarantulas come out on the field," reminisced Bobby Mitchell, a former Portland Beaver. "We'd get them and put them in players gloves. It was great sitting there in the locker room and waiting, knowing when they put the glove on they'd go crazy."

Handle with care

Few pieces of sports equipment get the same care and feeding as a baseball or softball glove, which are pretty much the same except the softball glove might have a slightly larger pocket.

Like a good pair of shoes, a glove should be formed to fit only you. I was angry and upset when someone broke into my car and stole the radio. When I learned the scoundrel had made off with my glove, a perfectly broken-in Wilson A-2000, I was ready to kill.

Gloves always are handled with care. The leather — they're all cowhide — is gently warmed by the hand, and the glove is caressed and massaged endlessly with soothing oils.

Oddly enough, all this tender attention

This represents some of that field-level humor. I wanted to get a feel for what it sounded like in the dugout. Oh, and I wanted an excuse to use a few colorful baseball nicknames.

Players get unusually attached to their gloves, which, as this Graig Nettles story shows, can illustrate how they feel about themselves and what they do. I really wanted to interview Nettles but could never reach him at spring training.

Here comes the how-to section. I wanted this to have practical uses but also to explore the things I did as a boy to break in my gloves. I never did get that Wilson A-2000 back.

comes after a traumatic breaking in phase.

There are various schools of thought on how to properly break in a new glove. Some suggest simply using it a lot. Use it in the field and pound your first into it while you're sitting on the bench. Pound it a lot.

But before most players use the glove, they go through some ritualistic steps to break it in. Breaking it in means just that: softening the leather, making it malleable, flexible.

Some ballplayers run over their gloves with their cars. Some throw their gloves against walls, or soak them in water, oil or even shaving cream. (The lanolin is supposed to soften the leather.)

One baseball fanatic said he knew someone who stuck his glove in a microwave oven. You youngsters out there shouldn't try this.

But the standard practice is somewhat more refined. The best way to break in a glove is to buy a bottle of mitt oil and slowly work it into the glove with a cloth.

There are lots of brands of mitt oil. Take your pick: Rawlings' Glovolium, Mizuno's Glove Oil, Louisville Slugger's Glove Softener, G-96 Glove Conditioner, Mink Oil.

Once you get the glove oiled up right, you must begin to form the pocket

Most of the methods used to form the pocket involve placing a ball or two in the glove and tying it up overnight or longer. A variation involves sticking the glove holding a ball under a pillow, a method which probably has resulted in a lot of sleepless nights for budding ballplayers.

Once it's broken in it should fit like a, well, glove.

The night I bought my Mel Stottlemyre glove, I greased it up right, put a ball in the pocket and tied it up with kite string. Then I pressed it underneath a bookshelf in the corner of my bedroom. I knew I was forming the perfect pocket.

I woke up a few times that night and peered across the room at the silhouette of the bookcase at that crazy, cockeyed angle.

It must have worked. I caught that line drive, didn't I?

Gloves become an extension of the hand, and this phase represents the beginning of that connection.

This closing segment was really about setting up that story of staring across my bedroom at that crooked bookshelf. Baseball always looks best when seen through a kid's eyes, and this was my chance to look through my inner child's eye again.

OPENERS
AN ANTHOLOGY OF LEADS

In preparation for tonight's poetry reading, Charles Bukowski is out in the parking lot, vomiting.

He always vomits before readings; crowds give him the jitters. And tonight there's a big crowd.

Glenn Esierly, *Rolling Stone,* using a startling-statement lead to begin this profile of poet Charles Bukowski

For two years, live music has boomed off the deck of a Beach Boulevard lounge and rolled down the Intracoastal Waterway into Donna Theiss' home across the water.

Sometimes the bands play so loud, she can hear every lyric from fives blocks away.

Big wheel keep on turnin',
Proud Mary keep on burnin'
Rollin', rollin', rollin' on the river.

That song, "Proud Mary," prompted Theiss' last call to a restaurant about a month ago. She said the employee who took her call wasn't very sympathetic.

"He said, 'If the music is so loud, then tell me what's playing right now,'" Theiss said. "I said, '"Proud Mary." I could stand here and sing the words to "Proud Mary" right now.'"

Caren Burmeister, *The Florida Times-Union* (Jacksonville, Fla.)

KANDAHAR, Afghanistan – Everywhere, the city is booby-trapped.

A woman returns to her home after five years in a refugee camp, opens a door and loses her life. A bus crammed with wedding day revelers runs over a mine and 45 die. A farmer wades into his field, walks around, loses a leg.

Six years after the shooting stopped in this city, the mines are still claiming victims. So are old grenades, unexploded shells and even bombs that look like toy butterflies. Children play among the mines, women step around them. A few times a week, another one explodes.

Dexter Filkins, *Los Angeles Times,* using a roundup lead to open a story on land mines in Afghanistan

Have you ever really embarrassed yourself? Don't answer that, stupid. It's a rhetorical question. Of course you've embarrassed yourself. Everybody has. I bet the pope has. If you were to say to the pope: "Your Holy Worshipfulness, I bet you've pulled some blockheaded boners in your day, huh?" he'd smile that warm, knowing, fatherly smile he has, and then he'd wave. He can't hear a word you're saying, up on that balcony.

Dave Barry, using a direct-address lead to begin a humor column

In the Northwestern lacrosse team's White House photo, four of nine women in the front row wear flip-flops. (President Bush, in the center, wears dark shoes.)

"YOU WORE FLIP-FLOPS TO THE WHITE HOUSE?!"

By Jodi S. Cohen and Maegan Carberry,
with additional reporting by Michael Kilian and Christi Parsons

Chicago Tribune — July 15, 2005

◄ MORE ON **STORY IDEAS** ON PAGE **67**

As Jodi Cohen explains it: "I got a call on my cell phone at about 12:15 p.m. to get back to the office and write about Northwestern University lacrosse team members wearing flip-flops when they met the President. I didn't know the team had been to the White House and thought the call, from one of the Metro editors, was a joke. I soon realized he was serious.

"The story idea came from the Chicago Tribune's top editor, who spotted the photo of the lacrosse team in the Tribune and thought there was an interesting fashion/trend story about wearing flip-flops to the White House. So I can't claim credit for the idea. Who knew that a photo in the back of the sports section would turn into a front-page story that would get picked up by media around the world? It was the most unlikely story during the summer of 2005."

COHEN'S COMMENTARY:

I decided to start the story this way to add drama and show that while she carefully planned her outfit, she didn't give a second thought to the decision to wear flip-flops. The contrast of wearing flip-flops and white pearls — the epitome of conservative dress — couldn't have been more perfect.

Kate Darmody was not the first player I talked to, but she definitely provided the best material. When she told me about her brother's e-mail, I knew I had hit the jackpot. His e-mail became the great headline and the reason, I believe, that the story got so much attention.

Figuring out the names of the players wearing flip-flops in the picture, then tracking them down within a few hours, was the key to this story. No photo caption identified the players. I learned their names from the Northwestern lacrosse Web site, which also listed their home towns. I used Nexis/ Lexis and Autotrack to get phone numbers and then started calling.

Before visiting the White House, Kate Darmody carefully planned her outfit. She bought a sundress from Ann Taylor. She put on a strand of white pearls.

And then she slipped on flip-flops to meet the president. So did about half of her teammates from the national championship Northwestern University women's lacrosse team, invited to the White House on Tuesday after a 21-0 season.

She didn't think twice about the footwear until she got an e-mail — in all capital letters — from her brother.

"YOU WORE FLIP-FLOPS TO THE WHITE HOUSE????!!!!" he wrote after seeing the picture on the team's Web site.

Aly Josephs' mother had the same reaction after seeing her daughter in the front row of the photo — the fifth person away from the president — wearing brown suede flip-flops with a skirt, sleeveless top and matching beaded jewelry.

"Don't even ask me about the flip-flops," her mother said when a reporter questioned her about the picture. "As somebody who is 52 years old, it mortified me. I don't go out of the house without pantyhose on."

Twenty- and 30-somethings will pair flip-flops with everything from shorts to cocktail dresses, with the footwear acceptable (at least to them) at work and at clubs, for a stroll down Michigan Avenue or even down the wedding aisle. For their moms, the shoes — best known for the flapping noise they make — are meant for places like the beach.

One of the hottest trends this summer, flip-flops are no longer a dime-store purchase, with some costing several hundred dollars. They come flat and with wedge heels. They have rhinestones and sequins and flowers. The straps are made of terry cloth and leather.

But in today's laid-back society, is there a distinction between ratty old flip-flops and ones from Neiman Marcus? Can they be worn at the White House, arguably the most formal setting in the United States?

Shoe expert Meghan Cleary, author of "The Perfect Fit: What Your Shoes Say About You," says no. In her chapter on flip-flops, where she weighs whether "to flip-flop, or not to flip-flop" for particular occasions, she would add a White House visit to the "not" category.

"For me, flip-flops are just not for a formal occasion," Cleary said. "But meeting the president, maybe this really speaks more to the worldwide acceptance of the flip-flop."

But Northwestern's lacrosse team members, dressed in skirts and dresses, thought nothing of it. Of the nine women in the front row with the president, four wore flip-flops. The rest wore heeled sandals.

This past season was only the fourth year that Northwestern has had a varsity lacrosse team, and the women were thrilled to join 14 other college championship teams at the White House.

These paragraphs get to the gist of why the lacrosse team wearing flip-flops became a story. Flip-flops had become acceptable almost anywhere. The question became: Are they acceptable at the White House?

Here's the "shoe expert" of the story. I found out about her while doing a search for other stories about the flip-flop trend. I Googled her, found her Web site and e-mailed her. She called back right before deadline. She was on the "Today" show a few days later — and was way more excited about that than being quoted in the Tribune.

Aly Josephs' mother gave me Aly's phone number. She lived with four or five other lacrosse players at Northwestern so they passed the phone around. They also identified which other players wore flip-flops and gave me some of their numbers.

"Nobody was wearing old beach flip-flops," said Josephs, 20, who wore $16 brown, flat flip-flops with rhinestones, one of about 15 pairs in her closet.

Darmody, 22, who decided on a wedge-heel flip-flop, said: "I tried to think of something that would go well with my outfit and at the same time not be that uncomfortable. But at the same not disrespect the White House."

She said that from May to September, "that is all I have on my feet all the time."

The teammates, and their athletic director, commented several times that it was actually the University of Michigan softball team — dressed in khaki shorts, polo shirts and sneakers — that was way underdressed.

"I would have felt out of place if that was what I was wearing," said Darmody, a lacrosse midfielder.

Flip-flops also pooh-poohed

Maegan Carberry, a co-reporter on the story, called etiquette experts to add another dimension to the story. She also talked to people on the streets of Chicago, but unfortunately, that didn't make it into the story.

But etiquette experts generally thought the flip-flops also were out of place.

"Many people are confused nowadays about when an occasion calls for dressing more formally. I'd say meeting a world leader is one of those occasions," said Charles Purdy, who writes the San Francisco Weekly's Dear Social Grace column.

Lesley Carlin, co-author of "Things You Need to be Told," said wearing flip-flops to the White House is a "huge no-no."

"You see them a lot more, but I've heard a lot of people remarking, 'Those belong at the beach and not at the office.' "

Even Joe Guidry, a salesman at the upscale Stuart Weitzman store on Michigan Avenue, said he wouldn't advise women to wear the company's $150 flip-flops to the White House.

"Meeting the president? I personally wouldn't wear them," he said.

Lindsey Munday, Northwestern senior and offensive player on the lacrosse team, chose to wear light blue sandals, but said the flip-flops were suitable too.

"I didn't look at any of my teammates and say, 'That was so inappropriate.' I think there is a line between certain flip-flops and others," she said.

Munday said she shopped for the White House outfit with her mother, and chose a sundress, cardigan, bag and shoes from Ann Taylor. "I think she was going more for the heel look than flip-flops," she said.

What's the dress code?

White House spokeswoman Erin Healy wouldn't comment on whether the White House has a dress code. Soon after President Bush took office, he suggested that men should wear a tie in the Oval Office, and staffers reportedly do not wear jeans in the West Wing.

Ann Stock, who was Hillary Clinton's social secretary, said that while there was no written dress code for White House guests, "people who visit the White House know they're going to a very special place and that one should dress appropriately."

Nancy Reagan's social secretary, Muffie Brandon, was aghast to discover that some female staffers routinely wore flip-flops to work in hot weather.

"We do not wear clogs at the White House," Brandon proclaimed.

Josephs, a junior on the lacrosse team who scored about 45 goals last season, had planned to wear a pair of heeled orange shoes to the White House but left them at home. She said the trip to the White House was "surreal."

The team gave Bush two "GWB43" lacrosse sticks. The teammates then shook his hand and posed for a picture, four rows of women standing tall with the president, who was dressed in a suit, blue tie and dark dress shoes.

Josephs' mother, Lydia, said her daughter's freshly pedicured toes were the first thing she noticed when she saw the picture.

"I called her up and screamed at the message machine, 'How could you go to the White House in flip-flops?' " she recalled. "She said, 'Mom, it didn't matter. Everybody was wearing flip-flops.' "

Tom Darmody, 38, also was surprised when he saw his sister in the picture.

"I was a little taken aback, to say the least," said Darmody, an attorney who admitted he might be jealous as his feet sweated in socks and leather shoes. "You are two people away from the leader of the most powerful country in the free world and you're wearing flip-flops?"

Michael Kilian, a Washington reporter, contributed this reporting about the current and former White House dress codes. After the story was published, Kilian told me that he thought the quote from Muffie Brandon sounded like a current quote when it was really from the time of the Reagan presidency. In retrospect, I would have explained that better.

I wanted to make sure the story acknowledged the team's athletic success as well as their flip-flop fashion. I worried that their success would be lost in this story.

The story took about six hours to report and write. The way it was displayed — with a long, narrow photo of just the players' feet — set the tone for the story. I never could have imagined the reaction that followed, with newspapers and TV stations around the country and even the world reporting on the flip-flops and the broader trend. I received more reader feedback than for any other story. One reader even sent her sister's wedding photo of the bridesmaids all wearing silver flip-flops! And I wore flip-flops to work for the rest of the week.

A PASSION FOR RAISING RABBITS

By Alana Baranick

The Plain Dealer — *Nov. 22, 2004*

◄ MORE ON **OBITUARIES** ON PAGE **92**

"People are dying to get into my columns," says Alana Baranick, winner of the 2005 award for best obituary writing by the American Society of Newspaper Editors. As the ASNE judges put it: "With vivid detail and direct language, Baranick creates richly textured portraits of everyday folks who become extraordinary through her words."

Baranick chooses the subjects for her feature obituaries based on their quirks and character, not on public prominence or fame. Take Patty Crites, for example.

"I read a short paid notice for 'Patty Crites, owner of Pat's Bunny Farm' in a small-town daily," Baranick recalls. "Other biographical details were sparse. In my quest for obit diversity — I had never written about a bunny farmer — I contacted her family for more info."

BARANICK'S COMMENTARY:

I like to start these "Life Story" obit features with something lively to grab the reader's attention.

She was only 63 — too young to die; I had to explain why she's dead. I use terms like "grandmother" rather than "Crites" or "She" to keep the text from becoming repetitive.

I could have listed all the events, fairs and bunny shows, but I used a generic phrase to save space.

I interview people who knew the deceased from various aspects of their lives. Some, like Renee Burns, are quotable. Others aren't worth quoting, but the information may be valuable.

I sat at a table at the Crites home, looking at pictures with her husband and daughter as they reminisced. I never would have thought to ask about the rabbits' names. It just popped out. So I asked where she got those names.

I didn't have enough space to say that Peggy ended up on the Crites' dinner table. This would not have been the place to address that anyway.

I thought it was nifty that she had everyday pets, farm animals, wildlife and exotic creatures.

SPENCER TOWNSHIP – Patty Crites' prize-winning rabbits were known for their long floppy ears, luxurious coats and unscheduled public demonstrations of bunny-birth.

The 63-year-old grandmother, who died of complications from congestive heart failure and other health problems Oct. 27, raised droopy-eared English lops and other breeds at Pat's Bunny Farm in Spencer Township for 30 years.

She showed her best bunnies at rabbit-club events and county fairs throughout Ohio.

At a few Medina County Fair rabbit contests, Crites entered pregnant rabbits who ended up giving birth before the judging began.

"She didn't realize how far along they were," said her friend Renee Burns. "People loved it, to see these little tiny pink things coming out."

Crites had as many as 250 rabbits at one time, and every one of them had a name.

"She read a lot of novels," said her daughter Regina Manos. "Every time she saw a good name, she'd write it down."

She also raised ferrets and Peruvian guinea pigs. Over the years, she had a Vietnamese pot-bellied pig and a de-scented skunk as house pets. She kept a goat, ponies, horses, dogs and cats. She took care of two crows, Igor and J.J., a pig named Peggy and her nine piglets.

Crites also had an African parrot and cockatiels. Her part-time jobs at a veterinarian's office in Litchfield and at a pet shop in Ashland yielded opportunities to adopt even more exotic animals.

"We almost ended up with a tiger," said her husband of 32 years, Jim. "One time she

Patricia Ann Crites

Nov. 9, 1940 - Oct. 27, 2004

Her mother, Helen Fetzer, lives in Spencer.

Former married name: Gerrick.

Enjoyed going with friends to movies, flea markets and country-music concerts.

tried to bring home an African anteater. She went to an auction in Wooster and brought an emu home. The only thing she never brought home was a monkey."

Crites, the daughter of a steel-hauling truck driver, was born Patricia Ann Fetzer at Berea Hospital. She started bringing stray animals home while growing up on Worthington Avenue near West 117th Street in Cleveland.

The location of her childhood home made Crites a city girl, but Crites really was a country girl at heart.

"We always used to go out to see my grandmother on the farm in Medina," said her younger sister, Beverly Magyar. "We weren't surprised when she started her bunny farm. She had trophies and all kinds of ribbons she'd won over the years. The hardest thing was for her to sell her rabbits when she was so sick."

Crites had three children – Brian Gerrick, Scott Gerrick and Regina – with her first husband, whom she married and divorced twice.

"They had some problems and were trying to patch things up," her sister said. "It didn't work. When I got married she said, 'Didn't you learn anything?' "

After her second divorce, she met Jim Crites, who also was divorced and had kids. They moved from Lakewood to a 17-acre

I stash little tidbits and unused quotes, which could have interrupted the flow of the story, into a bio box or in the photo cutlines.

This last line is pretty lame. I usually put some quirky saying or words to live by that the deceased was known to say. But I couldn't pump that sort of thing out of her relatives and friends.

Including what the parents did for a living helps define the person and shows how far the deceased moved away from or stayed close to her roots. Why did I give their address? See the next sentence.

The first husband did not want his name included in his ex-wife's story. He told me he really wasn't part of her life for long. Although I did not name him, I acknowledged his existence, because the kids' surnames were different.

farm in Spencer Township in the early 1970s.

Patty, her husband and her kids engaged in 18th-century re-enactments, where participants slept outdoors, wore pioneer garb, shot muzzle-loaders and paddled canoes.

"On all the campouts and everything, Patty always came out looking beautiful with perfect makeup on and never got dirty like the rest of us," said re-enactor Bob Wulff.

When she was younger, Crites hunted bear in Canada and deer in southern Ohio with her husband. She even went on rabbit hunts.

The only thing she ever shot was a fox.

But she was not averse to butchering the animals she raised — including bunnies that weren't suitable for show or too old or unattractive to be sold as pets — and cooking the meat for her family. The practice is common among rabbit breeders and farm folk.

"At rabbit shows, they'll have bunny-on-a-bun, creamed rabbit or barbecued rabbit," said Burns, a fellow bunny breeder. "How many animals can you raise and eat your mistakes?"

Crites grossed out her sister's kids one Easter when she tried serving them rabbit for dinner.

"They just thought that was amazing," her sister said. "You never knew what you were going to get on the holidays."

The hunting excursions sounded impressive —until we learn that she shot only one animal, and it was a predator. This is in stark contrast to Patty, the hopper chopper, in the next sentence.

I included the last sentence because urban and suburban readers might not understand the reality of life — and death — on the farm.

I love this woman. Burns freely spoke without regard to political correctness. But I did warn her that I intended to use the quote. She was cool with it. And then I moved in with the killer walk-off.

BGSU PROFESSOR A TALENTED SCULPTOR

The Toledo Blade — Aug. 8, 2002

Most obituaries, unlike the one above, are written on tight deadlines using information supplied by funeral homes and supplemented by phone calls to families or friends of the deceased. That's true of this one, as well. Like most ordinary obits, it supplies essential facts about the subject's interests and accomplishments along with details about survivors and funeral services.

BOWLING GREEN — Clifford Long, a mathematics professor at Bowling Green State University and gifted sculptor who used his talent to help students visualize math, died of cancer Tuesday in his home here. He was 71.

Dr. Long was born April 10, 1931, on the south side of Chicago. His father was a carpenter, and his influence may have been what first attracted Dr. Long to math, his son Steven Long said.

"He liked the angles, the measuring, the visual side of life," he said.

After high school, Dr. Long took a job as an order checker in the stockyards with Armour, Inc. He left the stockyards for the University of Illinois at Navy Pier in Chicago, where he studied math. Later, he transferred to the university's Champaign-Urbana campus, where he met his future wife, Patricia Marilyn Cline.

Dr. Long obtained his bachelor's degree, master's degree, and doctorate in mathematics from the University of Illinois. He took a teaching position at BGSU in 1959 and taught there for the next 35 years.

"So many people just want to do research and get grants," said his son, Thaddeus Long. "He wanted to teach people to love math."

Dr. Long carved the graphical displays of functions — mathematical relationships often too complex for the average person to visualize — in wood and marble for his students to see.

"People would see it and say, 'I always wanted to see what a trefoil knot would look like!'" Steven Long said.

Dr. Long took a special interest in computer graphics and the visualization of mathematical ideas. He was a pioneer in bringing the computer into classrooms at BGSU, and photographs of his sculptures were published in many science journals.

Despite a strong commitment to his work, Dr. Long found time to volunteer with Habitat for Humanity and Wheeled Meals, a meal delivery service he helped found.

He was devoted to his family, coaching his children's baseball teams and singing with his sons in a barbershop quartet.

Surviving are his wife, Patricia Marilyn Long; sons, Steven, Andrew and Thaddeus, and daughter, Melinda Gedeon.

Services will be at 2:30 p.m. Saturday in Bowling Green First Presbyterian Church, where the family will receive friends from 6:30 to 8:30 p.m. today and again from 1:30 p.m. until the service begins on Saturday. The Dunn Funeral Home is handling arrangements.

The family requests tributes to the BGSU Foundation Cliff & Lyn Long Scholarship Fund or to the Presbyterian Church Foundation Cliff & Lyn Long Local Benevolence Fund.

CHURCH BUS CRASH ON TURNPIKE KILLS 3

South Florida Sun-Sentinel
Aug. 8, 2004

◄ MORE ON **COVERING ACCIDENTS** ON PAGE **94**

Most accident stories are written by one reporter citing one or two sources. But for this tragic accident, five Sun-Sentinel staff writers contributed to the final report: Mike Clary, Neil Santaniello, Patty Pensa, Sallie James and Cadence Mertz.

As you study the story, notice how the additional reporting makes the coverage more comprehensive. At least eight different sources (including the reporters' own observations at the scene) describe the impact of the accident from a variety of dramatic perspectives.

Three people were killed Saturday night when a church bus was hit by an SUV on Florida's Turnpike, went out of control and crashed into the Boca Rio Canal just south of Glades Road.

The crash happened just before 10 p.m., and it wasn't until 1 a.m., when the white Girardin minivan was pulled from the 10- to 12- foot-deep canal, that authorities confirmed all of its occupants were accounted for.

The bus, from First Baptist Church Hillsboro in Coconut Creek, was bringing 23 passengers back from a water-park outing in Orlando.

Late Saturday, one seriously injured person had been airlifted to Delray Medical Center, six had been taken to West Boca Medical Center and two to Boca Community Hospital.

FHP Lt. Pat Santangelo said both the bus and a Ford Expedition were southbound on the turnpike when the Ford got a flat tire. Its driver lost control and bumped the bus, which was in the left lane.

The bus went out of control, swerving to the right and over about a 6-foot drop into the canal.

It was a section of the turnpike where the canal is not protected by a guardrail, Santangelo said.

The bodies lay on the west side of the canal, side-by-side and covered with plastic.

He said it was unknown whether the three people killed were children or adults.

Doug Doan, 53, of Davie, was one of the drivers who pulled over on the turnpike and jumped into the water to help rescuers.

Five or six people were on the roof of the vehicle, he said, and all were calling for help.

Doan, who was on his way home from a tubing trip, grabbed a diving mask from his car and jumped into the water. He helped pull out two children. He thought one was dead and one unconscious.

"Everybody was screaming from the bus," he said. "Somebody was shouting, 'Get my brother,'" but mostly he remembers a lot of shrieking.

Raymond Acevedo, 23, of Coral Springs, also stopped to help rescuers. He said a man who identified himself as the driver seemed consumed by remorse.

"I just acted on instinct," Acevedo said. He said a lot of people stopped along the turnpike to watch, but few jumped in.

Firefighter-paramedic Jeffrey Newsome, a member of Fire Rescue's Special Operations Team, was one of the first two divers in the water, which he said was 10 to 12 feet deep.

The bus was full of water, but no people were inside. Its horn was still sounding, its light and wipers still on.

While he was under water for 15 to 18 minutes, he saw the interior littered with book bags and shoes.

At one point, a near-hysterical woman ran up to the west bank of the canal, crying, "My son was on that bus!"

As a Palm Beach County sheriff's deputy consoled her, she looked up to spot her son on the other side of the canal.

"Greg!" she yelled.

But with the noise and commotion, her son could not hear her. She ran back to her car in an attempt to get onto the turnpike side of the road.

At West Boca Medical Center, at least two dozen family members and friends clustered around each other, hugging and crying. Some called on cell phones, trying to locate other members of the group.

Passengers with less-serious injuries, mostly children, were brought to the hospital by police cars and private vehicles. A boy walked in wrapped in a blood-soaked sheet. Highway Patrol troopers and sheriff's deputies talked to survivors as part of the investigation.

Sylvia Williamson, the wife of the Rev. Jerry Williamson, the church pastor, said most from the church youth group were in grades 7 to 12.

"It was the last hurrah before school starts," Williamson said, her voice faltering.

The church, at 5100 W. Hillsboro Blvd., has a small congregation of about 550. She said the accident has hit them hard.

The white top of the school bus gleamed beneath about 8 inches of water in the canal. The bus sat upright, its pop-up roof hatch open with divers peering in the top and swimming below.

Helicopters hovered above the scene while the red-and-blue lights of more than 25 emergency vehicles lit up the night.

The northbound lanes of the turnpike were opened to traffic just before midnight. Southbound lanes remained closed at 1:15 a.m.

On the turnpike side of the canal, medical teams treated dazed, wet survivors, while TraumaHawk helicopters lifted off with other victims.

FOR THOSE CUT OFF, A LIFE PRIMEVAL

By Vanessa Gezari

St. Petersburg Times — Sept. 12, 2005

◀ MORE ON **STORY STRUCTURE,** PAGE **48**

"I drove to New Orleans a week after Hurricane Katrina," Vanessa Gezari explains, "mainly to gather string for future stories. It was clear that the hurricane would transfigure the South, displacing tens of thousands of people, transforming a major city and altering the racial and economic composition of at least three states. I knew that as a national reporter, I'd be writing about these changes for months, and I didn't want to be forced to re-create damage I hadn't seen.

"But after I'd spent a few days in New Orleans, my editor and I decided that I should do a story right then to give readers a sensory picture of the empty city. The situation was strange enough, the sense of displacement powerful enough that even though I didn't feel I had a single blockbuster character or narrative, I thought I might be able to pull together an evocative piece that would put people in the ruins.

"I reported the story over about four days, drawing not just on my interviews and observations about other people, but very heavily on things I saw and felt, what I thought about driving through the deserted streets after nightfall, my own uneasiness, fear and wonder at what was happening. The hardest thing about writing it was stepping back from the reporting and getting clear about the idea I wanted to express, then choosing the best details to convey that idea to readers."

GEZARI'S COMMENTARY:

At first this story had a completely different lead. My editors unexpectedly held it a day, and sometime that night, I realized that the textbook wasn't just a nice detail but contained the central idea of the story. Then I knew I had to find a way to use it to bracket the rest of the reporting.

In the basement of a house on Panola Street, Armand Rodriguez's girlfriend moved the porcelain elephants and glass bells to the top shelf, along with a college textbook called "Society: the Basics."

The book says the Earth began 5 billion years ago, and for a long time, there was no life at all. Then came plants and animals, and finally people.

"We see that what we call 'civilization' is relatively recent indeed," the introduction says.

After introducing the big idea, I had to put readers back on the street. Clear, sharp details are usually the quickest way to do that.

Rodriguez hasn't read "Society: the Basics." He doesn't need to. Outside his window, Panola Street is a stagnant canal. Big blue dragonflies buzz over the water and magpies cry from the trees. The neighbors are long gone.

Despite a note from my editor, someone on the copy desk changed this quote. What he said, in true New Orleans fashion, was: "I been so lonely around here."

"I have been so lonely around here," says Rodriguez, who has been holed up with his dog since the day after Hurricane Katrina hit.

This isn't the New Orleans you know. It's not what you remember.

I wrote this section very early, knowing that many readers would come to the story with memories and preconceptions about New Orleans. I had to get rid of those before I could show them what the city had become. When you're writing about a big change, it's sometimes useful to tell people up front: Hey, this isn't what you think.

It's like nothing you've ever seen, though you might have imagined it, or you might have dreamed it. It is an abandoned city, where trees grow through windows, water laps under roof lines and the pavement is giving way to mud. Voices echo down flooded blocks, and fish swim in the streets. Cicadas are the new jazz.

Soldiers patrol the streets in Humvees, and convoys of police speed the wrong way down deserted highways. Helicopters drone overhead, carrying away the living, and along Interstate 10, trucks wait to ferry away the dead.

On Esplanade Avenue just north of the French Quarter, an Army truck rumbles past big old houses with white columns and gracious balconies.

"Attention citizens," a recorded voice booms. "If you are trapped or in need of medical assistance, please make as much noise as possible and you will be rescued. If you are not injured and are able to walk, please step out on your front porch and tell us you're OK."

No one steps out. The truck passes. The street is silent again.

I saw this on my last half-day of reporting. It's an important detail because it uses emptiness — the disembodied voice, the absence of human beings — to convey emptiness. In other parts of the story, I'm using solitary people to convey emptiness, which is trickier.

Only a few thousand people remain here, in a city that was home to some half-million two weeks ago. Emptiness has grown so ordinary that in some neighborhoods, the sight of another human being is like an electric shock. Civilization is a memory evoked by the Rite Aids with shattered windows and pried-open metal grates, the blocks of ruined houses, the flooded cemeteries with their moldering caskets and broken angels. At night, the sky is black and thick with stars. There's a 6 p.m. curfew, and by 9 p.m. it feels like anything could happen.

In a way, it already has.

Never has a modern American city emptied in a few days, leaving behind miles of ruins that are already giving way to the persistent decay of the bayou.

Here is some obligatory nut graf stuff — the change in population, the effects of looting, the fate of the city's tombs and the curfew — which I tried to write so it wouldn't seem like "information" and break the mood of the story. Don't settle for boring nut grafs. Work them over and they will sing.

While we were out on the water with rescuers, I wrote down everything, not knowing whether or when I would use it. If you meticulously describe what you see, detail by detail, you can put readers right there.

In the 9th Ward, a poor, mainly African-American neighborhood in Orleans Parish, the water is so deep that traffic lights barely clear the surface. At National Linen Service down Louisa Street, graying sheets are knotted around chain-link fences, and the Church of Christ is flooded halfway up its A-frame facade. A Pepsi machine floats by.

These are the archaeological remnants of New Orleans: Here was the city, here were its people. That's Muhammad Ali on the wall, there's a living room couch, a rocking horse, a basketball. These were their trophies, their photographs of births and marriages. This was the grocery store where they shopped, the sign still advertising fresh-cut meat and po' boy sandwiches and money orders. This was the liquor store, called In a Hurry, where they bought beer and cigarettes. There's the billboard for McDonald's, a restaurant they liked, and this painted sign is what's left of their local joint: "Down Home Cookin' 24 Hours."

Dogs still live here. A black beagle paddles weakly, trying to reach land in a neighborhood that has lost its boundaries. Pit bullterriers prowl porches, getting skinnier by the day, or perch on the roofs of pickups, growling and whining at passing boats. Sometimes rescuers pick them up, but no one knows which dogs are sick, which ones are dangerous. The large ones can tip a boat, so crews usually leave them behind.

At a school on Louisa Street, police in a boat try to convince a group of holdouts to leave. A man in the school says he still hears shooting at night. People say that armed looters paddle these streets in canoes, though there is little left to steal.

Across the parish in Uptown, the water is slowly receding. Ben Bernard, 62, is the last man on his block, maybe the last one on his street. He has been here the whole time with his dog, a sweet-tempered yellow puppy named Bling-Bling. He says he wouldn't have survived without her.

"God didn't make us to live alone," Bernard says, looking out over the mud and branches piled in the street. "He didn't make us to live on an island by ourselves."

His mother built this white frame house on Burdette Street; this is the address on his birth certificate. He's a retired electrician, but he says he doesn't need air conditioning or TV. He has a mosquito coil and a couple of cans of Chef Boyardee. He has a cell phone to call his daughter in New York. He has Bling-Bling.

He spends his days talking to the few people who happen by. He sits on the porch, and if the soldiers ask him to leave, he's polite. After all, he says, they work for him. He's not a criminal.

He feeds the birds and the cats. At twilight, his street is dead quiet. He sits on the porch with the dog, drinking water mixed with the juice of an aloe plant. He says aloe water can cure anything. A parakeet calls in the trees, and a mockingbird. Bernard listens, shudders.

"Kind of eerie," he says.

In the Carrollton neighborhood of Uptown a dozen blocks from the Mississippi River, the water is iridescent with chemicals. It smells of sewage and rotting garbage, but under all that is the smell of earth, the rich loam of a compost heap. Uptown is a swamp, and somewhere below the water, the mud is alive.

This is where Armand Rodriguez lives, in the pink wooden house on Panola Street with pictures of Ronald Reagan on the kitchen walls and Hunter S. Thompson novels on the shelves. He is 60, wiry and compact, as steady as a ship's captain. He was born here, and he has lived here since the hurricane on bottled water, canned milk and military meals-ready-to-eat. When soldiers came knocking last week, he didn't answer the door.

"I didn't want them to force me to leave," he says.

He's a carpenter for the Port of New Orleans, and he has been taking care of

I argued with my editor to keep the paragraphs long through this section because I wanted readers to feel the cascade of impressions as I had felt them. I saw myself in these flooded living rooms. I felt the futility of our efforts to organize the world and, at the same time, how deeply human those efforts were. You are not a machine. Don't be afraid to let your feelings illuminate your writing.

We identify with animals. After Katrina, when the lines between people and animals began to blur, the fate of dogs became really poignant. Whatever happened to dogs was happening to people, too.

Dogs again. Relationships with dogs had become the most important – often the only – relationships people had left.

This is probably the best quote in the story, partly because it's got the unmistakable ring of New Orleans speech. Look for quotes where you can hear the speaker's voice. Use them like drumbeats to punctuate the story's melody.

The aloe water, suggesting a resort to primitive remedies, was a gift. So was the dog's name, a reminder of materialism in a city that had lost everything it owned. Reporting is like that: if you work at it, good details will come naturally.

An environmental activist in New Orleans told me that the two basic components of a swamp are growth and decay, and that's just what was threatening about the emptiness after the flood: the feeling that nature was growing while human things melted away. I wanted to get both of those elements into the story.

Back to the guy we met at the beginning. This kind of ending should be a reminder and an expansion of the lead that takes the reader somewhere new. It's simple and has an intrinsic logic; it quietly asks the reader to think about where the story has taken him. I chose a simple structure on purpose. I didn't want anything to distract from the central idea of the story.

things around the house: painting screens, cutting a hole in the bedroom wall to hang the ironing board. He talks to Shemp, a big German shepherd. He tells him what a good boy he is, what a real good boy, and Shemp wags his tail so hard he nearly knocks over the trash can.

In these final grafs, I tried again to weave sharp details through the big idea. I wanted a fusion of abstract and concrete that would bring the force of the story home.

The day before Katrina hit, Rodriguez drove with his girlfriend, Cristina Louviere, to Texas. When they came back, a 4-foot alligator crawled across the road right in front of them. This was on Airline Highway in the middle of New Orleans. The water was already rising, and Cristina started to cry. She left soon afterward to stay with family outside the city. Her clothes and photographs are still here, along with her textbooks.

Thank God for the alligator. I needed Cristina's tears, not just Rodriguez's survivalism, to convey how unnerving the whole situation had become.

On the timeline inside the front cover of "Society: the Basics," Rodriguez has drifted backward. He is somewhere between the invention of the telephone in 1876 and the birth of the light bulb in 1879 — his phone works but he has no electricity. He has a radio that runs about half an hour before he has to wind it up again. He has a small silver .22-caliber pistol, but no bullets. There's a canoe in the back yard. He's out of Jack Daniels.

The loneliness is the worst part, and the stench of mold and death. The nights are quiet and hot, but when sleep finds him, it overtakes him completely.

I rewrote this ending about a dozen times before I got it to where it is. I'm still not entirely convinced. I wanted the story to end quietly, and I liked the idea that sleep had become a refuge. I think it achieves the feeling of an ending, which is half the battle.

OPENERS
AN ANTHOLOGY OF LEADS

Outlined against a blue-gray October sky, the Four Horsemen rode again. In dramatic lore they are known as Famine, Pestilence, Destruction and Death.

These are only aliases. Their real names are Stuhldreher, Miller, Crowley and Layden. They formed the crest of the South Bend cyclone before which another fighting Army football team was swept over the precipice at the Polo Grounds yesterday afternoon as 55,000 spectators peered down on the bewildering panorama spread on the green plain below.

Grantland Rice, *The New York Herald Tribune,* penning the most famous passage in sportswriting history (1924)

Much later, after nearly two years of searching for her killer, after the interviews at the station and the re-enactments in the dark and the lie-detector tests and the growing list of blind alleys and one sudden moment of stupid good luck — long after all that, they finally arrested a man and charged him with rape and first-degree murder.

An investigator asked a neighbor:
Does he look like a murderer to you?
The neighbor said:
What does a murderer look like?

Tom French, *St. Petersburg Times*

Ann Coulter is talking too loud. Sitting across from me at an outdoor table at a restaurant on Manhattan's Upper East Side, she's almost shouting, laughing, tossing her long blond hair, flailing her hands, her voice drowning out the people at the adjacent tables with her staccato one-liners. They gradually fall silent, turn, and stare.

John Colapinto, *Elle* magazine

GULF SHORES, Ala. – Sometimes Chucky has three-chicken days, and sometimes Chucky has six-chicken days. But Chucky does not enjoy no-chicken days — and yesterday was his second in a row.

So Chucky was hungry. And this was a problem, because Chucky, a 12-foot, half-ton American alligator that had spent the past 15 years at the Alabama Gulf Coast Zoo, was nowhere to be found.

Hurricane Ivan's eye blasted through the resort town of Gulf Shores early yesterday, ripping down the fence around Chucky's pond.

Zoo Director Patty Hall loves Chucky, as she loves every animal in her care, but she still dispatched a four-man crew with shotguns and pistols to kill him, if necessary. The heavily armed men sloshed their way through the waist-deep water that Ivan deposited on the zoo grounds, bringing a raw mix of the Wild Kingdom and the Wild West to the aftermath of the storm.

"As long as Chucky's been fed, Chucky's happy," said Hall, wearing hip boots and wielding a plywood board in case she encountered water moccasins — or Chucky. "Right now, I don't think he's happy."

— Michael Grunwald and Manuel Roig-Franzia, *The Washington Post,* opening a story that ran the day after Hurricane Ivan ripped through Alabama in 2004

"THIS ONE'S FOR REAL!"

By Mary Jo Patterson

Star-Ledger — Jan. 28, 2002

◄ MORE ON **COVERING FIRES** ON PAGE **96**

When a deadly fire struck Seton Hall University, the Newark (N.J.) Star-Ledger dispatched a team of reporters to the scene. This was the lead story in the paper's coverage; other related stories focused on the students, their families, the response at local hospitals and the investigation into the blaze. Notice how this story summarizes the essential facts about the fire while incorporating a variety of gripping anecdotes. Notice how many sources (and interviews) contributed to the story. And notice how, despite the horror and anguish, the reporter maintains a professional, objective tone.

A small but intense fire sent acrid black smoke through a dormitory at Seton Hall University in South Orange before dawn yesterday, killing three students and sending hundreds of others on a flight for their lives.

Fifty-eight students were injured, four critically, by the flames and thick smoke that billowed from a third-floor lounge. The smoke blinded and choked 18- and 19-year-olds as they felt their way, or crawled, to stairwells. Others, terrorized, remained in their rooms, crying and begging for help. At least one jumped from his window before firefighters could extend rescue ladders.

Nearly a score of false alarms in recent weeks had caused many students to disregard the fire alarm at first. Then, as the smoke filled the building, they realized this was no prank. "I heard people screaming. . . . 'This one's for real! This one's for real!'" said Jason Esposito, a resident of the dormitory, Boland Hall.

Alison Liptak was one of those who discounted the alert. "I just thought it was another false alarm. I just laid there, kind of ignoring it, until I heard someone running down the hall," said Liptak, 18, of Clifton. The pajamas-clad freshman escaped from her fourth-floor room to find another horror scene outside. She looked up to see students leaning out windows, pleading for help.

As of early this morning, investigators had not pinpointed the cause of the fire, but they had ruled out careless smoking and faulty electrical wiring.

Authorities identified the three dead students as John Giunta of Vineland, Aaron Karol of Green Brook and Frank Caltabilota of West Long Branch. Two of the three were found in the lounge, burned beyond recognition, according to sources at the scene. The third, whom fellow students tried to revive, was found in a bedroom nearby.

The most seriously injured were three of 12 victims admitted to the burn unit of Saint Barnabas Medical Center in Livingston, and one victim at University Hospital in Newark.

By day's end, 45 students had been treated and released from seven area hospitals, most suffering from smoke inhalation.

The six-story Boland Hall — built in 1952 as the university's first dormitory — is home to 600 Seton Hall freshmen.

University officials said that 18 false alarms had been registered at the 350-room structure since Sept. 1, fewer than in previous years. Still, a number of students buried their heads in their pillows at the sound of the alarm. "I didn't think anything of it," said Tom Semko of Howell. "We've had fire alarms going off all the time during finals week, and I figured, 'More of the same.'"

Hellish sights and sounds confronted fleeing students.

Anthony Neis, an 18-year-old from Staten Island, passed a young man who was clad only in shorts, covered with burns, and moaning. "He must have been in such pain," said Neis, who escaped unharmed.

Carrie Fleisher, a freshman from Hillsborough, saw a teenager on fire. "He was totally blackened. Some kids were hitting him with a jacket. He was conscious and hitting himself, too," she said.

Yatin Patel, 19, of Jersey City, trapped in his room, heaved mattresses out his window, with his roommate's help. Paralyzed with fear, he was standing at the window, contemplating jumping, when a firefighter burst into the room. Patel wet a sock, put it over his mouth and nose and — grabbing the kneeling fireman's left leg — began to crawl out into the corridor. His roommate held Patel's leg in turn and crawled behind them. The trio moved slowly through the darkness, under flames licking from ceiling tiles, to a stairwell.

Down the hall, Virginia Wannamaker dialed 911 on her cell phone as she waited in fear with her roommate. The 18-year-old from Irvington heeded the advice of the fire dispatcher, stuffing a comforter under the door and sealing it tight with packing tape. They opened windows and turned on a fan.

South Orange fire sources said they were alerted to the fire at 4:28 a.m. by the college's public safety department and had the fire under control by approximately 4:45 a.m. Officials on the scene could not pinpoint exactly when the blaze started, however. Seven other municipalities also responded to the general alarm fire.

University officials said the building's occupants included 18 paid resident assistants, one priest and four professional staffers. In the event of a fire, resident assistants are to knock on every door, said Lisa Grider, a spokeswoman for Seton Hall. South Orange firefighters conducted an extensive primary search of the dorm, followed by two more, she added.

Still, two freshmen slept through the entire ordeal undetected and emerged unscathed hours later, at 2 p.m.

The blaze was confined to a lounge area off the elevators, open on two sides to student rooms. Students use the area —

furnished with three plush velour sofas, a rug, a cork bulletin board and pay phones — to socialize and study. Sometimes they nap there, too.

University officials said smoking is allowed in dorm rooms but prohibited in the lounge. In the fire, the sofas were completely burned; the ceiling, cinderblock walls, and low-pile rug were singed. Fire officials speculated that the two dead students found in the lounge had left their rooms and became disoriented.

Boland Hall is one of six dormitories on campus and one of two without sprinklers. It is equipped with smoke detectors and 55 fire extinguishers, one of which was found, used, near the fire, university officials said.

"This is a heartbreaking tragedy for Seton Hall University, for our families, for all the Seton Hall family, and for the larger family of the state," said Msgr. Robert Sheeran, president of Seton Hall, a Catholic university founded in 1856. Some 2,200 of its 10,000 students live on campus.

Sheeran suspended all classes, activities, and events through Sunday pending further notice.

Gov. Christie Whitman, who visited the scene, called the fire a "huge tragedy."

By all accounts, the hours immediately before the fire passed like most nights at Boland Hall — except for the lingering air of jubilation caused by Seton Hall's unexpected win, 78-70, over basketball archrival St. John's. The winter semester, which began last Thursday, was fresh and new. Students were up late, as usual.

For example, Tiffany Hill, an 18-year-old from Maryland, had spent the night alternately studying her economics textbook and bouncing between friends across the hall and in the lounge. Around 3 a.m. she finally called it quits and retired to her room. She dozed for about an hour, when her roommate woke her, saying she needed to talk. Exhausted, Hill put her off and fell back asleep, but woke not many minutes later.

This time her friend was in her face. "Tiff, get up, get up," she yelled. "It's real." Hill had not heard the alarms, but she smelled smoke as soon as she shook herself awake. Someone banged at the door.

"We put on our stuff and ran," Hill said, interviewed hours later as she walked across campus, carrying the teddy bear slippers she had put on to escape the fire.

Michael McCaffrey, a roommate of victim Aaron Karol, was still awake when the alarms sounded. He was not in his third-floor room but on the floor above, watching movies with friends.

"My bed is on the other side of the lounge wall," McCaffrey said. "If I was there, I probably wouldn't be here right now. And when I heard the fire alarm, at first I didn't react much. I was very nonchalant. There's a fire alarm almost every night sometimes, it seems. It's those idiot frat pledges who are constantly pulling the alarms."

Rob Cardiello, who lived two doors from the lounge, was one of the few students to report actually seeing fire. He hadn't heard the smoke alarms, having put on earplugs before going to sleep. Suddenly he awoke, wet and sweaty.

"I looked to the right, to the lounge, and saw (orange) flames," he said. As he exited the building in the opposite direction, the sharp black smoke penetrated his lungs like acid. "I could feel the whole way down the hallway: Your lungs are burning," Cardiello said. The 18-year-old freshman from Clark was treated at Mountainside Hospital in Montclair for smoke inhalation.

As Cardiello ran toward safety, he smacked into two students who were running and screaming. He pushed one toward the right direction, grabbed the other, and charged down the hallway. The smoke was so thick, he said, that they ran past the exit, into a wall.

Once outside, Cardiello ran around campus, looking for a missing friend. "I didn't really realize how I was feeling until I stopped," he said hours later.

All four of the students listed as "very critical" were on respirators last night. The three at Saint Barnabas, all males, had second-degree burns covering from 15 to 56 percent of their bodies. Only one, Alvaro Ilanos, was identified.

At University Hospital, the patient was Dana Christmas, a resident adviser who suffered severe burns and respiratory distress. Christmas, 21, of Paterson was unconscious and attached to a ventilator to ease pressure on her smoke-damaged lungs. Doctors said she had burns over 60 percent of her body, including her face, back and extremities.

"She has fairly extensive injuries. Her condition is being monitored on a minute-to-minute basis," said Sanjeev Kaul, the trauma physician attending to her.

News of the fire hit the airwaves early, frightening parents.

In Teaneck, Roderico Sumilang and his wife, whose alarm radio had been set to an all-news station, heard about the fire the second they woke up. Sumilang turned on the TV. He dialed the number of the cell phone he had just given his son, Romil. The son's roommate answered.

"He said, 'I can't talk, the firemen are trying to get us out,'" the father recalled. "I said, 'Where's my son?' He said, 'He might have gotten out the back.'"

Sumilang called the college but got a recording. Again, he dialed his son's cell phone. This time, a different voice delivered the news: Romil had been taken away in an ambulance.

Many parents endured hours of agonizing uncertainty.

Others counted their blessings to find children alive. So did their kids.

"I think God had his arms around me this morning," said Nicole McFarlane, 19, a freshman from Summit who lived on Boland Hall's fifth floor. "That's why I got out. I had God's arms around me."

FAMILY LOSES ALL IN HOUSE FIRE

By Sanne Specht

Mail Tribune (Medford, Ore.) — June 1, 2005

◄ MORE ON **COVERING FIRES** ON PAGE **96**

Reporter Sanne Specht explains the origins of her story about fire victim Luis Davila:

"Davila's co-worker called the newsroom to pitch his friend's plight for one of our weekly 'Hometown Hero' stories. 'Can the community help?' he asked. We'd already done a brief on the structure fire. This story would demonstrate the family's material losses — and how close they came to losing their youngest child. It would also allow the community to be the 'hero' if they chose to help the family.

"I called Davila. In the initial telephone interview, he seemed anxious for publicity and eager to get cash donations. He was just back from the bank where he'd opened a special trust account, he said. We made an appointment to meet at the scene the next day.

"When the photographer and I arrived, the family was not there. The family dog — a young female Great Pyrenees — was tied to a large tree next to the burned-out trailer. The dog's brown eyes were red-rimmed and her normally white coat was greasy and black with smoke. She flinched when I went to pet her, then licked my hand."

Specht's journalistic skepticism becomes evident in her comments below. But as you'll see, she managed to conceal her doubts in the finished story.

SPECHT'S COMMENTARY:

In our phone conversation, Davila described his young son's rough night after the fire: "He was coughing and smoke was coming out his nose. He couldn't sleep all night. I was very worried." I was surprised when Davila told me he hadn't sought medical attention for the toddler. The EMTs had checked the boy out that morning, he replied.

I wanted the readers to go back to that morning, right before the fire — the "It was a day like any other, until…" scenario.

Davila was attempting to control the dialogue. It was clear he wanted to be the sole narrator. He would wander off with the photographer when I was quietly writing notes but immediately shadow me when I'd ask questions of family members. I wasn't having trouble understanding their comments, but his constant interruptions to "translate" derailed their answers — making it difficult to get their voices in the story.

CENTRAL POINT — Luis Davila picked up his young son, stepped over a melted Hula-Hoop and carried him into the burned-out husk of their former home.

The toddler squirmed in his father's arms.

"He was the one inside the house when the fire started," said Davila, looking at the charred wreckage — then back at his 22-month-old son, Abraham.

Davila's three older children were at school late on the morning of May 18. Davila was at a neighbor's house. Davila's wife, Silvia, popped in Abraham's favorite cartoon video: "Finding Nemo."

Silvia's plan was to keep the boy occupied while she slipped out to the yard to do some chores, he said.

"She put in 'Nemo' and was feeding the dog," said Davila, 39.

But looking back toward the house, Silvia saw a sight that sent her heart racing. Black smoke billowed out of the windows.

"She ran in and grabbed my son," said Davila. "Then she came running down the street crying 'Luis! Luis! Our house is on fire!'"

Davila, two doors away, responded quickly to his wife's calls. The trailer's phone lines, already melted, were useless. Neighbors called 9-1-1 as Davila used the garden hose in a futile effort to stem the furious blaze engulfing the 25-year-old single-wide mobile home. Silvia tried to calm her terrified son.

"He had smoke coming out of his nose," said Davila.

BOB PENNELL/MAIL TRIBUNE

Luis Davila carries his son, Abraham, though the charred remains of their home in Medford, Ore., after it was destroyed by fire.

Fire officials said the fire probably started in the family's wood stove. Although fire crews arrived within seven minutes, the home was already fully ablaze, said Central Point Deputy Fire Marshall Don Hickman.

"We have digital photos of the fire blowing out the windows," said Hickman. "They absolutely did lose everything."

Davila is grateful no one was hurt in the blaze, but the loss of their uninsured home and its contents — estimated at a total of $33,000 — has been a severe blow.

"That cute little boy was pretty upset," said Hickman. "Mr. Davila told me the stuff can be replaced, but his family can't."

The American Red Cross is working to provide some relief, while neighbors have donated clothes and food. But, for now, the six-member family is crammed into one of

I had already spoken to the fire officials before arriving at Davila's property. They validated the ferocity of the fire, the totality of the family's property loss and its monetary value. The fire-fighters' statements also painted a sympathetic portrait of Davila.

Davila continued interrupting my conversations with family members, so I waited for him to be distracted before approaching his daughter again. She was sticking close, and I wanted her story. If that hadn't worked, I would have told Davila I needed to talk to Diane without his "interpret-ations." However, I doubt she'd have spoken as freely.

the property's outbuildings, Davila said.

Davila's 9-year-old daughter, Diane, attends sixth grade at Scenic Middle School. She said living in relative homelessness in the aftermath of the fire "has been a nightmare."

"It's hard to sleep," said Diane. "I've been used to this house since I was born."

Willie Woolfolk has worked with Davila for the past seven years. Both are union laborers and Woolfolk said their union has raised about $500 to help the family. But

more is needed, he said.

"He's got a family," said Woolfolk. "Clothes, food, toys — all gone. I've never had anything like that happen. It must be devastating."

Davila said his priority is getting his family back on its feet. He admitted he's at a loss as to what to do next.

"I'm no rich man," said Davila. "I've been poor all my life. But we lost quite a bit."

Donations may be made to the Luis and Silvia Davila Fire Fund (555-5555). . . .

Willie Woolfolk provided the "Everyman" voice: someone who can relate but isn't directly related to the fire. Also, for the purposes of this story, it led into the "What can the community do to help?" section.

FINAL COMMENTS FROM SANNE SPECHT:

"Davila had a large number of roosters leg-staked on his property. He was evasive answering questions about the birds. But, when asked directly, Davila reluctantly admitted there'd been a lot more prior to the fire. He was clearly agitated by the topic. 'Why you want to know about my chickens, Sanne? Please don't talk about them, OK?'

"Back in the newsroom, I told the editor I had some concerns. As I did for all 'Hometown Hero' subjects, I ran Davila for criminal violations. He had a number of traffic violations, but nothing that dissuaded us from doing the story.

"Next, I called animal control to check for complaints. The animal control agent said they were watching the property, but no action had been taken. Ironically, prior to the fire, Davila had lodged his own complaint for the loss of several roosters. The birds had been killed by a neighbor's loose dog, he'd said. The agent said Davila had listed the birds as worth thousands of dollars — red-flagging the agent to suspect Davila may be involved in cockfighting.

"In the absence of hard evidence of current criminal activity, I wrote the story. I also gave the agent my name and number, requesting a call if their investigation turned up anything.

"This story brought forth a wave of folks offering donations. Even months later, community members continued calling to offer the family clothes and furniture.

"Animal control did not call."

OPENERS
AN ANTHOLOGY OF LEADS

Joe and M.A. Rowe are sitting in their kitchen at 11:43 on a cold Sunday morning when they hear a pickup truck in the gravel driveway of their large adobe house, RoweVista. "Oh, God," they say in unison, "They're here."

Through the wide windows of their kitchen, they see a man with a rifle run behind the truck and another man with a rifle run around the side of the house and aim through the sun-room windows. A third man crouches behind the short adobe wall in front of the Rowes' porch, only his rifle barrel visible.

"Go dial 911," Joe Rowe tells his wife. He picks up his Ruger 9 mm pistol and walks into the laundry room, peeking outside from behind the shaded glass of the laundry-room door. "What do you want?" he yells.

"We're from the Republic of Texas, and you're our prisoners of war," a voice calls out from behind the adobe wall.

Judd Slivka, *Arkansas Democrat-Gazette,* using a dramatic-action lead to open a story on violent Texas militias

Their house would collapse in a smoking ruin, and tears would stain their faces for hours afterward, but at least they had the family pictures.

"That was all we took," Miguel Mejia, a security guard in his 30s, said as he wiped his eyes.

On Sunday afternoon, he and his companion, Carmen Romero, sat in their Toyota 4-Runner across the street from what remained of their hilltop home above Claremont. Embers still blew off the gutted structure. The melted hulk of Romero's Lexus looked like it was fused to the driveway.

The couple had fled Saturday night with their two children, 14 and 3, when a wildfire charged up the canyon behind their home.

"Just the pictures," said Romero, her voice trailing off to a sob.

Paul Pringle, *Los Angeles Times,* opening a story headlined, "What Do You Save From a House Full of Memories?"

INTO THE FLAMES
By Stuart Tomlinson
The Oregonian — Oct. 4, 2001

◀ MORE ON **COVERING FIRES** ON PAGE **96**

Less than a month after the Sept. 11 attacks, firefighters had attained heroic status in American culture. When Oregonian editors heard about the dramatic rescue of a 3-year-old girl, they asked writing coach Jack Hart to work with reporter Stuart Tomlinson to create a chronological account of the event. The resulting piece provides a dramatic example of how a news story can be transformed into a gripping narrative.

TOMLINSON'S COMMENTARY:

We had many different ways to get into the story, but chose simple chronological order — starting at the beginning and then letting the action unfold and rise.

Lt. Jason McGowan was asleep when the call came into Gresham's Station No. 72 at 1:25 a.m. Wednesday: a fire at 2945 S.E. Ambleside Drive.

As he has a hundred or more times before, McGowan stepped into his grubby brown turnouts and jumped into Engine 72, with firefighter Fred Butler at the wheel and firefighter Eric Byrne in the third seat.

The exposition. The players have launched into action; one of them is a father.

As they rolled south on Kane Road toward Hogan Drive, the radio crackled, and dispatchers told them a 3-year-old girl was trapped in the basement. McGowan, a nine-year veteran, remembers that news making him think about his own 3-year-old daughter, Rylee.

But the situation wasn't good. McGowan knew by looking at his map that the house was at the far end of Ambleside Drive, a winding one-lane road that does indeed amble, through a stand of old cedars beside the green water of Johnson Creek.

They passed the hydrant at Hogan and Ambleside, the closest water source. The house was another 3,500 feet up Ambleside, and Engine 72 carried only 1,000 feet of hose.

Rising action. In the previous three grafs, the firefighters are presented with obstacles: the winding and narrow road, squeezing through old cedars, the extra 2,500 feet to the hydrant, the flimsy bridge.

Butler threaded the 20,000-pound fire engine down the road, clearing the hefty trunks of the cedars by inches. Then he neared the wooden bridge across Johnson Creek. He hesitated. McGowan knew about the bridge, and he knew it was rated to hold the heavy engine. But it looked flimsy.

The radio barked again: Battalion Chief Larry Fowler came on the air. He was already at the house, he reported, and the little girl was still trapped inside.

"There's a kid in there," McGowan shouted at Butler. "We're going."

And go they did, scuffing the rig's massive tires along the low railing of the narrow bridge.

They twisted up the road, past small houses tucked into the woods and through what one battalion chief referred to, with heavy irony, as "beautiful obstructions."

Then they arrived at a steel gate strung between brick pillars, the entrance to 2945 Ambleside. The truck would not fit through.

They've mostly cleared the obstacles getting to the house, but the truck won't fit. They make the decision: Go! Now it's full speed ahead.

Byrne and McGowan grabbed a 2½-gallon stainless-steel fire extinguisher, an ax, a prybar and a flashlight. Weighed down by their gear and the air tanks strapped to their backs, the two men ran up another 500 feet of driveway to the white clapboard house with the green trim.

The things they carried.

Fire and smoke streamed from the windows.

More obstacles; they're pumping adrenaline. Jack pulled these details out of me, stuff that might never make it into a first-day story about a fire rescue.

Fowler stood in the driveway holding 54-year-old Shirley Huddleston, who rents the house, in a bear hug. She was screaming.

It was Mrs. Huddleston who woke up to the smell of smoke and the insistent beep of a smoke alarm. She called 9-1-1 and hurried two of her grandchildren — Zane Langley-Harvey, 2, and Bryce Langley, 8 —outside. They were safe in Fowler's command rig.

How do you get in the basic facts of the fire — who lived there, how the fire was detected — without gumming up the narrative? This approach (what to call it — breathless?) seemed to work best.

Huddleston's daughter, 29-year old Melanie Langley, who also lives in the house, was away at work. But Huddlestone's 3-year-old granddaughter, Harley Langley-Harvey, was trapped in a basement bedroom.

Basement choked with smoke

Fowler told his two firefighters to go around the far right of the house. Byrne broke out a window and reached in to unlock the door. Fire rolled along the ceiling and glowed behind a wall. Smoke choked the basement all the way down to the floor. And the firefighters had no hose to beat back the flames.

Byrne went right; McGowan went left.

Byrne couldn't even see the floor he was crawling on. He had a hard time believing that anyone could be alive in the heat and

The climax. McGowan and Byrne actually enter the burning basement. They still have obstacles to overcome — they can't see, but they can hear. I must have called McGowan back 10 times at home for additional details about the rescue, the equipment he and Byrne used and how they felt during the rescue.

smoke.

But he heard a child cry, and he yelled, "Hey, kid, come to me, come to me."

And then he felt her head. He picked up the surprisingly lightweight form of the girl. Then he and McGowan ran out of the inferno into the forest, bathed in the cool light of the full moon. He laid little Harley on the ground, and she started to cry.

It was the sound of life. From the time the men sprinted to the house to the time they pulled Harley from the flames took four minutes.

But there was more to do. Fowler told them a man was still inside.

They went back into the burning basement and ran into the same hellish conditions. Again they crawled along the floor, sweeping back and forth. But the fire was too hot, and the ceiling was starting to buckle, starting to fall. Six minutes, seven. They had to retreat.

The denouement. They've made the rescue, but there is still someone inside. Unfortunately, they can't save them. It does not diminish what they've done, but adds a note of sorrow to an otherwise uplifting story. We tried to set that tone throughout.

Friend dies in fire

Terry L. Corcoran, 27, a friend of the Huddleston family who was only staying the night because his truck wouldn't start, died in the smoke and flames.

Harley was treated for smoke inhalation at Emanuel Hospital & Health Center and was released a few hours later. The American Red Cross put the family up in a hotel.

The fire apparently started when a candle was left burning on a wooden mantelpiece. The house is a total loss.

And Lt. Jason McGowan went back to work — he had another 24 hours on his shift. They call it "working a double," a 48-hour shift.

But he was still at the address on Ambleside Drive late Wednesday morning when the father of the three children, Peter Harvey, stopped by. Harvey shook McGowan's hand, gave him a hug and thanked him.

I was glad to do it, McGowan said.

Byrne slept and spent some time with his 3-year old daughter, Allison.

Everyone told them they were heroes: Photographers wanted pictures, perhaps with them holding their own daughters. Their emotions were mixed, the firefighters said. They wished they could have saved two lives.

Both men said they never once thought about the events of Sept. 11, when so many of their brother firefighters died doing the same thing they had just done: running into a burning building, trying to save lives.

"We don't make a habit of going into burning houses with only a fire extinguisher," McGowan said.

"But," he added, "we have a slogan around here:

" 'Whatever the day demands.' "

We struggled with the ending, and Jack, who has worked extensively with Pulitizer Prize-winning writer Tom Hallman, pushed for short, punchy sentences. Who was I to argue?

That final phrase from McGowan kept running around my head all day, and seemed the perfect kicker. In late 2004, McGowan, working as a reserve police officer, pulled a woman from a burning car.

OPENERS
AN ANTHOLOGY OF LEADS

In cold, wet blackness 240 feet below the world that didn't know if they were alive or dead, nine miners took turns snuggling each other for warmth. Since Wednesday night when they'd accidentally dug into a neighboring abandoned mine and their mine was inundated by an explosion of millions of gallons of water, they'd spent hours swimming, walking, standing and crouching in the frigid water that glowed orange in the intermittent light from their headlamps.

They found refuge in a chamber about 20 feet wide and 4 feet high. But when the water began rising, the men kept moving, hoping to find an even higher spot. Once they even tried to break through another rock wall to bring the water level down.

Instead, the water rose over their heads and they had to swim for a time in their heavy mining clothes.

At one point, they tore up a cardboard box, jotted last words to their loved ones and dropped them into a pail they affixed to a wall.

At another point, they built a dike of cinder blocks and tried to block the water with piles of canvas, but it was no use.

So the nine began tying themselves together. If they were going to drown, they were going to drown together, and their bodies could be found together, too.

The water kept coming. At one point it rose so high that the nine men strained to stretch their necks above it and gasped for air.

Then, the water stopped rising.

Bob Batz, *Pittsburgh Post-Gazette,* opening a story on the rescue of the Quecreek coal miners in Pennsylvania

FOUR CRIME BRIEFS

◀ MORE ON **COVERING CRIME** ON PAGE **98**

We've selected these crime briefs not because they're odd (although they are) but because they contain the kinds of facts, quotes and sources typical of most crime stories. Notice:

◆ *How that second story uses a chronological narrative, a "martini" structure, to re-create the incident. (For a longer example, see the next page.) Chronologies often provide the best way to explain* WHAT HAPPENED.

◆ *How some of these leads are more featurized than others, which makes the story more of a brite than a brief. That's a popular approach, provided the topic and tone are appropriate. Are they, in these cases?*

An Englewood woman has landed in jail after allegedly padding her bra with a rare greenwing parrot.

Jill Knispel, 35, faces felony charges for stealing the bird from her employer, Baby Exotic Birds of Englewood, after she traded it for a vintage 1964 Karmann Ghia automobile.

According to the Fish and Wildlife Conservation Commission, Knispel bragged to the car owners that she had flown the coop with the $2,000 bird after nesting it in her brassiere.

The car owners turned out to be close friends of the rightful owner, and squawked. After DNA tests confirmed the bird was the baby of parrots owned by Hobbs Guenther, Knispel was booked at the Sarasota County Jail under a $1,000 bond.

"The circumstances of the case are the most bizarre I've ever encountered," said veteran FWC investigator Lenny Barshinger.

But then, Barshinger may not have heard of Giraldo Wong, charged in August with smuggling two songbirds — tiny Cuban grassquits — into Miami by hiding them in his underpants.

The News-Press (Fort Myers, Fla.)

It's not every day that a robber gives instead of takes.

But Ambridge police said that's what happened yesterday when a man attempted to return a wad of cash to the bank he had allegedly robbed minutes earlier.

"He told us he knew he did wrong and he wanted to make it right," Ambridge police Sgt. Rick Bufalini said of suspect Andre Ellis.

Police said Mr. Ellis, 39, walked the nine blocks from his apartment to ESB Bank on busy Merchant Street yesterday morning.

Upon entering the bank, Mr. Ellis grabbed a withdrawal slip and scribbled a demand note on the back, Sgt. Bufalini said. At 9:57 a.m., the robber handed the piece of paper to a teller.

"Put the money on the counter," the note said. "Sorry I did this. God forgive me. I need help."

The teller handed the robber about $1,100. Police said Mr. Ellis left the bank and headed to a laundromat about a block away.

As police swarmed to the scene, something odd happened. Amid the washers and dryers and piles of dirty clothes, Mr. Ellis mulled over his predicament and apparently had some sort of revelation.

"He had a change of heart," Sgt. Bufalini said. "He saw all the police cars going around and got scared and knew that he did wrong. He decided to go back and give the money back."

Police said Mr. Ellis returned to the bank 20 minutes after the robbery, the cash stuffed in his jacket pocket. He could not get in, though.

After a bank is robbed, the institution usually locks its doors. Mr. Ellis tried banging on the window to get an employee's attention, but to no avail, police said.

Harmony police Officer Robert Santo, who used to work for Ambridge, spotted Mr. Ellis, matched him to the description of the robber, and notified other officers in the area. Mr. Ellis was arrested without a struggle.

Police charged him with robbery, theft and receiving stolen property. He was held on $100,000 straight bond and jailed.

Sgt. Bufalini said he had never heard of a robber returning his proceeds until yesterday.

"Too bad all bank robbers aren't like this," he said.

Jonathan D. Silver
Pittsburgh Post-Gazette

It's been more than a month since the clown last laughed.

That's how long Delmer Jefferson of Des Moines has searched for his miniature, flame-emblazoned, bright yellow tow truck. The one he built himself. The one the kids flocked to when he drove it in parades in his greasepaint, red nose and goofy shoes.

"It's a clown car. It shouldn't be hard to spot," Jefferson said. "They took the trailer, too. They took the whole thing."

Jefferson's pride and joy disappeared July 5 from a parking lot at the Za-Ga-Zig Shrine in Altoona. Police have been unable to pinpoint the culprit.

"I'm heartbroken," said Jefferson, who has been a Shriner clown for 34 years and manages the bar at the lodge.

Jefferson has crafted two other mini parade vehicles, a red semitrailer truck and a toilet-toting go-kart that looks like a bathroom on wheels. But the tow truck, fashioned from a riding lawn mower, was easily his favorite.

"I had it just the way I wanted it," he said, describing the various flashers and sirens that made children perk up along a parade route.

Don't even ask what the toy truck is worth.

"I can't replace it," Jefferson said. "And it's not worth anything to anyone else. It's a clown car."

Altoona Police Detective Jason Ferguson said he has looked into one tip that didn't pan out, but he hasn't abandoned hope of finding Jefferson's truck.

"This thing is so unique," he said. "What would anyone do with it?"

Larry Ballard
The Des Moines Register

[Note: This crime occurred Sunday, Dec. 25]

'Twas the morning after Christmas and all through the Coca-Cola bottling plant, not a creature was stirring — except for the would-be burglar hanging head-first from an air vent.

That's not exactly how the story goes, nor likely the way 23-year-old Jason Bibeau hoped things would end up.

But police said workers arriving Monday morning at the Coca-Cola Bottling Co., 912 E. Broadway in Bolivar, found the Urbana man stuck in the air vent, his legs dangling on top of the roof.

His bag, later recovered by authorities, contained no toys. Instead, it carried tools to aid the break-in, including a crowbar and pliers.

Police estimated Bibeau was hanging for one to two hours before he was found. They had to get the Bolivar Fire Department to extract him.

"He couldn't go backwards and he couldn't go forward," said Bolivar Police Chief Michael Seibert. "You had to see it. It was quite intriguing."

Bibeau was charged with second-degree burglary and first-degree property damage. He is being held in the Polk County Jail in lieu of $25,000 bail.

Bibeau told Bolivar police he gained access to the roof by placing a PVC pipe against the building and climbing it. He later "ripped out a vent" and tried to climb through it. That's how he got stuck.

"The guy was basically goofy," Seibert said. "He was like Santa Claus stuck in the chimney."

A T-shirt over his head hid Bibeau's identity from authorities at first. Seibert said an officer who knew Bibeau responded to the scene.

Bibeau told the officer he put the T-shirt over his head because he didn't want anyone to recognize him. He later told the officer he broke into the bottling company to steal money, police said.

A stocking cap that lay on the floor below Bibeau appeared to have fallen from the ceiling, police said. An orange bag of tools near Bibeau's feet was also recovered from the roof. Inside was a crowbar, flashlight and pliers.

An official at the bottling company told police that the damages would exceed $800.

Melissa DeLoach
The Springfield (Mo.) News-Leader

CHECK-WRITER SETS OFF CLERK'S INTERNAL ALARM

By Stuart Tomlinson

The Oregonian — Dec. 19, 2004

◄ MORE ON STORY STRUCTURE ON PAGE 48

This isn't a sensational crime story — no bullets, no thrilling chases, no dramatic rescues — but it's an excellent example of how engaging a crime story can be when the reporter re-creates events chronologically. "Without quite realizing it, I used the martini-glass style, a technique I picked up at a Bruce DeSilva workshop," Tomlinson says. "It's a variation on the inverted pyramid. As you work your way through the story, you reach the 'olive' — the story told in chronological order."

TOMLINSON'S COMMENTARY:

It seemed like sweet justice that a guy who ripped off so many people got caught and sent to the graybar hotel for writing an itty-bitty check for 80 bucks. So that was the lede right there.

What was his downfall? Not only an itty-bitty check, but an itty-bitty clerk with tons of experience.

We're getting the charges out the way early on, keeping the news up high before switching to the narrative.

This is the "turn," shifting into a juicy narrative of how the crime went down. Narrative can be quite effective, even on deadline. This required numerous callbacks to the detectives involved and to our spunky clerk, the protagonist in this narrative. Try and get as many small details as possible.

Looks nice . . . and a big fan of the turtleneck. These are details anyone other than a retail sales clerk might not remember. But they are nice scene-setters: the single check, the brand of turtleneck, the brand of shirt.

TROUTDALE — It was the check for $80.60 that put Brian Jake Parsons behind bars.

Parsons, 24, who police say wrote nearly $300,000 in bogus checks in three states, couldn't get that one past Judi Kramer.

"Maybe it's because I've been in retail for 36 years," said Kramer, manager of The Great Outdoor Clothing Store at the Columbia Gorge Outlet stores. "I've seen a lot."

Other clerks and store managers in Oregon, Washington and Alabama were less critical. An employee of a Kirkland, Wash., car dealership accepted a $44,000 check from Parsons for a new black BMW.

Parsons was arraigned Friday in Multnomah County Circuit Court on an indictment charging him with three counts of identity theft and three counts of second-degree forgery.

Parsons, who appeared on a video monitor during his arraignment, pleaded not guilty and is expected to next appear in court in January.

How did Parsons' journey of grandiose deception — that stretched from the Deep South to the Pacific Northwest — end in an outlet mall at the mouth of the Columbia River Gorge? Police said it was a classic, if unplanned, sting.

Just after 10:30 a.m. Dec. 8, the Kirkland, Wash., man — who has ties to Florida and Alabama — walked into the store Kramer manages. At 6 feet 4 and 230 pounds, Parsons came across as smooth and well-dressed, wearing a black turtleneck sweater, tan pants and a navy blue blazer.

But from the first Kramer was suspicious, she said, especially when Parsons pulled a single folded check from his pocket to pay for a Tommy Hilfiger turtleneck sweater, a plain white cotton turtleneck and a plaid Columbia shirt.

"I thought, 'Oh, here it comes,' " Kramer said. "He just had the single check and no checkbook. . . . Then he gave me an ID card that said he worked for the Department of Homeland Security. I said, 'You mean the national Department of Homeland Security?' He said, 'Yes.' "

Alarm bells went off in Kramer's head again when Parsons said he was a 38-year-old retired U.S. Army major.

"He looked 25, tops," she said.

Because of her experience with bad-check writers, Kramer knew she had to let Parsons write the check and leave the store with the merchandise for any charges to stick. After Parsons left, she ran the check through a verifying machine. The machine spit back numerous alerts and warnings.

An official at Bank of America confirmed what Kramer suspected: The check was no good, according to court records. Parsons had written more than $10,000 of bad checks on a nonexistent account, according to the records.

Kramer called 9-1-1. Troutdale Police watched Parsons as he went shopping, successfully writing two checks: one for $201.91 at the Levi's store and $129.97 to the Factory Brand Shoes store. He was arrested trying to write a fourth check.

He later admitted to police that he used his computer to print about 50 fake checks, according to court records.

Parsons was being held without bail at the Justice Center jail in Portland on an arrest warrant issued for theft in Wetumpka, Ala. He is also being held on a warrant for first-degree forgery in Hood River County.

And Judi Cramer is still selling turtlenecks and busting bad check writers.

"Judi was a little sharper, paid a little bit more attention than the other people he came across," said Troutdale Police Chief Dave Nelson. "She did a great job."

I love this quote. It shows not only how young Parsons looked, but raises the question how anyone else bought the story that he was a retired army officer, let alone a MAJOR?!

My editor at the time was a stickler for attribution, which really bogs the story down. Did we really need to say "according to court records" twice in the same paragraph? I think not.

The dollar amount of the bad checks at the other store came from the police report. Although these reports are usually chock-full of jargon and dry narrative, cops are trained to pick up small details, if not subtle nuance.

The closing kicker. Doesn't the chief have a nice way of saying the other clerks were brainless boobs not to see this guy coming from a mile away?

MURDERER CAUGHT IN TEXAS 15 YEARS AFTER ESCAPE

By Linda J. Johnson

Lexington (Ky.) Herald-Leader — Feb. 10, 2005

◀ MORE ON **INTERNET RESEARCH** ON PAGE **70**;
◀ MORE ON **COVERING CRIME** ON PAGE **98**

Imagine putting your Internet sleuthing skills to work . . . and capturing an escaped murderer. That's what Linda Johnson did.

Johnson, the computer-assisted reporting coordinator at the Lexington Herald-Leader, began investigating when the Kentucky corrections department posted a Web site listing escaped felons. "We focused on Annis," she said, "because he was the only escaped murderer still at-large, and he was from our coverage area."

Here's the story that resulted:

JOHNSON'S COMMENTARY:

Cops hadn't returned my calls for two days, then left a 5 p.m. voice-mail that Annis had been caught.

Once we decided to focus on Annis, I talked to the state patrol officer who investigated the escape, the cop currently in charge of the case and the cop who arrested Annis for murder in 1979. Between few police documents and 20-year-old memories, it made me wonder how hard they had looked for him.

At first, Moore refused to talk to me. She said she hadn't been able to sleep since I first contacted her and wasn't willing to dredge up old memories. I went to her job and convinced her to be interviewed.

We put this high up so cops couldn't claim credit — which they later tried to do. They were thrilled with me, and even joked about hiring me for other cases, until I wrote a follow-up story showing how little they apparently did to find Annis. Things got a little chilly after that.

Using the Web had never dawned on the cops.

Ralph Robert Annis, an escaped murderer who had eluded Kentucky police since 1990, was arrested yesterday in Corpus Christi, Texas. The arrest came just weeks after the Herald-Leader began questioning state officials about their failure to close the case.

Annis, who has been living under the alias Michael Winters, was convicted in 1979 of strangling his girlfriend's 10-month-old baby, Melanie Kaye Gifford, in Cynthiana. Two months before a scheduled parole hearing, he fled while on a furlough from the Marion Adjustment Center.

"Oh God, I am so glad," said Cathy Moore, Melanie's mother. She said she feels a huge sense of relief that he is back behind bars.

"It's good for Melanie, too," she said. "He did this, and he escaped, and now I feel like she can rest."

Police had made little or no progress in finding Annis until a former sister-in-law contacted authorities after she was interviewed recently by the Herald-Leader.

"We owe you one," Detective Sgt. Bobby Sullivan of the state police told a reporter. "I'm just glad to catch him."

Lt. Eric Wolford, the investigating detective at the state police's Columbia post, said last night that he was at a loss to explain why they hadn't been able to find Annis.

"I don't know," he said. "We should have been diligently looking for this guy, in my opinion."

They "probably should have been" using the Internet, and he did some searching in the last couple of weeks, but that wasn't until after he was contacted by the newspaper.

Clues on the Web

In a matter of days, the Herald-Leader located a man in Texas using the first five digits of Annis' Social Security number and the name Michael Winters. Wolford provided the alias to the paper, which was looking

into escaped prisoners in Kentucky.

The paper used information services such as Lexis-Nexis and AutoTrack, Internet telephone directories, people-finders and other tools. That particular Michael Winters had no driver's license, didn't vote and did not own a home.

Neighbors at a former address identified an old prison photo of Annis that the paper sent them.

Wolford, who transferred to the Columbia post last fall, has had the case for only a few months, and he declined to speculate on how things were handled in the past.

"It's an old case, there's not a lot of hard leads," he said in January. But nothing in the file showed where Annis' family or his wife's family had been contacted.

"I just think there's been a lack of documentation in the file," he said. "I've seen it before in some of these older cases."

Disappeared with wife, her son

Annis, 53, was the only Kentucky murderer imprisoned by the state who had never been caught or otherwise accounted for by officials — until now.

He escaped from Marion while on a 48-hour furlough with his wife, Jane Reichert Annis. Before leaving the prison, he closed a small bank account there, and sold a television for cash while on the furlough. Then he, his wife and her teenage son left the area for Texas.

He has been in the Corpus Christi area at least 12 years, possibly longer, working in construction and roofing, something he had done in Cynthiana before the murder. Jane Reichert Annis died in 2000, but they had not been together since the early 1990s.

The tip that resulted in the Texas arrest came from Annis' former sister-in-law. She contacted local police in Indiana shortly after she was interviewed by the Herald-

Even though the cops wouldn't release all their information, I had reams of documents from the corrections department, Annis' murder trial and his common-law wife's bankruptcy file. That turned out to be a gold mine of information.

The former neighbors cinched his ID. When the source described Winters to me, I knew we had Annis.

We're still waiting to see how thin this file is. The state patrol refused to release it until after sentencing, citing an ongoing investigation. I have an open records request ready to fax to them after the trial.

I found Reichert's parents through their marriage license — they married while he was in prison — which was in the prison file. Corrections had blacked out the family's names, so I ordered a copy from VitalChek.com and drove to Terre Haute, Ind., to talk to her mom. We found other family through Reichert's father's obituary online.

Leader.

The best information the Kentucky police ever had on Annis came in 1993, when they received an anonymous tip that he was living in a hotel room in Corpus Christi and using the alias Michael Winters.

"It was not an ambiguous tip," Wolford said in the January interview. "It was very specific. 'Ralph Annis is here, is living in Corpus Christi at this address.'"

But when Kentucky officials contacted Corpus Christi police with the information, they did not find Annis at that address.

Annis lived at several addresses in Corpus Christi and in nearby Bayside, Texas.

Wolford didn't think Annis would show up after all this time, unless there was a tip or he was arrested somewhere and fingerprinted.

The officer in Indiana did some searching on his own, using the alias and Annis' Social Security number provided by the former sister-in-law, which she found about 10 years ago while trying to find her sister. The Indiana officer then contacted the police in Texas, who called the Kentucky State Police.

Wolford hoped the story we planned would lead to a tip. He even offered to do an age-adjusted photo for the story. But we never got it.

This is when Wolford was not returning my calls. I think he was waiting to hear from Texas before talking to me again.

It panned out

About a week ago, the Nueces County Sheriff's Department contacted Detective Sgt. Bobby Sullivan at the Columbia post of the state police, asking for Annis' file. He e-mailed it to them and didn't hear anything back. "I kind of figured it didn't pan out," he said last night.

Yesterday, Corpus Christi officials called Sullivan to tell him Annis had been arrested.

He had changed one date on his birthday and his Social Security number by two digits, Sullivan said.

Annis is being held in the Nueces County jail on a charge of escape. He is being held without bond and was to appear before a magistrate this morning.

If Annis waives extradition, Wolford said, he should be back in Kentucky fairly quickly. If not, it could take a few weeks.

He faces a sentence one to five years for the escape, in addition to serving out the remainder of his sentence.

News researcher Linda Minch contributed to this report.

This has changed; sentence is now 10-20 years plus remaining time on his sentence.

Grant Cooper knows he lives in prison, but there are days when he cannot remember why. His crimes flit in and out of his memory like flies through a hole in a screen door, so that sometimes his mind and conscience are blank and clean.

OPENERS
AN ANTHOLOGY OF LEADS

He used to be a drinker and a drifter who had no control over his rage. In 1978, in an argument with a man in a bread line at the Forgotten Man Ministry in Birmingham, Ala., his hand automatically slid into his pants pocket for a knife.

He cut the man so quick and deep that he died before his body slipped to the floor. Mr. Cooper had killed before, in 1936 and in 1954, so the judge gave him life. Back then, before he needed help to go to the bathroom, Mr. Cooper was a dangerous man.

Now he is 77, and since his stroke in 1993 he mostly just lies in his narrow bunk at the Hamilton Prison for the Aged and Infirm, a blue blanket hiding the tubes that run out of his bony body. Sometimes the other inmates put him in a wheelchair and park him in the sun.

"I'm lost," he mumbled. "I'm just lost."

Rick Bragg, *The New York Times,* opening a story about an Alabama prison for aging and disabled inmates

She is throwing up again.

It's the fifth time this morning. There is nothing left in her stomach. Still, she leans over a toilet at the Grosse Pointe Woods Municipal Courthouse.

Call her Ann. Her real name won't be used, for the same reason she is vomiting.

In a few minutes, she and two other 15-year-old girls will walk in front of TV cameras, a judge, parents and dozens of their schoolmates, and talk about sex. They'll be asked about penises and penetration. Things whispered about while listening to a Brandy CD, but humiliating in front of strangers.

Cindy will go first, then Bonnie, then Ann. All wait in a small room near the courtroom. Out the window, across a lawn, they can see another waiting room where four boys in navy blazers pace nervously. One of the boys looks up and sees the girls. He shuts the blinds.

Ron French, *The Detroit News*

RAMPAGING ROOSTER ATTACKS GIRL

By Kelley Benham

St. Petersburg Times — Oct. 4, 2002

◀ MORE ON **COVERING CRIME** ON PAGE **98**

Kelley Benham wrote this story about a month after arriving at the St. Petersburg Times, her first newspaper job. She covered cops and city hall in Tarpon Springs, a funky city of about 20,000 on the Florida coast. "I had told the police public information guy that I wanted weird stuff," she explains, "not just the obvious press-release filler." After discovering the report on this attack, she visited the crime scene. "I walked up and there were all these people sitting under a tent outside, watching television and drinking Jack Daniel's. I thought: 'Right — they're either going to be really good, or they're going to run me off.'

"I said, 'Hey, does anybody know anything about a rooster?' "

BENHAM'S COMMENTARY:

I knew this story was going to have to have a great lead. I knew it had to have the word "rooster" in it.

The story is set up like a standard police story, or actually, like a parody of a police story, where the rooster is the good-kid-gone-bad. One of the first rules of journalism I learned is, in any animal story, get the name of the dog/cat/rooster, etc. In this case, asking if the rooster had a name led to "Was there a Rockadoodle One? Which led to the entire tragic story of the chicken's family.

Yep, I had to go back there to find out how tall the girl was, because I forgot to ask the first time. Now, this next part is where the straight narrative story part picks up. I had to go over these details with them about 47 times.

The best thing I know about quotes is that the right quote is usually the one that sounds the most natural. At first, people try to use formal language and they're self-conscious about how they speak. Wait until they loosen up. Get people talking in their natural voices. Those quotes are usually in the back of the notebook.

When they heard the screams, no one suspected the rooster.

Dechardonae Gaines, 2, was toddling down the sidewalk Monday lugging her Easy Bake Oven when she became the victim in one of the weirder animal attack cases police can recall.

In the cluster of beige houses at Lime Street and Safford Avenue where Dechardonae lives, man and chicken have coexisted peacefully for years in quiet defiance of city ordinance.

That ended Monday afternoon, when authorities apprehended the offending rooster, named Rockadoodle Two, and its sister, named Hen. Hen was not involved in the attack, police said.

The rooster struck around noon as Dechardonae ventured from her house in the middle of the cluster to visit her Uncle Tony, waiting in the driveway. It's a short walk, even if you're 3 feet tall and carrying a toy oven.

Tony Kramer, 44, heard the little girl shrieking, spun around and saw the rooster.

Rockadoodle Two had knocked the 27-pound girl flat on her belly and was pummeling her with beak, claws and blue-black wings.

"He was beating the crap out of her," said her mother, Lori Current, 27. "A freaking rooster, you know?"

Kramer ran for the girl, snatched her up by one arm and chased the bird off, waving his arms and shouting, "Oooh, get! Shoo! Shoo! Shoo!"

The man and the girl had taken about three steps when the rooster attacked again, knocking the screaming girl to the grass a second time.

Kramer swatted at the rooster, backhanded, and it shuffled off.

He could not pick up the girl because he has a bad hip, he said, so he took his niece by the hand and headed for her mother's house.

But Rockadoodle Two flew at the girl a third time, latched onto her narrow shoulders and hammered at her face from behind.

Kramer knocked the rooster down, but it didn't run away this time. It glared at him.

So he kicked it.

The bird flew to a porch nearby, still staring. It puffed its chest and ruffled its feathers.

"He just sat there, all bold," Current said.

"That chicken was not scared," Kramer said.

The neighborhood has never had any chicken trouble beyond the usual scratching and crowing, Kramer said.

Everybody there knew Rockadoodle Two. Neighbors described the rooster as a normally well-behaved bird from a good family. Its father, Rockadoodle, and mother, one-legged Henny Penny, lived in the neighborhood until their deaths by pit bull and heat stroke, respectively.

Everyone knows Dechardonae too. She travels door-to-door in her too-big flip flops chatting with neighbors. She used to pet Rockadoodle Two when it was a chick.

Kramer raised Rockadoodle Two's father. He did not own the son, but thought well of the bird until this, he said.

"I had known him since he was an egg," Kramer said.

That did not matter to Current when she called authorities.

The call surprised police, she said.

A chicken? they asked.

"Come and get him now," she told them. "I am not going to rest."

Hen was captured easily, but Rockadoodle Two led six people on a chase. They

---

I'm getting carried away with my one-sentence paragraphs here. Young writers use a lot of one-sentence paragraphs because they are very dramatic.

This used to say, "scratching, crowing, and pooping" but the copy editors cut out "pooping." So I would like to take this opportunity to put it back in. Thank you.

I wrote this sentence approximately 14 times until I got it right. When you have information that adds nothing to the story but is just interesting, you have to write it very economically.

This guy had a giant oil painting of roosters on his living room wall. He was wearing a hat with a rooster feather in it. The feather came from the attack rooster's father. My point is, usually if you do your job there is too much great stuff to fit in the story, and the hardest thing is choosing.

flushed the bird out from under a house with a cane fishing pole. But the rooster dodged the Humane Society officer's net, eluded a couple of flying grabs, shucked and bobbed and skittered through the sandspurs and weeds. Finally, the officer tackled him.

"This was no scrawny rooster," Current said.

Rockadoodle and Hen were taken to the Humane Society of North Pinellas, said executive director Rick Chaboudy. From there, they were sent for rehabilitation in Odessa, probably permanently, he said.

This is the city's first rooster attack in recent memory, said Tarpon Springs Police Sgt. Jeffrey Young.

"It does not appear to be epidemic," he said.

But keeping chickens in city neighborhoods is illegal, although police did not cite any residents in this case.

Rockadoodle is the second Tarpon

Springs rooster to make news in recent months. This year, a woman battling cancer befriended a stray rooster named Roosty and declared the bird her guardian angel.

The city told the woman the rooster had to go, and the controversy died only when Roosty did. It was killed by a raccoon in August.

Police were unaware of the chickens in Dechardonae's neighborhood, but residents there say the birds are scattered in back yards all over town.

"This right here is why we have those kinds of ordinances, so 2-year-olds can walk down the driveway safely," Young said.

Dechardonae was shaken after the attack but is recovering fine. Her scratches are almost gone; her right eye is barely puffy.

She hid in the house after the attack but said chickens don't worry her now.

"He gone," she said of the rooster. "The police got him."

OPENERS
AN ANTHOLOGY OF LEADS

Like a doctor feeling for a pulse, Dave Honaker lays his hands on the wide plastic hose. It begins to vibrate as pebbles and dirt rush through. It shudders a bit, then is still. Honaker smiles. The furry body of a prairie dog, still in its subterranean hole, is plugging the end of the hose. It's only a matter of time now.

You can feel when he's fighting back, Honaker yells over the roar of the powerful suction. He's got a good hold, and then he loses it.

Just then, the hose jolts, and with a rumbling whoosh, the rodent shoots up the hose. One! Honaker mouths, his eyes gleaming with excitement.

A moment later, another whoosh. Two!

It's like playing the violin, Honaker says modestly. After five years, you get a little better. Honaker is a master of the latest in rodent-control technology, the prairie dog vacuum.

Julia Prodis,
The Associated Press

Though it seems somehow improper to admit, Frank Cashi is 92 years old and he looks every second of it. Patches of white hair orbit a head that, otherwise, has been bald for 60 years. Four teeth, two on each side, are stationed apart like a 7-10 split. He's 5-foot-2, he weighs 125 pounds, and white stubble angles from his cheeks and chin, giving his face the appearance of an old pin cushion.

Chico Harlan, *Pittsburgh Post-Gazette,*
opening a story about a senior athlete

In a statement against student shortcuts, Villanova University administrators plan to stop selling Cliffs Notes at the school bookstore, drawing praise from faculty and barbs from student leaders and the guide's publishers.

(The foregoing was a brief synopsis of this story. Continue reading to learn the details and nuances, or you can stop right here and pretend you read the whole thing.)

Richard Sine, *The Philadelphia Inquirer,*
parodying a Cliffs Notes-style synopsis for this story on Cliffs Notes

---

Setting migration patterns back centuries, an incredibly lazy Arizona bird decided Friday to fly north for the winter.

Ken Fuson, *The Des Moines Register,* opening a story about a bird rescued from the baggage compartment of a Phoenix-to-Des Moines flight

COVERING THE MICHAEL JACKSON VERDICT

Celebrity trials often become media circuses — and the circus came to town in Santa Maria, Calif., during Michael Jackson's four-month trial for child molestation in 2005. Scores of reporters were on hand when the jury reached its verdict on June 13. And the stories they filed provided a study in contrasting styles, from the dry, distinguished New York Times to the more colorful flair of London's Daily Mail.

The examples below compare six different treatments of that court story.

◀ MORE ON **COVERING COURTS** ON PAGE **100**

THE NEW YORK TIMES

SANTA MARIA, Calif., June 13 — Michael Jackson was acquitted today of all charges in connection with accusations that he molested a 13-year-old boy he had befriended as the youth was recovering from cancer in 2003.

Mr. Jackson's complete acquittal — a stinging defeat for a retiring prosecutor who had spent more than a decade pursuing the singer on pedophilia accusations — ends a nearly four-month trial that featured 140 witnesses who painted clashing portraits of the 46-year-old international pop star as either pedophile or Peter Pan.

"Mr. Jackson, your bail is exonerated and you are released," Judge Rodney S. Melville said after the string of not-guilty verdicts were read.

Mr. Jackson stood for the verdicts and later embraced his chief lawyer, Thomas A. Mesereau Jr. One of Mr. Mesereau's assistants had quietly started sobbing as the first "not guilty" verdicts were read out in court.

Along with the verdict, the jury gave a note for the judge to read out in court. In it, they said they felt "the weight of the world's eyes upon us all" and that they had "thoroughly and meticulously" studied all the evidence. The note concluded with a plea "we would like the public to allow us to return to our lives as anonymously as we came."

The jury of eight women and four men delivered the verdict in California Superior Court here on their seventh day of deliberations, which began June 3. The jury was not sequestered and took weekends off. . . .

NOTICE HOW:
◆ The writing style is formal, unemotional, almost clinical (note the use of "Mr.").
◆ This excerpt focuses intently on the judicial proceedings. The story quotes the judge in the third paragraph, but it's a useless quote; Jackson, meanwhile, is hardly mentioned.

USA TODAY

SANTA MARIA, Calif. — Michael Jackson was acquitted Monday on charges he sexually molested a 13-year-old boy, ending a four-month trial full of lurid glimpses of the pop star's bizarre private life inside his Neverland Valley Ranch.

The onetime King of Pop wept softly and wiped his eyes as the jury's verdict was read inside a quiet courtroom.

Jackson said nothing after the verdicts of not guilty on all 10 charges were read. He walked from the courthouse, waved and climbed inside a waiting vehicle for the ride home.

"Justice was done. He was always innocent, and we proved it," defense attorney Tom Mesereau said.

Fans outside the courthouse jumped up and down, hugged and threw confetti. A woman released one white dove from a pen as each acquittal was announced. Jackson's family was ecstatic.

"Michael kept his strength, and he hung in there," his brother Tito Jackson told CNN.

A USA Today/CNN/Gallup poll taken after the verdict showed that 48% disagreed with the verdict and 34% agreed; 18% had no opinion.

The jury deliberated for 30 hours over seven days on charges that Jackson molested the boy in his home, a huge estate with carnival rides, circus animals and toys. . . .

NOTICE HOW:
◆ The lead for this story is very similar to the lead on MSNBC's story at right — but the wording ("lurid glimpses," "bizarre private life") is edgier. Which version do you think is more effective?
◆ Notice how the structure of both stories — the sequence of material — is similar (and logical), too.
◆ This is the only story to use those quotes from Jackson's brother and the defense attorney.
◆ USA Today's editors cleverly planned ahead for this moment, commissioning an instant poll to see if Americans agreed with the trial verdict.

MSNBC NEWS

SANTA MARIA, Calif. – Michael Jackson was found not guilty Monday on all counts in his trial on child molestation charges, ending a two-year legal saga for one of the world's most well-known pop stars.

The courtroom sat silently as Judge Rodney Melville opened the jury envelopes one by one and silently read the verdict forms to himself before allowing the court clerk to read the verdict out loud. Lead defense attorney Tom Mesereau Jr., who scored a dazzling legal victory in the case, patted Jackson on the shoulder after the verdict was read. Two jurors dabbed their eyes with tissues.

Jackson showed no visible reaction in court. He then slowly, silently walked out of court surrounded by family and his bodyguards, stone-faced and looking slightly stunned. The singer briefly waved to fans.

His fans, kept behind barriers at a distance from the courthouse, shouted and wept with joy over Jackson's acquittal, celebrating a complete victory for the singer's defense team, though one that may not repair his tarnished and ever more bizarre public image.

"I would never have married a pedophile. And the system works," Jackson's ex-wife Debbie Rowe said after the verdict in a statement given to "Entertainment Tonight." . . .

NOTICE HOW:
◆ Some emotions are described with verbs (as in the story at left), but most of the descriptions come from adjectives and adverbs.
◆ That second paragraph is long. Too long? The same could be said of the fourth paragraph, which ambitiously tries to merge at least three different ideas into one sentence.
◆ The third paragraph says Jackson showed no emotion in court, but the story at left says he wept and wiped his eyes. Which is it?
◆ The only quote comes from Jackson's ex-wife.

DAILY MAIL (LONDON)

There was no moonwalk and barely a smile from Michael Jackson as he was dramatically cleared of sexually abusing 13-year-old Gavin Arvizo.

The pop star sat silently as 10 "not guilty" verdicts rang out one by one across a hushed courtroom, ending the nightmare he has endured since charges were filed more than 18 months ago.

As he left Santa Maria court for the last time, the self-styled King of Pop held his hand to his heart and blew kisses to the screaming crowd.

Walking slowly under a large black umbrella, he stepped into a black SUV vehicle and was whisked home to his Neverland ranch without a comment, followed by legions of hysterical fans.

Just minutes earlier, the deathly quiet atmosphere was incredible as the world waited and watched for the verdict which would finally bring an end to a sensational 16-week trial.

A heavy silence hung over the court as each juror filed in one by one. Adding to the tension, Judge Rodney Melville delayed proceedings by warning he would tolerate no reaction, whether despair or jubilance, from anyone present.

As he opened each of 10 paper envelopes containing the verdicts, Jackson sat back in his chair, not glancing at his lawyer Tom Mesereau, and stared calmly ahead.

At least one juror openly sobbed as each acquittal was read out by the court clerk. Still, Jackson, who had faced almost 20 years in prison, did not flinch.

The frail star's demeanour was in complete contrast to the wild scenes of celebration outside.

Hundreds of fans punched the air, cheered, clapped and hugged each other as they heard that their idol was a free man. One woman released white doves for each not guilty verdict, another released white balloons into the sun-drenched sky and white confetti was showered over them all. . . .

NOTICE HOW:
◆ The lead names the victim. Most American papers withheld the boy's name to protect his privacy — but here, it's considered lead-worthy.
◆ Unlike the reserved, neutral tone of the New York Times excerpt, this one leans toward more dramatic interpretations and punchier phrasing: "ending the nightmare," "legions of hysterical fans," the "sensational" trial.
◆ This story uses no direct quotes.

THE ASSOCIATED PRESS

Linda Deutsch wrote two versions of this story. As she explains: "It's part of the AP's new policy of offering optional leads on major stories so that newspapers can have a choice of a more featurish approach if they want it. This makes sense particularly on a story that has been playing all day on TV and radio. On this particular story, the featurish approach (below right) recieved wide play."

SANTA MARIA, Calif. – A jury acquitted Michael Jackson on Monday of molesting a 13-year-old cancer survivor at his Neverland ranch — exonerating the pop star who insisted he was the victim of mother-and-son con artists and a prosecutor with a vendetta.

Jurors also acquitted Jackson of getting the boy drunk and of conspiring to imprison his accuser and the boy's family at the storybook estate — a total legal victory but one that may do little to improve his bizarre image. Jackson had faced nearly 20 years in prison.

The courtroom was deathly still as the verdicts were read. Jackson, as motionless as he had been throughout the trial, dabbed at his eyes with a tissue. One of his lawyers burst into tears as the first verdicts were announced, and Jackson later stood and was embraced by his chief lawyer, Thomas Mesereau Jr. Some of the women in the jury also wept and passed around a box of tissues.

As he left court, Jackson, looking drawn, held his hand to his heart and blew kisses to the screaming crowd. He was escorted by his aides into a black SUV, and made no immediate public statement. Jackson later arrived at Neverland, where applauding fans ran after his caravan as it disappeared behind the bunting-decorated gates.

"I would never have married a pedophile. And the system works," Jackson's ex-wife Debbie Rowe said in a statement given to "Entertainment Tonight."

Screams of joy rang out among a throng of fans outside the courthouse. Fans jumped up and down, hugged each other and threw confetti in celebration of the news. A woman in the crowd released one white dove as each acquittal was announced. . . .

NOTICE HOW:
◆ The first version uses a textbook news lead, opening with the news that "a jury acquitted Michael Jackson." The rewrite opens with a colorful description of Jackson leaving the trial.
◆ The second version includes more material about the significant, almost embarrassing defeat for the prosecutors.

SANTA MARIA, Calif. – Wanly blowing kisses of gratitude to his screaming fans, Michael Jackson left court a free man Monday and went back to Neverland after he was cleared of all charges in his child-molestation trial.

Jackson, 46, heard the words "not guilty" uttered 14 times in a deathly still courtroom. The Peter Pan of pop music could have gotten nearly 20 years behind bars if convicted.

A motionless Jackson dabbed at his eyes with a tissue as the verdicts were read, and he later was embraced by his chief lawyer, Thomas Mesereau Jr. Another member of his defense team burst into tears, and some of the women in the jury also wept and passed around a box of tissues.

Jackson, looking drawn, walked out of court minutes later to shrieks from fans, waved weakly and was driven home to his Neverland ranch, where applauding fans ran after his caravan as it disappeared behind the bunting-decorated gates. He made no immediate statement.

The acquittals marked a stinging defeat for Santa Barbara County District Attorney Tom Sneddon, who displayed open hostility for Jackson and had pursued him for more than a decade, trying to prove the rumors that swirled around Jackson about his fondness for children.

Sneddon sat with his head in his hands after the verdicts were read.

"We go back to work. We've got a lot of cases that we have pending. I have an office to run," he said. "I'm not going to look back and apologize for anything that we've done."

Fans outside the courthouse jumped up and down, thrust their fists in the air, hugged each other and threw confetti. A woman in the crowed released one white dove as each acquittal was announced.

◆ Descriptions of the charges against Jackson in the first version have now been replaced by more descriptions of the trial's aftermath.
◆ In all of these stories, the one quote we most wanted was Jackson's — but he never uttered a word. Thus, these stories use almost no direct quotes, relying instead on descriptions of events.

CITY MAKES A U-TURN: SPEED ZONE SET FOR COUNTRY CLUB

By Alandra Johnson

Lake Oswego Review — June 9, 2005

◄ MORE ON **COVERING MEETINGS** ON PAGE **104**

School board meetings, city council meetings, planning commission meetings — yes, meetings are a staple of community journalism. But here's an example of a city council story that avoids simply rehashing the minutes of a meeting. Instead, it focuses on the issue — changing the speed limit near a local school — and explains how it affects the neighborhood.

Notice how thoroughly reporter Alandra Johnson had done her homework before the meeting began. Her story recaps the history of the problem, introduces key players and condenses the debate into a few concise paragraphs. She punctuates the information with carefully selected quotes. And she summarizes the council's action without bogging us down in bureaucratic procedure.

After months of telling concerned parents that reducing the speed on Country Club Road was unnecessary to ensure student safety, officials with the city of Lake Oswego have changed their tune.

Tuesday night, the city council voted unanimously to reinstate a school speed zone on Country Club Road in front of Lake Oswego Junior High School.

The new speed zone, which will drop the speed from 40 to 20 miles per hour, will include flashing lights to alert drivers and will be enforced during high student traffic periods before and after school.

"I think it's an extremely reasonable solution that adds safety for both cars and pedestrians," said Lake Oswego Mayor Judie Hammerstad.

She said the solution settled long-standing debate between parents and police without abandoning the city's early commitment to motorist safety.

"What parents were looking at was the safety of the pedestrian and what the police were looking at was the safety of the motorist," said Hammerstad.

The solution, she said, is a win for both. Concerned parents also celebrated the victory.

"We won," said parent Tom Holder, an advocate for reinstating the school speed zone.

The flashing lights, which are expected to cost $10,000 and will be paid for by the city, will operate from 7 to 8:30 a.m. and from 2 to 3:30 p.m. They can also be programmed for student events such as basketball and football games.

Parents began clamoring for speed control on Country Club this spring after a junior high student darted into traffic and was struck by an oncoming vehicle.

Initially, officials at the city were reluctant to reinstate the school zone. The city first installed a school zone at the site in November 2002 and removed it in May 2004 — after studies revealed that most drivers didn't decrease speed in the area. Police argued that the speed limit was difficult to enforce and that the chance for rear-end collisions increased dramatically as a handful of vehicles slowed to 20 mph while others did not.

For more than two months after the accident on March 10, city officials maintained their initial position that reducing the speed on Country Club was unnecessary. They argued speed was not a factor in the accident involving the student and that the intersection in question did not have a history of pedestrian accidents over 20 years.

But parents continued to push for the change until Tuesday's decision.

"I've been badgering City Manager Doug Schmitz about this for three years," said Holder.

Holder has been one of the most vocal proponents of reducing speed along that stretch. He helped instigate the move to install the first speed zone and was one of the few to fight its removal in 2004. He credits the recent efforts of school committees and neighborhood associations with pushing through the issue.

Holder says Schmitz asked his opinion before taking the proposal to the city council, capping months of formal talks between city and school officials and residents championing the school zone. While Holder was pleased that the council agreed to implement the safety precautions, he said he didn't understand why it took so long.

"It was an awful lot of energy expended to get them to do the right thing," he said.

City officials don't see the plans as a reversal of a previous policy, but rather as a new tactic. Citizen Information Coordinator Josh Thomas, who spoke to many groups during the last few months, told the city council the new decision evolved out of talks, study and planning.

"We're trying to provide the least restriction but certainly want to provide the most protection," Thomas said.

He stressed that safety was still in the hands of drivers and pedestrians, no matter what tools were provided near schools.

"There is no magic panacea, or cure-all, that's going to solve everybody's problems," Thomas said.

PUTNAM COMMISSIONERS GET AN EARFUL OVER ABANDONED HOUSE

By Heather Svokos

The Charleston Gazette — Sept. 10, 1996

◄ MORE ON **COVERING MEETINGS** ON PAGE **105**

How do you cover a dull meeting in a lively way? By keeping an eye out for colorful characters and intriguing issues.

For example, take this story that Heather Svokos wrote for the Charleston Gazette. "It had all the markings of a standard county commission meeting," Svokos recalls — "a few hours steeped in boredom with occasional bickering. But then riled-up citizen Dodie Griffin came in with her complaint."

After Griffin's dramatic appearance, Svokos chased her out the door to get her phone number, then called her after the meeting to collect more details. "I had a feeling I could turn a blah commission meeting into an interesting vignette that would star one of the town's interesting characters," Svokos says.

"You won't meet a Dodie Griffin at every boring meeting. But when you find her, grab her. And get her phone number."

**SVOKOS'
COMMENTARY:**

I remembered the voice of Kate Long, the Gazette's writing coach, who said to try to think like a film director: Write your lead as if it were the opening frame of a movie. Doesn't get any more cinematic than this.

A somewhat startling visual — even if it didn't happen, it's interesting to imagine if it did.

Thought this was relevant because it established her as a veteran rabble-rouser, bolstered by the strong quote below.

And now, after we've established this character for the reader, we start to lay out the problem in more detail.

In retrospect, this might have been stronger if I'd used a quote or partial quote here.

D odie Griffin sits on her concrete porch, aims her Mossberg shotgun across the way and blasts her target.

Over the last few years, she's bagged a slew of snakes and rats that take refuge most of the time in an abandoned house next door.

She told Putnam County commissioners Monday how she had thought of gathering up her dubious bounty and plopping it onto the desk in their chamber.

But she thought better of it and addressed the commission without visual aids. This time.

Griffin recalled creating a stir 20 years ago when she brought commissioners a dead dog. It had apparently been mistreated at the county's animal shelter.

"I'm gonna be nice about this in the beginning," she said after Monday's commission meeting. "But if something isn't done about this, then I'm gonna be nasty."

Griffin said the house on Scott Lane has been abandoned for three years, and it's not only driving the varmints into her yard, it's a dangerous hazard for the children who often play there.

The basement of the rickety house is half-filled with water which floods it constantly, she said, because the lot used to be a swamp.

Children could easily fall through the floor and never be heard from again, Griffin told commissioners.

Another danger is the freezer and other appliances that sit on the porch with their doors open.

"They should be removed or turned toward the wall," Griffin said.

And don't get her started on the cockroaches. "I can spray cockroaches all day and I've got a dozen to deal with the next morning," she said.

Griffin is demanding action from the commission. She says she has been to the Health Department and the Solid Waste Authority, with little result.

She figures a recent state law regarding abandoned buildings should force commissioners into action.

The law, enacted June 1, gives counties and municipalities the power to sue property owners who have let their structures or property become rundown.

Previously, the only avenue was to put a lien against the property, a lengthy and often ineffective recourse. Now the county or city would be able to recoup cleanup and legal fees from the owner.

But in order to enforce the law, the commission needs to adopt a building code. They haven't and have indicated they won't until they've studied the matter in great detail.

Commissioner Jim Caruthers said it would be difficult to track down the owner, but he agreed to talk with members of the Solid Waste Authority about the problem. Likewise, Commissioner Steve Hodges said he would discuss it with officials at the Health Department.

If the commission doesn't do something within 10 days, Griffin says she will be back. "If it's a danger, they're supposed to take care of it immediately," she said.

"I'll be back over here with a pack of rats. I'll kill 'em, bring 'em here and dump 'em on their desk. If it takes shock treatment to get them to do something to that place, I can give 'em shock treatment."

If we wanted to write the story in a mind-numbingly boring way, we could have started here, with the legalese. Instead, we have a flesh-and-blood example that illustrates how this new law should be applied.

Hmm…the layers of red tape begin to reveal themselves. There's a law, but no building code to enforce it. This exposes a glitch in how the county has been operating.

With Dodie Griffin and her special promises, and a reporter sitting in the room, I'm guessing these commissioners probably did try to talk to authorities.

I wanted to close the story with a zinger. This was a stellar parting line.

THE CITY HAS $548 MILLION: WHAT DO YOU WANT?

By Bryan Gilmer

St. Petersburg Times — Aug. 21, 2002

◀ MORE ON **COVERING MEETINGS** ON PAGE **105**

The text below was the main component in a package that also included:
◆ A graphic providing a budget summary and a quick crash course in city spending.
◆ A breakdown of the three key budget issues facing the city council.
◆ A guide to getting involved, with links to council members, public speaking tips, etc.

"I remember where I was the morning I read the best city council budget story ever written," said Roy Peter Clark, writing coach at the prestigious Poynter Institute. "I was sitting at the breakfast table eating my Cheerios."

Clark had stumbled upon an experiment in the St. Petersburg Times: a budget story, written in the second person, urging YOU to help decide how the city spends its money.

"Wow," Clark wrote in his Poynter column. "This was remarkable. Perhaps even groundbreaking. I then did something I rarely do with such stories: I read it to the end. And then, because I could not believe my eyes, I read it a second time."

The reporter, Bryan Gilmer, admitted he'd dreaded writing another boring budget advance. "I thought, 'Readers must really hate these stories if I don't even enjoy doing them,'" he later said in an interview with Clark.

Gilmer further explained: "Newspapers often assume their readers know much more about how government works than they really do. And newspapers are really bad at interacting with their readers. So I wrote this piece in the second person. I used short sentences to make it an easy read for the government novices we pulled in with the graphics. And due largely to my strong feelings about the issue, it ended up… conversational, but with a point of view and a certain urgency."

Judge for yourself: Reader-friendly? Or too dumbed-down?

Do you live in St. Petersburg? Want to help spend $548 million?

It's money you paid in taxes and fees to the government. You elected the City Council to office, and as your representatives, they're ready to listen to your ideas on how to spend it.

Mayor Rick Baker and his staff have figured out how they'd like to spend the money. At 7 p.m. Thursday, Baker will ask the City Council to agree with him. And council members will talk about their ideas.

You have the right to speak at the meeting, too. Each resident gets three minutes to tell the mayor and council members what he or she thinks.

But why would you stand up?

Because how the city spends its money affects lots of things you care about.

It's the difference between whether the Walter Fuller Pool is open and heated in the winter or not. It determines whether there will be a new basketball court in North Shore Park. It determines whether the beloved volunteer coordinator at the Office on Aging for senior citizens gets laid off.

It's a tight budget year, and lots of things like insurance are costing the city more than before. The mayor and council have decided to cut services rather than raise the property tax rate.

But will the council listen to you?

"Absolutely," said council member John Bryan, adding that members of the public often change his mind on issues. "I'm looking to the people, hoping to hear information for my decision-making process."

Not everything can be done in one year, so council members may hear your idea Thursday but wait until next year to do it.

"It may not be able to be funded this year, but could be put into a queue for future years," council Chairwoman Rene Flowers said.

You can bring up any spending suggestion Thursday, but here are some major items that are in — or proposed to be cut from — the budget:

Boyd Hill Nature Park

Mayor Rick Baker proposes cutting a program specialist supervisor and three of the park's four full-time park rangers and replacing them with four part-time park rangers to save about $112,000. Baker notes that "we have been forced to make difficult decisions that impact both our employees and the services they provide to our citizens."

This would reduce the number of educational programs at the park south of Lake Maggiore from 850 per year to 400.

Lovers of the southern St. Petersburg park hate the idea, and many of them will be at Thursday night's public hearing to tell the council so.

"I am concerned about a proposal to shrink the budget of the Boyd Hill Park educational arm," resident Arlin Briley wrote to the mayor in a letter this week. "Thanks to its large acreage, Boyd Hill Park is a living lab, an invaluable opportunity to allow city kids a chance to learn about nature and life beyond shopping malls and sidewalks and classrooms.

Instead, Briley recommends pursuing county, state and federal educational grants to fund educational programs at the park.

Western St. Petersburg library plan

Baker proposes teaming up with St. Petersburg College to build a new library on the college's campus in western St. Petersburg. City residents and students would share the library, which would replace the current, smaller Azalea Branch.

The first of four $500,000 annual payments to the college for the cost of construction is in Baker's proposed city budget. After the library opened, the city would move the $300,000 it spends now on the Azalea Branch to the joint library instead.

A vocal group of city residents has blasted the idea of closing the Azalea Branch. If they could get the council to remove money for the new library the budget, they might be able to kill the idea.

"I'm not saying it's a bad idea. But I don't think we need to lose the library we currently have in the process," said Azalea neighborhood resident Mary Moser, who plans to remind the council of her position Thursday.

Parking meters

Baker is counting on a new revenue source to help balance the budget: parking meters. The city has had free on-street parking since it abandoned its expensive experiment with multispace, French-made "pay stations" in 1998.

Baker's staff estimates meters could bring in about $800,000 per year, on top of the $1-million the city expects from parking fines. For several years, part of that money would be needed to repay the $1.2-million he expects the meters to cost.

Some merchants like the idea that the meters will let people stay in spaces longer than the two-hour time limit common for street parking now. Others worry that the meters will clutter the street.

It was public outcry that got the pay stations yanked four years ago. And broad opposition could easily prevent the meters from being installed now. The council seems to be split about which way to go.

"No matter what the (council's) decision is, it's going to be pretty close to 50-50," member John Bryan said. "It's really a tough one."

Operating spending

◆ Pays workers' salaries and benefits, buys supplies, gasoline and other recurring expenses.

◆ Available: $488-million

◆ The most flexible pot of operating money is called the "general fund." It's used for things such as police, fire, parks and recreation and Midtown economic development.

◆ All the other operating money provides services such as water and sewer, sanitation and special projects such as the Pier, called "enterprise funds" or "special revenue funds." These services raise most or all of the money they spend, and money they raise generally cannot be spent in other areas.

◆ General fund money: $175-million, most of which comes from property taxes.

◆ Major general fund spending the mayor recommends: police $63-million, fire $26-million, recreation $11-million, parks $13-million.

Capital spending

◆ Pays for big-ticket items that can be used for several years, like new buildings, renovations, cars and trucks.

◆ Total capital money available: $60-million. About $21-million comes from the Penny for Pinellas 1-cent sales tax.

REPORTER REACTION

After Roy Peter Clark raved about this unconventional budget story on the Poynter Web site, he solicited feedback from journalists. Here's a sampling of opinions:

As a gov'ment writer, my only (minor) beef with this otherwise refreshing story is this: I fear it's a bit of a one-trick pony.

I suppose you could begin every year's budget-hearing-advance story with the sentence: "Do you live in (insert city name)? Want to help spend $ (insert figure) million?"

But before long, it's just another budget-hearing-advance story. So how do you keep it fresh from year to year?

A bit of news in the lead, I submit, would help: some detail other than the amount of the budget and the mayor's name.

The bullets at the end explaining operating budgets v. capital budgets, however, ought to run with stories like this in every paper, every year.
— **Alex Wayne**

Aside from several nitpicky matters (including the use of "beloved" in this story) there's a glaring problem that does the reader a disservice: In its cleverness, the story doesn't frame the issue at all correctly. St. Petersburg wouldn't have $548 million to debate; as with any government, I suspect it has fixed costs that devour huge amounts of the budget. Anyone who comes to a municipal budget public hearing with the impression that the entire thing is up for dissection will be dismissed (at least silently) as ignorant. The story needed to clearly and prominently explain what was truly available. And where is the deficit/surplus, if any? The story talked so far down to the readers that it forgot to raise them up with essential information they needed to make more effective arguments.
— **Jay Jochnowitz**

I can't believe people would criticize great, readable writing like this — it's what the public wants.

People want to read stories that affect them. And we as journalists need to bring awareness to the issues that readers may not even *know* they should care about. Some of the most important stories of the day involve budgets or seemingly boring meetings, but the language of the story gets the article skipped over.

People don't want to be treated like those of us in the newsroom know more or are better than they. They want to be just informed as we are — and then some.

I'm definitely going to take this advice and use it. I'm guilty of doing this to school board stories, but I didn't have the kind of editors who allow using narratives to describe what goes on . . . .
— **Williesha Lakin**

I know many people in the business have a big objection to using the second person in a story. I think it's one of those rules that stems from somebody's pet peeve way back when and just gets in the way of communicating with readers.

I've found it to be very useful in writing stories about government action and how it affects people. … It makes stories much less cold and impersonal, much less stilted.

By the way, I did like the story you wrote about. I try to do similar things myself. I try to give a short lesson in how government operates when I can, because many people don't understand the most basic things about public budgets and property taxes. Sometimes I explain by telling readers how this will affect "you." So far, my computer hasn't started smoking, and the God of Journalism hasn't struck me down with a bolt of lightning through the roof.
— **Linda Vanderwerf**

READINGS: ON "DEEP THROAT," WHISTLEBLOWERS AND ANONYMOUS SOURCES

◀ MORE ON ANONYMOUS SOURCES ON PAGES 69, 79, 107

In 2005, Mark Felt ended a 30-year mystery by revealing he was "Deep Throat": the unnamed source who helped Bob Woodward, Carl Bernstein and The Washington Post expose corruption in the Nixon White House, corruption that eventually forced Nixon to resign. But was Felt a hero or a traitor? Do government whistleblowers do the public a service by exposing secrets, or do they deserve public scorn for betraying confidences? Should news organizations publish accusations by unnamed sources — or forbid the practice entirely? Below, a selection of excerpts that debate the issues:

James Bettinger, director of the John S. Knight journalism fellowship program at Stanford University:

Deep Throat represents the kind of source that a lot of reporters would like to have. He served as someone that Woodward could go to on a regular basis and say, "Are we on the right track?" . . . That is a huge fear of every good reporter: "Do we have this right?"

There are certain kinds of reporting that cannot be done without sources who are unnamed, in particular reporting on national security or defense . . . because people jeopardize their careers and in some cases their legal status by disclosing things. That said, there is too great a reliance on anonymous sources. That's why every news organization I know of is trying to reduce their use or their reliance on anonymous sources.

Howard Kurtz, *The Washington Post:*

Sometimes reporters have no other way to ferret out vital information than by promising anonymity. In the war-against-its-enemies atmosphere of the Nixon administration, Felt not only would have lost his job had he gone public about White House skulduggery — he was threatened with firing just as a suspected leaker — but might well have been prosecuted for breaking the law.

The revelation also serves as a reminder that sources may have complicated motives for whispering to the press. Felt may have worried about the FBI's integrity but he also may have been resentful, as the bureau's No. 2 official, at being passed over for the top job, and according to Woodward he came to detest the Nixon White House. Inside sources rarely have clean hands.

Three decades later, the use and abuse of unnamed sources is rampant, especially in Washington, and the media all too often protect those with partisan agendas. It's a long road from Felt telling Woodward to "follow the money" to a Bush adviser telling the New York Times that John Kerry "looks French." But such potshots have become routine in daily reporting.

From an interview with Bob Woodward and Carl Bernstein on CNN's **Larry King Live,** June 2, 2005:

King: *What about those who are saying, Carl, that Mark Felt is a guy who wanted to be head of the FBI and all this was revenge?*
Bernstein: I think that's a much too simplistic way to interpret it. He obviously felt an obligation to the truth. He felt an obligation, I think, to the Constitution. He realized that there was a corrupt presidency, that the Constitution was being undermined, and he was disappointed about not being made head of

the FBI, and he was disappointed that the FBI that he loved and revered was being misused as part of a criminal conspiracy. . . .
King: *By today's standards, Bob, did Mark Felt break the law?*
Woodward: No, I don't think so. I think that he was careful to give us guidance. He didn't give us direct information from FBI files or reports, and at his insistence, we were not even supposed to say that we had such a source . . . technically, in journalistic terms, the conversations were on deep background.
King: *What do I do, as a reader, if a journalist I believe in writes that an informed source told him or her this?*
Bernstein: You need anonymous sources to get to the truth. Do reporters sometimes abuse that? Yes. Interestingly enough, really good editors today, more than when we were doing this story, demand of their reporters that the editors know who those anonymous sources are. There's much more identification of those sources in terms of — are they in the Army? Are they in the Navy? Are they men? Women? Are they Republicans? Are they Democrats? — so you can help guide the reader to see if the source has an ax to grind.
King: *Don't most sources have an ax to grind?*
Bernstein: Look, there's ambiguity in all human interaction, and we all have a point of view that we're trying to get across. And sure, the source does. But our job is to see that it's the best obtainable version of the truth, to keep looking for more information, compare it, find more sources. That's what this is about.

Patrick Buchanan, Nixon speechwriter and adviser:

And so it turns out that the two most famous investigative reporters of all time were a pair of stenographers for an FBI hack who was ratting out President Richard Nixon for passing him over as director.

That corrupt cop, Mark Felt, should be named co-winner of the 1973 Pulitzer Prize given to The Washington Post. For it appears Felt swiped the research for the Post's Watergate stories from FBI files, while Woodward did rewrite and Bernstein was on the coffee-and-Danish run.

And so the great mystery, "Who was Deep Throat?" reaches its anticlimax. He turns out to be a toady who violated his oath and, out of malice and spite, leaked the fruits of an honest FBI investigation to the nest of Nixon-haters at The Washington Post, then lied about it for 30 years.

Why did Felt lie? Because he knew he had disgraced himself and dishonored everything an FBI agent should stand for. He didn't want his old comrades to know what a snake he had been.

Charles Colson, former special counsel to President Nixon:

I am truly shocked that Mark Felt indeed turns out to be "Deep Throat." I knew him and worked with him closely and considered him completely trustworthy.

I am disappointed in Mark for choosing the media as the way to expose the corruption. If he felt that the wrongs of the Nixon administration had to be remedied, he should have walked into the FBI director's office and told him so, and if necessary walked in to the president.

No matter how Felt may justify his actions, it is not honorable to leak classified information to the press. Governments cannot function if the chief executive cannot trust people who hold sensitive positions, and there are few positions more sensitive than the deputy director of the FBI. A president has to be able to deal with someone in a sensitive position without worrying that his conversations will be disclosed to the press.

David S. Broder, *The Washington Post* columnist, responds to those previous comments by Pat Buchanan and Charles Colson:

In these comments, Americans born in the '70s, '80s and '90s can learn everything they need to know about the dangerous delusions of the Nixon era. The mind-set that created enemies lists, the blind loyalty to a deeply flawed individual, the twisting of historical fact to turn villains into heroes and heroes into villains — they are all there.

Such tendencies are not unique to one White House; they go with the territory. They must be consciously resisted by men and women of conscience working within an administration and checked by those on the outside — notably journalists — whose job it is to monitor the presidency.

Mark Felt did what whistleblowers need to do. He took his information to reporters who diligently dug up the evidence to support his well-founded suspicions.

The Republic was saved and the public well-served. That Colson and Buchanan still don't get it speaks volumes about them.

Howard Goodman, *South Florida Sun-Sentinel:*

If The Washington Post were running its Watergate stories today, each one would be followed by an unremitting battery of attacks from Limbaugh, Fox and Drudge to deliver the [White House] spin and sneer at the paper's lack of patriotism.

Even if those stories got traction with the public, they wouldn't lead to congressional hearings, as you saw in Watergate. Not with the same political party controlling Congress as the White House, as we have now.

Watergate was all about government secrecy, domestic spying, the push toward unchecked presidential power.

A lot of that is still with us. No less an expert than John Dean, who was Nixon's White House counsel, says the Bush administration is more secretive than Nixon's ever was.

What's changed is that today's public thinks less of the watchdogs than it does of the politicians.

Steven Winn, *San Francisco Chronicle:*

In her exhaustive and carefully reasoned study "Secrets: On the Ethics of Concealment and Revelation," Sissela Bok argues that secrecy is both fundamental to modern society and fundamentally dangerous. Police work, Greek tragedy, intelligence gathering, investigative journalism and a good deal of the pleasure in our social lives would wither without the power of secrets. . . . Quoting Woodrow Wilson, she cautions, "Everybody knows that corruption thrives in secret places."

History, in its customary role, will judge the Bush administration's arguments to justify the invasion of Iraq and conduct of the war more fully than we can. What was known, what was concealed and what was cloaked in secrecy by whom? However that story is eventually told, the air of widespread public skepticism about "national security" that surrounds it inevitably evokes the Nixon era. So does the current debate over the appropriate use of unnamed sources in investigative reporting.

How fitting, somehow, that Deep Throat should finally make his entrance now.

Al Neuharth, former publisher of *USA Today:*

In 1982, when we founded USA Today, we effectively banned all anonymous sources.

As competition for readers and viewers and listeners and prizes from peers has become greater, more and more publishers and editors and broadcast managers have relaxed their rules. More and more reporters have taken advantage of that environment.

It's so simple. Most anonymous sources often tell more than they know. Reporters who are allowed to use such sources sometimes write more than they hear. Editors too often let them get away with it. Result: Fiction gets mixed with fact.

The only way to win the war against this evil is for journalists at all levels to ban all anonymous sources.

Until or unless we do, the public won't trust us, and we put the First Amendment in jeopardy.

Michael Getler, *The Washington Post:*

Felt's story reaffirms the ability of smart and dogged reporters, courageous editors and owners, and truly informed yet anonymous sources to help get information before the public that is vital to a democracy's functioning.

Many of the recent attacks on the media have come because of the use of anonymous sources. In general, this is a healthy challenge because the use of such sources has become far too routine and has contributed to serious mistakes. But this attack is fairly easy to make and it is being used, in part, these days to undermine news organizations that report things some people don't want to hear.

Watergate revisited reminds us that it is naive to believe that important stories involving potentially serious danger to sources can always be reported on the record or should not be reported at all.

"MIDGET" ROBINSON GETS REVENGE, SLAMS FOR "OREGON FANS"

By Dan Raley

Seattle Post-Intelligencer — Feb. 13, 2004

◄ MORE ON **COVERING SPORTS** ON PAGE **108**

Veteran reporter Dan Raley began writing sports stories more than 30 years ago. He's spent most of his career at the Seattle Post-Intelligencer, where he currently covers the college basketball beat.

Deadline sportswriting requires speed and skill — especially for evening matchups like this one, which began at 7:30 p.m. "I never know how it's going to turn out," Raley says. "I have two unfair deadlines on game night: supplying a story right after the final buzzer sounds, and then a rewrite full of explanation within the hour for the final edition, which most people get on their doorstep and appears on the Web.

"It's often an exercise in endurance and luck. All I do is react and type throughout the action, run for quotes, type again furiously and hope for the best."

RALEY'S COMMENTARY:

I went with the moment, reminded of the well-documented football difficulties between the two neighboring schools and used that to describe a night of basketball friction. There really isn't time to consider options for the first-edition lead, so you pick something and go with it.

They push and they shove, and call each other names. This is Oregon and Washington in any sport.

Last night, the two rivals got together on the basketball court and did nothing to patch up their ill feelings, with an untimely love-pat down the stretch by the Ducks giving the home club a proper nudge in the right direction.

Once all the elbows had been put back in their respective holsters, the Huskies had emerged with an 83-74 victory last night before a crowd of 7,618 at Edmundson Pavilion.

True to form, this game did not end with the final buzzer, which came immediately after Nate Robinson's wind-up dunk that provided an exclamation point — and more words, and pushing and shoving.

Capping a 16-6 run to close it out, Robinson let loose some pent-up frustration with a windmill slam, one that came after everyone had conceded the game was all but over and stood waiting for the buzzer to sound. His antics brought a heated response from Oregon coach Ernie Kent and his players as everyone left the court.

When in a hurry, it's always best to seek out the glib one — in this case, Nate Robinson. He obviously has a biblical background, plus an increasing knowledge of sitcom TV. I walked away, silently mouthing the words "thank you" to myself.

"With 59 seconds left, I was thinking if I get it again, I'm going to go get another dunk," said Robinson, who led all scorers with 20 points. "(Mitch) Platt moved out of the way, and it was like Moses parting the Red Sea. All I could think about were those Oregon fans calling me Gary Coleman or midget. That dunk was for those Oregon fans."

Right or wrong, it capped a heady effort by the Huskies (11-9 overall, 6-6 Pac-10), who overcame a 13-point deficit in the second half and an earlier opportunity squandered with Oregon standout Luke Jackson

in foul trouble.

UW guard Brandon Roy gave his club the lead for good, 69-68, with a short jumper with 4:08 remaining. In another well-rounded team effort, Roy and forward Bobby Jones backed Robinson with 18 points each, while the Huskies' other big man, Mike Jensen, came up with his first double-double outing, serving up 14 points and a game-high 10 rebounds.

"The guys showed a lot of courage tonight," Huskies coach Lorenzo Romar said. "Multiple players stepped up and had good ballgames, and that's what we needed to beat Oregon."

Said Robinson, "The hungrier team won it, and we were 10 times hungrier."

The Ducks, however, provided plenty of help for the home team.

"We just folded," Kent said flatly.

His senior leader, Jackson, missed most of the first half with foul trouble. Sitting more than playing, the league's second-leading scorer had just 11 points — half of his average — and fouled out in the final moments.

Still, Oregon (11-7, 6-5) gave a decent preview of what's in store next season — of life without the flop top. Rather than give in to dire circumstances, the Ducks used superior height and intensity to gain a first-half advantage, then nearly put the UW away with a well-rested Jackson helping his club rush out to a 65-52 advantage with 9:10 left to play.

It all came unraveled when the rivalry and all of its trappings rose up and bit the Ducks in their tail feathers.

While holding a 65-57 lead and in-bounding the ball, Oregon reserve forward Jay Anderson was spotted giving Jones a

Some guys use a lot of stats; I think they're overrated and only use ones that say something, or I'll make a quick roundup of the leaders. Stats can be obtained off monitors in the press area and from stat sheets quickly distributed after the game.

I am extremely conscious of using the short impact quote, a lesson taught to me by Los Angeles Times columnist Bill Plaschke, a former Seattle teammate. Note the descending order of words in the first four quotations used. It created a rhythm unplanned.

We watched and wrote from a concourse halfway up the stands, behind the big-money fans. It's a cordoned-off area usually monitored by a guard, but I'm still fearful that I'll come back from quote-gathering and my laptop will be gone.

I try to avoid corn and cliché, but sometimes weird things sneak into my stories, especially when I'm in a rush. Tail feathers? Ugh.

healthy shove and was called for an intentional foul, the costliest of 26 turnovers for the Ducks.

"I'll have to look at that on tape and see why we shoved him," Kent said. "I don't know why we'd do that."

The Huskies got five points out of the jostling. Anderson was seated at the far end of the bench when his club next proceeded to cough up the ball once Jackson missed a shot and a free throw, and the UW rushed into a tie at 65. The next time down the floor, the Huskies had their first lead since early in the first half, 67-65, on Jones' fast-break lay-in.

Robinson, who hit 7 of 10 shots, had six rebounds and four assists as his usual pestering self, added to his extensive collection of highlight-film heroics in the opening half. Following up a Roy miss, the springy 5-foot-9 guard bounded down the lane, caught the ball in one electrifying motion

and jammed it through, putting considerable bend on the rim and putting a charge into the crowd.

But as was the case most of the half, the UW couldn't take advantage of Jackson's absence or Robinson's presence.

The Huskies' littlest player made sure everyone knew what he was about at the end with his other dunk. Kent had words for him, with his players eager to add some opinions of their own.

"I don't think they appreciated it, and I don't blame them," Romar said of Oregon's testy response. "I talked to him about it. I'm not mad at him."

"It was ridiculous, " Jackson said.

Robinson said he apologized to the Ducks coach and a few players, and he's ready to accept the consequences. Probably a lot of hate mail and an extra-rude reception in Eugene next year.

But first, he had some celebrating to do.

I obtained the quotes from the coaches in a media room, and from most players in their locker rooms. Pro teams will give you quote sheets, as do some colleges. I prefer to get my own, and ask my own questions.

Considering my time constraints, I wrote this description as it happened in the first half. Some reporters simply watch the game. Some watch and take notes. I watch, take notes and write. In my next life, I plan to be a courtyard juggler.

The Jackson quote was memorable because he was walking fast to his bus, and I was walking fast to my seat. I hollered at him and he hollered back, without anyone stopping. I got what I wanted.

OPENERS
AN ANTHOLOGY OF LEADS

He was on fire. It was three in the morning, and most of his classmates from the Kibimba school in Burundi were dead — beaten and burned alive by friends of theirs, kids and grown-ups they had known most of their lives. Smoldering bodies lay in mounds all over the small room. He had used some of the corpses for cover, to keep from being hit by the fiery branches tossed in by the Hutu mob outside. For hours he had heard them laughing, singing, clapping, taunting. Waving their machetes, they had herded more than a hundred Tutsi teenagers and teachers from his high school into the room before sunset. A couple dozen were still alive, moaning in pain, dreaming of death.

"There weren't that many of us left," he says. "A guy said, 'I'm going out — I don't want to die like a dog.' He jumped from a window. They cut him to pieces. Then they started a fire on the roof. After a while it started falling on me, and I held up my right arm as it came down, trying to pull bodies over me. My back and arm were on fire — it hurt so bad. I decided I had had enough. I decided to kill myself by diving from a pile of bodies onto my head. I tried twice, but it didn't work.

Then I heard a voice. It said, 'You don't want to die. Don't do that.' Outside we could hear Hutus giving up and leaving. I heard one say, 'Before we go, let's make sure everyone is dead.' So three came inside. One put a spear through a guy's heart; another guy tried to escape, and they caught him and killed him. I heard the voice say, 'Get out.' There was a body next to me, burned down to the bones. It was hot. I grabbed a bone — it was hot in my hands — and used it to break the bar on the window. The fires had been going for nine hours, so it was easy to break. My thinking was, I wanted to kill myself. I wanted to be identifiable. I wanted my parents to know me. I didn't want to be all burned up, like everyone else. I was jumping to let them kill me."

There was a fire underneath the window, set as an obstacle to escape. He jumped. And somehow, in the darkness, amid the uproar of genocide, at least for a few seconds, no one saw him. His back was on fire, his legs were smoking, and his feet were raw with pain. He ran.

If you could call it running.

Michael Hall, *Texas Monthly*, using this dramatic anecdote to begin a profile of distance-runner Gilbert Tuhabonye

ANNIKA HANGS WITH THE BIG BOYS

By Brian Murphy

San Francisco Chronicle — May 23, 2003

◄ MORE ON **COVERING SPORTS** ON PAGE **108**

In 2003, Annika Sorenstam became the first woman to compete with men in a PGA golf tournament. In the story below, notice how well Brian Murphy balances WHAT HAPPENED — the shots and scores — with HOW IT FELT for Annika to perform in such a pressure cooker.

Keep in mind that Murphy had no direct access to Annika. Most of the quotes were gathered at press conferences attended by swarms of reporters. A few were overheard on the golf course.

Notice, too, how the AT A GLANCE sidebar provides a home for the most significant tournament stats — freeing Murphy to focus his story on the emotional aspects of the match.

FORT WORTH, Texas — Her heart beat so loud inside her chest, she could nearly hear it. Her stomach, she admitted, was like a rough sea, swirling. Her hands, she said, were moist from sweat.

Annika Sorenstam stood at the 10th tee at Colonial Country Club, under a still morning sky, and needed a pep talk. As she walked to her ball, to start her historic day at the Colonial, she found just the right person to give it.

"Trust yourself," she said, out loud, under her breath.

She inhaled, exhaled and talked again, only to herself.

"You can do it," she said.

And then Annika Sorenstam did what she believed she could do. With a sure and smooth pass at her golf ball, with a 4-wood struck purely 243 yards down the fairway, she did it. Sorenstam became the first woman in 58 years to play in a PGA Tour event, and she didn't just settle for that.

She shot a beautiful 1-over-par 71, carving out not just a place in history but also a significant measure of respect and admiration from the best male golfers in the world. She smashed preconceived notions of impossibility and arrived at a place she always knew was there — a place where Sorenstam proved she can play golf, can play golf with the boys and can, perhaps, change the way people think about sports.

"I'm so relieved," Sorenstam said at a packed news conference after her round. "Oh, was I nervous on the tee. Actually, all day. It never went away. So I'm very happy. . . . It was a great day. More than I could ever have expected.

"I'll never forget this day."

TIE FOR 73RD PLACE

Sorenstam's 71 places her in a tie for 73rd, and because the top 70 players — and ties — qualify for the 36-hole cut, she is flirting with a massive achievement in today's second round. Obstacles, naturally, lurk all over: a later tee time today (11:43 a.m. PDT), firmer greens, and an uncooperative putter among them. But if Sorenstam proved anything Thursday, it is that obstacles are there to surmount, if you believe strongly

AT A GLANCE

HER ROUND
Score: 71
Birdies: 1
Pars: 15
Bogeys: 2
Average drive: 269 yards
Greens in regulation: 14
Missed fairways: 1
Total putts: 33
Birdie putts: 14

HER PLACE
Sorenstam is tied with 13 other golfers in 73rd place. In order to make today's 36-hole cut, she must be in the top 70, including ties.

HER TARGETS
First-round leaders:
Rory Sabbatini: 64
Patrick Sheehan: 65
Mark Calcavecchia: 65

HER EQUALS
A few other notable players who shot 71:
Skip Kendall
Lee Janzen
Scott Simpson

HER PURSUERS
Notable players who shot worse than 71:
Steve Elkington: 72
Stuart Appleby: 72
Peter Jacobsen: 72
Sergio Garcia: 72
Tom Lehman: 73

enough.

It helps, also, to smash drivers off the tee with regularity and hit 13 of 14 fairways. It also helps to hit second shots into small greens with a fluid swing so easily repeated, over and over, as Sorenstam did. Sorenstam hit 14 of 18 greens.

"I really didn't miss any shots at all today," she said.

And it helped Sorenstam tremendously to have two sympathetic playing partners — tour rookies Dean Wilson, 32, and Aaron Barber, 30. So it was that on her fourth hole of the day, the par-3 13th, she putted from the fringe from 15 feet away and watched it disappear into the cup. It was a birdie that rocked Colonial, and her wowed partners offered a fist-bump (from Barber) and a high-five (from Wilson).

"I've never done that before," Barber said. "But you can't help but root for her."

Said Sorenstam: "The guys were so nice to me, so supportive. . . . At least I made one birdie. It was a relief."

'SHE WAS AWESOME'

Can she play with the boys? Her score beat 27 of the 113 in the field, including Barber, who shot 72. But after watching Sorenstam work her way around Colonial with metronomic brilliance, Barber said he'll take the heat.

"I'm not ashamed," he said. "She was awesome."

As for that Vegas line, with the over-under on Sorenstam's first round at 76.5?

"I should have bet on myself," Sorenstam said.

Hole by hole, the world's best female golfer summoned up something special. Skeptics thought she would need something special not to embarrass herself, but Sorenstam leaned on age-old intangibles: moxie and the human element of competitive fire. Even the golf gods cooperated, with soft greens and no wind.

The gallery, meanwhile, swooned. She drew Tiger-esque crowds, and men and women alike wore green "Go Annika" buttons. One fan shouted, "You the woman!" on No. 5. A feel-good laugh rippled through the crowd. They roared upon her arrival at her last hole, a hero's welcome.

CENTER OF ATTENTION

Sorenstam cut a bright figure in snow-white pants and golf shoes set off by a navy blue and white top. She was easy to spot — usually on the fairway and always at the center of attention. The attention, though, produced a churning feeling in her gut, a tension that never left.

Though she consistently traded pleasantries with Barber and, especially, Wilson, she would stand over her ball and feel ill at ease. Tight pin placements on every hole, she said, tested her mettle.

"I've been nervous before, but this was more than usual," she said. "When I would look at the flag, I would get nervous again. … I feel like this is almost more than I can handle."

The pressure may explain her sketchy putting. Tucked pins meant her strategy was to hit at the middle of greens, leaving long birdie putts — eight times, she had birdie putts of 22 feet or longer. She made none. Only three times did she have legitimate birdie opportunities — within 12 feet — and she missed all three of them. The longest putt on the green she made was a 5-footer. Placing so much pressure on her lag putting eventually bit her, when Sorenstam bogeyed Nos. 5 and 9 (her 14th and 18th holes).

"When I get nervous," she said, "I get a little tentative with putts."

Nonetheless, the day resonated with a historic feel. Sorenstam slept well, woke at 6 a.m., got to the course at 7, then endured the longest 118 minutes of her life. She chipped, putted, hit balls and putted more. "Time," she said, "was going so slow." It seemed her tee time would never arrive. She chatted with Barber on the putting green, and they shared a moment.

Remember, he said, we're doing this together.

You're right, Sorenstam said.

Will our nerves go away? he asked.

I don't know, she said.

Well, this will be great preparation for future tournaments, he said.

Yes, Sorenstam said, this is what you'll see when you go in the last group at the Masters.

They laughed, new friends, new competitors, and they will show up again today at Colonial, to play golf.

QUOTED

From a Media Bistro article by Geraldine Hayward, recalling her days as the "Death Knock Queen" writing obituaries for British newspapers:

I sank into a sofa and started babbling questions about the dead guy. … They were bereaved, but I was anguished. Try as I might, I could not find one interesting thing this poor dead guy had ever done, and none of the 30-odd people in the room could say anything interesting about him, either. I was looking at the newspaper equivalent of dead airtime.

Eventually I had to admit defeat, and asked for a photograph — always a prelude to leaving. The dead guy was heading for an extended picture caption on page 7. The family got out a photo album and leafed through it as I tapped my mental foot impatiently and dripped sweat on their violently-patterned carpet.

"Here's one with his dog," the mother said, handing me a photo. "He loved his dog. Poor thing died of a broken heart three days after Mark was killed. Just curled up in his basket, refused to eat, and faded away. We're putting his dog lead in Mark's coffin so they can always rest together."

Ker-CHING! Now *that's* a story, madam. Quite worth the wait. It made a page three lead and an excellent addition to my clippings file.

OPENERS
AN ANTHOLOGY OF LEADS

This is grief: Your 11-year-old boy, your baby boy, is dead. You cannot find a suit that fits him, because he died too young and too short to fit into a nice funeral suit.

This is reality: Judah Benjamin Evans Smith died of epidural hematoma, of massive internal bleeding caused from a blunt blow to the head. He died Saturday evening, but was really dead before that, on life support, after two brain surgeries.

This is what you said to the boy's father when he got off the plane from Aberdeen, Miss.: "Joe, we've lost our son. They have him on life support, and I told them to leave him on it until you got here."

The details are still unclear, but this is what is known: While running, Judah apparently fell and hit his head on the bench-style seat attached to a cafeteria table at Dimitt Middle School Thursday afternoon.

Judd Slivka, *Seattle Post-Intelligencer*

Regrettably, unfortunately, lamentably and mournfully, Robert L. Chapman is deceased, demised, departed and dead at 81. The son, boy and male offspring of a West Virginia typewriter mechanic, Chapman once drove trucks, then studied poetry and medieval literature before editing the timeworn, antiquated, irreplaceable Roget's International Thesaurus.

Andrew Malcolm, *Los Angeles Times*

GIVE ME THE SIGN

By Dave Scheiber

St. Petersburg Times — July 5, 2005

◄ MORE ON **COVERING SPORTS** ON PAGE **108**

Great quotes, great anecdotes . . . collect enough of those and your story writes itself. Here's a sports feature that's as entertaining as it is educational, primarily because of the quotes and anecdotes reporter Dave Scheiber assembled from a variety of sources: books, newspaper articles, interviews with current ballplayers and phone calls to old-timers. The resulting feature is both an insider's guide to baseball strategy and an amusing collection of anecdotes any reader can enjoy.

From his coaching box alongside third base, Tom Foley's hands are a flurry of motion, as if he's brushing away a pesky fly.

They touch the bill of his Devil Rays ballcap, his chest, his wrists, his legs, his ears, his belt in no discernible pattern. Or they don't move at all.

It is the game within the game, the silent art of subterfuge and secret communication that is an intrinsic element of baseball and has been throughout its history.

The chief practitioners of the craft are third-base coaches, who get busy with their sleight of hand when a batter reaches base. The hidden messages they send to batters and runners — orders conveyed with equal stealth from the manager in the dugout — often dictate the flow and strategy of any given game.

Miss a sign and you may botch an at-bat or cost your team a win. Or maybe, as Foley once did while playing for Montreal, you dodge a bullet.

"I was in New York playing the Mets and facing Ron Darling," he said. "Man on first and second, nobody out. The bunt was on, but I missed the sign. Fortunately, I hit a three-run homer. When I came in the dugout and the manager, Buck Rodgers, said to me, 'You were supposed to bunt!' I said, 'Well, I saw the pitch pretty good. I thought I could hit it.' I was just joking around. But if you mess up and hit into a double play, well, man, that's a big mistake."

Given the importance of signs, it's no surprise that teams routinely look for ways to decode the hand and body language of third-base coaches — and why other teams frequently change signs to prevent them from being stolen. (Or, as legendary manager Casey Stengel was quoted in "The Hidden Language of Baseball" by Paul Dickson: "I ain't gonna change our signs. I'm just gonna change what they mean.")

But here's one trade secret to consider next time you watch Foley or one of his coaching counterparts with their hands flying rapid-fire:

Much of it means nothing.

"In the course of a game, say there are 100 pitches thrown or better, and of those 100 pitches, you only give signs when somebody's on base," Seattle third-base coach Jeff Newman said. "So if I give 40 signs a night, I'm really only giving probably no more than five real signs. The rest are decoys. So the key is making your decoys look like good signs.

"It's a cat-and-mouse game," he added. "And there are only so many places they'll allow you to touch without it being obscene."

Foley echoes the deception theme: "I may touch eight or 10 spots every pitch. And I may not put a sign on the whole game."

There's a good reason to always touch every spot.

"If it's late in the game and all of a sudden you might want to put a hit-and-run on, and you go to that one spot you never touched before, it's a red flag to the opponent," Foley said. "Because the other dugout is watching you. Somebody is always watching."

It could be anyone from a wily coach or bench player to stars such as former Milwaukee teammates Paul Molitor and Robin Yount, who prided themselves on winning some games for the Brewers in the '80s by swiping signs, Dickson wrote. "If you are able to steal a bunt, a hit-and-run, get an out and win an inning, you can win a game that you otherwise might have lost," Molitor told the author.

So how do third-base coaches ply their sign craft? Naturally, systems vary from team to team. But one common element is the indicator: a sign or touch that means the real signal is coming right up.

Foley gave some examples, stressing that none was part of his top-secret repertoire. "You could have an indicator where you touch a spot, and then it's not on unless you lock it in," he said.

And how do you lock in a sign?

"Well, let's say the left wrist is the lock-in," he said. "That means it's on if I touch it. If I put a sign on and I don't go to that left wrist, then it's not on. Then again, I could put no sign on and end up touching my left wrist and nothing's on."

Or say that belt stands for bunt and Foley's indicator is touching his right ear. His hands get in gear, moving this way and that, and suddenly he touches his right ear. "Then I go to my belt, and the bunt is on," he said. Well, not quite. "I might still hit a couple of more signs after that," he added, "and then I lock it in with my left wrist."

Sometimes, third-base coaches designate certain touched areas as "hot spots." You could have four hot spots, said Foley, and the one that you don't touch is the key to signaling a certain play.

What if Foley messes up a sequence?

"Then I've got a start-over sign," he said. "And I'm sure some clubs have a repeat sign. In other words, if they put the bunt on, and they want to put the bunt on again but not have to go through the same sign to do that, then there's a spot where it's a repeat."

The job would be tricky enough if it just required giving

signs to the batter and runners. But Foley and his third-base coaching colleagues have to make sure they get the signals correctly from the dugout, where they're sent — usually via a different set of signals — from the manager or his bench coach.

Rays senior adviser Don Zimmer was regarded as one of the game's great third-base coaches, but the job had its challenges.

"I had a manager who would relay the signs to me and I'd relay them to the players," Zimmer said. "So after we had just played this club for three days, he said to me, "You can keep your signs to the players, but I think so-and-so has stolen my signs to you. "'

So Zimmer went into the clubhouse and got new signs from his boss (whom he declines to identify). In the next inning, after one of his runners reached first, the manager signaled a hit-and-run. "But he gives me the old hit-and-run sign," Zimmer said.

"So I go through some signs and don't put on any play. Pitch is in the dirt, runner don't run and the hitter don't swing. My manager throws his arms up and is screaming and hollering at me.

"So all the players think I missed the sign from the act that he put on. I come in and he says, "I put on the hit-and-run!' And I said, "You put on the old hit-and-run!' And he says, "Ohhh, I forgot.' But in the meantime, I looked like the dummy."

Zimmer said he has seen plenty of costly gaffes result from missed signs, most often from batters who overlooked the squeeze sign and left the runner trying to score from third a goner at home plate. "I've seen that 20 times or more," he said.

Picking up signs simply requires staying focused, says Rays utilityman Eduardo Perez. But it can take some getting used to. In his book, "New Thinking Fan's Guide to Baseball," Leonard Koppett relates how former A's owner Charley Finley made his manager, Alvin Dark, break down all the team's signs for him. Dark did so for an hour until Finley had them. But when the owner asked Dark to give signs as they would be relayed in a game, Finley missed each and every one.

There have been countless classic sign moments.

Former American League umpire and crew chief Jim Evans remembered how Billy Martin, when managing the Texas Rangers in the 1970s, tried a league-approved walkie-talkie system with third-base coach Frank Lucchesi.

"With a runner on third, Martin told Lucchesi to put on the squeeze play," Evans said from his home in Colorado. "Evidently, Frank didn't hear Billy the first, second or third time he tried to communicate from the first-base dugout. Each time he ordered the squeeze, Martin got louder and louder as his temper boiled. So in disgust, Martin threw the walkie-talkie onto the dugout floor and it burst into a hundred

pieces. Luis Tiant, the Boston pitcher, stepped off the rubber and yelled at Lucchesi, "Hey, Frank! Billy wants you to bunt!"'

Mariners announcer and former Dodger first baseman Ron Fairly told the Seattle Times in 2003 about ex-first baseman Dick Stuart, who struggled to get signs from third-base coach Preston Gomez. One day, with Stuart on first, the frustrated coach moved his arms as if he were running and pointed to second. "That was his steal sign," Fairly said.

Base-stealing great Rickey Henderson had the green light in Oakland to run whenever he wanted, former first-base coach Jackie Moore said. "He didn't need any signs," said Moore, now manager of Houston's Triple-A team in Round Rock, Texas.

Baseball abounds with many more signs than those from the third-base coach and manager. There are the endless ones between pitcher and catcher, and the long tradition of stealing them to gain an edge — from spying in the scoreboard (a charge leveled against the '51 Giants in their amazing pennant-winning comeback) to eagle-eyed players and coaches on the field and in the dugout today.

As a batter, you can sneak a peek at the catcher to see how he's setting up for a certain pitch, but the consequence might be a mean brushback by the pitcher. Rays centerfielder Rocco Baldelli got an unintended lesson in the hazards of sign stealing shortly after being assigned to rookie ball in Princeton, W. Va.

"You know, I was so confused with what was going on in general, I had no clue," he said. "It was midway through the season and I got a hit, which was rare. So I was on second base. And the umpire called time and the opposing manager came out and pointed his finger at me and said, "If you keep doing that, you're going to get hurt, son.' Meaning, he thought I was looking in and giving the hitter the signs.

"Now, I'm going to tell you — I still didn't even know our signs, let alone trying to steal the other team's signs. But I was so nervous on base, freaking out a little from reaching base, I looked suspicious."

To Dickson, signs define the game. Among the nuggets in his book: In Indians manager Lou Boudreau's system, the same signs meant different things in each third of the lineup. And this Stengelism: "I have an ironclad system of signs. The other team can't steal 'em, and my fellows don't understand them."

"In one major-league game there are probably a thousand signs and signals," Dickson said by phone from his home in Maryland. "And that includes covert umpire signals, which there is a tradition of, besides the ones fans see. Sometimes the third-base coach isn't even giving the signs. There was a time when Billy Martin used to use a trainer to give the signs — the guy would use a tongue depressor.

"If you took signs and signals out of baseball, the game would fall apart."

VERMEIL SENSED IT WAS GO TIME

By Joe Posnanski

*The Kansas City Star —
Nov. 7, 2005*

◄ MORE ON **COVERING SPORTS** ON PAGE **108**

Joe Posnanski, named America's best sports columnist by the Associated Press Sports Editors, believes that columns, especially sports columns, should hit an emotion. "If a column doesn't make someone feel something — make someone laugh or cry or angry or curious — then it probably wasn't a very good column," he says.

Posnanski began writing columns at the Kansas City Star in 1996. Before that, he was a sports columnist in Cincinnati and Augusta. And for Posnanski, the column reprinted here exemplifies the difference between reporting and column-writing.

"When you write a story on an event or topic, you are trying mostly to inform," he explains. "It's all about those questions: who, what, when, where, how. A column needs to find the places in between those questions and give people a point of view that a game story cannot."

POSNANSKI'S COMMENTARY:

I had a different lead on this originally, a more complicated (i.e., confusing) one. I would imagine at least once while writing every column I remind myself "Keep it simple." This is as simple as it gets.

Kenny Chesney and Renée Zellwegger had split up two days before the column. I always look for ways to get goofy things like this into my column.

I normally do not like referring to us writers in the press box, but in this case I figured our debate — "Go or no" — was being played out by NFL fans across America.

Sometimes you get lucky. I went to Google and typed in "1,150 pounds." The first or second entry said: "Weight of an adult polar bear."

Chiefs president/CEO/general manager/disco king Carl Peterson stands up against the glass in his box at Arrowhead Stadium. He watches with some blend of excitement and panic. Numbers swirl in the air.

Ball on the Oakland 1.

Chiefs down 3.

Clock reads 0:05.

Time for one play.

A crowd of 79,033 goes mad.

A season teeters. This is one of those sports moments that tells you what's inside. What do you do? Go or no? In the press box, opinions split like Kenny and Renée. Half in the box demand the field goal — get the tie and send the game into overtime. The safe play.

Half in the box say go — win this game with one bold play.

"I just figured," Vermeil would say, "I'm too old to wait."

The Chiefs go for the win. They call their play 20-Z Blast, the simplest, straightest, most violent run in the playbook. The play begins with Will Shields, one of the greatest offensive guards in the game's history. He is supposed to turn a defensive lineman. Then, Jason Dunn, Brian Waters and Tony Richardson slam into the gap next to Shields. Altogether, that's 1,150 pounds of blocking — the weight of an adult polar bear.

At the same time, quarterback Trent Green takes the snap, hands the ball to running back Larry Johnson, 230 pounds himself. He takes the ball, runs to where the defense bends. He leaps into the end zone.

"I don't like to leap," Johnson would say.

That's 20-Z Blast. Basic as the multiplication table. If the Chiefs can move the

Raiders backward, they win. If not, they lose.

The ball is snapped. Shields turns his man. Dunn and Waters take out so many Raiders, Tony Richardson does not have anyone left to block. Johnson leaps into the end zone.

The Chiefs beat the Raiders. The season is alive again.

And up in his box, Carl Peterson smashes his hands against the window. The glass shatters and falls on him while the crowd flips out. The Chiefs rush the field; the place is madness. While the Chiefs kick the cherry-on-top extra point, Peterson washes the glass out of his hair and face. He rushes downstairs to hug everybody.

"How about the guts of the head coach?" he asks.

*   *   *

What a call. It's easy now to say that you would have done the same thing. I was one of those people in the press box saying the Chiefs should go for the win. Simple mathematics. If they had kicked a field goal, the game would have gone into overtime. That means winning was just about a 50-50 proposition.

I thought the Chiefs had a better than 50-50 chance to score from the 1.

But coaching pro football is about more than math. There were no talk shows when Sir Isaac Newton invented calculus (if there were, Louie from Louisville would have called in to say, "Oh man, you know Leibniz invented calculus first!").

The truth is, Dick Vermeil faced the quintessential coaching decision. Go or no? Take one bold shot at winning now or tie the game, take a deep breath and try to win

The form can be overused, but I like writing moments like this in the present tense. It can give the writing a little urgency.

Talk about lucky: Nobody knew about Peterson smashing the window. I just happened to be riding up the elevator with him, and I noticed his face was puffy. I asked him what happened, and he told the story. In the wild aftermath, no one else had noticed.

Many people think a column, especially a sports column, must be about an opinion. I think a column must present a point of view. In this case, I thought the Chiefs did the right thing by going for it. But I didn't think that would make a particularly interesting column. To me, my opinion on the subject was worth one or two lines.

A reader pointed out this had to be the first sports column to mention both Newton and Leibniz. I hope so.

it later? Go by the book (the book says kick) or roll the dice?

On another day, Vermeil admits, he might have kicked the field goal. Most coaches, I think, would have kicked there. Coaches, in general, do not let their games come down to one round of showdown poker. Too much luck involved. No, most coaches I know would rather keep the game going as long as possible. They figure the longer their teams are alive, the better chance they have of winning.

Vermeil is like that, too. He says he has never tried anything this bold in his coaching life. He says if the ball had been at the 2, he would have kicked. Gambling it all on one play goes against his nature.

But he could feel that this play was different. This game was different. This season was different. Go or no? The players wanted to go. Players always want to go. "If we had kicked there," Waters would say after the game, "then I would have wondered if there was something wrong with us. I would have wondered if they had lost faith in our offensive line."

The fans wanted to go. Fans always want to go, too.

But only Dick Vermeil would have endured the wrath had Larry Johnson not gotten into the end zone. He would have been skewered across the country. He knew it, too. "If we had not made it," he told reporters, "you guys would have had a lot of fun with that."

More than anything, though, Vermeil knew that a loss would have more or less killed this season. The Chiefs would have been 4-4, in last place in the AFC West. He would have had a hard time regrouping his players. The Chiefs would have been in line for another forgettable season.

Vermeil made the gutsy call. Vermeil said go.

"It was time," he said.

*   *   *

It is probably the happiest Chiefs locker room in 10 years.

"Did you block anyone on that last play?" Tony Richardson asks Will Shields.

"You have to ask me that?" Shields yells back. "Don't you know me?"

Laughter. Hugs. Insults.

"You have a smile on your face," Richardson says to tight end Tony Gonzalez. "You must have caught some passes."

"You're an instigator," Gonzalez says back.

More hugs. High-fives. Congratulations.

"This was one of the great ones," Chiefs founder Lamar Hunt says.

"I think we're as good as any team in the NFL," Gonzalez says.

"After this, there's no telling how good we can be," Waters says.

"I'm going to have a glass of wine," Peterson says.

There's no telling what would have happened had Dick Vermeil kicked the field goal at the end of the game. Maybe the Chiefs would have won in overtime. There's no way to express all the things that could have gone wrong with 20-Z Blast. Quarterback Trent Green might have fumbled the snap. Larry Johnson might have slipped. Someone might have been called for holding. The Raiders may have blown through the blocks.

"Wow, I was scared," Vermeil says. This was some gamble.

But really, football, life — it's all a gamble, isn't it?

"What did you think of the decision to go for it?" someone asks Will Shields.

"I'm not paid to think," he says.

Here's what I mean about point of view. Even though I thought it was right to go for the touchdown, I understand that it's a whole lot different being on the field and making that decision. I want to take the reader inside the decision and try to show, as best I can tell, what is really happening on the field.

I often use short quotes like "It was time" to punctuate a thought. Vermeil said a lot of things about his decision to go for the touchdown. But to me, all of it could be boiled down to those three words. "It ... was ... time."

Short. Punchy. Sentences. We're in the locker room now, and I'm trying to pick up the pace, get the reader to move a little quicker the way a movie director might with quick cuts.

I looked through my notebook after this game and saw a lot of quotes and a lot of thoughts I wanted to get into the column. So — and this is a bit unusual — I simply placed the quotes one after another. I hope each quote tells a bigger story.

I have had a constant argument with friends in column writing about what is more important, a good lead or a good ending. I've always been partial to the ending. To me, a good column has to have a payoff. When Will Shields said, "I'm not paid to think," I knew instantly that was the ending. The rest of the column was just of a way to get there.

GIRL'S LAST GIFTS BRING SMILES TO KIDS' FACES

By Colleen Kenney

Lincoln Journal Star — June 10, 2005

◀ MORE ON **FEATURE STYLE** ON PAGE **116**

Taped to Colleen Kenney's computer are four words from William Zinsser's "On Writing Well":
CLARITY
SIMPLICITY
BREVITY
HUMANITY
"This is my mantra when I'm writing," Kenney says. And those four qualities characterize the touching feature story reprinted below.

"I look for little stories that say big things," Kenney says. "A dying 8-year-old who's thinking of other kids' happiness — to me that's big news.

"Many reporters go into a story like this thinking they know what they're going to write. Stories like that turn out like clichés and have no heart.

"My best advice: Go into each story expecting it to be the best you've written. And see no story assigned to you as 'little.' "

KENNEY'S COMMENTARY:

My favorite phrase: "8 going on 9." Kids always say it this way, don't they? Even if their birthday's not for half a year. I wrote it this way for poignancy, because, as readers soon find out, Schuyler won't make it to 9.

After another reporter had passed on this story, I phoned the father, got the background on Schuyler and her death and a good sense of what a great child she was.

"The nice man with a beard." Schuyler's "very best friend." "Littlest to biggest." "Mommy." I chose words a kid would use rather than words a reporter would use. I'm telling this from a kid's perspective because I'm trying to put readers in Malorie's little shoes, so the payoff is greater.

Finding Malorie was the key. Once I did, I dropped everything and followed her around, focusing my note-taking on details that would advance her story. When I wrote this, I ignored pages of good details from other kids and parents.

Schuyler Peterson, 8 going on 9, lies in her daddy's bed.

She likes to do this, curl up to him and feel his breath on her head and his arms around her until she falls asleep. It makes her not so scared.

Daddy, she says, I still want to have a birthday party. I still want you to invite my very best friends and have them bring gifts.

But what should we do with all the toys?

Mike Peterson pauses now, recalling the conversation that night in January.

They both knew she'd never make it to her June 3 birthday.

"She said, 'Daddy, I want the poor kids to have them.' "

* * *

She sure didn't expect to get a toy today.

Malorie Underwood figured Thursday would be just another day.

She didn't see this coming, this nice man with a beard and toys for her and her four sisters and brothers and all the other kids here.

For the past month, Malorie has lived in Room 136 of the People's City Mission, in the family shelter, with her mom and siblings and grandma.

She sleeps on a bunk bed. There are two bunk beds in Room 136. Her 4-year-old sister, Makenna, sleeps on the other bed, a single bed under the window, a Barbie sleeping bag covering it.

Mommy told Malorie, don't expect any toys today. Maybe in a week, when money comes in. Sorry, baby.

The lounge fills with kids and their parents and mission workers, Malorie and her siblings.

"My little girl had cancer," the nice man begins.

He holds up a picture of a smiling girl, says her name was Schuyler and she died in February and she wanted kids here to have her toys.

He says her friends came to the birthday party last week with gifts for girls and boys, and they decorated cupcakes and let go of balloons at her grave.

He says this blond girl here is Morgan Bouwens, Schuyler's very best friend, and she'll help pass out all these gifts Schuyler wanted the poor kids to have.

"She was an awesome little girl."

The nice man stops talking, like he can't anymore, and other adults hug him. Everyone says a prayer for Schuyler. And him.

Mommy stands against a wall. She is wiping away tears.

Malorie stands in line quietly as kids, littlest to biggest, line up and the man returns to the toys and starts passing them out.

A white fuzzy kitty stuffed animal . . . a yellow "Power Puff" doll . . . a fat baby doll called "Lots of Love Babies."

Malorie sees what she wants. She hopes it'll be hers.

Makenna chooses a baby doll with its own pink diaper bag and supplies and carrier.

I didn't want to interview Mike Peterson at the mission because I wanted to focus on the kids' reactions to the gifts and take it from their point of view.

If it's clear who the speaker is, I leave off attribution. This makes it more real. You have my permission to argue with your editors on this one. Some of the best words of advice I ever got were from Joe Starita, a Pulitzer finalist and a former Journal Star city editor who now is a journalism professor at the University of Nebraska-Lincoln. "Remove the stink of journalism." (See, you know Joe said this, don't you? So why put in "he said"?)

The little boy clutching Tigger was adorable. A cute talker. I thought he'd be my subject. I was interviewing him when I overheard Malorie tell another little girl, "It's my birthday today." Malorie was standing quite a ways away from me when she said this. But I'd programmed myself going into this to keep looking for the best story, to keep my senses open (in this case, hearing), to keep seeing the big picture but also the little details. I have this theory that if you program yourself before each story, your subconscious will pick up stuff like this. (Kind of like how people can set mental alarm clocks at night and then wake up when they want.)

The minute I heard Malorie say it, I changed gears and followed her into Room 136 and met her mom, grandma and siblings. (I recognized Malorie's mom as the one I saw wiping away tears when the gifts were being passed out.)

A 5-year-old boy chooses a stuffed Tigger doll. He clutches it to his chest as he walks away.

A 6-year-old girl in front of Malorie chooses an art supply kit.

Her turn now.

She points to the Polly Pocket Spa Day package.

The nice man hands it to her.

She and Makenna show their mom and then rush across the hall to No. 136 to show Grandma.

"I got a Polly Pocket!"

"Let me see it," Grandma says, inspecting the toys. "Pretty nice."

"She's a pretty nice girl to give away all her toys," Malorie says.

And her daddy is a pretty nice daddy to bring them here, Grandma says.

* * *

Mommy enters No. 136. She's still crying.

She tells someone how thankful she is her own children are healthy and they have this place here at the mission —

they couldn't afford the $850 rent, so that's why they're all here.

She tells someone how thankful she is her kids got toys today—especially Malorie. What a blessing. The child support check doesn't come until next week, so she'd told Malorie not to expect anything today.

"This comes at a good time, huh, Malorie?"

Malorie walks back into the lounge, where kids are playing with their new toys. She walks up to the nice man, who is talking to a TV reporter.

She stands there, waiting, Polly Pocket Spa Day package in her hands.

"Hi, what's your name?"

"Malorie." Her voice is soft.

The nice man bends to her level.

"Malorie? Hi, Malorie. What toy did you get?"

She shows him Polly Pocket.

"I'm 7," she says. "And guess what? Today's my birthday."

"It is? Can she get an extra present? It's her birthday."

It was hard to ask her about finances. But the key is just to be sincere. If you're uncomfortable asking about finances, just say it. "I feel like a jerk asking you this, but..." In this case, I was able to tell the mom that I grew up poor, so I knew how happy the gift made Malorie and her.

I see Malorie walk over to Schuyler's dad and the TV reporter, who's putting away her camera. I'm screaming, "No, no, no," in my head. I'm holding my breath, acting like I'm not the least bit interested in Malorie or the fact it's her birthday. I didn't even write down the quote until later, just in case the TV reporter caught on. But she didn't. She just kept putting away her camera and missed the best possible story from this event. Any good reporter will tell you the best stuff often comes after you put away your notebook or think the interview is over.

The event was at 3 p.m. and I had this written by 5 or 6 p.m. I cried as I wrote. I walked over to my editor and said, with tears in my eyes, "This is such a great story, if I don't make it suck."

One was taken out by accident. Another with fanfare. A third by chariot.

But the winner of the Savannah-Chatham County Spelling Bee stayed plucky with yucky, sunk her teeth into incisor, and was at ease with acclimatize.

The eighth-grader at Oglethorpe Academy, Carissa Pfeiffer, won the bee for the third time in a row on "double entendre."

Mary Landers, *Savannah Morning News*

OPENERS
AN ANTHOLOGY OF LEADS

As Ron Borowiak tells it, Santa has the most fun with the adults who approach him with an all-grown-up, in-on-the-joke, wink-wink attitude. They sidle up with a certain chumminess and jovially assure him, "I still believe in you."

And Santa pauses, peers into their eyes, then whispers like a long-ago grandpa, "Good to see you again."

Makes the hair rise on the backs of their necks.

Kim Ode, *Star Tribune* (Minneapolis, Minn.)

It's still unclear why he was naked.

But there's no doubt it was Jody Lee Taylor, 1992 Virginia Lottery winner, who got high on crack cocaine and Crown Royal blended whiskey one night in June, drove his new Ford pickup the wrong way down U.S. 58 in Axton and then tried to run down a Henry County deputy.

Being a lottery winner didn't cause Taylor's problems, his friends and family say, but it sure didn't help.

Matt Chittum, *The Roanoke Times*

No multimillion-dollar contracts. No Sharpie-toting autograph seekers. No TV cameras or mouthy commentators. No trash talk. No blingbling. No big-time corporate sponsors, although goodness knows, the folks who make Clorox might want to consider the opportunity.

After all, this is croquet.

Katy Muldoon, *The Oregonian*, using a blind lead to lure you into a story about a successful croquet team

ALWAYS, ED

By Kelley Benham

St. Petersburg Times — Feb. 13, 2005

◀ MORE ON **FEATURE STORY STRUCTURES**, PAGE **118**

Always, Ed

In what manner can I describe our love?
Are there enough words in all languages and dialects to do so? (1994)

For breaking news, an inverted pyramid structure usually works best. But some stories — actual STORIES, with beginnings, middles and ends — need narratives that unfold chronologically. Especially love stories.

For "Always, Ed," Kelley Benham begins and ends with the present-day Ed, sitting alone as he struggles to write a love letter. But in between those opening/closing bookends lies the heart of the story: a long chronological flashback that conveys the significance of Ed's letters.

Benham explains how the story came about:

"When I was a college junior, my boyfriend bought me one of those Valentine's Day Love Lines in the University of Florida student newspaper, the Alligator. I can't remember what it said.

"I remember another letter on another page. 'JUDY,' it began, in 24-point type. At the end it said, 'Come closer, let me explain it another way.'

"Ed must be an English major, I thought. I hoped Judy wouldn't dump him.

"Over the years — I stayed at UF six years, OK? — I pieced together a love story about these two strangers. The letters became, as I said in the story, annual evidence of what is possible.

"My earnest boyfriend one year tracked down Ed. He found out it was the Alligator's general manager, Ed Barber. In Gainesville, everyone knows Ed Barber.

"Years later, all grown, I heard Judy died. I was in the newsroom, checking e-mail. I was on deadline for a funny story about North Dakota and I felt wrecked.

"My very wise editor, Mike Wilson, told me I needed to write about them, but I wasn't sure I wanted to. What if their marriage was as screwed up as everyone else's? I didn't want to know. What if I fumbled the story and ruined the legacy of their 48 years?

"I waited until January. Waited a while longer. Waited until Mike was teasing me about it. Then I called Ed."

BENHAM'S COMMENTARY:

This is the feature story version of a nut graf. Tells what the story is about, but tries to do it in a graceful way.

He knows how the letter will end. Every letter has ended the same way since their letters were high-school locker notes.

    Always,

    Ed

What comes before that is just a fumbling attempt. Ed Barber is 65, and he has loved Judy for 48 years. For more than three decades, he has written her a love letter for Valentine's Day. In his mind, he has never gotten one right.

He's a logical man, and he has tried, in other years, to explain in these letters what can't be explained. He has described love using science and mathematics, compared her to music, wind and water.

But this defies logic. He is just a man. These are just words.

JUDY, it begins.

I knew early on, maybe before I even picked up the phone to dial Ed's number, certain things about the shape of the story. I knew it would have a JUDY at the top and an Always at the end, like all of the letters. I knew it would be filled and shaped by Ed's letters, somehow. I think I knew his words were as important as mine. The work was half done before I dialed.

He plucks softly at the keys. He misses the clattering of manual typewriters. It is so quiet in the house. He stops every so often and puts his chin in his hands, wipes his eyes. Any minute he imagines he might feel her hand on his shoulder. But he is alone in his wingback chair by the big window. Outside the birds are pecking under the tall pine. The humming of the air conditioner is the only sound.

The antique Regulator on the wall has not ticked in almost a year. It is frozen at 9:45. Last March, Ed rewound the hands, a reminder he does not need.

He knows he can't stop time, but he wishes he could. If he could, maybe he could make it go back.

From chaos you flew to me,
On beauty's butterfly wings. (2004)

When he tells it, and he loves to tell it, he always lingers on the moment he saw her.

She was barely 15, coming back from majorette practice. She was carrying a pile of books, her baton and her crinolines through the empty halls of Hialeah High School. He was a senior, almost 17. He can't say why she stunned him the way she did, why he still remembers the way her curls stuck to her forehead, the way her cheeks flushed pink. She wasn't the girl every guy wanted, but after he saw her, he never wanted anyone else.

He stole her baton to get her to walk

This scene comes from the last day of reporting I did. It took a long time to get this close to Ed, to get inside his house and inside his head. This was three trips to Gainesville, which is a three-hour drive, and spending the whole day. Going to the newspaper office, going to lunch, visiting Judy's grave, eating Ed's tofu meatballs, hanging out while he wrote.

To guide my reporting, I kept reminding myself that the story is about the letters. Otherwise, it's just another (yawn) love story about old people who were married a long time. I went through every letter, pulled out my favorite parts and put them into rough order on my computer screen and sort of filled in an outline in between. To start, I looked for one that sounded like a beginning.

with him. The next day he hung around her locker and was late to class. She wouldn't give him her phone number, so his friend Jack spied on her in the phone booth as she dialed her house, copied down the number and auctioned it on the spot. Ed's bid was highest. He asked her out that weekend.

He was her first real date. They saw "The Unguarded Moment" at the theater on Miracle Mile. It was a titillating movie for its time, featuring degenerate youths and a teacher's bra strap.

Ed turned to Judy in the dark and kissed her, a brazen move for a first date in 1956.

"I can't believe it to this day," he says. Just as surprising, she kissed him back.

On their second date, in a back seat at a drive-in, they kissed so much that the front-seat couple fled the car. When they were alone, he told her he loved her. "Because I felt it," he says. Judy said nothing. Ed repeated himself. Still nothing. He tried not to worry.

On their third date, a chilly fall night, she snuggled beside him and whispered "I love you" into his ear.

From then on they were Ed and Judy, Judy and Ed.

For me, it was love at first sight. Like a bolt of lightning! You didn't believe me in the beginning. But I persisted, and eventually you returned my love. Then, adults said we were too young to know what real love was. That angered us. Now I have to admit that in one sense they were right. Because our love has grown so tremendously through the years, swelling and bursting forth in marvelous and complicated ways. Our love then . . . as true and real as it was . . . holds no measure to today's or tomorrow's, or our thousands of tomorrows. (1993)

After graduation he went into the Coast Guard. She wrote him every day for three years. He wrote her back almost as often. He still has the letters, somewhere, and he's a little nervous about

their children finding them. "Let's just say there was a lot of wishful thinking in those letters," he says.

He'd come home in his uniform and meet her at school. One night over dinner, he asked her to marry him, and, believing he did not deserve her, said, "Please."

Their daughter Janet was born 10 months after the wedding.

They moved to Gainesville in 1962 so he could attend the University of Florida. He majored in journalism but spent most of his time at the student newspaper, the *Florida Alligator.* He worked his way from reporter to executive editor. He earned next to nothing and sold his blood for extra money. Judy worked, but he couldn't stand to see her go without, so he quit school to work at the *Alligator* full time.

The newspaper, which eventually moved off campus and became the *Independent Florida Alligator,* became his second great love. He has never left it.

Now he is its general manager, with a cluttered little office upstairs. Students run the paper downstairs. He is also the publisher of the High Springs Herald, a community paper 25 miles north.

In 1972, when he was assistant general manager, the *Alligator* started a Valentine's Day tradition called Love Lines. They are mostly silly messages between infatuated classmates, loaded with lust and sickening nicknames. Last year, J-Dogg wrote to H-Money and a Mongolian Horse Princess wrote to her hairy barbarian.

Somewhere in that first edition was the first of Ed's public letters to Judy. Just 21 words.

"JUDY, my love and best friend. Our love is earth and air and FIRE . . . and wonderfully crystal-caved. Your husband . . . Always, Ed."

They'd settled into a comfortable life by then. She worked for the school system. Janet was 10 and their son Chris was 3. Ed still felt he didn't deserve Judy, but she built his confidence by being steady, never complaining about the things they could not afford.

They had a little starter house in a shady neighborhood. He built a tree house in the live oak in the back yard. They liked to feed the birds out there. They made dinners for friends and worked on a screenplay together on Sunday mornings. The Love Lines, just a couple of sentences each, became their yearly gift to each other.

In 1980, he appealed to her affection for Kermit the Frog: *"You are my rainbow connection! I'm glad you love green because I'm weird!"*

And she wrote back: *"Ed, You put flowers in my life just by being there."*

When the newspaper came out, he'd grab a copy, read her letter first, then check his for typos. He'd cut it out and paste it on a piece of paper and try to tape it to her door at work when she was out.

Often Ed would come home and show the letters to Chris, who loved to read them but couldn't do it in front of his dad. He'd take them off somewhere by himself. Even the embarrassing ones made him happy.

He noticed the way his parents looked at each other. Their eyes would lock across the room and his heart would jump. Then he'd feel a little sad, because he knew by then how rare that was.

Upon reading this, the sophisticated may chuckle, or even sneer, at what I have said. But that's okay. A thousand, thousand years from now when their cynicism is less than dust, our union will still be joyously winging through the time and space of endless love. (1991)

Something must have happened in 1991, but if so, no one can remember what it was.

When Ed sat down at the computer to write his annual Love Line, something took hold of him.

"Surely no others have ever known anything like the love and intimacy we have shared for more than three decades," he wrote. "We enjoy the passion and freshness of romance. But also we have the rich comfort and wonderful warmth of our true friendship."

For 266 words, he described the way their hands unconsciously slipped together when they walked, how he could read her mind in a glance, the bond they felt after 30 years of births and deaths and joy and sorrow. And her: her voice, her spirit, her laugh, on and on.

He doesn't remember how she reacted, except that she thanked him, as always. She usually called him from her office and cooed with gratitude.

He remembers that Trish Carey, the *Alligator*'s assistant general manager, asked him about his love letter in advance the next year. She told him the people in production were asking for it. He hadn't busted deadline yet, as he was inclined to do. They just wanted to read it.

That year, he wrote more than 300 words: "Over decades the fabric of our lives has been woven one small thread at a time. Those strands of shared moments, anguished or ecstatic, quiet or electric, were interlaced in such a way that nothing can cut, tear or rip apart."

By then they were grandparents. He'd grown out his beard, twisted and waxed his mustache into curls. She had the same laugh she had when they met. They looked a little like Santa and Mrs. Claus. Everywhere they went, they stood close and held hands, and people noticed something about them.

The letters became legend at the little newspaper. Whoever had the job of guiding them to publication without errors sweated over the task. It was Trish Carey's job for several years. "I was so nervous," she said. And she couldn't help but think, as countless readers no doubt did, that if her husband ever wrote her something so beautiful she'd fall over dead.

Janet wrote Love Lines to her husband when they dated. Chris never had the

Judy wrote Ed every year, and you have to mention that, but it would have been a distracting mistake to quote her letters too many times. You have to make choices and keep the story line simple.

I had lots of material from Ed and Judy's kids, but it would be a mistake to quote them talking about their parents much. It would interrupt the flow of the story. Picture a jarring quote from Chris here.

Yes, Ed's writing is over the top. "Joyously winging through the time and space of endless love?" That's what's so great about it. If he were a polished, perfect writer, it would just be a story about a good writer, and so what? Ed is self-conscious about his writing. I told him the story was not about his talent or lack of it, but about an ordinary guy trying to elevate himself for his girl. He got that.

Ed's writing is such an important part of the story that it was critical I interview him about it. I put every letter in front of him and asked what he remembered about writing it. I learned how his mind works. I saw him wrestle with the rational and irrational. With love and death. That stuff appears near the beginning and end of the story.

I noticed it about them, because I met them one time, at a wedding. I talked to Judy for about five minutes. I didn't know it was an interview.

nerve. He was waiting for a girl who inspired him the way his mom inspired his dad.

Ed doesn't know how many people noticed. But from time to time he'd hear that, for people he didn't even know, the letters had become annual evidence of what is possible.

I have heard your heart. For more than 40 years, its rhythm beneath my cheek has been soft, murmured comfort. . . . Your heart surges with the strength of virtue. It has thundered with our passion. Your heart has soared with joy and laughter, and has been shattered in sorrow. . . . Recently, my darling, you have been ill and doctors say your heart is physically weak. I am greatly afraid. But as I sat silently by your hospital bed, within mine your silken hand pulsed its familiar, sweet whispers . . . forever . . . together . . . forever . . . together . . . forever . . . together. (1997)

She had heart trouble in 1997. He imagined losing her, and wrote that he felt as if he were inside a dark cave, in a darkness so intense his eyes strained until they hurt.

But she recovered and he felt safe again. His heart was more troublesome than hers. Sometimes he'd try to talk to her about what she would do after he died. She never wanted to discuss it. In March 2004, driving back from the annual *Alligator* picnic, he brought up the subject again. She brushed him off.

"Babe," she said, "we're going to go together."

The next morning, Sunday, she slept late. He made her coffee as always – with cream, two sugars – and took it to her in bed, but could not wake her.

He doesn't know how long he stayed with her, but he knows he screamed. It was 9:45 a.m.

Love through a mirror darkly, through a crystal clearly, through a prism brightly. The brilliance that is your beauty faints the sky's silvered stepping stones. Your hair is rippled light and your aroma is sunned roses. To hold you is to meld with the passion of the sun and the gentleness of the moon. . . . Our love has viewed more than fifteen thousand sunrises and one less sunset. You are the first flush of the new horizon and the dazzling of each day's last flash. There will never be a setting of our love. You are my fixed star. You guide my way. (1999)

He is in that cave he imagined eight years ago.

"A hole in the universe," he says.

He reads, but his mind drifts. He listens to music, but it doesn't sound the same. He gets up and puts on a suit and goes to work at the newspaper, but even that is a duller joy.

He is surrounded by her face in photographs, but he doesn't have to look at them. He doesn't have to think of her to see her. She's just with him in a way he can't explain.

She's nursing a child. She's teasing him after one of his smarty-pants jokes. She's leaning into him, and her scent is like the soft wrinkles of a baby's neck. She's in his arms in a dark school gym, they're swaying to the Platters, he's out of step and she's whispering, "Slow down, slow down."

People tell him he'll feel better. He doesn't believe that. He doesn't even want it.

It has been almost a year. "It gets harder," he says. "The longer she's gone . . . the longer she's gone."

She had retired from her job as an auditor for the school system so they could travel. They were finally going to sell their starter house. He won't do either without her. She deserves to be grieved.

He tends the flowers at her grave: pink roses, pansies, wild violets, creeping fig. He takes water there in his car when he's feeling well enough. Sometimes he sings. The song is called "Always."

People say he should move on, see Europe, publish his book, that she would want that. He believes she would.

Margin notes:

I would be one of those people.

Even before I interviewed him, I knew this section of the letter about her heart would go with the scene that follows.

Look for ways to use dialogue when you can. It lets you hear Judy's voice. Don't you love that she calls him "babe?"

I wanted the reader to find out about her death the way Ed did. That's why that moment doesn't come until now. And when it does come, I felt like the man ought to have some privacy. The time ties back into the beginning of the story where we see the clock stopped on the wall.

I like the connection between her being his fixed star and him being lost.

I asked him these questions that first day in his office. He was surrounded by her pictures. In one she was 15, in another she had gray hair. I asked how she looked when he remembered her. Maybe the best question I asked.

I drove him to Judy's grave. We spent about an hour there. I asked what he'd be doing if I weren't there, and he told me he sings to her. He sang some of the lyrics to "Always."

I got this happy feeling when he said this. Didn't they read the valentines? It validated my concept of the story. I thought, OK, these letters meant something. They mattered and they still matter. This story was not a stupid idea.

But she was half of every plan he ever made. He wonders, when people say these things, didn't they read the valentines?

I may feebly string words together as an attempt to translate all that you are . . . and all that you mean to me. But no matter what I write . . . you are the true author. It is only because of the wonder of your being that our love exists. (1994)

He is still at his keyboard, her letter before him. Writing it is harder than it has ever been. He types with her wedding ring on his pinky, next to his. The rings are inscribed "Always." He keeps lifting his glasses so he can wipe his eyes.

He didn't want me to come to the house. But Ed's in the newspaper business, so he knew we wanted to see him really writing the letter, not faking writing the letter. And he knew we wanted to come when he'd naturally be doing it. We don't ever fake stuff or set up stuff.

Maybe it's not even logical for him to write it if she can't read it. But it's Valentine's Day, so how can he not? He feels compelled to remind people who she was, what she meant.

"I just wish with all my heart I could truly express it," he says. "If I was able to write a whole book, I couldn't do it."

He confronts the hole in the room in every line. He feels left behind.

I wrote a lot of this story as if I was inside Ed's head. I felt confident doing that because I was constantly asking him what he was thinking, and because everything I used came straight out of his mouth or went straight into his letter.

He is recovering from heart surgery. He can't help but wonder why she died so unexpectedly while he and his rickety heart keep living. Death is no more easily understood than love.

Did he lose her because he was too proud? Did he put her before God?

He doesn't believe those things. But he thinks them. He believes he lost her to a virus that weakened her heart, and nothing more.

The letter is too stiff. He has been redundant. The words should be stronger. It should be lyrical and emotional and magnificent and worthy of her. He'll keep trying. All he has is time.

He fantasized once that he might write the Great American Novel or win the Pulitzer Prize.

But his greatest efforts have gone into these little tributes, paid for by the letter. She is his richest material. She is epic.

He is just a rational man, with a patched heart, writing a letter about things that are not rational.

He gets to the bottom and he signs it the usual way.

Always.

Sometimes he thinks it turned out not to be. In another way, it is the truest thing he ever wrote.

When I die, I don't care what may be carved on my tombstone. Or what is said over me. Or even how I am remembered. Except. Except I hope someone of those gathered may turn to another and softly whisper something like, "You know . . . Judy and Ed. Now that was a great love story!" (1993)

I heard at a workshop that the material you use in a story usually comes from the back of the notebook. That was true here. When we arrived, Ed had already started the letter. He finished it as Cherie Diez took photos and I scribbled notes in the corner. Periodically, I'd look over his shoulder to see if he was struggling. I wouldn't have done that if I thought it would interrupt him, but he was lost in the letter and seemed to have forgotten we were there. We noticed the clock stopped on the wall – that's in the top of the story. In the letter he wrote that he felt like she might lay her hand on his shoulder any minute. That's in the top of the story too. Ed talked a little — he asked out loud if he lost her because he put her before God — but for the most part the room was uncomfortably quiet. I noticed every sound. The air conditioner, ticking clock, his fingers on the keys.

It was thoughtful of Ed to write me such a nice ending. But he's been working on this story for 48 years, so he had time to get it right.

This was published with the story:

Here is one of our favorite letters from Ed to Judy. It is from 1996.

JUDY,

How is it our love lives so? It is the fragile murmur of memories, the delicate whisper of just now. So to abbreviate our love to words of explanation, even most tender, would seemingly shred it by that fashion. If we split its nucleus, or magnified it through a lens, could it bring us closer to an answer? God forbid that it could.

Yes, it is true our love could stand the dissection. For the paradox is, that for all its sweet tenderness, our love has the strength of the winds of stars! But to reduce it to the symmetry of a mere explanation, to bring it down to the level of reason, would be a manner of its corrupting. Our love is far beyond explanation. It is not reasonable that you are the embodiment of all that is good and sweet and beautiful. Yet you are. It is not reasonable that you should love me. Yet you do. The human comedy is much better for the wise use of rationality. But our love? Although it encompasses reason, it has evolved to a much higher plane beyond logic, to that of faith and tender passion. Come closer, my darling, and let me explain in another way.

Always,
Ed

There's no rule that requires every story to be structured in a linear sequence of paragraphs. Sometimes form drives content. The design of a page — like this Valentine's Day layout — can determine how the story is presented. Free-form, illustration-intense pages are often designed first, before the text is written. The reporter then writes to fit, often squeezing in words line by line.

THE PLAIN DEALER

The perfect kiss

All hands on deck

Lips get all the credit, but never underestimate the importance of engaging the hands while the lips sing their sweet song. As **Auguste Rodin's lovers** helpfully demonstrate, winding limbs around one another can be so much fun you completely forget to cover up for your audience.

Baby love

Few things in life feel better than planting a soft kiss on the head of a **newborn**. Try it. It'll change your life.

For you, my sweet

Alone on Valentine's Day? The perfect kiss might be as close as your nearest drugstore, on sale in 1-pound bags. **Chocolate** isn't love, but it's a darned fine substitute when your pickings are slim.

Hair and tear

Ashton Kutcher's **razor stubble** probably looks better than it feels after 15 minutes of necking. Then again, maybe Demi Moore likes the burn. As the master chief told her in "G.I. Jane," "the best thing about pain is it lets you know you aren't dead yet." Well, yeah, or the guy can shave.

Oh! You again!

Second only to first kisses for relieving pent-up desire, the **welcome-home kiss** is reason enough to travel more often.

no.1

Auspicious debuts

Whether it happens by the swing set in second grade or in the moment you know you've met your One True Love, **first kisses** are the best. Choirs of angels have been known to hum a little Handel to celebrate the end of all that anticipation.

Make your maw meticulous

Few lovers ever wished their partners would smoke more cigarettes, eat more hot dogs or gargle with garlic. Perfect kisses thrive in fresh, clean environments. Care for a **Tic Tac**?

BY KAREN SANDSTROM

Consider three smoochable truths. Nothing beats a first kiss. Practicing on a pillow does nothing to prepare a novice for reality. And, according to kissing expert Michael Christian, 96 percent of women "rave" about neck kisses.

That about exhausts the list of universal kissing laws. But with the help of Christian, author of "The Art of Kissing," and another expert or two, we've assembled some thoughts about the who, what, when, where and how of the perfect kiss. In honor of the season, we decided to share them with you.

Kiss-kiss. Happy Valentine's Day.

Dangerous liaisons

Some folks are just too dangerous to kiss. **Poison Ivy** from "Batman," for instance. Certain members of organized-crime families of Sicilian descent for another. Your neighbor's wife. Must we go on?

If we wanted 5 pounds of tongue, we'd go to the deli counter

The success of a **French kiss**, like the success of French cuisine, depends on understanding the difference between just enough and way too much. If your amorous advances inspire pursed lips, your technique might feel too much like a tonsillectomy. Breathe, man, breathe!

Rim shots

Love isn't always blind, but it's often myopic. A clash of **eyeglasses** during a kiss can be as startling as a cymbal crash. So shed the specs, close your eyes and see the world with your lips. It's better than Lasik surgery.

Kissable quote

"I believe in the sweet spot, soft-core pornography, opening your presents Christmas morning rather than Christmas Eve, and I believe in long, slow, deep, soft, wet kisses that last three days."

— Kevin Costner as Crash Davis in **"Bull Durham"** (1988).

Three great cinema smackers

Vivien Leigh and Clark Gable in the parlor in "Gone With the Wind"; Burt Lancaster and Deborah Kerr by crashing waves in **"From Here to Eternity"**; James Stewart and Donna Reed while sharing a telephone receiver in "It's a Wonderful Life."

ALL THIS ICE, AND THE CAPTAIN IS HOT
By Judd Slivka
Seattle Post-Intelligencer — Jan. 4, 2000

◄ MORE ON **WRITING PROFILES** ON PAGE **120**

Reporter Judd Slivka spent two weeks aboard a Coast Guard icebreaker, filing a story a day as part of a series titled "From the End of the Earth."

"Looking back," he recalls, "I remember not really wanting to write this story at first. We were so caught up in the day-to-day of the other stories we were doing that writing a short profile didn't appeal to me. At the time, I was worried that either we'd be seen as pandering or the captain was going to be so pissed at me that he'd leave me on an ice floe. The photographer convinced me to do it by saying, 'I've got 50 really good pictures of him. Write something.'"

SLIVKA'S COMMENTARY:

I lucked out standing on the bridge talking to Julich one day in late December. We were just chatting and he was the nicest guy in the world and then he sensed something wrong and it was like talking to a different guy.

This is one of my favorite grafs that I wrote from that trip. It's probably the best-reported 83 words I've ever written. There's a lot of depth here that came from spending time with the captain over the previous few weeks.

I love cause-and-effect pairings. This was one. And it gives me the chance to transition into the nut graf.

This graf and the previous two are my nut grafs, but there's really two sentences that matter. The one that defines his roles and the "nothing more like God" line. I could have just used those two lines and been fine.

Now we're leaving the moment, back to an earlier incident. The scene on the bridge is your introduction to Terry Julich. Now here's the background.

ABOARD USCGC POLAR STAR — So here is the captain on the bridge. His bridge, and he is angry. Not screaming-angry. He is blue-eye-glaring, jaw-tightening, prominent-cheekbones angry.

But he is the captain, he sets the tone, and this day as the Polar Star crunches through a field of ice that it shouldn't be in, the captain is doing what test pilots aim for in emergencies, "maintaining an even strain."

So Capt. Terry Julich politely excuses himself from the conversation he's in after a few minutes of the icebreaker's hull grinding against the ice. And with the easy walk of someone at sea the better part of the past 20 years, goes over to the center control console, picks up the phone and begins to talk to the officers driving the ship from far above in the aloft conn, officers who have put the ship into the ice it shouldn't be in.

But he speaks in low and quiet tones, so that no one else will hear him. The problem should not happen again.

That much is clear. He is the captain. This is his ship.

The captain of any military ship has plenty of roles: Father. Warden. Manager. Figurehead. Safety observer. The man who eats alone.

Commander.

The captain sets the tone for the ship and its company. There is nothing more like God on Earth than a captain at sea, and Julich knows this, which is why he speaks in low tones when the news is bad.

He does not always speak in low tones; the news is usually not bad.

In his at-sea office, he laughs out loud, deliriously and deliciously, when talking about his three children back on Mercer Island, and he points out the artwork they've given him, the photo collages they've made.

The artwork is standard-kid, something on construction paper that should look like a house, a car, a cow, a bunny, a daddy, but looks more like a bunch of colored lines.

He loves them. He loves the collage, with pictures of him and his wife and his children at different ages. He loves the videotapes his wife gave him of his children's birthday parties, and he pops them into his VCR at night when the ship's movie selection offers no joy.

He laughs – alone – in his stateroom.

His wife and children hung the artwork themselves while the ship was still in Seattle. They came into his cabin and chose the wall space, the tape, the whole bit.

He has three children – Jake, 4, Juliana, 7, and Jenna, 8 – and a wife who, when she went on vacation in Vermont, went to the local public library so she could still e-mail her husband at sea.

He has been on this ship before, two tours, and knows it well. He has been in the ice before — this trip makes four times he has sailed through Antarctica's Ross Sea. But this is his first cruise commanding the Polar Star, and it's an adjustment for everyone, captain and crew.

But the ship still sails, and Julich has been on the bridge during most of the heavy ice-breaking, observing what his officers are doing in the aloft conn, because when it comes down to it, the officer who sets the tone is the officer who is responsible if the ship sinks into a freezing sea.

Life goes on. He finishes his instructive phone call to the officer in aloft conn, the blue eyes stop glaring, the jaw loosens up, the cheekbones retreat. He walks back to his chair on the starboard side of the bridge, sits back and politely resumes the conversation.

He was telling a story, wasn't he? It was about his kids, God bless them.

Would you like to see the video?

Here, I'm basically drawing a not-so-subtle contrast between "icy commander" and "family guy." The details are what stood out after several conversations in his cabin. I don't think I opened my notebook for this part.

This story lacks quotes. It's by design. I didn't want Julich talking about himself or his officers talking about him. The story was strictly an observational sketch. Besides, the quotes I had sucked.

I love the detail about his wife. It speaks to love, and I'm a big fan of love. Julich's voice softened whenever he talked about his wife, but that's the sort of detail that you can't demonstrate very well in print. So I chose to write it from his wife's perspective.

I love present tense. I think it moves the story along a lot faster; it makes readers feel like they're there.

Back to the original scene. I call it a "tie-back," and at times I've done them so much they're clichéd. But in a profile, I like the idea of taking the reader back to where we started.

I'm showing how Terry Julich talks. I wanted to end on something that was totally his personality.

THE GOOD DOCTOR

Orthopedist James Andrews circulates among the stars but he always keeps his feet on the ground

By Manish Mehta

The Star-Ledger — Feb. 29, 2004

◀ MORE ON **WRITING PROFILES** ON PAGE **120**

"Dr. James Andrews is the most compelling figure I've ever covered," recalls Manish Mehta, sports enterprise reporter for the Newark (N.J.) Star-Ledger. "His name is everywhere, popping up in newspapers across the country nearly every day. In fact, a simple Google search of 'Dr. James Andrews' yields 4.39 million hits.

"Yet few people knew much about the man beyond the fact he was the most respected sports doctor in the country. Whenever a star pitcher or quarterback was injured, he would visit Dr. Andrews.

"I was intrigued by the man, and fortunate enough to have a close friend who had a fellowship with Dr. Andrews at his office in Birmingham, Ala. I pitched the story idea to my editor, who immediately loved it. We were interested in extracting every bit of detail about this man. How did he become this almost mythical figure in the world of sports medicine, this guru that every athlete NEEDED to see if he were injured?

"After my friend put in a good word for me and I was granted permission by Dr. Andrews' personal public relations guy, I flew to Birmingham for a few days. Before I knew it, I was chatting with Andrews for hours about everything under the sun. I witnessed a few surgeries and was invited to see his home. I was fortunate enough to fly to Auburn with the doctor, where I got more insight into his colorful and charming personality, and even shared a burger with him.

"It was the most memorable three days of my career."

MEHTA'S COMMENTARY:

It was a no-brainer to open the story with this amusing anecdote. It's fun. It's different. It grabs your attention and draws you into the story. Thank goodness all of us were wearing our seat belts!

BIRMINGHAM, Ala. — The old man behind the wheel was raving about a burger joint down the road when he nearly collided with a car in the parking lot.

"Lord have mercy!" he whooped, raking his fingers through a forest of silver hair. "That was a close one!"

He pushed down on the gas, jolting the passenger in the back seat, as a downpour suddenly broke over them. The old man, starving now, raced around the bend and pulled up in front of the neon lights.

"Y'all jump out . . . and I'll park."

Three men piled out and skipped over puddles before entering the restaurant. Moments later James Andrews pulled up a chair, his lavender sports coat and silk tie sprinkled by raindrops, ready to scarf down dinner.

The nut graf. Explain who Andrews is and why we're writing about him before getting back to the dinner story.

Dr. Andrews has treated nearly every marquee athlete of this generation and the procedures he has perfected have forever changed professional sports.

None of that mattered now.

Andrews' belly was screaming for food.

I squeezed plenty of detail into this attribution to highlight how Andrews treats all members of the community, not just athletes. I also needed to clarify that the opening scene took place at Auburn, not his home base of Birmingham.

"We used to go to Burger King," he said shortly after treating athletes, senior citizens and teachers at the new sports medicine rehabilitation complex at Auburn University, some 110 miles from his base of operation in Birmingham. "But I like this place a lot more."

Cheeburger Cheeburger lives by the motto Big Is Better. Its walls are plastered with Polaroids of customers who have pol-

ished off cantaloupe-sized mounds of beef.

There is no such snapshot of Andrews.

Still, coeds at a nearby table gawked for several minutes at the sparkling championship ring wrapped around his finger.

"Who is that guy?" a girl whispered. "I think he played in the Super Bowl or something . . . didn't he?"

Andrews was too busy lifting his burger from a wicker basket to notice. He reached for the community pool of fries and drained a Coke bottle before unraveling his 61-year-old body.

"Let's go, men," he announced after the last bite, dropping a folded $20 bill on the table for the server.

This girl was sitting at the adjacent table with friends. She was only a few feet away, but Andrews was so hungry and focused on scarfing down his food that he didn't hear her!

I included the exact amount of the tip to foreshadow his generosity in his professional life.

TIME FOR EVERYONE

TJD (Top Jock Doc) to some, Sawbones to others, this paunchy man with sleepy eyes has repaired the admired, the adored and the ignored. He has crossed paths with bonus babies, movie stars and foreign dignitaries.

He has mended injured elbows, shoulders, hips, knees and fractured spirits. And never once has he promised a miracle. "In all the years I've gone to Dr. Andrews, he's never lied to me," said Charles Barkley, whose relationship with the doctor started during the former basketball star's days at Auburn. "He always gave me confidence to come back stronger than before."

Michael Jordan, Jack Nicklaus, Derek Jeter and Bo Jackson were patients. So were

I transitioned away from the opening scene because I thought it was necessary to blend in some of Andrews' credentials at this point. I wanted to give the reader a better idea of just who this man was. Although I don't have a universal set of guidelines I follow, I usually make a rough outline before I write to give me direction as I piece together the details of the story.

the San Diego Chicken, Jane Fonda, Hulk Hogan and members of the Saudi royal family.

Twenty years after hobbling into Andrews' office, Nicklaus still vividly recalls the morning Andrews changed his life.

"It was Election Day," the golf legend said. "Jim operated on my knee. And I came home and voted that afternoon."

To become one of the most important men in all of sports and medicine, Andrews worked under Jack Hughston, widely considered the father of sports medicine, in Columbus, Ga., for 13 years. From there, Andrews moved to Birmingham in 1986, where he co-founded the Alabama Sports Medicine and Orthopaedic Center (ASMOC) and the nonprofit American Sports Medicine Institute (ASMI) at the HealthSouth Medical Center in Birmingham.

"I'm lucky our lives intersected," said Roger Clemens, who went to Andrews for arthroscopic shoulder surgery in 1985. "Any time I see guys upset or worried about their future because of an injury, I tell them that before you do a thing, you need to go see this man."

Clemens' ensuing Hall of Fame career enhanced Andrews' reputation to the point where he ultimately became the most sought-after surgeon in the sports world.

Today, Andrews sees about 60 patients every Monday and Wednesday, bounding from room to room, examining wounded joints. He also travels to Auburn every other Wednesday night as part of an outreach program for the townsfolk.

On Tuesdays and Thursdays, he slips into knee-high white rubber boots, blue scrubs and a matching mask to perform as many as 20 surgeries a day — including the ulnar collateral ligament (UCL) reconstruction, or Tommy John surgery, for pitchers with ailing elbows.

If that's not enough, he also drives 60 miles to Tuscaloosa to tend to athletes at the Alabama rehab clinic on Tuesday nights.

AT THEIR CALL

The red minivan rolled into Auburn

Opelika Airport at 8:16 p.m. after dinner at Cheeburger Cheeburger. Four men hopped out and cut across the open field.

"It's as cold as a devil tonight," Andrews said in a soft Southern drawl, boarding the cramped, six-seat company plane.

His private jet — a refurbished Falcon 10 with two TVs, DVD player and coffee maker — was on the fritz. He sunk into the seat, flipped on the light switch, and pulled out his cell phone.

"It's a constant battle trying to keep up with all the calls," said Andrews, who permanently keeps his phone on vibrate.

Physicians and patients, some of whom he doesn't even know, will ask for his opinion on everything from a bum shoulder to a trick knee. He returns every call.

"I'd say I get about 50 calls a day on this cell phone. Well, maybe not 50 . . . but it sure seems like 50." He checked his messages before reaching into a leather satchel that serves as his roving office to scan some paperwork before takeoff.

"I get tired just watching him sometimes," said Chuck Bowie, Andrews' personal pilot who spent nearly 150 hours in the air with him last year traveling to college and pro football games.

The flight back to Birmingham will take 25 minutes — enough time for Andrews to unwind and leaf through the neatly folded copies of the Wall Street Journal and USA Today beside him. After a few minutes of silence, however, he again springs to life.

"Did I tell you about that celebrity quail hunting trip I'm taking this weekend down in Texas?" he asked the man sitting across from him. "It's going to be a good time. You ever been quail hunting?"

Andrews passed the man a packet with a list of items up for silent auction: A Bob Knight autographed basketball. A "Men of Dallas" poster signed by Larry Hagman. Four episodes of "SHAZAAM!" on VHS.

"They got some pretty good stuff," Andrews said.

The two-day trip would be a break from the wave of consultations and surgeries. "The last time Dad took a vacation and tried to relax," said Andrews' daughter, Amber, "he got sick."

Reaching these high-profile athletes took a few days, but it was well worth the effort. I contacted Barkley through his employer (TNT). Andrews' personal PR contact put me in touch with Nicklaus. I reached Roger Clemens through his team's media relations department. When I received a call from Clemens, I could barely hear him since so many people were screaming in the background. Clemens was sitting in the bleachers at his son's baseball game, eager to talk about Andrews. For each of the conversations, I learned how much of an impact Andrews truly had on their lives, not just their careers.

Not many people can keep such a hectic schedule, let alone 61-year-olds.

Andrews gave me all the specifics on his training in Georgia, the number of surgeries he performs weekly, the trips to Tuscaloosa. I had the good fortune of watching him slip into those rubber boots and perform the operations from the viewing room at the hospital.

Choosing to go back to the scene after dinner just made sense to me. Andrews' colorful personality shines through on the plane ride home. Again, we see the incredible amount of responsibility he carries each day.

I try to be as unobtrusive as possible when I'm reporting. I was sitting on the plane having a conversation with Andrews. I'm never "interviewing" a subject. I'm chatting with them, breaking down the barriers, making them feel as comfortable with me as possible. I've found that people are much less likely to be themselves if you're constantly sticking a tape recorder in their face. I carry a slender notepad and jot things down here and there. Very informal. People tend to say great stuff in settings like cars or airplanes.

I couldn't resist this bit of irony.

WHERE IT ALL BEGAN

In a long piece like this, it's always a good idea to splash in the back story. Andrews' childhood had never been written about before in detail.

By the turn of the 20th century, Jim Nolen owned cotton fields and oil wells throughout Northern Louisiana, even though his formal education ended with the first grade.

Nolen, whose wife later taught him how to read and write, became a makeshift medicine man along the countryside. He concocted homemade remedies — oils, potions, ointments — for anybody who needed care.

When his daughter, Mozelle, gave birth to a baby boy, he knew his grandson's career path: "You're going to be my doctor one day," Nolen, known as Grandy to the family, would say as he rocked the little boy to sleep.

Jimmy Andrews grew up with his grandparents on the outskirts of Homer, La., 50 miles northeast of Shreveport. When Andrews' father, Rheuben, returned from World War II, the family moved into a three-bedroom brick house and opened a dry-cleaning store. Jimmy doubled as a delivery boy and steam presser in the sweltering shop.

"That's where I was encouraged to get a good education, working in that laundry," he said with a smile.

Andrews volunteered these childhood stories, but I got wind of his wild college days from his daughters. He confirmed all of it with a hearty laugh when I asked him about it later.

Andrews, an Eagle Scout, spent hours building model airplanes and soapbox cars. He also had a penchant for playing Tarzan, using a bamboo rod to leap over a fishing pole nailed to two trees in the back yard. The lanky teenager played football, baseball, basketball and track before accepting a scholarship to pole vault at Louisiana State University. Andrews, a Kappa Alpha man, always kept busy.

When he wasn't winning the Southeastern Conference pole-vaulting championship, he was riding a horse through the college library to deliver invitations to a fraternity formal.

The wild and crazy side of Andrews that most people never knew he had.

"If you're not having fun, you might as well do something different," Andrews said. "Sometimes, I had too much fun."

One night, long after finishing medical school, Andrews broke his hand at a local watering hole.

"I think he operated on his own hand… somehow," his oldest daughter, Amanda, said. (Another physician set the cast, but Andrews removed the pins himself several weeks later when others were too scared to do so.)

There was also the day when Andrews' love for the open road landed his high-priced Ferrari in a nearby ditch.

"My wife said I couldn't drive any more red or yellow cars," Andrews said with a wink. "She wouldn't put up with all that nonsense."

Andrews now drives a silver Aston Martin Vanquish.

Another example of Andrews' humor.

PASSION FOR SPORTS

Jenelle Andrews still laughs at the framed painting hanging in her husband's study. The doctor, outfitted in a navy-blue pinstriped suit, is sitting beside his grandson, Jamie. The young boy has a soft, innocent smile on his lips.

The one thing that separates good features from great ones is detail. The more detail you can infuse into your story, the livelier it will be. I was struck by all the memorabilia and photos at Andrews' home. I scribbled down everything I saw as I got the grand tour.

Both are gripping a tiny red race car. "I'm afraid Jamie's got the curse too," she said, shaking her head.

Andrews lives with his wife and two youngest daughters, Amber and Abby, in an extravagant Italian villa set off a quiet street a few minutes from downtown Birmingham. Memorabilia that tell of the doctor's life are sprinkled throughout the five-bedroom house.

A crisp, color photo of Andrews huddled with Jerry Pate, Emmitt Smith and Troy Aikman at a charity golf event rests under a glass case.

The Abracadabra Room — devoted to Andrews' passion for yacht racing — reveals his greatest conquest out at sea: a Blue Marlin that hangs over the doorway. The area also commemorates his role as co-chair of a syndicate that raced in the 2000 America's Cup in New Zealand.

"All of his boats are named Abracadabra," Jenelle Andrews said. "He's got this thing for A's if you hadn't noticed." Andrews has six children — three with his first wife and three with Jenelle — Andy, Amanda, Archie, Ashley, Amber and Abby. He also has two grandchildren named Allie and Jamie. Andrews, of course, calls his

Another one of Andrews' quirks that makes him such a compelling figure. His explanation as to why all his kids' names begin with 'A' is priceless.

grandson Ace.

"There are a lot of advantages to having your name start with "A,"" he said, his face widening to a grin. "The kids get their names called first. And at graduation, they go down the aisle first... so I can get up and go home."

The doctor rarely lounges at home, though.

When not treating patients, Andrews likely can be found at a high school sporting event, voicing his displeasure with referees. "That wasn't traveling! ... What are you looking at?"

"I just saw him at a basketball game last week," said Mountain Brook High School athletic director Terry Cooper. "He comes to different events all the time."

Andrews, who paces the sideline at Mountain Brook football games, has become the unofficial doctor for the school that Amber and Abby attend. He even operated twice on Amber to repair torn anterior cruciate ligaments - battle wounds from competitive cheerleading.

Somehow, Andrews always has tried to remain an integral part of his children's lives. He once showed up in dress shoes to work out with Amber, who was rehabbing her torn ACL, during a vacation in Panama City. He even lived through the humiliation of flopping face-first during a family bowling excursion.

And his son, Archie, 32, still remembers his father traveling across the Southeast for his football games.

"Every Friday night, he'd find the nearest airport, fly in, rent a car and drive as long as it took to watch me play high school football," Archie said. "That was real special for me."

EVERY MAN'S HERO

Mary Jane Robinson edged forward in her seat, slowly looked both ways, and raised her palms to the sky.

"I don't know where he could have gone," the nurse said.

"You can try his office," Pat Jones cut in, "but I doubt he's in there."

"I didn't even know he had an office," said Craig Rubenstein, a sports medicine

fellow training under Andrews. "I don't think he does either. There's not a lot of down time to hang out there."

Andrews' clinic — six exam rooms decorated with framed autographed pictures of former clients — is typically a whirlwind of activity, with nurses transporting charts and fellows chatting into mini-tape recorders. Andrews, an advocate of research and education in his field, has mentored nearly 200 doctors through the ASMI Sports Medicine Fellowship Program.

But it's deserted on surgery day.

Instead, the clan gathers in an area with views of all four operating rooms. Andrews often sneaks away between surgeries to check up on his patients without breakaway speed or multimillion dollar contracts.

Professional athletes make up 15 percent of his clientele.

"I can't say that I'm just going to take care of high-profile athletes," said Andrews, a member of the Alabama Sports Hall of Fame. "That's skipping over a bunch of people — the high school kids, the elderly — who are very important to me. I'll never let that happen."

Jones, Andrews' nurse for more than 20 years, has seen countless teenagers from poor, rural towns limp through the doors with no health insurance.

Andrews never turned them away.

"We have to take care of these kids," he would tell her. "The only way they're going to make it in this life is if they go to college. And the only way they can do that is by getting an athletic scholarship. They may never play pro ball, but that doesn't matter. College will give them a chance to lead productive lives."

So Andrews routinely scribbled NO CHARGE along the bottom of their charts.

"That's just something he does," Amanda Andrews said. "He doesn't ever talk about it."

Now, Andrews was threading through the halls once again en route to the physical therapy center on the first floor. He stopped short of the entrance, balled up his right fist, and gently tapped Mike Davis on

I can't stress enough how important it is to leave no stone unturned. Of course, we're confined by deadlines, but I recommend calling as many sources as possible. Old friends. Family. Coaches. Teachers. Anybody. You never know when you're going to uncover that one anecdote that's going to make your story sing. Having too much information is a good problem to have.

Shifting to this final scene at the office made perfect sense to me. This is where we see Andrews in action. In a long piece, it's beneficial to break the story into sections to inject new life into it. Readers get bored reading a 3,000-word story without a break. This technique allows for vignettes, or mini-stories, which gives readers a chance to view a subject through different lenses. Once again, splash as many details as possible into these re-created scenes. It adds color to your story.

Few people realize this. Andrews' national reputation as a doctor who solely deals with pro athletes couldn't be further from the truth.

A clear example of Andrews' selflessness and generosity.

the chest.

"You know, this man's a hero," Andrews said, pointing to Davis. "Y'all should really talk. I gotta check up on some people in here. Be right back."

Davis, a 63-year-old engineer, entrusted Andrews with his achy joints long ago.

"He scoped my knees when I was 46, and said he'd replace them when I was 60," Davis said. "When I turned 60, I came to replace my knees, and Dr. Andrews said, 'No.'

"I said, 'Wait a minute, you promised me.' So he said he'd do it only if I lost 40 pounds and put up three pints of blood. So six weeks later, I lost the weight and donated the blood ... and he replaced both knees at the same time. How about that?"

A few minutes later, Andrews swept out of the room.

A stranger standing nearby looked up at Davis and asked, "Is Dr. Andrews ever going to slow down?"

Davis casually wrapped his arm around the young man and began to chuckle.

"What do you think?"

This is a fitting end to the story. If you noticed, I never quoted anybody describing Andrews as a "great dad" or a "generous man" or a "tireless worker." I simply gave examples that allowed the reader to come to his own conclusion about the man.

This sidebar offered a quick way for readers to take a peek into Andrews' hectic schedule. We cobbled the details together for a typical day. (It was indeed one day, not a composite of several days.) When writing longer pieces, it's great to have extra "furniture" — charts, bio boxes, etc. — to enhance the overall presentation of the package.

A WORKDAY IN THE LIFE OF JAMES ANDREWS

6:32 a.m. – Rolls out of bed and hops into the shower for a quick rinse. "It's like Superman in a phone booth," a friend says. "He's in and out in a flash."

6:39 – Slips into slacks, a collared shirt and sports jacket.

6:41 – Pulls out of the circular driveway in his silver Aston Martin Vanquish and heads to work. He rolls into the parking lot 15 minutes later at the Alabama Sports Medicine and Orthopaedic Center on 13th street.

7:01 – TJD (Top Jock Doc, as he's known to his son Archie's friends) ambles into the locker room of the doctors' lounge. He changes into his uniform: blue scrubs, white rubber boots and a matching mask and cap.

7:05 – He grabs a cup of coffee and shovels down bacon, eggs and toast.

7:10 – Reviews his workload of 11 scheduled surgeries. "This is a pretty light day for him," nurse Pat Jones says.

7:20 – Starts seeing patients, hopping between four operating rooms.

8:14 – Downtime to return calls. Already there are three urgent messages pinned to a board in the viewing room.

9:21 – He readies for another wave of patients.

10:07 – John Iverson Jr., a 19-year-old pitcher for Arkansas Tech, is about to have Tommy John surgery and "get fixed." Andrews eases any concerns with his Southern charm.

10:46 – Repairs a torn rotator cuff on Steve Gardner, a 39-year-old dentist from nearby Huntsville, Ala. Gardner's father waits in the hallway. Jimmy Gardner visited Andrews 10 years ago after being kicked in the knee by a cow on his Mississippi farm. The doctor repaired his torn ACL. "Dr. Andrews treated me like I was Roger Clemens," he says.

11:48 – Speaks to Iverson's parents, John and Marsha, over the intercom system in the viewing room. The Iversons drove 120 miles from Meridian, Miss., to witness the surgery. John Iverson Sr. says "Dr. Andrews has helped keep our son's dream alive."

12:25 p.m. – Blazes through the halls en route to the physical therapy center. He's talking about a recent charity golf event where he played alongside Alice Cooper and Marshall Faulk.

12:36 – Heads back upstairs to the surgery room.

2:48 – The doctor is missing. "He'll show up . . . eventually," nurse Jones says.

2:49 – Andrews drowns his hamburger with ketchup in the doctors' lounge.

3:51 – Lounges on the diamond-shaped couch in the viewing room, legs crossed, returning messages and examining an MRI of an NFL Pro Bowl player. "He's the king of multitasking," says Craig Rubenstein, a fellow studying under Andrews.

4:35 – A day full of ACL, rotator cuff and elbow repairs winds down.

4:42 – Walks across the street in scrubs to the American Sports Medicine Institute looking for new Mets pitching coach Rick Peterson. (The Mets were testing pitchers in the biomechanics lab.)

4:46 – Talks baseball with reporters. "Let me show you around this place," he says.

5:05 – Heads back to ASMOC and changes out of his scrubs.

5:12 – Hops in a black suburban with Dr. Lyle Cain to visit patients 60 miles away at the University of Alabama.

6:05 – Arrives on campus and treats injured Alabama athletes for the next hour or so before heading back to Birmingham.

8:04 – Pulls up to his Italian-style villa in Mountain Brook. He's home.

8:10 – Throws down steak and potatoes for dinner with his wife, Jenelle.

9:10 – Catches up with his daughters, Amber and Abby.

10:24 – Heads upstairs to call it a day.

IF I DIE

By Diana K. Sugg

The Sun, Baltimore, Md.
Dec. 21–24, 2004

◀ MORE ON **WRITING ENTERPRISE
PROJECTS** ON PAGE **122**

To read this entire series, view
Monica Lopossay's photographs
and hear detailed comments on
the project, visit www.poynter.org
and search for *Angels and Ghosts*.

*Diana Sugg's medical reporting won a Pulitzer Prize in 2003. And "If I Die," her poignant look at critically ill
children written in 2004, provides a dramatic example of "immersion" reporting — and journalistic perseverance.*

*"It took me two years to get the hospital to agree to let me in with a family," Sugg recalls. "I started with just
permission for one conversation, and followed the family's lead. The boy's mother allowed me to stay, and I was
in the room just about every day for 25 days, usually from about 11 a.m. to 3 a.m. or later. I watched, I took
notes, I asked questions, I listened, I absorbed."*

*Sugg's efforts produced an achingly intimate profile of R.J. Voigt, a boy dying of a rare, aggressive cancer.
The story ran in four parts; Part Three is reprinted below.*

*"This was the hardest story of my career," Sugg says. "I spent many nights and weekends of my own time
reporting and writing the story. I had to face down critics who thought I was a vulture, or that the story would
be too depressing for people to read. Emotionally, it was tough ground, particularly because so much time with
the family in one room made me close to them. For months, I was haunted with nightmares. But all along, I
knew the story would help other children, and I was convinced the great cost was worth it. I still believe that."*

No one knew why the boy started shimmying, going for
the corners of his hospital bed. R.J. Voigt was suddenly restless, agitated. The 12-year-old kept calling out for
his mom. But he didn't seem to know what he wanted. She
kept asking the doctors, "Is this a sign?"

His mother, Michele Voigt, grew afraid to leave his room or
fall asleep for just a minute, for fear she would miss the
moment. She knew there were many ways R.J.'s life could end:
stroke, cardiac arrest, even the tumors eating away at the arteries in his neck. Already, there had been a few false alarms.

After three years of high-tech medicine, R.J. was spiraling
into his last days. It was a time when the scariest questions had
no answers, when every emotional detail would echo for a
family's lifetime.

But as countless families have experienced, there are no
guidelines for this final, often frantic stage.

In Room 817 at the Johns Hopkins Children's Center in
mid-July 2003, the questions were no longer about how to
treat the boy's aggressive cancer. Instead, oncologists, nurses, a
priest and a bereavement coordinator were doing their best to
help R.J. and his family prepare for death.

Michele Voigt was taking no chances. Tumors and treatment
had made it hard for him to talk, so she'd already set up two
ways for him to get her attention in the hospital. One was a rat-
tle they called the "Mommy Clicker." The other was a baby
monitor for when she was down the hall. Now, she decided
they needed another signal. She asked him to wave goodbye.

People want to believe that youth protects dying children,
that they don't grow anxious or have thoughts related to the
end. But those who work closely with children say those ideas
are misconceptions.

Even as the adults around R.J. were trying to catch up, he
had been quietly working out specifics of his death, and
beyond. In the spring, he asked for his own autopsy, befud-
dling his mother, who couldn't believe that it would come to
that. When he described the funeral he wanted, the level of
detail surprised even his oncologist. He asked to be buried on
Deal Island, next to his Great-uncle Wayne. For his funeral, he

preferred stuffed animals. Flowers, he said, were for girls.

He wondered what heaven was like, and whether his dogs,
Greedy and Muffin, who had both died, would be with him.
When the time had been right, in May, during his last short
stay at home in Pocomoke City, he asked the one person he
knew would tell him.

"Grandmom," he said, cuddling against her while watching
The Flintstones in Viva Rock Vegas, "what do you think?"

Carol Wisnom had sweated out a hard 61 years, but she'd
never seen anything like the cancer that had attacked her
grandson. She told him what she thought, that animals and
people have different heavens, but that if he asked real nice,
God might let him bring the dogs.

"OK, then," R.J. said, leaning his head on her. "I think that's
what I'll do. I'm tired." That afternoon, he developed a high
fever and was taken back by ambulance to Baltimore, never to
go home again.

A PROTOCOL FOR DYING

In a broader effort to change the culture around critically ill
children, the Johns Hopkins Children's Center and other children's hospitals have ventured into this difficult territory to
craft a better ending for the children and everyone around
them.

The Hopkins project, Harriet Lane Compassionate Care, is
working to make the death of children less frightening and
mysterious. Led by a physician and a nurse, the palliative care
group aims to help doctors and families to acknowledge earlier on in a child's illness that he might die — to try to make the
family's time together, and the child's death, reflect their values
and wishes.

R.J. Voigt was among the few dying children to get attention
in this little-explored arena.

In medicine, for all the scientific protocols that have been
mapped — plans of treatment that doctors follow for heart
attacks, even for strep throat — there is no plan for handling
the death of a child. Almost all the research and attention is
poured into saving lives.

Later, after their child dies, many parents say they didn't realize how close it was. For months, often years, they'd pushed for treatments. They'd seen their children live longer than anyone once thought they could. Now, they were shocked that no one could tell them what would happen next.

"Has no child died before?" one mother asked.

The children are uncertain, too, but it is often worse for them. Because of their age, they often have incomplete or inaccurate ideas about death. Doctors say many believe they did something to deserve it. Many want to know if it will hurt. And just as anyone would, these children often feel anxious, angry and lonely. But, sensing these questions would upset their parents and others, kids often won't say anything.

Just as their parents worry about them, the children are concerned about their parents. To protect them, the children often do not talk to their parents directly about their fears and doubts, said Myra Bluebond-Langner, a Rutgers University anthropologist who has studied chronically and terminally ill children and their families for more than 30 years. Hopkins staff members tell of a 9-year-old girl who, near death, called her younger siblings into her hospital room to tell them to take care of their mother.

WORRIES AND WISHES

In R.J.'s last weeks, nurse Laurie Rome noticed one day that he had been listening to his mother's phone conversation as she was saying she didn't know if she could go on if he died. After she left, Rome said, she gently asked him how he felt.

R.J. answered in his hoarse voice, tears streaming down his swollen face. He said he was scared for his mother.

"You know, we're not just taking care of you; we're going to take care of her, too," Rome told him. It was one of the few times he reached out to a nurse. He pulled her arm toward him and held onto it. He cried. The nurse cried, too.

They never knew which day would be his last. And even as R.J. was fading, the team and family around him were in a race. All along, the child life specialists, who provide psychological and emotional support to the children, had been trying to give R.J. the chance to do what he wanted.

For one 14-year-old boy, that meant driving his grandmother's red Mercedes-Benz. In another case, when it became known that all that a teenage boy wanted was to graduate from high school, they called his teachers, who rushed to the hospital. Then, just before withdrawing life-sustaining treatment, they held an impromptu ceremony, with cap and gown and "Pomp and Circumstance."

On R.J.'s list were things as simple as going to Ocean City and bowling. Neither was possible, because he could barely walk or move around. Another, seeing a movie that was only in theaters, first seemed out of the question. But that he wouldn't be alive by the time "Daddy Day Care" came out on video helped Hopkins staff persuade the studio to send a courier with a copy of the comedy.

They would have the movie for one night. But by the time the film arrived, R.J. was too sleepy. A nurse, not knowing the plans, had given him an anti-nausea drug that sedated him. They tried Pepsi, Ritalin, a cold cloth, moving him to a chair. R.J. even slid his fingers under his glasses, trying to hold his eyelids open.

They rewound "Daddy Day Care" seven times. Seven times, they restarted. But he never really got to see it. R.J., who rarely cried, let out a few tears. "Just forget it, Mom," he said, frustrated. "I can't watch it."

Because they knew that one of the biggest fears of children is being forgotten, Hopkins staff made sure R.J. got visits from people important to him, like his second-grade teacher, Jamey Landon, who inspired him to be a physician, and a family friend, Wayne Brisco.

Other visitors seemed intrusive, but turned out not to be. Among them were a former Mrs. Maryland and a troop of seventh- and eighth-grade girls.

That day, R.J. was too ill and hurting to even watch his cartoons. His head was covered in heat packs and cold packs, and all that could be seen of his face was one blue eye. The girls took turns getting close to him and giving him presents, but they weren't sure how to talk with him.

Later, he wrote a secret note to his mother, one she would cherish as a glimpse of him as a teenager. "When are the girls coming back?"

In addition to making those memories, the staff helped the children to create mementos.

During the last week of her life, one Howard County teenager, Kelly Petrlik, created a photo album of herself to leave behind for her family. She worked on it from her hospital bed at Hopkins after getting her sisters to sneak in pictures from home. The 16-year-old also left behind a journal for each of her parents, instructions for her gift for a sister's far-off wedding, and a request that at every family celebration they buy a special candle for her.

Nurses have long made white plaster molds of the children's hands as a keepsake for parents, but that used to be done after the child had died. During R.J.'s time in the hospital, with impetus from the palliative care staff, molds were made earlier. R.J. was able to help mix up the plaster from the kit and press his hand into it. He made one for his mother and signed the back. Later, Michele could put her hand in those cool spaces, and feel him.

In his own way, R.J. was getting ready. He designated certain belongings for his sister and cousins. Some children even write wills. Later, R.J. asked his mother for a pen and paper and laboriously scrawled out a thank-you note to his doctors, nurses, his mother and family. It was the morning after he'd first called out to his mother, "The angels are coming."

CHRISTMAS IN JULY

He told her there were six of them. One angel stayed with him all the time, sitting or lying in his bed. The other five came and went. They were big, and fit in the room like a puzzle. Neither male nor female, he told his mother, they were "beyond beautiful."

Not until he started talking often about the angels could Michele bring herself to do the hardest thing. For awhile, those working with the palliative care project had been encouraging her to celebrate R.J.'s favorite holiday right away.

So one night, before bed, Michele told R.J. if he wanted, he could have a Christmas in July, just in case he didn't make it to December. If he did make it, he'd get two Christmases. "Are we going to have a tree and everything?" he asked.

Over the next few days, an assistant at the nursing station brought in a string of colored lights and a small artificial tree for the corner. Michele made snowmen for the door and cut snowflakes and taped them on the room's one big window. The big, blue, inflatable alien, which R.J. had won at a festival his last time out of the hospital, got a Santa cap.

But Michele just couldn't bear to sit down with R.J. to make his wish list. Sitting in the hallway one night, she told R.J.'s pediatric oncologist, Dr. Meghan A. Higman, "I just don't feel like I'm a good mom anymore. I couldn't change anything for R.J."

Sometimes, she couldn't stand being in his room. So that night, after he had eaten, she left the baby monitor at the nurses' station, went downstairs, bought a fried fish sandwich and charged out of the hospital.

Michele popped into a cab. As it pulled away, she rolled the window down. It seemed like the first time she'd breathed all day. She ate some of her sandwich and stared bleary-eyed out at the muggy, gray Baltimore night. She let the wind blow through her hair. It was a short trip over to the Ronald McDonald House to check for mail, but enough time for her to gather her courage.

Back in R.J.'s room, she set up the laptop on his bed. Usually, she tapped out e-mails, sharing grief and advice with the makeshift sorority of mothers around the country who were sitting by the bedsides of their own dying children.

But this night, July 10, was about presents.

"OK, R.J.," she said, firing up the Toys "R" Us Web site. He'd been dozing, but he pepped up. He pulled his legs up to his chest, tapped his skinny finger on his forehead. His mother started making a neat list on a clipboard.

"Oooh, what about this?" she said, her voice brightening, but sounding as if it might break. "Finding Nemo for X Box?"

He seemed skeptical. He wasn't feeling good. Every few minutes, his eyelids drooped closed, or she needed to suction his mouth, and they had to stop. But he got into it, picking out an alien-mission video game, hockey games and action figures. Eventually, he took over the computer mouse.

Michele planned to celebrate Christmas on July 28, the day Dr. Higman returned from a trip. But in the next few days, R.J.'s condition would worsen.

That hot night, sitting side by side at the computer, would be their Christmas.

It ended with a dispute typical of any mother and her nearly adolescent son. He kept trying to click on one button on the Web site, while she called him off. "That's for 14-year-olds."

He persisted, and a moment later, she sighed. "OK," she said, "we'll go where you want to go."

THE BOTTOM BUNK

In their final days, young patients like R.J. often know what they want. Disproving a common misconception, the children are aware they will soon die and have specific concerns about how and where.

Dr. Nancy Hutton, a Hopkins pediatrician and co-director of the compassionate care program, was surprised when she interviewed children about what was important to them at the end of life. Delving into issues like resuscitation and treatment preferences, she discovered feelings that had been bottled up.

One adolescent patient specified that she wanted every aggressive treatment, including a ventilator, as long as there was even a 1 percent chance she might recover. Others decide they're done.

Kelly Petrlik wrote her parents a letter, saying she wanted to stop antibiotic treatments for her cystic fibrosis. The Woodbine teenager revealed that, for some time, she had only been going through them for her family. Her mother had noticed how she pepped up for her father and grandparents, how she put on a good front. But she was tired. Her parents agreed with her. Kelly died a few weeks later, in the summer of 2002, her family gathered around her bed at Hopkins.

R.J. had already helped set up limits on his care, paring back to antibiotics, fluids and pain medicine. He had also said he wanted to die in Pocomoke City, at home, in his bottom bunk. That was something Michele wished she could have done for her son. She discussed it with Dr. Higman and Elizabeth Reder, the Hopkins bereavement coordinator. But emotionally, like many other parents, Michele didn't feel she could handle her son dying at home.

There were practical reasons, too. To take R.J. home, Michele and her family would have to leave the place that had cared for her son for so long. It meant she would have to do much of the medical care herself, in a house that wasn't well-equipped.

Many parents don't accept hospice care because they equate it with giving up. Insurance policies require a prognosis of only six months to live. They also stipulate that the patient must stop any curative treatment for the illness. Yet for some of these kids that kind of treatment, like a blood transfusion, can be palliative, bringing them a better quality of life.

Another problem is the difficulty of finding hospice care for children. With the number of children's deaths relatively low and many families opposed to the concept, there isn't much of a market for it. Citing a lack of expertise, most adult hospices won't take children as patients. Health care workers who are willing to deal with dying adults also say that, emotionally, they are reluctant to care for dying children.

All told, only about 1 percent of dying children get hospice care. Usually, it is very late. One local hospice nurse described going to a home to start a new case. She talked with the parents in the kitchen, and then they took her upstairs to meet the child. By the time they entered her bedroom, their daughter had died.

ANGELS WITH NO WINGS

R.J. had been motioning and talking, as if conversing with someone at the end of his bed. When his mother asked what he was doing, sometimes he didn't seem to hear her, or wouldn't answer. But eventually he told her he was talking to the angels. It is something nurses and doctors say children often tell them.

In R.J.'s case, he said the angels had told him the cancer was all through him, something that would later be proved accurate on autopsy. And he said the angels were picking at the tumors, trying to heal him.

Five days before R.J.'s death, when the family's favorite hospital chaplain, the Rev. Salvatore Livigni, arrived, he hugged Michele and put his hand on R.J.'s head. Then he took out a box, carefully unwrapping a porcelain statue. It was an angel, one of hundreds the priest has given to sick children at Hopkins in his five years there.

Holding it up, Father Sal, 69, turned the statue side to side, so R.J. could get a good look. Then the priest leaned closer to him, inquiring earnestly. "Do the angels look like this?" he asked R.J.

R.J. shook his head no.

"Do they have wings?" Again, R.J. shook his head no.

"What do the angels look like?" R.J. didn't answer. A few moments later, the boy said something, but his speech was so garbled that even after four tries, Father Sal couldn't understand him.

Sighing, Father Sal said, "He's an angel himself."

In those last days, doctors were balancing R.J.'s medical problems with his looming death. Solving one problem would create another. The cancer had grown so much in his mouth and throat that he could barely open his mouth to chew, and when he got even a little food in, it fed the tumors. Doctors couldn't give him nutrition in fluid form because that would mean more swelling in his face. Sometimes that swelling got so bad around his cheeks and eyes that he couldn't see.

His pain was getting worse. He kept calling his mother, motioning to his abdomen, then his arm. When the resident sketched a quick picture of the body, asking him which part

hurt, he circled his whole body. They gave him more morphine. His mother was growing frantic.

"Is it hurting really bad, Baby Bear?" she asked.

That night, July 20, his blood pressure was plunging, and he cried out in his hoarse voice, "Mom, help!"

He was trembling. His eyes rolled back in his head. "Help me. Help me."

"Help what, honey?" Michele said, panicking. "I don't know what to do." She fiddled with his "trache," the breathing tube in his throat, with his suction tube. She put a hot pack on his face. He shook his head no. He kept moving around in the bed, reaching out his long arm to her. "Mom! Mom!"

The red numbers on the monitor hanging near the door started to flash. His oxygen level, tracked from the monitor he wore on his finger, had fallen too low that night. She was afraid to hold him, just like when he was a newborn with a collarbone broken during delivery.

Michele was confused, her voice breaking. "I thought they were quiet and peaceful."

SLEEP, SLEEP AWAY

Somehow, when death comes, many parents think it will be calm. But like so much around a child's dying, little has been said about what the final moments would look or sound like. Some doctors call this stage the final crescendo. It is the pace of death.

Dr. Joanne Hilden, a pediatric oncologist at The Children's Hospital at The Cleveland Clinic, wrote a book to give parents the basics, after she'd talked to several families about what they wished they'd known. For example, one couple didn't realize that putting their child on a ventilator meant he would not be able to talk with them.

Hilden explains that near death, children may be restless, agitated or have seizures. Others get the hiccups. Although some colleagues chastised Hilden for being too blunt in the 2003 book, "Shelter From the Storm," she said many parents reported that it helped them.

Many parents either don't or can't grasp how close their child is to death. In a 2000 study, Dr. Joanne Wolfe of the Dana-Farber Cancer Institute found that parents' awareness that the child probably wouldn't be cured lagged behind the physicians' by three months. And often even the doctors don't know, for as difficult as it is to forecast survival in adults, experts say it's tougher in children, because there are fewer studies about their often-rare illnesses, and their resilience makes for unpredictable courses.

When her critically ill daughter was in the hospital, Diane Irwin always had the sense that death was a week away. Irwin, who lives in Parkville, said because of that false idea, she wasted some of the last hours of her 4-year-old girl's life washing her baby blanket and searching hospital vending machines for Casey's favorite cereal. Now she wishes someone had alerted her to keep vigil.

Casey, who had cancer, died at Hopkins in 1998. Irwin said she is still haunted by her daughter's moaning in her last days. "I wanted her to sleep, sleep away," she said.

Now, she yearns for the chance she missed, to hold her daughter one last time. She dreamt once about how it might have been, that instead of being afraid to pick her up, she had cradled Casey and whispered in her ear, "I love you."

"The parents are crying out," Irwin said. "This could be so beautiful. This could be a gift."

Some of the children seem to sense when the end is near. Ryan King had been sick with leukemia for two years, and in late 2000, he was expected to live several more months. But one night, just before bed in their Glen Arm home, he called to his mother as she was about to leave his room. He thanked her for taking care of him. Ryan died the next morning.

She said she now believes he must have known he was about to die.

LET IT BE

By Thursday, July 24, when Hopkins' pediatric oncologists presented R.J. with an honorary medical degree and a white coat, he couldn't stand the square of summer sunlight coming from the window. Some children at this point can't even bear to be touched, said Reder, the hospital's bereavement coordinator. They're cocooning, pulling inward.

"I am ti-red," he sputtered.

After the days of agitation and restlessness, R.J. had become quiet and still. His skin looked duskier. His jaw and face, so swollen and hard before, had shrunk down. It made his eyes look bigger, bluer.

For R.J., there was a plan. Nurses had a list of people to call when the end got near. Counselors were available for Michele and her family.

It seemed that everything was falling into place. His mother was playing country gospel music, and some of his favorites, like the Beatles' "Let It Be." The Catholic chaplain, Father Sal, showed up to tease and pray with him, and that night, his grandmother came bustling in the door.

"Grandmom's here, love!" Carol Wisnom called out. She brought a container of homemade mashed potatoes and snapshots of his dog, Muffin. R.J.'s swollen lips moved in and out. It was his way, Michele said, to blow his grandmother kisses.

If his grandmother and sister had known it was the last night, they wouldn't have gone back to the Ronald McDonald House. If his mother had known it was his last night, she would have stayed up and talked to him until morning. But she didn't, and he became restless again. He kept talking about his white coat and honorary medical degree. He wanted to make sure his mother had told some of his favorite physicians and nurses.

"I'm the youngest doctor in history. I'm younger than Doo-

gie Howser," he said, referring to the television character.

LAST ONE

The nurse gave him Benadryl to help him settle down, and he and his mother slept. When Michele awoke on her fold-out chair at 5:15 a.m., a resident was checking R.J. His body was twitching.

"Ronald Joseph Frank Voigt," his mother remembers saying, her voice rising, "answer me. You're scaring me." But that familiar call couldn't reach him this time. He kept staring straight ahead.

Michele had already assembled CDs she wanted him to hear, and she put on "Amazing Grace." She held him and sang to him. A young physician, on her first night supervising several floors of children, found herself chiming in. R.J., she said, was calm, comfortable. The room had a sense of serenity.

"It seemed like everything was all right in the world, like it was the way it was supposed to be, and maybe it was, for that brief moment in time, because a mother was loving her son," said Dr. Lola Stavroudis. "When you see something that pure and beautiful, it gives you hope for the rest of us."

His grandmother, his sister, Kimberly, and two close friends arrived, and one by one, they told him how much they loved him, that he could go.

"I told him I could not stand to see him suffer no more," his grandmother said shortly afterward. Then it was up to his mother. She'd heard the tales of other dying children at Hopkins, the ones who managed to stay alive for their parents. Dr. Higman had told her that R.J. was probably hanging on for her. Now, as Michele lay at her son's side, crying, holding him, she looked into his face.

She said she could see he was holding on. "I knew it was for me," she said. And this last hour of R.J.'s last day, July 25, 2003, she summoned the words. She told him to go with the angels.

A few minutes later, as his breathing became shallow, Dr. Stavroudis walked up to his bed. Part of her hoped she'd hear a heartbeat; part of her didn't. She listened. She bowed her head. For the first time in her career as a physician, she uttered the words. "I'm sorry, he's gone."

It was 7:37 a.m.

Within an hour, the blinds were pulled up, the lights unplugged on the little tree. A nurse stood on either side of R.J. One warmed his hand between her palms, so she could make one last hand mold. The other, Brigid Gilmore, his favorite, dipped a washcloth in warm water and rubbed it with Ivory soap. She gently wiped his cheeks and cleaned his arms, his legs, every last finger.

The machines had been turned off. It was quiet, so quiet, except for the splashing of the water and Gilmore's voice, as she worked with the other nurse to carefully pull out the needle in his chest, the one he hated.

"Last one, R.J."

WHY DO WE SPEED?

By Rick Hampson and Paul Overberg

USA Today — Feb. 23, 2004

◄ MORE ON **ENTERPRISE PROJECTS** ON PAGE **122**

This terrific enterprise project was written by Rick Hampson using statistical research provided by Paul Overberg. Overberg recalls the story's inception:

"An editor noticed a story about how the California Highway Patrol was writing lots more tickets for driving over 100 mph. He proposed a national look at speeding, and whether and how it was increasing. His idea sparked lots of personal story-swapping among editors, a good sign that readers would be interested, too. I knew that we had done just such a project in 1997, using electronic files of speeding tickets from 1991 and 1996. We had archived that data. When I told the editor we could use it with new data to track this trend over a full decade, we got the green light."

As you read the story, notice:

◆ The organization — an introductory overview frames the issue, then five different sidebar stories focus on different aspects of the problem.

◆ The writing style — Hampson writes with a clean, clear, accessible voice. But notice, too, how he subtly adds a wry sense of humor to his delivery, a balancing act that's not always easy to pull off considering how serious (grim, even) some of his material is.

◆ The masterful blend of statistics and anecdotes, which combine to make the story authoritative and personable at the same time.

LANCASTER, Pa. — Barry Landis was doing 109 mph when the radar detector on the dash of his '97 Dodge Avenger started to beep and blink. That's when he saw the police cruiser.

Why was he driving so fast? Because he was in such a good mood.

Why was he in such a good mood? Because he was driving so fast.

"It's a cyclical kind of thing," he says.

To Landis, who once pushed his little Dodge to 130 mph, it boils down to this: "I like to go fast on a snowboard. I like to go fast on a bike.

"I just like to go fast."

So do many other drivers — so many that the state police here have started releasing to the news media the names of speeders ticketed at 90 mph or more. The idea: shame them into slowing down.

At another time in another land, it might work. But not today. Not in Lead Foot Nation, where drivers hit speeds that once seemed out of reach to everyone but race-car drivers, stuntmen and moonshiners. Here, many drivers regard the posted limit as a minimum, not a maximum.

USA Today analyzed 1.2 million speeding tickets issued in 2002 on interstate highways in 18 states — or about 40% of the interstate system. When compared with similar tickets from 1991 and 1996, they confirm what many suspect:

◆ We're speeding faster than ever — in some cases, much faster.

◆ Even though highway speed limits have been raised by as much as a third over the past decade, we speed further above these new limits than we did above the old ones.

◆ Despite official promises that higher limits would be more strictly enforced, we're getting more leeway from the police, who all but ignore speeders 10 to 15 mph over the limit.

Most striking is the rise in extreme speeding — driving over 90 mph, or 15 mph above any speed limit. In 1991, just 2% of ticketed drivers topped 90 mph; in 2002, 10% did.

Even what police call "The Century Club" — those driving 100 mph or faster — is getting much less exclusive. In 1991, just one driver in 300 was ticketed at or above 100; in 2002, the ratio was down to one in 100.

In an attempt to slow traffic, judges in Sutter County, Calif., have tripled the fine for driving 100 mph to almost $1,000.

So many Sutter commuters use triple-digit speeds to shorten their morning drives to Sacramento or the San Francisco Bay Area that the state police have added a 5 a.m. patrol. It's the great paradox of the American road. Traffic is getting heavier, there's less open road, and gasoline costs more. That should slow us down.

But we want to drive faster, and we do it every chance we get.

So why do we speed?

Because we have a full bladder or an empty cooler. Because the cake is in the oven. Because class starts in five minutes. Because the day care center is closing, and it's a dollar a minute after 6 o'clock.

We speed because we want to get away or because we want to win a race. Because we think we're James Dean or James Bond. We speed because we believe *F=ma:* Fun equals mass times acceleration.

We speed because our engines are bigger, our tires better, our suspensions firmer, our cabins quieter, our roads smoother.

We speed because we don't realize how fast we're going —

at least, that's what we tell the trooper.

Here in Lancaster County, where the Amish still travel by horse and buggy, the state police say they get so many complaints about speeding that they've borrowed an old vice squad tactic: fight prostitution by embarrassing the johns.

But the strategy assumes people are ashamed to speed.

When friends of Barry Landis found his name in the local newspaper, they cut out the story, presented it to him for his scrapbook with their congratulations and offered their own tales of high-speed brushes with the law. "It sorta made me a celebrity," Landis, 26, says sheepishly.

The trooper who stopped him, Phillip Matson, acknowledges the limits of publicity: "People's feelings aren't hurt by it. Some of 'em take pride in it."

WHY DO WE SPEED?

Because everyone else does, especially our leaders

A decade ago, South Dakotans who had never met or seen the governor knew Bill Janklow was a speeder. He had received a dozen speeding tickets and had been involved in a half-dozen accidents.

Part of it was functional. He had a lot of ground to cover between church suppers and county fairs.

Part was political. Speed seemed to be Janklow's trademark; he even made light of it in his State of the State speech in 1999. It was a populist calling card that helped make him a man of the people, even after he went to Washington last year to serve in the House of Representatives.

But in August, Janklow ran a stop sign while driving at least 16 mph over the speed limit and hit and killed a motorcyclist. He was convicted in December of manslaughter and sentenced last month to 100 days in jail and fined $5,750. He resigned his House seat.

One of the surest measures of speeding's social acceptance is that politicians feel free to do it. An analysis of the driving records of a million motorists done for insurance companies ranked the occupations of drivers most likely to speed. Politicians finished fourth. Only students, military personnel and laborers beat them.

No surprise, then, that a proposal to reduce the speed limit on Interstate 80 in Nebraska probably will die in committee; or that Texas legislators last year refused to increase fines for driving more than 25 mph over the limit; or that in half the states drivers cannot block others in the left lane — even if they're at or above the limit.

We all vote with our right foot, and that includes moms in minivans and pops in pickups.

Comparing tickets issued in 1991 with those issued in 2002, the percentage of highway speeders who were ticketed for driving over 75 mph rose from 52% to 83%. A speeding

THE JUMP PAGE — *Page 4A of USA Today shows the layout of the speeding package: five sidebars, two information graphics and the conclusion of the front-page story.*

ticket has roughly the same stigma as an overdue notice from the library. There's no Mothers Against Fast Driving. But there is the Speed Channel.

Speed kills, but it also sells: cars, beer, movies, songs. That's how it is in Lead Foot Nation, home to Larry Ford of Franklin, Ind., who souped up his 1940 Ford Coupe with a 396-cubic-inch engine that gets it up to 100 mph. And to C.J. "Pappy" Hart, who was 87 a few years ago when stopped for going 85 in a 55 mph zone. He wasn't driving his motor home at the time, but he has done 85 in that, too.

Most highway safety advocates focus on "belts and booze" — seat belt laws and drunken driving — and ignore speeding. "Everybody sort of does it," says Alan Williams of the Insurance Institute for Traffic Safety. "It's a folk crime."

Marion Emslie made this discovery when her 15-year-old daughter was killed six years ago.

Talia was riding in a car driven by a high school classmate when it left Interstate 495 outside Boston and hit a tree. Police estimated that it was going about 85 mph.

Emslie says she demanded that criminal charges be filed against the 18-year-old driver, who allegedly had been switching lanes recklessly. The response: "People thought I should forgive him."

"People in town didn't want to talk about speeding," she says. "They said the driver wasn't drinking. They put themselves in the driver's seat, not my daughter's."

The driver was convicted and sentenced to 21 weekends in jail. But Emslie says her condemnation of speed aroused such hostility in town that she began to feel uncomfortable. Finally, she moved.

Her conclusion: " There is no stigma to speeding. Parents don't want to go there because they'd have to look at themselves and ask, 'Do I obey the speed limit?' "

WHY DO WE SPEED? *Because we're sure we won't crash — or get hurt*

Speed is a cause of many crashes; the trouble starts when you try to determine whether it was *the* cause, or even a primary one.

So whether higher speeds necessarily mean more accidents is surprisingly hard to prove. Many other factors contribute to crashes: weather, drinking, distractions . . .

But when something does go wrong at high speed, the result can be a catastrophe of cinematic proportions. Such was the fate of Michael Hanson, 23, a mortgage banker. His license, revoked because of a speeding ticket in 2002, had been reinstated last June.

On July 22, he had dinner at a restaurant with his business partner. Afterward he pulled his silver Porsche — so new it didn't have plates — onto California Highway 55, the Costa Mesa Freeway, southeast of Los Angeles.

Witnesses say he quickly accelerated to 100 mph. And when a small black car passed him, he gave chase — even though at 10 p.m. there still was plenty of traffic.

Hanson reached an overpass when he suddenly veered right to avoid hitting a vehicle. He lost control. His Porsche smashed through a guardrail, left the freeway, soared through some trees and crashed 23 feet below, on the southbound lanes of the San Diego Freeway. There, it clipped a Toyota Corolla, crossed several lanes, smashed into the median and exploded.

Even though his seat belt was buckled, Hanson was thrown into the northbound lanes, run over by several vehicles and decapitated.

A motorist, Adam Swain, saw a Cadillac roll over Hanson. "It's one thing to see this stuff on TV," he told The Orange County Register. "But when you see something like this, it makes you think differently."

Four days later, a generally admiring story about Hanson's life appeared in the Register. It began: "Michael Allen Hanson didn't believe in boundaries."

We can change the speed limits, but we can't change the laws of physics. They dictate that the force of a crash does not increase proportionately with its speed, but geometrically. The 25% increase in crash speed from 40 to 50 mph increases the risk of a fatality by 100%.

Assume, as USA Today's ticket analysis suggests, that significant enforcement of 65-mph limits now begins around 80, instead of 75, the rough enforcement line a decade ago. In a crash, that 5-mph difference translates into an increase in impact force of 14%. And that means more broken bones, punctured organs and severed arteries.

At very high speeds, the protective technology with which we have crammed our cars can't save us; the collision is too violent, the vehicle too crumpled. A seat belt, for instance, can stop you from being thrown through the windshield, but it won't stop you from being crushed into the windshield.

At 100 mph, says Chuck Hurley of the National Safety Council, "you don't need a seat belt. You need an ejection seat."

WHY DO WE SPEED? *Because we think we have a good excuse*

Two judges stand outside their chambers in Ellicott City, Md., exchanging tales from traffic court. If you wonder why people speed — why they say they speed — listen to what Sue-Ellen Hantman and Louis Becker hear.

"I was going 75 in a 55 zone because I thought the limit was 65, and the cops always give you 10 miles an hour."

"I was picking up a sick child."

"I had a sick child in the back seat."

"I had to make a midnight curfew."

"I didn't know how fast I was going because it wasn't my car."

"I was going downhill."

Judge Hantman has a soft spot for just one excuse: "I was going with the flow of traffic." On highways in Howard County, that often means 80 mph.

Speeding has become such a concern that the judges have

begun ordering some speeders to attend an evening class at the courthouse on its dangers.

There is no Speeders Anonymous ("My name is Bill, and I drive 95 in 65 zones") but if there were, its meetings might feel something like these classes in Ellicott City.

Here's what one is like: It's a Monday evening; about 60 drivers are enrolled in the class. Most are young men in their 20s and early 30s — the drivers most likely to speed. Their average ticket: 22 mph over the speed limit.

During the next three hours, the reluctant students are subjected to gory video of accidents and amputations, graphic explanations of what trauma teams do to keep accident victims alive, and hair-raising testimony from survivors. A crippled, brain-damaged woman tells them, "I'm the real thing, folks; we don't all die."

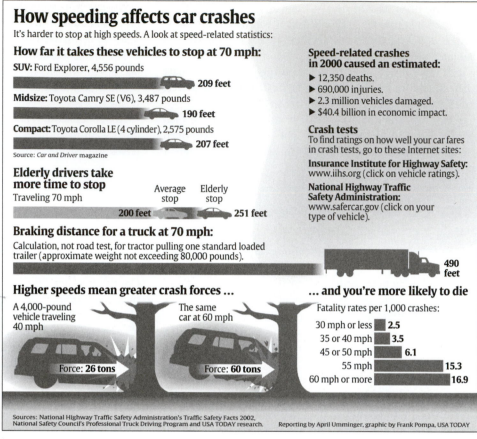

How speeding affects car crashes

It's harder to stop at high speeds. A look at speed-related statistics:

How far it takes these vehicles to stop at 70 mph:

SUV: Ford Explorer, 4,556 pounds — **209 feet**

Midsize: Toyota Camry SE (V6), 3,487 pounds — **190 feet**

Compact: Toyota Corolla LE (4 cylinder), 2,575 pounds — **207 feet**

Source: *Car and Driver* magazine

Elderly drivers take more time to stop
Traveling 70 mph — Average stop **200 feet** — Elderly stop **251 feet**

Braking distance for a truck at 70 mph:
Calculation, not road test, for tractor pulling one standard loaded trailer (approximate weight not exceeding 80,000 pounds). **490 feet**

Higher speeds mean greater crash forces ...
A 4,000-pound vehicle traveling 40 mph — Force: **26 tons**
The same car at 60 mph — Force: **60 tons**

... and you're more likely to die
Fatality rates per 1,000 crashes:
- 30 mph or less **2.5**
- 35 or 40 mph **3.5**
- 45 or 50 mph **6.1**
- 55 mph **15.3**
- 60 mph or more **16.9**

Speed-related crashes in 2000 caused an estimated:
- 12,350 deaths.
- 690,000 injuries.
- 2.3 million vehicles damaged.
- $40.4 billion in economic impact.

Crash tests
To find ratings on how well your car fares in crash tests, go to these Internet sites:

Insurance Institute for Highway Safety: www.iihs.org (click on vehicle ratings).

National Highway Traffic Safety Administration: www.safercar.gov (click on your type of vehicle).

Sources: National Highway Traffic Safety Administration's Traffic Safety Facts 2002, National Safety Council's Professional Truck Driving Program and USA TODAY research. Reporting by April Umminger, graphic by Frank Pompa, USA TODAY

The trauma nurses who lead the class have ice packs, blood-pressure cuffs and high-sugar drinks ready for the faint. They treat the students with resigned detachment, as if they are just so many future organ donors.

Shane Williams, 20, a college student from Eldersburg, Md., was caught driving 95 in a 55-mph zone. He doesn't need this class to tell him speed is dangerous. Three days before, his cousin was killed when he smashed his Eagle Talon into a utility pole while driving 100 mph.

Nevertheless, Williams has to admit it: He loves speed. As a young man in his 20s, he fits the profile of a fast driver. It's partly a social thing, he explains, especially when the weather gets nice. "When it's the speedin' season, if you have a nice car you can meet nice people, interesting people. You can be with the 'in-crowd.'"

But it's more than that. He recalls the time he "buried" his silver '94 Mustang's speedometer, which goes up to 150 mph. "I went up on (Interstate) 70 with a few people in the car, and we just took off. It usually takes 10 minutes to get to the next exit, and it took about two minutes."

Now he's smiling, in spite of himself. He can't fake it. "When you're going that fast, you're flyin'. It feels good" — he pauses — "while you're doin' it."

While you're doing it.

Is he alluding to the danger of speed? Or lamenting the transience of its delight?

WHY DO WE SPEED? *Because we think we have a right to*

The classic debate between state troopers and the speeders they stop has shifted. Once, drivers would deny they were speeding; increasingly, they deny the state's right to stop them from speeding.

"They tell you about the German autobahn," says Capt. Steven McDaniel, the troop commander in Lancaster, Pa.

The German highway system, about two-thirds of which has no speed limit, is a beacon of freedom to those who view speeding as a civil right.

One is Chad Dornsife, 57, who drives between San Diego and Lake Tahoe. He has spent his life as a builder and traveling salesman traversing the American West, where "you always have that 10-mile horizon," he says. "Anything you can do to shorten it, you do."

Dornsife feels safest going far above the speed limit in his Subaru station wagon in the far left lane of a freeway. He's a lane or two from merging traffic.

Dornsife also claims an unusual distinction: For years now, he has hit 100 mph every day he has been on the highway.

It's a matter of principle; he feels his right to speed is infringed upon by government agencies, which need the ticket fees, and insurance companies, which use speeding violations to increase rates.

He and other speed-limit abolitionists believe that speeds well over 100 mph are safe on many freeways. Eventually, Dornsife predicts, drivers will cruise at 100 — thanks to intelligent cruise control. Cars will sense when other vehicles get close and will automatically slow down.

Leon James, a University of Hawaii psychologist, says that because children now grow up riding at such high speeds, by the time they're adults, extreme speeds won't seem so fast.

Some of us already drive like there's an American autobahn. Jay Leno talked last year to Playboy about midnight cruises in his McLaren F1 sports car. "I constantly find myself going 100-110 on the freeway," he said, "when the car feels like it's going 50."

WHY DO WE SPEED? *Because no one's gonna stop us*

A ritual is played out whenever a state increases the speed limit.

Officials, having bowed to public pressure for higher limits, acknowledge that the old ones were widely disregarded and promise to enforce the new ones rigorously. They sound like a parent telling an incorrigible child, "This time I really mean it."

Last August, North Dakota raised its speed limit on interstate highways to 75 mph, from 70.

Gov. John Hoeven vowed that troopers would "properly enforce" the new limit, and the head of the state highway patrol promised "enforcement action on any speeds over 75." That month, troopers wrote 1,881 speeding tickets, up from 1,549 in the same month a year earlier.

But since then, enforcement has eased. In the month after the initial anti-speeding effort, state police wrote 100 fewer tickets than in the same month the previous year.

Jason Klesch, 27, of Fargo predicted last summer that the speed line could not be held at 75. "Cruisin' at 80," he told an Associated Press reporter at the time.

These days, he puts his black '97 Pontiac Grand Prix SE on cruise control and drives 80 — along with almost everyone else, he says.

The national speed limit of 55 mph was abolished in 1995 largely because Congress agreed that an artificially and unreasonably low limit was turning America into a "nation of lawbreakers."

But higher limits haven't ended the public's Prohibition-scale disobedience. Americans still feel free to drive 10 to 15 mph over the limit, even though the limit now usually is 65, 70 or 75.

Take highways with a 65-mph limit. Significant ticketing of speeders in such zones began around 75 mph a decade ago. Now, the USA Today ticket analysis suggests, it starts at 80.

In 1991, a quarter of tickets written in those 65-mph zones cited speeds up to 75. In 2002, only 7% of those ticketed were speeding within 10 mph of the limit.

In fact, we're surpassing the new limits by even wider margins. In 1996, 38% of interstate highway speeders were ticketed at 15 mph or more above the speed limit. Seven years later, even though many of these limits had increased, those 15 mph or more over the limit had risen to 52%.

At a minimum, North Dakota driver Klesch says, "if you set the limit at 75, people will go 80. If you set it at 80, they'll go 85. I don't see many police on the highways."

The police are playing a game they can't win. There are too many of us, and too few of them.

So they focus on the fastest speeders and leave the speed limit itself virtually unguarded.

"If you stop a guy going 75," Pennsylvania State Trooper A.B. White says, "you're going to miss one going 90 or 100."

But extreme speeders are more dangerous to catch — especially on busy urban highways without wide shoulders.

And more difficult. "It's hard to catch a car going 90 if you're starting from zero," says Lt. Armand Bilodeau of the Rhode Island State Police

The police try to play the game. They use airplanes and unmarked sports cars. In Pennsylvania, troopers have started hiding radar inside yellow state Department of Transportation trucks.

But we're too smart for them. We have radar detectors — legal almost everywhere — and we know to stay in our lanes, to accelerate only when we're in the open, to watch how fast the truckers are going and to never, ever antagonize them, or they'll call the Smokies and sic 'em on us.

The police understand. They don't take it personally.

Last May, the annual, unauthorized coast-to-coast speedathon known as the Gumball Rally started in San Francisco and tore through Reno and Las Vegas en route to Miami. But the Nevada police didn't get too excited about the Ferraris and Lamborghinis roaring by at 100 mph and up.

"You have a fast car," observed Angie Wolff, a spokeswoman for the Nevada Highway Patrol, "it's hard to go slow."

Contributing: Bruce Rosenstein and Emma Schwartz

ONE HAPPY BIG-BOX WASTELAND

Oh my yes, there is indeed one force that is eating away the American soul like a cancer

By Mark Morford

San Francisco Chronicle — Aug. 17, 2005

◀ MORE ON **WRITING COLUMNS** ON PAGE **131**

Mark Morford began creating cultural commentary for the online edition of the San Francisco Chronicle in 2000 — "via a strange cocktail of serendipity, sheer nerve, good timing, oddball mentors and divine cataclysm," as he explains. After a few years and steadily increasing popularity, he moved into the print edition of the paper, where his columns run twice a week.

"Boring writing makes my soul curdle," says Morford, who describes his writing style as "wry and sexy and fun and incendiary and thoughtful and winking and open-thighed and highly literate and well-informed and self-deprecating and well-lubricated and happy to buy you a drink."

MORFORD'S COMMENTARY:

Vibrant opinion writing is, to me, all about getting to the damn point ASAP, conveying the tone and attitude at the outset, hooking the reader right in. I like how this lead aims the reader toward a specific action, adds a visual (well, automotive) element, as if you're now on a verbal road trip with me. Which, in fact, you are.

The litany. The list. More specific. It's all immediately familiar, all of a piece. Everyone knows these names, everyone has seen these stores, knows their nasty aesthetics and how they breed like bloated bunnies in the same corners of the nation. Readers are a part of the story now; we are standing side by side, lookin' around, and I'm pointing at noteworthy stuff.

Visceral language to get the attitude flowing a little more powerfully. "Garbage," "toxic," "poison," "hospitals" — can you tell how I feel about fast food? Obviously, we are focusing on the negative. Later, I give hints of the positive, of what it used to be like, for contrast. Eternal Rule #1: Rub opposing energies together, create sparks. And don't forget to look for subtleties. They're vital.

Do you want to feel like you might as well be in Tucson or Boise or Modesto or Wichita or Muncie and it no longer freakin' matters, because we as a nation have lost all sense of community and place? Why, just pull over, baby. Take the next exit. Right here, this very one.

Ah, there it is, yet another massive big-box mega-strip mall, a giant beacon of glorious community decay, a wilted exclamation point of consumerism gone wild. This is America. You have arrived. You are home. Eat it and smile.

There is the Target. There is the Wal-Mart and there is the Home Depot and the Kmart, the Borders and the Staples and the Sam's Club and the Office Depot and the Costco and the Toys "R" Us and of course the mandatory Container Store so you may buy more enormous plastic tubs in which to dump all your new sweatshop-made crap.

What else do you need? Ah yes, food. Or something vaguely approximating it. There is the Wendy's and the Burger King and the Taco Bell/KFC hybrid (ewww) and there is the Mickey D's and the Subway and the Starbucks and the dozen other garbage-food fiends lined up down the road like toxic dominoes, all lying in wait to maul your arteries and poison your heart and make you think about hospitals.

And here's the beautiful part: This snapshot, it's the same as it was 10 miles back, same as it will be 10 miles ahead, the exact same massive cluster of insidious development as you will find in roughly 10,000 noncommunities around the nation and each and every one making you feel about as connected to the town you're in and the body you inhabit as a fish feels on Saturn. In the dark. In a hole. Dead.

You have seen the plague. I have seen the plague. Anyone over 30 has seen the plague evolve from a mere germ of disease in the late '80s to a full-blown pestilence of big-box shopping hell. I was recently up in northern Idaho, where my family has owned a beautiful house on a lake in a tiny burg near the Canadian border for 40 years, and to get to this region you must pass through the explosively grown resort town of Coeur d'Alene, and the plague is there perhaps worse than anywhere within a 75-mile radius.

I am officially old enough to remember when passing through Coeur d'Alene meant stopping at exactly one — one — traffic light on Highway 95 on the way north, surrounded by roughly one million pine trees and breathtaking mountain vistas and vast, calming open spaces, farms and fields and sawmills and funky roadside shops and gorgeous lakes for miles.

There are now about 20 traffic lights added in as many years, scattered down a 10-mile stretch of highway and each and every one demarcates a turnoff into a massive low-lying horribly designed strip mall, tacky and cheaply built and utterly heartless, and clearly zero planning went into any of these megashops, except to space them so obnoxiously that you have to get back in your goddamn car to drive the eighth of a mile to get to the Target to the Best Buy to the Wal-Mart to the Super Foods and back to your freakin' sanity.

Do you want to know what depresses the American spirit? Do you want to

I don't recall planning it, but "germ," "plague" and "disease" all tie quite nicely into the hospital punch line, above. Once you take on an attitude, the appropriate language tends to flow around it. Note the eyeblink shift into personal anecdote midway through this graf. Eternal Rule #2: Personal anecdote always trumps general impression. Adds reader trust; they believe you know what you're talking about because you were there, you saw it. Be specific: name names, years, roads, etc., as specifically as possible.

Again, lots of detail here. I didn't have enough of this in the first draft; my editor suggested more descriptives for better sensory effect. Hence, the quick pastoral vista. It worked.

I am just tremendously fond of the well-crafted breathless run-on sentence. This one, by my standards, is relatively petite. I call it a style, voice. Others may call it annoying lack of punctuation and unbearable use of polysyndeton (the repetitious stacking of "and" conjunctions for delirious effect). I do not care. If you lack something like this in your opinion/satire writing (a trademark sense of wordplay, a joy in the malleable sentence), something is deeply wrong and you might want to consider stronger coffee, kinkier sex or better scotch. Or med school.

know why it feels like the center cannot hold and the tyranny of mediocrity has been loosed upon our world? Do you want to know what instills more thoughts of suicide and creates a desperate, low-level rage the source of which we cannot quite identify but which we know is right under our noses and which we now inhale Prozac and Xanax and Paxil by the truckload to attempt to mollify?

I have your answer. Here it is. Look. It is the appalling spread of big-box strip malls, tract homes like a cancer, metadevelopments paving over the American landscape, all creating a bizarre sense of copious loss, empty excess, heartless glut, forcing us to ask, once again, the Great All-American Question: How can we have so damned much but still feel like we have almost nothing at all?

Oh and by the way, Coeur d'Alene has a distinct central portion of town, well off the toxic highway. It is calm and tree lined and emptily pretty and it is packed with, well, restaurants and art galleries. And real estate offices. For yuppies. Because, of course, there are no local shops left. No mom-and-pops, few unique small businesses of any kind. No charm. No real community per se. Just well-manicured food and mediocre art no true local can actually afford and business parks where the heart used to be.

I have little real clue as to what children growing up in this sort of bizarre megaconsumerist dystopia will face as they age, what sort of warped perspective and decimated sense of place and community and home. But if you think meth addiction and teen pregnancy and wicked religious homogeny and a frightening addiction to blowing s--- up in violent video games isn't a direct reaction to it, you're not paying close enough attention.

This is the new America. Our crazed sense of entitlement, our nearly rabid desire for easy access to mountains of bargain-basement junk has led to the upsurge of soulless big-box shops which has, in turn, led to a deadly sense of pre-

fabricated, vacuous sameness wherever we go. And here's the kicker: We think it's good. We think it helps, brings jobs, tax money, affordable goods. We call it progress. We call it choice. It is the exact opposite.

Result No. 1: Towns no longer have personality, individuality, heart. Community drags. Environment suffers. Our once diverse and quirky and idiosyncratic landscape becomes ugly and bland and vacuous and cheap.

Result No. 2: a false sense of safety, of comfort, wrought of empty sameness. We want all our goods to be antiseptic and sanitized and brightly lit and clean. In a nation that has lost all sense of direction and all sense of pride and whose dollar is a global joke and whose economy is running on fumes and whose goods are all made overseas and whose incompetent warmongering leader makes the world gag, that toxic sameness is, paradoxically, reassuring.

Result No. 3: We are trained, once again, to fear the different, the Other, That Which Does Not Conform. We learn to dislike the unique, the foreign, foreigners. We lose any sense of personal connection to what we create and what we buy and I do not care how cheap that jute rug from Ikea was: When they are mass-produced in 100,000 chunks in a factory in Malaysia, it ain't quirky.

Sameness is in. Sameness is the new black. It is no different than preplanned Disney World vacations or organized religion or preplanned cruises or themed restaurants where all edges have been filed off and every experience has been predigested and sanitized for your protection because God forbid you have an authentic experience or nurture genuine individual perspective or dare to question the bland norm lest your poor addled soul shudder and recoil and the Powers That Be look at you as a serious threat.

I have seen the plague and so have you. Hell, you're probably shopping in it. After all, what choice do you have?

OLD MAN SAT, STARED UNTIL A CHILD HAPPENED TO PASS

By Charles Kuralt

The Charlotte News — Oct. 11, 1956

◄ MORE ON **WRITING COLUMNS** ON PAGE **131**

Charles Kuralt (1934-1997) is best remembered as a CBS television correspondent and host of "CBS Sunday Morning." During his broadcast career, he won 10 Emmys and three Peabody Awards for journalism.

But Kuralt started out as a newspaper reporter and columnist in North Carolina, where he honed his distinctively pure, simple writing style. Kuralt loved human interest stories — sweet, quirky, touching slices of life that captured the dreams and dramas of ordinary folks. Some of his best columns are charmingly old-fashioned narrative vignettes, like this one. Notice how Kuralt's sparse style and short sentences create an effect that's as much poetry as journalism.

It was five o'clock in the afternoon, that was part of the reason. The elegant lady in the fur cape, the four businessmen and the two young housewives stood at the Tryon St. bus stop with the vacant look of people thinking about their own affairs, tired of working, tired of shopping and eager to get home.

So they didn't notice the old guy in the alley.

He wasn't much to notice. He sprawled against a brick wall and raised his stubble-covered face to the people who passed by and lifted a shaking arm to offer them a pencil.

Some stared at him curiously. Nobody stopped.

The people waiting for the bus didn't even look his way. The lady in fur stepped out to the curb impatiently and looked up the street to see if the bus was coming.

One of the four businessmen leaned against a plate glass window, took a newspaper from under his arm and turned to the sports page.

One of the housewives glanced uncomfortably at the old man in the alley, and looked away.

They all waited.

That was when the little girl walked up. She was a few steps ahead of her mother, whose arms were full of packages. The little girl walked straight up to the old man in the alley and looked at him. He looked back. The little girl's mother took her place with the others, shifted the packages in her arms and began waiting for the bus.

"Come here, Annie," she said.

The little girl walked over.

"He's selling pencils," her mother said.

The man with the newspaper stared over at the little girl.

The little girl walked back over to the alley and peered down at the man.

She didn't say anything and neither did he.

She turned back to her mother and tugged at her arm.

"I want a pencil," she said.

Her mother smiled, took her pocketbook from her arm and reached into it awkwardly, without putting down the bulky packages. She gave the little girl a nickel.

The girl took it over to the alley and put it in the man's hat. She looked at him once more, then walked quietly back to her mother's side.

"God bless you," the old man mumbled. She didn't hear him.

The bus arrived and its doors opened.

Everybody got on.

But before they did, two of the businessmen and the lady with the furs dropped coins in the old guy's hat.

A little child had led them.

TWO EDITORIALS

These award-winning editorials demonstrate how to express strong opinions in a compelling style. The first attacks the pettiness of a city politician; the second defends the contributions of a statewide group of citizens. Each, in its own way, makes its case eloquently — without badgering readers.

By Stephen Henderson

The Sun (Baltimore, Md.) — Jan. 5, 2000

Now comes Martin O'Malley, taking his place in the pitiful queue of Baltimore mayors who have thought small and acted smaller with regard to city schools.

Mr. O'Malley has wasted no time using his school board appointive power to exact petty political revenge. He booted board member Edward J. Brody last week — basically because Mr. Brody worked vigorously on the mayoral campaign of Carl Stokes, one of Mr. O'Malley's chief rivals.

It wasn't possible to work with Mr. Brody, Mr. O'Malley said. Too much political history. Too many bad feelings.

Huh? Are we back in third grade on the playground?

Some advice for His Honor: Grow up. There's a reason they don't let kids be mayors.

The mayor's action might be more defensible if Mr. Brody were a slouch on the board. He's not.

On a board where everyone boasts some expertise and shoulders the work of five people (pro bono), Mr. Brody is a standout.

Mr. Brody, founder of one of the city's largest trucking companies, brings a business sense to school matters. He engineered many of the labor negotiations that yielded concessions from city teachers. He led the search for the schools' chief executive.

It wasn't uncommon for Mr. Brody — like other members — to spend upward of 30 hours a week working on school matters. Even if Mr. O'Malley finds an executive with Mr. Brody's experience to replace him, how likely is he to unearth one who will give so freely of his or her time?

Mr. O'Malley made his tantrum even more juvenile by leveling absurd accusations that Mr. Brody had something to do with literature on zero tolerance that called him a racist during the campaign.

Of course, Mr. O'Malley offers no proof. But on the playground, who needs proof? The bully always gets his way.

This isn't the first time Mr. O'Malley has shown himself to be more petulant than mayoral. He offered departing police Commissioner Thomas C. Frazier a foot in the rear on his way out. And as a member of the City Council, he built a reputation for making sure his "enemies" got what he thought was coming to them. The school system doesn't need a mayor like that. Neither does the rest of the city.

If Mr. O'Malley can't see past political vendettas and act in the best interests of the people and institutions that can help save Baltimore, we're in for a rocky administration.

By David Barham
Arkansas Democrat-Gazette — Oct. 18, 2002

The spinners tried to make good news from our poll. We didn't see it in the same rose-colored way.

A survey the *Democrat-Gazette* paid for and published this week showed that 46.8 percent of Arkansas residents think the Hispanic influx in the state has been a good thing.

That's mighty white of us.

Hispanic leaders praised the numbers. Said they're making progress, etc., etc.

But we're more worried about the 35.6 percent who said Hispanics are a problem, and we're worried about those who didn't know or wouldn't answer. When those who say Arkansas newcomers are doing the state good don't get even 50 percent in a poll, we have to worry.

What's the problem? Is it that them Hispanics are taking away jobs from good old Arkies who've been here forever? Or at least since the Indians were pushed out?

No, that can't be it. These immigrant workers have been flowing toward the increase in jobs and some of those jobs are not the kind others want.

Maybe Hispanics are putting too much pressure on schools and other public services. . . .

But who would complain about that if the immigrants were from, say, Mississippi, Louisiana or Germany? Is a booming economy — one that attracts workers, and their wives and children — a bad thing? We can't imagine many would prefer the alternative.

Those of us who have been here a while — as the song says, "Red and Yellow, Black and White" — might pause and consider the defining characteristic of any American immigrant: They're immigrated. They've freely chosen to be here. Because their hopes and dreams and ambitions match ours. That's why they left their land and came to America. In a way, they were American even before they left — in their minds, hearts and hopes.

The lazy, unimaginative, self-satisfied aren't about to leave the comforts, or even noncomforts, of home.

Englishmen didn't brave the dangerous sea to move here because they were lackadaisical. Italians didn't leave their families to move here because they were dullards with no dreams. Chinese and Japanese folk didn't uproot their families and move to a strange land with strange customs because they were unindustrious.

And dreamers who move here from Mexico or Honduras don't strike out on their own because they are unambitious or don't want to work. On the contrary, they're looking for work. They may not know the phrase "American Dream," but they've dreamed it. Just like so many of our pioneering forefathers.

These new Americans have a better life here, working on farms and washing cars. They hope, too, that their children will get a better education in America, and they want their children's future to be bright. So the Hispanic immigrant will gut chickens for slaughter at midnight because he can make more money here than he can across the Rio Grande. And, yes, he'll wash dishes and mop restaurant floors and do all kinds of jobs others will not.

These migrants aren't the only folks moving around, either. These days, your daughter may live on the west coast, and your son on the east coast — of Australia. Travel is easier these days, and uprooting and replanting is a way of life, all over the globe.

But still, like always, it is the ambitious who do it.

Those who are content — no matter how poor their circumstances — stay on the same hill they were raised on. Whether that hill is in France, Mexico or Drew County.

Many immigrants, thankfully, have chosen to call Arkansas home. We had one of the fastest-growing Hispanic populations in the nation during the 1990s, with a 337 percent increase. That's a more than three-fold increase in a group known for its appetite for work, religious fealty, and its dream of a better life.

We should be proud.

We're definitely better off.

SPEARS' STRIPPER ACT AN UNFOCUSED BORE

By Doug Elfman

Las Vegas Review-Journal — March 8, 2004

◄ MORE ON **WRITING REVIEWS** ON PAGE **132**

Doug Elfman was the music columnist at the Las Vegas Review-Journal when he found himself reviewing his third Britney Spears concert — "the third time I skewered her on my Bic," as Elfman puts it.

"What I like about this review is it's fun and breezy and heartfelt," he says. "The review is implicitly intellectual while also being conversational. That's my voice, and not just in print. I really do speak like this. My theory about writing is it's easy to do, as long as you learn how to talk well — funny, interesting — and then just talk to people in the paper.

"As Dave Barry puts it: Write with your mouth open."

ELFMAN'S COMMENTARY:

I got the idea for my lead while I was watching B.S. pretend to perform various acts of onanism in front of all these people. I was thinking something, like: Oh my God, Chris Rock would hate Britney's parents.

Notice how my editors let me describe humping and masturbation and orgasm, plus a scattering of "B.S." references. We fielded a few complaints. But do they really measure up against the hundreds of thousands of readers who didn't complain? No. The Review-Journal understood that I was writing in the year 2004 for human beings who are quite familiar with humping and masturbation.

"It's so bad it's bad" came to me while I was waiting for the show to suck more than it was presently sucking. I wanted it to super-blow so it'd entertain me, like Britney's previous tours did. Alas. I try to write reviews that are better than what I'm reviewing. This time, it was easy.

Clear Channel is such a hypocrite that this was the most obvious observation to make.

On Friday night, the comedian Chris Rock stood on stage at the MGM and said his only job in life is to keep his daughter "off the pole": "They don't grade fathers, but if your daughter is a stripper, you (messed) up."

The very next night on the same stage, Britney Spears slid down a stripper's pole in front of 13,300 people, then walked over to a bed and pretended to hump a dude.

This came right after she sang a ballad called "Touch of My Hand," during which she stripped off a white robe, revealing a nude body suit, and rubbed both hands over herself while on her back in a motion simulating masturbation.

There's nothing wrong with that in my book, in theory. But in reality, B.S.'s new tour is an unfocused bore of false sexuality, horrible songs, trite choreography, unfocused themes and less ambition than a house cat that sits around licking itself all day.

It's not even so bad it's good. It's so bad it's bad.

It's so bad that B.S., who's 22, signed up to sing this masturbation song on tour, and she pretends to masturbate for something like three minutes, and yet she has done such a poor job of executing a catchy chorus/orgasm that she hasn't generated any marketable controversy.

You'd think there would be some controversial whining at least from Clear Channel, the friend-of-Bush entertainment company that is now endorsing governmental bans on forms of entertainment that are not Puritanical.

But, uh-oh, Clear Channel is B.S.'s tour promoter, so don't expect it to shut down her money-making tactics. Clear Channel is an example of what Chris Rock calls "the hypocrisy of democracy."

In B.S.'s defense, few kids were there. The crowd looked nothing like the stereotype of her previous tours of preteens, Maxim subscribers and gay men. It looked more like a convention of women in their 20s, 30s and 40s, wearing blond dye and short skirts.

Those fans whooped their biggest cheer when B.S. seductively dropped her robe. If you are a sociologist or some other -ologist, please e-mail your theory of why at least 8,000 adult women went manic to see this woman naked.

I'm not even sure you can call her the woman she was meant to be. Look at those booby boobs. Her teeth are white like bleach. And those hair extensions, and that weird tan: You're kidding me, right?

As for her singing, she told The New York Times she does not lip-sync, but one of her managers told the Times her vocals are a mix of recorded and real-time sounds. Either way, those vocals were unfortunate.

B.S. tried to croon cabaret versions of her pop hits, "…Baby, One More Time" and "Oops…I Did It Again." But her style and meter were troubled. Shaking your thing in a bustier and ruffled panties does not automatically make anyone a cabaret singer.

To say her new songs — especially "Showdown," "Boom Boom, (I Got That)" and "Outrageous"— are immediately forgettable is giving them credit they don't deserve. They were hardly "songs" to begin with. They were annoying, short, moronic keyboard loops, punctuated with tiny vocals tricked out electronically.

B.S. talked twice. Once, she alluded to tough personal times that were caused by her recent, 55-hour marriage in Vegas. But her experiences "made me who I am right now" and made her "realize how beautiful life can be," she said.

The other time she talked to the crowd, she goo-goo-gah-gahed, "Oh, my goodness,

No one ever e-mailed me to explain why women love seeing Britney fake-naked.

You know, this may be my favorite part of the review: "booby boobs." I've never used that term before or since. But it makes me laugh whenever I read it. By the way, tons of newspapers won't allow the word "boobs."

I wish I'd used the word, "underpants," instead of "panties." "Panties" is pervy. "Underpants" is funny.

I could have described more of the music in detail. I was a partial-scholarship violinist once, and a singer and a keyboardist in a garage band that never got out of the garage. But I prefer to write for a general audience, so I wasn't about to deconstruct B.S.'s "music" with words that would fall on deaf ears — or is it blind eyes, since we're talking about readers?

B.S. says the onyx is a gem that changes colors when light hits it. But my sister, who knows about voodoo stuff in New Orleans, says B.S. is thinking of something totally different. And yet, strangely, I do not care enough anymore to Google this.

I love referring to Britney as B.S. If I have one regret in journalism, it is that the B.S. nickname for her royal stupidhead has not caught on with the rest of the media. Come on, it's natural. It's fun. Give it a whirl.

a lot of cute guys (are) in the audience tonight. Are you guys feeling lucky? Who knows? ... Maybe, I'll marry you!"

B.S. called this charade "The Onyx Hotel Tour," because she fancies herself as an onyx, a gem that changes colors when light hits it. So, a few stage props appeared hotel-ish. And an emcee insulted audience members and farted. I'm still not sure why the Onyx hotel wants this gassy guy as its concierge.

B.S. claimed a "portion" of her $48.50-$98.50 tickets was donated to her Britney Spears Foundation. I asked several tour people to comment on what that "portion" is and how it gets spent. They did not respond.

A source told me attendance was as high as it was because a huge number of tourists were in town for a NASCAR event and other stuff and they bought tickets on the day of the show.

But there was an abundance of serious fans. A 21-year-old guy insisted I write that B.S. is "gorgeous" and that he loves her videos: "She pushes it to the edge."

But after the show, nonfanatics who were walking behind me griped how hideous she was. "She sucked," one woman said. "I really thought she would have more talent than that."

I agree. B.S. didn't just suck, she suckity-suck sucked. I'm grading her a "D-," and not an "F," because I think she has room to degrade. If you think B.S. can't get any worse, you're selling her short.

So here's the line everyone quoted the most: B.S. "suckity-suck sucked." It's like one of my legacies at this point. And here's a little secret. When I was editing the story, I had to cut a half-inch for space, and "suckity-suck sucked" was the first thing I sliced, because I wasn't sure people would get it, and I didn't know how to spell it. But then I thought, "Aw, screw it," and put it back in. You should always trust your first instincts and question your reservations.

AN ASSORTMENT OF CYNICAL REMARKS

"Journalists play an important role in society, which is to take real life, and somehow make it boring."
Dave Barry

"Every journalist who is not too stupid or too full of himself to notice what is going on knows that what he does is morally indefensible. He is a kind of confidence man, preying on people's vanity, ignorance, or loneliness, gaining their trust and betraying them without remorse."
Janet Malcolm

"I don't know why anyone would ever talk to the press. The press is like a lamprey that latches on to a subject and just sucks and sucks and sucks until your brain and your soul is as dry as a crouton. Because they need what you have inside you to make their story. And they don't care anything about YOU, they care about their story. I've advised everyone in my family to never ever ever talk to the press, for any reason."
Stephen Colbert, satirist, *The Colbert Report*

"Managing a newsroom is like managing a daily disaster. Good newspapers are put out by a collection of scruffy, recalcitrant characters that would make most normal business people shudder. News folks don't like to be managed. If we did, we'd all be doing something else.
"We are great at gang-tackling a good old natural disaster. Give us a triple ax murder or a chain-saw dismemberment, and we love it. We're good at scandal; we love Watergates and Iranscams and public officials who fudge on their expense accounts. We love to go nuts."
Deborah Howell, ombudsman, *The Washington Post*

"If I were a father and had a daughter who was seduced, I would not despair over her. But if I had a son who became a journalist and continued to remain one for five years, I would give him up."
Soren Kierkegaard, philosopher

From an article in Quill magazine by Michelle Dally, a veteran newspaper reporter who spent a semester teaching a college journalism class:

When I wasn't attempting to teach them things they should have learned long before, I was attempting to unteach things they actually had learned long before.

In one editing exercise, I discovered a number of students deleting every "But" that began a sentence in a standard AP article.

"You can't just take these out," I said. "You need these for transition."

I was greeted with perplexed stares.

"But what about my English teacher?" one senior asked. "She told me never to start a sentence with But or And."

"This isn't English," I heard myself saying. "This is journalism."

News gathering wasn't much better. For one assignment my students had done background research on legislators and then went and interviewed them. One student — a particularly talented one — came back and reported, "I read that this guy was an alcoholic, but I didn't want to ask him about it."

"Why not?" I asked.

"I didn't want to be a jerk."

"It's your job to be a jerk," I reminded him, and then bit my tongue.

MOVIE REVIEW: THE RETURN OF THE KING

By Claudia Puig

USA Today — Dec. 16, 2003

◀ MORE ON **WRITING REVIEWS** ON PAGE **132**

Claudia Puig began her reporting career on the police beat. She then spent a decade covering the entertainment industry at The Los Angeles Times. Now she reviews movies for USA Today.

"My critical approach is a populist one," Puig explains. "Because USA Today is read across the nation (and internationally), I am always mindful that I am writing for a very large and diverse audience. Because our reviews are not lengthy, I try to cover a lot of ground in limited space. I want my critiques to have something for everyone, from the movie buff to the person who only sees a couple movies a year."

PUIG'S COMMENTARY:

I chose this lead because of the connections between king and crown, to emphasize that this was the finest of the three films, and also to stress that the entire trilogy was superb. It was concise and stated my perspective with authority and no equivocation.

It's important to put a film that is part of a larger series in context and refer to its predecessors, especially because not everyone reading has seen the previous two films — hence this introduction to the entire trilogy.

Again, more context. It's essential to judge the entire three-part work as one, just as it is also important to focus on the independent piece — the third movie — that is analyzed for review. One can't give short shrift to either the entire package or the individual part. Also, when judging this final installment, character development, emotional heft, plot continuity and a spiraling of the saga were what viewers would focus on, and that is what a critic needs to examine and address. In other words, a critic must assess if Jackson's efforts provided the payoff that viewers would expect, when he had already set a pretty high bar in the previous two films. And though the work is being judged on its artistic merit and not on its commercial value, in the case of such a costly, sprawling and high-profile set of films, it's germane to mention box office figures as context, as well.

"The Lord of the Rings: The Return of the King" (★★★★ out of four) is the jewel in the crown of the masterful trilogy.

The three-part story of courage, friendship, honor and duty — spanning "The Fellowship of the Ring" (2001), "The Two Towers" (2002) and "The Return of the King," which comes to theaters tonight — is ideally suited to epic filmmaking. It is steeped in fast-paced action and grand adventure, yet still grounded in humanity — a rare combination among large-scale film extravaganzas.

It isn't until now that director Peter Jackson's efforts can be fully and fairly judged, notwithstanding the monumental box office success of the first two films, which have grossed $1.8 billion worldwide. As good as each individual movie is, the third film vaults the work into the stratosphere of classic movies. Key characters are enhanced, new civilizations visited and battles fought more intensely, while feelings and motivations are plumbed more deeply and movingly.

After the release of the first and second films, one wondered how the trilogy, as a nine-hour film fest, might compare with other cinematic watermarks. In its entirety, "The Lord of the Rings" surpasses other multi-part sagas such as "Star Wars" or even "The Godfather." Both "Star Wars" and "The Godfather" had weak links, whole movies that didn't work as well as the best of the series. "Rings" maintains the same standard of excellence with each film and grows more assured with each installment. Of course, some of that escalating power is attributable to the storytelling prowess of J.R.R. Tolkien, upon whose classic novels the trilogy is based.

The books depict the odyssey of the humble hobbit Frodo, whose quest is to destroy a powerful ring that could enslave all the inhabitants of the fictional land of Middle-earth. Helping him accomplish his mission is a heroic cadre of creatures: Gandalf the wizard; Legolas the elf; Gimli the dwarf; Aragorn and Boromir, both men; and three other hobbits, Sam, Merry and Pippin. This unlikely alliance comes together in a spirit of acceptance and tolerance to fight the satanic Sauron and his devilish henchmen.

Those of us who do not consider ourselves fans of fantasy initially may have thought to dismiss the movies as farfetched, overblown silliness. It was hard to imagine the films as relevant or transcending their genre.

But many of us have come around to another point of view: The films tell a classic story that espouses the virtues of love, hard work and compassion and decries greed, deceit and abuse of power in a mighty struggle against temptation and the corrupting forces of power. The story's message about conserving natural resources has profound significance for our times, as does the notion of taking up arms against an evil tyrant and the importance of overcoming prejudice to work toward a common goal of peace.

Ironically, these simple messages were massively complicated to pull off, requiring a budget of nearly $300 million, a crew of 26,000 extras and a production team of 2,400, which included medieval weapons designers, stone sculptors, linguists, blacksmiths and model builders. Bringing to life such a wide-ranging story with technical proficiency and visual dazzle is an unprecedented achievement, one that likely will define Jackson, much as George Lucas is forever linked to the "Star Wars"

All reviews must summarize the plot, usually as broadly as possible, avoiding minutiae (unless it offers a telling detail or intrinsic point). With other reviews, I might not list as large a cast of characters, but since the novels are so well known and thus the characters so familiar, it seemed appropriate here.

This was a personal note. I am not a fan of Tolkien, and fantasy literature is something I've never warmed up to. But, despite that, I found the films riveting. I felt that needed to be noted, as it is a testament to the ability of Jackson as a director and his co-writers to create an epic that transcends the genre.

Some of the finest works in literature, art or film have powerful, timeless messages. The fact that "Return of the King" has an environmentalist theme and dissects corruption, prejudice and politics needed to be stated, as it gives the movie additional resonance and makes it more than just an entertaining story of adventure and peril.

Again, the making of a film is not always essential to note in a review of its merits, but in the case of something as gargantuan and complex as this trilogy, it was worth mentioning, providing still more context.

movies he directed.

Though the acting ensemble is strong, the movie does not belong to any one of them. While Elijah Wood capably carries off Frodo's transition from boy to man, his is not the most indelible performance.

Gollum, voiced by and physically patterned after the movements of British actor Andy Serkis, is the most realistic other-worldly character since E.T. and similarly will remain etched in moviegoers' collective memories. Ian McKellen's Gandalf has a larger role in the third film, morphing from wizard/prophet to army general, and one cannot imagine the role played by anyone else. Viggo Mortensen's principled Aragorn is the king to whom the third film's title refers.

A key character is the landscape of Middle-earth. The movies feel mythical but look historical. In the third installment, for example, Minas Tirith, a seven-tiered city of kings, looks European, Byzantine and fantastical at the same time.

There is a bittersweet quality in the tril-

In most other reviews, I might spend more time analyzing various aspects of the actors' performances. With a film such as this one — that is built on an ensemble cast and where the production design can be almost as important as the individual characters in moving the viewer — it was necessary to look at the portrayals, but also to acknowledge the importance of the visual scenery.

ogy's coming to an end — even if "The Return of the King" seems ready to conclude at least three times before the movie finally comes to a rather anticlimactic close. Many moviegoers, like Jackson and the cast — who grew quite close during filming — may understand, and even appreciate, the lingering goodbye. And while scores of filmgoers clamor to see the final installment, no one is eager for the journey to end.

Jackson's masterpiece will no doubt have a long life on DVD and be the subject of countless revivals over the years. The director's next project is a remake of "King Kong," which seems a bit like hiring Michelangelo to paint an office building. Though if anyone can make something out of that tired vehicle, Jackson can.

But what Rings fans may be most excited about are the rumors that Jackson may attempt "The Hobbit," a prequel to the Tolkien trilogy. Should Jackson sign on to make "The Hobbit," the Rings finale might feel more like a temporary "till we meet again" than a formal goodbye.

If I had it to do over again, I think I would emphasize a little more strongly that the film doesn't seem to know where to end — or want to end. I cut Jackson some slack on that one for the reasons stated above, but I believe the film would have benefited from some additional editing. One ending, or maybe two, if there's a twist. But four?

Ordinarily, I might not mention a filmmaker's next project, but in this case it was such a high-profile subject that it seemed to be warranted.

Again, because there was so much speculation about Jackson tackling "The Hobbit," this seemed like the best note to end the review on. Since "Rings" fans are such a numerous and rabid bunch, I felt their concerns were germane to the review.

QUOTED
ON LIBERAL BIAS IN THE MEDIA

"Right-wing partisans . . . have always attacked aggressive reporting as liberal. We were biased, all right — in favor of uncovering the news that powerful people wanted to keep hidden: conflicts of interest at the Department of Interior, secret meetings between Vice President Cheney and the oil industry, backdoor shenanigans by lobbyists at the FCC, corruption in Congress, neglect of wounded veterans returning from Iraq, Pentagon cost overruns, the manipulation of intelligence leading to the invasion of Iraq. . . .

"If reporting on what's happening to ordinary people thrown overboard by circumstances beyond their control and betrayed by Washington officials is liberalism, I stand convicted."

Bill Moyers, former PBS journalist/commentator

"Are media liberal? Maybe media were liberal in some ways in the days of family newspaper ownership in some places. Not anymore. These are big media conglomerates, for the most part. Primarily, they care about performance and returns, not about politics.

"Abandon the illusion that there's a socialist behind the curtain manipulating the media levers. That clanking sound is just a cash register."

Charlie Madigan, columnist, *Chicago Tribune*

"I think it's the demonstrable presence of so many liberals in the big-city news media — and their coverage of anti-war activities and the civil rights, feminist, gay rights, consumer and environmental movements — that has enabled the conservatives to make their case for liberal bias.

"To many conservatives, the very fact that the media covered these movements means the media were sympathetic to them and the coverage was tainted by a liberal bias.

"Moreover, journalists are skeptical, confrontational and iconoclastic, which means they challenge the establishment, while conservatives want to conserve it.

"So the better journalists do their job, the more likely conservatives are to see them as liberal."

David Shaw, *Los Angeles Times*

"Conservatives also know that if the press is effectively intimidated, either by the accusation of liberal bias or by a reporter's own mistaken belief in the charge's validity, the institutions that conservatives revere — the military, corporate America, organized religion and the powerful conservative groups themselves — will be able to escape scrutiny and increase their influence. Working the refs works."

Eric Alterman, from his book, *What Liberal Media?*

POLYPEPPERS AND PORK RINDS

By David Sarasohn

The Oregonian — June 18, 2004

◄ MORE ON **WRITING REVIEWS** ON PAGE **132**

David Sarasohn is a nationally syndicated political columnist at The Oregonian, a newspaper that takes food seriously. He's one of several critics who write restaurant reviews for the paper's weekly entertainment guide.

"I have been writing about restaurants – now this is scary – for 25 years, or approximately 4,239,872,975 calories," Sarasohn says. "I got into it when I got a job at a magazine and the reviewer had just quit, and I suggested I do it. At the time, my major qualification was liking to eat; after doing it for about 10 years, I figured I could claim to be as pompous as anyone about it. (Although when I remind my wife, as I am occasionally obliged to, that I am a food professional, she makes a rude and unpleasant noise.)

"Typically, I go out two or three times a week – some not for reviews but for our restaurant news column. Generally, it's two visits with four people for each restaurant, both to sample enough of the menu and because restaurants have good and bad nights. I went to Nuestro Cocina because a friend whose taste I respect liked it, which is one of many ways the choice is made."

SARASOHN'S COMMENTARY:

The first line, in a review as in anything, is to grab the readers. Pork rinds popping up in a restaurant review should do that.

You so rarely get to feel suave while ordering fried pork rinds.

Often, in fact, even the guy behind the counter at the minimart snickers.

A restaurant where you can order fried pork rinds with an apple martini — and they're accompanied by two sauces with both fire and subtlety, and you can feel like you're layering not just your arteries but your taste buds — is not just a statement of a skilled and unexpected kitchen. It's a reason to praise the lard.

Three snappers, 50 words. Now we can get to the theme and the substance.

Nuestra Cocina is a bold, impressive Mexican restaurant, a long way from a combination plate. It offers Mexican dishes that you don't run into regularly — red snapper in banana leaves with roasted poblano chiles, and we'll get back to the pork rinds — and dishes that seem more familiar but still have an unexpected spin. It achieves its impact not with fire that sears away the flavor of the ingredients, but with a polypeppered richness that still lets the core flavors through.

The core assessment paragraph, in which the review assesses the restaurant and the reader assesses the reviewer, who needs to show that he knows what he's talking about.

The new line is set out early with the appetizers. This version of seviche minces red snapper into small pieces, each permeated with lime, tomato and chiles, filling up a cocktail glass with a pungent freshness. Nuestra Cocina is hardly the first place to pile up a tortilla with spiced, shredded pork, but the pile here is both tall (watch your fingers picking it up) and savory with chile and cinnamon.

We're going to be describing dishes for a while now, and the language needs to be vivid to keep readers reading.

Grilled prawns marinated in tamarind are charred in their shells but after peeling are sweet and fresh, with a little smoke from the grill and a little fire from the dipping sauce. Piles of chorizo, black beans and chile, with

---

RESTAURANT REVIEW

Nuestra Cocina

Grade: B+

Cuisine and scene: Benjamin Gonzales puts his own skillful spin on Mexican dishes you've seen before and comes up with some striking ones you haven't. A relaxed, casual atmosphere suggests that there are worse ways of spending a summer's day than open-air consumption of spiced-pork tacos and Tequila Sunrises.

Must-have dishes: Seviche of red snapper; masa cakes with chorizo, black beans and chile; carne asada; white prawns in garlic and pasilla chiles; chocolate pound cake with cinnamon ice cream; lemon empanada.

Sound level: Quiet enough to hear lips smacking, even near the bar.

Service: Engaging and highly enthusiastic about the food.

Price range: Moderate; entrees $9-$16

Extras: Full bar; major credit cards; wheelchair accessible; smoking only on patio; street parking.

Serving: Dinner 5-10 p.m. Tuesday-Thursday; 5-11 p.m. Friday-Saturday.

The numbers: 2135 S.E. Division St.; 503-232-2135.

A sidebar box, running alongside the review, conveys information important to the reader that would slow down the review. There's always an unease about the short rating, whether a grade or stars or a one-word assessment, because it over-simplifies everything and encourages some readers to skip reading the review itself. But readers want it — and that's the key issue of a service feature like a review.

texture and tang, rest on masa cakes, circles of puff pastry with body and heft that make you wonder about the shortening involved.

Which brings us back to the pork rinds. They're actually more texture than flavor, something like big porcine shrimp chips. But they're ideal carriers for chile arbol and avocado sauces — the latter not guacamole but something thinner in texture and thicker in flavor.

Like all Mexican chefs, Nuestra Cocina's Benjamin Gonzales paints with peppers, but he stresses rich colors instead of burning ones: poblanos and pasillas instead of

We started the review with the pork rinds, we'll be circling around and ending with them, and we need them to reappear around the middle so readers will remember them for the finish.

This is all the reader needs to know about Gonzales, namely what his cooking style is — unless there's something striking in his biography, like winning the Nobel Peace Prize.

jalapenos and habaneros. So red snapper keeps its melting fishiness intact among the poblanos, while tender, outsized prawns burst through their escort of garlic and pasillas. But restraint doesn't come at the expense of flavor, and Gonzales puts his own vivid spin on Mexican standards.

His carne asada never forgets that it's a steak, and in a pungent preparation it stays remarkably juicy, as much carne as asada. His chicken mole has a deep chocolatey tinge to it, with the pieces simmered but not inflamed.

A soup of meatballs — and it's just nice to say "albondigas" — is no longer on the regular menu but occasionally surfaces as a special. In it, the broth actually has more body than the meat; it's a powerful infusion of stock, spices and cilantro, the kind of essence that could be given intravenously if it weren't so pleasant to take it orally.

For a Mexican restaurant, Nuestra Cocina also puts an unusual emphasis on desserts. Its flan actually is surprisingly forgettable, unduly rough-edged in texture. But its pastries — notably a lemon-filled empanada with an endearing crust, and wedges of chocolate poundcake with cinnamon ice cream — are admirable and especially useful for settling down a system still wrestling with a peck of peppers.

The closing of the Pearl District's Cafe Azul left an empty spot for a sophisticated Mexican restaurant. Nuestra Cocina may be no Cafe Azul — its dishes are considerably less complex and elaborate, but also less expensive. Its prices are firmly in the moderate range, with entrees from $9 to $16. Avoiding the more elaborate inspirations of the bar, two people could engage in a considerable meal and a pitcher of clove-scented sangria for around $60.

The space itself is stark but cozy, built around a lively open kitchen and a livelier bar area defined by a nonstop shaking of margaritas. An outdoor dining area peering onto Southeast 21st Avenue could come into season this weekend. Servers generally seem excited about the whole idea and about what they're serving.

Nuestra Cocina is a skillful, reasonably priced Mexican restaurant, with both its own ideas and intriguing renditions of the standards. From its handmade tortillas to squash and gruyere tamales, it spins both expectations and its customers.

And nobody snickers when you order the pork rinds.

At least not after the first time.

Art or opera critics can speak from above, but in a restaurant review, pomposity is poison. Everybody eats. With luck, the offhand reference to carne asada as a spicy steak will make its identity clear to anyone who doesn't know.

A reference to an unusual word being unusual tells the reader that you're seeing things the same way.

How do four diners decide what to order? Simple. I tell them. I might ask politely if there's anything they'd particularly like, but I know what I need to try, and besides, we'll share everything anyway. You need to get a range of dishes – not just fish, not just red meat – and be careful to hit whatever looks like a specialty, or something so bizarre you've never seen it anyplace else.

You've got to get the prices in, both because a restaurant review is a service piece and because you're reassuring the reader that just like him, you notice the size of the bill.

Now we're at the final judgment, tying everything up, reminding the reader that you've now gone through the menu together.

Back to our opening theme. Even after authoritatively discussing different peppers and Mexican sauces, reviewer, like reader, still realizes that pork rinds are a little strange.

OPENERS
AN ANTHOLOGY OF LEADS

Cops call it "Collars for Dollars." It's how they turn arrests on the streets into money in their pockets. Until now, it has been a courthouse secret.

It works like this: Police list each other as witnesses in drunk driving and misdemeanor cases even if they did little or no police work. Then they all get to go to court, where they make overtime they don't deserve.

"That is stealing," said former Miami Police Capt. Nate Harris, who tried unsuccessfully to stop it in his department two years ago. "It's embezzlement, is what it is."

An eight-month Miami Herald investigation documented Collars for Dollars abuse involving hundreds of officers in thousands of cases. It happens so often that it costs Dade County taxpayers millions. It burdens the courthouse with thousands of unnecessary witnesses, leads to lost cases and even traps some innocent people.

From **Collars for Dollars,** a 1998 investigative series in the *Miami Herald* by Jeff Leen, Gail Epstein and Lisa Getter

Florida is letting thousands of chronic drunken drivers, killers in car accidents and other unfit motorists take the wheel again, with disastrous results.

These motorists have received permission to drive again despite terrible driving records that had caused their licenses to be revoked for five years, 10 years or even permanently.

The result: Dozens of people have been maimed or killed.

Lawmakers decided to give second chances to remorseful drivers as a way to help people who would not be able to support themselves and their families if they could not drive.

Yet, The Orlando Sentinel found during a three-month investigation that many fail to reform, continuing to drive drunk and causing deaths and injuries.

From **Florida's License to Kill,** a 1998 investigative series in the *Orlando Sentinel* by Debbie Salamone, Liz Gibson and Greg Miller

JOURNALISM'S STRANGE SECRET: THE OCCULT HAND SOCIETY

Imagine there's a secret society of journalists — a society so secret, only a few readers, reporters or newsroom bosses even know it exists.

No meetings, no dues, no club officers, no funny hats. Want to join? All you have to do is sneak an oddball seven-word phrase into one of your stories, and you're a member.

Welcome to the Occult Hand Society.

No one really knows how the society got started. Some say it was founded back in the 1930s by legendary journalist Heywood Broun and his boozy pals. Others claim it began in 1965, when Charlotte News reporter Joseph Flanders buried this sentence deep in a crime story:

"It was as if an occult hand had reached down from above and moved the players like pawns upon some giant chessboard."

Flanders' drinking buddies were impressed. "Now *that*," said one, "is what I call prose."

As the story goes, Flanders' friends vowed that they, too, would find a way to slip that pretentious, pulp-fiction phrase (*it was as if an occult hand. . .*) into their stories. Before long, their inside joke spread to newsrooms across the country.

A quick Web search reveals "occult hand" references popping up everywhere, from a bowling feature in The Washington Post ("it was as if an occult hand had guided the black sphere down the narrow lane and into the triangle of pins") to a story in the Los Angeles Times about the Oscars ("it was as if an occult hand had hurled a raspberry at Hollywood").

It's always been a forbidden thrill for reporters to hide secret messages in their stories. Some troublemakers have succeeded in spelling out vulgarities using, say, the first letter in each line of type. By reading vertically, you'd see the words "eat my shorts," or something nastier.

But gaining entry into the Occult Hand Society, at least, won't get anybody fired — we hope. In uptight newsrooms, it's just a harmless prank that lets repressed reporters take revenge on their fuddy-dud copy editors.

A few classic moments from the OHS archives:

AN OCCULT HAND READER

Kristin Tillotson in the Minneapolis *Star Tribune* (1998):

It was as if an occult hand had reached down and given the nation's television critics a pinch on the tush. Since the HBO series "Sex and the City" premiered four years ago, it has been praised by most female critics, but bashed by many male critics.

Tony Russomanno, reporting for San Francisco's CBS5.com (2004):

If the mosquito-born virus continues to spread as expected, the Bay Area may see a massive death of crows, hawks, owls, sparrows and finches. It's already happened around Los Angeles, where it was as if an occult hand had swept crows from the air.

Jason Harris, *Burlington County Times* (2004):

Stetson took an unconventional stance over the tee, reared back with his driver and hit the ball with a satisfying thwack. For a second, the ball looped into the sky. Then, as though swatted down by some occult hand, it dropped back into the grass about 100 yards short of the pin.*

*Some Occult Hand purists would argue that entries such as this are flawed and unacceptable because they fail to respect the proper wording: i.e., *"it was as if an occult hand..."*

Don Stoneman, on a stinky substance used to keep coyotes away from sheep, in Canada's *Farm & Country* (1998):

Martin knows from looking at tracks that coyotes "sit and look at it and then try to find a way around it." It is as if an occult hand prevented them from crossing an invisible line.

Douglas LeBlanc in *Christianity Today* (2004):

For nearly a decade, J.K. Rowling's Harry Potter series has been a litmus test of evangelicals' commitment to defying popular culture. Some churches have consigned Potter novels to bonfires because of the series' portrayal of magic spells and wizardry. For some Christians, it was as if an occult hand had nudged unknowing children toward pop witchcraft.

Ed Culhane, from an ice-fishing story in the Appleton, Wis., *Post-Crescent* (2003):

Pottner said he was heading back to his sack and had just turned for the door when this great, huge sturgeon simply materialized in the back left corner of my hole, no more than 16 inches under the surface.

I thought, "Shark!" Then, "No, sturgeon." It seemed impossible. It was as if an occult hand had simply reached through from some invisible dimension and placed it there. For a millisecond, I couldn't speak, couldn't move.

I'd lost touch with reality. My brain disbelieved my eyes.

Ed Culhane, striking again in the Appleton, Wis., *Post-Crescent* (2001):

It was as if an occult hand struck Jerry Lee Lewis down with strep throat just before he was to take the stage in front of 2,000 expectant fans on a recent rainy night in Green Bay.

Marty Levine, on a brewhouse clock that came to life after being stuck for years at 6:30, from the *In Pittsburgh* newsweekly (1998):

A few weeks ago, the clock changed to 6:35 overnight — as if an occult hand had reanimated its innards.

Mark Lane, in the Daytona Beach, Fla., *News-Journal* (1998):

We are now in the final innings of the 1990s. Zero Decade is almost upon us, and as though an occult hand has hit the jukebox selector, the '80s acts are warming up the old routines to take out again on the road.

William Bunch on how Florida hurricanes caused more damage in Republican counties, in the *Philadelphia Daily News* (2004):

As if by an occult hand, each seemed to batter the Bush-backing bastions while sparing the guardians of Gore.

— Thanks to Charles Stough for his diligence in archiving OHS entries

THE BOOK OF ALWAYS

By J. Taylor Buckley

J. Taylor Buckley — veteran reporter, sports columnist and writing coach at USA Today — has compiled a definitive list of journalistic clichés, which he calls his ALWAYS list. "It's the only guide you'll ever need to keep your newspaper copy enriched with the clichés of authenticity," Buckley boasts.

Here's a sampling from Buckley's vast collection:

◆ Economies, particularly local ones, always *sag,* even though money is always *pumped into them.*

◆ Government budgets are always *unveiled.*

◆ Funds are always *earmarked.*

◆ Votes in Congress are always *crucial.*

◆ Committee chairmen and chairwomen in Congress are always *powerful.*

◆ Battle lines are always *drawn.*

◆ Negotiators are always *cautiously optimistic.*

◆ Deadlines are always *around the corner.*

◆ Races are always *tight.*

◆ Reality is always *harsh.*

◆ Truces and labor agreements are always *hammered out.*

◆ A wait-and-see attitude is always *adopted.*

◆ Debates are always *spirited;* arguments are *heated.*

◆ Details are always *sketchy.*

◆ Security is always *beefed up.*

◆ Power lines never fall; they're always *downed.*

◆ Fires always *rage;* smoke always *billows.*

◆ Rain always *fails to dampen the spirits* of parade-goers.

◆ Thunderstorms always travel in *bands,* as do rioting teenagers.

◆ Tornadoes always *hopscotch* through counties. Storms in the plains always *rumble.* Hurricanes are always *brewing.*

◆ People always *dig out* after snow-storms, *thaw out* after ice storms.

◆ Disaster victims are always taken to *makeshift morgues.*

◆ Investigators always *sift through wreckage.*

◆ Buses always *plunge* off the roadway.

◆ Takeoffs by malfunctioning aircraft are always *aborted.*

◆ Plane crashes, especially those involving celebrities, are always *fiery.*

◆ The deck of an aircraft carrier is always measured in *football fields.*

◆ Lawns are always *well manicured.*

◆ Prep schools are always *prestigious.*

◆ Machine guns are always *toted.* They are never *wielded* or *brandished.* It's knives that are always *wielded* or *brandished.*

◆ SWAT teams always carry *high-powered rifles,* never pistols, low-powered rifles or just rifles.

◆ Neighbors of crime victims are always *shocked and saddened,* while neighbors of mass murderers are always *shocked and appalled.*

◆ The bodies of teenage women sexually victimized or murdered are always found *scantily clad,* while older women in similar circumstances are always found *partially nude.*

◆ Denials of wrongdoing are always *vehement.*

◆ Mistaken identity, like beer, always comes in *cases.*

◆ Felons who receive subpoenas or errant motorists who get tickets are always *slapped* with them.

◆ Suicide victims are always *despondent.*

◆ Death is always *sudden, unexpected* or *premature.*

◆ Failing newspapers always die, just as failing businesses always *close their doors.* No enterprise just closes or shuts.

◆ The family farm always *goes on the auction block.*

◆ The shots one must get after being bitten by an animal suspected of carrying rabies always come *in a painful series.*

◆ Cigars are always *chomped* — rarely, if ever, smoked.

◆ Contract talks that stagnate or drag on always go into *marathon sessions* that end in *11th-hour settlements.*

◆ Crisis-induced press conferences are always *hastily called.*

◆ A newsmaker caught fending off obnoxious reporters and ridiculous questions is always said to be *keeping the media at bay.*

◆ Among the performers in any media circus are always the ever-present *hordes of photographers.*

◆ Running backs always *find daylight* after blockers create a hole *big enough to drive a truck through.*

◆ Errors made by baseball players are always *costly.*

◆ Teams that win in tournaments, especially high school teams, always *came to play.*

◆ Rookies always come in only one color: *green.*

THE 12-STEP PROGRAM TO GOOD WRITING

A speech by Michael Gartner

Michael Gartner is a journalism legend. He's been president of NBC News, Page One editor of The Wall Street Journal, editor of The Des Moines Register, general news executive of USA Today — and in 1997 Gartner won the Pulitzer Prize for editorials he wrote in the Ames (Iowa) Tribune, of which he was editor and co-owner.

In this speech, delivered at a writer's workshop a few years ago, Gartner summarizes what it takes to be a good writer. It's advice every new reporter would be wise to heed.

I'm told I am talking about The Fun of Writing. But writing isn't always fun. Sometimes, it's painful. Sometimes, it's frustrating. Sometimes, it's embarrassing. The fun of writing? That, sometimes, is like the fun of a headache. Or the fun of cavities. Or the fun of divorce.

I have been associated, off and on, with USA Today, so I tend to make lists and charts and graphs. This morning, let me give you a list. I'll call it, with a bow to Alcoholics Anonymous, the 12-Step Program to Good Writing.

Step 1: Report.

Words alone aren't enough. Good writing needs facts. You cannot be a good writer if you are not a good reporter. You need facts and details, quotes and descriptions.

Even if you're writing fiction, you need facts. Think about the mystery novels you read. They all have good plots, of course, but they have something else, too: they all teach you something. John Grisham will teach you about the law, or about the death penalty, or about New Orleans. Elmore Leonard will teach you about Florida or racing. Tom Clancy loads his books with fact.

Writing is just the pie crust; facts are the pie. So report, report, report. Then throw away the meaningless, the redundant, the unnecessary. (Don't do the opposite. Adlai Stevenson said journalists are people who separate the wheat from the chaff — then print the chaff.)

Keep the good stuff. Then sit down to write. So, first, report.

Step 2: Read.

You cannot be a good writer if you don't read. Read great stuff. Read awful stuff. Read classics. Read trash. And think about the writing that you're reading. Why did he say it that way? Why did she put it this way? Why is that so awful? Why is this so good?

Do you want to read some beautiful writing? Read the essays of Dr. Lewis Thomas, read the editorials of Vermont Royster, read the columns and essays of Calvin Trillin. Read Sports Illustrated. Read "Winnie the Pooh." Read — and reread and reread and reread — anything by E.B. White. Read the Page One articles in The Wall Street Journal, the science articles in The New York Times, the sports articles in The Boston Globe. So, second, read.

Step 3: Listen.

You cannot be a good writer if you don't listen.

I used to work at NBC News, and there was a wonderful woman there. She was smart and personable and telegenic, and I always thought she was going to be a zillion-dollar star. But she had a fatal flaw. She didn't listen.

She might be interviewing you, and she'd say, "Now tell me, Mr. Gartner, I understand your second rule of good writing is to read. Is that right?" and you'd say, "Yes, but before I get to that, I should tell you that on the way up to the show this afternoon I saw 18 masked men come into the lobby of this building, and they grabbed Tom Brokaw and Bryant Gumbel and have kidnapped them, and they killed four guards as they left the building." And she'd say, "Yes, and what is your third rule of good writing?"

She didn't listen. And I should add, she is no longer at a network.

The good writer must listen for the nuance, the emotion, the detail, the odd fact. The good writer must listen for the great quote — a quote, after all, is just the print version of a sound bite — must listen for the evasive answer, must listen for the heartfelt reply. The good writer must listen so carefully that he, or she, can follow through on a dropped hint, a fumbled answer, a punted reply. So, third, listen.

Step 4: Simplify.

The best piece of newspaper advice I ever got in my life I got, fortunately, when I was just 21 years old. I was just out of college, a newly hired copy editor at The Wall Street Journal. I was working nights and late one evening I looked up and this big, gentle man was standing there watching me. He introduced himself as Barney Kilgore.

Barney Kilgore was the man who invented the modern-day Wall Street Journal. He was a genius. He had been a reporter and editor, but by this time he was president of the company — though, like all good managers, he spent a lot of time walking around the place.

"What are you doing?" he asked me. I explained that I was trying to rewrite a story I'd been given, because it was murky. "Good," he said, and then he added: "Remember, the easiest thing for the reader to do is quit reading."

Oh, what wonderful advice to a newspaperman. I pasted it on my typewriter, and I've kept it written on my computers and notebooks — and etched in my brain — ever since.

"The easiest thing for the reader to do is quit reading." So you have to keep the reader interested. You must not bore him. You must not confuse him. You must not alienate him. Or her.

You must cut the complex to the simple, you must turn the simple into the eloquent. You cannot be lazy, and you cannot be careless. Or you will lose the reader. And if you lose the reader often enough, you will lose your job. So, fourth, simplify.

Step 5: Collaborate.

You cannot be a good newspaper writer if you don't have a good working relationship with your editor. Talk about ideas. Talk about structure. Talk about sources. Talk about length. Talk about everything.

You cannot have an adversarial relationship with your editor. In the first place, that wastes too much of your energy, thinking constantly of her as a bitch or him as a son of a bitch. In the second place, that deprives you of a great sounding board. In the third place, it gets you lousy play for your stories.

Everyone needs an editor. But just as good lawyers go forum shopping for good judges, good reporters should go forum shopping for good editors. (You know what Lord Keynes said of lawyers and writing: They turn poetry into prose, and prose into jargon.) Look around your newsroom, find an editor you admire and attach yourself to him or her. For a bad editor can turn poetry into prose, can ruin good writing.

Once, when I was a young editor on the Page One desk at the Journal, my boss wandered over to the fellow at the next desk and tossed back a piece he had been working on for a day or two. "Redo it," he said. "What's wrong?" the writer asked. The reply was simple: "You've got all the words but none of the music."

Find an editor who can recognize the music, fine-tune it, even add it. A good writer must have a good editor. So, fifth, collaborate. Which brings me to …

Step 6: Trust.

You cannot be a good writer, a good reporter or a good editor if you don't work in an atmosphere of trust.

Let me explain it with another story from my days — it seemed like a lifetime, but it was only five years — at NBC. One afternoon, Tom Brokaw and I were arguing. I can't remember what it was about, but I remember we were sitting in my office, and we had strong views — strong and opposing. He thought something should be on the air, and I thought it shouldn't, but maybe it was the other way around.

"Look," I said, "if we do this, we could end up with egg on our face."

"No," he said. "If we don't, we could end up with egg on our face."

And he added, "And the thing you've got to realize is this: it's your egg, but it's my face."

And that's the way it is in newspapers, too — sometimes it's the editor's egg, sometimes the reporter's; sometimes it's the editor's face, sometimes the reporter's. But if you don't trust one another — respect one another — one of you is going to end up with egg on your face, and it might not be your egg.

Trust means honesty and respect, openness and courtesy. You simply cannot work with someone you don't trust. So, sixth, trust.

Step 7: Experiment.

There is, in London, a borough called Hackney. Centuries ago, it was known for the horses that were bred there. A Hackney horse was often hired out, so eventually the word "hackney" came to describe any horse kept for hire. Horses that are hired out are often used for dull, plodding work, and that's why today we say anything — a phrase, a practice, a style — that's dull, overworked or worn out is *hackneyed*.

That's why a writer whose assignments are boring or whose writing is stale is called a hack. And the way you keep from being boring or dull or stale is to experiment.

Don't let your writing get in a rut. I realize that this is especially hard at newspapers and magazines that have unbreakable formulas for writing articles and features. But fight the system.

Peter Kann was probably the best writer in the history of The Wall Street Journal. (And, as his editor, I should add, "and the worst speller.") He was always experimenting, always forcing me to break the mold of those Page One stories. He'd go to far-off corners of the world, gather wonderful detail, telling anecdotes and pithy quotes, then assemble them into something beautiful that looked not at all like the formula Page-One stories of then or now. They were just too beautiful to touch, so beautiful and delicate that I feared if I even breathed heavily on just one paragraph the whole arrangement would crumble. So I'd run them as Peter wrote them — except, of course, for the spelling — and the readers were thrilled.

Try new techniques, new arrangements, new gimmicks, though that's a lousy word to use. So, to avoid being a hack, seventh, experiment.

Step 8: Talk.

Talk to others, but talk to yourself. Chip Scanlan of the Poynter Institute once asked me how many times I write a lead for an editorial before I find the right one. Just once, I said. But then I admitted I write 50 in my head, on the 35-mile drive to work in the morning or home in the evening. I compose as I drive, and then I say the leads out loud, listening for the rhythm and cadence, hunting for the lyric — much the same way, I suspect, a songwriter taps out different notes on his piano in search of just the right tune. Sometimes, I make up whole editorials — 400 or 500 or 600 words — as I drive, and I talk them to myself, often out loud. I work, especially, on the leads and the endings. For I think the biggest flaw in newspaper writing is a lack of endings.

In television, I constantly heard producers talking about how a story had to have a beginning, a middle and an end. So do newspaper stories — even the briefest, most mundane. A story has to have an end, a closing. The reader can't feel she has been left hanging. You have to have a graceful way to say, as Porky Pig used to say, "That's all, folks." In editorial writing, the ending has to make the point one final time, add the final punctuation. In news stories, it has to be the final ribbon wrapping up the package of information.

Remember how, a while ago — it might seem like hours to you — I said Step No. 3 was "listen." Well, listen to yourself, too. The good writer develops his own voice. You just can't do that if you don't listen to yourself. And the best way to listen to yourself is to read to yourself — out loud. Listen for the cadence — or the discordance. Listen for the beat — and the offbeat. Listen for the rhyme and the reason. Sometimes, you'll hear the jarring word, the awkward phrase — the word that looked just fine but sounded junky, the phrase that typed nice but sounded clunky. So, eighth, talk.

Step 9: Pounce.

My partner at the Ames newspaper, the guy I own the paper with, had a party when I won the Pulitzer Prize. He had the whole staff in, of course, and some townfolk, and he invited my father, a retired newspaperman who turned 95 that very day.

Everyone was having a good time, and I saw, out of the corner of my eye, a Des Moines Register reporter talking to my father. They talked for several minutes. The next day, in the Register story, there was one paragraph about my father. After noting that the youngest person at the reception was a 5-year old, the reporter wrote: "The oldest was Gartner's father, Carl, whose 95th birthday coincided with the announcement that his son had won the most prestigious prize in journalism. 'I taught him to dangle his first participle,' Carl Gartner said."

That was a great quote, and the reporter pounced on it. The good writer knows how to use quotes. He knows to use them as punctuation, as transition, as reinforcement. He knows never to use them redundantly, long-windedly, or

confusingly. The quote, as I said earlier, is just newspaperdom's sound bite — a device to move the piece along, to get the reader from here to there — by adding a dollop of fact or a dash of amusement. The good writer always uses quotes and always uses them sparingly. But it takes a good ear to get a good quote. So, ninth, pounce.

Step 10: Love.

You cannot be a good writer if you do not love writing and love reporting. It's simply impossible. If you do not love what you are doing, quit now and find another job, another line of work. For you'll never be happy — and you'll never be good.

I have this rule about work. No job is perfect, I believe. Every job has some tasks that are disagreeable or distasteful or dismaying. But no one should stay in a job where more than 20 percent of the duties are unpleasant and unsatisfying. When the bad-part index hits 20, quit. Every job should be at least 80 percent fun. You can't love a job that's no fun, and you can't succeed in a job you don't love. That's especially true if the job is writing. To be a good writer, you just absolutely have to love writing — you have to love the meanings and sounds of words, you have to love the rhythms of phrases, the cadence of sentences. You have to love, even, the look of paragraphs as they sit atop one another.

You have to love facts, too. You simply cannot be a good newspaper person if you are not curious. I remember, once, when my daughter, who now is 26, was in kindergarten, and the teacher called us in. "I'm worried about Missy," the teacher said. "She seems so immature." "Well, what the hell," I responded, "she's only 5 years old." My wife, more rational as always, asked the teacher what she meant. "Well," the teacher said, "she just walks around all the time and asks everyone else what they are doing."

"I hate to tell you this," I said to the teacher, "but that's what I do all day, too."

You cannot be a good writer if you do not love facts. You cannot get facts if you are not curious. Therefore, as your logic teacher would tell you, you cannot be a good writer if you are not curious. So, tenth, love.

Step 11: Care.

You cannot be a good writer — or reporter — if you do not care what you are writing about. You have to have a genuine interest.

I'm not saying you should have an agenda — indeed, if you have an agenda you should not be in the newspaper business. And let me stop here, for a minute, and explain. If you want to change the world, you are in the wrong business. If you want to change the world, become a teacher or a politician or a sociologist or a mom. Do not be a reporter.

I have a friend who 40 years ago was a summer intern on

the Baltimore News-American, which doesn't exist any more. Soon after my friend got there, a wise and wizened old city editor called him over.

"Son," he said, "there are two million people in this town, and every one of them has a story to tell." My friend thought he knew what was coming, and he sort of rolled his eyes. But the old editor continued: "And the thing for you to remember, son, is that most of those stories are crappy."

Well, anything can be made interesting, but it's a whole lot harder to write interestingly about people with boring stories than people with charming ones. So pick your stories carefully, for it's hard to care about something crappy. And you cannot be a good writer if you do not care about what you are writing about. So, eleventh, care.

Step 12: Balance.

You can be a good writer and write terribly unfair stories, but you can't be a good newspaper writer and do that. Not, at least, for a mainstream newspaper. Fairness is vital for every story and every newspaper, for the unfair story hurts the credibility of the reporter and the editor and the newspaper.

What this means is that the good writer avoids cheap shots. And I know that is hard to do. Cheap shots are just so much fun. Sometimes, they just roll out of the computer like Fords off an assembly line. They are sharp and snappy and pretty and appealing. But they're also deadly — for the writer.

All I can tell you is what I do — keep writing them, because they're so much fun to write — but then take them out. I have a drawer full of the greatest cheap shots in Iowa, words and phrases that I savor, that I chuckle over, that I read to my friends. But they've never made it to print — well, most never have — because I, or sometimes one of my editors, decided they just weren't fair. And good newspaper writing, as I said, demands fairness. So, twelfth, balance.

Today, for you to get into the brains of my children — and of me and my father — you must report more thoroughly than ever and write more gracefully than ever. You must report. Read. Listen. Simplify. Collaborate. Trust. Experiment. Talk. Pounce. Care. And balance.

It is an enormous challenge — and it can be enormous fun. Who else in the world is paid just to ask questions, to think and to write?

There simply is nothing more satisfying, nothing more fun.

What's your IQ?

Answers to the journalism fact-and-folklore quiz on page 7.

1) Frank Zappa.

2) Perry White, editor of The Daily Planet (where Clark Kent and Lois Lane worked).

3) DEWEY DEFEATS TRUMAN (see photo at right). As it turned out, it was actually Truman who defeated Dewey in the 1948 presidential election.

4) Ann and Abby (Ann Landers and Abigail Van Buren).

5) The launch of USA Today.

6) The Atlanta Journal-Constitution; the

Detroit Free Press; the Toronto Globe and Mail.

7) Walter Cronkite.

8) "Dr. Livingstone, I presume?"

9) Japan (a paper called Yomiuri Shimbun).

10) 30.

11) In 1974, Barbara Walters was hired by ABC as its first permanent news anchor (though Marlene Sanders had anchored some newscasts years before).

12) 4,400.

13) Sex columnist.

The STUDENT JOURNALISTS' NEWS ATTITUDE SURVEY

Results from the survey on page 14, based on responses received in February 2006 from 569 students enrolled in a variety of journalism courses at 10 U.S. colleges ranging in size from small (Cerritos College in California) to large (Michigan State University).

---

1) I think news stories usually:

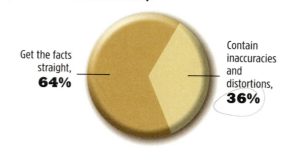

Get the facts straight, **64%**

Contain inaccuracies and distortions, **36%**

2) I prefer to get my news:

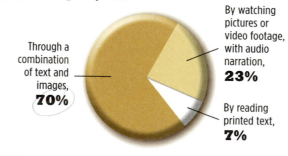

Through a combination of text and images, **70%**

By watching pictures or video footage, with audio narration, **23%**

By reading printed text, **7%**

3) Generally, I think the government:

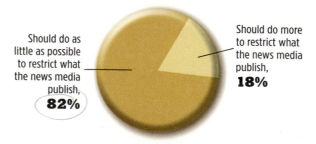

Should do as little as possible to restrict what the news media publish, **82%**

Should do more to restrict what the news media publish, **18%**

---

4) The president is assassinated. What would you be most likely to do? (You can choose more than one):

Turn on the TV, then leave it on constantly to monitor the situation	**58%**
Turn on the TV, see what's happening, then get on with my life	**33%**
Track developments online by monitoring news Web sites	**22%**
Buy a newspaper as soon as I saw one with a big assassination headline	**17%**
Listen to radio news and talk shows	**15%**
Avoid the news as much as possible to escape the hype and overkill	**5%**

5) Which of these people do you consider to be journalists?

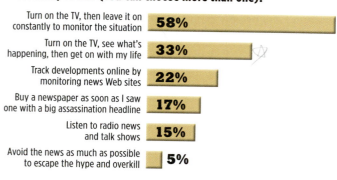

Bill O'Reilly	**44%**
Bob Woodward	**39%**
Oprah Winfrey	**18%**
Rush Limbaugh	**24%**
Katie Couric	**54%**
Jon Stewart	**36%**

THIS QUESTION WAS BASED ON A POLL DISCUSSED ON **PAGE 130**

6) In general, the news is biased in favor of:

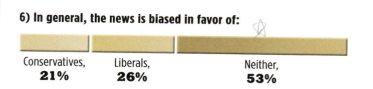

Conservatives, **21%**	Liberals, **26%**	Neither, **53%**

7) If you heard conflicting versions of a news story, which version would you be most likely to believe?

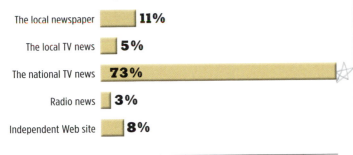

The local newspaper **11%**

The local TV news **5%**

The national TV news **73%**

Radio news **3%**

Independent Web site **8%**

8) Which of these adjectives would you generally use to describe most news today? (You can select more than one):

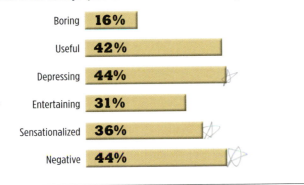

Boring **16%**

Useful **42%**

Depressing **44%**

Entertaining **31%**

Sensationalized **36%**

Negative **44%**

9) How often do you generally watch TV news?

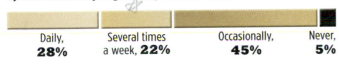

Daily, **28%** | Several times a week, **22%** | Occasionally, **45%** | Never, **5%**

10) How often do you generally read newspapers?

Daily, **30%** | Several times a week, **30%** | Occasionally, **35%** | Never, **5%**

11) How often do you generally read news online?

Daily, **25%** | Several times a week, **23%** | Occasionally, **36%** | Never, **16%**

12) A news reporting career seems like it would be (check all that apply):

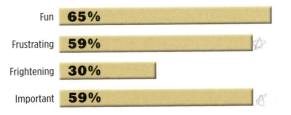

Fun **65%**

Frustrating **59%**

Frightening **30%**

Important **59%**

CONFIDENTIAL SOURCES

What would you do if a judge ordered you to reveal the name of a confidential source — if refusal meant you'd be sent to jail for contempt?

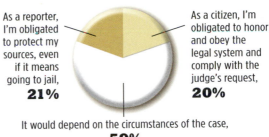

As a reporter, I'm obligated to protect my sources, even if it means going to jail, **21%**

As a citizen, I'm obligated to honor and obey the legal system and comply with the judge's request, **20%**

It would depend on the circumstances of the case, **59%**

WHICH OF THESE STATEMENTS DO YOU MOST AGREE WITH?

(Those answering "neither" are represented by the thin white pie slice.)

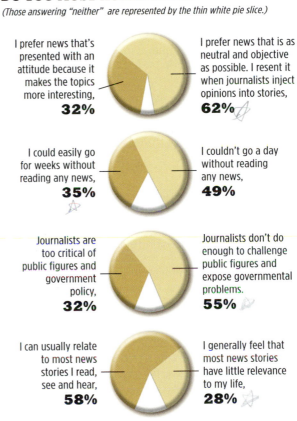

I prefer news that's presented with an attitude because it makes the topics more interesting, **32%**

I prefer news that is as neutral and objective as possible. I resent it when journalists inject opinions into stories, **62%**

I could easily go for weeks without reading any news, **35%**

I couldn't go a day without reading any news, **49%**

Journalists are too critical of public figures and government policy, **32%**

Journalists don't do enough to challenge public figures and expose governmental problems. **55%**

I can usually relate to most news stories I read, see and hear, **58%**

I generally feel that most news stories have little relevance to my life, **28%**

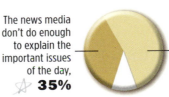

The news media don't do enough to explain the important issues of the day, **35%**

The news media do a good job explaining important issues; the problem is, people just don't pay attention, **54%**

Generally, I prefer to read news about serious issues and major events, **52%**

Generally, I prefer to read celebrity news and lighter, offbeat stuff, **36%**

1 WHICH STORY IS MORE NEWSWORTHY?

1) An earthquake struck **San Diego** today, killing at least 50.

Both events would be tragic, but San Diego has greater proximity to Americans, and the story would have a much greater emotional connection.

2) The office of **Oprah Winfrey** was evacuated today after a clerk opened a letter believed to contain anthrax.

Readers crave celebrity news, and such a dramatic death threat to a popular public figure would warrant media attention. Foreign diplomats don't have quite the prominence (in America) that Oprah does, although any political incident involving bioterrorism is still newsworthy.

3) Police arrested 20 suspected terrorists in downtown Toronto today **after a three-hour gun battle.**

The more violent the conflict, the more newsworthy it becomes. A gun battle in the heart of any city makes a dramatic story.

4) An ebola victim is being treated at a local hospital.

Yes, the governor's son has a certain amount of celebrity, but the ebola virus is a rare and fatal disease with terrifying implications for everyone in the community.

5) A local policeman died last weekend after **he tried to rescue a young boy from drowning.**

A plane crash in the wilderness is tragic, but remote. A losing battle to save a child's life in the line of duty is a gripping story that demands to be told.

6) A drunk driver was killed after his car hit a tree **on the way to his 100th birthday party.**

The story becomes much more compelling once we grasp the cruel irony of a 100-year-old man dying that way.

7) Convicted double murderer Arthur Itis escaped from prison **last night.**

A murderer on the loose *now* gives this story urgency. If he escaped a year ago, we assume he's probably long gone and no longer a threat.

8) A new local pooper-scooper law takes effect at midnight tonight.

Yes, a legislative pay hike affects our tax dollars, but the consequences are abstract and distant. A new pooper-scooper law, on the other hand, has an immediate impact on the daily activities of pet owners throughout the community.

2 WOULD YOU RUN THESE STORIES?

1) Former Yankee legend and baseball Hall-of-Famer Bo Linball died last night in a Brooklyn nursing home at age 103.

A: Yes, this would run in the sports section, probably as a news brief, unless there was a substantial local connection.
B: No. Not relevant to campus listeners.
C: No. No connection to the community.
D: No. Wrong kind of celebrity; not an odd-enough death.

TEST YOURSELF
Answers to the questions on page 32
EXERCISES FOR CHAPTER 2

2) Rhoda Rooter, a local botanist, stunned the state flower show last weekend by unveiling Sapphire Serenity, the first naturally hybridized blue rose.

A: Yes. This would make a terrific photo story for the Living section; might even provide an opportunity for a big color photo on Page One.
B: No — unless Rhoda has a connection to the botany department at the college, in which case her achievement deserves coverage.
C: Yes. Again, a terrific photo story.
D: No. Too dull and ordinary for our readers.

3) A Springfield College professor resigned Tuesday after winning $5 million in the state lottery.

A: Yes. This could make an interesting profile.
B: Yes. On campus, this is a story that students and faculty can easily relate to.
C: Only if the daily paper didn't write the story — or if the reporter discovers another angle that makes the story interesting. Ordinarily, weekly papers won't waste time and energy covering stories that have appeared earlier in competing publications.
D: No. Too bland and ordinary for our readers.

4) A man claims that a prostitute he hired in a Springfield hotel turned out to be an alien who tried to suck his brain.

A: No. Too idiotic and unverifiable. You can't print every bizarre fantasy that people dream up or you won't have room for real news.
B: No. Too idiotic and unverifiable.
C: No. Too idiotic and unverifiable.
D: Yes. This is just the kind of material we're looking for.

5) A new fad on Canadian college campuses: "pumping," where students stick bicycle pump nozzles up their sphincters to give themselves a rush of air.

A: Possibly, depending on the editors' tastes. Some will argue that this fad is too crude to publicize. (Although if deaths result, it becomes a fatal health-fad story worth covering.)
B: Yes. Our own students love hearing about crazy students on other campuses.
C: No. Too distant, too tasteless.
D: Yes. Possible cover story? With photos?

6) A typhoon struck Borneo this morning, killing more than 400 and leaving thousands homeless.

A: Yes. Breaking international news; deserves a story.
B: Yes. Breaking international news; deserves at least a mention in a news-headline roundup.
C: No. Too distant, too timely for a weekly publishing schedule.
D: No. Our readers want escape, not depressing reality.

7) The Springfield County commissioners approved permits for a new waste-disposal site yesterday.

A: Yes. This is dull-but-important news for local readers.
B: Probably not. Too bureaucratically disconnected from campus life.

C: Yes. This is dull-but-important news for local readers.
D: No. Never.

8) A doctoral psychology student at Springfield College believes that tattoos lower your IQ.

A: No. Without scientific evidence, this is just another crackpot theory. Conduct legitimate research and produce trustworthy data — *then* we'll talk.
B: No. We don't consider unprovable opinions to be news.
C: No. We don't consider unprovable opinions to be news.
D: Yes. And let's illustrate the story by showing some dumb-looking guy with lots of tattoos.

③ WHAT'S IT CALLED?

1. Cutline (or caption)
2. Attribution
3. Beat
4. Headline
5. Byline

6. News
7. Lead
8. Liftout quote
9. Dateline
10. Jump

---

① CHOOSE THE BEST LEAD

1) The best lead is *b*. It's simple and straightforward, putting the basic facts in the right order.

Example *a:* You shouldn't lead with the *where* (Lyman Airport).

Example *c:* The word "tragic" is unnecessary. Most editors would remove it.

2) The best lead is *c*. Example *a* uses a weak topic lead, telling readers that *the city council met*. Big deal. The wording is awkward (*to improve a plan to increase*).

Example *b* offers more detail, although that 4-3 vote tally isn't really worth including in the lead. And the wording makes it seem as though the water rates go up on Tuesday.

But *c* is the most effective, reader-friendly approach. *If you live in Oakdale* will immediately grab your attention (if you live in Oakdale, that is; if you don't, you may tune out the story, but that's fine). The lead then explains why this matters to you: *Your water bill is increasing.* And to Oakdale citizens, that's the ultimate meaning of this story. In subsequent paragraphs, the story will explain why the council took this action.

Some editors and instructors will balk at using a direct-address lead here, on a news story. But as we'll see in Chapter 5 (on covering meetings), it's a useful way to alert readers that this news affects *you.*

3) The best lead is *c*. Example *a* begins clumsily with the date, including the unnecessary *June 3*. Example *b* leads with the girls' names — but ordinary news stories will usually use delayed-identification leads, as *c* does. And the phrase *twirled to victory* is vague and possibly condescending: If you spent hundreds of hours honing your dancing skills, would you want them described as *twirling?*

4) The best lead is *b*. Why? We can't legally prove that Robbin Banks is guilty of any crime, so it's wrong to say *he was arrested after robbing a bank;* we can't say *his crime was robbing banks.* Both of those sentence constructions brand him as guilty, which could lead to accusations of libel. To be safe, as we'll explore in Chapter 5 (on covering crime), the best wording is found in example *b.*

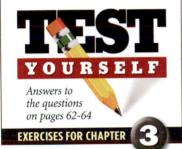

Answers to the questions on pages 62-64

EXERCISES FOR CHAPTER ③

One other problem: Example *b* spoils the punch line. The guy's name looks like it could be *Robbin Banks Friday.*

5) The best lead is *c*. It's short. Simple. It sets up the story without clutter. The details — his name, the pneumonia, the all-time record — will follow in paragraphs two and three.

Neither *a* nor *b* is bad, however. But a delayed-identification lead is preferable if the name isn't recognizable (or humorous, as in question 4).

Other problems: Example *a* begins with the word *pneumonia,* which simply isn't a crucial element of the story. And there's no *when* in that sentence.

Example *b* uses the word *prison* twice in the same awkward phrase (*the oldest prisoner ever to serve in a Florida prison*).

② TOO MUCH OPINION?

1) Moe Mentum's futile campaign came to a disappointing end last night as the candidate conceded defeat before 200 loyal supporters.

There's too much opinion in this sentence, making it more commentary than newswriting. Three adjectives are to blame:

Futile: His campaign was hopeless? Doomed? That's an opinion, and a negative one.

Disappointing: To whom? Obviously, the majority of the voters in this election aren't depressed.

Loyal: If you can't look into the hearts of all of his supporters, you can't judge if they're all truly loyal, can you? (Some of them might be spies from his opponent's campaign staff.)

2) Moe Mentum's grassroots campaign came to an end last night as the exhausted candidate conceded defeat before 200 cheering supporters.

This sentence is more accurate. Three adjectives provide description, but in an acceptably neutral way:

Grassroots: This isn't meant as an insult; it describes a campaign that relies on citizen involvement instead of major political-party support.

Exhausted: If it's clear that the candidate is acting fatigued — or better yet, if he admits it — it's appropriate to note it here.

Cheering: If you observe that everyone in the room is, in fact, clapping and yelling, this observation is accurate.

3) Logging continued in Conifer National Forest yesterday, despite howls of protest from liberal legislators and environmental radicals who assailed timber workers as "rapists."

This lead unfairly favors the loggers. Its wording creates the kind of negative spin that talk-show radio hosts do best: It discredits the opposition by unfairly labeling them all as either *liberals* or *radicals,* trivializing complex arguments to *howls of protest.* We're not told who called timber workers *rapists,* but highlighting such a sensational-yet-unsourced quote seems deliberately inflammatory. One ugly word hurled by one angry protester does not fairly characterize the reasoning of the entire group.

It would be just as biased — and unfair — to word that lead in a way that favors the environmentalists. For example:

Hundreds of concerned citizens gathered in Riley Plaza yesterday to protest the timber industry's continued destruction of giant redwoods in Conifer National Forest.

4) Legendary geezers the Rolling Stones will rock Memorial Coliseum tonight as they kick off the first of three highly anticipated weekend concerts.

In feature writing, especially in stories about popular culture, you're usually permitted to adopt a more playful personality than straight news stories would allow — but it's a fine line, hard to define. Overt bias or negativity is inappropriate, but it's OK to reflect prevailing cultural attitudes.

For instance, the Stones *are* pop-music legends, virtually everyone would agree. And their age is a factor in all news coverage about the band: it's ironic and amusing to see 60-somethings continuing to act like teenagers. Here, the word *geezer* is used with affection toward major celebrities; it would have an entirely different, crueler meaning if you called your aging school superintendent a geezer.

In subsequent paragraphs, this story will quote fans who are excited about the concert — so describing the show as *highly anticipated* accurately reflects the content of the story.

5) This is a parody of a traditional news report, something "The Daily Show" has mastered brilliantly over the years. It's satire, as biased as humanly possible (but notice how terrific those descriptions are).

UNSCRAMBLE THE FIVE W'S

Here are the *only* logical ways to combine those five W's — and the leads that result:

1) At midnight tonight, Abner Hoobler will become the first Nebraskan to reach the age of 115.

Notice that we led with the *when* — which is a bit unusual — because this story is based on time and timing. We've also identified Abner by name in our lead (instead of calling him *a Dayton man*) because Abner is a local celebrity, and it makes this neighborly news story a little more folksy and friendly.

Notice, too, that we'll save the local *where* for the second or third paragraph; the big *where* (Nebraska) is more essential than the nursing-home *where.*

2) A dog named Victor plunged over Niagara Falls Saturday — and emerged victorious.

Playing with the dog's name gives the story greater appeal than simply saying *a dog.*

Or to take a different approach:

While his family ate breakfast Saturday, Victor the dog went for a swim — over Niagara Falls.

Notice how using a dash forces the reader to pause a moment before reading that final phrase. The lead is set up like a joke, where a slight delay gives the punchline greater pizazz.

3) A Dayton woman decided her husband spent too much time clowning around with his friends, so she glued a clown mask to his face while he was sleeping.

We left the *where,* the *when* and the woman's name for later paragraphs. The most important thing is to communicate the clown angle as clearly and tightly as possible.

4) A local minister was bitten in the leg Sunday after leaping into the lions' den at the Dayton Zoo.

Rev. Faith Christian, a minister at the Dayton Zealotic Church, said she was trying to convert the lion to Christianity by shouting "Jesus loves you."

Conveying all that information in one sentence is extremely difficult; you run the risk of writing a "suitcase lead," one that bulges like an overstuffed bag. The solution above saves the *why* for the second paragraph while using a delayed-identification lead.

To write a slightly longer one-sentence lead, you could try this:

A local evangelist who leapt into the Dayton Zoo lions' den and shouted "Jesus will save you" was lucky to escape with just a bite in the leg when she tried converting the king of beasts to Christianity.

But some editors would argue that this lead is too long, so saturated with information that it bogs down.

BOIL DOWN THESE LONG-WINDED LEADS

1) The editor of the Catholic magazine America was forced by the Vatican to resign Wednesday after publishing articles critical of church positions.

2) Student drinking may be to blame for damage to campus windows, lights and doors last weekend, a school official said.

Or, if you want to lead with the damage:

Damage to campus windows, lights and doors last weekend may have been the result of student drinking, a school official said.

⑤ SUPPLY THE MISSING NUT GRAF

When Tad Pole left the Lawton Library last Tuesday afternoon, he couldn't believe his eyes.

"My bike was gone," he said. "That's the third bike I've had stolen this year. I had a huge honkin' lock on it, too."

Pole isn't alone. Campus bicycle thefts have hit an all-time high this year. On average, 50 bikes are reported stolen annually, but so far this year, that number is 230.

"I've never seen anything like this," said Seymour Butts, campus security chief. "Whether it's one thief or a whole gang, we can't be sure. But it's an epidemic."

Lynn O'Leum had an expensive mountain bike stolen from outside Hoobler Hall last week. "I know at least three other people whose bikes have been boosted this year," she says. "That's it. From now on, I'm walking."

Even Helmut Laws, president of the campus cycling club, had his bike stolen during a club meeting last month. . . .

6 WRITE THIS NEWS BRIEF

Some people would just take the money and run.

But when Laura Lynn Hardy found $300,000 lying on the street, she bicycled 20 miles through a Christmas Eve snowstorm to return the cash to its rightful owner.

After lunching in Lincoln on Friday, Hardy spotted an envelope on the sidewalk in front of Lincoln Federal Savings. The 19-year-old yoga instructor tossed it in her backpack and pedaled home to Locust Valley.

When she opened the envelope, Hardy discovered $300,000 in cash and checks payable to Fenster Ford, the area's largest car dealer.

Hardy alerted the bank, hopped back on her bike and raced to Lincoln just as snow was starting to fall. She was greeted at the bank by its president, Xavier Mooney, and by Fred Fenster, owner of Fenster Ford.

The trio posed for photos, shook hands and exchanged holiday wishes. And as darkness fell, Hardy hopped back on her bike and rode home.

Her reward for being so honest? A handshake.

"It's enough just to do the right thing," Hardy said.

There are other ways to begin this story. You could try a direct-address lead:

What would you do if you found $300,000? If you're Laura Lynn Hardy, you'd give the money right back.

Though questions leads are often lazy and obvious (which is why editors warn against them), they can hook readers into stories if they're skillfully worded.

You could also adopt the point of view of the men whose money was lost:

Two Lincoln businessmen were relieved to receive a last-minute gift from a good Samaritan on Christmas Eve.

The gift? A missing envelope worth $300,000.

But the most logical focus for the lead is Laura Lynn Hardy. She's the star of the story — and once your lead sets up the situation, no matter what approach you take, most of your story will become a chronological narrative that describes her actions.

Now, many readers might feel that this story is *really* about something that's not explicitly stated in the facts: Laura Lynn Hardy got gypped. After all she went through — bicycling 20 miles in the snow as darkness fell — on Christmas Eve, yet — the two wealthiest men in town didn't even *insist* on some kind of reward? A hundred dollars? A car? Free checking? *Anything?*

After finding $300,000 on the street, Laura Lynn Hardy bicycled 20 miles through a Christmas Eve snowstorm to return the money to two of the wealthiest men in town.

The reward for her honesty? A handshake.

Yes, many readers will agree that those two rich men *should* have insisted on rewarding Hardy. And many journalists will be offended by the sexism in Fenster's condescending quote. Still, some editors will find that lead is too judgmental; it crosses the line from news reporting to commentary. To learn more about the difference between the two, see page 130.

7 CHOOSE THE CORRECT GRAMMAR, PUNCTUATION AND STYLE

1) *Correct answer: a.* The AP stylebook says that it's *OK*, not *okay* or *o.k.* People wear *T-shirts.* And *coach* is a job description, not a formal title, so it does not need to be capitalized.

2) *Correct answer: b.* Military titles are abbreviated before proper names, so it's *Gen.*, not spelled out as *General.* Numerals 10 and above use figures; below 10, they're spelled out. And *vice president* is a formal title that's capitalized (but not abbreviated) before someone's name.

3) *Correct answer: b.* Compass directions (*east, west*) are generally lowercase; they're capitalized when they indicate regions (*the South*). Long state names are capitalized and set off by commas when they follow city names; short state names (*Ohio, Idaho, etc.*) aren't capitalized.

4) *Correct answer: a.* *FBI* uses no periods. Numbered streets use words (*First, Third*) if they're lower than 10; higher-numbered streets use numerals (*12th, 42nd*). Street addresses use no commas. And *avenue* is abbreviated when it's part of a street address.

5) *Correct answer: b.* Decades are abbreviated with apostrophes before the numeral, not after (*'90s*, not *90's*). Single letters are made plural by adding *apostrophe s* (*A's*), although multiple-letter combinations don't add apostrophes (*ABCs*). And speaking of apostrophes: it's written as *rock 'n' roll.*

6) *Correct answer: a.* When the abbreviation for *junior* follows a complete name, it's written *Jr.* but not set off by a comma. *Who*, not *that*, is the pronoun used for people (and animals with names). And *mayor* is a formal title that's capitalized only when it precedes a name.

7) *Correct answer: b.* When a number begins a sentence, it's generally spelled out. Use *from* and *to* together, as a pair, rather than adding a hyphen. It's redundant to say *10 a.m. in the morning.* Use figures and dollar signs (*$5*) in most references to money.

8) *Correct answer: b.* *Over* usually refers to spatial relationships (*the bird flew over the lake*); for numerals, use *more than.* Capitalize *World Series.* When plural nouns end in *s*, just add an apostrophe to make them possessive. And sports scores use hyphens (*5-2*), not the word *to.*

9) *Correct answer: a.* Spell out the word *percent* (one word, not *per cent*). And it's *Alzheimer's disease.*

10) *Correct answer: b.* Use numerals for all ages. After age 18, refer to *boys* and *girls* as *men* and *women.* Abbreviate September when it's used in a date.

8 CRAFTING CLEVER LEADS FOR BRITES

Here are the leads that originally began those four brites. There are other possibilities, of course — and yours may be more clever than these.

1) Linc and Helena Moore may have finally learned the answer to that age-old question: Why did the chicken cross the road?

Because the chicken doesn't know jaywalking is illegal.
— The Associated Press

2) Computer programmer Steve Relles has the poop on what to do when your job is outsourced to India.
— Reuters

3) Rick O'Shea was listed in serious condition Sunday at Park West Hospital — but he's in better shape than earlier, when he was declared dead.
— The Associated Press

4) At the London Zoo, you can talk to the animals — and now some of them talk back.
— The Associated Press

⑨ REWRITING THE EMANCIPATION PROCLAMATION LEAD

We sent this exercise to dozens of professional reporters at newspapers across the country, giving them the same instructions that *you* were given.

After reviewing their results, we selected the eight finalists shown below. We sent these eight leads back to the reporters, asking them to choose the best one (and to provide critical comments on all the entries).

Reprinted below are those eight finalists. As you read them, ask yourself:

◆ *How do these leads compare to* YOUR *solution?*
◆ *What do you like or dislike about each entry?*
◆ *Which one would you choose as the best of the batch?*

1

President Abraham Lincoln made a stand against slavery today, ordering freedom for more than 4 million people held in bondage in the secessionist states.

With Union forces making gains in the South, Lincoln's "Emancipation Proclamation" will take effect Jan. 1, 1863. His statement emphasized that a goal of the war under way was the "immediate or gradual abolishment of slavery."

The proclamation does not affect the status of slaves in border states loyal to the Union. And a seceding state may avoid the freedom measure if it rejoins the Union before Jan. 1.

> **JUDGES' COMMENTS:** "Ho-hum. None of the big picture, all of the details too soon."
>
> "I don't like the imprecise *made a stand.* And as I understand it, it does affect slaves in other areas if they escape there from the South."
>
> "I would have used *took* rather than *made,* and I'm not sure what the connection is between Union forces making gains in the South and the date the proclamation takes effect."
>
> "Tells the story. Wouldn't mind seeing this on the desk as a first take from AP."

2

President Abraham Lincoln signed an order Monday aimed at ending the 145-year-old institution of slavery in 10 secession states, affecting the fates of at least 4 million slaves and redefining the purpose of the nation's Civil War.

The executive order takes effect in three months, on Jan. 1. It does not address slaves living in Union states, border states or states that join the Union before the new year deadline.

Lincoln's move comes one week after the Union army's bloody victory in Antietam, Md., and 1½ years into the war between the North and South.

> **JUDGES' COMMENTS:** "Nice and straightforward, though *affecting the fates of* is imprecise – how? Also, readers at the time probably didn't need the *1½ years into the war* part, not on such a huge story."
>
> "Brisk, good rhythm and reflects a grand sense of history. It includes most major points and puts Antietam in better perspective."
>
> "This is the longest lead (37 words, including three numbers). A classic "suitcase" lead. (Was this from a *New York Times* reporter?)"
>
> "It's clear, direct and seems to be the shortest. I also think it is the best blueprint to guide a writer organizing a complex story."

3

President Lincoln declared four million U.S. slaves free as of Jan. 1, but his order carries little legal authority and probably will do little for those held in bondage in the 13 rebellious states.

Nonetheless, his Emancipation Proclamation, which goes into effect Jan. 1, marks the first serious American effort to limit the practice of slavery, which started on this continent in 1619 and was one of the root causes of the bloody rebellion, which now enters its 17th month.

> **JUDGES' COMMENTS:** "It's good, but not good enough. Repeated use of the word *little* in the lead grates on me. Not sure if it's accurate to say this was *the first serious American effort* to end slavery."
>
> "A little too much editorializing for me. I can almost live with *carries little legal authority,* but *probably will do little for those held in bondage* is a bit much on the opinion front."
>
> "I like the idea, but the words get muddled. It's not as tight as it needs to be (words like *nonetheless* and *on this continent* detract from the central meaning)."

4

Slaves will be "forever, free" and slavery abolished in states still rebelling against the United States on Jan. 1, according to an order signed yesterday by President Abraham Lincoln.

Owning slaves is not yet outlawed in states that are loyal to the Union. But the "emancipation proclamation," which also frees slaves who escape from or are captured from rebel states, makes clear the president's determination to keep fighting the war to reunite a nation where all people are free.

> **JUDGES' COMMENTS:** "Kind of clunky."
>
> "Wordy and tortured."
>
> "This one made me dizzy and nauseous."
>
> "It's too narrow, concentrating only on the issue of slavery and not what slavery means. And it errs in stating that slavery was not outlawed in states loyal to the Union. Only in the border states was it legal."
>
> "That comma in the quote is grammatically weird, but it was part of the quote, so . . ."

5

In a gesture likely to inflame both sides in the year-long war of secession, President Abraham Lincoln Monday enlisted a new army four million strong.

In an Emancipation Proclamation, the president announced that all slaves held in the secessionist states will be free, as of New Year's Day, 1863.

"Hereafter, the war will be prosecuted for the immediate or gradual abolishment of slavery," Lincoln declared. How this can be accomplished, and how the slaves might even hear of this declaration is unclear, but the President is clearly buoyed by last week's victory at Antietam and anxious to narrow the focus of the conflict.

The Declaration is also riddled with loopholes: Slaves held in the five border states of Delaware, Kentucky, Maryland, Missouri and West Virginia are not included, and any state that rejoins the Union before the measure takes effect may continue slavery for the present. Critics were swift to note this.

"We show our sympathy with slavery by emancipating slaves where we cannot reach them and holding them in bondage where we can set them free," said Secretary of State William Seward.

> **JUDGES' COMMENTS:** "I like the *enlisted a new army four million strong* in the lead. Nice image."
>
> "This one just does not work; it starts out with an odd declaration of a new army. In fact, several hundred thousand freed slaves did serve in the Union army, but not 4 million."
>
> "The reporter saying the president is *clearly buoyed* and *anxious* seems to be going out on a limb."
>
> "This one starts with a dependent clause and rambles for 25 words, none of which is *free* or *slaves,* which might tell readers what the story is about."

6

President Lincoln freed the slaves yesterday.

Lincoln signed an executive order yesterday that will free about 4 million slaves living in the Confederacy on Jan. 1, but will have the practical effect of freeing them now.

The proclamation is largely symbolic, however – slaves in the border states were not freed, and any Confederate state that re-enters the Union will be able to retain slavery there, as well.

So while Lincoln hailed the emancipation – "(A)ll persons held as slaves ... are, and henceforward shall be free" – his own Secretary of State, William Seward, belittled the executive order as symbolic and hypocritical.

"We show our sympathy with slavery by emancipating slaves where we cannot reach them and holding them in bondage where we can set them free," said Seward, who was a noted New York abolitionist before joining Lincoln's cabinet.

Lincoln's action, however, has confirmed to many, both in the North and the South, what they've long suspected: the war is being fought to end slavery, not over states' rights.

> **JUDGES' COMMENTS:** "If you're going to be historic, be historic. *President Lincoln freed the slaves yesterday* has all the flash of *Mary went to the store to buy milk.* If the grand and glorious idea is what constitutes your first sentence, be grand and glorious."
>
> "Best of the bunch. Short, to the point, with proper context. I especially liked the last graf, which puts the entire issue into its broad context."
>
> "I like the start, but didn't need the two *yesterdays* so close. The lead see-saws with *largely symbolic* – which is it? And the last graph is a good idea, but might need more precise wording: They more than *suspected* – they debated, etc. The proclamation didn't just come out of left field."

7

President Abraham Lincoln today pledged to free millions of slaves in the rebellious states of the South by Jan. 1, a decision that changes the very argument for the war. The Emancipation Proclamation is certain to elate abolitionists and ensure fierce debate in next year's presidential election.

Perhaps most critically, by changing the war's goal from preservation of the union to the abolition of slavery, the Emancipation Proclamation ends any chance of European intervention in favor of the cotton states. All of Europe outlawed slavery decades ago.

> **JUDGES' COMMENTS:** "Too intellectual for a daily newspaper."
>
> "I like the content, but the language is a little bookish. That's not necessarily a bad thing, but it's something to be aware of."
>
> "Clean. Summarizes the historical context succinctly and accurately."
>
> "This sounds more like analysis than straight news, especially to put the expected effects on next year's presidential race and Europe so high up. Just the news of the proclamation itself would have been huge."

8

After more than a year of war sparked by a state's right to allow slavery or the nation's power to abolish it, President Lincoln freed the slaves Monday. Sort of.

Lincoln signed a proclamation ending slavery "then . . . and forever" on New Year's Day in the states of the rebel confederacy. Left untouched by his so-called Emancipation Proclamation are slaves in five states that have not seceded from the Union and those in any state that rejoins the Union before the war ends.

Even Secretary of State William Seward acknowledged the inconsistency of Lincoln's move: "We show our sympathy with slavery by emancipating slaves where we cannot reach them and holding them in bondage where we can set them free."

> **JUDGES' COMMENTS:** "Too flip."
>
> "This sounds like something I'd read in sports: *The Patriots are a dynasty. Sort of.* To the guy with the whip marks on his back, I bet he wouldn't find it very amusing."
>
> "First sentence starts in a way that delays the big news."

THE WINNER: The lead that received the most votes from our judges was entry number 2, submitted by Todd Frankel of the St. Louis Post-Dispatch. (If it's any consolation, many veteran reporters came to realize that this was *not* an easy lead to write.)

THE FINALISTS: 1) Steve Paul. 2) Todd Frankel. 3) Don Hamilton. 4) Bob Batz. 5) Paul Duchene. 6) Judd Slivka. 7) Peter Sleeth. 8) Jim Camden.

HOW MUCH EDITTING DO YOU NEED?

Answers to the quiz on page 53.

❶ *Which would you print?*

a) Police arrested the rapist, Levon Coates, who sheriff Smith described as a homeless drug addict.

> This sentence uses the word *who* incorrectly; it should say *whom,* instead. And the title of *sheriff* should be capitalized. But worse: You're calling Leavon Coates a rapist when he hasn't been convicted. That invites a libel lawsuit. And speaking of lawsuits:

b) Police arrested the alleged rapist, Levon Coates, whom Sheriff Smith described as a homeless drug addict.

> Calling Coates an *alleged* rapist is considered sloppy and potentially defamatory by libel experts. Better rework the sentence to say that Coates was arrested and charged with rape.
>
> The big problem? Both sentences include the sheriff's statement that Coates is a drug addict. That is the sheriff's opinion, and it's a dangerous, unprofessional remark. Print it, and Coates can sue both the sheriff AND YOU for defamation of character unless you can *prove* he's a drug addict. Which you probably can't.
>
> The correct answer is "c" — neither one.

❷ *Which would you print?*

a) The $4,400,000 grant is allocated into three areas: $1,700,000 for research, $1,900,000 for new oscilators, and $1,800,000 for salaries.

> *Oscilators* is misspelled. There's no comma needed before the word *and.* And when it comes to printing numerals in the millions, most publications abbreviate with decimal points and spell out the word *million,* as example "b" does. But wait — there's more:

b) The $4.4 million grant is allocated into three areas: $1.7 million for research, $1.9 million for new oscillators and $1.8 million for salaries.

> This example is correctly written and punctuated. But the problem with both "a" and "b" is that the numbers add up to $5.4 million, not $4.4 million.
>
> The correct answer is "c" — neither one.

❸ *Which would you print?*

a) The terrorist will be hanged at midnight.

b) The condemned terrorist will be hung at 12 midnight.

> *Hanged* is the correct past tense of *hang* when

the verb refers to execution. Saying *12 midnight* is redundant. Some editors would also consider the word *condemned* to be redundant, too.
> The correct answer is "a."

❹ *Which would you print?*

a) By the time Lincoln became President, seven states had succeeded from the union: South Carolina, Florida, Mississippi, Alabama, Louisiana and Georgia.

> Capitalize *president* when it's used before Lincoln's name (to form the title *President Lincoln*) but not elsewhere in the sentence. Capitalize *Union.* It's *seceded,* not *succeeded.* And in addition:

b) By the time Lincoln became president, seven states had seceded from the Union: South Carolina, Mississippi, Florida, Alabama, Louisiana and Georgia.

> Though this sentence is written correctly, it lists only six states, not seven. (The seventh state, for those keeping score, was Texas.)
> The correct answer is "c" — neither one.

❺ *Which would you print?*

a) Melman is the candidate that is very heavily favored.

> It should be *who,* not *that: Melman is the candidate who is most heavily favored.*
> And most editors will urge you to avoid using the bland adverb *very.*

b) Melman is the heavily-favored candidate.

> No hyphen is needed after *heavily.* You should write: *Melman is the heavily favored candidate.*
> The correct answer is "c" — neither one.

❻ *Which is correct?*

a) Between you and me, she is a better reporter than I.

b) Between you and I, she is a better reporter than me.

> The correct answer is "a." If you need to know why, consult a good grammar guide.

❼ *Which would you print?*

a) Jim and his friend, Jack, were chased by his dalmatian puppy, Rex, which bit him.

b) Jim and his friend Jack were chased by his Dalmatian puppy, Rex, who bit him.

> To understand this one, look in The AP stylebook under "essential phrases." In a nutshell: If Jack is Jim's only friend in the world, you can call him *Jim's friend, Jack.* But if Jim has more than one friend, use no comma: *Jim's friend Jack.*
> The same applies to the puppy: Is Rex his only puppy, or one of many? We don't know. But because of all the pronouns in this sentence, we don't know whose dog it is or who got bit.
> What's more, the sentence should be active

(the puppy chased them), not passive (they were chased by the puppy). A good editor would ask you to rework this sentence for clarity.
> By the way, *who* is correct. And Dalmatian is capitalized.
> The correct answer is "c" — neither one.

❽ *Which would you print?*

a) The boys' golf team won their first play-off.

b) The boys golf team won its first playoff.

> The correct answer is "b." *Boys* doesn't take an apostrophe. The singular subject of the sentence *(team)* uses the pronoun *its* (no apostrophe). And *playoff* isn't hyphenated.

❾ *Which would you print?*

a) 20,000 helpless villagers died in the tragic volcano eruption.

> Don't begin sentences with numbers. But more importantly:

b) Twenty thousand helpless villagers died tragically in the volcano eruption.

> Give us facts, not emotions and opinions. Were all 20,000 villagers truly *helpless?* Did they all die *tragically?* In whose opinion?

c) The volcano killed 20,000 helpless villagers.

> A volcano will not kill you unless it erupts; it's the eruption that kills, not the volcano.
> One other note: A "village" is a small town with a small population. When 20,000 people die, that's a lot of victims — and editors might quibble about using the term "villagers."
> The correct answer is "d"— none of the above.

❿ *Which would you print?*

a) More than 50 anti-war churchgoers carried handmade signs.

b) Over 50 antiwar church-goers carried hand-made signs.

> The correctly hyphenated and nonhyphenated words are in "a." And when modifying numbers, *more than* is usually preferred.

⓫ *Which would you print?*

a) Prof. Anne Benson said, "Dr. Wormer is a blackmailing faggot, like my ex-husband."

b) Professor Anne Benson alleged that Dr. Wormer was "a blackmailing faggot" like her ex-husband.

> Please say you answered "c." Never mind that "a" abbreviates *professor,* which you shouldn't do. The big problem here is that Professor Benson is using *you* to call both her ex-husband and Dr. Wormer blackmailers and faggots. Not only is that language highly offensive, but it exposes you to two defamation lawsuits. This ugly, libelous quote will cause you terrible pain.
> The correct answer is "c" — neither one.

① WHAT WOULD BE YOUR BEST SOURCES FOR THESE STORIES?

a) *Best sources for the Cara Mehl story:*

◆ **Cara's parents:** to talk about Cara's condition and plans for the trip.

◆ **Cara:** to get her reaction to the gift and to talk about her illness.

◆ **The church minister:** to talk about Cara's family and the fund-raising drive. He can also put you in touch with:

◆ **The coordinator of the fund-raising drive:** to get reactions and hear their future plans.

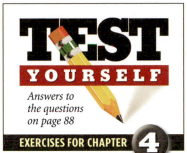

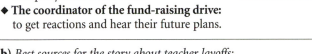

Answers to
the questions
on page 88

EXERCISES FOR CHAPTER 4

b) *Best sources for the story about teacher layoffs:*

◆ **The school superintendent:** to explain why the layoffs were necessary.

◆ **Book, Kuehl and Matrix:** to get their reactions and learn their future plans.

◆ **A representative from the teachers' union:** to comment on the layoffs.

◆ **Students taking classes from Book, Kuehl and Matrix:** to get reactions to their teachers' layoffs.

◆ **Other teachers and staffers at the high school:** get reactions to their colleagues' layoffs.

c) *Best sources for the campus crime story:*

◆ **Statistics:** The key to reporting this story *isn't* finding good quotes; it's uncovering data that accurately details the incidence of campus crime. For that, you'd begin by tracking down documents that provide statistics, both at your local college and at other key colleges, keeping in mind:

— You'll want to compare crime on your local campus to crime on other similar campuses. Avoid comparing apples to oranges. If you're a suburban community college, you'd want to analyze crime rates at other similarly sized suburban community colleges; if you're a large urban university, you'd want to track crime at other large urban universities.

— Sort crimes appropriately. Compare thefts to thefts, rapes to rapes; don't just lump everything into a pile called "crime."

— Some schools are reluctant to release crime data. If you encounter obstacles, try other sources: city police departments, the FBI — even the U.S. Department of Education tracks campus crime data.

You'll also want to speak to:

◆ **Campus police officials** for their data, opinions and anecdotes.

◆ **School administrators and spokespeople** for their observations and opinions.

◆ **Students,** ideally those affected by crime, to provide personal opinions and anecdotes.

◆ **Criminologists and other experts** who focus on campus crime or work for watchdog groups. (For instance, a Web search would turn up a nonprofit organization called Security on Campus, a clearinghouse for campus crime statistics and resources.)

d) *Best sources for the tiger story:*

◆ **First, general research:** Read past news stories on the Web to

see how common this situation is and to learn how these cases have been resolved in the past. Consult reliable sources about tigers for a quick crash course on their diet, lifestyle and personality. Then talk to:

◆ **Hugh Jass:** to explain the situation.

◆ **His neighbors:** to see what kind of problems Jass and his tiger have created.

◆ **The police:** the public information officer can tell you about the charges, but the arresting officer will probably have a better first-person story to tell you.

◆ **A tiger expert** (a zookeeper, a director of a wildlife sanctuary, a veterinarian who specializes in big cats) to comment on tigers confined in these living conditions.

◆ **Other government officials** who may be involved in the case, whether from the county health department or the USDA.

◆ **Hugh Jass' landlord,** to see if Hugh's lease allows him to have pets.

e) *Best sources for the logging story:*

◆ **First, general research:** Read past news stories on the Web to gain perspective and study the history of this controversial issue. As you begin gathering reliable statistics and insightful quotes, you'll also get a better sense of which human sources you should contact, including:

◆ **Forest service representatives,** to comment on the new decision.

◆ **Forestry experts,** to explain both sides of the issue.

◆ **Environmentalists,** to respond to the government's policy.

◆ **Homeowners** near the national forest who would be endangered by wildfires.

◆ **Local/state legislators** with a stake in the outcome.

f) *Best sources for the Claire Annette story:*

◆ **First, general research:** Visit her Web site. Study her biography. Read previous interviews she's given. Keep an eye out for any references to her childhood or teen years. (In fact, check all her lyrics to see if she reminisces in any of her songs.) Listen to as much of her music as you can. Then contact:

◆ **The concert promoter,** who can give you details about the concert — prices, dates, expectations of ticket sales — as well as contact information for Claire. If the promoter can't help you, contact Claire's record company or manager.

◆ **Claire,** to talk about her music, her life since leaving town, her memories of living here, her feelings about returning.

◆ **Claire's family,** if any relatives still live here, to see how they feel about her career. Will they loan you some old photos to print with the story? You can also ask them for the names of:

◆ **Friends Claire had** while growing up, to share old memories (and photos).

◆ **Local fans** buying concert tickets, to talk about Claire's music.

◆ **An old high school yearbook** will usually provide an old photo as a last resort.

Important hint: If you read that brief interview with Claire in question #2, she reveals a source that could turn this into a terrific story.

WHAT QUOTES WOULD YOU USE FROM THESE THREE INTERVIEWS?

On this page, we've reprinted each of those three interviews, adding comments and highlighting the remarks we'd quote directly.

CLAIRE ANNETTE

Preliminary chitchat. Not newsworthy.

"Hi. This is Claire. I've gotta catch a plane in, like, two minutes. Talk fast."

"OK. Thanks. How does it feel to come back home after all these years?"

She's stating an obvious fact. It's not necessary to quote her saying this.

"Home? Oh, yeah. We're playing two shows at Adler Auditorium. God, it's gonna be funny. . . I don't know. I mean, I lived there til I was, what? Eighteen? But even

This is her best quote about leaving home. Begin with the word "even" and end with the word "heart."

though I really needed to get away — to start over, to find my true voice — I've always kept that little town in my heart, I guess, even though it sounds corny to say it. And

A nice thought here, but it's just too inarticulate to use.

you know, it's true that everybody sort of fantasizes, you know, about fame and hitting it big. Well, hell, I

Eliminate the word "hell" unless you want it to add color. This reveals how she feels about herself, then and now.

may be famous, but I'm still basically the same lonely nerd I was back in high school. So, coming home. It's

Too much fumbling to quote directly. Best to paraphrase, though the phrase "painful reminder" might come in handy as a partial quote.

sad. Well, maybe not. See, all my family has sort of moved away, or died, so it's really just sort of a painful reminder of, you know, life goes on, things change.

Here it is: the best quote of the interview, and it tips you off to a great source who might otherwise have been left out of the story.

"I'll tell you, though: I'd love to see Mrs. Washburn again. She was my piano teacher for seven years. I still catch myself, in the middle of a concert, thinking, Boy, if only Mrs. Washburn could see me now. Yeah, I suppose I should really try to get ahold of her. I mean, if I

Best to end the quote before Claire starts babbling again.

have time. We'll see.

"Anyway, I gotta go catch a plane. Talk to you in a few weeks, OK? Bye."

ANITA BATH, *a devoted local fan:*

"Are you excited about finally getting to see Claire in concert?"

A bit of a cliché, but an honest reflection of her joy. Well worth quoting.

"Oh, come on. I mean, Jesus, this is like a dream come true for all of us here. I can't, you know, afford to

Fly to Japan? Interesting idea, but not worth quoting.

fly to Japan or some big stadium concert someplace else."

Best to start the quote after the word "Jesus," to avoid offending readers unnecessarily.

"What is it you like about her?"

"Gosh, her songs are so beautiful. Her lyrics are like poetry. And coming from the same place, geographically, it's like we speak the same language, you know what I mean?"

This summarizes the appeal Claire has for many local fans. It's a good quote, but it should end at the word "language."

"Will you get to sit up close for the concert?"

This isn't worth repeating. No one cares. Sorry.

"No. We're in the nosebleed seats. Our tickets suck."

"Any chance you'll get to meet her face to face while she's in town?"

This "uncle" thing may or may not be true. Everybody says stuff like this, but it means nothing.

"I've got a friend whose uncle used to live next door to her. But no, Claire's too important, and too busy. We'll go to the airport, though. We'll wave hello when she lands, and we'll wave goodbye when she leaves."

A nice sentence, and it encapsulates the loyalty some of her fans will express when Claire is here.

RAMONA WASHBURN,
Claire's childhood piano teacher:

"I taught Claire for seven years. She studied classical piano, along with a little jazz and ragtime. I had a studio in my living room, and she'd come once a week.

Good background information to include in the story, but too basic and ordinary to use as a direct quote.

She was a very . . . a very . . . oh, I don't know . . . a very clean girl. I mean, the way she played. I recall

"Clean"? Probably best not to quote Ramona here, since she seems to be fumbling for the right word. Wait until she starts making sense.

she had a very precise way of fingering the notes — she hated to make mistakes — and I used to tell her, Claire, dear, it's not enough just to hit the notes. You've got to put joy, and pain, and love into everything you play. Now, I

Again, it's probably best not to quote Ramona using the word "overboard" — or calling herself "old." Wait until she hits her stride with the word "some."

guess, she's really, you know, gone a little — well, I was going to say overboard, but maybe it's just me. I'm old, and I think perhaps some of her songs are a little too loud and vulgar for my taste. But when she plays soft and slow — oh, it's a sweet thing to hear, isn't it?"

Here's the memory you're waiting for: where Ramona reveals the young girl that eventually flowered into an artist. Great stuff.

A lovely sentiment, and it answers an important question readers will have: What does the teacher think of the student's music?

3 **QUOTES: PUNCTUATION AND ATTRIBUTION**

a) Gov. Lew Swires said he'll support a tax increase on Tuesday. "It's long overdue," said Gov. Swires.

What's wrong:

◆ The placement of the word *Tuesday* makes this quote confusing. Did Swires say this on Tuesday? Or will he support the tax increase next Tuesday? Or — most peculiarly — will he support tax increases that occur on Tuesdays?

As a general rule, try to place the *when* of an event as close as possible to the sentence's *verb.* In other words:

A giant asteroid destroyed Mars on Friday. OR:

Coach Smith announced Sunday that he was retiring. OR:

Gov. Lew Swires said Tuesday he'll support a tax increase.

Now, some might still find that last sentence confusing and interpret the news this way: *The governor said that next Tuesday he'll support a tax increase.* In this case, then, perhaps the best solution is to begin the sentence with a prepositional phrase:

On Tuesday, Gov. Lew Swires said he'll support a tax increase.

◆ The attribution for that direct quote is incorrect. Once we've identified Gov. Swires, we need only use his last name in all subsequent attributions. And the preferred form is *Swires said,* not *said Swires:*

"It's long overdue," Swires said.

b) "I adore Elizabeth Taylor," gushed student actor Art Major. "Did you ever see her classic performance in "Who's Afraid of Virginia Woolf?"

What's wrong:

◆ Most editors will consider the verb *gushed* a little too flowery. Better to let the quotation do the gushing and simply use the word *said* in the attribution.

◆ You must enclose the title of the movie, *Who's Afraid of Virginia Woolf?*, in single quotation marks, since it appears as a title inside a direct quote.

◆ Notice, too, that Art Major's quote is actually a question, so the quote needs to end in a question mark. Thus, to correctly punctuate the end of the quote, you'll need to run, in order:
1) the question mark that ends the movie title;
2) the single end-quotation mark that encloses the movie title;
3) the question mark that punctuates Art's quote; and
4) the double end-quotation mark that encloses Art's quote.

The corrected quote:

"I adore Elizabeth Taylor," said student actor Art Major. "Did you ever see her classic performance in 'Who's Afraid of Virginia Woolf?'?"

c) "Assaults on campus increased from 20 in 2004 to 33 in 2005," Penn State University deputy director of university police Ben Z. Dreen said. "That's an increase of 75 percent."

What's wrong:

◆ To avoid confusingly complex attributions, long job descriptions should *follow* the speaker's name, not precede it. The preferred order, in such cases, is this:
1) the word *said;*
2) the speaker's name;
3) the long, wordy job title.

Thus, the correct attribution here would be:

"Assaults on campus increased from 20 in 2004 to 33 in 2005," said Ben Z. Dreen, Penn State University deputy director of university police.

◆ However, there's a bigger problem: Dreen's math is incorrect. An increase from 20 to 33 is a 65 percent increase. Either his data is incorrect or his method of calculating percentage increases is faulty. Don't run this information until he's double-checked his math.

◆ This is a dull, dry statement that shouldn't even be a direct quote. Avoid using quotes to present statistics or simple facts; it's your job as a journalist to find the cleanest, clearest way to convey that information. Use quotes to add color, emotion or insight to the facts you gather.

d) The mayor complained, off the record, that Smith was "a rat" for betraying him, he said.

What's wrong:

◆ You generally need only one verb of attribution per sentence. Here, the mayor *complained* that Smith was "a rat." It's redundant to add the phrase *he said* at the end of the sentence.

◆ There's a much bigger problem here, however: If the mayor told you this off the record, why are you quoting him at all? You're betraying his confidence. This is called *burning your source.* The mayor will soon be calling your editor, demanding that you be fired. How will you defend yourself?

e) Ray Cleaves said, "When I was a boy, I saw Muhammad Ali battle George Foreman on Wide World of Sports. He was always my favorite boxer."

What's wrong:

◆ "Wide World of Sports" was the title of a TV show. It should appear in single quotes.

◆ Generally, you should avoid beginning a quote with the attribution. Instead, look for a logical pause — either at the end of a clause, or the end of a sentence — and insert the attribution there:

"When I was a boy," Ray Cleaves said, "I saw Muhammad Ali battle George Foreman on 'Wide World of Sports.' He was always my favorite boxer."

OR: "When I was a boy, I saw Muhammad Ali battle George Foreman on 'Wide World of Sports,' " Ray Cleaves said. "He was always my favorite boxer."

◆ But which boxer is Cleaves' favorite: Ali or Foreman? That pronoun *(he)* could apply to either man. You need to ask Cleaves to clarify his quote, then insert the proper name in parentheses to avoid confusing readers. Like so:

"When I was a boy, I saw Muhammad Ali battle George Foreman on 'Wide World of Sports,' " Ray Cleaves said. "He (Ali) was always my favorite boxer."

f) "I hate rap music," April Schauer says, "most of the time. It's repetitive and annoying."

"It's the poetry of the street. It can be hypnotic and imaginative," Mike Raffone says.

What's wrong:

◆ That first attribution is awkwardly positioned. It needs to move to the end of the first quoted sentence:

"I hate rap music most of the time," April Schauer says. "It's repetitive and annoying."

It's also possible that her original quote might actually have said this:

"I hate rap music," April Schauer says. "Most of the time, it's repetitive and annoying."

You would need to check your notes — or listen to the tape-recording of the interview — or, as a last resort, call April and read the quote to her — to be sure of her meaning.

◆ Notice how that second quote appears to be a continuation of April speaking; we don't realize it's a new speaker (Mike) until we reach the end of the paragraph. To avoid colliding quotes, it's best to introduce the second speaker's quote by using its attribution as a buffer. Like this:

"I hate rap music most of the time," April Schauer says. "It's repetitive and annoying."

Mike Raffone disagrees. "It's the poetry of the street," he says. "It can be hypnotic and imaginative."

◆ Notice how we added an attribution *(he says)* to show that Mike uttered that quote; the word *disagrees* is not an adequate synonym for *says.* (And yes, present-tense attributions are perfectly acceptable in feature stories like this.)

"All too often, a story free of any taint of personal opinion is a story with all the juice sucked out. Keeping opinion out of the story too often means being a fancy stenographer."

— **Geneva Overholser,** *journalism professor at the University of Missouri*

◆ **To use these remarks as a direct quote:**

"All too often, a story free of any taint of personal opinion is a story with all the juice sucked out," said Geneva Overholser, a journalism professor at the University of Missouri. "Keeping opinion out of the story too often means being a fancy stenographer."

◆ **As a paraphrase:**

Stories stripped of all opinion often become too lifeless, said Geneva Overholser, a journalism professor at the University of Missouri. According to Overholser, by keeping personal opinions out of their stories, reporters often become mere stenographers.

◆ **As partial quotes:**

The two best sound bites from Overholser's complete quote are the colorful phrases *juice sucked out* and *fancy stenographer.* (Notice how she uses those phrases as the punchlines to her sentences.) Thus, to use them as partial quotes, you'd write something like:

Stories stripped of all opinion often become stories "with the juice sucked out," said Geneva Overholser, a journalism professor at the University of Missouri. By keeping stories free of opinions, a reporter often becomes "a fancy stenographer," Overholser said.

---

❶ WHAT'S WRONG WITH THIS LEAD?

1) That *the jury reached a verdict* is not the news; the *actual verdict* is the news. What was the verdict? Don't make readers wait.

To say the verdict is *shocking* may only be true for some; for others, the trial may not have been *dramatic* at all. Avoid tired clichés. If you must add adjectives, make sure they're based on facts.

2) Half a dozen spectators isn't a crowd. It probably isn't even a story. Why are you even writing about this? You call this news?

Was his vacation last year? Or was the slideshow last year? This is a confusing sentence construction.

3) When reporting traffic accidents, general vehicle descriptions are usually sufficient (*a truck, a station wagon, a motorcycle*). Don't bog readers down in unnecessary model numbers unless it factors into the event for some reason.

The injury to the motorcycle driver should lead the story, not the fact that a collision occurred.

4) That opening dependent clause is just too rambling and wordy. It takes too long to get to the point.

And when that clause finally ends, we fail to learn whether the commissioners even passed a new tax ordinance — or, if they did, what it means to us, the citizens. The *meeting* is not the story; the *new tax* is.

5) Beginning a lead with a quote is rarely the best solution, and this quote is a worn-out cliché which probably doesn't belong *anywhere* in the story. Later in the sentence, we recycle yet another cliché: *it's do or die.*

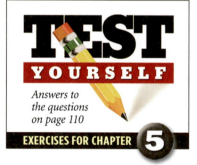

TEST YOURSELF

Answers to the questions on page 110

EXERCISES FOR CHAPTER 5

Why not tell us which day the game is, instead of vaguely saying *this weekend?*

6) To say police *were called* is a passive sentence structure. Better to say *police responded.*

But having said that: Police responding to a serious accident is not newsworthy; police respond to *all* serious accidents. What's newsworthy is that the accident was a hit-and-run. What happened to that victim? *That's* your lead.

The exact time is not necessary in accident stories unless, for some reason, it's a factor in the events. And nobody can keep track of dates; use the day of the week, unless the accident happened more than a week ago.

7) In the lead for most obituaries, you should emphasize some noteworthy accomplishment by the deceased. Suffering from diabetes is not an accomplishment. And though the cause of death is worth mentioning, try not to use negative, subjective words like *suffering* or *crippling.*

Don't say *passed away.* Simply say *died.*

8) You could say that this man was *arrested and charged with murder.* Or you could say he was *arrested in connection with a string of murders.* But to say he was *arrested for a string of murders* makes him appear guilty — which is both unfair and potentially libelous. Even though he isn't specifically named, he could easily be identified by anyone connected with Madison High.

Notice, too, the awkward syntax: Were the murders based on tips, or was the arrest based on tips?

Finally, if the tips were confidential, why are we identifying their source? Aren't we putting his ex-wife in danger by exposing something that she might want to remain a secret? Check with the police before you publicize this information.

❷ COVER THIS SPEECH STORY

Here's one suggested solution. Yours may be different, of course — but are the details complete? Is the summary accurate? Have you added enough quotes to capture Gartner's personality?

Distinguished journalist Michael Gartner insists you can't be a writer if you don't love writing.

"It's simply impossible," he said. "If you do not love what you are doing, quit now and find another job, another line of work. For you'll never be happy — and you'll never be good."

Gartner spoke Tuesday morning to a responsive crowd of nearly 200 in the Memorial Union ballroom as part of a lecture series sponsored by the school of journalism.

Gartner's speech — "The 12-Step Program to Good Writing" — combined anecdotes and advice from his long career as Page One editor of The Wall Street Journal, editor of The Des Moines Register and Pulitzer Prize-winning editor of the Ames (Iowa) Tribune.

Gartner admitted that, as a former executive at USA Today, "I tend to make lists and charts and graphs." As a result, his speech became a Top-12 list that urged writers to:

◆ **Report.** "Writing is just the pie crust," Gartner said. "Facts are the pie. So report, report, report. Then throw away the meaningless, the redundant, the unnecessary."

◆ **Read.** "You cannot be a good writer if you don't read," Gartner said. "Read great stuff. Read awful stuff. Read classics. Read trash. And think about the writing that you're reading."

◆ **Simplify.** Gartner recalled working late one night in the Wall Street Journal newsroom. He unexpectedly encountered the president of the company, Barney Kilgore, and explained that he was rewriting a story because it was murky. "Good," Kilgore said. "Remember, the easiest thing for the reader to do is quit reading."

That advice, Gartner says, has been printed on his notebooks and pasted on his computer ever since.

Other suggestions from Gartner's 12-step list: Listen. Collaborate. Trust. Experiment. Talk. Pounce. Love. Care. And balance.

"It is an enormous challenge," Gartner concluded, "and it can be enormous fun. Who else in the world is paid just to ask questions, to think and to write?"

After his speech, Gartner was awarded the William Henry Fox Prize by Eaton X. Benedict, dean of the journalism school. The Fox Prize is given annually by the university to honor a distinguished journalist.

"Gartner is a national treasure," Benedict said. "His speech really hit a nerve."

Journalism major Forrest Ranger agreed: "This is the kind of stuff you never read in textbooks," he said. "But it's valuable to hear it."

Next month, the lecture series will sponsor a speech by former NBC anchor Tom Brokaw.

❸ WRITE THIS CRIME STORY LEAD

1) Let's start with the most basic possible solution:
Stormy Snowe has been murdered.

That's simple. Urgent. Attention-getting. But it's incomplete. And it assumes you've watched enough local TV to recognize Stormy by her name alone. To be safe, we could add a modifier:
Weathercaster Stormy Snowe has been murdered.
To make it even clearer, we could say —
WUGH meteorologist Stormy Snowe has been murdered.
— but some of us don't recognize TV-station call letters. For many readers, too, *meteorologist* is just a fancy name for *weather forecaster*. So it might be best to simply say:
Channel 2 weathercaster Stormy Snowe was murdered last night.

Adding the time element is smart. Web site readers will have access to this story *only* on Thursday morning, since a new, updated version may replace this one later in the day.

But we should add more details about the crime. For instance, you should find a more appropriate word to replace *murdered*:
Channel 2 weathercaster Stormy Snowe was bludgeoned to death last night.

Too sensational? Maybe. But it's more accurate. The AP stylebook warns that "murder" is premeditated homicide; thus, you should avoid the word until someone is convicted in court.

Another way to word the same information is to deliberately use a passive construction. Ordinarily, of course, you should avoid passive sentences. But sometimes they can be effective:
The body of Channel 2 weathercaster Stormy Snowe was found beaten to death in a downtown alley this morning.

That's a good lead. And if you wanted to, you could stop right there, let the horrific news sink in, then answer the *why* questions (about how it happened) in the second paragraph.

But readers will want more juicy details as soon as possible. Since this murder was committed by Stormy's jealous ex-boyfriend, we could try squeezing him into the lead:
Channel 2 weathercaster Stormy Snowe was bludgeoned to death by a jealous ex-boyfriend last night.

Warning: We don't know the circumstances of the boyfriend's confession. Maybe police beat it out of him; maybe he's innocent but just seeking publicity. We only know he confessed because the cops *told* us he did. So to be safe, we should attribute our facts to the police:
Channel 2 weathercaster Stormy Snowe was bludgeoned to death by a jealous ex-boyfriend last night, police said.

That "*police said*" attribution gets the job done, but it seems a bit awkward. We could reconstruct that sentence to read:
Channel 2 weathercaster Stormy Snowe was bludgeoned to death last night by her ex-lover, who police said stalked the popular TV personality before attacking her in a jealous rage.

That's acceptable, though it's wordy and complex. To smooth things out, we could recast the lead in two sentences:
Channel 2 weathercaster Stormy Snowe was found dead in a downtown alley this morning. Police say her ex-lover confessed to beating her with a crowbar after seeing her kiss another man.

Lead-writing is subjective; different reporters would try different approaches. Did your solution match any of those above?

2) When stories like this get big play in competing media, you can usually assume that readers are familiar with the *who* and the *what:*

Stormy Snowe has been murdered.

So for later stories — or for follow-ups running the next day — you wait and hope for new information to emphasize in your lead:

Just hours after she secretly married her high-school sweetheart, Stormy Snowe's dream of a new life ended in tragedy.

But if we have no new information — and so far, we don't — then you'll often need to write a lead that uses a different approach than stories you've written previously. You could play up the other *who,* for instance — the murderer, rather than the victim:

Police say it was Stormy Snowe's ex-lover who stalked the popular TV weathercaster early Thursday morning and — after watching her kiss another man — used a crowbar to bludgeon her to death in a downtown alley.

Or you could exploit the *why* of the murder:

A night of stalking, a kiss and a fit of rage ended in the bludgeoning death of Channel 2 meteorologist Stormy Snowe in a downtown alley early Thursday morning.

 WRITE THIS ACCIDENT STORY

Here's one suggested solution. Yours may be different, of course — but are the details complete? Is your wording as tight as possible?

Two teenagers died and a third was injured Saturday after their all-terrain vehicles slid on ice in a mountainous area five miles west of Butteville.

Cooper Black, 13, and Arial Bookman, 13, were killed after their vehicle skidded off an icy bridge on U.S. Highway 111, the Benson County Sheriff's Office reported. The vehicle plunged over a cliff and crashed into a tree, and the teens were hurled onto a rocky creek bed about 100 feet below the road. They were wearing helmets.

A second ATV carrying two other teenagers slipped off the roadway but didn't go over the cliff. The driver, Geneva Franklin, 16, ran about a mile to a house to summon help. Meanwhile, his passenger, Gill Sans, 13, tried to reach the teenagers in the creek bed but slipped and fell onto the rocks, fracturing his leg.

All four teens were from Green Lake in Benson County.

Rescue crews spent four hours removing the teenagers from the creek bed, the sheriff's office said. Sans was taken by helicopter to Providence Hospital in Dawson, where he was listed in satisfactory condition.

— Adapted from a story originally published in *The Oregonian*

 GENERATING IDEAS FOR FEATURE STORIES

PERSONALITY PROFILE:
◆ Profile the mysterious billionaire Elvis Trump. Score an exclusive, in-depth interview to explore his colorful past, his exotic lifestyle, his reasons for rebuilding the cathedral, etc.
◆ Profile Barney "Boom-Boom" Rubble. Learn about his past triumphs, failures, concerns, motivation, etc.

HUMAN-INTEREST STORY:
◆ Talk to the old priest who's lived in the cathedral for 40 years (or some other colorful church-related figure), and see what emotional impact the demolition will have.
◆ Find out who or what will be disrupted by the demolition of the church — the homeless who are fed there, the faithful parishioners who attend Mass every day, the old caretaker who feeds cats in the alley — and see what stories can be told.
◆ Attend the last wedding that takes place in the cathedral. Or the last funeral. The last baptism. The last church service.

COLOR STORY:
◆ As the building is imploded, describe the reactions from onlookers, neighbors, cops, priests and nuns who watch it collapse.

BACKGROUNDER:
◆ Urban renewal in the heart of downtown. Is the rebirth of the cathedral part of a larger pattern?
◆ This is a good opportunity to analyze the state of the Catholic

TEST YOURSELF

Answers to the questions on page 134

EXERCISES FOR CHAPTER 6

Church today. When the cathedral was built, most residents were Catholic; the church had tremendous cultural and political influence. But today, the collapse of the old cathedral is almost a metaphor for the declining status of the church. What lies ahead?

TREND STORY:
◆ Goodbye, wrecking ball: Big-city stadiums, hotels and apartment buildings are no longer knocked down; they're blown up. A look at cost/labor/time-saving advantages that support this trend.
◆ Trends in religious architecture. What do 21st-century churches look like? Have churches changed to suit their congregations' lifestyles? Discuss new megachurches, attendance trends, etc.
◆ Souvenirs: Will local vendors hawk T-shirts, bumper stickers and other memorabilia to the crowds gathering to watch the implosion?

REACTION PIECE:
◆ Death of the old cathedral: Talk to neighbors, church officials, local business owners, priests, nuns and parishioners to see how they're reacting to the news, and what effect it will have on their lives or careers.
◆ The new cathedral: Show architectural plans for the new, ultramodern church. Get reactions from architects, city planners, priests, nuns and parishioners. Ask your readers to write in and sound off.

FLASHBACK:
◆ Recap, through quotes, anecdotes and photos, the colorful his-

tory of the cathedral. (This could be packaged as a giant time-line.)

HOW-TO:
◆ How to implode a building. Create a diagram of the church showing where the explosives will be planted and how they'll be detonated.

CONSUMER GUIDE:
◆ Where to watch the implosion: the best viewing locations, when to arrive, what to bring (binoculars, folding chairs, a face mask to keep from inhaling dust from the implosion).

PERSONAL NARRATIVE:
◆ Get a job on Barney Rubble's crew, so you can view the final setup and countdown from the inside.
◆ Conduct an extensive interview with Barney himself, so you can construct a first-person narrative after the implosion.

 GENERATING IDEAS FOR SIDEBARS AND INFOGRAPHICS

A FAST-FACTS BOX:
◆ For stories previewing the implosion, create a box telling readers the time, place — even the TV stations that might telecast the event.
◆ For stories on the church building, create a box describing the cathedral's size, date of construction, initial cost, repairs that have been done, historical highlights, etc.

A TIMELINE:
◆ The year-by-year history of the cathedral.
◆ A chronology of highlights from the career of Elvis Trump.
◆ A timeline of historic downtown buildings (and what became of those that are now gone).

A DIAGRAM
◆ A cross-section of the cathedral showing architectural high-lights (stained glass windows, statues, etc.).
◆ A cross-section of the cathedral showing structural problems.
◆ A cross-section of the cathedral showing where the explosives will be placed for implosion.
◆ A cross-section of the new, modern cathedral.

A STEP-BY-STEP GUIDE
◆ How to implode a cathedral, from site preparation to the final push of the button.

A MAP
◆ Showing where to view the implosion, and where trespassing will be forbidden.

A LIST
◆ Oldest churches in the city
◆ Biggest churches in the city
◆ Oldest buildings in the city
◆ Other city structures facing major renovation or destruction

AN OPINION POLL
◆ Are you sorry to see the old cathedral die?
◆ What do you think of the new cathedral design?

A BIO BOX
◆ Personal data/career highlights of Barney "Boom-Boom" Rubble

◆ Personal data/career highlights of Elvis Trump

A CHECKLIST
◆ What to take along if you're viewing the implosion (binocu-lars, folding chairs, a face mask to keep from inhaling dust from the implosion, etc.)
◆ Barney Rubble's official pre-implosion checklist: all the safety/technical issues he needs to resolve before pushing the button.

A QUOTE COLLECTION
◆ Are you sorry to see the old cathedral die?
◆ What do you think of the new cathedral design?
◆ Reactions from those witnessing the implosion.

3 **HARD NEWS vs. SOFT NEWS**

1) The Burger King slaying is the hardest of these stories, a breaking news story involving a serious crime: murder.

2) Though it may seem frivolous at first glance, the bikini-bar story has the makings of a news controversy. It could grow into one of those continuing dramas that stirs up community reac-tion.

3) Giving $2 million to the Humane Society will have an effect on both humans and pets in the community. Barbie dolls may seem like childish toys, but that amount of money is significant.

4) Fans lining up for a movie always provide an amusing pop-culture diversion. The story is soft, but timely — though it doesn't have much actual impact on the lives of ordinary folks.

5) Recipes are helpful, but there's not much about turkeyburgers that's urgent or crucial to the public interest.

4 **WHAT'S WRONG WITH THESE REVIEWS?**

1) When it comes to food, everyone has likes and dislikes. But to call the most popular dish at a restaurant "unpalatable" just because you don't like asparagus? That makes you appear petty and close-minded, and it calls your other judgments into ques-tion, too. Good critics rise above their prejudices. If necessary, solicit the opinion of a reliable colleague whose tastes are more objective than yours.

2) Avoid arcane references to artistic trivia that nobody will get (or even care about). You may think you're illuminating us with your vast historical expertise; to most readers, however, you sound like a guitar geek who needs to get a life. If you must refer-ence past works, at least ensure that they mean *something* to most readers.

3) Panning a children's play? At Christmas? That's cold, Scrooge. Pick on someone your own size. Smart journalists try to build rapport with readers, not shred every ounce of goodwill.

4) There's no need to add phrases like *I think* or *in my opinion*. It's a review. We'll recognize your opinions without being alerted.

5) Thanks. Now that you've given away the plot twists and spoiled the ending, we don't need to see the movie. Next time, keep the plot details to a minimum. And beware of "spoilers" that ruin the story line's surprises.

PRINT *it or* **PULL** *it ?*

YOU MAKE THE CALL

Answers to the quiz on page 141.

Our panel of experts:

Jay Bender, an attorney in Columbia, S.C., specializes in media law and First Amendment issues. Among his clients are The State newspaper (in Columbia) and the South Carolina Press Association.

Barbara Mack is a media law attorney who teaches journalism at Iowa State University.

James Tidwell is an attorney, professor of journalism at Eastern Illinois University and author of "Media Law in Illinois."

John D. Zelezny is a communications lawyer, lecturer and author of "Communications Law: Liberties, Restraints and the Modern Media."

❶ Our experts unanimously agreed that you'd need to **PULL** at least *part* of that quote.

"The 'lazy and stupid' and 'partying' comments would be considered loose, figurative language that can't be proved true or false," Tidwell said. "But the 'getting laid' comment *can* be proved true or false, and could be construed as claiming the quarterback has loose morals. So unless you can independently verify the accuracy of the statement, I'd pull it."

Zelezny agreed. "Though 'lazy' is protected opinion," he said, "the factual implication of reckless sexual behavior is defamatory."

Trying a different angle, Mack pointed out that "the weenie way to approach this is to say the coach is an 'official source' (a public employee who is paid, in part, to speak to the press) and as such, reporting his comments doesn't rise to 'actual malice.'" Thus, she reasoned, you *could* get away with printing the whole quote.

"This is a great example," she added, "where what is *legal* (get-away-withable) isn't *ethical*."

Good point. Is the quote really that essential and newsworthy, given all the ill will, hurt feelings and litigation that could result? After all, it's just *a football game.*

❷ *PRINT IT.* Professor Jones' remark refers to the theory — not the author.

As Bender observed, "Smith is a public figure by virtue of entering a continuing public debate, and the response is protected as part of a vigorous debate on matters of public interest."

Besides, the term "racist" is so overused, it has lost its literal meaning, Tidwell said. "Today, such a claim would be considered figurative language that couldn't be proved true or false."

❸ *PRINT IT.* You can't libel the dead, our experts all agreed — but they also expressed some concerns about the ethics of running that quote.

"What good would derive from printing such comments?" Tidwell asked.

More importantly, Bender said, "you would need to know if the musician left a husband because publishing that statement would damage his reputation." Which means that, conceivably, he could sue.

Most editors would be wary of printing such extreme comments about *anyone,* living or dead, without more factual support. Taking the word of just one opinionated source is a dangerous risk.

❹ *PRINT IT* — but only if Lickt has actually been charged with the crime.

There's some gray area here, so pay close attention: Until people are convicted of crimes, in court proceedings, you cannot call them criminals; you can't refer to them as *rapists* or *murderers* or *car thieves.* If you do, and if they're acquitted (or charges are dropped), they can turn around and sue you for defaming them.

Make sense? Well, many attorneys also insist that simply adding an adjective such as *alleged* offers no legal protection; calling someone an *alleged rapist,* they say, is similar to calling him a *young rapist* or a *potential rapist* — whatever adjective you use, you're still calling him a *rapist.*

But not all attorneys see it as a problem. "Ah, the old 'alleged' trick," Mack said. "I've never seen a winning lawsuit on this issue. Print it."

Others argue that, until a person has been formally charged with a crime, you should avoid the risk of using *alleged.* As Bender explained: "If the allegation is taken from a public record, such as an arrest warrant or indictment, I believe publication is protected under the privilege of fair report. If the person is merely a suspect, and has not been named in a warrant or indictment, *alleged* will provide no protection."

Zelezny offered another way to consider the problem: "If police arrested the guy because they suspect he's connected with a homicide, but they're not yet sure how he's connected, then it would be legally risky to label him either a *murderer* or an *alleged murderer.*

"On the other hand, if they obtained an arrest warrant specifically on suspicion that he committed murder, then I think it's accurate to say *alleged murderer,* and I would be fine with that."

❺ *PULL IT,* our experts all agreed. "I didn't know we were training students to report rumors," Bender wryly observed. "Unless there were a factual basis for publishing the allegation, don't print it."

❻ Our experts were divided on this one. Zelezny said **PULL IT:** "Allegations of professional incompetence and code violations are defamatory," he said.

"More facts, please," said Mack. "If she's making a report to the school board, it's one story. If she's bitching at a cocktail party, it's another. I'd pull it unless she is some kind of 'expert' who has knowledge of the food and is commenting on it for some purpose."

For Tidwell, this was a close call, but he voted to **PRINT IT:** "I would argue that the claim in this context is loose, figurative language that can't be proved true or false," he said. "This claim is similar to stating the cooks' food isn't fit to eat. It's fair comment and criticism."

❼ Three of our experts said **PRINT IT.** "If the story is true, run it," Mack said. "You didn't insinuate anything."

"No, I *do* think we're insinuating that he's likely gay," Zelezny argued. "But I think we're safe here because we're accurately reporting his behavior, and readers have the opportunity to draw their own conclusions — as long as we're correct about calling it a gay club."

Tidwell advised pulling the story to avoid "a clear insinuation that the quarterback is gay."

And finally, as Bender noted: "I don't think there would be any liability, but that's not to say there would be no suit. You might be concerned that the quarterback would demonstrate his macho cred by bopping the columnist on the nose."

① LIBEL, COPYRIGHT, PRIVACY: SOME HYPOTHETICAL SITUATIONS

a) That remark is not libelous. Calling someone "crazy," "nuts" or "a lunatic" is an opinion, uttered as an emotional outburst — not as a statement of fact. Calling someone a "menace" is a generic insult, too. It can't be either proved or *disproved*.

But why print that quote in your story? We all constantly hurl curses and insults at real and imaginary wrongdoers. So unless that "lunatic" driver is dramatically blameworthy, treat this quote as meaningless background noise, not news. Repeating it in your story may just stir up unnecessary hostility.

b) You could lose this libel suit. Business at the store could suffer because of your story. The owner could rightly claim that he's losing customers, especially other devout Christians who mistakenly assume that the store sells pornography and now refuse to shop there.

c) No, she couldn't win her libel suit. The quote is defamatory, but it doesn't specifically identify Paine by name; if you say "Acupuncturists are all quacks," you're talking about thousands of them in a general way. If, instead, the quote had called all *local* acupuncturists quacks, that would target Paine more directly — thus becoming more dangerously defamatory.

d) No. The mistake was made by the police, not you. As long as you accurately convey what's in that police report — a public record — the "fair report" privilege protects your story.

e) Everybody criticizes referees and umpires; it's an accepted part of the job. In a way, game officials are public performers; they do their job in front of hundreds, thousands, sometimes even millions of loud, opinionated fans, players and coaches. Like athletes, their performance is subject to harshly negative reviews. As long as that coach doesn't utter false statements of fact about the ref, he's safe (though the league may fine him for unsportsmanlike conduct). Saying "he's blind" is a vague generalization, like saying "he's crazy."

f) You could lose an intrusion invasion of privacy claim. The professor, working in his office with the door closed, had a reasonable right to expect privacy — to conduct a private conversation without a reporter eavesdropping and printing his remarks without his permission. The substance of his remarks makes no difference; you intruded on his privacy.

g) Print the jokes. They're not just jokes — they've become *news*, and your readers have a right to know what's said over the public airwaves about their community. You're not reprinting those jokes to sell on T-shirts; you're quoting a public figure who said something newsworthy. That's fair use.

h) According to the Supreme Court, outspoken social activists become public figures when they "thrust themselves to the forefront of particular public controversies in order to influence the resolution of the issues involved." For a public figure to win a libel suit, she would have to prove that you deliberately twisted the facts about that court case. That correction you ran doesn't

Answers to the questions on page 152

EXERCISES FOR CHAPTER 7

erase the damaging facts in your original story, but it does indicate your remorse and sincerity. Most likely, she couldn't win this libel suit.

i) If you had learned about this abortion from reading her confidential medical records, you'd be guilty of violating her privacy. But you obtained the information from police arrest reports. Reporting on public documents is not an invasion of privacy.

j) It doesn't matter *where* you obtain libelous misinformation. If it's truly defamatory, both you and that Web site are liable for publishing it.

② LEGAL CONCEPTS AND DEFINITIONS

a) *False.* A damaging statement becomes libelous only if the facts are *untrue*.

b) *True.* If they're in a public place and involved in a legitimate news story, you don't need their permission to shoot their photo.

c) *False.* There are no federal libel laws; what wins a case in one state may lose in another.

d) *False.* This is one of those rare exceptions to what's considered plagiarism. Some news outlets run press releases verbatim; others insert a sentence here, a paragraph there. For example, in a story announcing an award given to a teacher, you might lift a few sentences of background biography from the news release; in a story about an upcoming concert, you might lift a paragraph on ticket information.

Generally, recycling press-release material is allowed for short, generic news stories. For longer stories — *especially any story that uses your byline* — you should make every sentence original, citing a press release as your source if you paraphrase from it.

e) *True.*

f) *True.*

g) *False.* "Actual malice" is when you deliberately lie or disregard the truth.

h) *False.* A shield law protects journalists from being forced to reveal the identities of their sources.

i) *True.*

j) *False.* A libel plaintiff needs only to prove that he or she is identifiable by description, occupation, street address — even after being recognized in a photo.

k) *False.* To safely reprint copyrighted material, you need permission from the owner of the copyright. Simply crediting your source isn't enough. (Besides, many Web sites illegally reproduce images from other sources, so giving them credit may be both meaningless and incorrect.)

l) *False.* You can express whatever opinions you want in a review — but you could lose a libel suit if you introduce false statements of fact (*Ann Thrax is so convincing playing a drug addict because she spent years snorting coke*), or if you make allegations you can't support (*Thanks to steroids, Harry Rump has become a handsome Hollywood hunk*).

1 WRITE THE LEADS FOR THESE TELEVISION NEWS STORIES

a) This actually happened to Joe Donlon, anchor at KGW-TV in Portland, Ore. He describes how he wrote his lead-in to that story:

"While I was working in Tucson, Ariz., we had a deadly police shooting. A man had a gun and wouldn't put it down, so the officer on the scene shot and killed him. It was the second time it had happened in two weeks.

"There are a number of ways this story could be written for broadcast. Chances are, you would hear something like this:

A SHERIFF'S DEPUTY SHOT AND KILLED A MAN TODAY. THAT MAN HAD A GUN, AND REFUSED TO PUT IT DOWN. (REPORTER'S NAME) IS LIVE WITH OUR REPORT TONIGHT.

"I took a step back and tried to insert myself into that scene. Here's the introduction I went with:

IT HAS TO BE ONE OF THE TOUGHEST SITUATIONS AN OFFICER WILL EVER FACE… SOMEONE HAS A GUN, AND THEY'RE POINTING IT -- RIGHT AT YOU. IN A MATTER OF SECONDS, YOU HAVE A DECISION TO MAKE … DO YOU SHOOT -- OR TAKE A CHANCE ON GETTING SHOT? WELL, FOR THE SECOND TIME IN TWO WEEKS, A LOCAL OFFICER …DECIDED TO SHOOT.

"That seemed like a much more effective and compelling way to communicate the story and draw viewers in."

b) POLICE ARE LOOKING FOR A SMALLVILLE MAN ACCUSED OF STABBING HIS WIFE AND TRYING TO SET HER ON FIRE.

c) WANT TO MAKE YOUR FEET MORE SWEET? THEN EAT MORE BEETS.

2 WHAT'S WRONG WITH THIS BROADCAST NEWSWRITING?

a) "I've got a really painful cramp in my groin," said OSU halfback Bud Weiser, explaining why he's sitting out tonight's game.

The improved version:

O-S-U halfback Bud Weiser (WHY-zer) says he's sitting out tonight's game because of a painful cramp in his groin.

What we fixed:

◆ Remember that broadcasting axiom: *Attribution before assertion.* First, tell us *who* has the medical problem. Otherwise, listeners or viewers will be startled to hear the newscaster exclaim out of the blue, "I've got a really painful cramp in my groin." The attribution must precede that information.
◆ O-S-U should be hyphenated to make sure nobody pronounces it "Oh-sue." Weiser's name may need a pronouncer, too, to make sure nobody says "WEE-zer."
◆ We've paraphrased Weiser rather than trying to quote him.
◆ We've eliminated the word *said.* The sentence is now in the present tense.

b) The victims were taken to St. Vincent Hospital, where they are now recovering. The hospital lists them in critical condition.

The improved version:

The victims are in critical condition at Saint Vincent Hospital.

What we fixed:

◆ That first version was too wordy. We assume the victims are recovering in the hospital — that's what patients in hospitals *do.* (Obviously, they had to be *taken there*, too.)
◆ Spell out *Saint.* Avoid abbreviations.
◆ The sentence is now in the present tense.

---

c) The thieves stole $17,900,500, bank officials reported.

The improved version:

The bank says the thieves stole nearly 18-million dollars.

What we fixed:

◆ We rounded off the number and expressed it properly.
◆ We placed the attribution first and streamlined the phrasing.
◆ The sentence is now in the present tense.

---

d) Library officials announced that patrons under the age of 18 will no longer be permitted to check out any of the library's movie videotapes or DVDs.

The improved version:

The library says — if you're under 18, you can't check out videos.

What we fixed:

◆ The original phrasing was too formal and wordy. We compressed the meaning as much as possible ("videos" conveys the same idea as "movie videotapes or DVDs").
◆ It's written in the second person. It's now about *you.*
◆ The sentence is now in the present tense.

---

e) A 10-year-old skateboarder was struck and killed by a truck at 1120 Baker St. this morning. Police haven't yet identified the driver of the truck.

The improved version:

Police are looking for a truck driver who struck and killed a 10-year-old skateboarder on Baker Street this morning.

What we fixed:

◆ We've streamlined the phrasing.
◆ That first sentence was originally written in passive voice and past tense. The new version is in present tense, active voice.
◆ *Street* should not be abbreviated.

---

f) The earthquake, which struck at 7:01 a.m., caused no reported damage, just rattling windows and setting off car alarms throughout the city.

The improved version:

The earthquake struck just after 7 this morning. It rattled windows and set off car alarms, but no damage has been reported.

What we fixed:

◆ The time of the quake is now phrased more conversationally.
◆ One long, complex sentence has become two shorter ones.

---

g) President George W. Bush has announced a new plan to cut estate taxes by 9%.

The improved version:

President Bush is promoting a new plan to cut estate taxes by nine percent.

What we fixed:

◆ We've replaced the verb to make it sound more current.
◆ It should be written *nine percent* in words, not *9%.*
◆ In broadcast newswriting, you don't need to say the entire name of well-known public figures. It's enough to say simply *President Bush.*

TEST YOURSELF
Answers to the questions on page 174
EXERCISES FOR CHAPTER 9

3 TURN THIS NEWSPAPER STORY INTO A RADIO BRIEF AND A TELEVISION PACKAGE

An example of a 45-second radio story:

Every dog has his day — but on Bilford's campus, those days may soon be over. A petition drive by Students Against Dogs has asked the administration to outlaw dogs on campus. Ferris Wheeler is the group's president.

Wheeler: *"This stinks. I mean, this school smells like dog doo. Irresponsible pet owners are letting their dogs chase cyclists, bark and crap all over campus."* **(:12)**

Not all students agree, however. Dog owner Juliet Sims says a dog ban would be unfair.

Sims: *"I admit there's too much poop on the sidewalks, but it's wrong to let a few bad apples ruin it for everybody."* **(:07)**

The Board of Trustees will debate the issue at their Thursday meeting.

An example of a 90-second television package:

Lead-in **(:10)**	**(Anchor)** DOGS — AND DOG DROPPINGS — ARE RAISING A STINK ON BILFORD'S CAMPUS THESE DAYS. WUGH'S (REPORTER'S NAME) HAS DUG UP THIS REPORT.
Video cover of dogs roaming around **(:10)**	**(Reporter v/o)** SOME SAY THAT BILFORD COLLEGE IS GOING TO THE DOGS. YOU SEE THEM EVERYWHERE -- RUNNING. FETCHING. BARKING. AND YES -- POOPING.
Stand-up showing reporter on campus with dogs in the background **(:12)**	**(Reporter on-cam)** UNTIL NOW, DOGS HAVE BEEN ALLOWED TO ROAM FREELY AROUND THE CAMPUS, EVEN THOUGH THEY'RE SUPPOSED TO BE KEPT ON A LEASH. SOME STUDENTS, LIKE FERRIS WHEELER, HAVE HAD ENOUGH.
SOT, with name line: FERRIS WHEELER, President, Students Against Dogs (:12)	**(Wheeler)** *"This stinks. I mean, this school smells like dog doo. Irresponsible pet owners are letting their dogs chase cyclists, bark and crap all over campus."*
More video cover of dogs roaming around and sniffing at the signs **(:18)**	**(Reporter v/o)** IN RESPONSE TO A PETITION FILED BY STUDENTS AGAINST DOGS, SCHOOL ADMINISTRATORS HAVE POSTED SIGNS THAT SAY "NO DOGS ALLOWED." AND THE BOARD OF TRUSTEES IS CONSIDERING BANNING DOGS FROM THE CAMPUS. SOME DOG OWNERS, LIKE JULIET SIMS, OPPOSE THE IDEA.
SOT, with name line: JULIET SIMS, Bilford junior (:13)	**(Sims)** *"This proposal is ugly and unfair to responsible dog owners like me. I admit there's too much poop on the sidewalks, but it's wrong to let a few bad apples ruin it for everybody."*
Reporter stand-up **(:15)**	**(Reporter on-cam)** EVERY DOG HAS HIS DAY — AND FOR DOGS HERE AT BILFORD, THAT DAY IS THURSDAY, WHEN THE BOARD OF TRUSTEES WILL ASK, WHO LET THE DOGS OUT? AND SHOULD WE LET THEM <u>STAY</u> OUT? THIS IS (REPORTER'S NAME) REPORTING.

---

4 WHAT'S IT CALLED?

a) *Radio:* cut or actuality. *TV:* sound on tape (SOT)

b) out-cue

c) reader

d) natural sound

e) toss

f) tease

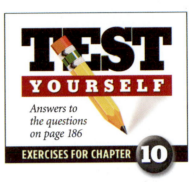

TEST YOURSELF

Answers to the questions on page 186

EXERCISES FOR CHAPTER **10**

 1 GENERATE A NEWS RELEASE

Here's one suggested option for that news release:

ZOO MOURNS THE LOSS OF HOMER, THE POLAR BEAR

The Midland Zoo's oldest polar bear was found dead in its exhibit this morning. The zoo is investigating the cause of death.

"We will do everything in our power to determine how this bear died," zoo director Chris P. Bacon said. "Animal welfare and the preservation of species are our primary goals here at the zoo."

The zoo will perform an necropsy to try to determine the cause of death, zoo veterinarian Dr. Shanda Lear said. The results will not be available for several weeks.

Zookeeper Sara N. Getty found the dead bear, a 16-year old male named Homer, floating in the exhibit pool.

"Homer was a very curious and playful polar bear and we will miss him terribly," Getty said.

Zoo staff responded immediately to the incident. The remaining polar bears, a 9-year-old male named Yukon and a 10-year old female named McKenzie, were removed from the exhibit and are being monitored by veterinary staff.

Polar bears have thrived at the zoo since 1985. This unique exhibit allows the bears to engage in natural behaviors, playing in manufactured snow, digging in gravel and hunting trout in the chilled pool. The bears are ambassadors for their wild relatives, educating zoo visitors about these threatened animals.

Notice how:

◆ The goal of the press release is to make the zoo look as caring, responsive and responsible as possible. We reinforce that message in a positive way throughout the story, from the second sentence of the lead to the statement that "zoo staff responded immediately."

♦ We put the zoo's main message in a quote from the zoo director, a credible authority figure.

♦ We put a human face on the loss of the bear by quoting the zookeeper. We also put Homer's name in the headline to appeal to your emotions. (Did it work?)

♦ The lead of the release suggests that the polar bear might have died of old age. That may not be true, but it deflects suspicion that carelessness or mistreatment may have contributed to Homer's death or the deaths of those other two animals.

♦ We did not include information about the previous deaths at the zoo because we don't want to suggest that they were related.

♦ The closing paragraph recycles details about the zoo's educational mission that reinforce the message that the zoo is responsive and dedicated to the welfare of the animals in its care.

2 NOW TURN THAT RELEASE INTO A NEWS STORY

One possible solution:

For a third time in two weeks, an animal has died at the Midland Zoo.

A 16-year-old polar bear named Homer was found floating in the exhibit pool an hour after his morning feeding Friday. The cause of death is unknown.

The zoo will perform a necropsy to try to determine the cause of death, zoo veterinarian Dr. Shanda Lear said. The results will not be available for several weeks.

The zoo's remaining polar bears, a 9-year-old male named Yukon and a 10-year old female named McKenzie, were removed from the exhibit and are being monitored by veterinary staff.

Two other animals have recently died at the zoo. Last week, a 10-year-old bobcat named Regina died of renal failure. Two weeks ago, a 6-year-old giraffe named Kenya died from a broken neck when her horns got caught in her stall.

Zoo officials said the deaths are unrelated.

Notice how:

♦ The lead reveals our story angle — not just the death of this bear, but the fact that it's the third death this month. The polar bear's death is not an isolated incident.

♦ We chose not to use those quotes from the zoo director and the zookeeper. Neither quote supplies any solid information. Reporters should be wary of appeals to emotion and authority. It's best to let the facts speak and let readers draw their own conclusions.

♦ We chose not to add that boilerplate information about the zoo's educational mission. It seems too self-promotional.

♦ Bottom line: A typical editor might read this story and say, "You're playing up the serial-death angle. And I can see where there's a possiblity that something is amiss over at the zoo. Three animals dead in two weeks? Is that normal? Is there neglect or abuse? How often do animals die at the zoo? How long should animals live when they're in captivity?

"Do you have time to research this further right now? Because if not — if you can't flesh out this story with more interviews and statistics — then you should do a follow-up as soon as you can. Crunch some numbers, talk to some more experts and find out if there's a bigger story worth chasing here."

WHAT'S WRONG WITH THIS NEWS RELEASE?

1) The quote lead is a bad idea for either news stories or news releases — especially a quote that makes your client look like a jerk.

2) The boastful, self-serving language continues in paragraphs two and four. Using your release as shameless advertising is a sure way to turn off journalists reading it.

3) In paragraph three, there's an improper lack of objective newswriting style: "you can't miss our concert."

4) The time of concert has been omitted.

5) There's no name or contact information.

4 PLAN A MEDIA KIT

Remember, the more items you include and the more media kits you produce, the more expensive this project becomes. So your first question should be: What's our budget?

Once you know how much money you can spend, you'll be able to decide what to include. A list of options to choose from:

♦ News release announcing the new product and the tasting event.

♦ Backgrounder and/or fact sheet on your company.

♦ Byliner on the health and environmental benefits of organic chocolate.

♦ Previously published reviews of the company's established line of chocolates.

♦ Brochure promoting the new chocolates.

♦ Fact sheet on organic chocolate.

♦ Timeline or calendar listing dates and locations of upcoming chocolate-tasting events.

♦ Invitation to the press for a behind-the-scenes chocolate tasting and factory tour.

♦ Photos of the new chocolates.

♦ Samples of the new chocolates.

Where to send the media kit: Of course, you'll send it to local media outlets and interested businesses, but you want to make sure it lands on the right desk. Your list could include:

♦ Feature editor and business editor of the city newspaper. (At big papers, send one to the food writer and any business reporter who writes stories about new local products.)

♦ Feature editor of any local monthly magazines, weekly community newspapers or campus papers.

♦ Editor of any local/regional business journal.

♦ National food magazines (*Food & Wine, Bon Appetit, Gourmet magazine,* etc.).

♦ National trade journals (*Chocolatier, Candy Industry, Confectioner, Art Culinaire, Tea & Coffee Trade Journal*).

♦ Any local/regional TV and radio stations that report soft news like this.

♦ Candy buyers for local grocery store chains.

♦ Local merchants who sell upscale candy, including candy stores, coffee shops, gift and card shops, luxury hotels, day spas, wine shops, bakeries and florists (who often deliver both flowers and candy).

♦ Local culinary schools.

GLOSSARY

absolute privilege The right of legislators, judges and other public officials to speak without threat of libel when carrying out their duties.

actuality (also called a *cut, sound bite or bite*) The recorded voice of someone in the news, or sound from a news event. Actualities include statements from public officials, interviews with eyewitnesses, comments from experts — even the shouts of an angry mob.

actual malice Reckless disregard of the truth; printing something you know to be false. This is a condition that must be proved in libel cases filed by public figures or public officials.

ad An advertisement.

advance A story explaining an upcoming meeting or event.

advertorial Part advertising, part editorial; an advertisement section in a publication that contains stories and photos.

advocacy journalism A type of reporting in which journalists take sides in a controversial issue, promoting a particular point of view.

agate Small type used for sports statistics, stock tables, classified ads, etc.

anchor The person who reads the news during a newscast and provides transitions between stories.

anecdotal lead A humorous, dramatic or revealing incident that's used to begin a story.

anecdote A brief recounting of an entertaining or informative incident within a story.

angle The focus, emphasis or "slant" of a story; a distinctive way of viewing and writing about a topic.

AP The Associated Press, a worldwide news-gathering cooperative.

assignment Designation by an editor for a reporter or photographer to cover an event.

attribute Identify the source of a fact, opinion or quote.

attribution The written phrase that identifies the source of a fact, opinion or

quote in a story.

B copy A section of a story that's written ahead of time for an event that will occur close to deadline.

B-roll (or *cover*) Video images shot at a news scene that are later used to illustrate (or cover) a sound bite or reporter's track that was recorded separately.

background Information gathered by reporters to help them understand a story's history, meaning, context, etc. Also refers to quotes or facts that can be used in a story without disclosing the source's name.

backgrounder A story that explains the basics of an issue or event. Also refers to an interview in which a source provides information, though not necessarily for publication.

beat The area or subject that a reporter is responsible for covering. A beat can be a topic (crime), an institution (the state legislature) or a location (Lincoln County).

bias Unfairly favoring one side over another when writing a story.

blog A Web log; an online journal providing commentary and/or links to related Web sites.

blogger Someone who writes a blog.

blogosphere The interconnected community of blogs and bloggers who post comments and link to each other's blogs.

blotter Newsroom slang for the crime reports that summarize facts about local arrests.

break To publish an important or dramatic story for the first time. To cover *breaking news* is to report on an event still in progress.

brief A short news story.

brite (or *bright)* A short, amusing news story.

broadcast Sending information to many destinations simultaneously via radio, television or computer network.

broadsheet A full-size newspaper, measuring roughly 14 by 23 inches. Most dailies (The New York Times, USA Today)

are broadsheets. If you fold a broadsheet in half, it becomes a *tabloid.*

budget A roundup of stories by each department of a newsroom (news, sports, business, etc.), which is then discussed at news meetings as editors plan coverage.

browser A software program (such as Internet Explorer or Netscape Navigator) that enables you to view Web pages.

bullet A type of dingbat, usually a big dot (●), used to highlight items listed in the text.

bump To delay or relocate a story.

bureau A news-gathering office separate from the main newsroom. A major newspaper, for instance, might have bureaus at the state capital, in Washington, D.C., and in foreign countries.

byline The reporter's name, usually printed at the beginning of a story.

caption A sentence or block of type providing descriptive information about a photo; used interchangeably with *cutline.*

change of venue Transferring a court proceeding to another jurisdiction after the prosecution or defense claims that potential jurors have been prejudiced by local media coverage.

clip A story clipped from a newspaper.

closed-ended question A direct question intended to elicit a yes-or-no answer ("Should the president be impeached?") — as opposed to an *open-ended question* intended to encourage a lengthy answer.

color *Giving a story color* means adding description or human interest; *coloring a story* means slanting it unfairly by adding bias.

column Advice or commentary by a columnist writing in a distinctive style on a consistent topic (sports, music, current events).

column inch A way to measure the depth of a story; it's text that, when printed, is 1 inch long and one column wide.

column logo A graphic device that labels regularly appearing material by packaging the writer's name, the column's name and a small mug or drawing of the writer.

conflict of interest A situation where a journalist's personal interests (family, friends, finances, etc.) affect the coverage of a story.

convergence Combining a variety of media (text, images, audio, video) to cover a story.

copy The text of a story.

copy desk The newsroom department responsible for editing stories, writing headlines and designing pages.

copy editor A newsroom staffer who edits stories and writes headlines.

copyright The legal protection given to authors preventing others from copying or selling their work.

correspondent A reporter who files stories from outside the newsroom — usually someone assigned to cover events in another city, state or country.

cover To gather news about an event.

cq A phrase inserted into a story (but not printed), usually following a phone number or a peculiar spelling, to advise copy editors that "this information has been checked." Example: *Police arrested a construction worker named Vladimir Schroughmfk (cq).*

credibility The public's perception of the reliability of a reporter or news outlet.

crusade A campaign by a news outlet to bring about reform or encourage government action.

cub A rookie or trainee reporter.

cut To delete part of a story.

cutline A sentence or block of type providing descriptive information about a photo; also called a *caption*.

daily A newspaper that prints a new edition every day.

dateline Words appearing at the start of the first paragraph of a story that identify where the story was filed.

deadline The time by which a reporter must finish a story.

deck A small headline running below the main headline; also called a *drop head*.

deep background Information that may be used in a story but which cannot be attributed in any way, in order to protect the source's identity.

delayed identification lead A type of news lead that withholds a significant piece of information — usually a person's name — until the second paragraph.

developing story A story in progress; an event or situation that will require additional time to unfold.

dialogue The use of quotes to re-create a conversation between two or more people.

dig To question or investigate in depth.

dingbats Decorative type characters (■ ◆ ● ★) used for lists or graphic emphasis.

draft An early version of a story, before it's rewritten and polished for publication.

dummy A small, detailed page diagram showing where all elements (text, photos, headlines, etc.) go.

editor A person who assigns, approves or corrects stories for publication or broadcast.

editorial Commentary that expresses opinion about a current event or issue (usually the opinion of an editor, publisher or owner); the department of the newspaper that gathers, writes, edits and publishes news.

editorialize To inject the reporter's opinion inappropriately into a news story or headline.

embargo A restriction placed on a news story or press release that specifies when the information can be made public.

enterprise story An article or project that's more creative, original and ambitious than typical news stories.

exclusive A story reported by only one news outlet; a *scoop*.

fact sheet A page distributed by public relations practitioners highlighting key data about a product, project or event.

fair comment and criticism The right of journalists to print their opinions on the performance of public figures or entertainers. Such criticism is legally protected as long as writers do not falsify facts.

feature A non-breaking-news story on people, trends or issues. A feature story isn't necessarily related to a current event;

it appeals to readers because of its topic, angle or writing style.

flag The name of a newspaper as it's displayed on Page One; also called a *nameplate*.

follow or **follow-up** A story supplying additional details about an event that's been previously covered.

font A typeface.

Freedom of Information Act (FOIA) A 1966 law requiring federal agencies to make most of their records available to the public upon request.

freelancer A self-employed writer who sells stories to publications.

futures file A collection of clips, press releases, notes and story ideas, arranged by date, to remind editors of upcoming stories to assign.

general assignment Where a reporter covers a wide range of stories rather than focusing on a specific beat.

grabber An attention-getting lead.

graf Short for "paragraph."

gutter The space running vertically between two columns.

handout See *news release*.

hard news Factual coverage of serious events (crime, accidents, speeches, government action). Soft news, on the other hand, refers to lighter, less urgent feature stories.

header A special label for any regularly appearing section, page or story; also called a *standing head*.

headline Large type running above or beside a story to summarize its content; also called a *head*, for short. Headlines are usually written by copy editors, but occasionally by reporters.

hit The term used for counting the number of visitors to a Web page. (Technically, it refers to the number of elements on each Web page; accessing a page with text and three images would count as four hits.)

home page The main page of a Web site, providing links to the rest of the site.

hole An unanswered question in a story; a significant missing fact that's identified when a story is edited.

human-interest story A feature that provides drama or emotional impact for readers.

home page The main page of a Web site, providing links to the rest of the site.

HTML HyperText Markup Language, the coding used to format and display Web pages.

immediate identification lead A lead in which the "who" is identified by name, usually because the person is recognizable to most readers (as opposed to a *delayed identification lead*).

in-cue The first words of a cut or wrap.

information graphic Any map, chart or diagram used to analyze an event, object or place. (Called an "infographic" for short).

intro (or *anchor intro*) The lead to a reporter's wrap, read by an anchor.

invasion of privacy Violating the right of an ordinary person to be left alone — to stay out of the news.

inverted pyramid A news story structure that presents the most important facts first; the rest of the information is organized in descending order of importance.

investigative journalism Reporting that requires extensive research to uncover information on misconduct or corruption that has been concealed from the public.

italic Type that slants to the right, *like this.*

jargon Specialized technical or bureaucratic language that's often confusing or meaningless to ordinary readers.

journalese Tired clichés that are recycled by lazy reporters (*solons hammered out a last-minute agreement in a marathon 11th-hour session*).

journalism The business and craft of producing content for the news media.

jump To continue a story on another page; text that's been continued on another page is called the *jump.*

justification Aligning lines of text so they're even along both the right and left margins.

kicker An ending that concludes a story

in a clever way: a surprise, a punch line or a memorable quote.

kill To delete (or refuse to run) a story, or something within a story.

layout The placement of art and text on a page; to *lay out* a page is to design it.

lead The first sentence or paragraph of a story. It's pronounced *lede* (and journalists often spell it that way, too).

lead-in Words that introduce some element in a broadcast news story.

leading questions Questions intended to steer an interviewee in a particular direction.

lead story The story deserving the biggest headline and best display on Page One, or at the start of a newscast.

libel Publishing or broadcasting a false statement that maliciously or carelessly damages someone's reputation.

liftout quote A graphic treatment of a quotation taken from a story, often using bold or italic type and a photo. Also called a *pull quote.*

link A clickable word or image on a Web page that directs you to another page or site.

live Not prerecorded; usually refers to stories filed from a news scene.

localizing Providing a community angle on a national story by discussing its connection to local people, issues or events.

logo A word or name that's stylized in a graphic way; used to refer to standing heads and column labels in a newspaper.

maestro A staffer who works with reporters, editors, photographers and designers to plan and create special treatments for stories.

masthead A block of information, including staff names and publication data, often printed on the editorial page.

media kit A package of information about a product, group or event, often containing background information, photos, news releases and so on.

median The middle number or halfway point in a series of numbers arranged by size; it's used whenever calculating an *average* would be confusing or misleading. In the series *1, 2, 4, 11, 13,*

the median — the middle number in the series — is *4.*

morgue A news library, where published stories and photos are stored for reference.

mug shot A small photo showing a person's face.

multimedia Presenting information using more than one medium, combining text, graphics, audio and video.

narrative A storytelling style where events unfold chronologically.

narrative lead A lead that begins a story by placing readers in the middle of the action.

natural sound (or *ambient sound*) In radio or TV new stories, sounds recorded to capture the flavor of a news scene — birds singing, crowds cheering, planes landing.

news conference An interview session where someone fields questions from a group of reporters; also called a *press conference.*

news director The top news executive in a television newsroom, responsible for news content, budget decisions, hiring and firing staff, etc.

news release Information sent out by a group or individual seeking publicity; also called a *press release* or handout.

nut graph (or *nut graf*) An explanatory paragraph near the top of the story that summarizes what the story is about — or tells readers why they should care.

obit Short for *obituary,* a story about someone who has died.

off the record An agreement by a reporter and a source specifying that information revealed in an interview cannot be printed in any form.

op-ed page The page opposite a newspaper's editorial page, usually reserved for columns and letters to the editor.

open-ended question A question phrased in a way that encourages a source time to give a lengthy, in-depth answer ("Why do you think the president should be impeached?") — as opposed to a *closed-ended question* designed to elicit a yes-or-no answer.

open-meeting laws State and federal laws that guarantee public (and press) access to meetings of government bodies.

open-record laws State and federal laws guaranteeing public (and press) access to most government records.

out-cue *(OQ)* The final words of a cut or wrap.

package A story that uses multiple points of entry (text, sidebars, graphics, photos, etc.) to make complex topics more accessible to readers; also, a story that's prepared by a TV news reporter, usually taped, featuring the reporter's narration, one or more sound bites and often a stand-up.

pad To lengthen a story by adding unnecessary material, usually so it fits a predetermined length.

paginate To design a page on a computer.

paraphrase An indirect quote that summarizes, in your own words, what someone else said.

partial quotation A section or fragment of a longer quote that you insert into another sentence: *The answer, as Dylan once sang, is "blowin' in the wind."*

plagiarism Passing off someone else's words or ideas as your own.

play The emphasis given to a story or an element within a story. News can be "played up" (emphasized) or "played down" (de-emphasized).

podcast An audio version of a news story made available for downloading on a Web site.

pool A group of reporters and photographers selected to cover a story where access is limited; their reports and photographs are then shared with other media outlets.

press box The section of a sports arena or stadium reserved for reporters covering the event.

press conference An interview session where someone answers questions from a group of reporters; also called a *news conference.*

press release Information sent out by a group or individual seeking publicity; also called a *news release* or *handout.*

privilege A journalistic defense against

libel that allows reporters to print what's said in legislative or judicial proceedings *(fair report privilege)*, to express opinions *(opinion privilege)* or to review public performances *(fair comment and criticism).*

profile A feature story that uses interviews and observations to paint a picture of someone newsworthy.

prompter A device that projects a news script in front of the camera lens for an anchor to read. (*TelePrompTer* is a well-known brand name.)

public figure In libel cases, a person who has acquired fame or notoriety (a performer or athlete, for example) or has participated in some public controversy (a protester or social activist).

public official In libel cases, someone who exercises power or influence in governmental affairs (a police officer, mayor or school superintendent, for example).

public relations The skills and tactics used to convey information and maintain a positive public image about a person, product, event or organization.

publisher The top-ranking executive of a newspaper, who oversees all departments (editorial, advertising, circulation, etc.).

puff piece A flattering story written to provide gratuitous publicity.

Pulitzer Prize The most prestigious award in journalism, established by publisher Joseph Pulitzer at Columbia University.

Q and A An interview printed in question-and-answer form.

quote (n.) The exact words spoken by a source; (v.) to print a source's exact words inside quotation marks.

readership The estimated number of readers who view a publication (as opposed to *circulation,* which is the number of copies distributed).

reporter A person who gathers and writes news stories for publication or broadcast.

running story A story that is continuing to unfold, necessitating follow-up stories as events develop.

scoop (n.) An exclusive story no other news outlet has; (v.) to beat the competition to a juicy story.

script The written version of a radio news story.

second-day story A "follow-up" story that provides additional details about an event that was previously covered.

sedition Activities or writings that incite resistance or hostility toward the government.

series Two or more stories on the same topic, usually published in a scheduled sequence.

shield laws Statutes that give journalists the right to protect the identity of sources when questioned during judicial proceedings.

sidebar A small story, graphic or chart accompanying a bigger story on the same topic.

slander Defamation by the spoken word. (Defamation by the printed word is *libel.*)

slideshow A series of photos and captions — often incorporating audio commentary — that illustrates a topic or event on a Web site.

slug The name given to a story for newsroom use.

soft news Stories that are lighter and less urgent than serious breaking news events.

SOT, sound-on-tape A recorded sound bite (usually audio and video) played during a TV news story.

sound bite A recorded comment from a news source (usually audio and video).

sources Records or people providing journalists with information. (The term usually refers to *people.*)

spike To kill or withhold a story from publication.

spin The slanting of information by a source, usually in an attempt to make someone look good.

stand-up A shot of a reporter at a news scene reporting a story.

spot news A timely event covered by journalists as it happens.

spread A story layout designed across two facing pages.

staffer Someone who works for a news organization: a reporter, editor, photographer, etc.

stet A proofreading comment that means

"leave it – ignore any editing notations."

story The word journalists use to refer to a published article.

stringer A part-time correspondent who is not a regular newsroom employee but gets paid by the story.

style A writer's unique blend of syntax, vocabulary and perspective that gives his or her writing its characteristic personality; also, a news organization's rules for punctuation, capitalization, abbreviation, etc.

stylebook A compilation of newsroom rules for punctuation, capitalization, abbreviation, etc., with guidelines on everything from handling profanity to recording sports scores.

subhead Lines of type, often bold, used to divide text into smaller sections.

suitcase lead An excessively long lead that's overstuffed with facts, like a bulging suitcase.

summary lead A news lead that summarizes the most significant of the five W's *(who, what, when, where, why)*.

syndicated columnist A writer whose commentary is sold and distributed by a news organization for reprinting in other publications.

tabloid A newspaper format that's roughly half the size of a standard (broadsheet) page; also, a derogatory term for a type of sleazy, sensational journalism (made infamous by tabloid-sized newspapers back in the early 20th century).

tag (or *sign-off, sig-out, lockout, standard out-cue*) The closing line where reporters say their names and station call letters (*"Ella Funt, Newsradio 920"*).

takeout A longer analysis piece that attempts to put a complex issue into perspective.

talent Reporters, anchors, disc jockeys — those paid to appear on the air (as opposed to engineers or office staff).

target audience A particular demographic (a segment of the public) at which media producers or advertisers aim their message.

tease A brief headline or promo for a coming radio or TV news story.

transition A word or phrase used by a writer to move a story from one point (or topic, or idea) to another. Common transitions include *however, meanwhile, on a related issue, nevertheless,* etc.

trend story A feature story on the culture's latest fads, fashions and ideas — from fashions and technological gizmos to social customs and lifestyles.

typo A typesetting mistake.

Video news release A press release, complete with images and sound, ready to be used in a televised newscast.

VO or *voice-over:* When the anchor speaks over video, or when a reporter narrates over video cover.

voicer A news story by a reporter that doesn't use actualities; when it's delivered by an anchor reading a script, it's called a *reader.*

wire service An organization (such as The Associated Press) that compiles news, features and photos and distributes them, for a fee, to subscribing publications.

wrap A radio news story that begins and ends with a reporter's voice "wrapped" around one or more sound bites. (TV reporters call this a *package.*)

yellow journalism Reporting that's sleazy or sensational.

THE REPORTER'S
WEBLIOGRAPHY

Here's our list of recommended Web sites, arranged alphabetically. For a more up-to-date list (with links), visit **www.mhhe.com/harrower1**.

BIOGRAPHICAL INFORMATION

Biographical Dictionary
www.s9.com
A good site for a quick (but brief) biographical check on almost any famous person.

Biography
www.biography.com
The Biography Channel Web site. Provides data on public figures and (especially) celebrities.

BLOGS

Romenesko
www.poynter.org/column.asp?id=45
The best Web roundup of media industry news and gossip.

Robot Wisdom
www.robotwisdom.com
Boingboing
www.boingboing.net
Looking for feature story ideas? Tracking trends? Or just hoping for oddball, interesting reading? These two respected sites demonstrate how the best blogs monitor what's new and cool.

Naples News blogs
www.naplesnews.com/blogs
More examples of the effective format we displayed on page 159.

CRIME AND COURTS

Covering Crime and Justice
www.justicejournalism.org/crimeguide/toc.html
Helpful articles on covering the crime and justice beat compiled by Criminal Justice Journalists.

FBI's Uniform Crime Reports
www.fbi.gov/ucr/ucr.htm
Statistics on all types of crime occurring throughout the United States.

Bureau of Justice Statistics
www.albany.edu/sourcebook
Criminal justice statistics from over 100 sources.

U.S. Department of Justice
www.usdoj.gov

U.S. Courts
www.uscourts.gov/allinks.html
Offers links to all courts throughout the U.S.

ENVIRONMENT

Environmental Protection Agency (EPA)
www.epa.gov
Includes the EPA Newsroom, regulations and educational resources for the public.

National Oceanic & Atmospheric Administration
www.noaa.gov
Data on oceans, the atmosphere, ecosystems, climate change and weather forecasts.

WorldWatch Institute
www.worldwatch.org
News and features on environmental issues and problems from around the world.

EXPERT SOURCES

ProfNet Experts
profnet3.prnewswire.com/enter/index.jsp
A site connecting journalists with experts and information officers around the world.

National Press Club
npc.press.org/newssources/index.cfm
The National Press Club's online directory of experts in nearly 400 topics.

US Newswire
www.usnewswire.com/links/slink.html
Connects journalists with expert sources in public policy, academia, government and industry.

GOVERNMENT AND POLITICS

Fed World
www.fedworld.gov
Links to a vast array of federal government sites.

Voter Information Sevices
www.vis.org
Offers analysis of Congressional voting records.

Campaign Finance Information Center
www.campaignfinance.org
Part of the Investigative Reporters and Editors (IRE) Web site, to help you follow the money.

Federal Election Commision
www.fec.gov/disclosure.shtml
Official campaign finance reports and statistics.

U.S. Government Statistics
www.fedstats.gov

U.S. Bureau of Census
www.census.gov

U.S. Federal Government Directory
www.searchbeat.com/fed-usa.htm
A collection of links to federal and state Web sites, agencies, news, weather, businesses, etc.

State and Local Government on the Net
www.statelocalgov.net
A directory of Web sites for state, county and local governments across the country.

U.S. Government Printing Office Access
www.gpoaccess.gov
The Web site to view or order documents printed by the U.S. government.

HISTORY

Best of History Web sites
www.besthistorysites.net
Links to more than 1,000 history Web sites.

The History Channel
www.historychannel.com
Speeches, videos, timelines and maps.

The Library of Congress
www.loc.gov/index.html
Access to maps, documents, photos, video.

JOURNALISM ORGANIZATIONS

American Association of Sunday and Feature Editors
www.aasfe.org

American Copy Editors Society (ACES)
www.copydesk.org

American Press Institute
www.americanpressinstitute.org

American Society of Journalists and Authors
www.asja.org

American Society of Newspaper Editors
www.asne.org

Asian American Journalism Association
www.aaja.org

Associated Press Sports Editors
www.apse.dallasnews.com

Association for Education in Journalism and Mass Communication
www.aejmc.org/

Association for Women in Communications
www.womcom.org

Association of Health Care Journalists
www.healthjournalism.org

Black Journalism Review
www.blackjournalism.com

Center for Media and Public Affairs
www.cmpa.com

Columbia Scholastic Press Association
www.columbia.edu/cu/cspa

Committee to Protect Journalists
www.cpj.org

Committee of Concerned Journalists
www.journalism.org

Criminal Justice Journalists
www.reporters.net/cjj/index.html

DART Center for Journalism & Trauma
www.dartcenter.org

Fairness and Accuracy in Reporting
www.fair.org

First Amendment Center
www.firstamendmentcenter.org/

Freedom Forum
www.freedomforum.org

International Center for Journalists
www.icfj.org

Investigative Reporters and Editors
www.ire.org

Journal of Mass Media Ethics
www.jmme.org

Journalism Education Association
www.jea.org

Media Info Center
www.mediainfocenter.org/

National Association of Black Journalists
www.nabj.org

National Association of Hispanic Journalists
www.nahj.org

National Association of Science Writers
www.nasw.org

National Conference of Editorial Writers
www.ncew.org

National Federation of Press Women
www.nfpw.org

National Institute for Computer-Assisted Reporting
www.nicar.org

National Lesbian & Gay Journalists Association
www.nlgja.org

National Scholastic Press Association
studentpress.journ.umn.edu/

National Society of Newspaper Columnists
www.columnists.com

Native American Journalists Association
www.naja.com

Newseum — Interactive Museum of News
www.newseum.org

Online News Association
www.journalists.org/

Quill & Scroll
www.uiowa.edu/~quill-sc/

Poynter Institute for Media Studies
www.poynter.org

The Pulitzer Prizes
www.pulitzer.org

Radio–Television News Directors Association
www.rtnda.org/

Religion Newswriters Association
www.rna.org

Reporter's Committee for Freedom of the Press
www.rcfp.org

Society of American Business Editors and Writers
www.sabew.org

Society for Environmental Journalists
www.sej.org

Society for News Design
www.snd.org

Society of Professional Journalists
www.spj.org

South Asian Journalists Association
www.saja.org

Unity: Journalists of Color
www.unityjournalists.org

LAW AND ETHICS

Freedom of Information Act
www.usdoj.gov/04foia/

The Reporter's Privilege:
www.rcfp.org/privilege

Shield laws by state, from the Reporters Committee for Freedom of the Press.

Student Press Law Center
www.splc.org

Journalism codes of ethics
www.asne.org/ideas/codes/codes.htm
Links to dozens of news organizations' codes.

NEWS AND NEWS SITES

Mondo Times
www.mondotimes.com

Newslink
newslink.org

NewsVoyager
www.newspaperlinks.com/voyager.cfm
Need a link to a newspaper, magazine, TV or radio station? If it exists, one of these three sites will get you there.

10 X 10
tenbyten.org
An innovatively designed news site that ranks the day's top stories visually and numerically.

NewsTrove
newstrove.com/index.html
Links to news sources filtered to suit your own viewpoint. Is this the future of news delivery?

Newspaper Archives
www.newspaperarchive.com
Need to track down an old story? This site boasts access to millions of back issues.

U.S. News Archives on the Web
www.ibiblio.org/slanews/internet/archives.html
A clearinghouse of links to the archives of many U.S. newspapers.

PUBLIC RELATIONS

All About Public Relations
aboutpublicrelations.net/toolkit.htm
A toolkit of helpful columns and articles compiled by Steven R. Van Hook.

PR News Wire
prnewswire.com
International clearinghouse of news releases.

Public Relations Society of America
www.prsa.org

RADIO AND TELEVISION

Television Newswriting Workshop
www.mervinblock.com/tips.html
Articles, tips and columns by the outspoken and entertaining Mervin Block.

Broadcast Education Association
www.beaweb.org/

National Association of Broadcasters
www.nab.org

RESEARCH SITES FOR JOURNALISTS

Refdesk.com
www.refdesk.com
A comprehensive one-stop information source. For a reporter, this makes a good home page.

Journalist Express
www.journalistexpress.com
Another all-purpose home page with links to reference material, publications, headlines, etc.

The Journalist's Toolbox
www.americanpressinstitute.org/pages/toolbox/
Hundreds of helpful links from the American Press Institute.

Power Reporting
powerreporting.com
A Web site listing "thousands of free research tools for journalists."

Reporter's Desktop
www.reporter.org/desktop
Another one-stop collection of links to reference materials, Web sites, maps and search engines.

Cool calculators
www.madison.com/library/LEE/calculators.html
A broad assortment of tools to help you calculate percentages, money, speed, temperature, etc.

Fagan Finder Quotations and Proverbs Search
www.faganfinder.com/quotes/
Need to track down a quote or proverb? This is usually the best place to start.

Search Systems
www.searchsystems.net
A free directory that allows you to search public record databases of all kinds.

The Smoking Gun
www.thesmokinggun.com
Want to see how entertaining public records and legal documents can be? This stuff is priceless.

Internet Movie Database
www.imdb.com
The best source for information about movies, videos — even television shows.

CIA — The World Fact Book
www.cia.gov/cia/publications/factbook/
Information on every country on the planet, from illicit drug use to number of telephones, courtesy of U.S. intelligence agencies.

TELEPHONE AND ADDRESS SERVICES

Anywho Online Directory
www.anywho.com/rl.html

Switchboard
www.switchboard.com/

The Global Yellow Pages
www.globalyp.com/world.htm

Zip Codes
zip4.usps.com/zip4/welcome.jsp

URBAN MYTHS AND LEGENDS

Health–Related Hoaxes and Rumors
www.cdc.gov/doc.do/id/0900f3ec80226b9c
The Centers for Disease Control posts information on most health hoaxes here.

Urban Legends Reference Pages
www.snopes.com

Urban Legends and Folklore
urbanlegends.about.com/library/blhoax.htm
These two sites help separate fact from folklore.

SOURCES AND CREDITS

① THE STORY OF JOURNALISM

Newsroom heroes, legends and folklore (pages 6-7)

Image credits:

Photos of Twain, Bly, Mencken, Hemingway and Truman from the Library of Congress Prints and Photographs Division.

Thompson photo by Rick Giase of the Rocky Mountain News.

Woodward and Bernstein photo © Bettmann/Corbis.

The birth of journalism (pages 8-9)

Text credits:

Stone excerpt reprinted from "History of American Journalism" by James Melvin Lee, Garden City Publishing Co. 42.

Thomas excerpt reprinted from "A Treasury of Great Reporting," edited by Louis L. Snyder and Richard B. Morris, Simon and Schuster, 2nd edition. 29.

Image credits:

Franklin and Thomas illustrations from the Library of Congress Prints and Photographs Division.

Engraving of medieval printers courtesy of St. Bride Printing Library, London.

Colonial printer illustration from photos.com.

Stamp Act stamp and post rider engraving from Peter C. Marzio, "The Men and Machines of American Journalism." The Smithsonian Institution, 1978.

Additional sources:

Emery, Edwin. "The Press and America." 3rd ed., Prentice-Hall, 1972.

Hudson, Frederick. "Journalism in the United States." Harper & Brothers, 1873.

Lee, James Melvin. "History of American Journalism." Garden City Publishing Co.

Marzio, Peter C. "The Men and Machines of American Journalism." The Smithsonian Institution, 1978.

Starr, Paul. "The Creation of the Media." Basic Books, 2004.

Stephens, Mitchell. "A History of News." Viking, 1988.

Tebbel, John. "The Compact History of the American Newspaper." E.P. Dutton, 1969.

Mott, Frank Luther. "American Journalism, A History: 1690-1960." 3rd ed.

News in the 19th century (pages 10-11)

Image credits:

Newsboy from a painting by James Henry Cafferty, "Newsboy Selling The New York Herald," 1857. Rubin Collection of American Art.

Yellow Kid from Peter C. Marzio, "The Men

and Machines of American Journalism." The Smithsonian Institution, 1978.

Bennett and Douglass photos from the Library of Congress Prints and Photographs Division.

Steam press and typewriter from photos.com.

Telegraph by Ryan McVay/Getty Images.

News in the modern age (pages 12-13)

Text credits:

Cronkite quote from "A Reporter's Life" by Walter Cronkite, Alfred A. Knopf. 305.

Pulitzer quote from "The College of Journalism" in The North American Review, 1904.

Murrow quote from "In Search of Light: The Broadcasts of Edward R. Murrow, 1938-1961." Alfred A. Knopf, 1967. 37.

CNN quote from CNN. com.

Image credits:

Photo of Pulitzer © Bettmann/Corbis.

Antique radio and TV from PhotoDisc/Getty Images.

Cover of first Time magazine © 1923 Time, Inc./Getty Images.

② HOW NEWSROOMS WORK

What is news? (pages 16-17)

Image credits:

Newspaper page courtesy of The Virginian-Pilot.

Newspaper-reading couple © Bettmann/Corbis

Text credits:

Statistics sources:

◆ Serious issues v. crime news: from a media poll conducted by Ipsos-Public Affairs, Aug. 26, 2003.

◆ Self-censorship: from a Pew Research Center poll, April 30, 2000.

◆ Americans' emotional reactions to the news: from Thomas E. Patterson's 2000 study conducted by the Joan Shorenstein Center on the Press, Politics and Public Policy.

◆ Political story percentage: The Readership Institute, 2004.

◆ Under-30 readers: from a poll by the Project for Excellence in Journalism.

◆ Media being out of touch: CNN/Gallup Poll. Feb. 4-8, 1999.

Man Bites Dog, The Associated Press, June 4, 2004. Copyright © 2004 Associated Press. All rights reserved. Distributed by Valeo IP. Reprinted by permission.

What readers want (pages 18-19)

Text credits:

"How to Read the Newspaper Faster" from

Esquire magazine, February 2003.

Statistic on reader multitasking from the Simultaneous Media Usage Survey (SIMM), conducted by BIGresearch in October 2003.

Kris McGrath quote from "State of the American Newspaper: What Do Readers Really Want?" by Charles Layton, American Journalism Review, March 1999.

Image credits:

Focus group photo by Felix Adamo, The Bakersfield Californian.

Photo of the monitoring device from Eyetools, Inc.

How a story gets written (pages 20-21)

Illustrations by Steve Cowden, with special thanks to Harris Siegel for being such a good sport.

How the news comes together (pages 22-23)

Adapted from an information graphic by Steve Cowden with text by Bill Graves, published in The Oregonian, Dec. 4, 2000.

Who's who in the newsroom (pages 24-25)

Image credits:

Photo of Scott Byers by James McKenzie.

Photo of Susan Page courtesy of Susan Page.

What it's called (pages 26-27)

Image credits:

Pig photo by Kraig Scattarella of The Oregonian.

All other photos from Photodisc except the tornado, nurse and happy couple © Bettmann/Corbis.

Both page examples adapted from "The Newspaper Designer's Handbook" by Tim Harrower, McGraw-Hill. 14, 34.

Tools, talent and temperament (pages 28-29)

Thanks to John M. Baer for a few of the ideas expressed in the introduction.

Image credits:

Reporter illustration and photos of cameras, cell phone and laptop computer from photos.com.

Test yourself (page 32)

Image credits:

Photos of screaming woman and squirrel © Bettmann/Corbis.

Woman trapped in dryer from Thinkstock.

NEWSWRITING BASICS

Just the facts (pages 34-35)

Image credits:
Photo of Lincoln from the Library of Congress Prints and Photographs Division.

Text credits:
Excerpt from the Staunton Spectator can be found at http://valley.vcdh.virginia.edu — part of the Valley Project, a fascinating Civil War-era archive of letters, diaries and newspapers.

"Simpsons"/First Amendment survey results from a 2006 McCormick Tribune Freedom Museum survey.

The inverted pyramid (pages 38-39)

Text credits:
Schwarzenegger Gets an Austrian Licking, July 17, 2004. Copyright © 2004 The Associated Press. Reprinted by permission of Reprint Management Services.

Image credits:
Civil War photo © Royalty-Free/Corbis.

Writing basic news leads
(pages 40-41)

Text credits:
Buried lead example from a column by Hal Taylor in the National Observer, original date unknown.

Image credits:
Dickens illustration by Joe Spooner.

Airplane photo © AP/Wide World Photos.

Beyond the basic news lead
(pages 42-43)

Text credits:
Lincoln Mabry lead written by Rick Senften in The Repository (Canton, Ohio).

Thanks to Ken Fuson for allowing yet another author to resurrect his classic springtime lead.

Image credits:
Poe illustration by Joe Spooner.

After the lead . . . what next?
(pages 46-47)

Text credits:
Robbery story reprinted from The Oregonian.

Milk-squirting brite adapted from a story by The Associated Press, Sept. 1, 2004.

Image credits:
Melville illustration by Joe Spooner.

Story structure (pages 48-49)

Text credits:
Transition excerpt adapted from an example in "Newswriting From Lead to '30' " by William Metz. Prentice-Hall, 1991. 93.

Barnett, Bella and Hamilton excerpts from The Oregonian.

Image credits:
Pencil photo from photos.com.
Photo of the two guys © Bettmann/Corbis.

Rewriting (pages 50-51)

Image credits:
Beethoven illustration from the Library of Congress Prints and Photographs Division.

Delete-key photo from photos.com.

Text credits:
Linda Marvin excerpt adapted from a story by Tim Harrower in The Oregonian.

Editing (pages 52-53)

Image credits:
Photo of editing hands by Andy Piper of the Rocky Mountain News.

Photos of Oregonian staffers by Mike Lloyd.

Newswriting style (pages 54-55)

Image credits:
Uncle Sam parody poster by Steve Cowden.

Excerpt reprinted from "The Associated Press Stylebook." Basic Books, 2004. 69.

Text credits:
AP style highlights written by Wally Benson, adapted from "The Associated Press Stylebook."

Making deadline (pages 56-57)

Image credits:
Reporter illustration (top) by Tony Champagne.

Deadline comic (bottom) by Joe Spooner, adapted from an illustration by Michael Atchison.

Text credits:
Some ideas in the deadline checklist adapted from a list by Michelle McLellan.

Star Tribune quotes from a compilation of tips by Laurie Hertzel at www.notrain-nogain.org/Train/Res/Write/conq.asp

66 newswriting tips (pages 58-59)

Image credits:
Reporter illustration from photos.com.

④ REPORTING BASICS

Where stories come from
(pages 66-67)

Text credits:
Lipinski quote from a column in the Chicago Tribune by Eric Zorn, July 21, 2005.

Image credits:
Photos from photos.com except firemen photo by Michael Lloyd, The Oregonian; Mick Jagger photo by Ross Hamilton, The Oregonian.

Finding and using sources
(pages 68-69)

Text credits:
Fire story written by Alice Klement.

Image credits:
Jail cell photo by Thomas P. Costello, Asbury Park Press. Dormitory fire © AP/Wide World Photos. Einstein photo from the Library of Congress Prints and Photographs Division.

Using the Internet (pages 70-71)

Image credits:
Lead photo from photos.com.

Text credits:
Kenneth G. Wilson quote from "The Columbia Guide to Standard American English." Columbia University Press, 1993.

Berger quote from "Citizen falls into tsunami trap" by Ellen Hollemans, Mail & Guardian Online, Jan. 10, 2005.

Movie-title quote by New York Times reporter James Sterngold reprinted from a column in the Washington Post by Howard Kurtz, Dec. 4, 1998.

Observation (pages 72-73)

Text credits:
Charles Wallace excerpt from the Los Angeles Times via "Newswriting from Lead to '30' " by William Metz. Prentice-Hall, 1991.

Milton Bracker excerpt from "A Treasury of Great Reporting," edited by Louis L. Snyder and Richard B. Morris. Simon & Schuster, 1962.

Excerpt from Tom Wolfe, "The Me Decade and the Third Great Awakening," from "Mauve Gloves & Madmen, Clutter & Vine," pp. 115-116, published by Farrar, Straus and Giroux/Bantam Books.

Susan Orlean excerpt from "My Kind of Place." Random House, 2004.

Justin Davidson excerpt from Newsday, March 29, 1997, quoted in "1998 Best Newspaper Writing," edited by Christopher Scanlan. The Poynter Institute and Bonus Books Inc.

Bill Blundell excerpt from The Wall Street Journal, quoted in "1998 Best Newspaper Writing," edited by Christopher Scanlan. The Poynter Institute and Bonus Books Inc.

Excerpts by David Rhode and Corey Kilganon from "Tales From the Times, Real-Life Stories to Make You Think, Wonder, and Smile, from the Pages of The New York Times," edited by Lisa Belkin. St. Martins Griffin, 2004, 32.

Bob Greene excerpt from "Cheeseburgers: The Best of Bob Greene." Atheneum, 1985.

Image credits:
Photo by Ross William Hamilton.

Taking notes (pages 74-75)

Image credits:
Photo of Christina Leonard by Pat Shannahan, Arizona Republic.

Note-taking photos: (top) Tanya Breen, Asbury Park Press; (middle) ©Rodrigo Arangua/AFP/Getty Images; (bottom) Andy Piper, Rocky Mountain News.

Text credits:
Fishel anecdote from "Reunion: The Girls We

Used to Be, The Women We Became" by Elizabeth Fishel. Random House, 2000. 156.

Interviewing (pages 76-79)

Image credits:

Holyfield photo by Sara A. Fajardo, Orlando Sentinel.

Acrobat interview photo © Gideon Mendel/Corbis.

Flood photo by Josh Meltzer, The Roanoke Times.

Gibson photo © Frank Micelotta/Getty Images.

Football coach photo by Hal Stoelzle, Rocky Mountain News.

Text credits:

Gibson excerpt from "The Art of the Interview" by Lawrence Grobel, copyright © 2004 by Lawrence Grobel. Used by permission of Three Rivers Press, a division of Random House Inc. and Lukeman Literary Management.

Quotations (pages 80-81)

Image credits:

Bush photo by Michael Lloyd, The Oregonian.

Hemingway photo © Bettmann/Corbis.

Text credits:

Scanlan quote from "The Quote Diet," a "Chip on Your Shoulder" column posted Aug. 23, 2004, on Poynteronline.

Bush quote via Maureen Dowd, "The Language Thing," The New York Times Magazine, July 29, 1990.

Attributions (pages 82-83)

Text credits:

"Citizen Kane" review excerpt from David Thomson on Salon.com, July 28, 2000.

LaRocque quote from her article in Quill magazine, March/April 1999.

Catron quote from "Keep Attribution Simple," Writers Digest, March 1991.

Pit bull story by Chuck Slothower from The Oregonian, Feb. 19, 2005.

Math for journalists (pages 84-85)

Image credits:

Adding machine photo by C Squared Studios/Getty Images.

Scanlan quote from "Writing With Numbers," a "Chip on Your Shoulder" column posted April 3, 2001, on Poynteronline.

⑤ COVERING THE NEWS

Fire photo on chapter opening page by Andrew Skinner, Oceana's Herald-Journal.

Covering a beat (pages 90-91)

Image credits:

Photos by Michael Lloyd.

Writing obituaries (pages 92-93)

Text credits:

Tucker obituary by Gerald S. Goldstein, Providence Journal-Bulletin.

Hinch comments extracted from a series of tips on writing obituaries at www.notrain-nogain.org/ListARC/ obit.asp

Image credits:

Cemetery photo © Royalty-Free/Corbis.

Covering accidents and disasters (pages 94-95)

Image credits:

Car photo by Mark R. Sullivan, Home News Tribune.

Volcano photo: © U.S. Geological Survey.

Tornado photo: NOAA Photo Library, OAR/ERL/National Sever Storms Lab (NSSL).

Earthquake photo: Mark Downey/Getty Images.

Storm damage: C. Lee/PhotoLink/Getty Images.

Hurricane: © Royalty-Free/Corbis.

Snowstorm: Walter Hodges/Brand X Pictures/Getty Images.

Victim photo: © AP/Wide World Photos.

Text credits:

Josh Meyer quoted from his undated memo, "Some Basic Tips on Disaster Coverage."

Covering fires (pages 96-97)

Image credits:

Barn fire: Marshall Gorby, Springfield News-Sun.

Fire aftermath: Bob Pennell, Medford Mail Tribune.

Covering crime (pages 98-99)

Image credits:

Gun, police car photos © Royalty-Free/Corbis.

Interview photo by Al Podgorski, Chicago Sun-Times.

Covering courts (pages 100-101)

Image credits:

Justice statue photo © Royalty-Free/Corbis.

Covering speeches (page 102-103)

Text credits:

"Ann Coulter causes stir at KU" by Mike Belt from Lawrence Journal-World, March 30, 2005. Reprinted by permission of Lawrence Journal-World.

Image credits:

Annan photo © Fabrice Coffrini/AFP/Getty Images.

Covering meetings (page 104-105)

Image credits:

City council photo by Tim Harrower.

Text credits:

"Putnam Commissioners Get Earful Over Abandoned House" by Heather Svokos from Charleston Gazette, Sept. 10, 1996. Reprinted by permission of Charleston Gazette.

"City Has $548-Million: What Do You Want?" by Bryan Gilmer from St. Petersburg Times, Aug. 21, 2002. Copyright © 2002 St. Petersburg Times. Reprinted by permission.

Clark quote from "The Greatest Story Never Told," a column by Roy Peter Clark posted Nov. 10, 2003, on Poynteronline.

Covering politics (pages 106-107)

Image credits:

Kennedy/Helen Thomas photo © Bettmann/Corbis.

Kerry photo © Nathaniel Welch/Corbis Outline.

Bush press conference photo © Chuck Kennedy.

Text credits:

Wolff quotes posted on a NewsLab Web site covering his workshop. "Equipping the Desk for Campaign 2002" at www.newslab.org/resources/politics.htm

Covering sports (pages 108-109)

Image credits:

Muhammad Ali photo © Bettmann/Corbis.

Molly Yannity photo by Grant Haller.

Text credits:

Dwyer quote from "The Associated Press Sports Writing Handbook" by Steve Wilstein. McGraw-Hill, 2002.

⑥ BEYOND BREAKING NEWS

The world of features (pages 112-113)

Image credits:

Feature pages reprinted by permission of the Detroit Free Press.

Pageant photo by Michael Lloyd.

Generating story ideas (pages 114-115)

Text credits:

Stein quote orginally appeared in the introduction to "1001 Article Ideas" by Frank A. Dickson. Writer's Digest Books, 1979.

Image credits:

Light bulb photo from PhotoLink/Getty Images.

Carpenter ant story reprinted from The Oregonian.

Feature style (pages 116-117)

Image credits:

Tom Wolfe photo © Lynn Goldsmith/ Corbis.

Text credits:

Tom Wolfe excerpt from "The Girl of the Year," reprinted in "The Kandy-Kolored Tangerine-Flake Streamline Baby." Farrar, Strauss and Giroux, 1965. 204.

French excerpt from "4UREYESONLY" by Thomas French, Monique Fields and Dong-Phuong Nguyen, St. Petersburg Times, May 18, 2003.

Feature story structures

(pages 118-119)

Image credits:

Rose photo by Steve Cole/Getty Images.

"Always, Ed" page reprinted by permission of the St. Petersburg Times.

"The Perfect Kiss" page reprinted by permission of the Cleveland Plain Dealer.

Text credits:

Harrigan quote from "Organizing Your Material" in "The Complete Book of Feature Writing." Writer's Digest Books, 1991.

Writing profiles (pages 120-121)

Image credits:

"Stars and Stripes Wherever" photo by J. Kyle Keener, Detroit Free Press.

Painter photo by Mel Curtis/Getty Images.

Text credits:

Ager tips adapted from "Hearts and Guts: Writing the Personal Profile," a column posted Aug. 20, 2001, on Poynteronline.

Enterprise projects (pages 122-123)

Image credits:

Deadline journalist illustration by Tony Champagne.

Photo of Diana Sugg by Monica Lopossay, The Sun. Reprinted by permission.

Investigative reporting (pages 124-125)

Text credits:

Boardman and Barstow quotes from "Tips From the Trenches," The Quill, March 1, 1999.

Uhrhammer quote from "Reporting/Writing/Editing," Ron Lovell, editor. Kendall/Hunt, 1982. 117.

Excerpt from "The 30-Year Secret" by Nigel Jaquiss in Willamette Week, May 12, 2004. Reprinted by permission.

Short-form alternatives (pages 128-129)

Image credits:

Darth Vader illustration by Daniel Dulhunty, The Border Mail, Wodonga, Australia.

Writing editorials and columns

(pages 130-131)

Image credits:

Limbaugh photo © Robert Giroux/Getty Images.

Commentary page reprinted by permission of

the Chicago Sun-Times.

Text credits:

Journalist/commentator survey conducted in 2005 by the University of Pennsylvania's Annenberg Public Policy Center. (Incidentally, 48 percent of both ordinary Americans *and* journalists thought Katie Couric was "very close" or "somewhat close" to their ideas of what a journalist is.)

Quindlen excerpt from "Loud and Clear" by Anna Quindlen. Random House, 2004. 56.

Kuralt excerpt from The Charlotte News, Oct. 31, 1956.

Ivins excerpt from "The Current State of American Energy Policy," May 5, 2005.

Waterhouse quotes from a column posted by Tom Coates on his blog, plasticbag.org.

Writing reviews (pages 132-133)

Image credits:

Jagger photo by Ross Hamilton, The Oregonian.

Ebert photo by Patty Williams, reprinted with permission of Roger Ebert.

Test yourself (pages 134)

Image credits:

Michael Gartner photo provided by the Iowa State Daily.

7 LAW AND ETHICS

Press rights (pages 136-137)

Special thanks to Mark Witherspoon for providing the inspiration for that "big blowhard" rant. In a *good* way.

Image credits:

Photo of reporter from punchstock.com.

Press wrongs (pages 138-139)

Image credits:

Photo© AP/Wide World Photos.

Illustrations in "Trouble" chart by Steve Cowden.

Understanding libel (pages 140-141)

Image credits:

Cruise/Kidman photo © AP/Wide World Photos.

Cherry Sisters photo from the collection of George Mills. American Heritage, October/November 1982.

Text credits:

List of "explosive" words adapted from a list compiled by Bruce Sanford in "Libel and Privacy." Aspen Law and Business, 1998.

Franklin quote from "An Account of the Supremest Court of Judicature in Pennsylvania, viz., The Court of the Press," Sept. 12, 1789.

DeFord quote from an untitled 1926 article on libel.

Invasion of privacy (page 142)

Image credits:

Cartoon by Steve Cowden, adapted from a 1985 cartoon in The New Yorker by Ed Fisher.

Copyright law (page 143)

Image credits:

Cover image from "Barry Trotter and the Unauthorized Parody" by Michael Gerber. Fireside, 2002.

Taste and decency (pages 144-145)

Image credits:

Nooky's photo by Daniel Kramer, Houston Press.

Dick Cheney photo © AP/Wide World Photos.

The Seven Deadly Sins (pages 146-147)

Image credits:

Evil reporter illustration by Tony Champagne.

Jayson Blair photo © The New York Times.

Text credits:

Blair quote from "Burning Down My Master's House: My Life at The New York Times" by Jayson Blair. New Millenium, 2004. 1.

Journalistic ethics (pages 148-149)

Image credits:

Ape illustration from the Rick Marshall collection. American Heritage, October/November 1982.

Text credits:

The first case study on page 148 was derived from actual events described in the excellent ASNE Credibility Handbook, available at asne.org.

Sources for credibility statistics: Harris Poll (Jan. 2005); Pew Research Center (2004); Harris Poll (2004).

"Code of Ethics" from Society of Professional Journalists, 3909 N. Meridian St., Indianapolis, Indiana 46208, www.spj.org. Copyright © 2005 by Society of Professional Journalists. Reprinted by permission.

8 ONLINE REPORTING

From print to the Web (pages 154-155)

Text credits:

Stevenson quote from "What You See Is Not What You Get" by Thomas Lang, posted on cjrdaily.org, March 3, 2004.

Media convergence (pages 156-157)

Image credits:

Converged reporter illustration by Steve Cowden.

Photo of Wilma Colon by Ken Lyons.

Images from "UAB's 'hell' hath no fury" in the Lawrence Journal-World, March 27, 2004. Reprinted by permission of Lawrence Journal-World.

Text credits:

Stone quote from "The Backpack Journalist Is a 'Mush of Mediocrity'" by Martha Stone, USC Annenberg Online Journalism Review, posted April 2, 2002.

Curley quote on p. 156 from a Q-and-A with Jay DeFoore in Editor & Publisher, Dec. 19, 2005.

Curley quote on News Center seating from an NPR story, "Watchful Eyes on Kansas Media Innovations" by David Folkenflik.

Online storytelling options
(pages 158-159)

Text credits:

Daniel Weintraub's blog can be found at www.sacbee.com/static/weblogs/insider/

Tom Hanson's blog can be found at www.naplesnews.com/blogs/talk_town_tom_hanson/

Image credits:

Slideshow photos by Mike Sypniewski and Daryl Stone. Reprinted by permission of the Asbury Park Press.

BROADCAST JOURNALISM

Broadcast news (pages 164-165)

Image credits:

Photo illustration of radio tower uses images © Borland/PhotoLink/Getty Images and © Brand X Pictures/PunchStock.

Photos of Mitchell and Barry by Michael Lloyd.

Text credits:

Cohler quote from "Broadcast Journalism: A Guide for the Presentation of Radio and Television News" by David Keith Cohler. Prentice Hall, 1993.

Writing for broadcast (pages 166-167)

Text credits:

Pam Zekman quote first appeared in "What Newspaper Writers Can Learn From TV," an undated article written by Valerie Hyman for the Poynter Institute. Contacted by phone, Zekman verified the accuracy of the quote.

Image credits:

Newscast illustration by Tony Champagne.

Photo provided by Pam Zekman.

Radio news reporting (pages 168-169)

Text credits:

Radio news stories reprinted with permission from the news directors at KXL, KEX and KPAM.

Fire story by Boaz Herzog, The Oregonian, Jan. 26, 2006.

Image credits:

Mesaros photo by Michael Lloyd.

Television news reporting
(pages 170-171)

Text credits:

KGW news stories reprinted with permission of KGW-TV.

Image credits:

Bradley photo ©Louise Gubb/Corbis SABA.

PUBLIC RELATIONS

What is public relations?
(pages 176-177)

Text credits:

Bernays quote from his 1992 essay, "The Future of Public Relations," posted on the Web site of The Museum of Public Relations.

Prejean-Motanky quote from her "Advice and Perspective" column posted on the Publicity Club of Chicago Web site, September, 2003.

Planning a public relations strategy (pages 178-179)

Image credits:

MacKnight photo by Tim Harrower.

Writing news releases (pages 180-181)

Image credits:

News release provided by Oregon Health & Science University.

Man and woman with notepad © Index Stock Photography Inc./PhotoDisc/Getty Images.

Text credits:

Laermer quote from "Full Frontal PR" by Richard Laermer and Michael Prichinello. Bloomberg Press, 2003. 117.

Balance, bias and media manipulation (pages 182-183)

Text credits:

"Basic flaws led FBI to bungle Mayfield case, report finds," by Anne Saker and Susan Goldsmith, The Oregonian, Jan. 7, 2006.

Bill Press quote from "Spin This!" by Bill Press. Pocket Books, 2001. 22.

Van Hook quote from his undated column "Ethical Public Relations: Not an Oxymoron" posted on his Web site, All About Public Relations.

Image credits:

Illustration by Paul Lachine.

Scott McClellan photo © AP/Wide World Photos.

THE MORGUE

"Old Constan" reprinted with the permission of Scribner, a division of Simon & Schuster Adult Publishing Group, from "Ernest Hemingway, Dateline: Toronto" by Ernest Hemingway, edited by William White. Copyright ©1985 by Mary Hemingway, John Hemingway, Patrick Hemingway, and Gregory Hemingway. All rights reserved.

"The Constitution" by H.L. Mencken from The Baltimore Evening Sun, Aug. 19, 1935. Copyright 1935, reprinted with the permission of The Baltimore Sun.

"The Kentucky Derby" reprinted with the permission of Simon & Schuster Adult Publishing Group from "The Great Shark Hunt" by Hunter S. Thompson. Copyright ©1971, 1979 by Hunter S. Thompson.

"Oregon Pays Tribute to Its Vietnam Vets" by Don Hamilton from The Oregonian, Nov. 12, 1987. Reprinted by permission.

"Mail Species" by Dave Philipps from Page 1, Life Section, Colorado Springs Gazette, Dec. 11, 2003. Reprinted by permission of Colorado Springs Gazette.

"Glove Story" by Don Hamilton from The Oregonian, April 12, 1986. Reprinted by permission.

"You wore flip-flops to the White House?!" by Jodi S. Cohen and Maegan Carberry with contributions by Michael Kilian and Christi Parsons. Copyrighted July 15, 2005, Chicago Tribune Company. All rights reserved. Used with permission.

"A passion for raising rabbits" by Alan Baranick from The Plain Dealer, Nov. 22, 2004. Copyright ©2004 The Plain Dealer. All rights reserved. Reprinted with permission.

"BGSU Professor a Talented Sculptor" Obituary from the Toledo Blade, Aug. 8, 2002. Reprinted with permission of the Blade.

"Church bus crash on turnpike kills 3" by Mike Clary, Neil Santaniello and Patty Pensa from the South Florida Sun-Sentinel, Aug. 8, 2004. Reprinted by permission of South Florida Sun-Sentinel.

"For those cut off, a life primeval: A few solitary souls pass the days watching nature reclaim sections of New Orleans" by Vanessa Gezari from St. Petersburg Times, Sept. 12, 2005. Reprinted by permission of St. Petersburg Times.

"This one's for real! Fire kills 3 in Seton Hall dorm prone to false alarms" by Mary Jo Patterson from The Star-Ledger, Jan. 20, 2000. Copyright © 2000 The Star-Ledger. All rights reserved. Reprinted with permission.

"Family loses all in house fire" by Sanne Specht from Medford Mail Tribune, June 1, 2005. Reprinted by permission of Medford Mail Tribune, Medford, Ore.

"Into the flames" by Stuart Tomlinson from The Oregonian, Oct. 4, 2001. Reprinted by permission.

"Woman accused of unorthodox theft of rare parrot" from The News-Press (Fort Myers, Fla.), Nov. 7, 2005. Reprinted by permission.

"Bank robbery suspect in Ambridge nabbed while trying to return wad of cash" by Jonathan D. Silver from Pittsburgh Post-Gazette, Nov. 9, 2005. Reprinted by permission.

"Clown doesn't find truck theft funny" by Larry Ballard from Des Moines Register, Aug. 9, 2004. Copyright 2004, reprinted with permission by the Des Moines Register.

"Man dangles for hours in botched burglary attempt" by Melissa DeLoach from the News-Leader, Dec. 30, 2005. Reprinted by permission.

"Check-writer sets off clerk's internal alarm" by Stuart Tomlinson from The Oregonian, Dec. 19, 2004. Reprinted by permission.

"Murderer caught in Texas 15 years after escape" by Linda J. Johnson from the Lexington Herald-Leader, Feb. 10, 2005. Reprinted by permission of the Lexington Herald-Leader.

"Rampaging rooster attacks girl" by Kelley Benham from the St. Petersburg Times, Oct. 4, 2002. Copyright © 2002 St. Petersburg Times. Reprinted by permission.

Michael Jackson story from The New York Times, June 13, 2005. Copyright © 2005 The New York Times Co. Reprinted by permission.

Excerpt from "Juror: Victim, family not credible" by Martin Kasindorf from USA Today, June 14, 2005. Reprinted with permission.

Michael Jackson story as appeared in the Daily Mail (London), June 13, 2005.

Michael Jackson stories by Linda Deutsch, June 13, 2005. Used with permission of The Associated Press. Copyright © 2005. All rights reserved.

"City makes a U-turn: speed zone set for Country Club" by Alandra Johnson. Used by permission of the Lake Oswego Review.

"Putnam Commissioners Get An Earful Over Abandoned House" by Heather Svokos from the Charleston Gazette, Sept. 10, 1996. Reprinted by permission of the Charleston Gazette.

"The city has $548-million: What do you want?" by Bryan Gilmer from the St. Petersburg Times, Aug. 21, 2002. Copyright © 2002 St. Petersburg Times. Reprinted by permission.

"'Midget' Robinson gets revenge, slams for 'Oregon fans'" by Dan Raley from the Seattle Post-Intelligencer, Feb. 13, 2004. Reprinted by permission.

Excerpt from "Running for His Life" by Michael Hall reprinted with permission from the August 2003 issue of Texas Monthly.

"Annika hangs with the big boys" by Brian Murphy from the San Francisco Chronicle, May 23, 2003. Copyright © 2003 San Francisco Chronicle. Reprinted by permission.

"Give me the sign" by Dave Scheiber from the St. Petersburg Times, July 5, 2005. Copyright © 2005 St. Petersburg Times. Reprinted by permission.

"Vermeil sensed it was go time" by Joe Posnanski from the Kansas City Star, Nov. 7, 2005. Reprinted by permission.

"Girl's last gifts bring smiles to kids' faces" by Colleen Kenney from the Lincoln Journal Star, June 10, 2005. Reprinted by permission of the Lincoln Journal Star.

"Always Ed" by Kelley Behham from the St. Petersburg Times, Feb. 13, 2005. Copyright © 2005 St. Petersburg Times. Reprinted by permission.

"The Perfect Kiss" by Karen Sandstrom from The Plain Dealer, Feb. 14, 2004. Copyright © 2004 The Plain Dealer. All rights reserved. Reprinted with permission.

"All this ice, and the captain is hot" by Judd Slivka from the Seattle Post-Intelligencer, Jan. 4, 2000. Reprinted by permission.

"The Good Doctor" by Manish Mehta from The Star-Ledger, Feb. 29, 2004. Copyright © 2004 The Star-Ledger. All rights reserved. Reprinted with permission.

Part 3 of the four-part series, "If I Die" by Diana K. Sugg from The Baltimore Sun, Dec. 21-24, 2004. Copyright © 2004. Reprinted with the permission of The Baltimore Sun.

"Speeders Outgun New Limits" by Rick Hampson and Paul Overberg from USA TODAY, Feb. 23, 2004. Copyright ©2004. Reprinted by permission of USA Today.

"One Happy Big-Box Wasteland" by Mark Morford from the San Francisco Chronicle, Aug. 1, 2005. Copyright © 2005 San Francisco Chronicle. Reprinted by permission.

"Old Man Sat, Stared Until a Child Happened to Pass" by Charles Kuralt from "Charles Kuralt's People." Reprinted by permission of Kenilworth Media.

"O'Malley's pettiness shines through again" by Stephen Henderson from The Baltimore Sun, Jan. 5, 2000. Copyright © 2000, reprinted with the permission of The Baltimore Sun.

Editorial by David Barham from the Arkansas Democrat-Gazette, Oct. 18, 2002. Used with permission, © 2002, Arkansas Democrat-Gazette.

"The Onyx Tour: Spears' stripper act an unfocused bore" by Doug Elfman from the Las Vegas Review-Journal, March 8, 2004. Copyright © 2004. Reprinted by permission of Las Vegas Review-Journal.

"The Return of the King" by Claudia Puig from USA Today, Dec. 16, 2003. Reprinted by permission.

"Polypeppers and Pork Rinds" by David Sarasohn from The Oregonian, June 18, 2004. Reprinted by permission.

"The Book of Always" by J. Taylor Buckley reprinted with permission.

"The 12-Step Program to Good Writing" by Michael Gartner, reprinted with permission.

INDEX